MARVEL
ARTHUR

writers
CHRIS CLAREMONT & WALTER SIMONSON
pencils
ARTHUR ADAMS
inks
TERRY AUSTIN, BOB WIACEK & ART THIBERT
with AL GORDON, MIKE MIGNOLA, AL MILGROM & ARTHUR ADAMS

letters TOM ORZECHOWSKI & BILL OAKLEY
colors CHRISTIE SCHEELE, STEVE BUCCELLATO,
PETRA SCOTESE & GLYNIS OLIVER
color reconstruction AVALON STUDIOS
cover colors AVALON STUDIOS
editors ANN NOCENTI, RALPH MACCHIO & BOB HARRAS

collections editor JEFF YOUNGQUIST
associate editor CORY SEDLMEIER
assistant editor JENNIFER GRÜNWALD
book designer JEOF VITA
editor in chief JOE QUESADA
president BILL JEMAS

I could say I don't like to think of my past work, that I only look to the glorious future, to my next world-shattering, mind-bending project. You know, to my next visionary masterpiece. Or maybe I should say prophetic, my next prophetic masterpiece...I like the sound of the phrase "Arthur Adams: X-Men PROPHET!"

I could say that the heavy responsibility of being a prophet, especially an X-Men prophet, means I don't have time to look into my past.

But that would be a lie.

The truth is I don't really remember much at all of what went into the stories in this collection that you, dear reader, now hold in your hands. So I've decided that what I will do is share with you what little I do remember and then just make up the rest.

Okay?

Good.

with my life!?!" He then dissolved into inarticulate sobbing. After about twenty minutes of trying to calm Chris down, he pulled himself together a bit and said in a shaky voice, "I'm sorry. I shouldn't have called. I'll call back later," and hung up.

I went back to watching the end of *Star Trek* TOS, Episode #29 "Operation Annihilate" (the one with the "fried egg" alien amoeba things that possess Spock).

At about 11:00 PM California time, meaning it was 2 AM in New York, Chris called back. He was clearly drunk.

"Hey Arthur, buddy, you gotta get over here! This place is full of the most amazing chicks I ever saw! You gotta get over here! WOOOO!"

"Chris, I live in California."

"What? Oh yeah. But dude... chicks!"

With some effort I was able to convince Chris that I was not going

Luckily, it turned out that 900,003 pages of the plot dealt with the personal and professional challenges facing Loki's plain but spirited Filipino housekeeper, Lupe. It really hurt to lose that plot thread, but it seemed the right choice at the time. After cutting that, I was down to around 100,000 pages of plot. So, 1,000 pages of plot per page of pencil art—this still seemed like too much story, so I randomly selected 104 pages from the remaining 100,000 and, you know, I think it worked out pretty well.

The following spring, I was supposed to be working on a *Longshot Graphic Novel* or a *Longshot* continuing series or some other darn thing that may or may not have had "Longshot" in its title, but I was instead sitting at my drawing desk staring blankly at the TV, waiting for a Popeye cartoon to come on (I think he ate spinach

The truth is I don't really remember much at all of what went into the stories in this collection that you, dear reader, now hold in your hands. So I've decided that what I will do is share with you what little I do remember and then just make up the rest.

—Arthur Adams

So there it was, January of 1985, and I, Arthur Adams, sat in my studio/bedroom in Vacaville, California, munching on a nice chunky peanut butter and apple butter sandwich while happily watching a rerun of *Leave It to Beaver* on channel 20. In this episode, Beaver gets in trouble. During commercial breaks, I worked on issue 6 of *Longshot*. All was right with the world.

The phone rang. It was a telephone call from *Longshot* writer and *X-Men/New Mutants* editor Ann Nocenti.

"Chris [Claremont] wants you to draw the next *New Mutants Annual*. What do you think?"

I'd met Chris once or twice before at various comic book conventions and he had seemed like a nice enough guy so I said, "Sure, why not, sounds great, have Chris give me a call."

Later that afternoon (During *Star Trek* TOS, Episode #29 "Operation Annihilate!"), Chris called. "Oh Arthur!" He moaned pitifully, "What am I going to do

to fly to Manhattan that night. Finally we got to talking about the *New Mutants Annual*.

He talked about this really cool project he was working on with Paul Smith. It was going to be two issues of X-Men and Alpha Flight versus Loki, Asgardian God of Evil.

"That sounds great!" said I.

After a long silence, during which I thought that perhaps Chris had passed out, a frightening voice growled out of the receiver, "If you EVER tell ANYONE about...about...Earlier...I. WILL. CRUSH. YOU! Click." Yes, he actually said, "Click."

About a week later, while I was watching *Die Monster Die*, the biggest Fed-Ex truck I had ever seen, then or since, pulled up in front of the house. The Fed-Ex man, Javier, unloaded 93 document boxes from it onto my front lawn as I looked on in horror. Javier, looking over the release form, laughed and said, "Oh. Marvel Comics. Must be another Claremont job."

I got to work.

and behaved violently in this one), when the phone rang.

"Hi Arthur! Want to draw *X-Men Annual #10*?" Said Ann in a voice that said I had better respond "yes" if I knew what was good for me.

The theme song to Popeye had started, so I mumbled distractedly, "Sure, have Chris give me a call."

Seconds later, just as Popeye started, the phone rang again.

"Hi, may I speak to Arthur Adams?"

"Speaking."

"Hi Arthur! This is Chris Claremont. I'm a really big fan of your stuff. Ann just told me you might be interested in working on an X-Men annual with me and I'm really excited about finally being able to work with you!"

"Um, what? Listen, there's a Popeye on..."

"You know, X-MEN!!! I'm really looking forward to working with you! I think it'll be great!"

"Chris, we have worked together."

Silence on the other end of the line, (Well, there might have been the sound of a chicken clucking, but I'm not really sure.)

"On *New Mutants? X-Men Annual #9?*" I asked.

Silence.

"In Asgard? Last Year?" I said.

"In Asgard?! I've never been to Asgard, Arthur!"

And it went on like that for some time, till finally he said he did remember working with me in the past. I could tell he didn't, but that's OK, he's a really busy guy, and I needed to get back to my Popeye cartoon.

A week later, I got the script. This one was a measly 86,000 pages long. 85,152 of those were about a Spanish gigolo named Jorge. (I think Chris thought that was funny.) It was good stuff, but as we were having Longshot join the X-Men, I thought we might be better off focusing on that. Also, it was much more fun to draw Longshot and Mojo and Spiral again.

Two years later, I get a call from Chris.

"X-Babies!" He exclaimed.

"Uh, what?" I was just settling down to a showing of *One Million Years B.C.*, which I had heard featured dinosaurs, and maybe a girl in a bikini.

"X Babies! We'll make millions!"

"Chris, what are you talking about?"

"You draw *X-Men Annual #12!* The first half of the book will be set in the Savage Land, and then you can draw dinosaurs! You love dinosaurs!" I did, and so he had my full attention.

"The last part of the book is, from outta nowhere... X-BABIES! Can you stand it?!? We'll make millions!!!"

"Chris, have you been drinking?"

"Just my usual 12 cups of coffee! Can you hear your heart beating? I can hear mine right now!!! Thump! Thump! Thump! It's SOOOO LOUD!!!"

Marvel never made X-Baby toys, and disillusioned, I considered for awhile leaving comics and entering the fast paced world of dish washing at the local Pizza Hut.

Finally, there were the three issues of *The Fantastic Four*. "What?" You may ask. The FF in an *X-Men Visionaries* collection? It don't make no sense do it? No, my friend, it do not.

But who cares?

It's fun!

One day in June of 1991, I was sitting at home watching a video tape of *Destroy All Monsters*, a Godzilla film I'd seen a gazillion times, but of course I was sitting there studying it as though my very life depended on it. (Clearly I'm not that smart.)

The phone rang.

It was Walter Simonson.

I stopped the video tape.

Once I was talking to Ann Nocenti about something amazing Walt had just done and Ann said, "I think Walt could do a book called *Potato-Salad Man*, and it would be great!"

I think Ann was right.

Anyhow, on the phone, Walt told me that he was was working on the Fantastic Four, but he was way behind schedule on it. He wanted to know if I could help him out by pencilling three issues so he could get caught up.

But wait, you may be thinking, Arthur Adams? Helping to get a monthly book back on schedule?

That's crazy!

Well, it seemed like a good idea at the time.

So Walt asked what FF villians I might wanna draw.

I said "Uuuh, maybe the Sub-Mariner, or...the Skrulls...or the Mole Man...or, maybe some big monsters...I don't know..."

Walt then suggested that we kill the FF (Don't worry, they got better.) and replace them with Marvel's four most popular characters at that time, Wolverine, Spider-Man, Ghost Rider, and the Punisher. I suggested the Hulk instead of the Punisher.

Walt then said, in a Barry White sorta voice, "Solid."

Somehow, poor ol' Ralph Macchio of *Karate Kid* fame agreed to be our Editor. Ralph was full of himself from his recent Hollywood success. Too full of himself.

He'd learn.

We were lucky enough to get Art Thibert to ink my pencils. Apparently, he had not talked to Terry, or Bob, or any one else that had inked me, and had no idea of the perils his fingers now faced.

Anyhow, we had gotten it all done. The stress had aged Ralph Macchio's baby-faced features at least ten years! His movie career was over, and never again would he know the embrace of young nubile starlets, but he didn't mind! He didn't mind because *FF #347* sold like crazy!

I'd better go see what's on T.V.

Reveling in TIVO,

ARTHUR ADAMS
Arthur Adams
May 2003

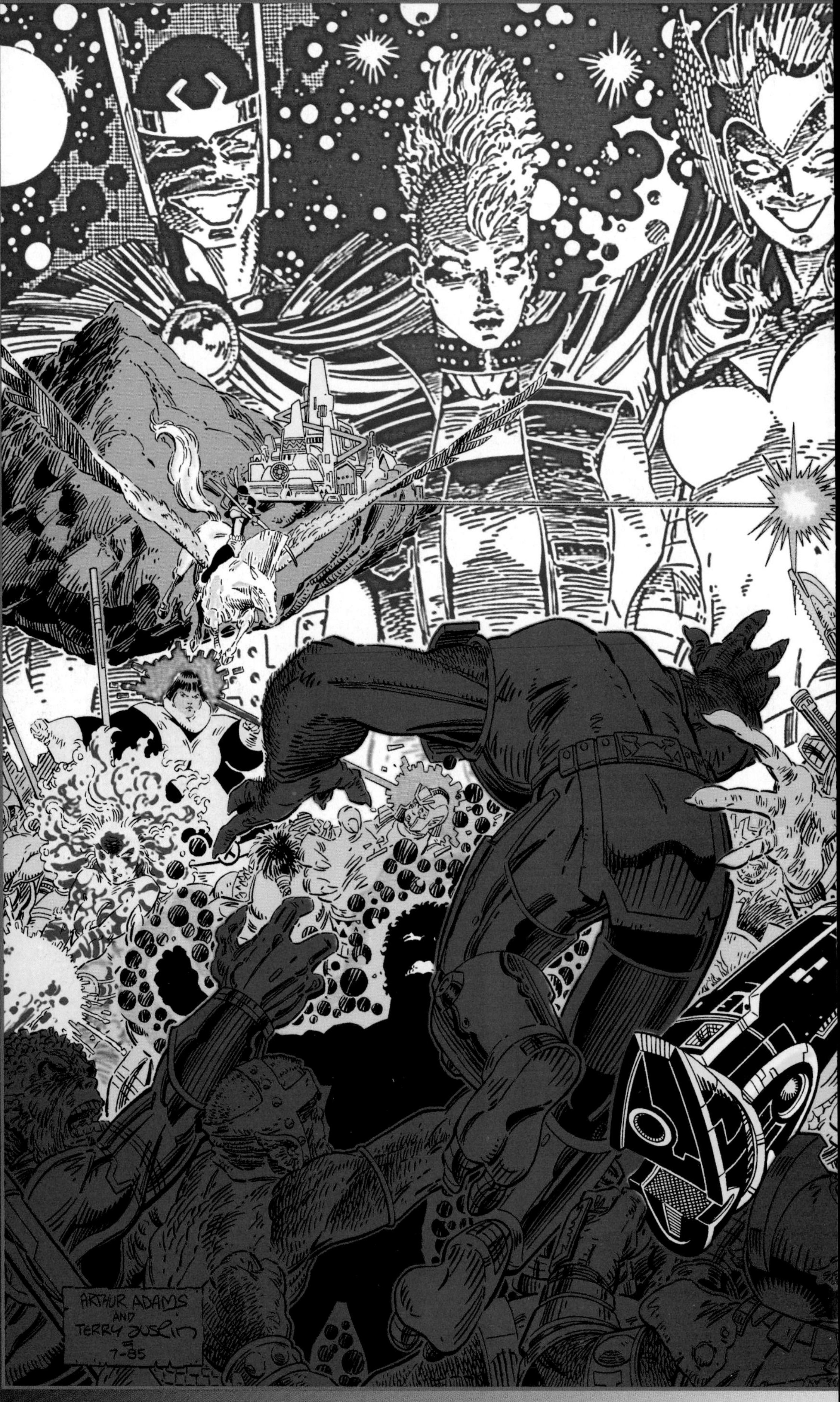
ARTHUR ADAMS
AND
TERRY AUSTIN
7-85

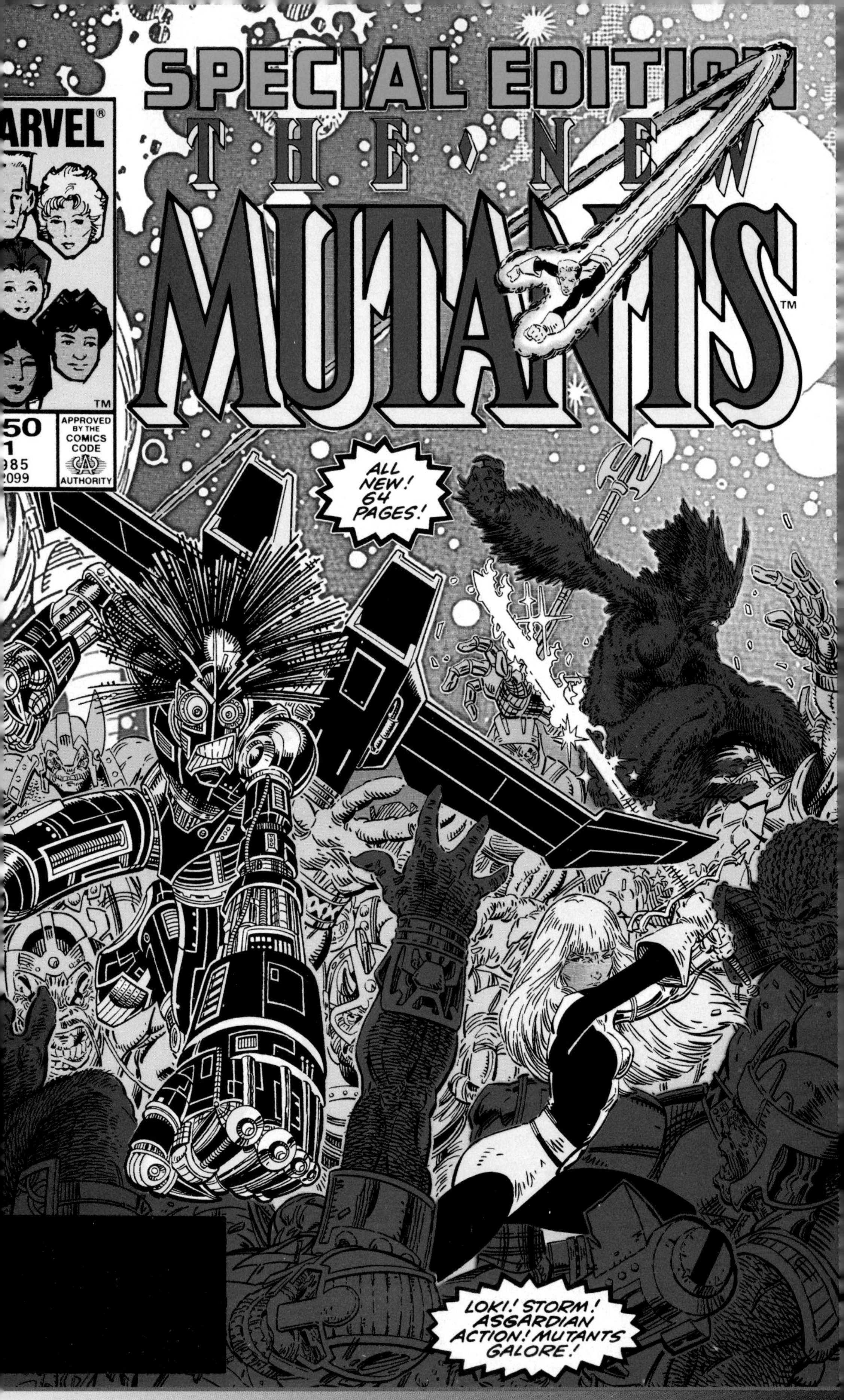
SPECIAL EDITION
THE NEW
MUTANTS™
MARVEL®
TM
APPROVED BY THE COMICS CODE AUTHORITY
ALL NEW! 64 PAGES!
LOKI! STORM! ASGARDIAN ACTION! MUTANTS GALORE!

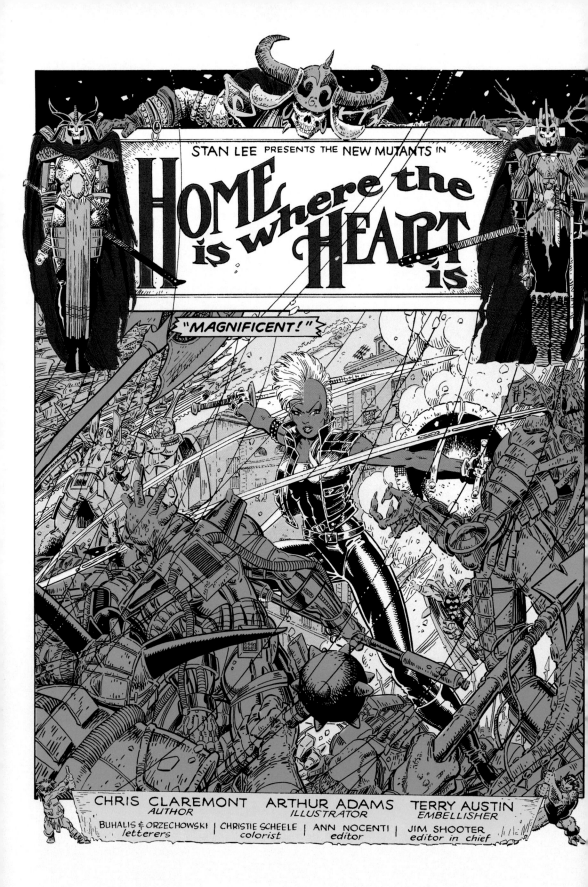

STAN LEE PRESENTS THE NEW MUTANTS IN

HOME is where the HEART is

"MAGNIFICENT!"

CHRIS CLAREMONT
AUTHOR

ARTHUR ADAMS
ILLUSTRATOR

TERRY AUSTIN
EMBELLISHER

BUHALIS & ORZECHOWSKI
letterers

CHRISTIE SCHEELE
colorist

ANN NOCENTI
editor

JIM SHOOTER
editor in chief

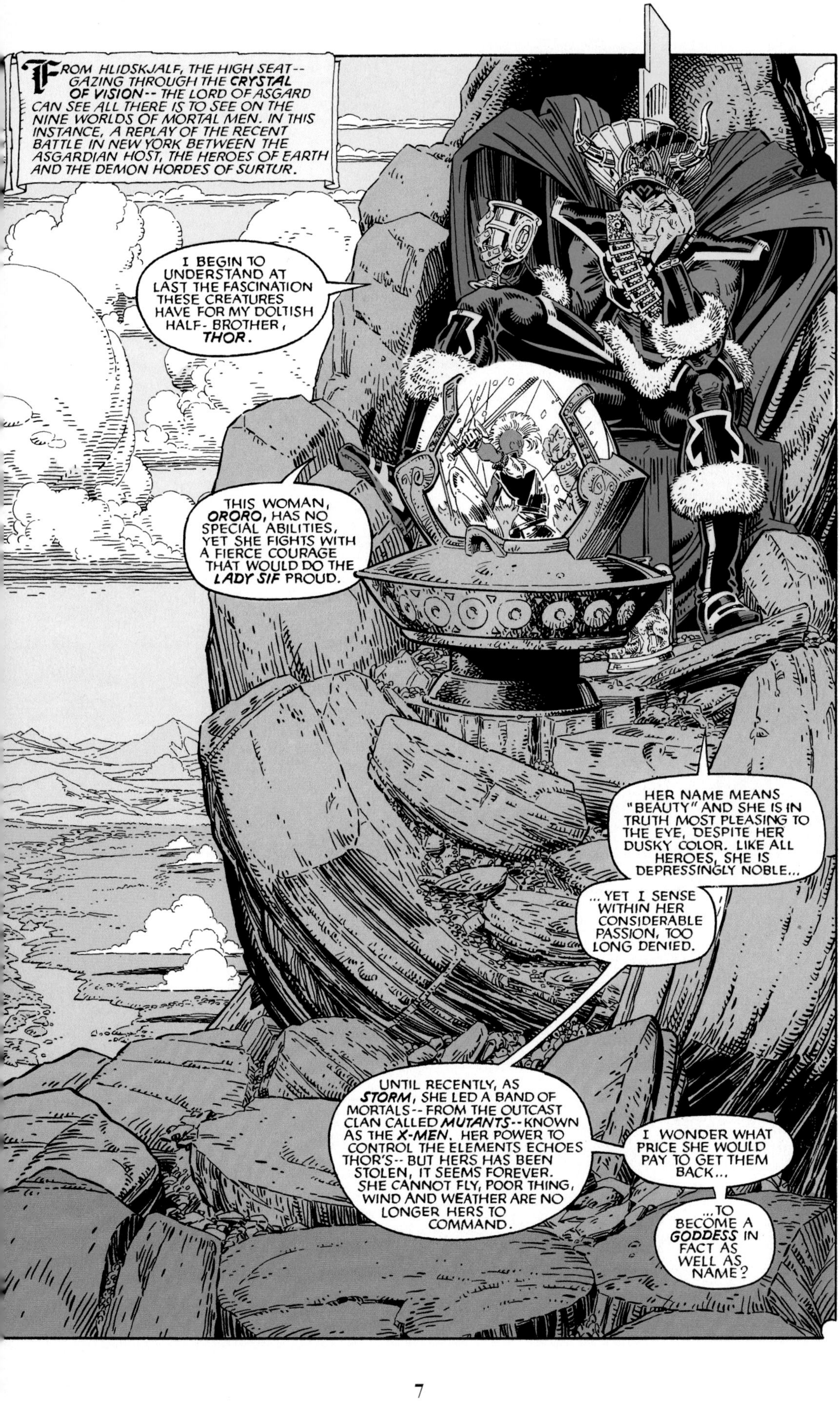
FROM HLIDSKJALF, THE HIGH SEAT-- GAZING THROUGH THE CRYSTAL OF VISION-- THE LORD OF ASGARD CAN SEE ALL THERE IS TO SEE ON THE NINE WORLDS OF MORTAL MEN. IN THIS INSTANCE, A REPLAY OF THE RECENT BATTLE IN NEW YORK BETWEEN THE ASGARDIAN HOST, THE HEROES OF EARTH AND THE DEMON HORDES OF SURTUR.
I BEGIN TO UNDERSTAND AT LAST THE FASCINATION THESE CREATURES HAVE FOR MY DOLTISH HALF-BROTHER, THOR.
THIS WOMAN, ORORO, HAS NO SPECIAL ABILITIES, YET SHE FIGHTS WITH A FIERCE COURAGE THAT WOULD DO THE LADY SIF PROUD.
HER NAME MEANS "BEAUTY" AND SHE IS IN TRUTH MOST PLEASING TO THE EYE, DESPITE HER DUSKY COLOR. LIKE ALL HEROES, SHE IS DEPRESSINGLY NOBLE...
...YET I SENSE WITHIN HER CONSIDERABLE PASSION, TOO LONG DENIED.
UNTIL RECENTLY, AS STORM, SHE LED A BAND OF MORTALS-- FROM THE OUTCAST CLAN CALLED MUTANTS-- KNOWN AS THE X-MEN. HER POWER TO CONTROL THE ELEMENTS ECHOES THOR'S-- BUT HERS HAS BEEN STOLEN, IT SEEMS FOREVER. SHE CANNOT FLY, POOR THING, WIND AND WEATHER ARE NO LONGER HERS TO COMMAND.
I WONDER WHAT PRICE SHE WOULD PAY TO GET THEM BACK...
...TO BECOME A GODDESS IN FACT AS WELL AS NAME?

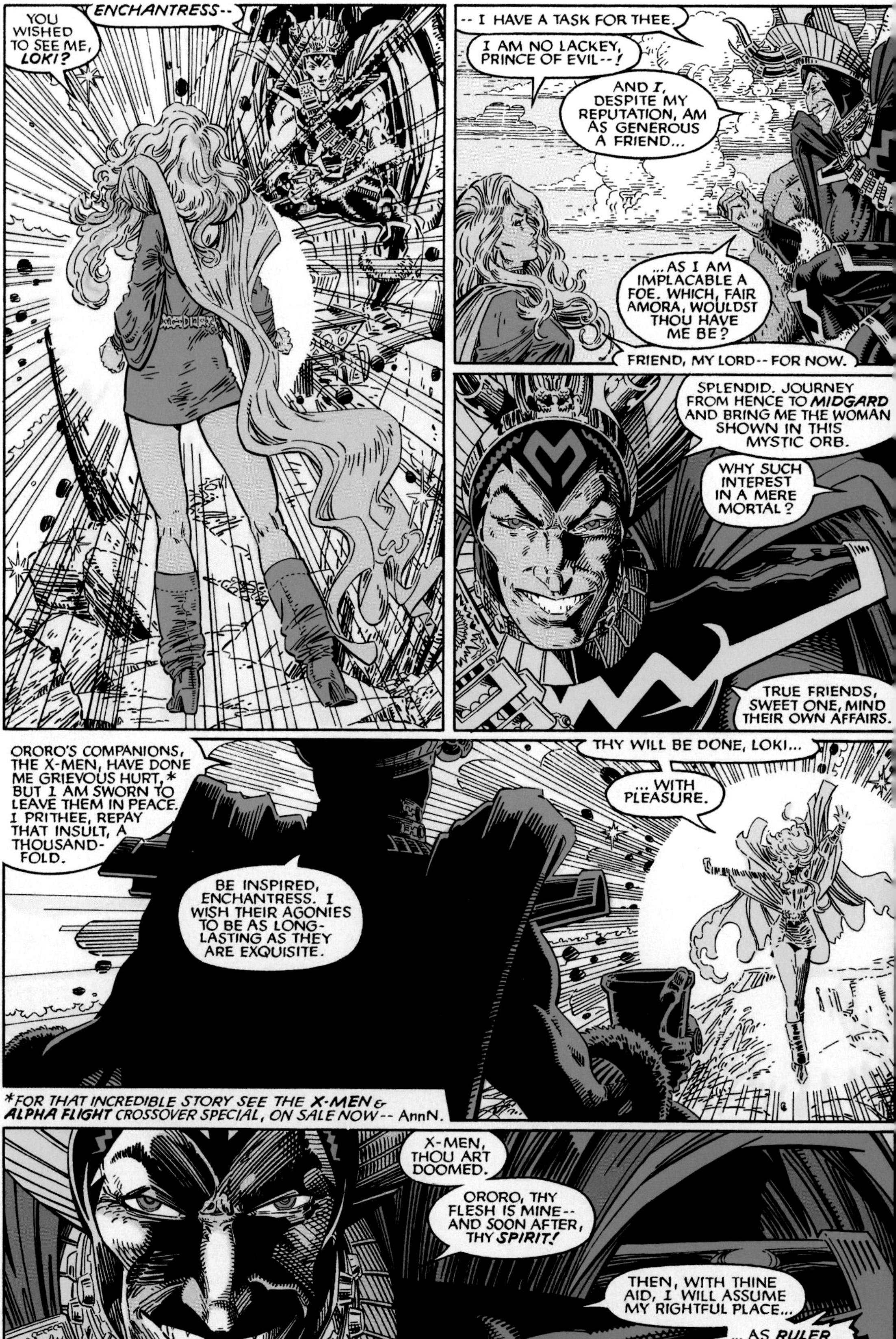
YOU WISHED TO SEE ME, LOKI?
ENCHANTRESS--
-- I HAVE A TASK FOR THEE.
I AM NO LACKEY, PRINCE OF EVIL--!
AND I, DESPITE MY REPUTATION, AM AS GENEROUS A FRIEND...
...AS I AM IMPLACABLE A FOE. WHICH, FAIR AMORA, WOULDST THOU HAVE ME BE?
FRIEND, MY LORD-- FOR NOW.
SPLENDID. JOURNEY FROM HENCE TO MIDGARD AND BRING ME THE WOMAN SHOWN IN THIS MYSTIC ORB.
WHY SUCH INTEREST IN A MERE MORTAL?
TRUE FRIENDS, SWEET ONE, MIND THEIR OWN AFFAIRS.
ORORO'S COMPANIONS, THE X-MEN, HAVE DONE ME GRIEVOUS HURT,* BUT I AM SWORN TO LEAVE THEM IN PEACE. I PRITHEE, REPAY THAT INSULT, A THOUSAND-FOLD.
BE INSPIRED, ENCHANTRESS. I WISH THEIR AGONIES TO BE AS LONG-LASTING AS THEY ARE EXQUISITE.
THY WILL BE DONE, LOKI...
...WITH PLEASURE.
*FOR THAT INCREDIBLE STORY SEE THE X-MEN & ALPHA FLIGHT CROSSOVER SPECIAL, ON SALE NOW-- AnnN.
X-MEN, THOU ART DOOMED.
ORORO, THY FLESH IS MINE-- AND SOON AFTER, THY SPIRIT!
THEN, WITH THINE AID, I WILL ASSUME MY RIGHTFUL PLACE...
...AS RULER OF ASGARD!!

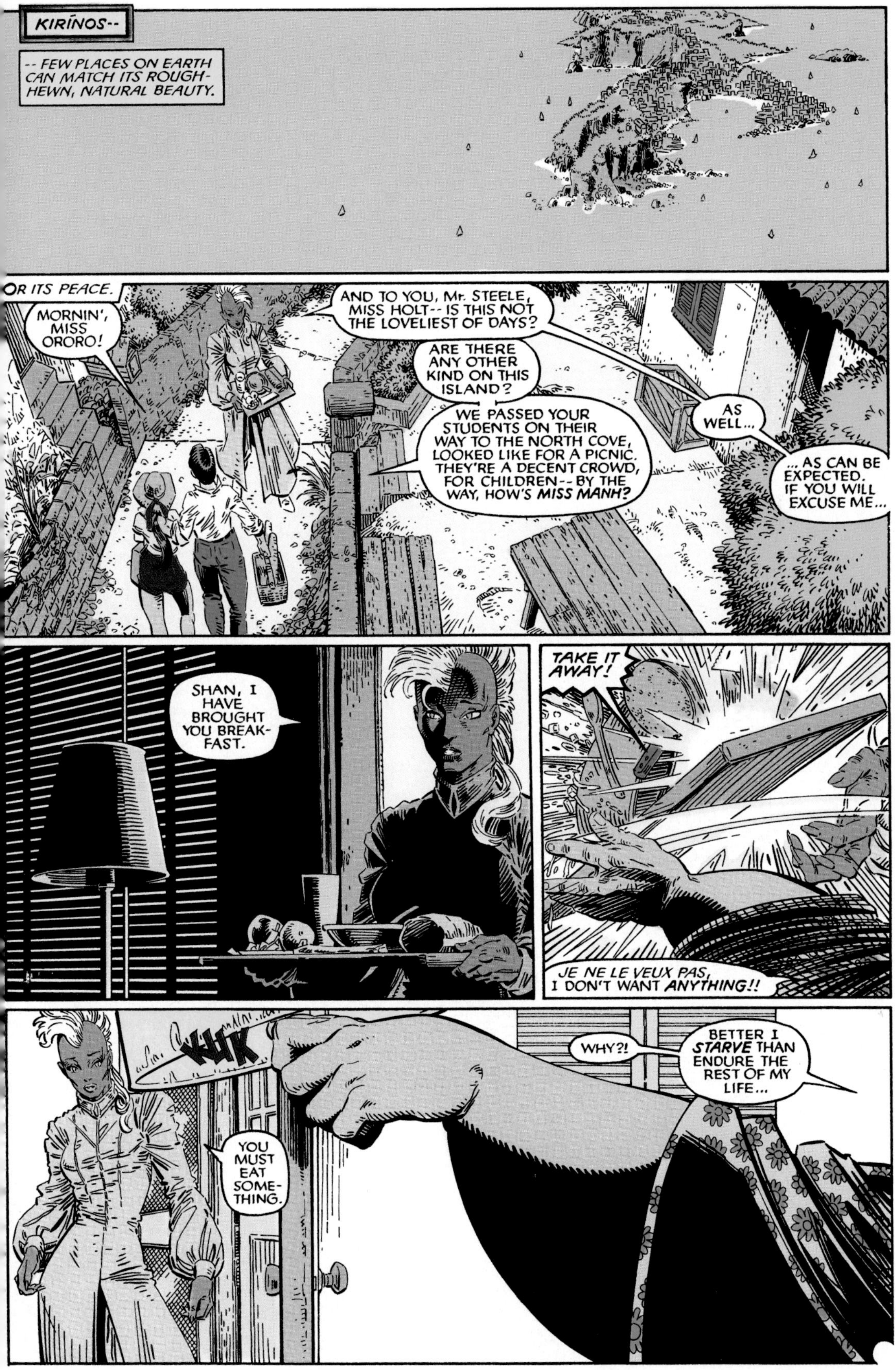
KIRÍNOS--
-- FEW PLACES ON EARTH CAN MATCH ITS ROUGH-HEWN, NATURAL BEAUTY.
OR ITS PEACE.
MORNIN', MISS ORORO!
AND TO YOU, Mr. STEELE, MISS HOLT-- IS THIS NOT THE LOVELIEST OF DAYS?
ARE THERE ANY OTHER KIND ON THIS ISLAND?
WE PASSED YOUR STUDENTS ON THEIR WAY TO THE NORTH COVE, LOOKED LIKE FOR A PICNIC. THEY'RE A DECENT CROWD, FOR CHILDREN-- BY THE WAY, HOW'S MISS MANH?
AS WELL...
... AS CAN BE EXPECTED. IF YOU WILL EXCUSE ME...
SHAN, I HAVE BROUGHT YOU BREAK-FAST.
TAKE IT AWAY!
JE NE LE VEUX PAS, I DON'T WANT ANYTHING!!
KUK
WHY?!
BETTER I STARVE THAN ENDURE THE REST OF MY LIFE...
YOU MUST EAT SOME-THING.

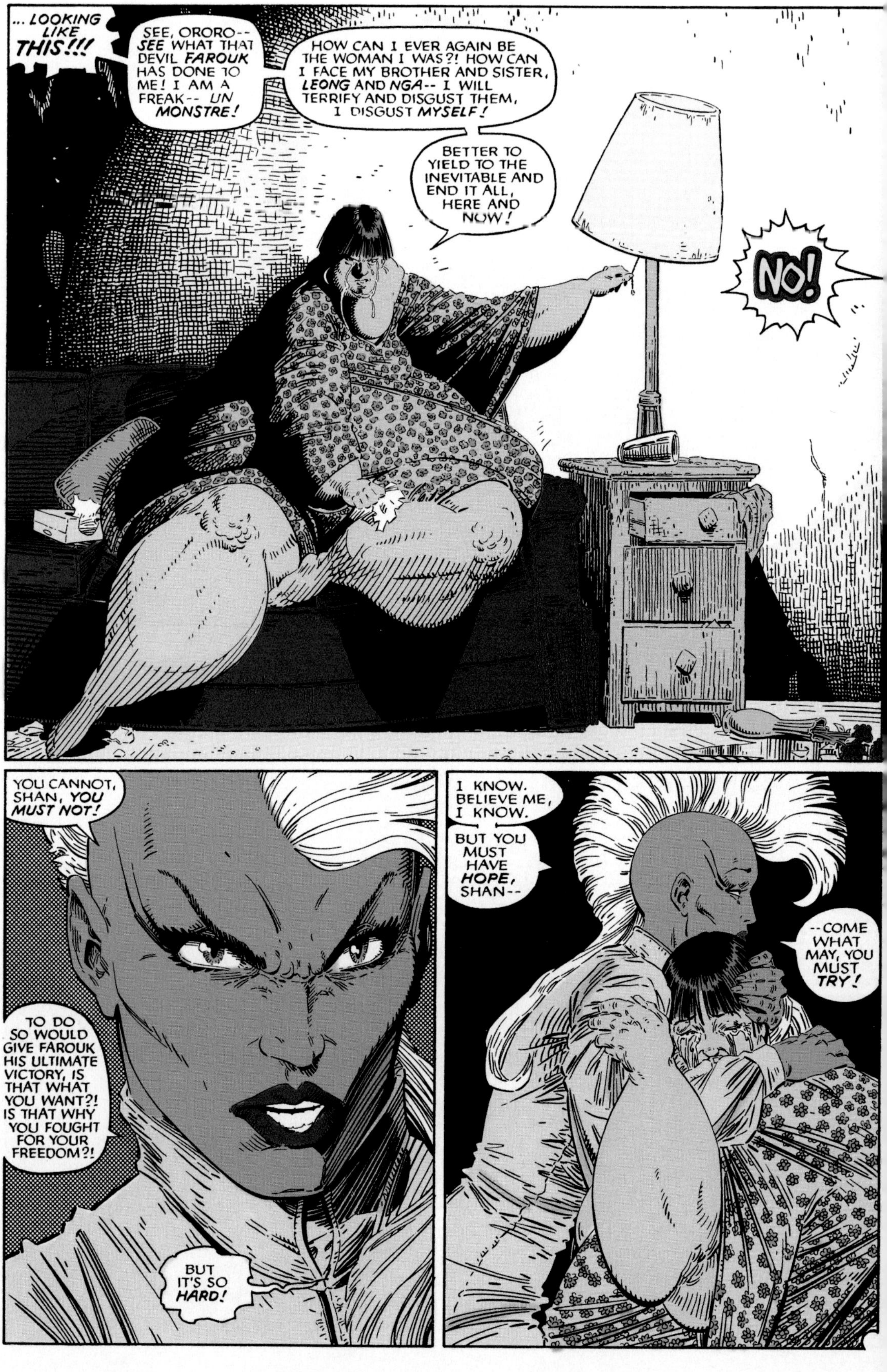

...LOOKING LIKE THIS!!!
SEE, ORORO-- SEE WHAT THAT DEVIL FAROUK HAS DONE TO ME! I AM A FREAK-- UN MONSTRE!
HOW CAN I EVER AGAIN BE THE WOMAN I WAS?! HOW CAN I FACE MY BROTHER AND SISTER, LEONG AND NGA-- I WILL TERRIFY AND DISGUST THEM, I DISGUST MYSELF!
BETTER TO YIELD TO THE INEVITABLE AND END IT ALL, HERE AND NOW!
NO!
YOU CANNOT, SHAN, YOU MUST NOT!
TO DO SO WOULD GIVE FAROUK HIS ULTIMATE VICTORY, IS THAT WHAT YOU WANT?! IS THAT WHY YOU FOUGHT FOR YOUR FREEDOM?!
BUT IT'S SO HARD!
I KNOW. BELIEVE ME, I KNOW.
BUT YOU MUST HAVE HOPE, SHAN--
--COME WHAT MAY, YOU MUST TRY!

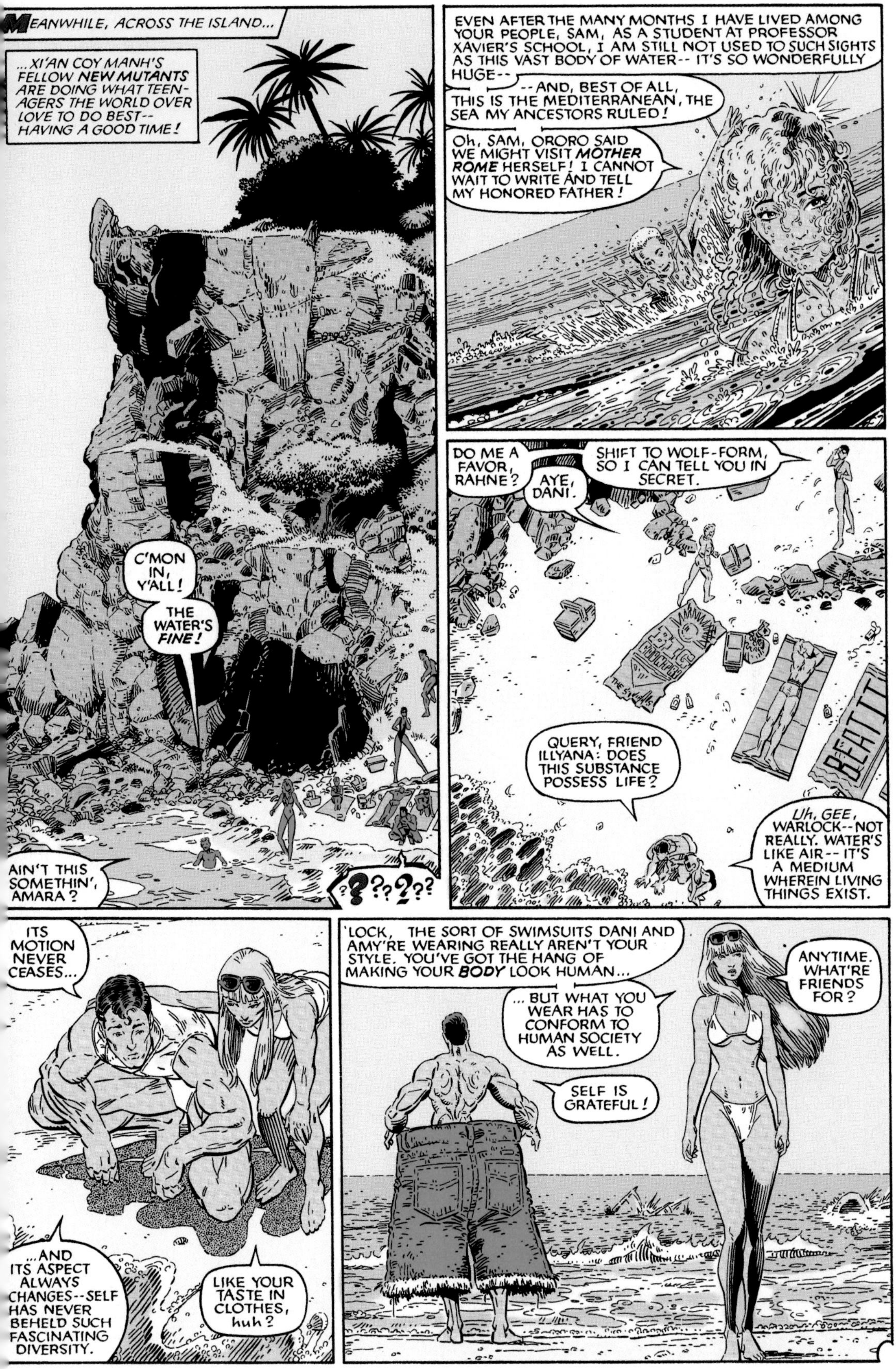
MEANWHILE, ACROSS THE ISLAND...
...XI'AN COY MANH'S FELLOW NEW MUTANTS ARE DOING WHAT TEEN-AGERS THE WORLD OVER LOVE TO DO BEST--HAVING A GOOD TIME!
C'MON IN, Y'ALL!
THE WATER'S FINE!
AIN'T THIS SOMETHIN', AMARA?
?????
EVEN AFTER THE MANY MONTHS I HAVE LIVED AMONG YOUR PEOPLE, SAM, AS A STUDENT AT PROFESSOR XAVIER'S SCHOOL, I AM STILL NOT USED TO SUCH SIGHTS AS THIS VAST BODY OF WATER-- IT'S SO WONDERFULLY HUGE--
--AND, BEST OF ALL, THIS IS THE MEDITERRANEAN, THE SEA MY ANCESTORS RULED!
Oh, SAM, ORORO SAID WE MIGHT VISIT MOTHER ROME HERSELF! I CANNOT WAIT TO WRITE AND TELL MY HONORED FATHER!
DO ME A FAVOR, RAHNE?
AYE, DANI.
SHIFT TO WOLF-FORM, SO I CAN TELL YOU IN SECRET.
QUERY, FRIEND ILLYANA: DOES THIS SUBSTANCE POSSESS LIFE?
Uh, GEE, WARLOCK--NOT REALLY. WATER'S LIKE AIR-- IT'S A MEDIUM WHEREIN LIVING THINGS EXIST.
ITS MOTION NEVER CEASES...
...AND ITS ASPECT ALWAYS CHANGES--SELF HAS NEVER BEHELD SUCH FASCINATING DIVERSITY.
LIKE YOUR TASTE IN CLOTHES, huh?
'LOCK, THE SORT OF SWIMSUITS DANI AND AMY'RE WEARING REALLY AREN'T YOUR STYLE. YOU'VE GOT THE HANG OF MAKING YOUR BODY LOOK HUMAN...
...BUT WHAT YOU WEAR HAS TO CONFORM TO HUMAN SOCIETY AS WELL.
SELF IS GRATEFUL!
ANYTIME. WHAT'RE FRIENDS FOR?

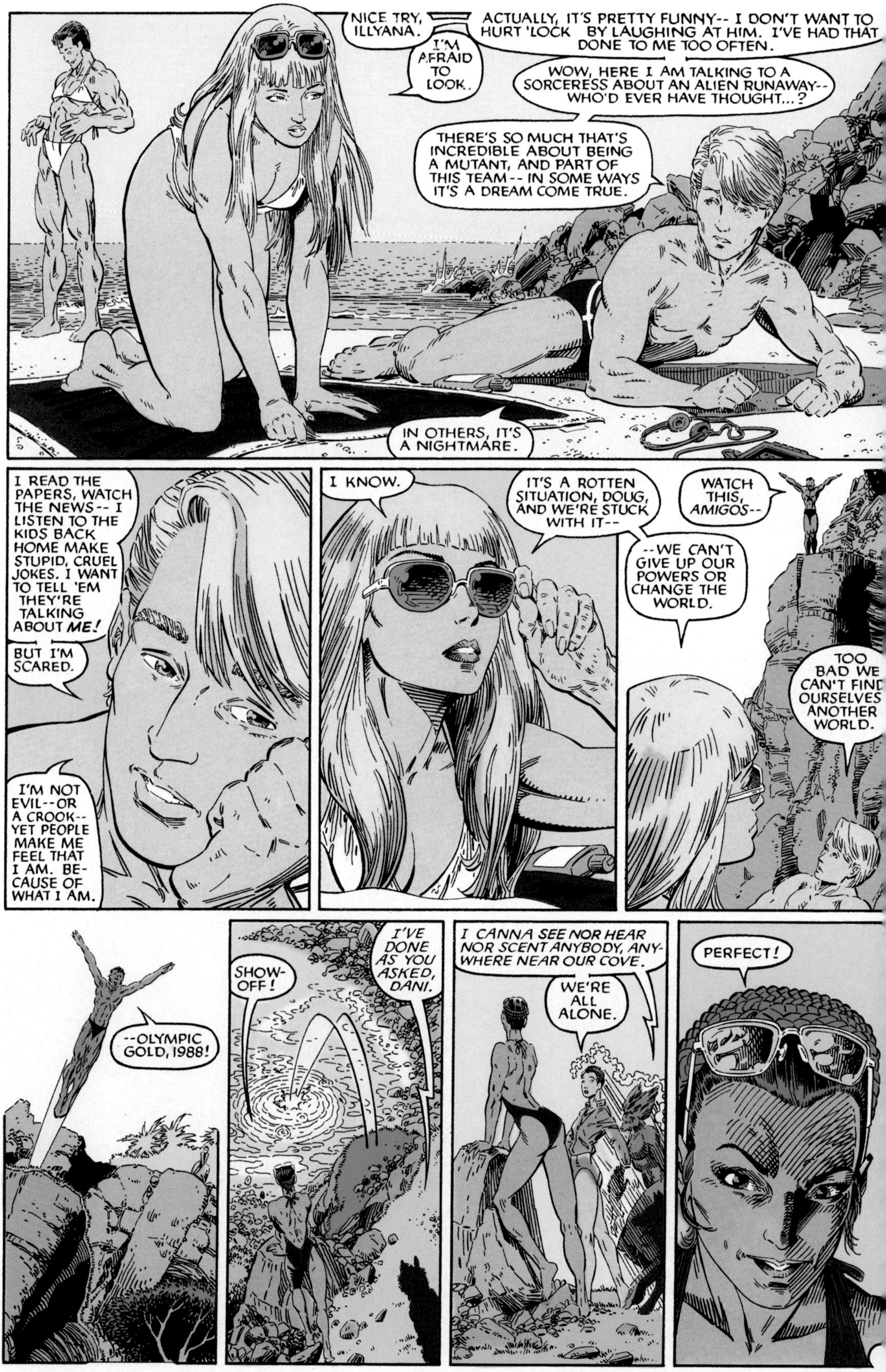

NICE TRY, ILLYANA.
I'M AFRAID TO LOOK.
ACTUALLY, IT'S PRETTY FUNNY-- I DON'T WANT TO HURT 'LOCK BY LAUGHING AT HIM. I'VE HAD THAT DONE TO ME TOO OFTEN.
WOW, HERE I AM TALKING TO A SORCERESS ABOUT AN ALIEN RUNAWAY-- WHO'D EVER HAVE THOUGHT...?
THERE'S SO MUCH THAT'S INCREDIBLE ABOUT BEING A MUTANT, AND PART OF THIS TEAM -- IN SOME WAYS IT'S A DREAM COME TRUE.
IN OTHERS, IT'S A NIGHTMARE.
I READ THE PAPERS, WATCH THE NEWS-- I LISTEN TO THE KIDS BACK HOME MAKE STUPID, CRUEL JOKES. I WANT TO TELL 'EM THEY'RE TALKING ABOUT ME!
BUT I'M SCARED.
I'M NOT EVIL--OR A CROOK-- YET PEOPLE MAKE ME FEEL THAT I AM. BE-CAUSE OF WHAT I AM.
I KNOW.
IT'S A ROTTEN SITUATION, DOUG, AND WE'RE STUCK WITH IT--
--WE CAN'T GIVE UP OUR POWERS OR CHANGE THE WORLD.
WATCH THIS, AMIGOS--
TOO BAD WE CAN'T FIND OURSELVES ANOTHER WORLD.
--OLYMPIC GOLD, 1988!
SHOW-OFF!
I'VE DONE AS YOU ASKED, DANI.
I CANNA SEE NOR HEAR NOR SCENT ANYBODY, ANY-WHERE NEAR OUR COVE.
WE'RE ALL ALONE.
PERFECT!

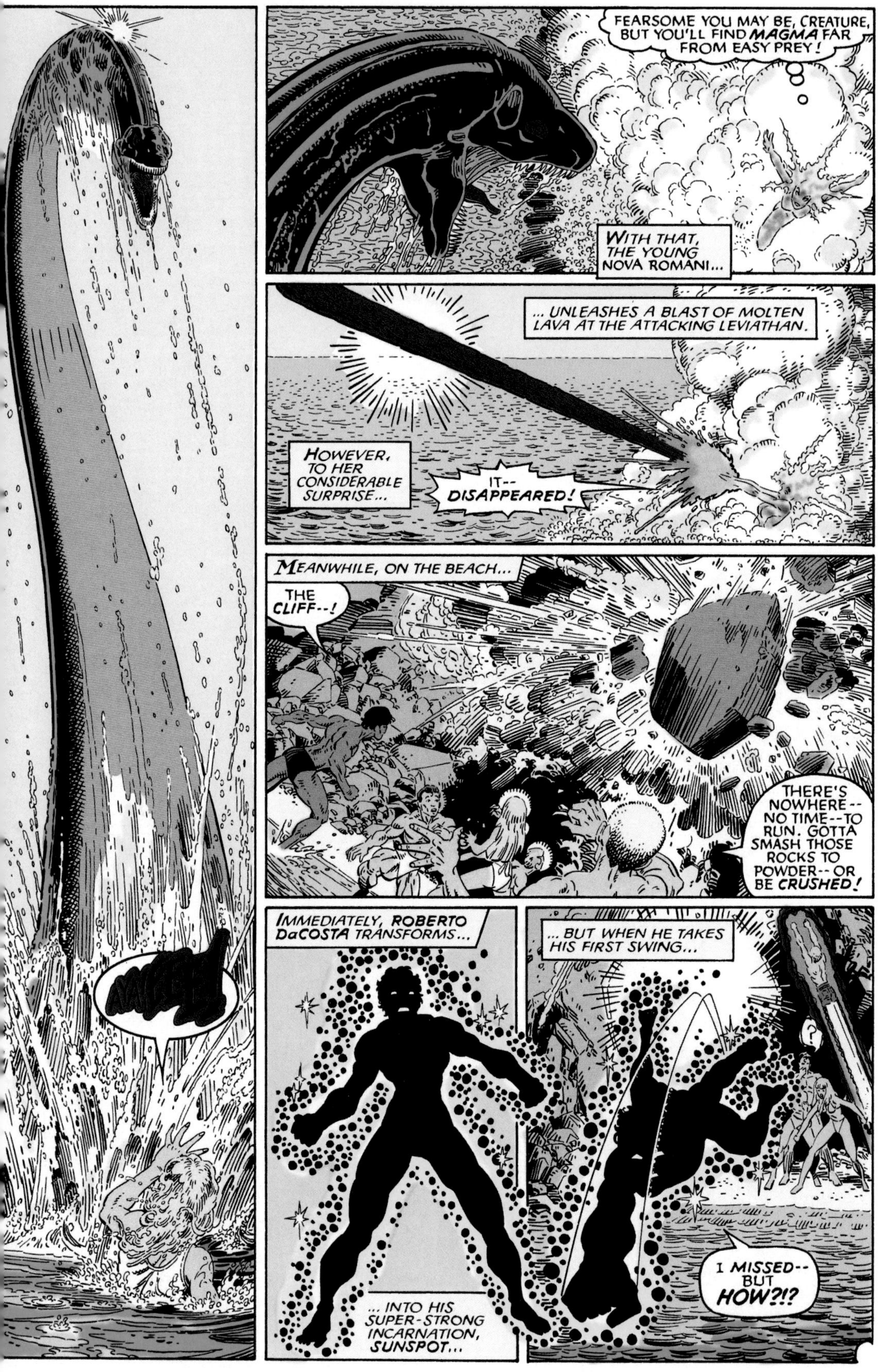

FEARSOME YOU MAY BE, CREATURE, BUT YOU'LL FIND MAGMA FAR FROM EASY PREY!
WITH THAT, THE YOUNG NOVA ROMANI...
... UNLEASHES A BLAST OF MOLTEN LAVA AT THE ATTACKING LEVIATHAN.
HOWEVER, TO HER CONSIDERABLE SURPRISE...
IT-- DISAPPEARED!
MEANWHILE, ON THE BEACH...
THE CLIFF--!
THERE'S NOWHERE-- NO TIME--TO RUN. GOTTA SMASH THOSE ROCKS TO POWDER-- OR BE CRUSHED!
IMMEDIATELY, ROBERTO DaCOSTA TRANSFORMS...
... INTO HIS SUPER-STRONG INCARNATION, SUNSPOT...
... BUT WHEN HE TAKES HIS FIRST SWING...
I MISSED-- BUT HOW?!?

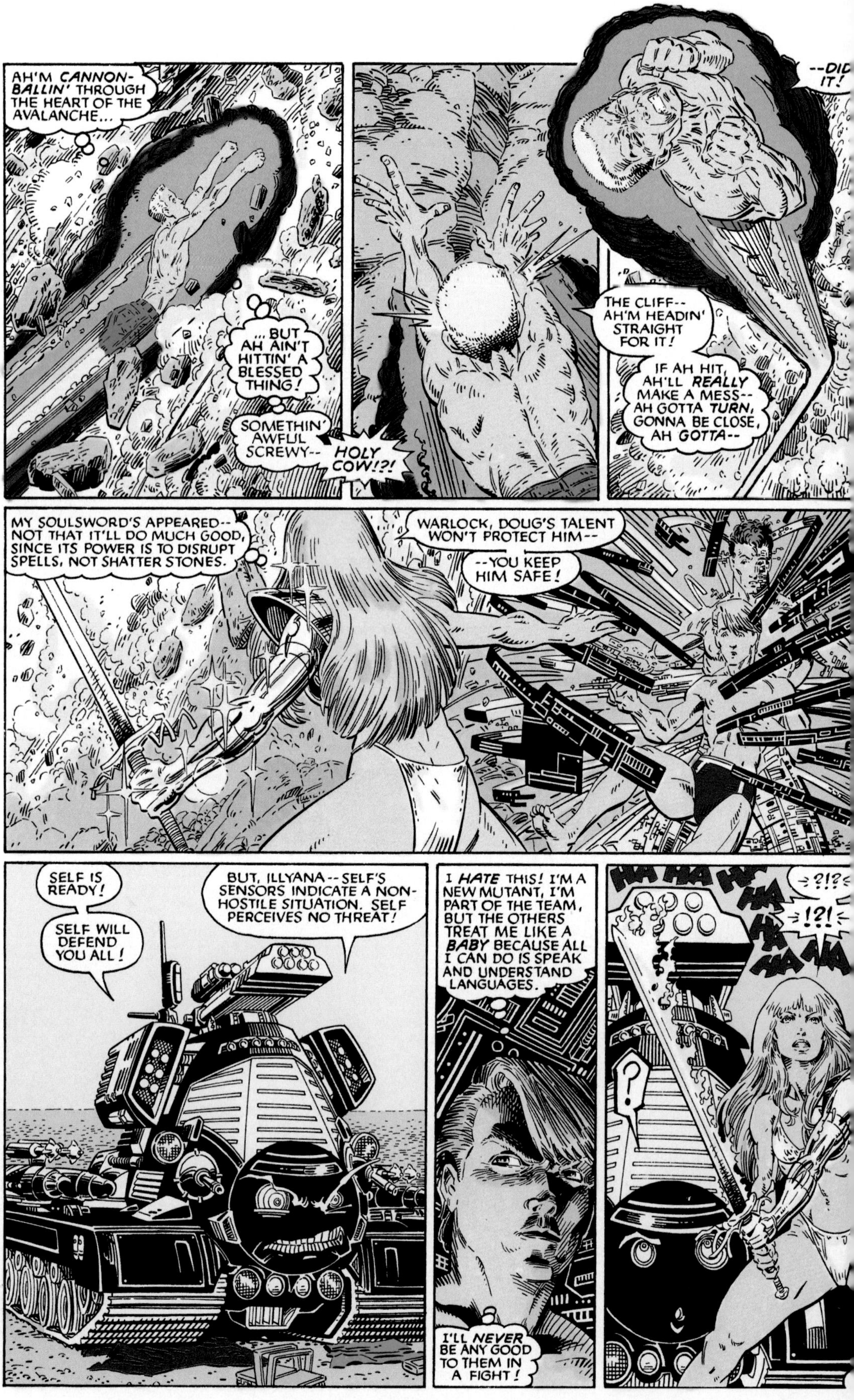
AH'M CANNON-BALLIN' THROUGH THE HEART OF THE AVALANCHE...
...BUT AH AIN'T HITTIN' A BLESSED THING!
SOMETHIN' AWFUL SCREWY--
HOLY COW!?!
--DID IT!
THE CLIFF-- AH'M HEADIN' STRAIGHT FOR IT!
IF AH HIT, AH'LL REALLY MAKE A MESS-- AH GOTTA TURN, GONNA BE CLOSE, AH GOTTA--
MY SOULSWORD'S APPEARED-- NOT THAT IT'LL DO MUCH GOOD, SINCE ITS POWER IS TO DISRUPT SPELLS, NOT SHATTER STONES.
WARLOCK, DOUG'S TALENT WON'T PROTECT HIM--
--YOU KEEP HIM SAFE!
SELF IS READY!
SELF WILL DEFEND YOU ALL!
BUT, ILLYANA--SELF'S SENSORS INDICATE A NON-HOSTILE SITUATION. SELF PERCEIVES NO THREAT!
I HATE THIS! I'M A NEW MUTANT, I'M PART OF THE TEAM, BUT THE OTHERS TREAT ME LIKE A BABY BECAUSE ALL I CAN DO IS SPEAK AND UNDERSTAND LANGUAGES.
?
I'LL NEVER BE ANY GOOD TO THEM IN A FIGHT!
HA HA HA HA HA HA HA HA
?!?
!?!

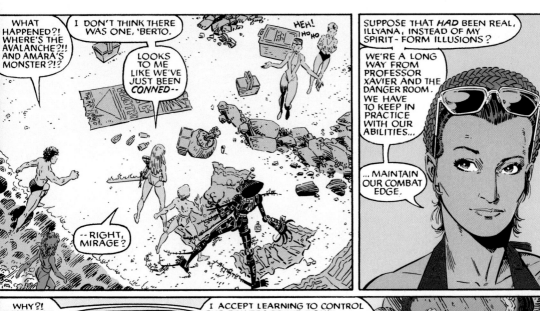

WHAT HAPPENED?! WHERE'S THE AVALANCHE?!! AND AMARA'S MONSTER?!?

I DON'T THINK THERE WAS ONE, 'BERTO.

LOOKS TO ME LIKE WE'VE JUST BEEN *CONNED*--

HEH! HO HO

--RIGHT, MIRAGE?

SUPPOSE THAT *HAD* BEEN REAL, ILLYANA, INSTEAD OF MY SPIRIT-FORM ILLUSIONS?

WE'RE A LONG WAY FROM PROFESSOR XAVIER AND THE DANGER ROOM. WE HAVE TO KEEP IN PRACTICE WITH OUR ABILITIES...

...MAINTAIN OUR COMBAT EDGE.

WHY?! WE'RE NOT THE X-MEN, DANIELLE, WE AREN'T MEANT TO GO LOOKING FOR TROUBLE.

THAT'S RIGHT-- BUT WHAT IF TROUBLE FINDS US, 'BERTO, WHAT THEN?! WE HAVE TO BE ABLE TO HANDLE OURSELVES.

I ACCEPT LEARNING TO CONTROL OUR POWERS SO WE DON'T BECOME A THREAT TO ANYONE, BUT WHY CAN'T WE LIVE NORMAL LIVES IN THE BARGAIN?! IS THAT ASKING SO MUCH?!!

BOBBY HAS A POINT, DANI.

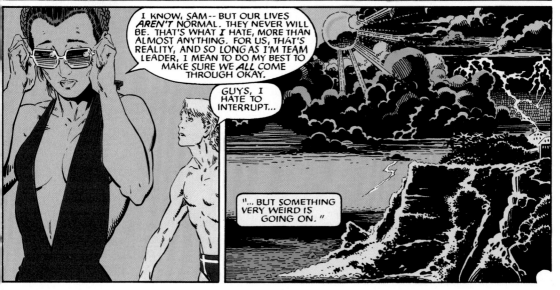

I KNOW, SAM-- BUT OUR LIVES *AREN'T* NORMAL. THEY NEVER WILL BE. THAT'S WHAT *I* HATE, MORE THAN ALMOST ANYTHING. FOR US, THAT'S REALITY, AND SO LONG AS I'M TEAM LEADER, I MEAN TO DO MY BEST TO MAKE SURE WE *ALL* COME THROUGH OKAY.

GUYS, I HATE TO INTERRUPT...

"...BUT SOMETHING VERY WEIRD IS GOING ON."

15

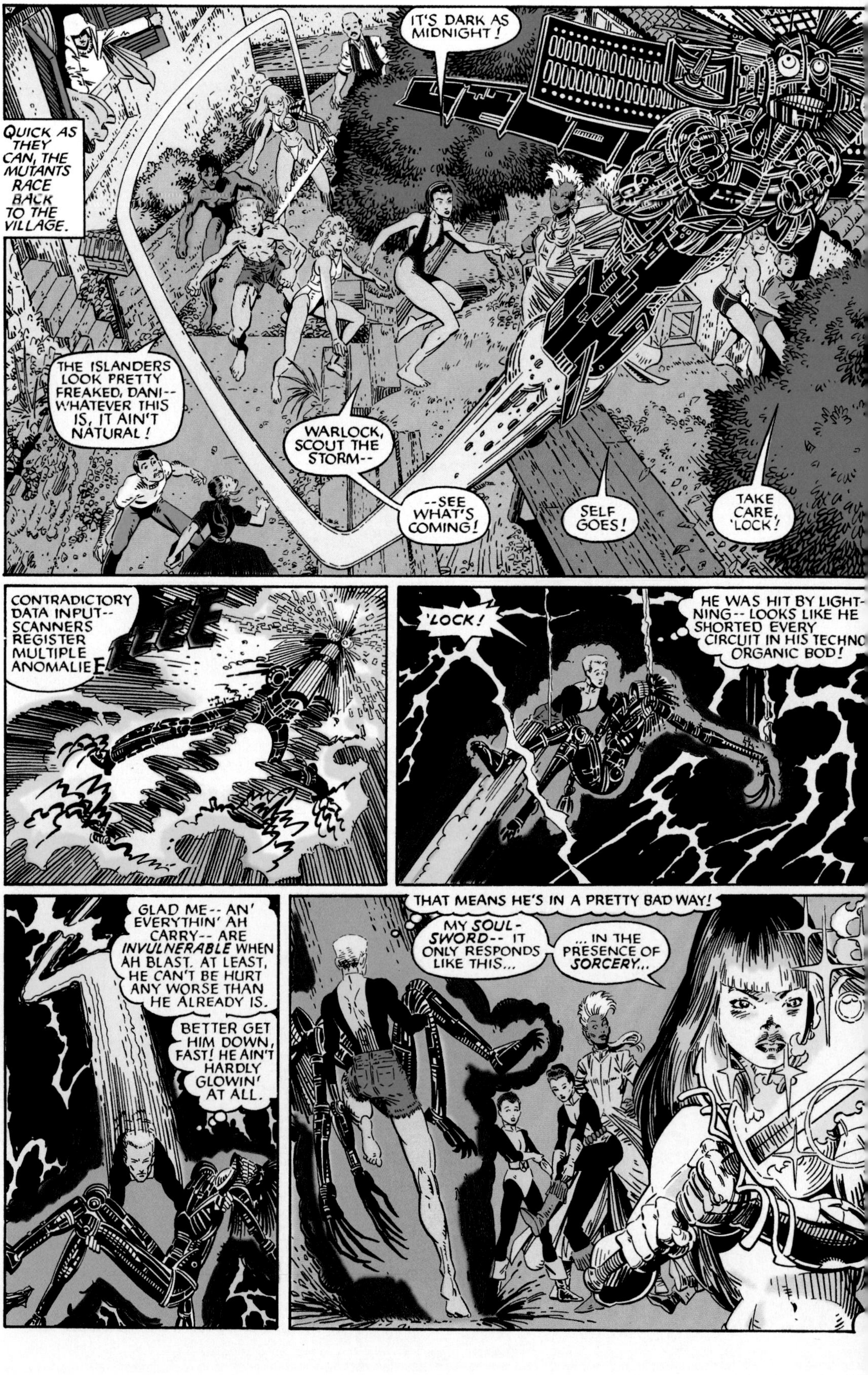
QUICK AS THEY CAN, THE MUTANTS RACE BACK TO THE VILLAGE.
IT'S DARK AS MIDNIGHT!
THE ISLANDERS LOOK PRETTY FREAKED, DANI-- WHATEVER THIS IS, IT AIN'T NATURAL!
WARLOCK, SCOUT THE STORM--
--SEE WHAT'S COMING!
SELF GOES!
TAKE CARE, 'LOCK!
CONTRADICTORY DATA INPUT-- SCANNERS REGISTER MULTIPLE ANOMALIEE
'LOCK!
HE WAS HIT BY LIGHTNING-- LOOKS LIKE HE SHORTED EVERY CIRCUIT IN HIS TECHNO ORGANIC BOD!
GLAD ME-- AN' EVERYTHIN' AH CARRY-- ARE INVULNERABLE WHEN AH BLAST. AT LEAST, HE CAN'T BE HURT ANY WORSE THAN HE ALREADY IS.
BETTER GET HIM DOWN, FAST! HE AIN'T HARDLY GLOWIN' AT ALL.
THAT MEANS HE'S IN A PRETTY BAD WAY!
MY SOUL-SWORD-- IT ONLY RESPONDS LIKE THIS...
...IN THE PRESENCE OF SORCERY...

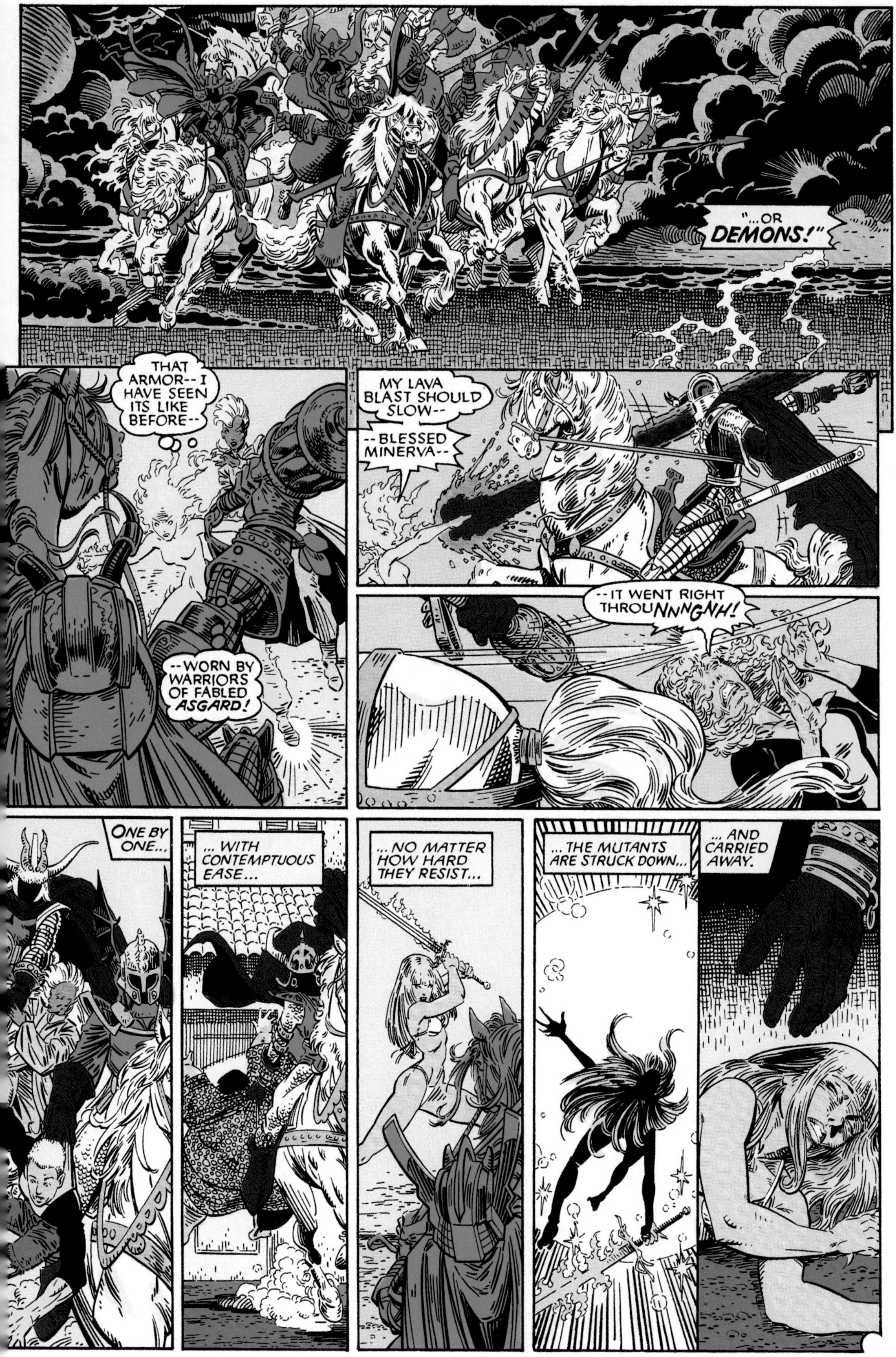
"...OR DEMONS!"
THAT ARMOR-- I HAVE SEEN ITS LIKE BEFORE--
--WORN BY WARRIORS OF FABLED ASGARD!
MY LAVA BLAST SHOULD SLOW--
--BLESSED MINERVA--
--IT WENT RIGHT THROUNNNGNH!
ONE BY ONE...
...WITH CONTEMPTUOUS EASE...
...NO MATTER HOW HARD THEY RESIST...
...THE MUTANTS ARE STRUCK DOWN...
...AND CARRIED AWAY.

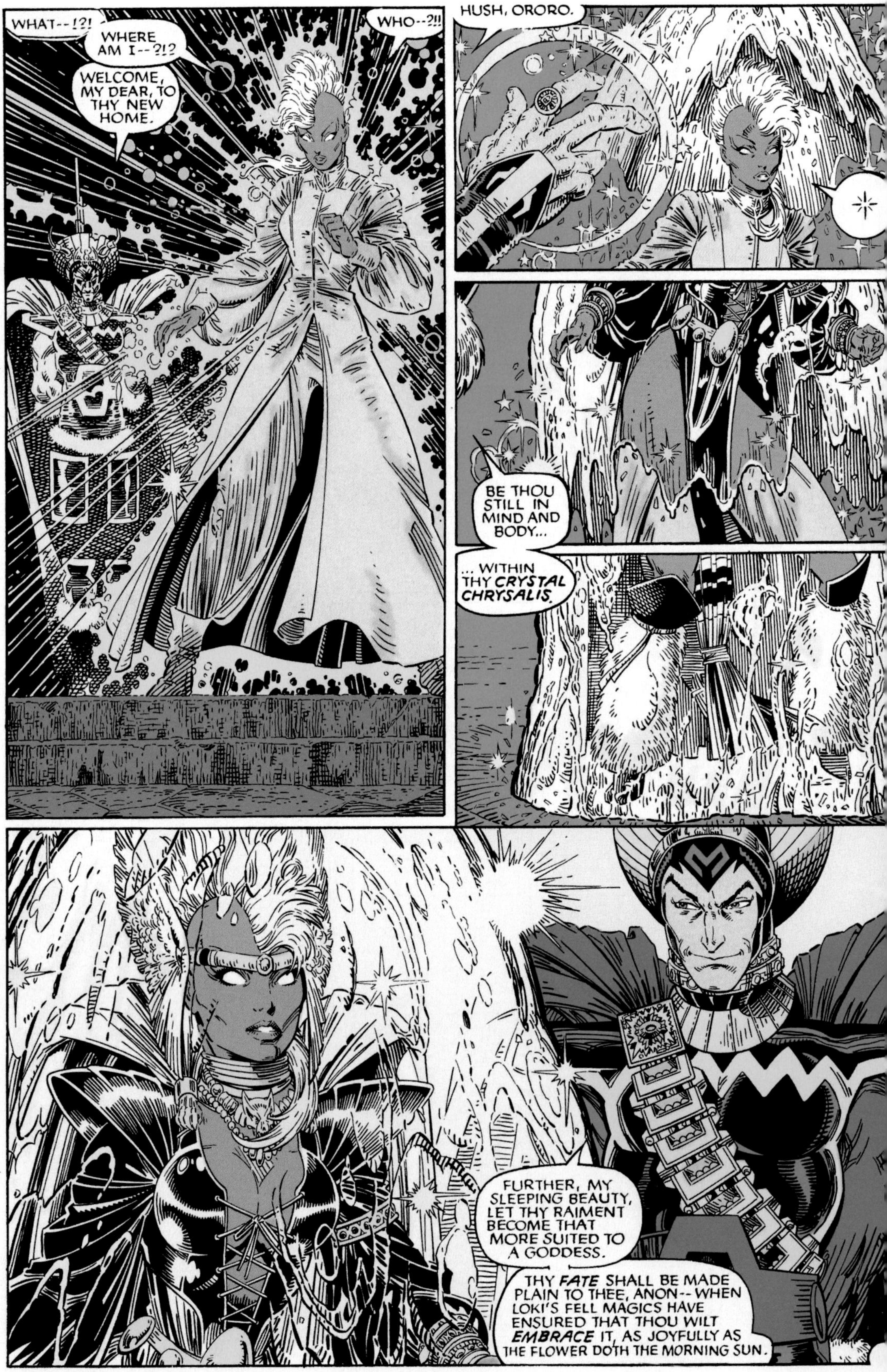
WHAT--!?!
WHERE AM I--?!?
WELCOME, MY DEAR, TO THY NEW HOME.
WHO--?!!
HUSH, ORORO.
BE THOU STILL IN MIND AND BODY...
... WITHIN THY CRYSTAL CHRYSALIS.
FURTHER, MY SLEEPING BEAUTY, LET THY RAIMENT BECOME THAT MORE SUITED TO A GODDESS.
THY FATE SHALL BE MADE PLAIN TO THEE, ANON--WHEN LOKI'S FELL MAGICS HAVE ENSURED THAT THOU WILT EMBRACE IT, AS JOYFULLY AS THE FLOWER DOTH THE MORNING SUN.

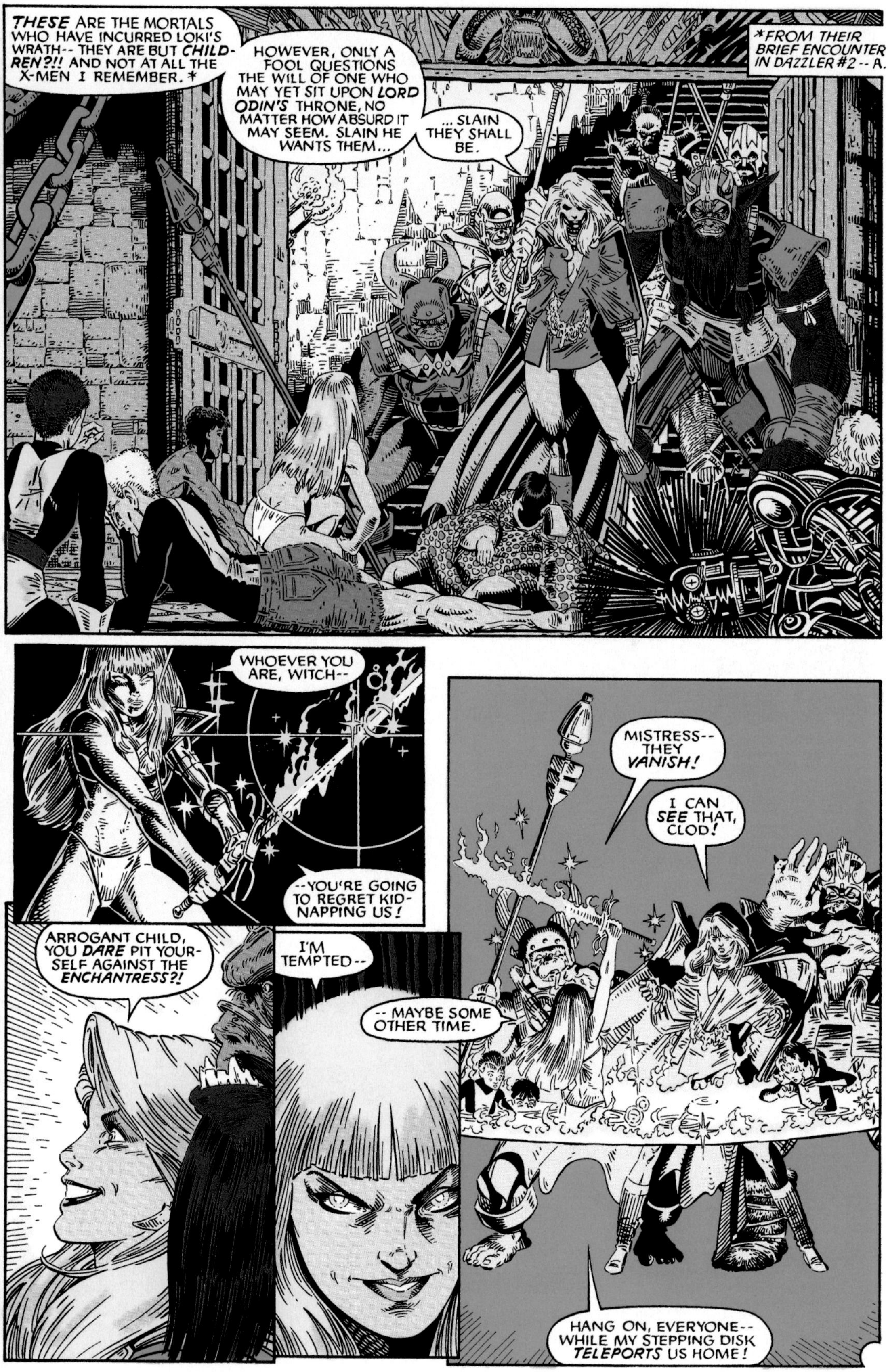
THESE ARE THE MORTALS WHO HAVE INCURRED LOKI'S WRATH-- THEY ARE BUT CHILD-REN?!! AND NOT AT ALL THE X-MEN I REMEMBER.*
HOWEVER, ONLY A FOOL QUESTIONS THE WILL OF ONE WHO MAY YET SIT UPON LORD ODIN'S THRONE, NO MATTER HOW ABSURD IT MAY SEEM. SLAIN HE WANTS THEM...
... SLAIN THEY SHALL BE.
*FROM THEIR BRIEF ENCOUNTER IN DAZZLER #2 -- A.
WHOEVER YOU ARE, WITCH--
--YOU'RE GOING TO REGRET KID-NAPPING US!
ARROGANT CHILD, YOU DARE PIT YOUR-SELF AGAINST THE ENCHANTRESS?!
I'M TEMPTED--
-- MAYBE SOME OTHER TIME.
MISTRESS-- THEY VANISH!
I CAN SEE THAT, CLOD!
HANG ON, EVERYONE-- WHILE MY STEPPING DISK TELEPORTS US HOME!

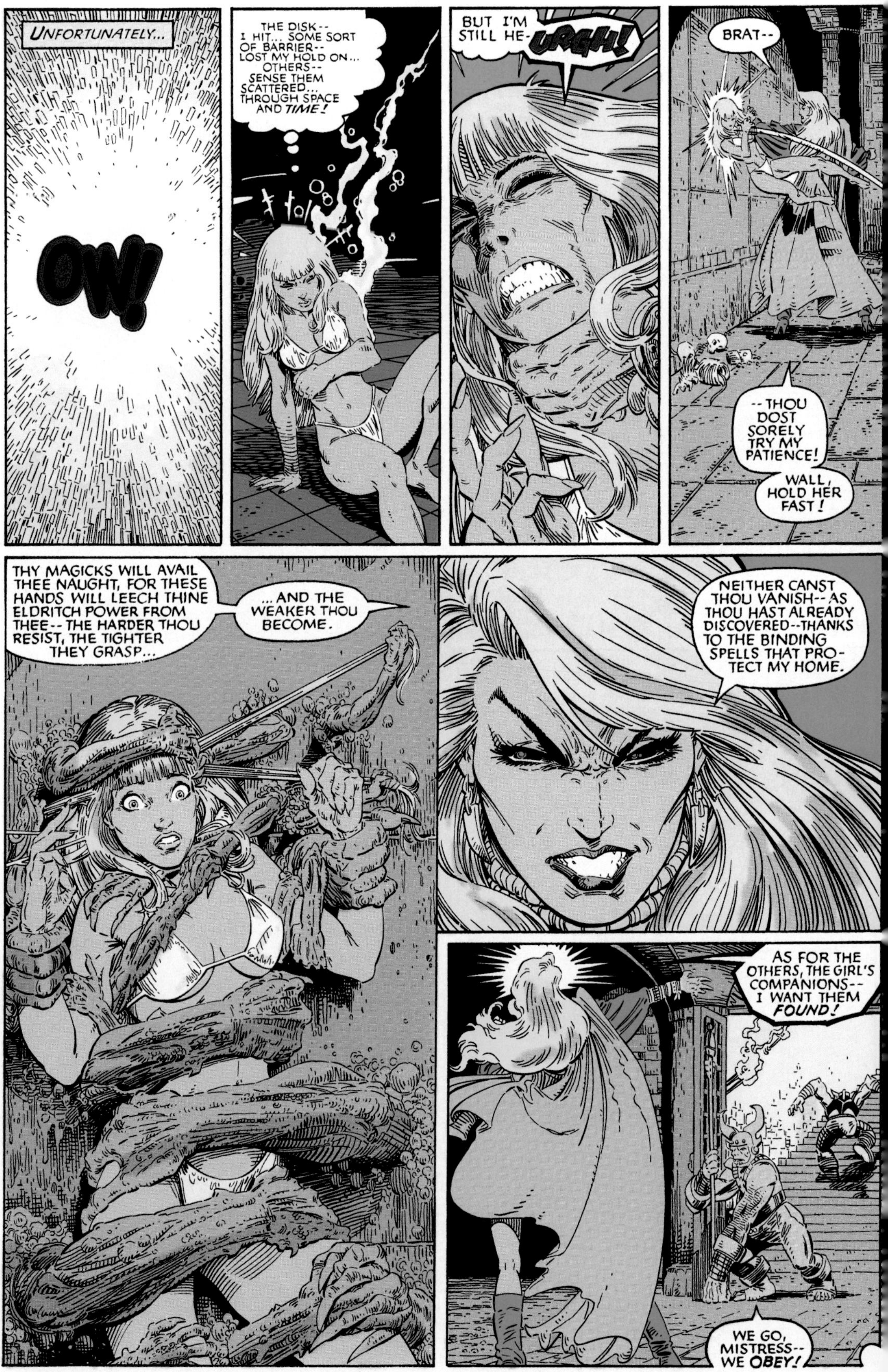

UNFORTUNATELY...
OW!
THE DISK-- I HIT... SOME SORT OF BARRIER-- LOST MY HOLD ON... OTHERS-- SENSE THEM SCATTERED... THROUGH SPACE AND TIME!
BUT I'M STILL HE-
URGH!
BRAT--
--THOU DOST SORELY TRY MY PATIENCE!
WALL, HOLD HER FAST!
THY MAGICKS WILL AVAIL THEE NAUGHT, FOR THESE HANDS WILL LEECH THINE ELDRITCH POWER FROM THEE-- THE HARDER THOU RESIST, THE TIGHTER THEY GRASP...
...AND THE WEAKER THOU BECOME.
NEITHER CANST THOU VANISH--AS THOU HAST ALREADY DISCOVERED--THANKS TO THE BINDING SPELLS THAT PROTECT MY HOME.
AS FOR THE OTHERS, THE GIRL'S COMPANIONS-- I WANT THEM FOUND!
WE GO, MISTRESS-- WE OBEY!

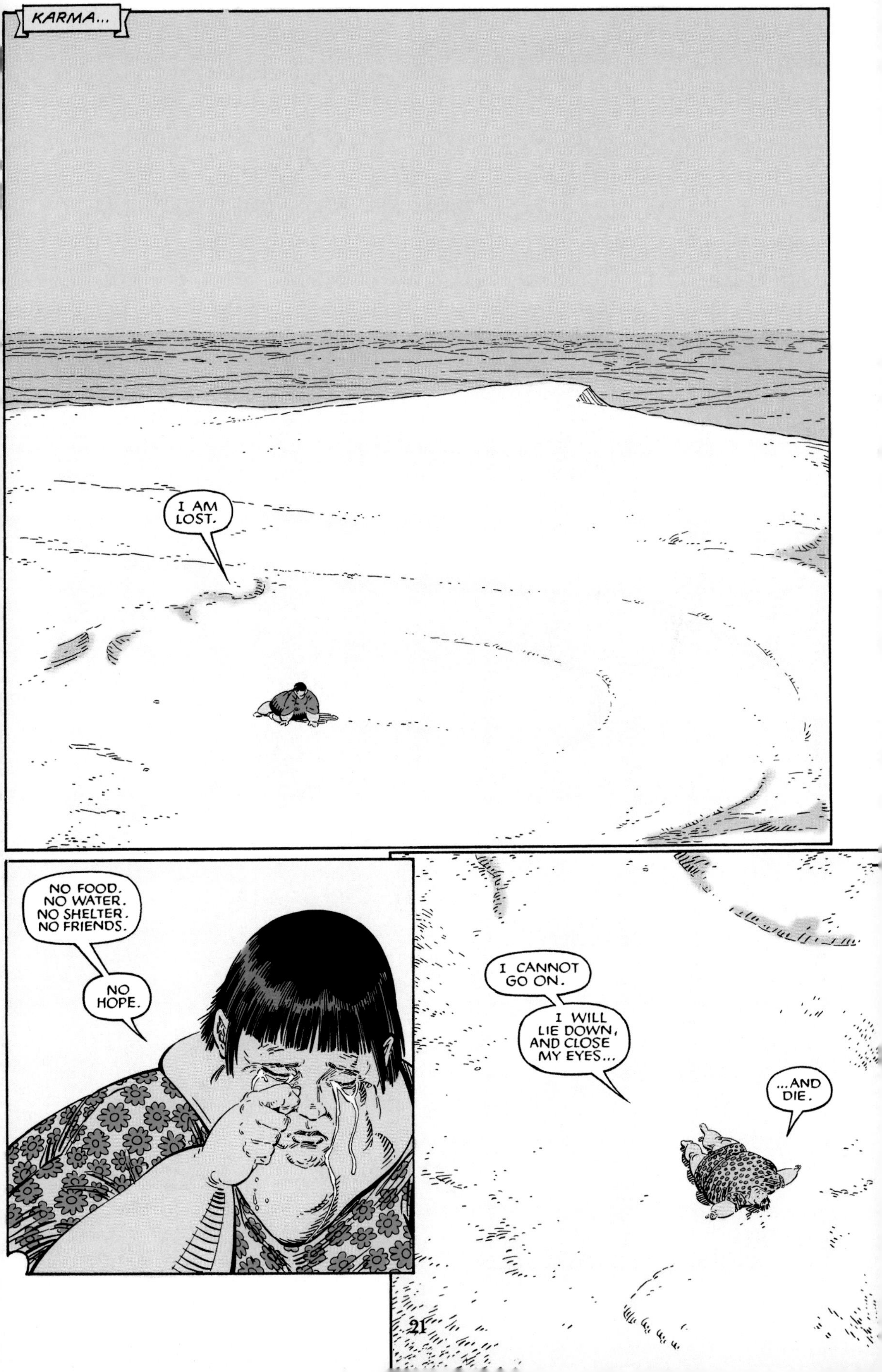
KARMA...
I AM LOST.
NO FOOD. NO WATER. NO SHELTER. NO FRIENDS.
NO HOPE.
I CANNOT GO ON.
I WILL LIE DOWN, AND CLOSE MY EYES...
...AND DIE.

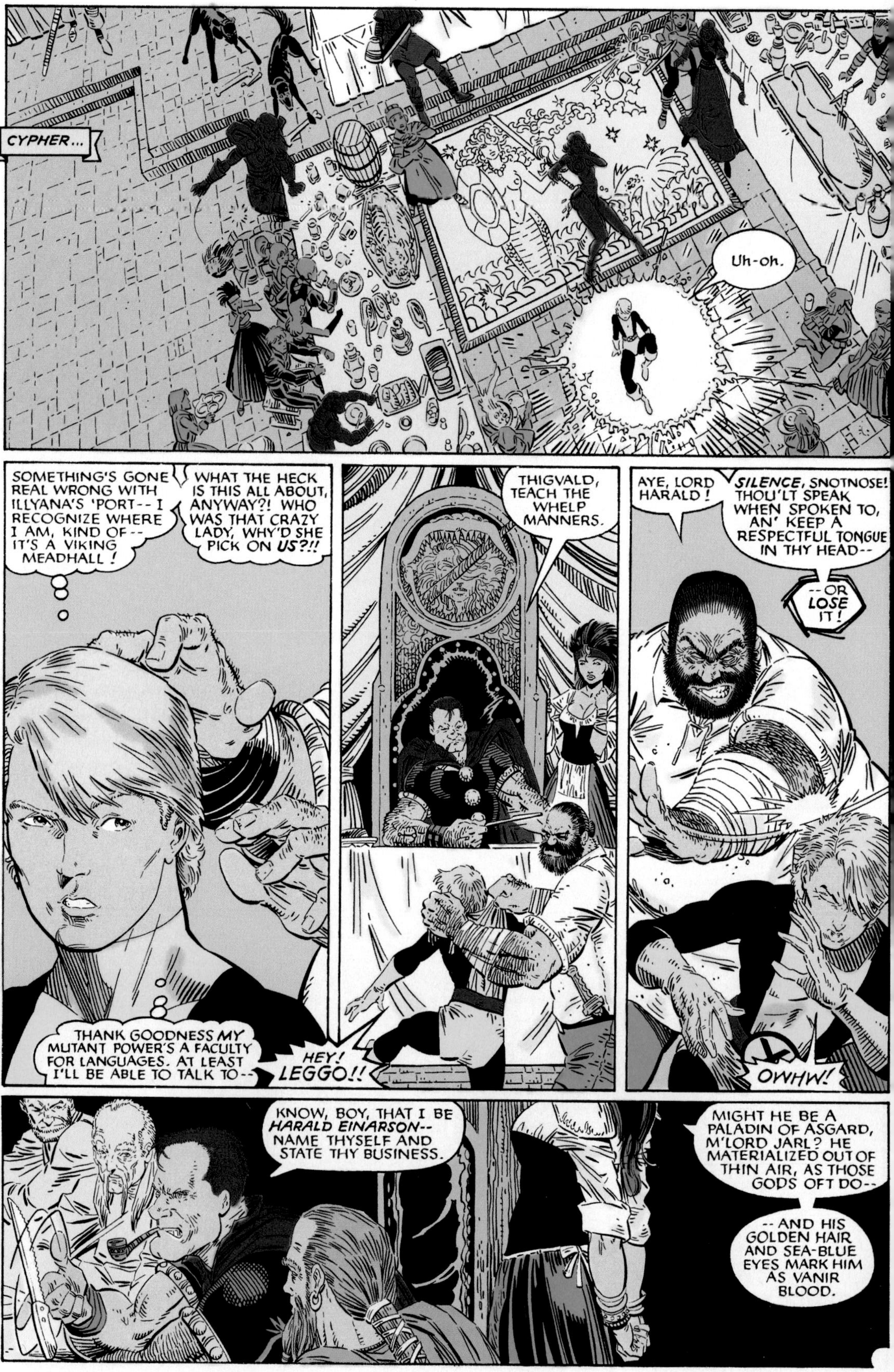
CYPHER...
Uh-oh.
SOMETHING'S GONE REAL WRONG WITH ILLYANA'S 'PORT-- I RECOGNIZE WHERE I AM, KIND OF-- IT'S A VIKING MEADHALL!
WHAT THE HECK IS THIS ALL ABOUT, ANYWAY?! WHO WAS THAT CRAZY LADY, WHY'D SHE PICK ON US?!!
THANK GOODNESS MY MUTANT POWER'S A FACULTY FOR LANGUAGES. AT LEAST I'LL BE ABLE TO TALK TO--
THIGVALD, TEACH THE WHELP MANNERS.
HEY! LEGGO!!
AYE, LORD HARALD!
SILENCE, SNOTNOSE! THOU'LT SPEAK WHEN SPOKEN TO, AN' KEEP A RESPECTFUL TONGUE IN THY HEAD--
--OR LOSE IT!
OWHW!
KNOW, BOY, THAT I BE HARALD EINARSON-- NAME THYSELF AND STATE THY BUSINESS.
MIGHT HE BE A PALADIN OF ASGARD, M'LORD JARL? HE MATERIALIZED OUT OF THIN AIR, AS THOSE GODS OFT DO--
--AND HIS GOLDEN HAIR AND SEA-BLUE EYES MARK HIM AS VANIR BLOOD.

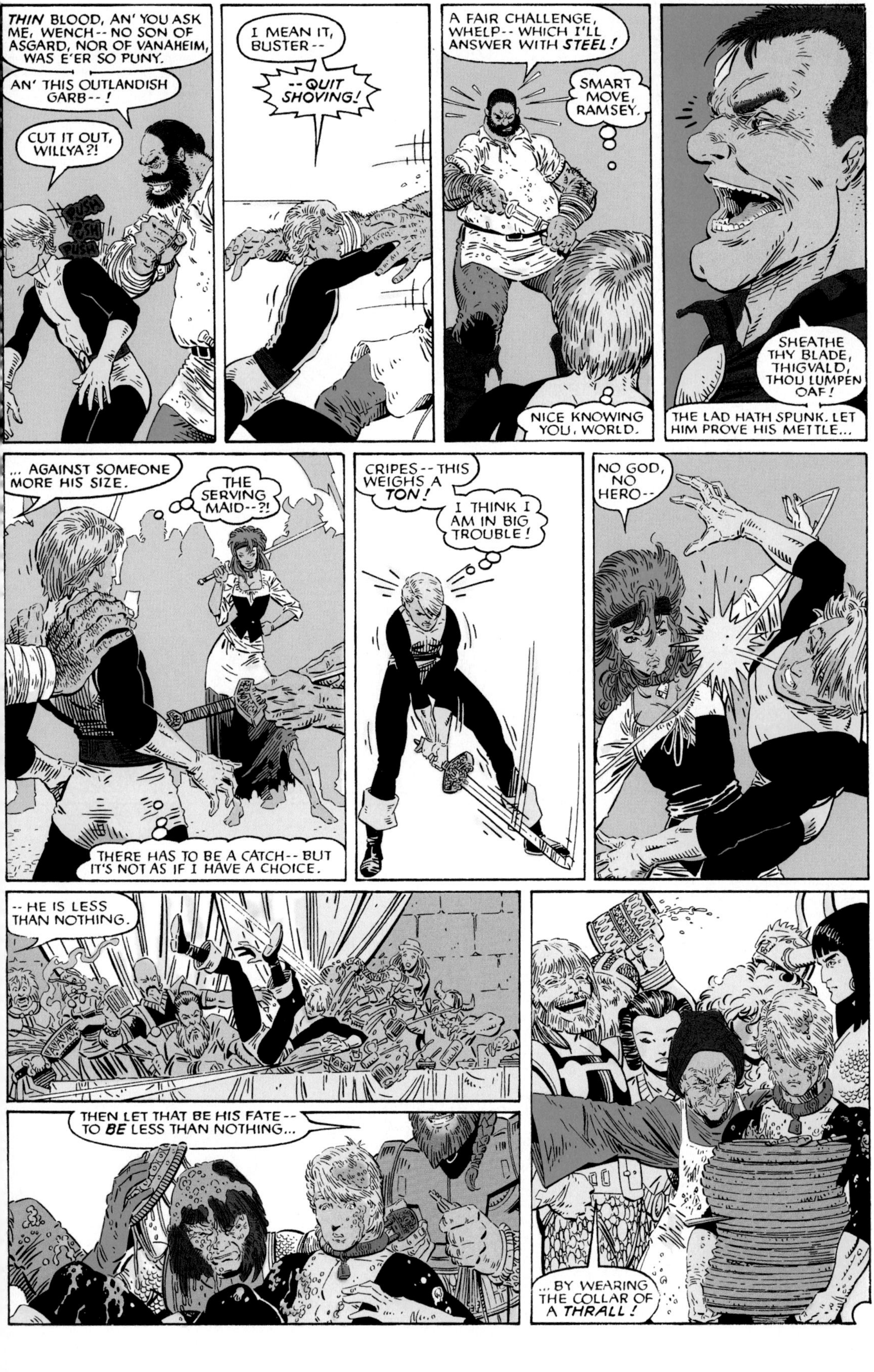
THIN BLOOD, AN' YOU ASK ME, WENCH-- NO SON OF ASGARD, NOR OF VANAHEIM, WAS E'ER SO PUNY.
AN' THIS OUTLANDISH GARB--!
CUT IT OUT, WILLYA?!
PUSH
PUSH
PUSH
I MEAN IT, BUSTER--
--QUIT SHOVING!
A FAIR CHALLENGE, WHELP-- WHICH I'LL ANSWER WITH STEEL!
SMART MOVE, RAMSEY.
NICE KNOWING YOU, WORLD.
SHEATHE THY BLADE, THIGVALD, THOU LUMPEN OAF!
THE LAD HATH SPUNK. LET HIM PROVE HIS METTLE...
...AGAINST SOMEONE MORE HIS SIZE.
THE SERVING MAID--?!
THERE HAS TO BE A CATCH-- BUT IT'S NOT AS IF I HAVE A CHOICE.
CRIPES-- THIS WEIGHS A TON!
I THINK I AM IN BIG TROUBLE!
NO GOD, NO HERO--
--HE IS LESS THAN NOTHING.
THEN LET THAT BE HIS FATE-- TO BE LESS THAN NOTHING...
...BY WEARING THE COLLAR OF A THRALL!

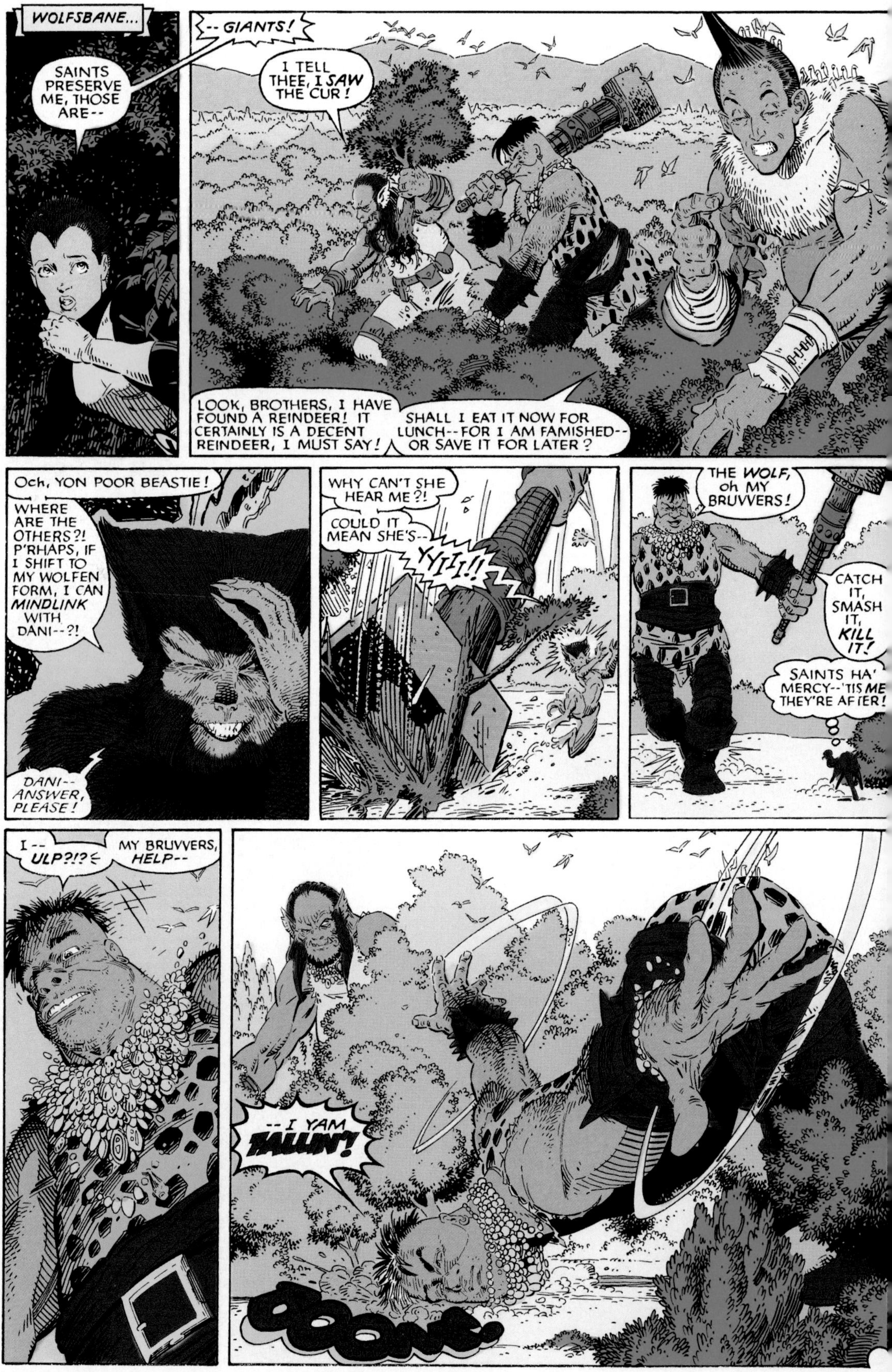
WOLFSBANE...
SAINTS PRESERVE ME, THOSE ARE--
--GIANTS!
I TELL THEE, I SAW THE CUR!
LOOK, BROTHERS, I HAVE FOUND A REINDEER! IT CERTAINLY IS A DECENT REINDEER, I MUST SAY!
SHALL I EAT IT NOW FOR LUNCH--FOR I AM FAMISHED--OR SAVE IT FOR LATER?
Och, YON POOR BEASTIE!
WHERE ARE THE OTHERS?! P'RHAPS, IF I SHIFT TO MY WOLFEN FORM, I CAN MINDLINK WITH DANI--?!
DANI--ANSWER, PLEASE!
WHY CAN'T SHE HEAR ME?!
COULD IT MEAN SHE'S--
YYIII!!
THE WOLF, oh MY BRUVVERS!
CATCH IT, SMASH IT, KILL IT!
SAINTS HA' MERCY--'TIS ME THEY'RE AFTER!
I--ULP?!?
MY BRUVVERS, HELP--
--I YAM FALLIN'!
DOOM!

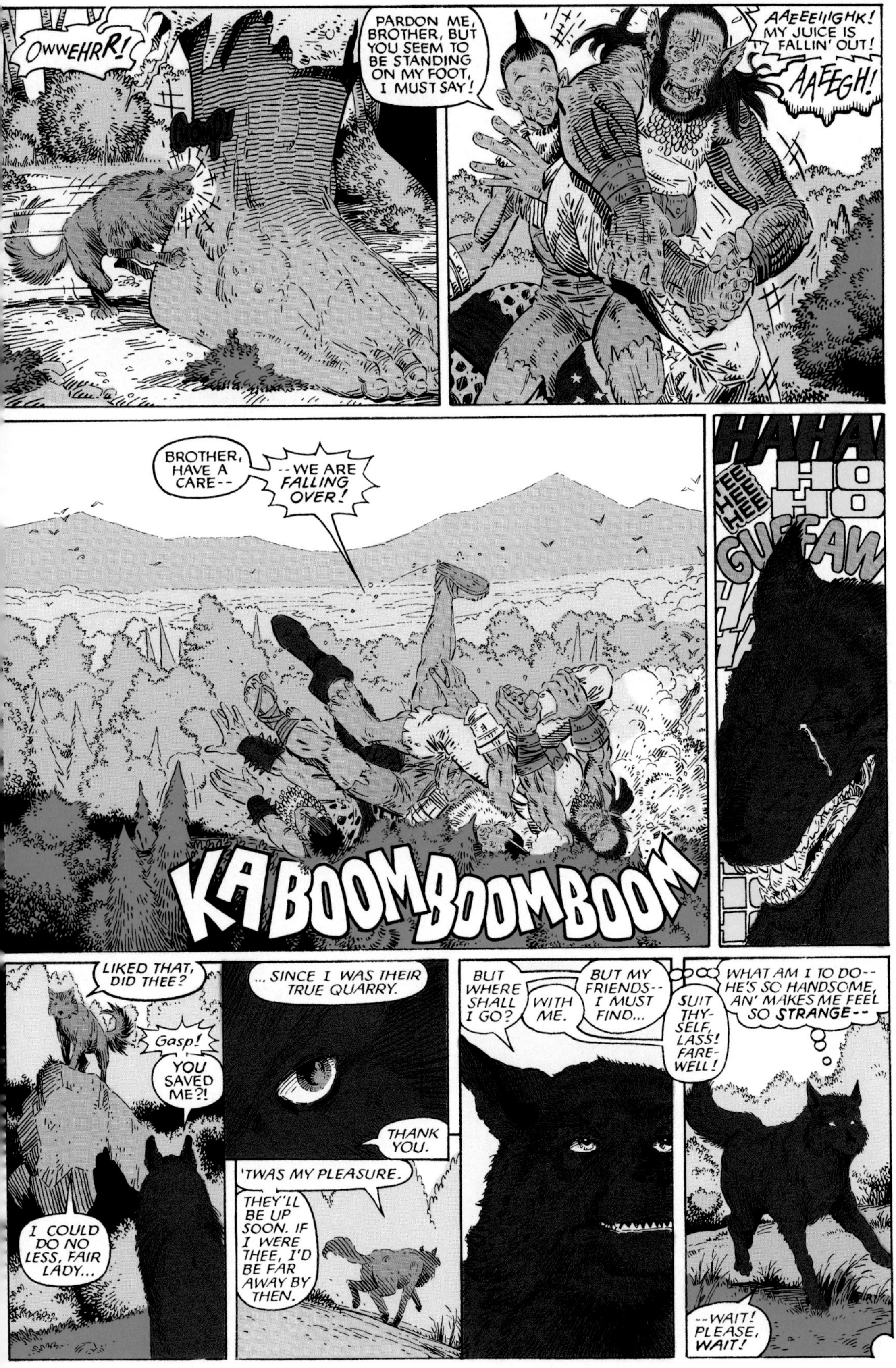
OWWEHRR!
GOMP!
PARDON ME, BROTHER, BUT YOU SEEM TO BE STANDING ON MY FOOT, I MUST SAY!
AAEEEIIIGHK! MY JUICE IS FALLIN' OUT!
AAEEGH!
BROTHER, HAVE A CARE--
--WE ARE FALLING OVER!
KA BOOM BOOM BOOM
HAHA
HO HO
HEE HEE
GUFFAW
LIKED THAT, DID THEE?
Gasp!
YOU SAVED ME?!
I COULD DO NO LESS, FAIR LADY...
...SINCE I WAS THEIR TRUE QUARRY.
THANK YOU.
'TWAS MY PLEASURE.
THEY'LL BE UP SOON. IF I WERE THEE, I'D BE FAR AWAY BY THEN.
BUT WHERE SHALL I GO?
WITH ME.
BUT MY FRIENDS-- I MUST FIND...
SUIT THYSELF, LASS! FAREWELL!
WHAT AM I TO DO-- HE'S SO HANDSOME, AN' MAKES ME FEEL SO STRANGE--
--WAIT! PLEASE, WAIT!

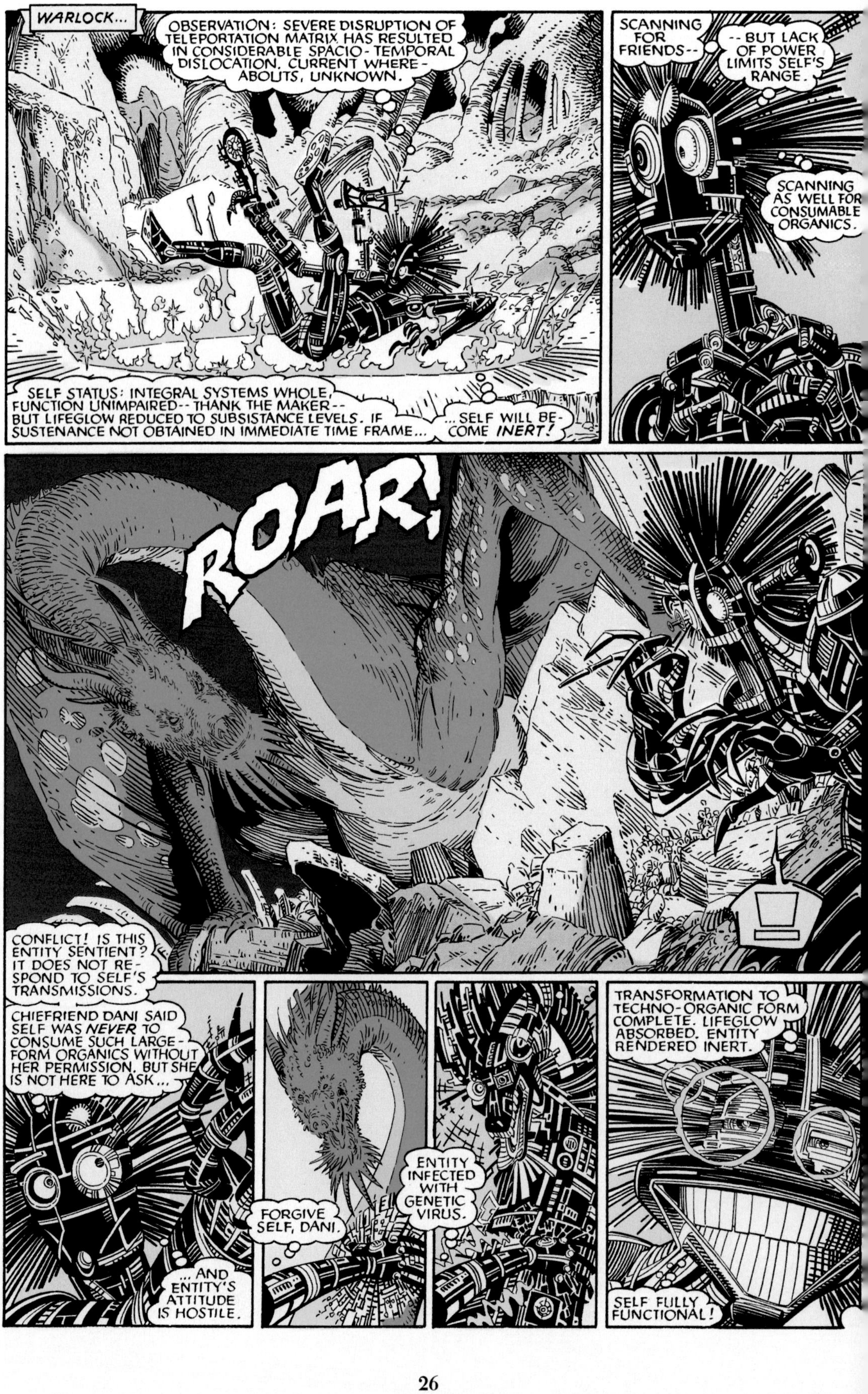
WARLOCK...
OBSERVATION: SEVERE DISRUPTION OF TELEPORTATION MATRIX HAS RESULTED IN CONSIDERABLE SPACIO-TEMPORAL DISLOCATION. CURRENT WHEREABOUTS, UNKNOWN.
SELF STATUS: INTEGRAL SYSTEMS WHOLE, FUNCTION UNIMPAIRED-- THANK THE MAKER-- BUT LIFEGLOW REDUCED TO SUBSISTANCE LEVELS. IF SUSTENANCE NOT OBTAINED IN IMMEDIATE TIME FRAME...
...SELF WILL BECOME *INERT!*
SCANNING FOR FRIENDS--
--BUT LACK OF POWER LIMITS SELF'S RANGE.
SCANNING AS WELL FOR CONSUMABLE ORGANICS.
ROAR!
CONFLICT! IS THIS ENTITY SENTIENT? IT DOES NOT RESPOND TO SELF'S TRANSMISSIONS.
CHIEFRIEND DANI SAID SELF WAS *NEVER* TO CONSUME SUCH LARGE-FORM ORGANICS WITHOUT HER PERMISSION. BUT SHE IS NOT HERE TO ASK...
...AND ENTITY'S ATTITUDE IS HOSTILE.
FORGIVE SELF, DANI.
ENTITY INFECTED WITH GENETIC VIRUS.
TRANSFORMATION TO TECHNO-ORGANIC FORM COMPLETE. LIFEGLOW ABSORBED. ENTITY RENDERED INERT.
SELF FULLY FUNCTIONAL!

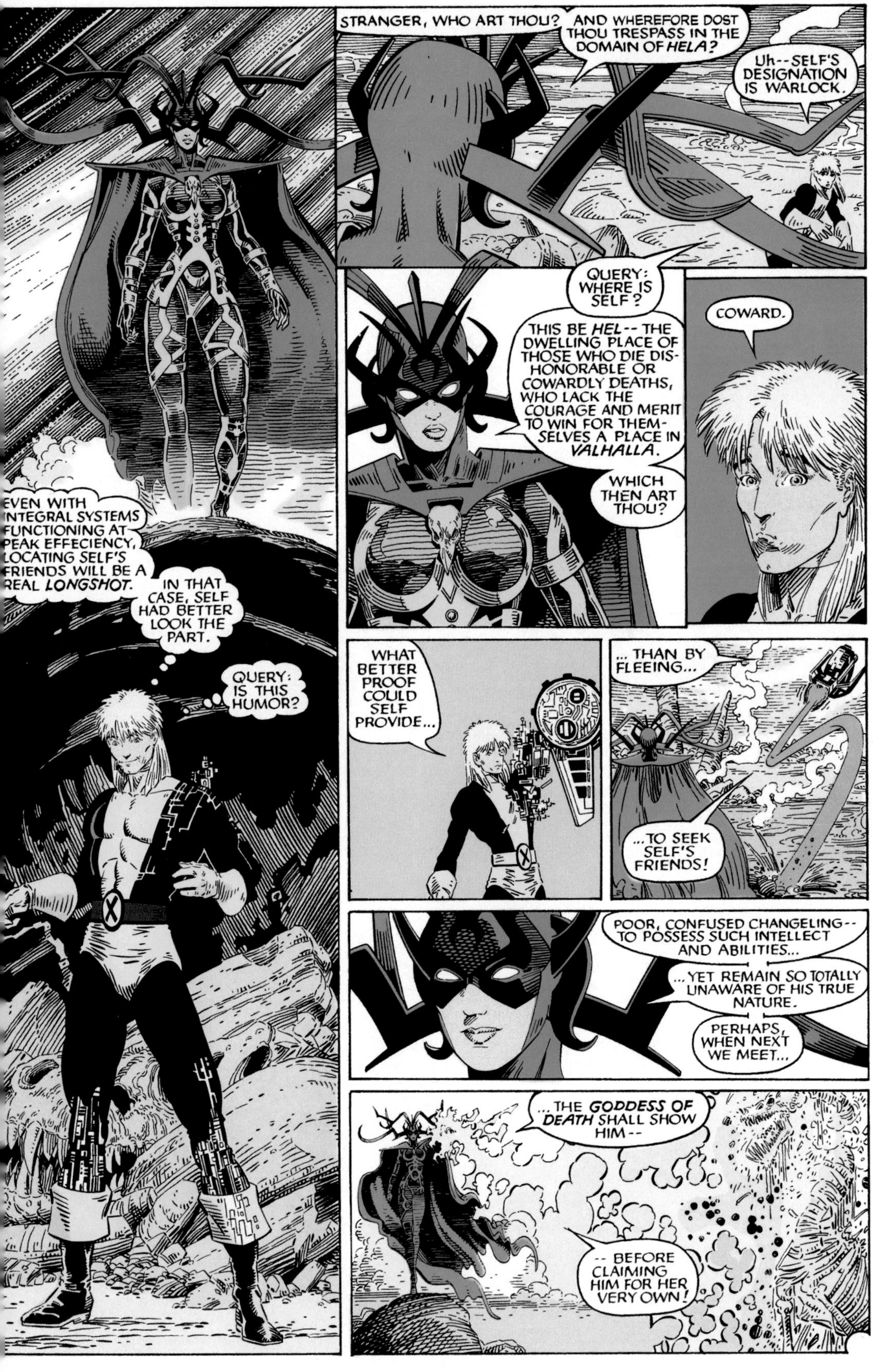

STRANGER, WHO ART THOU?
AND WHEREFORE DOST THOU TRESPASS IN THE DOMAIN OF HELA?
Uh--SELF'S DESIGNATION IS WARLOCK.
QUERY: WHERE IS SELF?
THIS BE HEL-- THE DWELLING PLACE OF THOSE WHO DIE DIS-HONORABLE OR COWARDLY DEATHS, WHO LACK THE COURAGE AND MERIT TO WIN FOR THEM-SELVES A PLACE IN VALHALLA.
WHICH THEN ART THOU?
COWARD.
EVEN WITH INTEGRAL SYSTEMS FUNCTIONING AT PEAK EFFECIENCY, LOCATING SELF'S FRIENDS WILL BE A REAL LONGSHOT.
IN THAT CASE, SELF HAD BETTER LOOK THE PART.
QUERY: IS THIS HUMOR?
WHAT BETTER PROOF COULD SELF PROVIDE...
... THAN BY FLEEING...
...TO SEEK SELF'S FRIENDS!
POOR, CONFUSED CHANGELING-- TO POSSESS SUCH INTELLECT AND ABILITIES...
...YET REMAIN SO TOTALLY UNAWARE OF HIS TRUE NATURE.
PERHAPS, WHEN NEXT WE MEET...
...THE GODDESS OF DEATH SHALL SHOW HIM--
-- BEFORE CLAIMING HIM FOR HER VERY OWN!

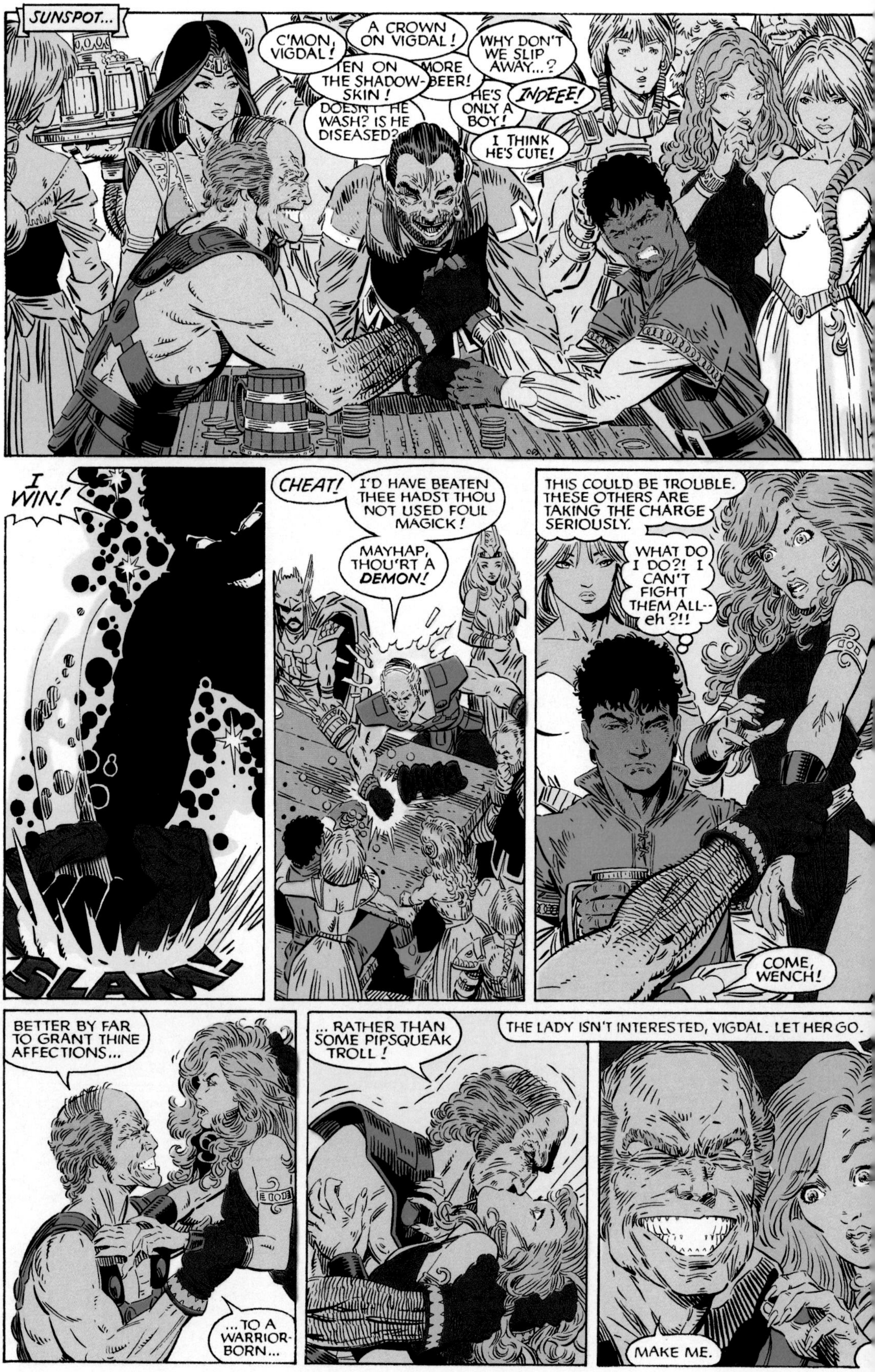
SUNSPOT...
C'MON, VIGDAL!
A CROWN ON VIGDAL!
TEN ON THE SHADOW-SKIN!
MORE BEER!
DOESN'T HE WASH? IS HE DISEASED?
WHY DON'T WE SLIP AWAY...?
HE'S ONLY A BOY!
INDEEE!
I THINK HE'S CUTE!
I WIN!
SLAM!
CHEAT!
I'D HAVE BEATEN THEE HADST THOU NOT USED FOUL MAGICK!
MAYHAP, THOU'RT A DEMON!
THIS COULD BE TROUBLE. THESE OTHERS ARE TAKING THE CHARGE SERIOUSLY.
WHAT DO I DO?! I CAN'T FIGHT THEM ALL--eh?!!
COME, WENCH!
BETTER BY FAR TO GRANT THINE AFFECTIONS...
...TO A WARRIOR-BORN...
... RATHER THAN SOME PIPSQUEAK TROLL!
THE LADY ISN'T INTERESTED, VIGDAL. LET HER GO.
MAKE ME.

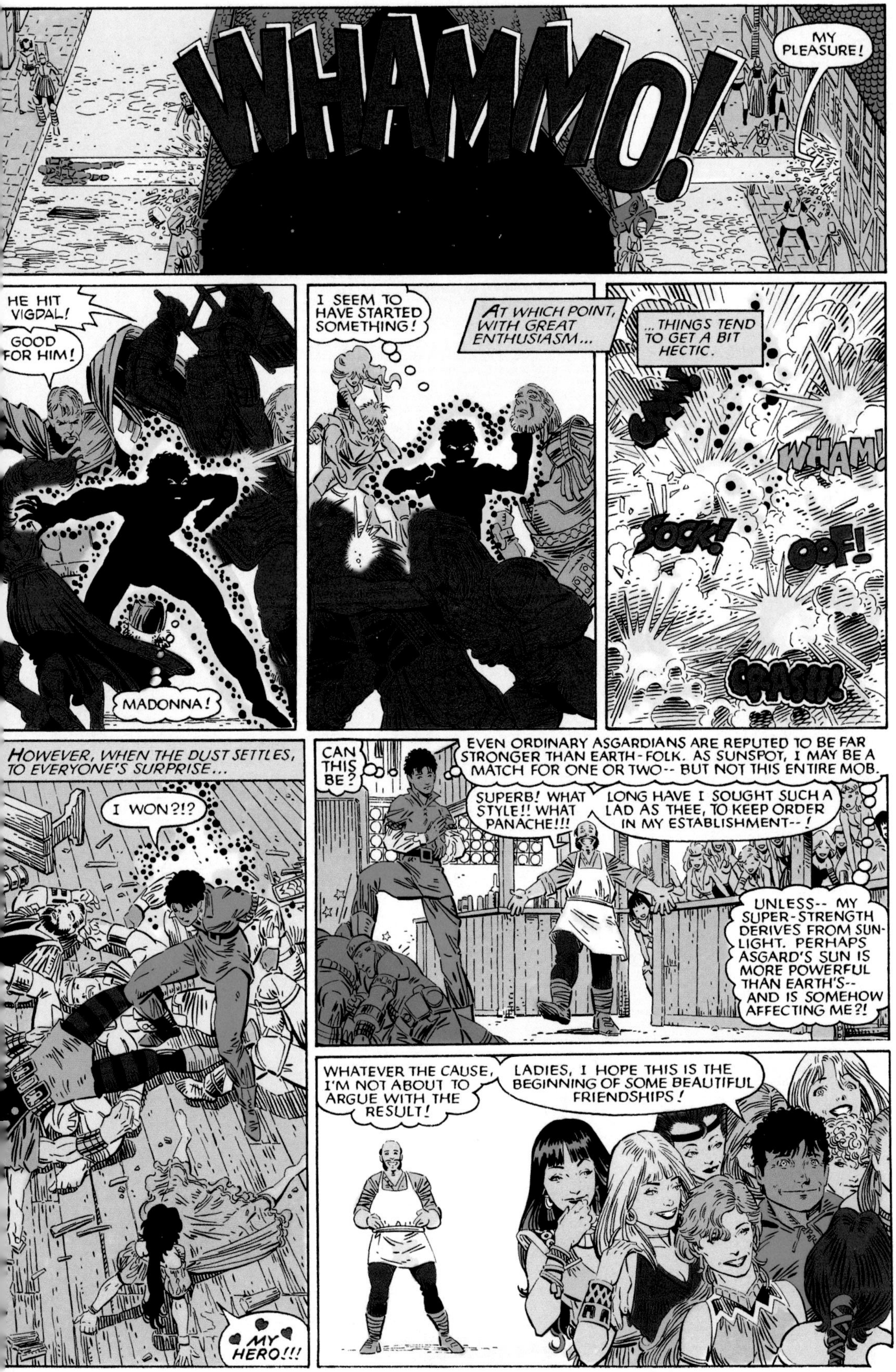
WHAMMO!
MY PLEASURE!
HE HIT VIGDAL!
GOOD FOR HIM!
MADONNA!
I SEEM TO HAVE STARTED SOMETHING!
AT WHICH POINT, WITH GREAT ENTHUSIASM...
...THINGS TEND TO GET A BIT HECTIC.
WHAM!
SOCK!
OOF!
CRASH!
HOWEVER, WHEN THE DUST SETTLES, TO EVERYONE'S SURPRISE...
I WON?!?
MY HERO!!!
CAN THIS BE?
EVEN ORDINARY ASGARDIANS ARE REPUTED TO BE FAR STRONGER THAN EARTH-FOLK. AS SUNSPOT, I MAY BE A MATCH FOR ONE OR TWO-- BUT NOT THIS ENTIRE MOB.
SUPERB! WHAT STYLE!! WHAT PANACHE!!!
LONG HAVE I SOUGHT SUCH A LAD AS THEE, TO KEEP ORDER IN MY ESTABLISHMENT-- !
UNLESS-- MY SUPER-STRENGTH DERIVES FROM SUNLIGHT. PERHAPS ASGARD'S SUN IS MORE POWERFUL THAN EARTH'S-- AND IS SOMEHOW AFFECTING ME?!
WHATEVER THE CAUSE, I'M NOT ABOUT TO ARGUE WITH THE RESULT!
LADIES, I HOPE THIS IS THE BEGINNING OF SOME BEAUTIFUL FRIENDSHIPS!

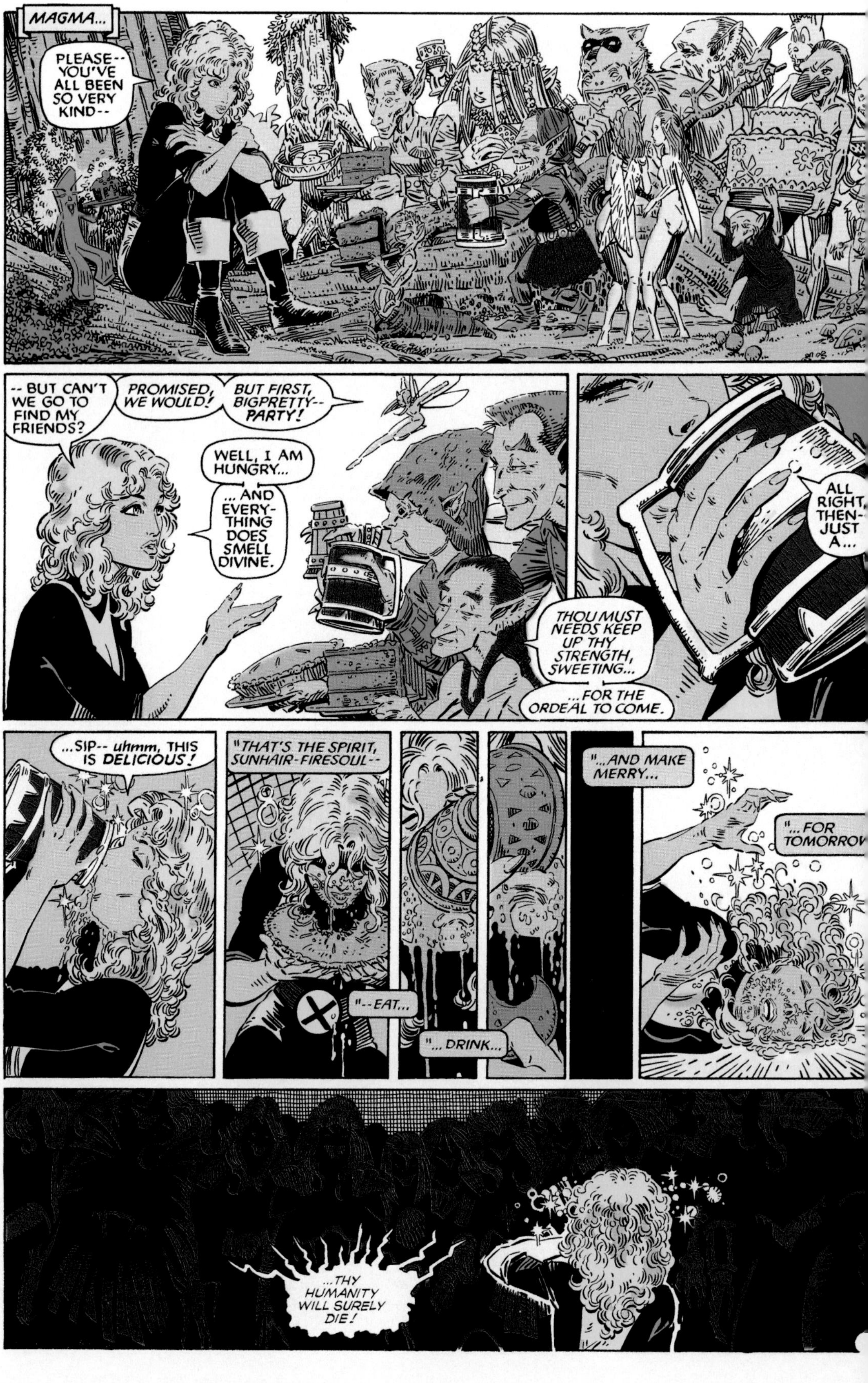
MAGMA...
PLEASE-- YOU'VE ALL BEEN SO VERY KIND--
-- BUT CAN'T WE GO TO FIND MY FRIENDS?
PROMISED, WE WOULD!
BUT FIRST, BIGPRETTY-- PARTY!
WELL, I AM HUNGRY...
... AND EVERYTHING DOES SMELL DIVINE.
THOU MUST NEEDS KEEP UP THY STRENGTH, SWEETING...
... FOR THE ORDEAL TO COME.
ALL RIGHT, THEN-- JUST A...
... SIP-- uhmm, THIS IS DELICIOUS!
"THAT'S THE SPIRIT, SUNHAIR-FIRESOUL--
"--EAT...
"... DRINK...
"... AND MAKE MERRY...
"... FOR TOMORROW
... THY HUMANITY WILL SURELY DIE!

CANNONBALL...

WHERE THE HECK *AM I*?!

NO WAY TO TELL TIME -- FOR ALL AH KNOW, AH BEEN WANDERING THROUGH THESE TUNNELS FOR WEEKS! PROBABLY BEEN GOIN' IN CIRCLES, TOO!

HOTTER'N HADES HERE -- AH NEED TO FIND SOME WATER, AN' SALT, BEFORE AH PASS OUT FROM DEHYDRATION!

WOULDN'T MIND A BITE TO EAT, NEITHER --

HEY!?!

WHO ART THOU, BOY?!

AND WHYFORE DOST THOU TRESPASS IN *NIDAVELLIR* --

-- THE REALM OF THE *DWARFS*!

MY NAME'S SAMUEL GUTHRIE, SIR.

AH'M AFRAID AH'M HERE BY ACCIDENT. AH'LL BE GLAD TO LEAVE, IF SOMEONE'D KINDLY SHOW ME THE WAY.

AH'D BE OBLIGED AS WELL IF Y'ALL COULD SPARE SOMETHING TO DRINK. AND MAYBE SOME FOOD?

SUCH GIFTS ARE PRECIOUS -- ESPECIALLY WHEN THE NEED IS SO GREAT -- CANST THOU PAY FOR THEM?

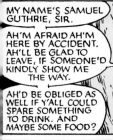

AIN'T GOT NO MONEY.

SERVICE WILL DO.

EEIIRRII!!!

EGVANDA -- MY *WIFE*?!!

A WOMAN'S VOICE -- SCREAMIN' IN PURE TERROR!

THESE TROLLS MAY BE THE WORST CREEPS IN CREATION --

-- BUT AH CAN'T STAND BY AN' LET *ANYONE* BE HURT LIKE THAT. MY DADDY, BLESS HIM, TAUGHT ME BETTER!

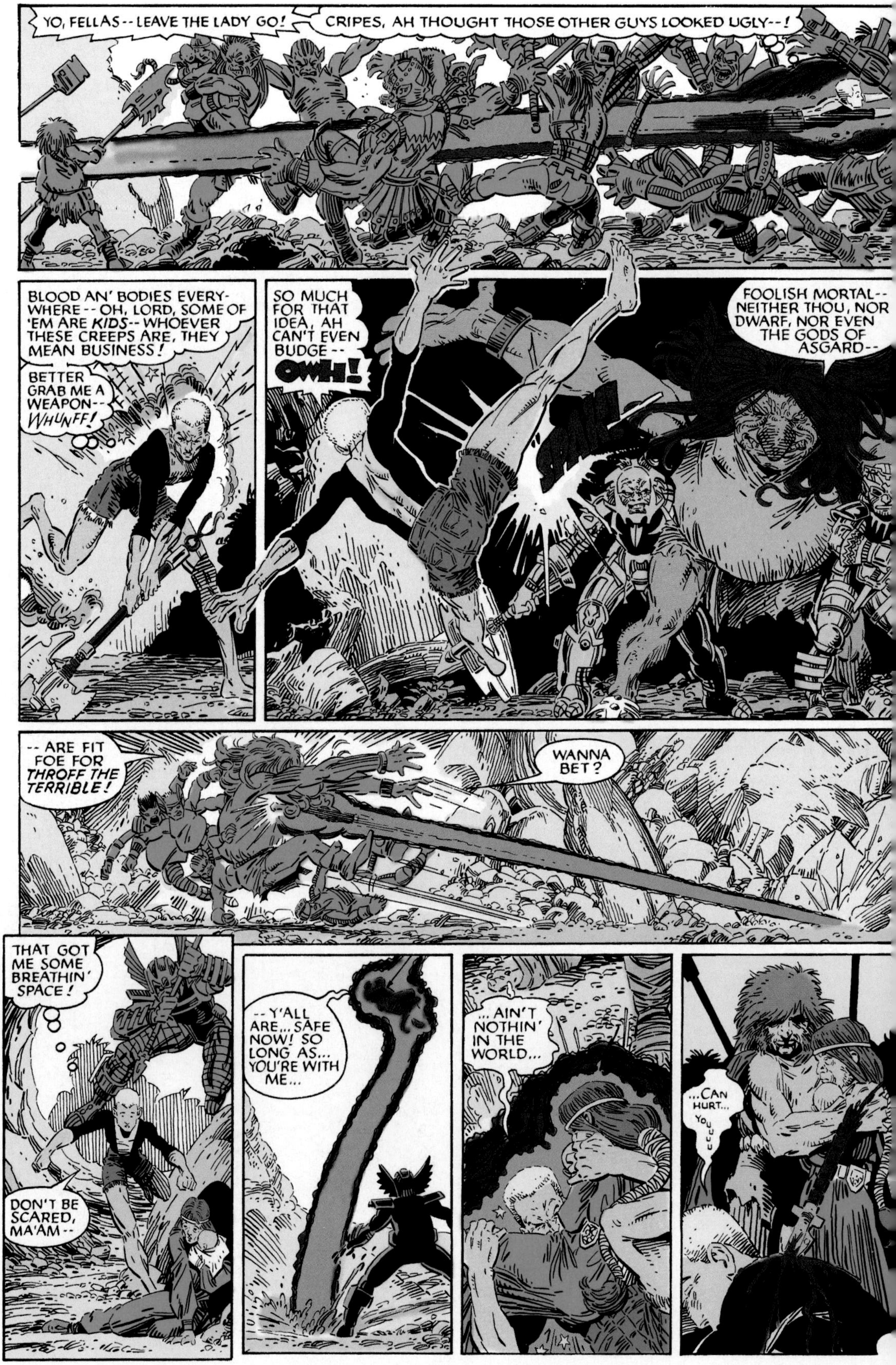
YO, FELLAS -- LEAVE THE LADY GO!
CRIPES, AH THOUGHT THOSE OTHER GUYS LOOKED UGLY--!
BLOOD AN' BODIES EVERYWHERE -- OH, LORD, SOME OF 'EM ARE KIDS -- WHOEVER THESE CREEPS ARE, THEY MEAN BUSINESS!
BETTER GRAB ME A WEAPON-- WHUNFF!
SO MUCH FOR THAT IDEA, AH CAN'T EVEN BUDGE --
OWH!
FOOLISH MORTAL-- NEITHER THOU, NOR DWARF, NOR EVEN THE GODS OF ASGARD--
-- ARE FIT FOE FOR THROFF THE TERRIBLE!
WANNA BET?
THAT GOT ME SOME BREATHIN' SPACE!
DON'T BE SCARED, MA'AM --
-- Y'ALL ARE... SAFE NOW! SO LONG AS... YOU'RE WITH ME...
... AIN'T NOTHIN' IN THE WORLD...
...CAN HURT... YOUUUU

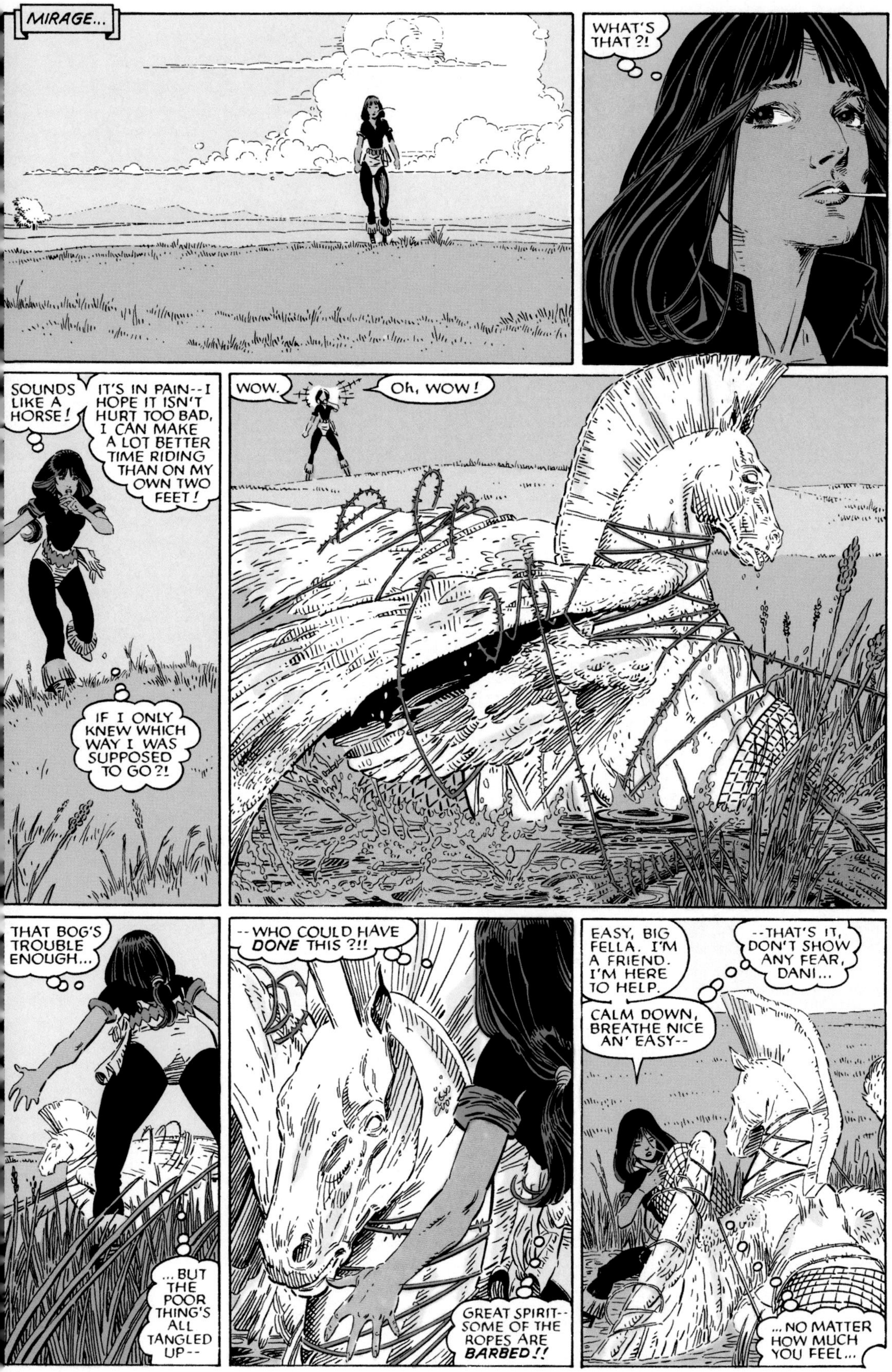

MIRAGE...
WHAT'S THAT?!
SOUNDS LIKE A HORSE!
IT'S IN PAIN--I HOPE IT ISN'T HURT TOO BAD, I CAN MAKE A LOT BETTER TIME RIDING THAN ON MY OWN TWO FEET!
IF I ONLY KNEW WHICH WAY I WAS SUPPOSED TO GO?!
WOW.
Oh, WOW!
THAT BOG'S TROUBLE ENOUGH...
...BUT THE POOR THING'S ALL TANGLED UP--
--WHO COULD HAVE DONE THIS?!!
GREAT SPIRIT--SOME OF THE ROPES ARE BARBED!!
EASY, BIG FELLA. I'M A FRIEND. I'M HERE TO HELP.
--THAT'S IT, DON'T SHOW ANY FEAR, DANI...
CALM DOWN, BREATHE NICE AN' EASY--
...NO MATTER HOW MUCH YOU FEEL...

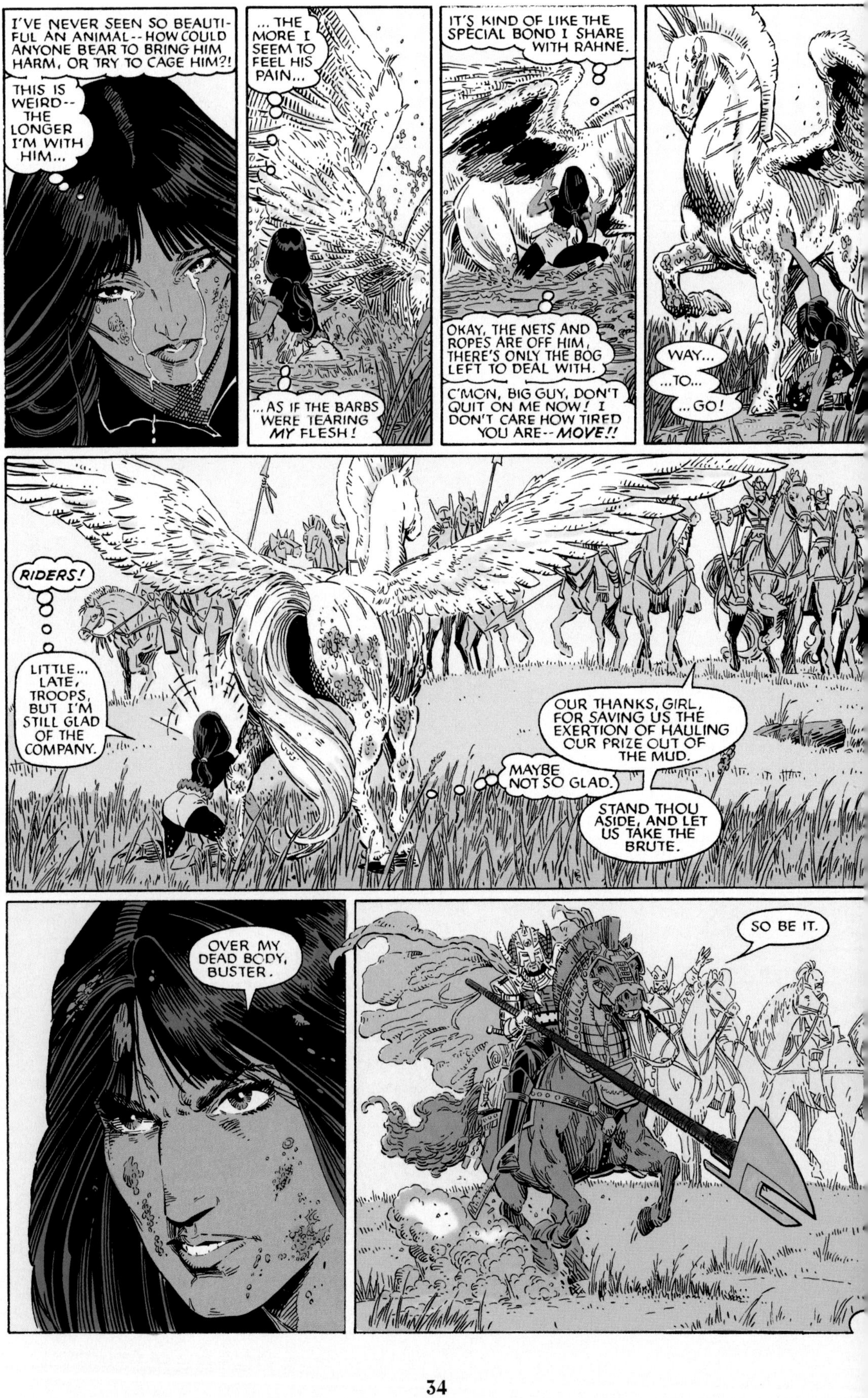

I'VE NEVER SEEN SO BEAUTIFUL AN ANIMAL--HOW COULD ANYONE BEAR TO BRING HIM HARM, OR TRY TO CAGE HIM?!
THIS IS WEIRD--THE LONGER I'M WITH HIM...
...THE MORE I SEEM TO FEEL HIS PAIN...
...AS IF THE BARBS WERE TEARING MY FLESH!
IT'S KIND OF LIKE THE SPECIAL BOND I SHARE WITH RAHNE.
OKAY, THE NETS AND ROPES ARE OFF HIM, THERE'S ONLY THE BOG LEFT TO DEAL WITH.
C'MON, BIG GUY, DON'T QUIT ON ME NOW! I DON'T CARE HOW TIRED YOU ARE--MOVE!!
WAY...
...TO...
...GO!
RIDERS!
LITTLE... LATE, TROOPS, BUT I'M STILL GLAD OF THE COMPANY.
OUR THANKS, GIRL, FOR SAVING US THE EXERTION OF HAULING OUR PRIZE OUT OF THE MUD.
MAYBE NOT SO GLAD.
STAND THOU ASIDE, AND LET US TAKE THE BRUTE.
OVER MY DEAD BODY, BUSTER.
SO BE IT.

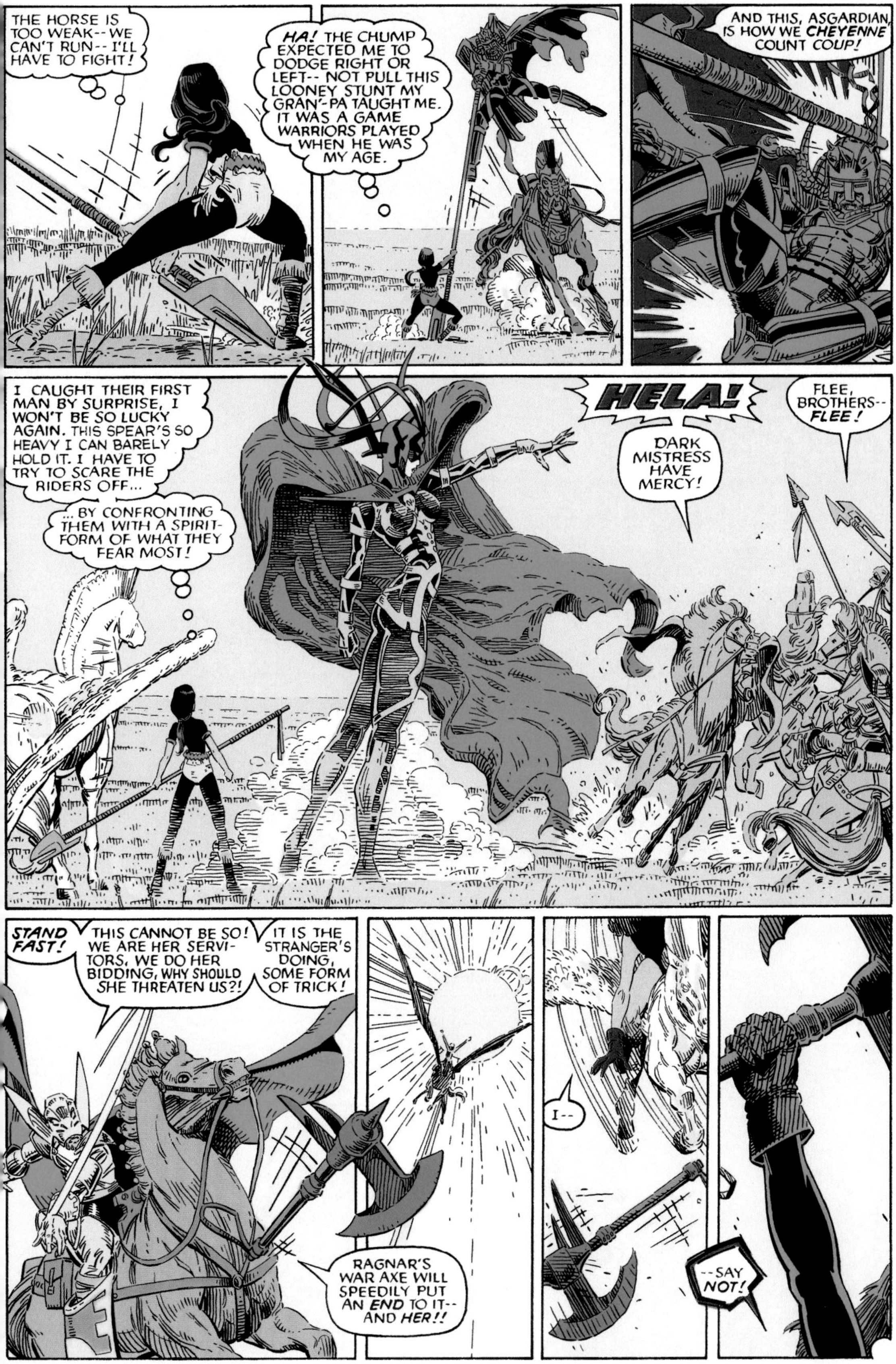

THE HORSE IS TOO WEAK-- WE CAN'T RUN-- I'LL HAVE TO FIGHT!
HA! THE CHUMP EXPECTED ME TO DODGE RIGHT OR LEFT-- NOT PULL THIS LOONEY STUNT MY GRAN'-PA TAUGHT ME. IT WAS A GAME WARRIORS PLAYED WHEN HE WAS MY AGE.
AND THIS, ASGARDIAN, IS HOW WE CHEYENNE COUNT COUP!
I CAUGHT THEIR FIRST MAN BY SURPRISE, I WON'T BE SO LUCKY AGAIN. THIS SPEAR'S SO HEAVY I CAN BARELY HOLD IT. I HAVE TO TRY TO SCARE THE RIDERS OFF...
... BY CONFRONTING THEM WITH A SPIRIT-FORM OF WHAT THEY FEAR MOST!
HELA!
DARK MISTRESS HAVE MERCY!
FLEE, BROTHERS-- FLEE!
STAND FAST!
THIS CANNOT BE SO! WE ARE HER SERVITORS, WE DO HER BIDDING, WHY SHOULD SHE THREATEN US?!
IT IS THE STRANGER'S DOING, SOME FORM OF TRICK!
RAGNAR'S WAR AXE WILL SPEEDILY PUT AN END TO IT-- AND HER!!
I--
--SAY NOT!

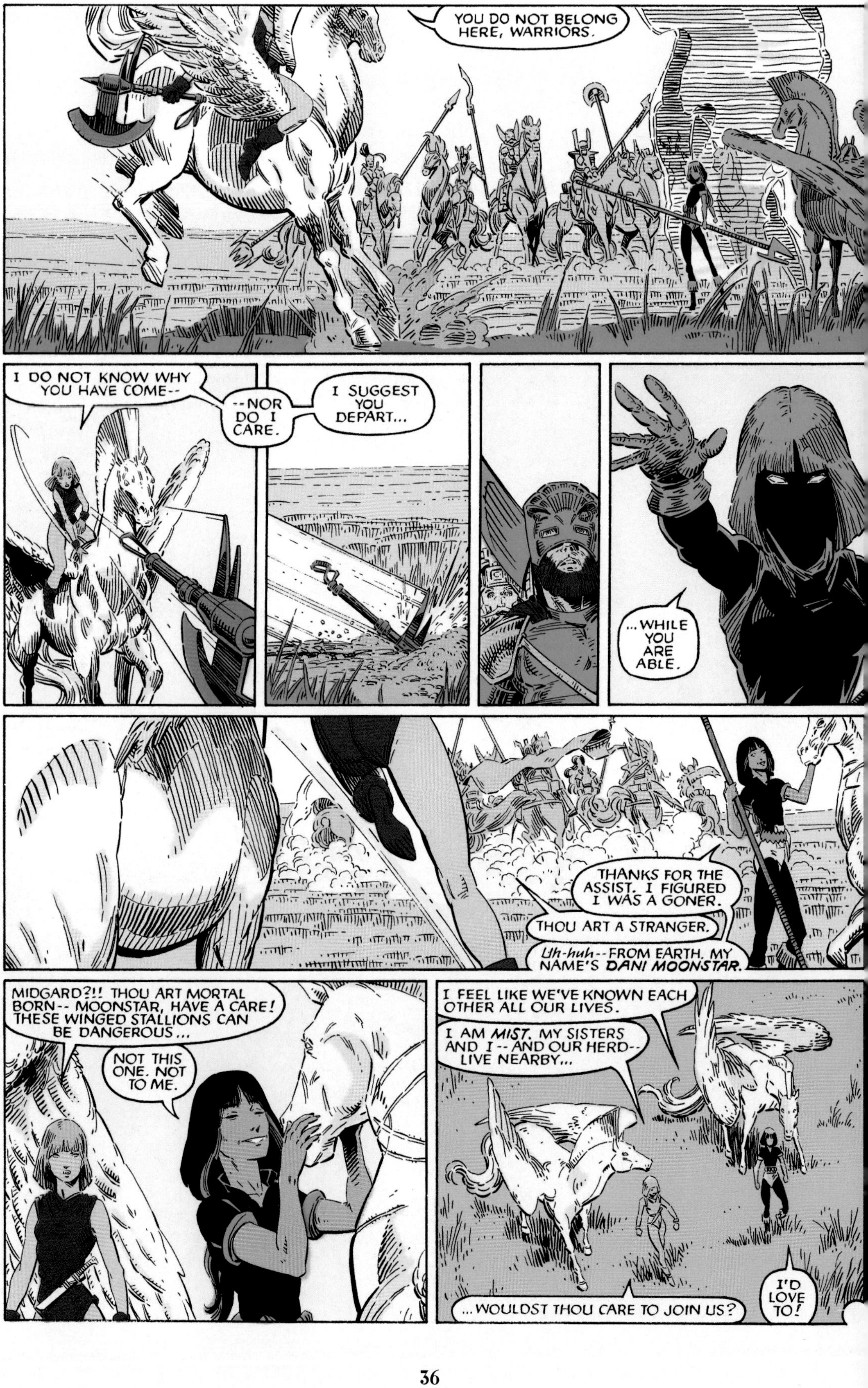

YOU DO NOT BELONG HERE, WARRIORS.
I DO NOT KNOW WHY YOU HAVE COME--
--NOR DO I CARE.
I SUGGEST YOU DEPART...
...WHILE YOU ARE ABLE.
THANKS FOR THE ASSIST. I FIGURED I WAS A GONER.
THOU ART A STRANGER.
Uh-huh--FROM EARTH. MY NAME'S DANI MOONSTAR.
MIDGARD?!! THOU ART MORTAL BORN-- MOONSTAR, HAVE A CARE! THESE WINGED STALLIONS CAN BE DANGEROUS...
NOT THIS ONE. NOT TO ME.
I FEEL LIKE WE'VE KNOWN EACH OTHER ALL OUR LIVES.
I AM MIST. MY SISTERS AND I -- AND OUR HERD-- LIVE NEARBY...
...WOULDST THOU CARE TO JOIN US?
I'D LOVE TO!

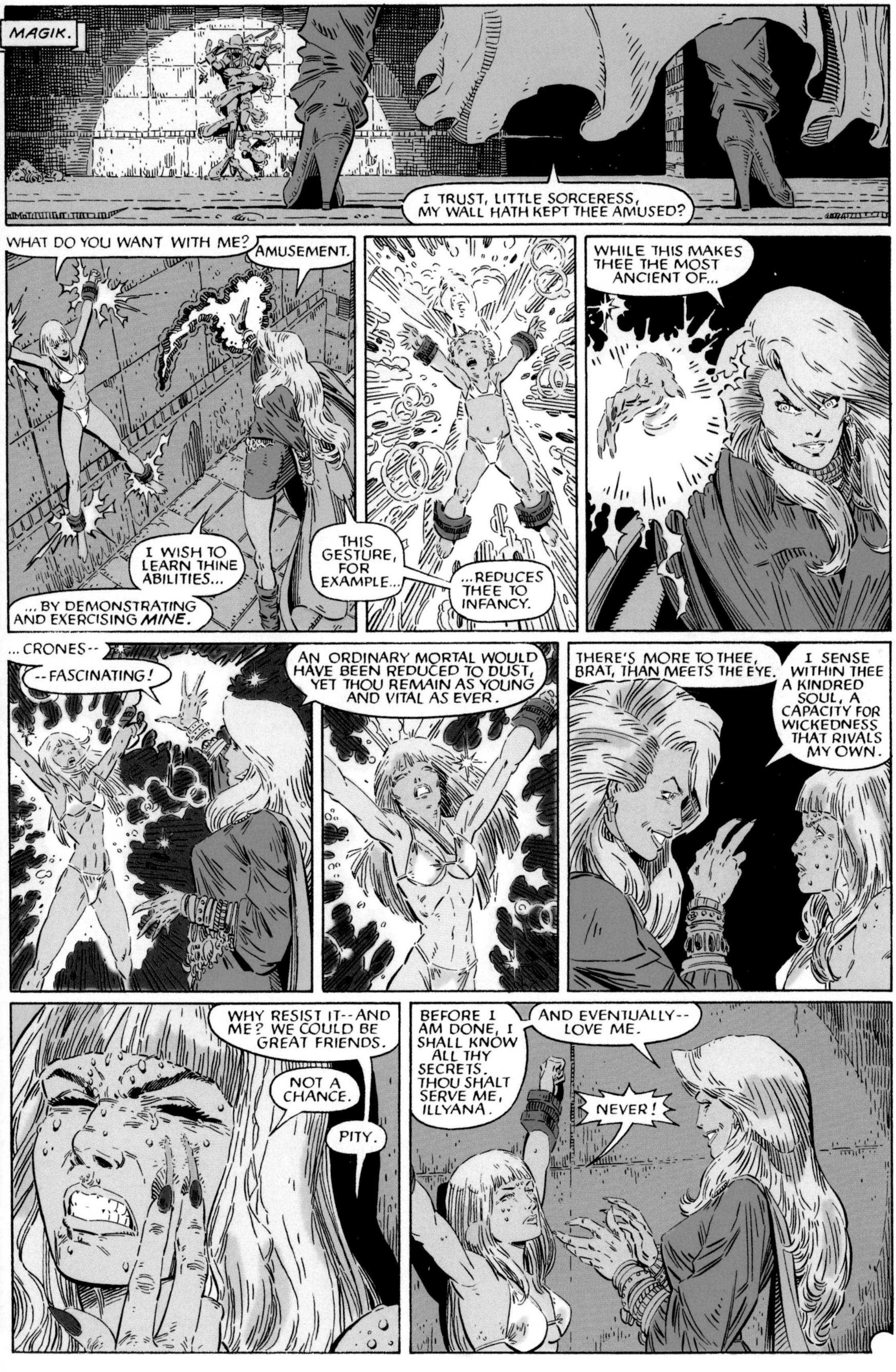
MAGIK.
I TRUST, LITTLE SORCERESS, MY WALL HATH KEPT THEE AMUSED?
WHAT DO YOU WANT WITH ME?
AMUSEMENT.
I WISH TO LEARN THINE ABILITIES...
...BY DEMONSTRATING AND EXERCISING MINE.
THIS GESTURE, FOR EXAMPLE...
...REDUCES THEE TO INFANCY.
WHILE THIS MAKES THEE THE MOST ANCIENT OF...
...CRONES--
--FASCINATING!
AN ORDINARY MORTAL WOULD HAVE BEEN REDUCED TO DUST, YET THOU REMAIN AS YOUNG AND VITAL AS EVER.
THERE'S MORE TO THEE, BRAT, THAN MEETS THE EYE.
I SENSE WITHIN THEE A KINDRED SOUL, A CAPACITY FOR WICKEDNESS THAT RIVALS MY OWN.
WHY RESIST IT--AND ME? WE COULD BE GREAT FRIENDS.
NOT A CHANCE.
PITY.
BEFORE I AM DONE, I SHALL KNOW ALL THY SECRETS. THOU SHALT SERVE ME, ILLYANA.
AND EVENTUALLY--LOVE ME.
NEVER!

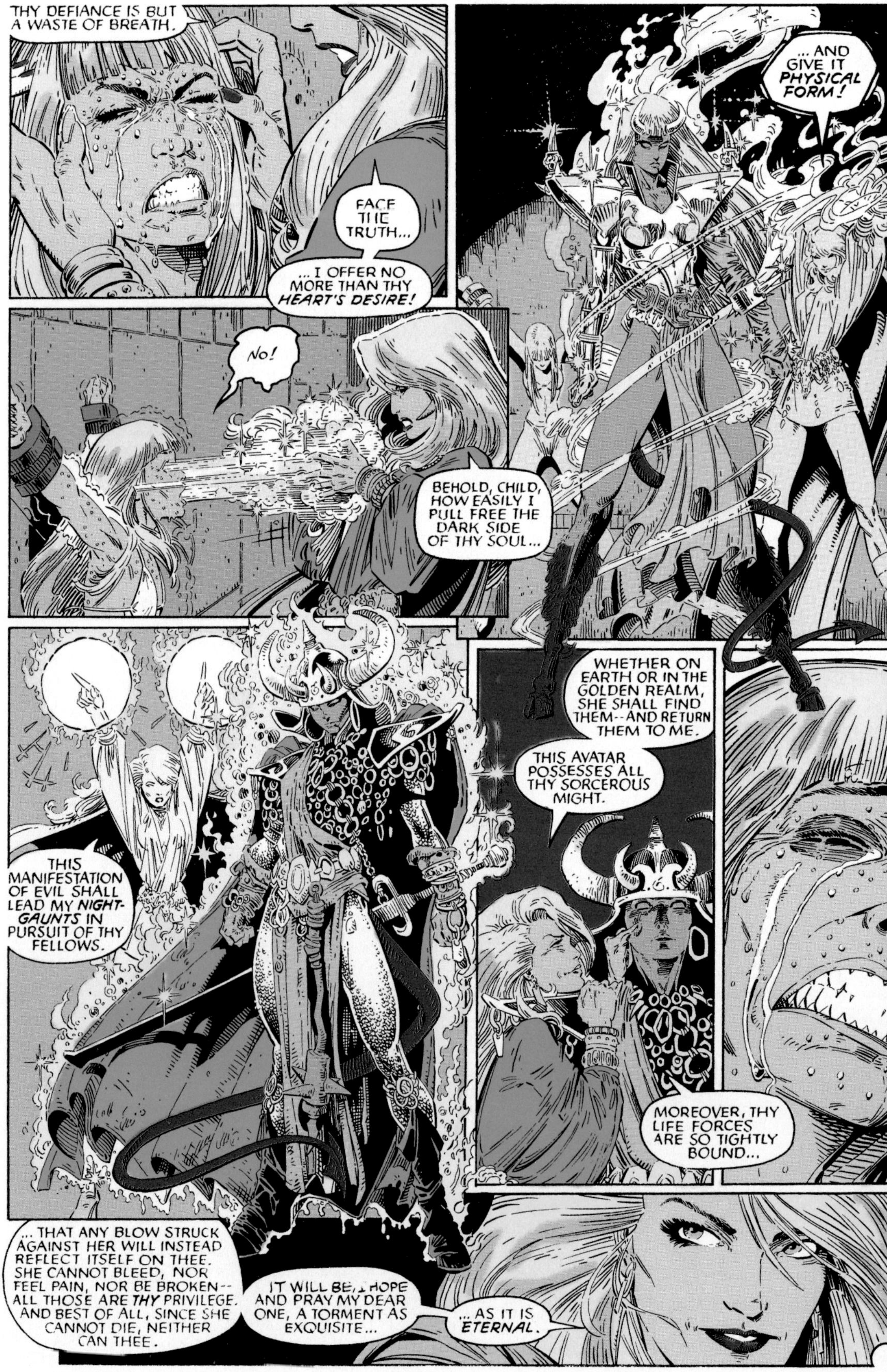

THY DEFIANCE IS BUT A WASTE OF BREATH.
FACE THE TRUTH...
...I OFFER NO MORE THAN THY HEART'S DESIRE!
...AND GIVE IT PHYSICAL FORM!
No!
BEHOLD, CHILD, HOW EASILY I PULL FREE THE DARK SIDE OF THY SOUL...
THIS MANIFESTATION OF EVIL SHALL LEAD MY NIGHT-GAUNTS IN PURSUIT OF THY FELLOWS.
WHETHER ON EARTH OR IN THE GOLDEN REALM, SHE SHALL FIND THEM--AND RETURN THEM TO ME.
THIS AVATAR POSSESSES ALL THY SORCEROUS MIGHT.
MOREOVER, THY LIFE FORCES ARE SO TIGHTLY BOUND...
...THAT ANY BLOW STRUCK AGAINST HER WILL INSTEAD REFLECT ITSELF ON THEE. SHE CANNOT BLEED, NOR FEEL PAIN, NOR BE BROKEN-- ALL THOSE ARE THY PRIVILEGE. AND BEST OF ALL, SINCE SHE CANNOT DIE, NEITHER CAN THEE.
IT WILL BE, I HOPE AND PRAY MY DEAR ONE, A TORMENT AS EXQUISITE...
...AS IT IS ETERNAL.

KARMA.
...NOT DEAD YET--?!!
WHY IS IT TAKING SO LONG?!
QU'EST-CE QUE C'EST-- WHAT IS THAT?!!
A VOICE?!? THEN-- I AM NOT ALONE IN THIS WILDERNESS!
SACRE COEUR!
SUCH THINGS CANNOT BE REAL--C'EST UNE HALLUCINATION-- I AM DREAMING! THE SUN HAS ADDLED MY BRAINS!
HELP ME!
THE SAND DEMON-- FOR THE LOVE OF FATHER ODIN--SAVE ME!!!
I CANNOT REFUSE THE CHILD-- BUT WHAT AM I TO DO?!
THIS BLOATED BODY IS OF NO USE-- BUT IF THAT CREATURE HAS A BRAIN, THEN PERHAPS WITH MY MUTANT POWER...
...I CAN POSSESS IT!

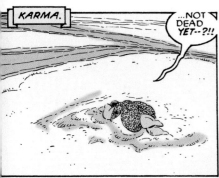

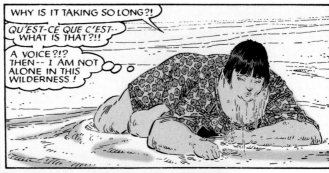

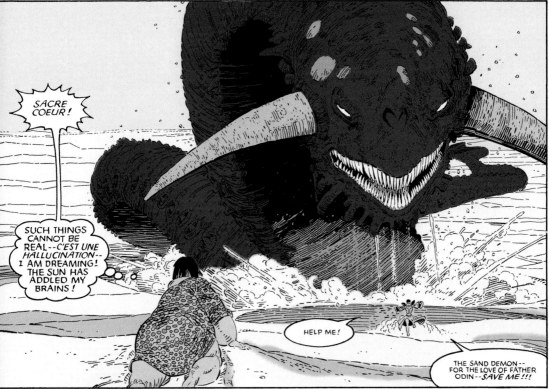

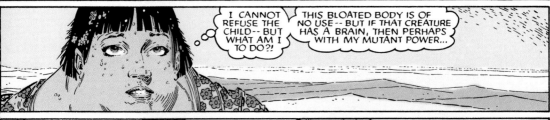

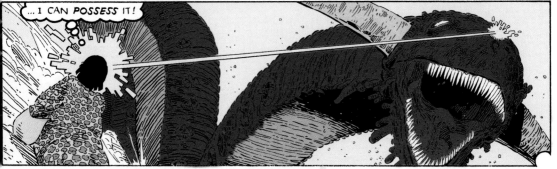

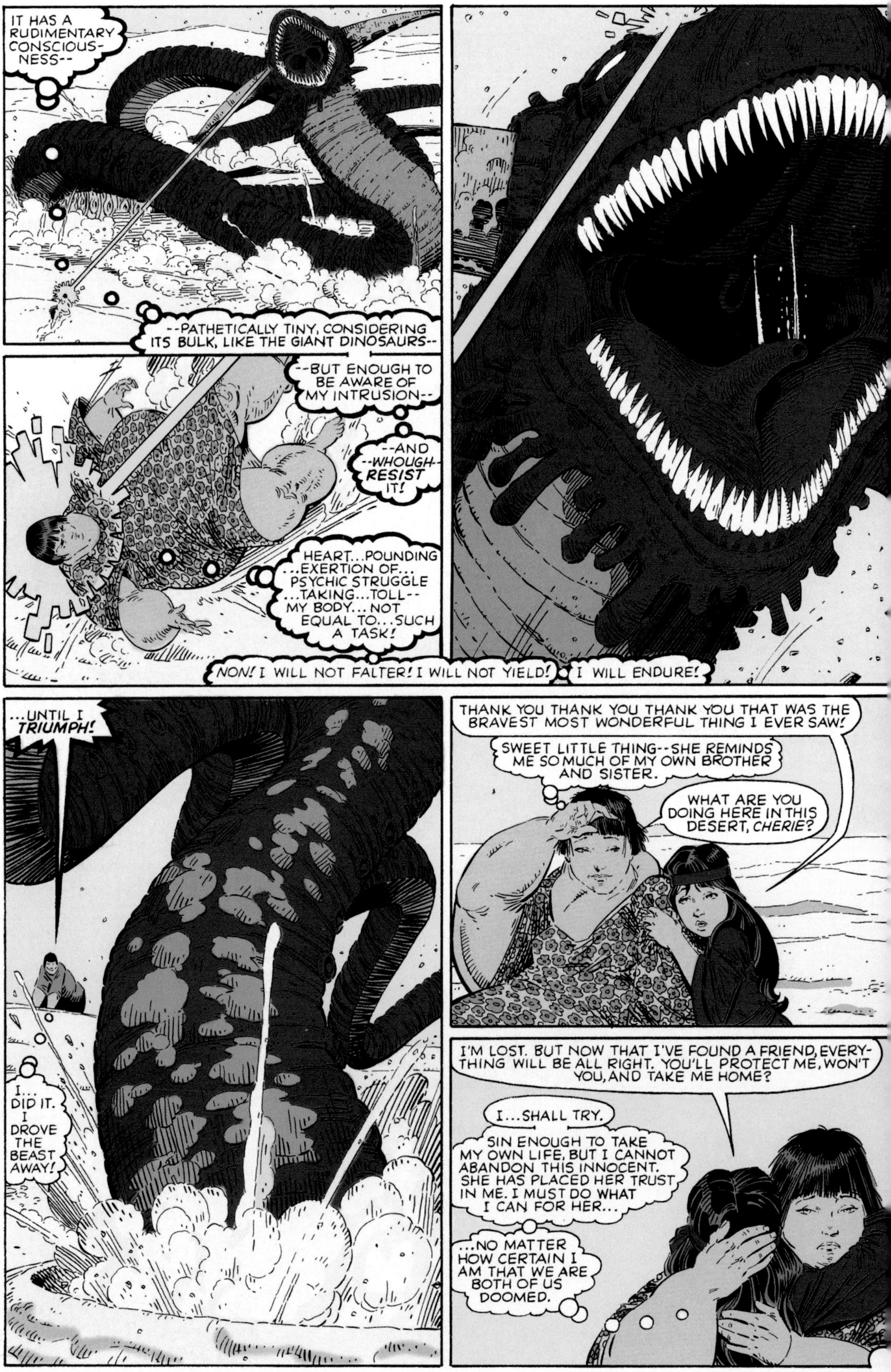
IT HAS A RUDIMENTARY CONSCIOUS-NESS--
--PATHETICALLY TINY, CONSIDERING ITS BULK, LIKE THE GIANT DINOSAURS--
--BUT ENOUGH TO BE AWARE OF MY INTRUSION--
--AND --WHOUGH-- RESIST IT!
HEART...POUNDING ...EXERTION OF... PSYCHIC STRUGGLE ...TAKING...TOLL-- MY BODY...NOT EQUAL TO...SUCH A TASK!
NON! I WILL NOT FALTER! I WILL NOT YIELD!
I WILL ENDURE!
...UNTIL I TRIUMPH!
I... DID IT. I DROVE THE BEAST AWAY!
THANK YOU THANK YOU THANK YOU THAT WAS THE BRAVEST MOST WONDERFUL THING I EVER SAW!
SWEET LITTLE THING--SHE REMINDS ME SO MUCH OF MY OWN BROTHER AND SISTER.
WHAT ARE YOU DOING HERE IN THIS DESERT, CHERIE?
I'M LOST. BUT NOW THAT I'VE FOUND A FRIEND, EVERYTHING WILL BE ALL RIGHT. YOU'LL PROTECT ME, WON'T YOU, AND TAKE ME HOME?
I...SHALL TRY.
SIN ENOUGH TO TAKE MY OWN LIFE, BUT I CANNOT ABANDON THIS INNOCENT. SHE HAS PLACED HER TRUST IN ME. I MUST DO WHAT I CAN FOR HER...
...NO MATTER HOW CERTAIN I AM THAT WE ARE BOTH OF US DOOMED.

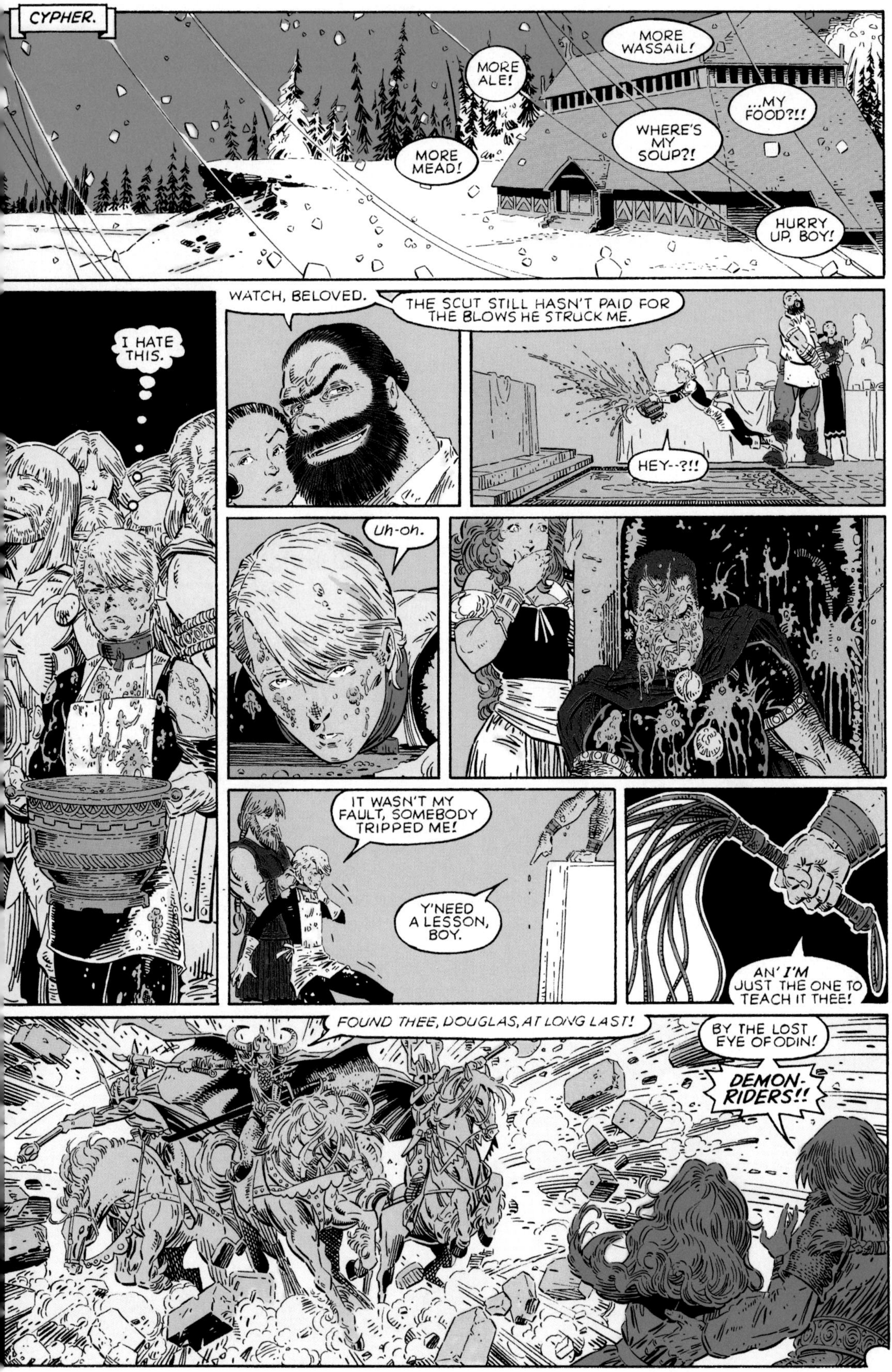
CYPHER.
MORE ALE!
MORE WASSAIL!
...MY FOOD?!!
WHERE'S MY SOUP?!
MORE MEAD!
HURRY UP, BOY!
I HATE THIS.
WATCH, BELOVED.
THE SCUT STILL HASN'T PAID FOR THE BLOWS HE STRUCK ME.
HEY--?!!
Uh-oh.
IT WASN'T MY FAULT, SOMEBODY TRIPPED ME!
Y'NEED A LESSON, BOY.
AN' I'M JUST THE ONE TO TEACH IT THEE!
FOUND THEE, DOUGLAS, AT LONG LAST!
BY THE LOST EYE OF ODIN!
DEMON-RIDERS!!

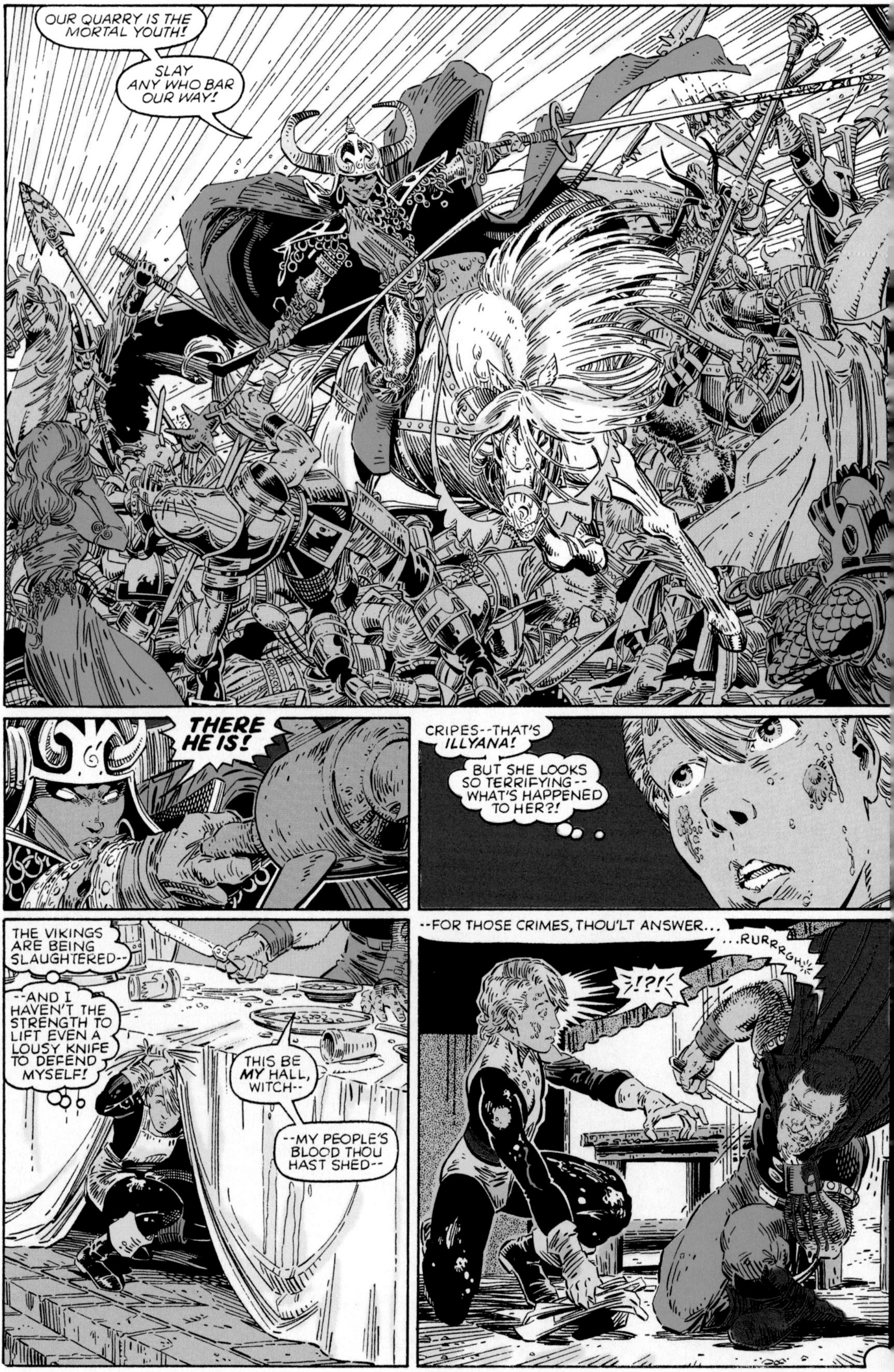

OUR QUARRY IS THE MORTAL YOUTH!
SLAY ANY WHO BAR OUR WAY!
THERE HE IS!
CRIPES--THAT'S ILLYANA!
BUT SHE LOOKS SO TERRIFYING-- WHAT'S HAPPENED TO HER?!
THE VIKINGS ARE BEING SLAUGHTERED--
--AND I HAVEN'T THE STRENGTH TO LIFT EVEN A LOUSY KNIFE TO DEFEND MYSELF!
THIS BE MY HALL, WITCH--
--MY PEOPLE'S BLOOD THOU HAST SHED--
--FOR THOSE CRIMES, THOU'LT ANSWER...
...RURRRGH!
!?!

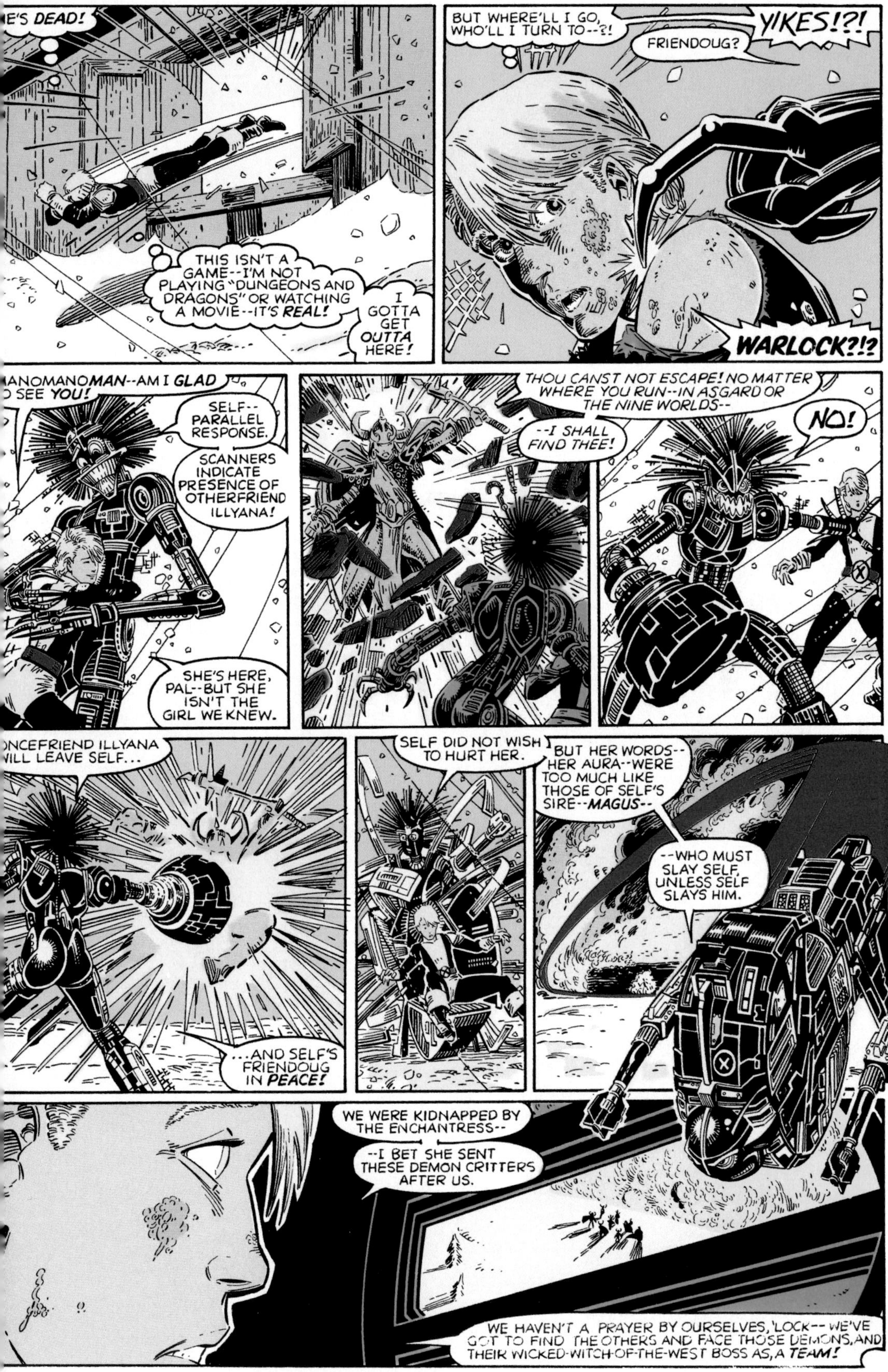

E'S DEAD!
THIS ISN'T A GAME--I'M NOT PLAYING "DUNGEONS AND DRAGONS" OR WATCHING A MOVIE--IT'S REAL!
I GOTTA GET OUTTA HERE!
BUT WHERE'LL I GO, WHO'LL I TURN TO--?!
FRIENDOUG?
YIKES!?!
WARLOCK?!?
ANOMANOMANOMAN--AM I GLAD O SEE YOU!
SELF--PARALLEL RESPONSE.
SCANNERS INDICATE PRESENCE OF OTHERFRIEND ILLYANA!
SHE'S HERE, PAL--BUT SHE ISN'T THE GIRL WE KNEW.
THOU CANST NOT ESCAPE! NO MATTER WHERE YOU RUN--IN ASGARD OR THE NINE WORLDS--
--I SHALL FIND THEE!
NO!
NCEFRIEND ILLYANA WILL LEAVE SELF...
...AND SELF'S FRIENDOUG IN PEACE!
SELF DID NOT WISH TO HURT HER.
BUT HER WORDS--HER AURA--WERE TOO MUCH LIKE THOSE OF SELF'S SIRE--MAGUS--
--WHO MUST SLAY SELF, UNLESS SELF SLAYS HIM.
WE WERE KIDNAPPED BY THE ENCHANTRESS--
--I BET SHE SENT THESE DEMON CRITTERS AFTER US.
WE HAVEN'T A PRAYER BY OURSELVES, 'LOCK-- WE'VE GOT TO FIND THE OTHERS AND FACE THOSE DEMONS, AND THEIR WICKED-WITCH-OF-THE-WEST BOSS AS, A TEAM!

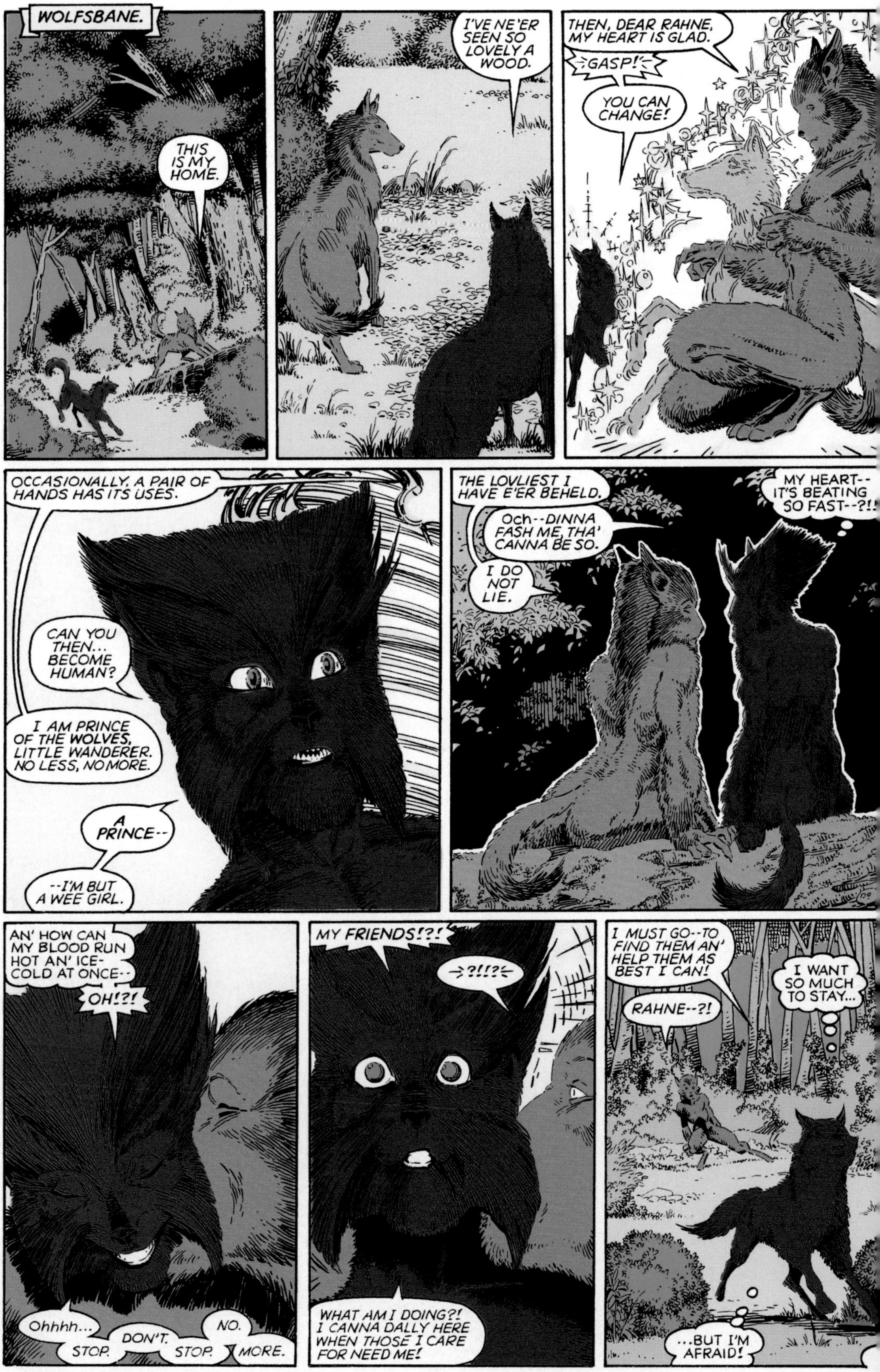
WOLFSBANE.
THIS IS MY HOME.
I'VE NE'ER SEEN SO LOVELY A WOOD.
THEN, DEAR RAHNE, MY HEART IS GLAD.
GASP!
YOU CAN CHANGE!
OCCASIONALLY, A PAIR OF HANDS HAS ITS USES.
CAN YOU THEN... BECOME HUMAN?
I AM PRINCE OF THE WOLVES, LITTLE WANDERER. NO LESS, NO MORE.
A PRINCE--
--I'M BUT A WEE GIRL.
THE LOVLIEST I HAVE E'ER BEHELD.
Och--DINNA FASH ME, THA' CANNA BE SO.
I DO NOT LIE.
MY HEART-- IT'S BEATING SO FAST--?!
AN' HOW CAN MY BLOOD RUN HOT AN' ICE-COLD AT ONCE--
OH!?!
Ohhhh... STOP. DON'T. STOP. NO. MORE.
MY FRIENDS!?!
?!!?
WHAT AM I DOING?! I CANNA DALLY HERE WHEN THOSE I CARE FOR NEED ME!
I MUST GO--TO FIND THEM AN' HELP THEM AS BEST I CAN!
RAHNE--?!
I WANT SO MUCH TO STAY...
...BUT I'M AFRAID!

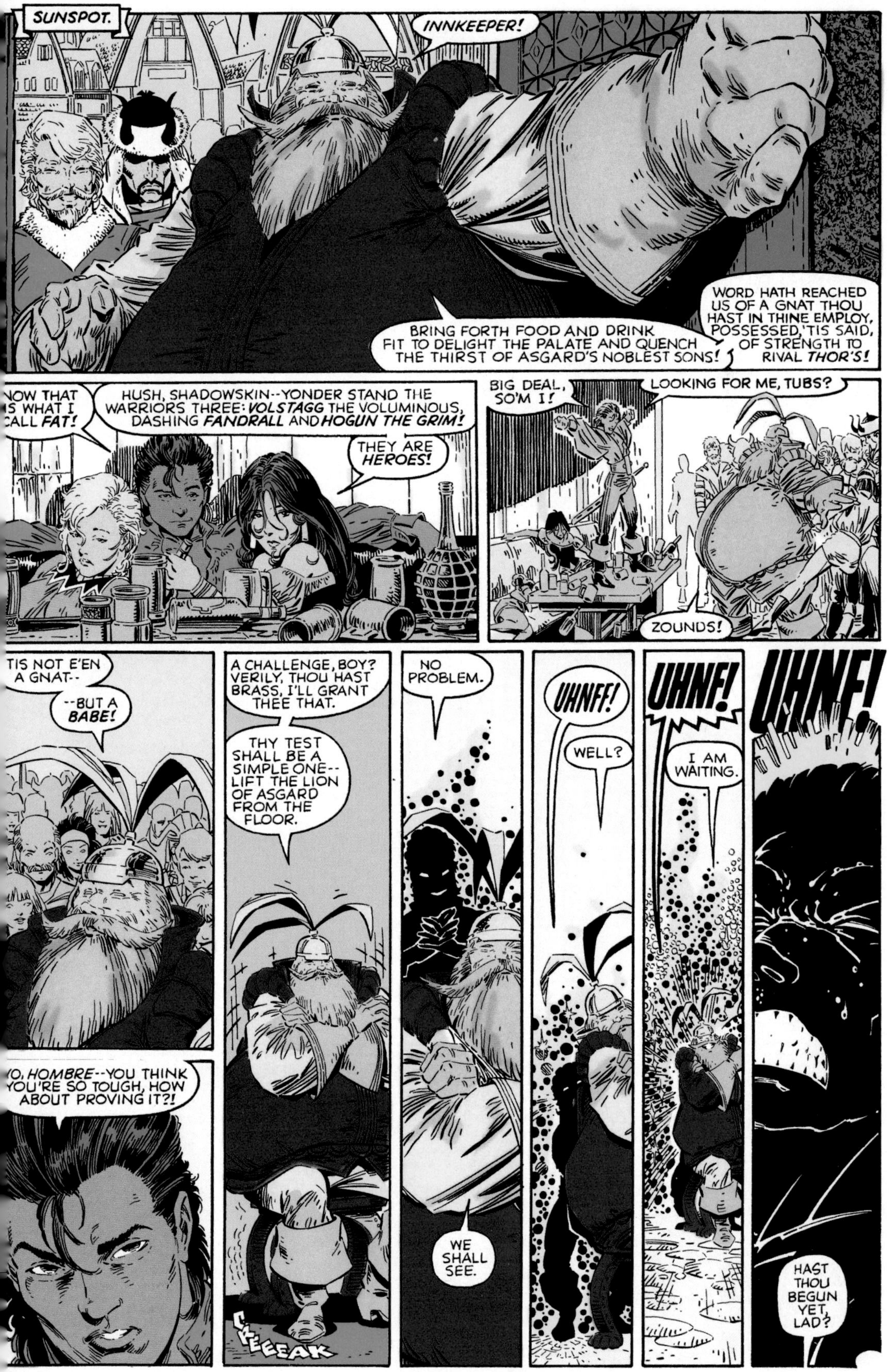
SUNSPOT.
INNKEEPER!
BRING FORTH FOOD AND DRINK FIT TO DELIGHT THE PALATE AND QUENCH THE THIRST OF ASGARD'S NOBLEST SONS!
WORD HATH REACHED US OF A GNAT THOU HAST IN THINE EMPLOY, POSSESSED, 'TIS SAID, OF STRENGTH TO RIVAL THOR'S!
NOW THAT IS WHAT I CALL FAT!
HUSH, SHADOWSKIN--YONDER STAND THE WARRIORS THREE: VOLSTAGG THE VOLUMINOUS, DASHING FANDRALL AND HOGUN THE GRIM!
THEY ARE HEROES!
BIG DEAL, SO'M I!
LOOKING FOR ME, TUBS?
ZOUNDS!
TIS NOT E'EN A GNAT--
--BUT A BABE!
YO, HOMBRE--YOU THINK YOU'RE SO TOUGH, HOW ABOUT PROVING IT?!
A CHALLENGE, BOY? VERILY, THOU HAST BRASS, I'LL GRANT THEE THAT.
THY TEST SHALL BE A SIMPLE ONE--LIFT THE LION OF ASGARD FROM THE FLOOR.
CREEEAK
NO PROBLEM.
WE SHALL SEE.
UHNFF!
WELL?
UHNF!
I AM WAITING.
UHNF!
HAST THOU BEGUN YET, LAD?

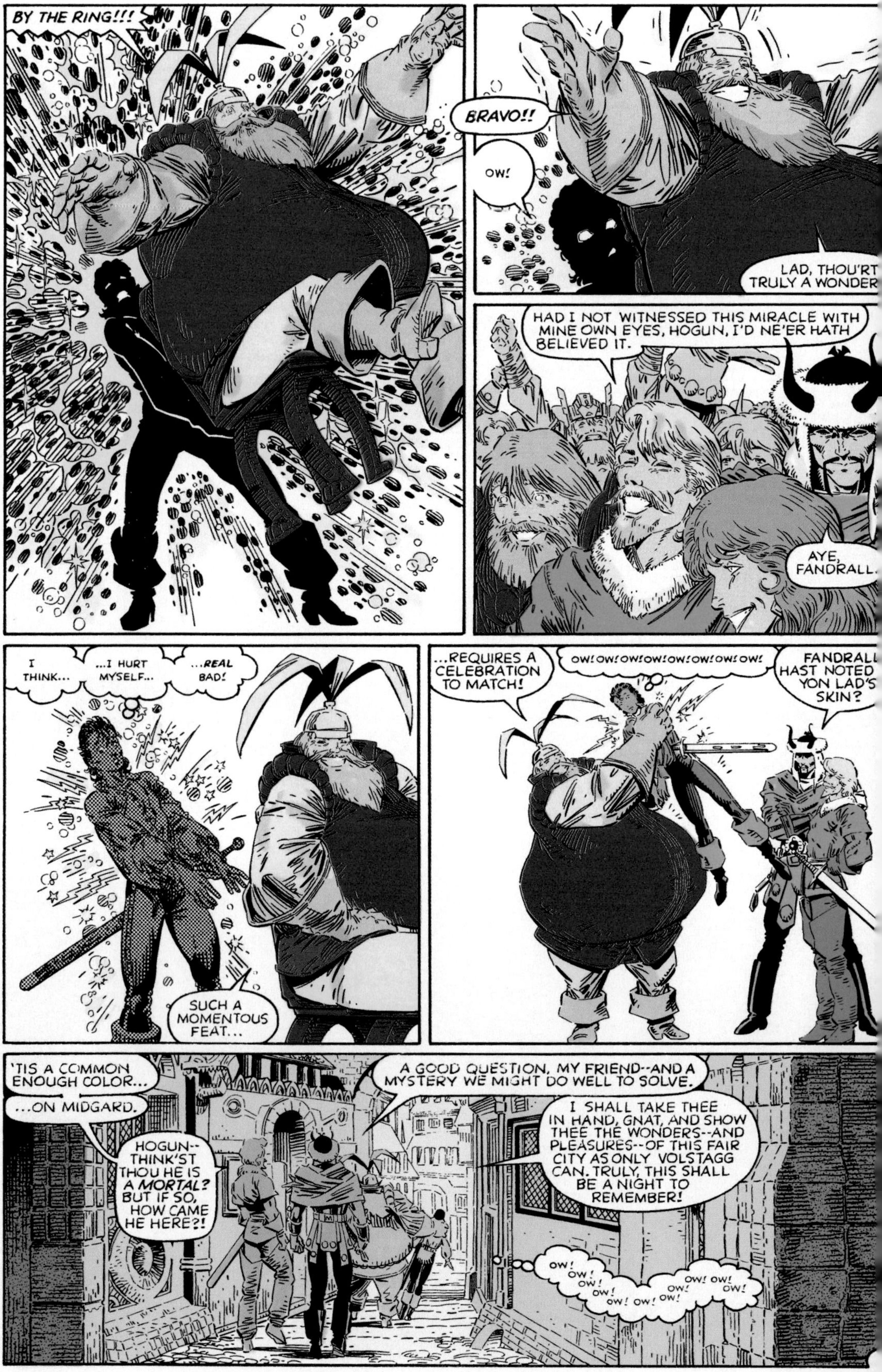
BY THE RING!!!
BRAVO!!
OW!
LAD, THOU'RT TRULY A WONDER
HAD I NOT WITNESSED THIS MIRACLE WITH MINE OWN EYES, HOGUN, I'D NE'ER HATH BELIEVED IT.
AYE, FANDRALL.
I THINK...
...I HURT MYSELF...
...REAL BAD!
SUCH A MOMENTOUS FEAT...
...REQUIRES A CELEBRATION TO MATCH!
OW! OW! OW! OW! OW! OW! OW! OW!
FANDRALL HAST NOTED YON LAD'S SKIN?
'TIS A COMMON ENOUGH COLOR...
...ON MIDGARD.
A GOOD QUESTION, MY FRIEND--AND A MYSTERY WE MIGHT DO WELL TO SOLVE.
HOGUN-- THINK'ST THOU HE IS A MORTAL? BUT IF SO, HOW CAME HE HERE?!
I SHALL TAKE THEE IN HAND, GNAT, AND SHOW THEE THE WONDERS--AND PLEASURES--OF THIS FAIR CITY AS ONLY VOLSTAGG CAN. TRULY, THIS SHALL BE A NIGHT TO REMEMBER!
OW! OW! OW! OW! OW! OW! OW! OW! OW! OW!

CANNONBALL.

THOU WERT SORELY WOUNDED, SAM. THAT ELVEN SPEARPOINT NEAR PIERCED THY BRAVE AND NOBLE HEART.

WHY SO GLUM, SAM?

IS LIFE SO HARD A TRIAL TO FACE? SHOULD WE HAVE LEFT THEE TO DAME HELA'S EMBRACE?

AH JUST FEEL LIKE AH'VE BEEN IN THIS BED FOREVER.

NO SIR. AH'M GRATEFUL TO Y'ALL FOR PULLIN' ME THROUGH.

PATIENT THOU MUST BE. WITH LOVING CARE, THOU'LT SOON BE WELL...

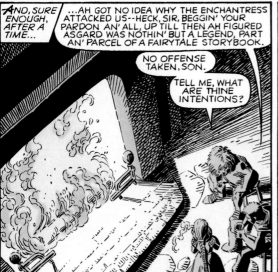

AND, SURE ENOUGH, AFTER A TIME...

...AH GOT NO IDEA WHY THE ENCHANTRESS ATTACKED US--HECK, SIR, BEGGIN' YOUR PARDON AN' ALL, UP TILL THEN AH FIGURED ASGARD WAS NOTHIN' BUT A LEGEND, PART AN' PARCEL OF A FAIRYTALE STORYBOOK.

NO OFFENSE TAKEN, SON.

TELL ME, WHAT ARE THINE INTENTIONS?

SOON AS AH'M FIT, AH'LL GO AFTER MY FRIENDS, TRY TO GET US ALL HOME.

THE ENCHANTRESS IS A FORMIDABLE FOE.

THOU COULDST STAY WITH US, PALADIN.

AND MAKE OUR HOME THINE OWN.

PEACE, KINDRA--LEAVE THE LAD BE!

IN HAPPIER TIMES, SAM, AN APPEAL TO LORD ODIN WOULD HAVE SET THIS MESS A'RIGHT. BUT WITH HIS DISAPPEARANCE AFTER THE SURTWAR, THE VERY FABRIC OF THE REALM HATH BEGUN UNRAVELING.

MY PEOPLE ARE BESET WITH DARK ELVES--THOSE WHO FOL-LOWED ACCURSED MALEKITH--SEEKING TO CONQUER US, SO THAT WE, WITH OUR METAL-WORKING SKILLS, MIGHT FORGE THEM THE WEAPONS NEEDED TO OVERTHROW THE GODS.

I'VE LITTLE LOVE FOR ASGARD--IT WOULDN'T BREAK MY HEART TO SEE THOSE PROUD AESIR HUMBLED--BUT BY MY HEARTH-FIRE RUNES, I'LL DIE BEFORE I SEE MY RACE ENSLAVED!

I FEAR, MY BOY, THEE AND THINE HAVE STUMBLED HEADLONG INTO A BEARPIT--EH?!!

FATHER-- THE CAVERN WALL!

GLORY--?!

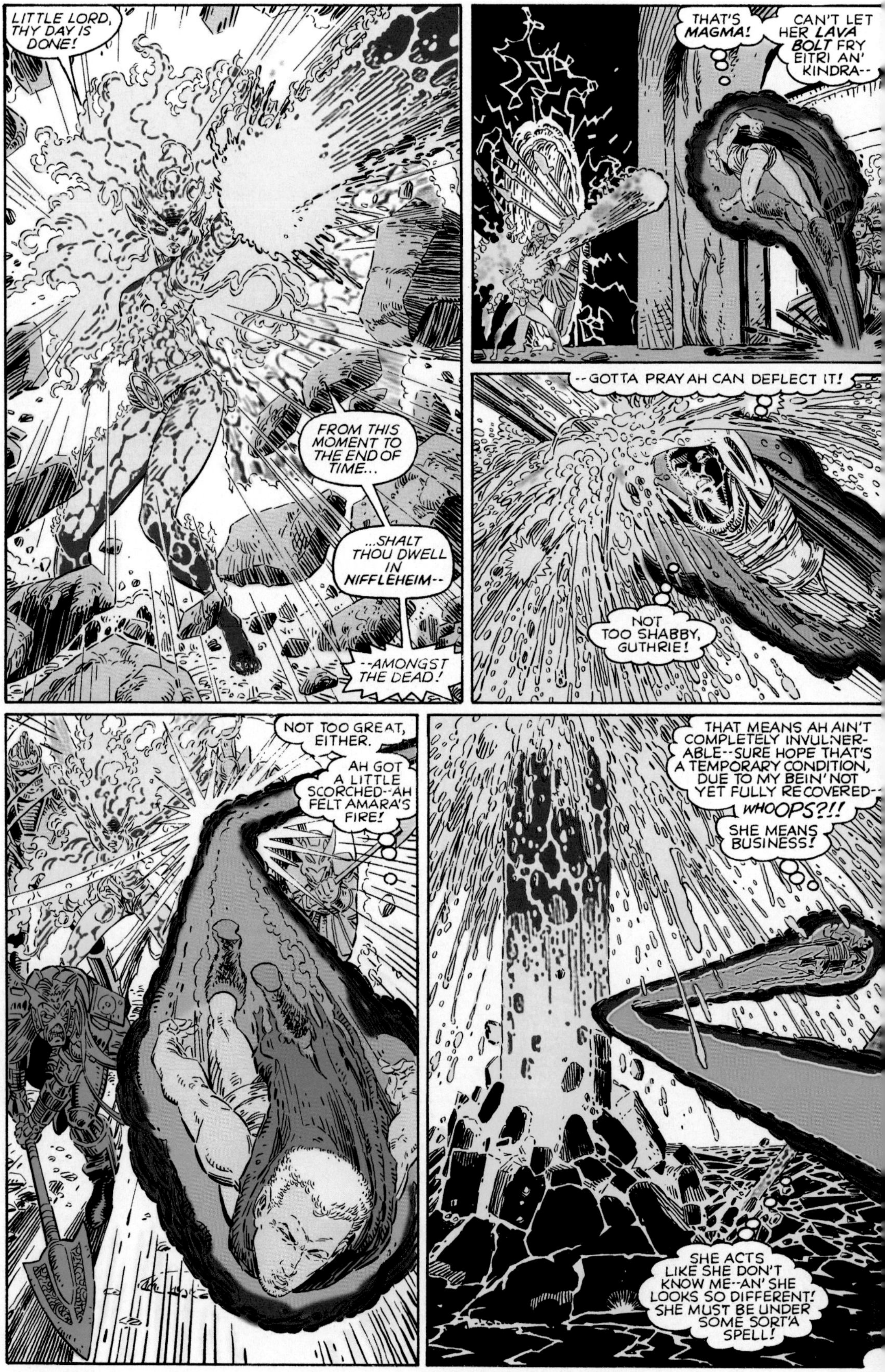
LITTLE LORD, THY DAY IS DONE!
FROM THIS MOMENT TO THE END OF TIME...
...SHALT THOU DWELL IN NIFFLEHEIM--
--AMONGST THE DEAD!
THAT'S MAGMA!
CAN'T LET HER LAVA BOLT FRY EITRI AN' KINDRA--
--GOTTA PRAY AH CAN DEFLECT IT!
NOT TOO SHABBY, GUTHRIE!
NOT TOO GREAT, EITHER.
AH GOT A LITTLE SCORCHED--AH FELT AMARA'S FIRE!
THAT MEANS AH AIN'T COMPLETELY INVULNER-ABLE--SURE HOPE THAT'S A TEMPORARY CONDITION, DUE TO MY BEIN' NOT YET FULLY RECOVERED--
WHOOPS?!!
SHE MEANS BUSINESS!
SHE ACTS LIKE SHE DON'T KNOW ME--AN' SHE LOOKS SO DIFFERENT! SHE MUST BE UNDER SOME SORT'A SPELL!

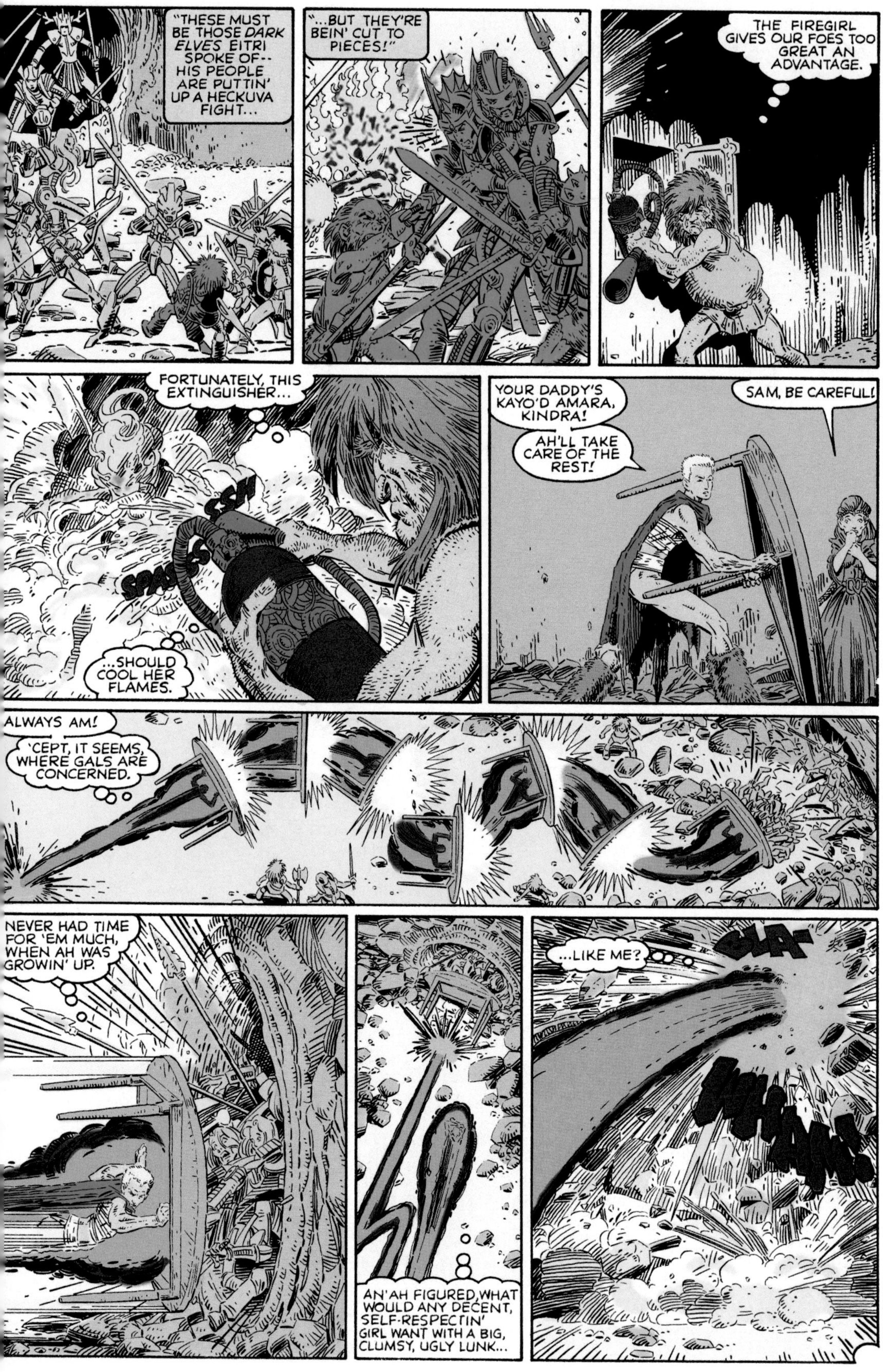
"THESE MUST BE THOSE *DARK ELVES* EITRI SPOKE OF-- HIS PEOPLE ARE PUTTIN' UP A HECKUVA FIGHT...
"...BUT THEY'RE BEIN' CUT TO PIECES!"
THE FIREGIRL GIVES OUR FOES TOO GREAT AN ADVANTAGE.
FORTUNATELY, THIS EXTINGUISHER...
SSSH
SPASSS
...SHOULD COOL HER FLAMES.
YOUR DADDY'S KAYO'D AMARA, KINDRA!
AH'LL TAKE CARE OF THE REST!
SAM, BE CAREFUL!
ALWAYS AM!
'CEPT, IT SEEMS, WHERE GALS ARE CONCERNED.
NEVER HAD TIME FOR 'EM MUCH, WHEN AH WAS GROWIN' UP.
AN'AH FIGURED, WHAT WOULD ANY DECENT, SELF-RESPECTIN' GIRL WANT WITH A BIG, CLUMSY, UGLY LUNK...
...LIKE ME?
GLA-
WHAM!

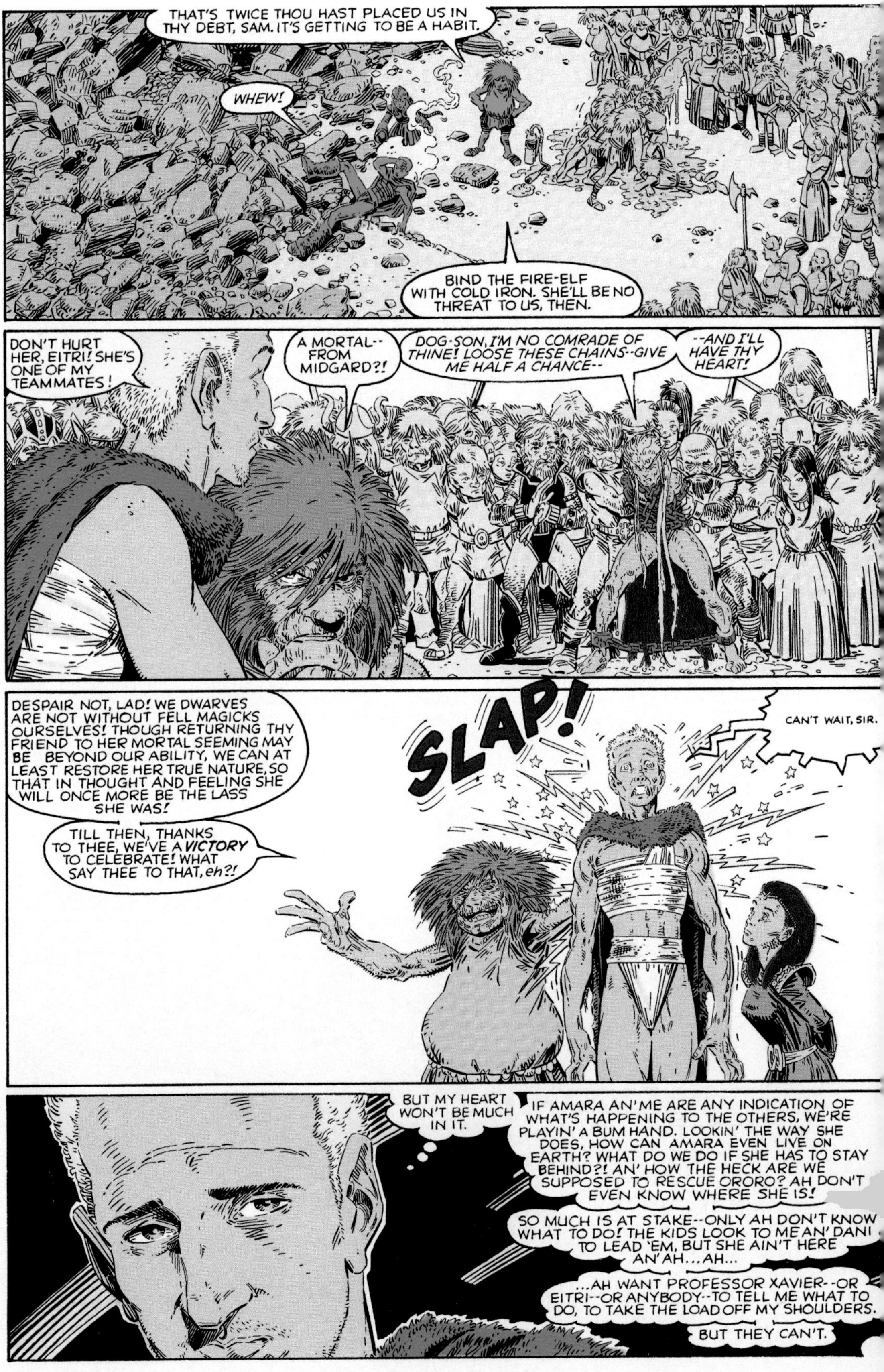

THAT'S TWICE THOU HAST PLACED US IN THY DEBT, SAM. IT'S GETTING TO BE A HABIT.
WHEW!
BIND THE FIRE-ELF WITH COLD IRON. SHE'LL BE NO THREAT TO US, THEN.
DON'T HURT HER, EITRI! SHE'S ONE OF MY TEAMMATES!
A MORTAL--FROM MIDGARD?!
DOG-SON, I'M NO COMRADE OF THINE! LOOSE THESE CHAINS--GIVE ME HALF A CHANCE--
--AND I'LL HAVE THY HEART!
DESPAIR NOT, LAD! WE DWARVES ARE NOT WITHOUT FELL MAGICKS OURSELVES! THOUGH RETURNING THY FRIEND TO HER MORTAL SEEMING MAY BE BEYOND OUR ABILITY, WE CAN AT LEAST RESTORE HER TRUE NATURE, SO THAT IN THOUGHT AND FEELING SHE WILL ONCE MORE BE THE LASS SHE WAS!
TILL THEN, THANKS TO THEE, WE'VE A VICTORY TO CELEBRATE! WHAT SAY THEE TO THAT, eh?!
SLAP!
CAN'T WAIT, SIR.
BUT MY HEART WON'T BE MUCH IN IT.
IF AMARA AN' ME ARE ANY INDICATION OF WHAT'S HAPPENING TO THE OTHERS, WE'RE PLAYIN' A BUM HAND. LOOKIN' THE WAY SHE DOES, HOW CAN AMARA EVEN LIVE ON EARTH? WHAT DO WE DO IF SHE HAS TO STAY BEHIND?! AN' HOW THE HECK ARE WE SUPPOSED TO RESCUE ORORO? AH DON'T EVEN KNOW WHERE SHE IS!
SO MUCH IS AT STAKE--ONLY AH DON'T KNOW WHAT TO DO! THE KIDS LOOK TO ME AN' DANI TO LEAD 'EM, BUT SHE AIN'T HERE AN' AH...AH...
...AH WANT PROFESSOR XAVIER--OR EITRI--OR ANYBODY--TO TELL ME WHAT TO DO, TO TAKE THE LOAD OFF MY SHOULDERS.
BUT THEY CAN'T.

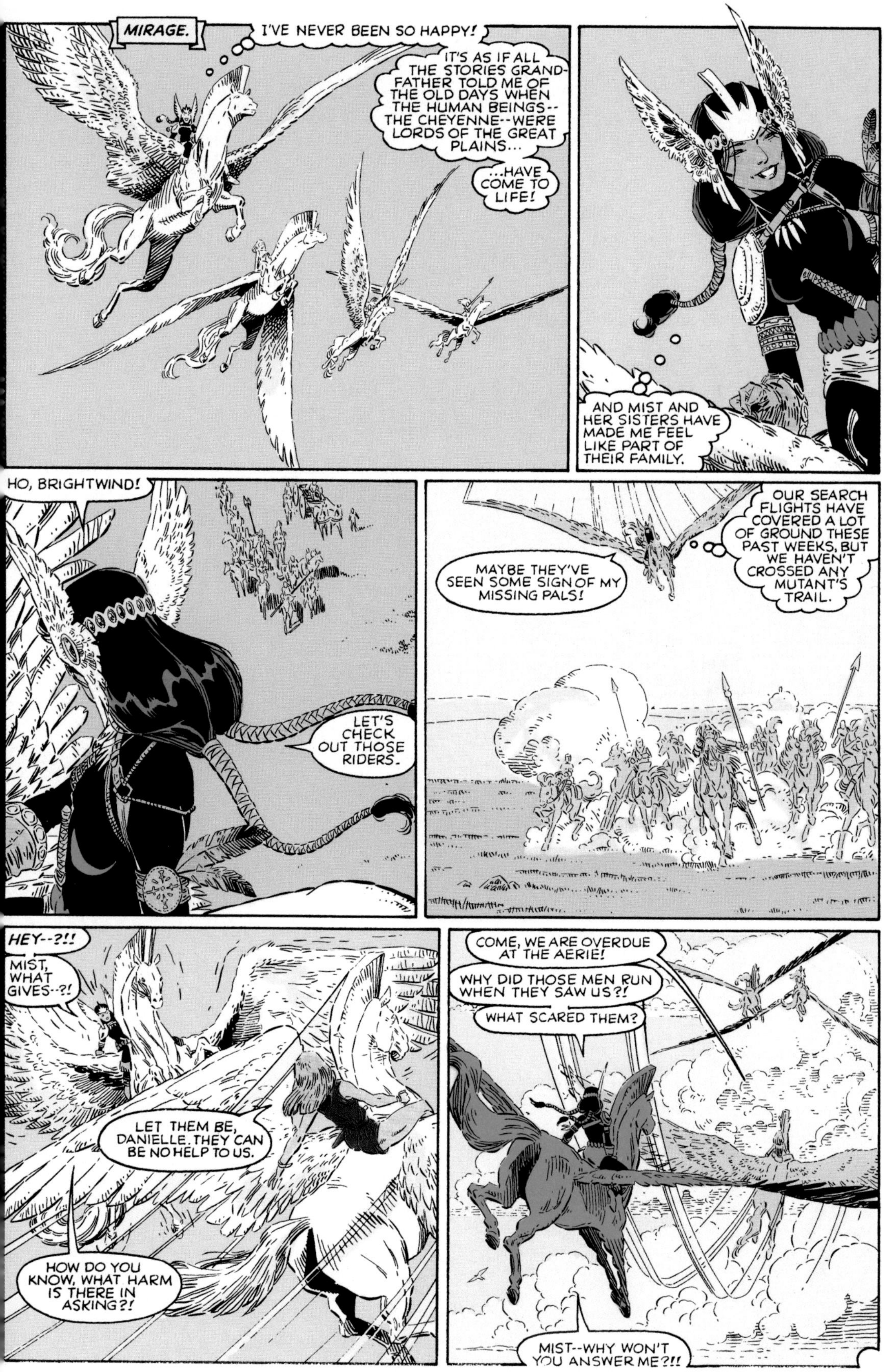
MIRAGE.
I'VE NEVER BEEN SO HAPPY!
IT'S AS IF ALL THE STORIES GRAND-FATHER TOLD ME OF THE OLD DAYS WHEN THE HUMAN BEINGS--THE CHEYENNE--WERE LORDS OF THE GREAT PLAINS...
...HAVE COME TO LIFE!
AND MIST AND HER SISTERS HAVE MADE ME FEEL LIKE PART OF THEIR FAMILY.
HO, BRIGHTWIND!
LET'S CHECK OUT THOSE RIDERS.
MAYBE THEY'VE SEEN SOME SIGN OF MY MISSING PALS!
OUR SEARCH FLIGHTS HAVE COVERED A LOT OF GROUND THESE PAST WEEKS, BUT WE HAVEN'T CROSSED ANY MUTANT'S TRAIL.
HEY--?!!
MIST, WHAT GIVES--?!
LET THEM BE, DANIELLE. THEY CAN BE NO HELP TO US.
HOW DO YOU KNOW, WHAT HARM IS THERE IN ASKING?!
COME, WE ARE OVERDUE AT THE AERIE!
WHY DID THOSE MEN RUN WHEN THEY SAW US?!
WHAT SCARED THEM?
MIST--WHY WON'T YOU ANSWER ME?!!

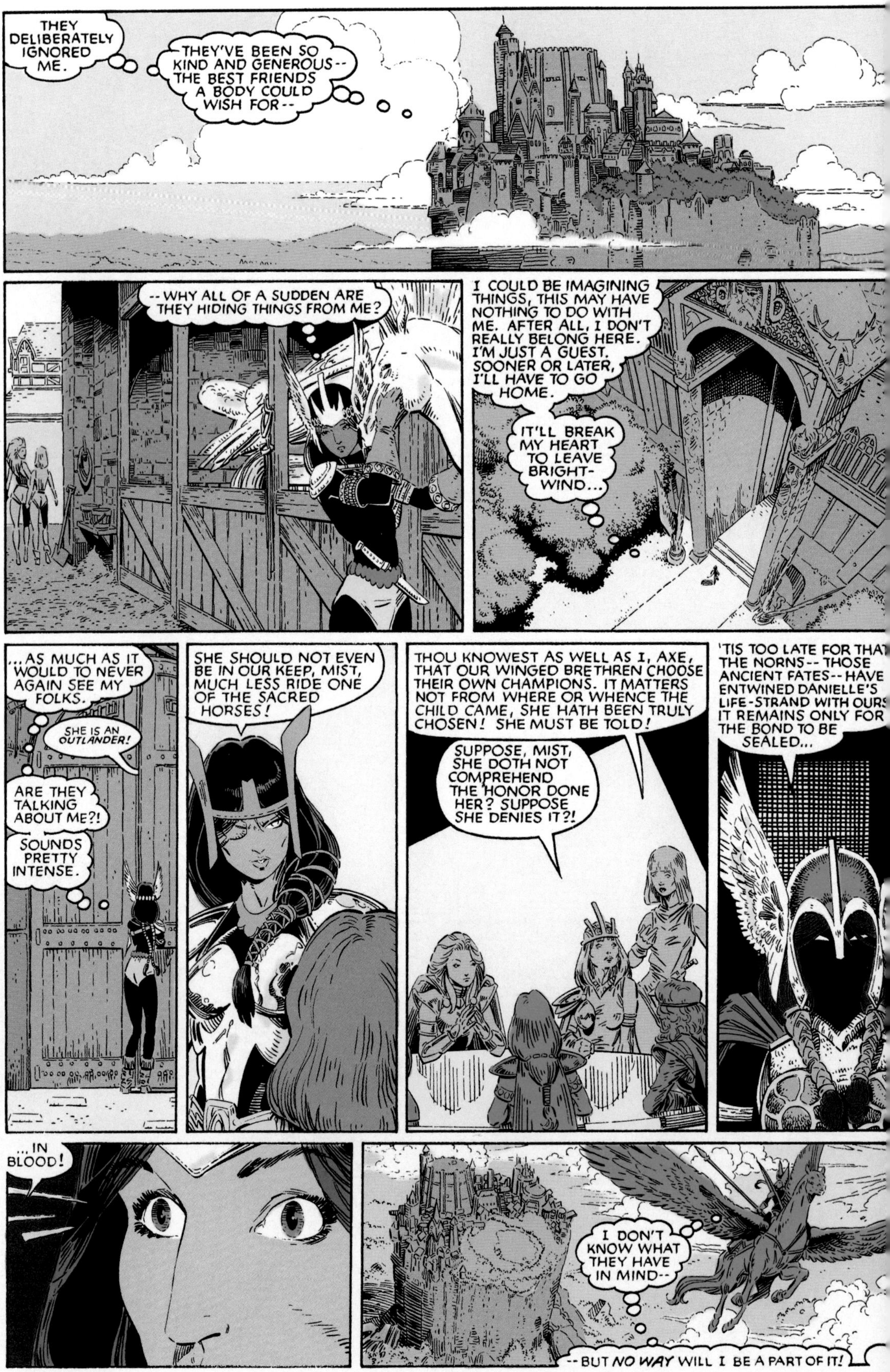
THEY DELIBERATELY IGNORED ME.
THEY'VE BEEN SO KIND AND GENEROUS-- THE BEST FRIENDS A BODY COULD WISH FOR--
--WHY ALL OF A SUDDEN ARE THEY HIDING THINGS FROM ME?
I COULD BE IMAGINING THINGS, THIS MAY HAVE NOTHING TO DO WITH ME. AFTER ALL, I DON'T REALLY BELONG HERE. I'M JUST A GUEST. SOONER OR LATER, I'LL HAVE TO GO HOME.
IT'LL BREAK MY HEART TO LEAVE BRIGHT-WIND...
...AS MUCH AS IT WOULD TO NEVER AGAIN SEE MY FOLKS.
SHE IS AN OUTLANDER!
ARE THEY TALKING ABOUT ME?!
SOUNDS PRETTY INTENSE.
SHE SHOULD NOT EVEN BE IN OUR KEEP, MIST, MUCH LESS RIDE ONE OF THE SACRED HORSES!
THOU KNOWEST AS WELL AS I, AXE, THAT OUR WINGED BRETHREN CHOOSE THEIR OWN CHAMPIONS. IT MATTERS NOT FROM WHERE OR WHENCE THE CHILD CAME, SHE HATH BEEN TRULY CHOSEN! SHE MUST BE TOLD!
SUPPOSE, MIST, SHE DOTH NOT COMPREHEND THE HONOR DONE HER? SUPPOSE SHE DENIES IT?!
'TIS TOO LATE FOR THAT THE NORNS-- THOSE ANCIENT FATES-- HAVE ENTWINED DANIELLE'S LIFE-STRAND WITH OURS IT REMAINS ONLY FOR THE BOND TO BE SEALED...
...IN BLOOD!
I DON'T KNOW WHAT THEY HAVE IN MIND--
--BUT NO WAY WILL I BE A PART OF IT!

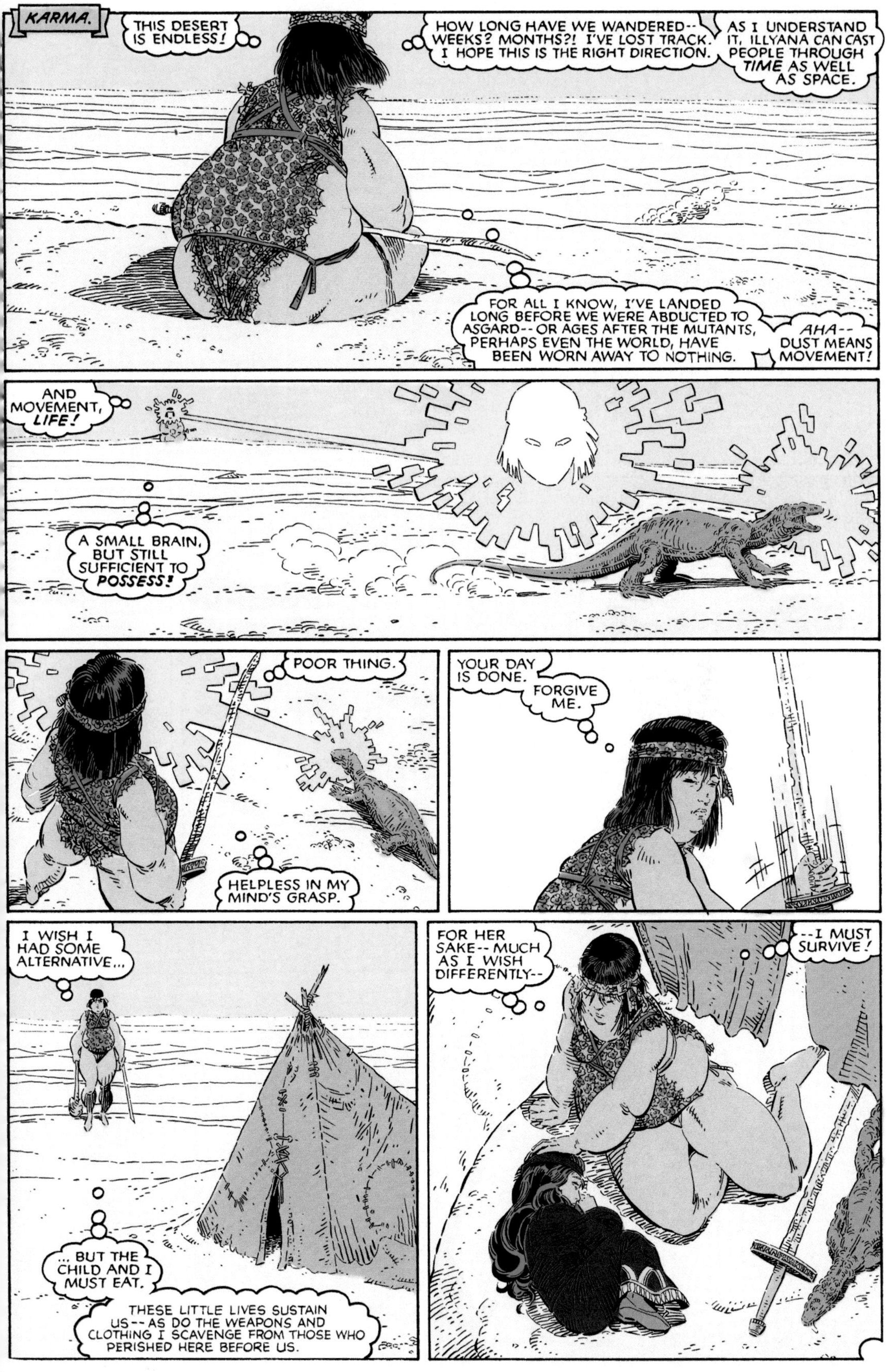
KARMA.
THIS DESERT IS ENDLESS!
HOW LONG HAVE WE WANDERED-- WEEKS? MONTHS?! I'VE LOST TRACK. I HOPE THIS IS THE RIGHT DIRECTION.
AS I UNDERSTAND IT, ILLYANA CAN CAST PEOPLE THROUGH TIME AS WELL AS SPACE.
FOR ALL I KNOW, I'VE LANDED LONG BEFORE WE WERE ABDUCTED TO ASGARD-- OR AGES AFTER THE MUTANTS, PERHAPS EVEN THE WORLD, HAVE BEEN WORN AWAY TO NOTHING.
AHA-- DUST MEANS MOVEMENT!
AND MOVEMENT, LIFE!
A SMALL BRAIN, BUT STILL SUFFICIENT TO POSSESS!
POOR THING.
HELPLESS IN MY MIND'S GRASP.
YOUR DAY IS DONE.
FORGIVE ME.
I WISH I HAD SOME ALTERNATIVE...
... BUT THE CHILD AND I MUST EAT.
THESE LITTLE LIVES SUSTAIN US-- AS DO THE WEAPONS AND CLOTHING I SCAVENGE FROM THOSE WHO PERISHED HERE BEFORE US.
FOR HER SAKE-- MUCH AS I WISH DIFFERENTLY--
--I MUST SURVIVE!

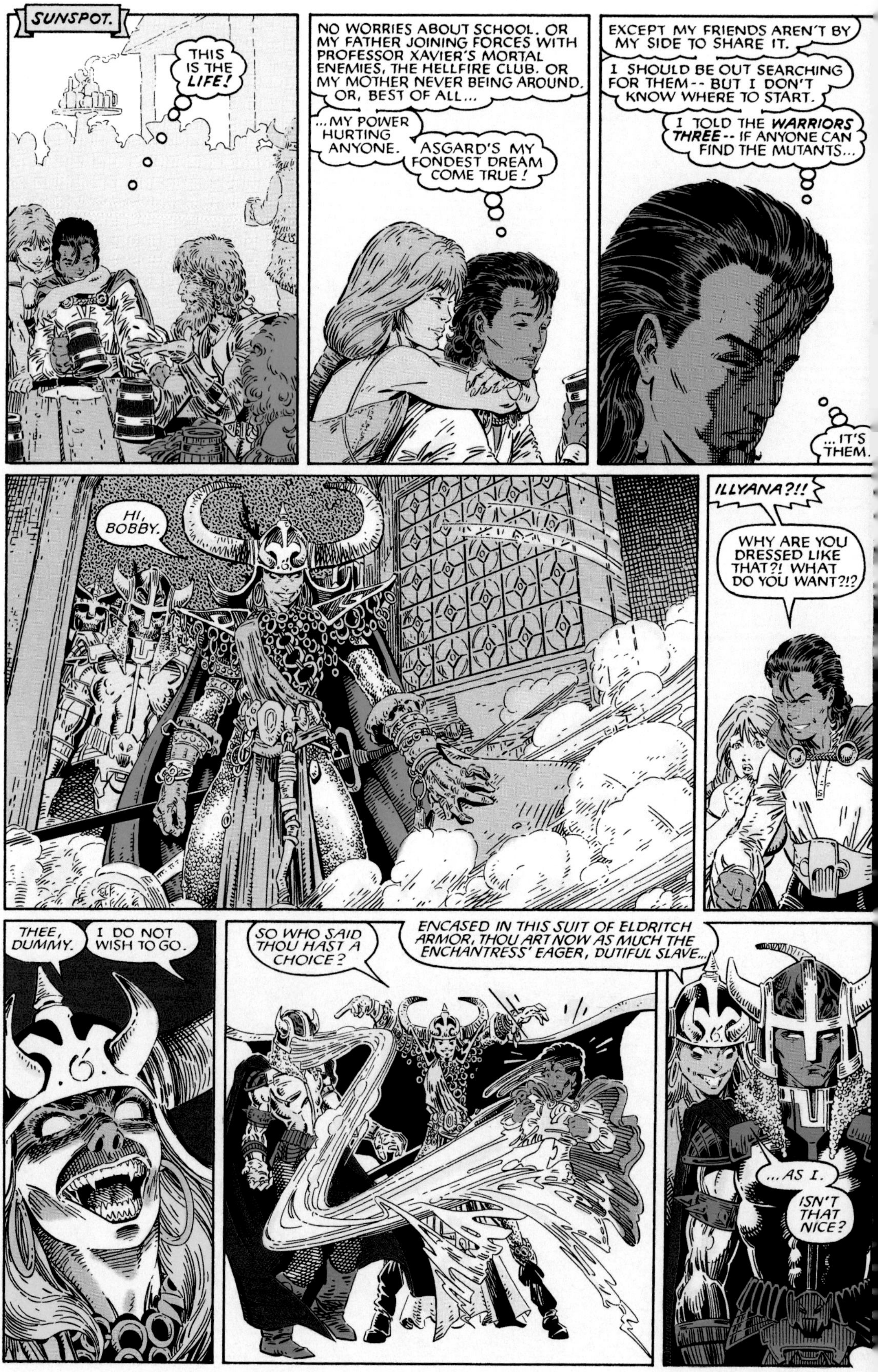
SUNSPOT.
THIS IS THE LIFE!
NO WORRIES ABOUT SCHOOL. OR MY FATHER JOINING FORCES WITH PROFESSOR XAVIER'S MORTAL ENEMIES, THE HELLFIRE CLUB. OR MY MOTHER NEVER BEING AROUND. OR, BEST OF ALL...
...MY POWER HURTING ANYONE.
ASGARD'S MY FONDEST DREAM COME TRUE!
EXCEPT MY FRIENDS AREN'T BY MY SIDE TO SHARE IT.
I SHOULD BE OUT SEARCHING FOR THEM -- BUT I DON'T KNOW WHERE TO START.
I TOLD THE WARRIORS THREE -- IF ANYONE CAN FIND THE MUTANTS...
...IT'S THEM.
HI, BOBBY.
ILLYANA?!!
WHY ARE YOU DRESSED LIKE THAT?! WHAT DO YOU WANT?!?
THEE, DUMMY.
I DO NOT WISH TO GO.
SO WHO SAID THOU HAST A CHOICE?
ENCASED IN THIS SUIT OF ELDRITCH ARMOR, THOU ART NOW AS MUCH THE ENCHANTRESS' EAGER, DUTIFUL SLAVE...
...AS I.
ISN'T THAT NICE?

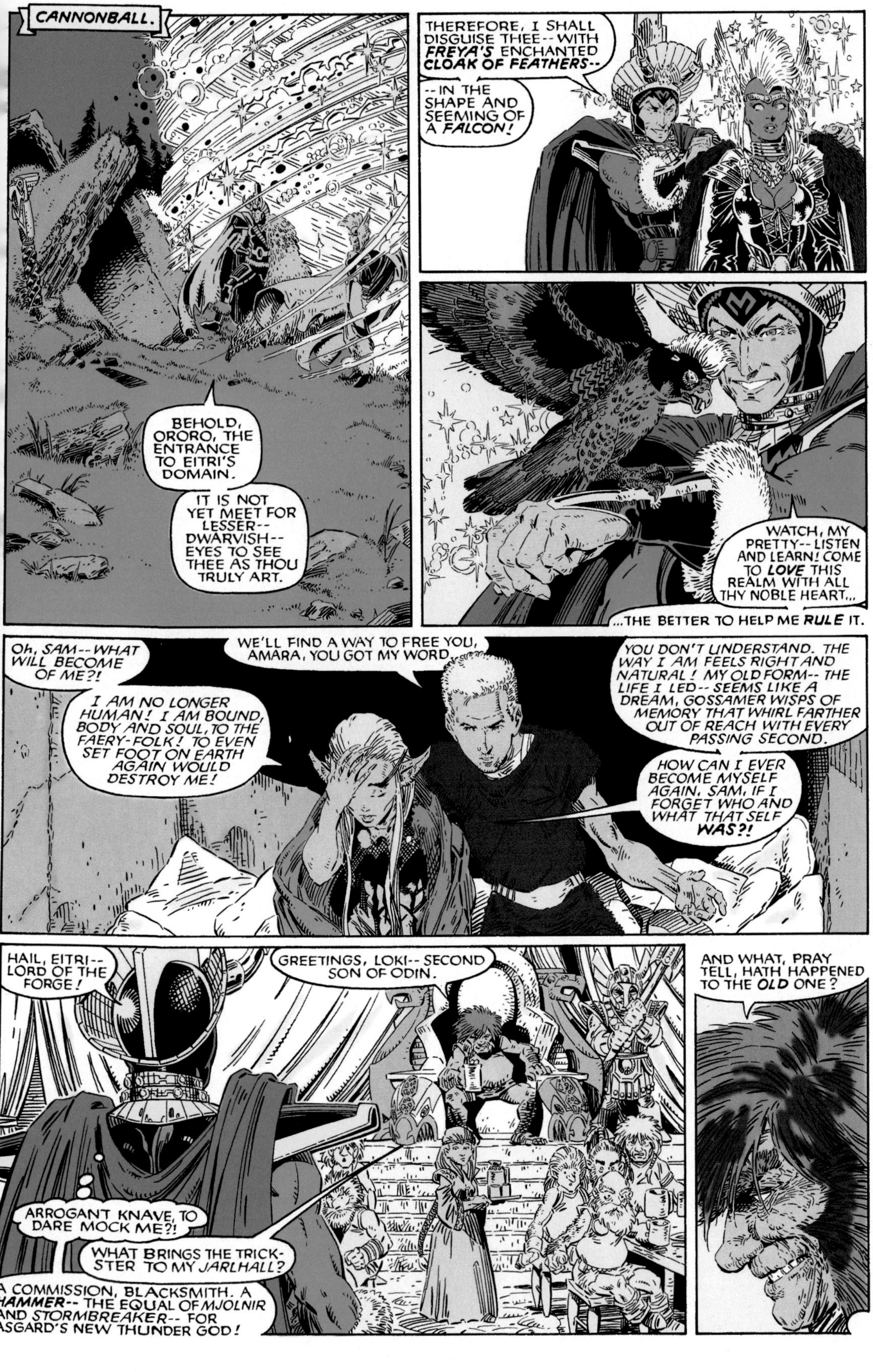
CANNONBALL.
BEHOLD, ORORO, THE ENTRANCE TO EITRI'S DOMAIN.
IT IS NOT YET MEET FOR LESSER-- DWARVISH-- EYES TO SEE THEE AS THOU TRULY ART.
THEREFORE, I SHALL DISGUISE THEE-- WITH FREYA'S ENCHANTED CLOAK OF FEATHERS--
--IN THE SHAPE AND SEEMING OF A FALCON!
WATCH, MY PRETTY-- LISTEN AND LEARN! COME TO LOVE THIS REALM WITH ALL THY NOBLE HEART...
...THE BETTER TO HELP ME RULE IT.
Oh, SAM-- WHAT WILL BECOME OF ME?!
I AM NO LONGER HUMAN! I AM BOUND, BODY AND SOUL, TO THE FAERY-FOLK! TO EVEN SET FOOT ON EARTH AGAIN WOULD DESTROY ME!
WE'LL FIND A WAY TO FREE YOU, AMARA, YOU GOT MY WORD.
YOU DON'T UNDERSTAND. THE WAY I AM FEELS RIGHT AND NATURAL! MY OLD FORM-- THE LIFE I LED-- SEEMS LIKE A DREAM, GOSSAMER WISPS OF MEMORY THAT WHIRL FARTHER OUT OF REACH WITH EVERY PASSING SECOND.
HOW CAN I EVER BECOME MYSELF AGAIN, SAM, IF I FORGET WHO AND WHAT THAT SELF WAS?!
HAIL, EITRI-- LORD OF THE FORGE!
GREETINGS, LOKI-- SECOND SON OF ODIN.
ARROGANT KNAVE, TO DARE MOCK ME?!
WHAT BRINGS THE TRICKSTER TO MY JARLHALL?
A COMMISSION, BLACKSMITH. A HAMMER-- THE EQUAL OF MJOLNIR AND STORMBREAKER-- FOR ASGARD'S NEW THUNDER GOD!
AND WHAT, PRAY TELL, HATH HAPPENED TO THE OLD ONE?

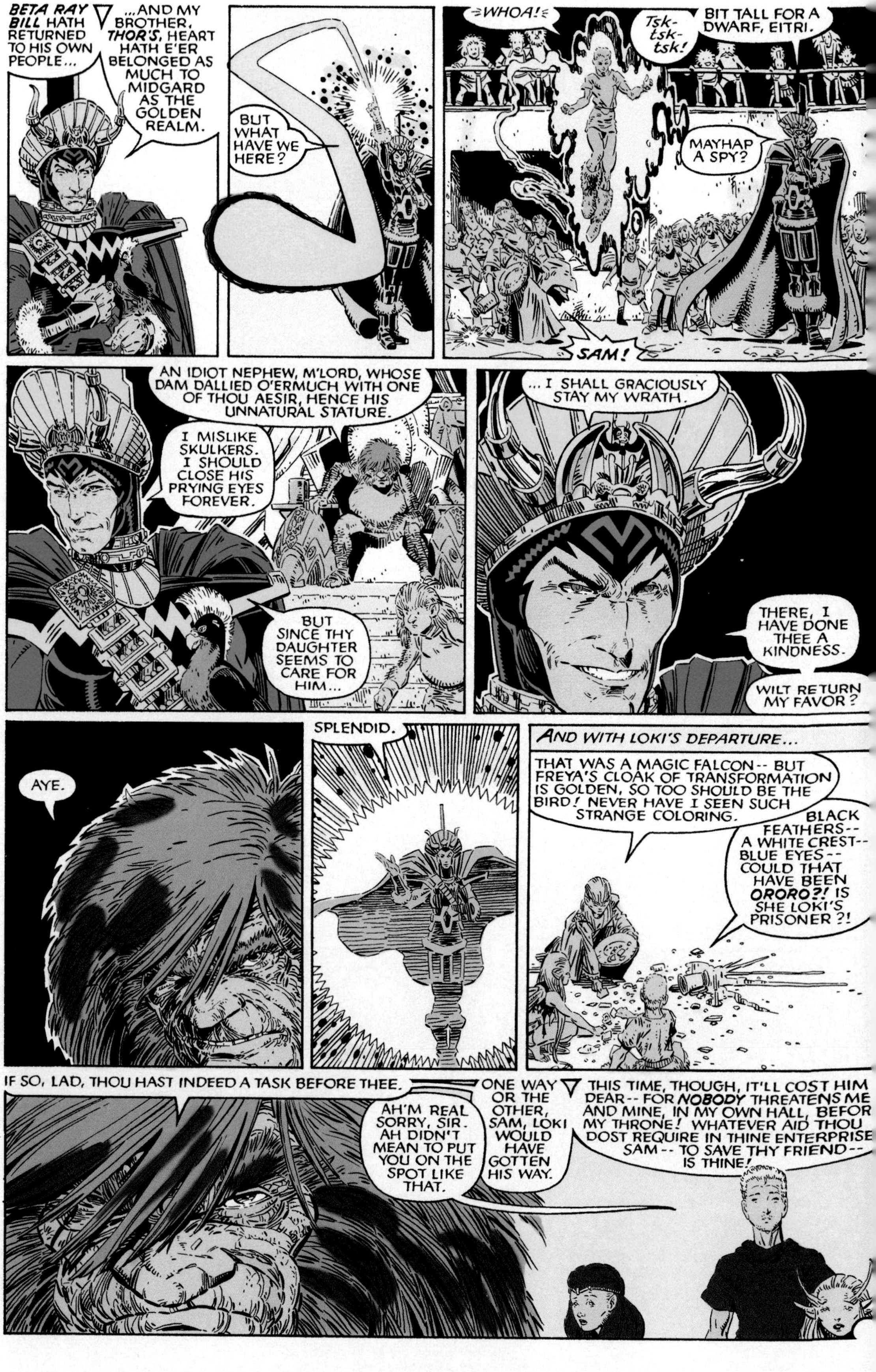
BETA RAY BILL HATH RETURNED TO HIS OWN PEOPLE...
...AND MY BROTHER, THOR'S, HEART HATH E'ER BELONGED AS MUCH TO MIDGARD AS THE GOLDEN REALM.
BUT WHAT HAVE WE HERE?
WHOA!
Tsk-tsk-tsk!
BIT TALL FOR A DWARF, EITRI.
MAYHAP A SPY?
SAM!
AN IDIOT NEPHEW, M'LORD, WHOSE DAM DALLIED O'ERMUCH WITH ONE OF THOU AESIR, HENCE HIS UNNATURAL STATURE.
I MISLIKE SKULKERS. I SHOULD CLOSE HIS PRYING EYES FOREVER.
BUT SINCE THY DAUGHTER SEEMS TO CARE FOR HIM...
... I SHALL GRACIOUSLY STAY MY WRATH.
THERE, I HAVE DONE THEE A KINDNESS.
WILT RETURN MY FAVOR?
AYE.
SPLENDID.
AND WITH LOKI'S DEPARTURE...
THAT WAS A MAGIC FALCON -- BUT FREYA'S CLOAK OF TRANSFORMATION IS GOLDEN, SO TOO SHOULD BE THE BIRD! NEVER HAVE I SEEN SUCH STRANGE COLORING.
BLACK FEATHERS -- A WHITE CREST -- BLUE EYES -- COULD THAT HAVE BEEN ORORO?! IS SHE LOKI'S PRISONER?!
IF SO, LAD, THOU HAST INDEED A TASK BEFORE THEE.
AH'M REAL SORRY, SIR. AH DIDN'T MEAN TO PUT YOU ON THE SPOT LIKE THAT.
ONE WAY OR THE OTHER, SAM, LOKI WOULD HAVE GOTTEN HIS WAY.
THIS TIME, THOUGH, IT'LL COST HIM DEAR -- FOR NOBODY THREATENS ME AND MINE, IN MY OWN HALL, BEFOR MY THRONE! WHATEVER AID THOU DOST REQUIRE IN THINE ENTERPRISE SAM -- TO SAVE THY FRIEND -- IS THINE!

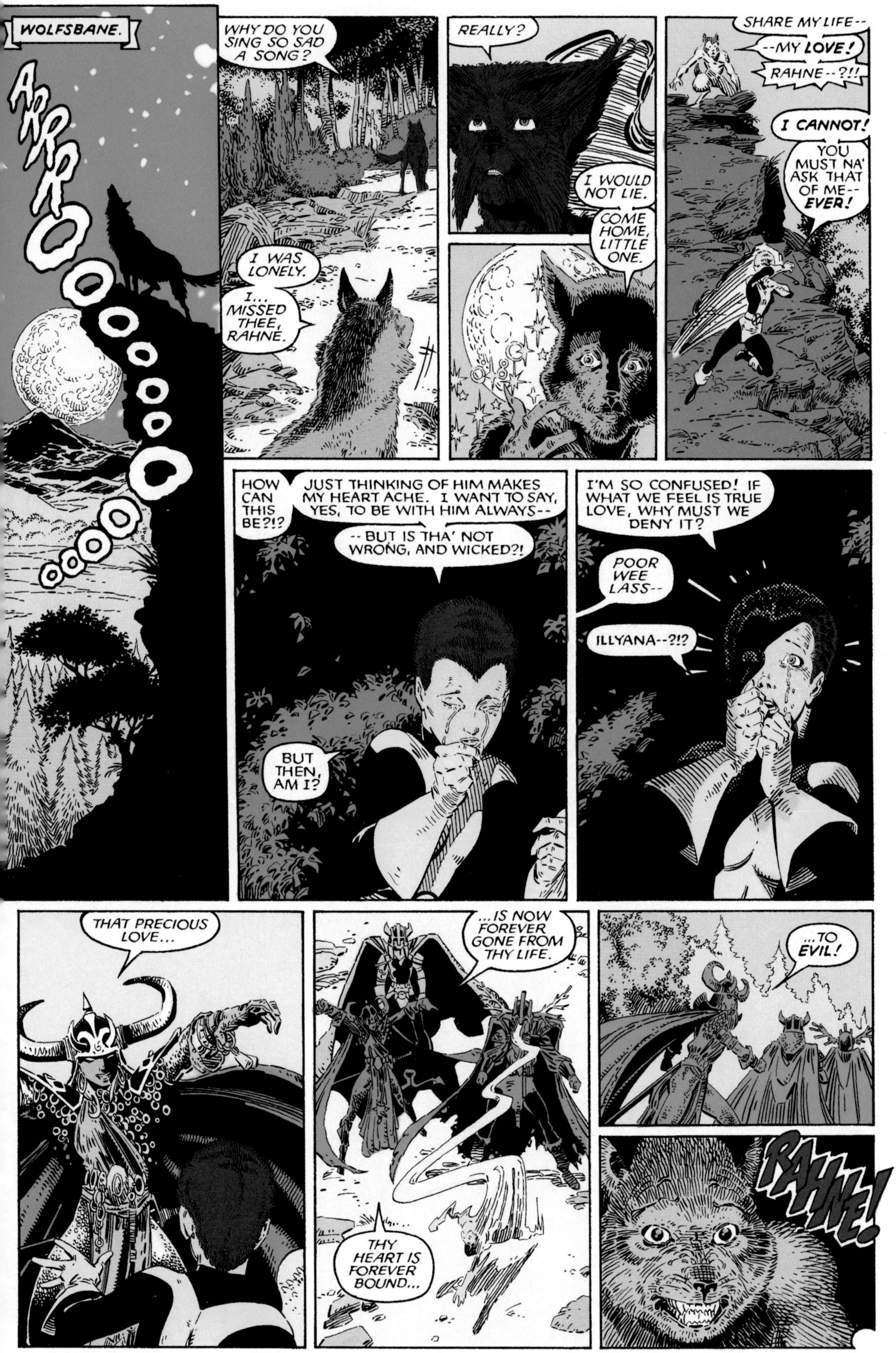
WOLFSBANE.
ARRROOOOOOOOOOOOOOO
WHY DO YOU SING SO SAD A SONG?
I WAS LONELY.
I... MISSED THEE, RAHNE.
REALLY?
I WOULD NOT LIE.
COME HOME, LITTLE ONE.
SHARE MY LIFE--
--MY LOVE!
RAHNE--?!!
I CANNOT!
YOU MUST NA' ASK THAT OF ME--EVER!
HOW CAN THIS BE?!?
JUST THINKING OF HIM MAKES MY HEART ACHE. I WANT TO SAY, YES, TO BE WITH HIM ALWAYS--
--BUT IS THA' NOT WRONG, AND WICKED?!
BUT THEN, AM I?
I'M SO CONFUSED! IF WHAT WE FEEL IS TRUE LOVE, WHY MUST WE DENY IT?
POOR WEE LASS--
ILLYANA--?!?
THAT PRECIOUS LOVE...
...IS NOW FOREVER GONE FROM THY LIFE.
THY HEART IS FOREVER BOUND...
...TO EVIL!
RAHNE!

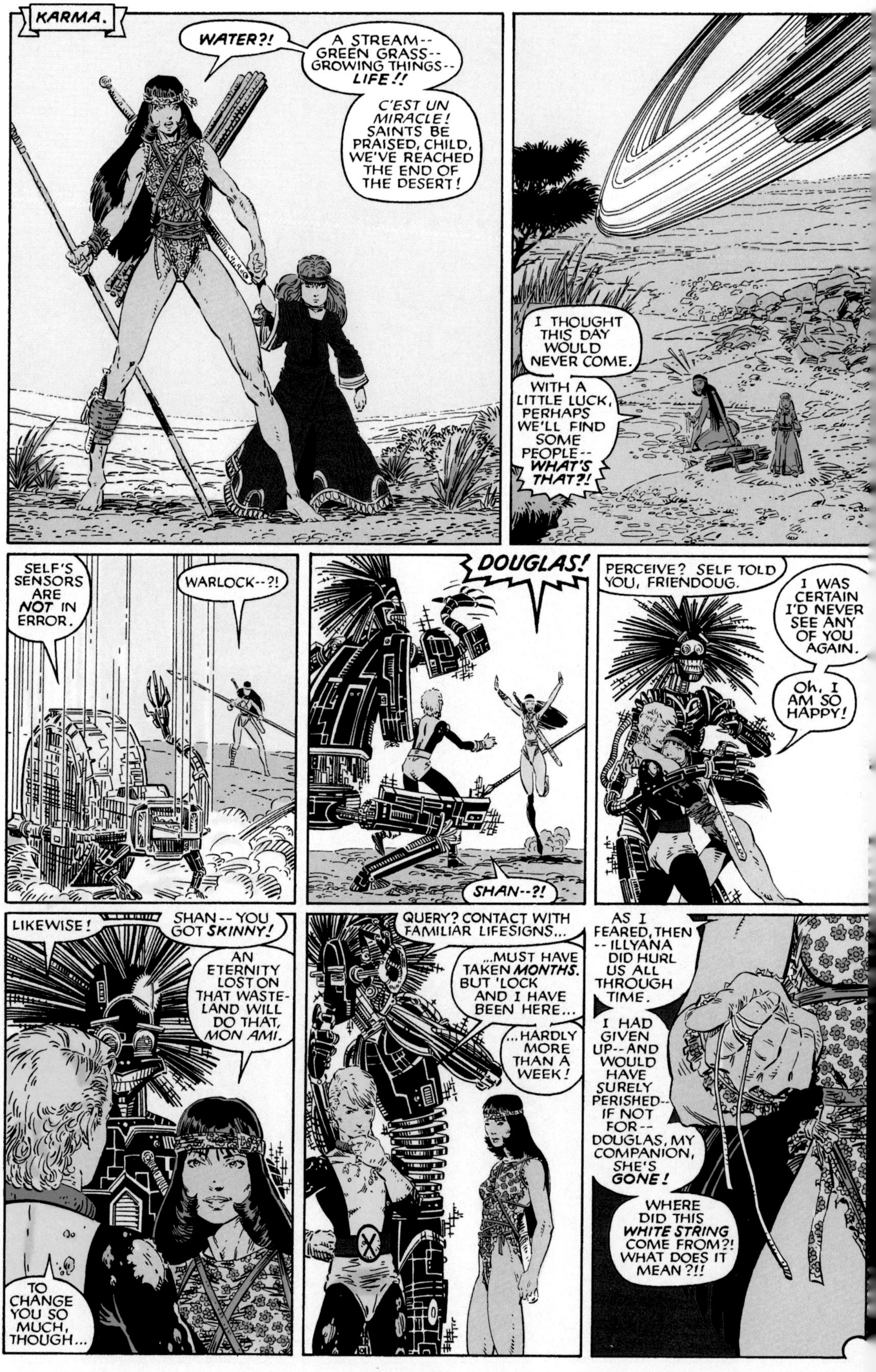

KARMA.
WATER?!
A STREAM-- GREEN GRASS-- GROWING THINGS-- LIFE!!
C'EST UN MIRACLE! SAINTS BE PRAISED, CHILD, WE'VE REACHED THE END OF THE DESERT!
I THOUGHT THIS DAY WOULD NEVER COME.
WITH A LITTLE LUCK, PERHAPS WE'LL FIND SOME PEOPLE-- WHAT'S THAT?!
SELF'S SENSORS ARE NOT IN ERROR.
WARLOCK--?!
DOUGLAS!
SHAN--?!
PERCEIVE? SELF TOLD YOU, FRIENDOUG.
I WAS CERTAIN I'D NEVER SEE ANY OF YOU AGAIN.
Oh, I AM SO HAPPY!
LIKEWISE!
SHAN-- YOU GOT SKINNY!
AN ETERNITY LOST ON THAT WASTE-LAND WILL DO THAT, MON AMI.
TO CHANGE YOU SO MUCH, THOUGH...
QUERY? CONTACT WITH FAMILIAR LIFESIGNS...
...MUST HAVE TAKEN MONTHS. BUT 'LOCK AND I HAVE BEEN HERE...
...HARDLY MORE THAN A WEEK!
AS I FEARED, THEN -- ILLYANA DID HURL US ALL THROUGH TIME.
I HAD GIVEN UP--AND WOULD HAVE SURELY PERISHED-- IF NOT FOR-- DOUGLAS, MY COMPANION, SHE'S GONE!
WHERE DID THIS WHITE STRING COME FROM?! WHAT DOES IT MEAN?!!

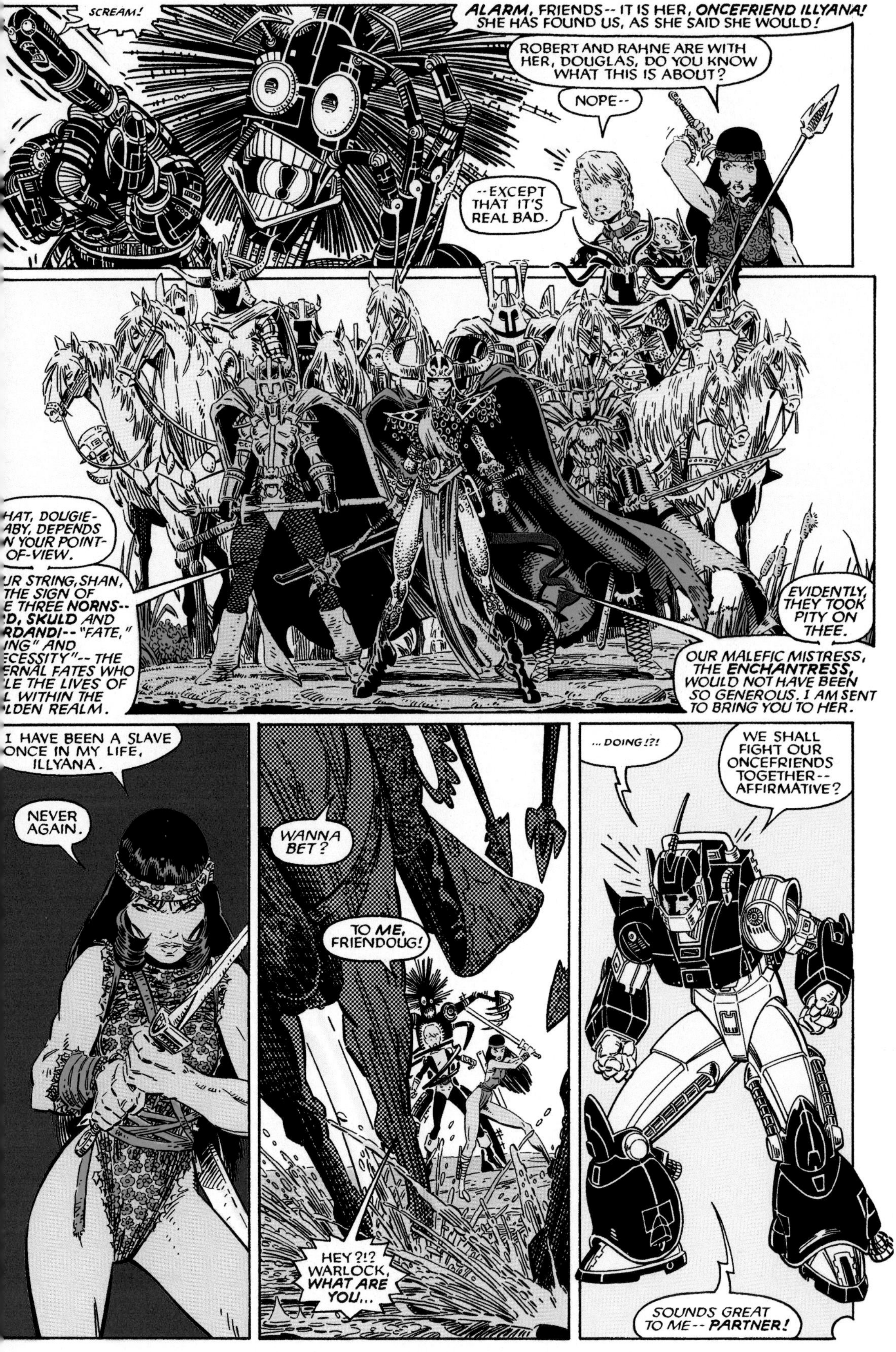
SCREAM!
ALARM, FRIENDS-- IT IS HER, ONCEFRIEND ILLYANA! SHE HAS FOUND US, AS SHE SAID SHE WOULD!
ROBERT AND RAHNE ARE WITH HER, DOUGLAS, DO YOU KNOW WHAT THIS IS ABOUT?
NOPE--
--EXCEPT THAT IT'S REAL BAD.
HAT, DOUGIE-ABY, DEPENDS N YOUR POINT-OF-VIEW.
UR STRING, SHAN, THE SIGN OF E THREE NORNS-- D, SKULD AND RDANDI-- "FATE," ING" AND ECESSITY"-- THE ERNAL FATES WHO LE THE LIVES OF L WITHIN THE LDEN REALM.
EVIDENTLY, THEY TOOK PITY ON THEE.
OUR MALEFIC MISTRESS, THE ENCHANTRESS, WOULD NOT HAVE BEEN SO GENEROUS. I AM SENT TO BRING YOU TO HER.
I HAVE BEEN A SLAVE ONCE IN MY LIFE, ILLYANA.
NEVER AGAIN.
WANNA BET?
TO ME, FRIENDOUG!
HEY?!? WARLOCK, WHAT ARE YOU...
... DOING!?!
WE SHALL FIGHT OUR ONCEFRIENDS TOGETHER-- AFFIRMATIVE?
SOUNDS GREAT TO ME-- PARTNER!

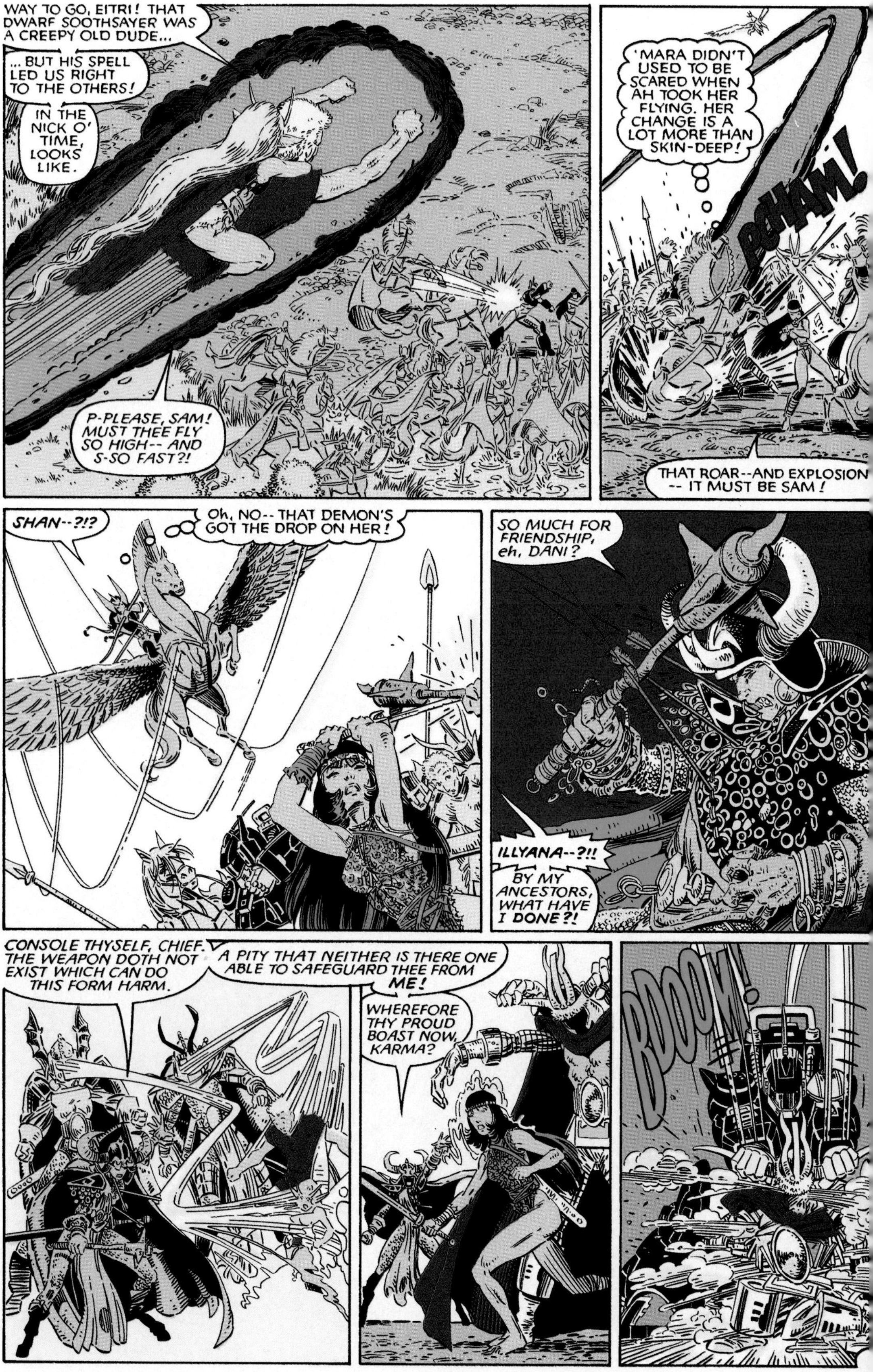

WAY TO GO, EITRI! THAT DWARF SOOTHSAYER WAS A CREEPY OLD DUDE...
...BUT HIS SPELL LED US RIGHT TO THE OTHERS!
IN THE NICK O' TIME, LOOKS LIKE.
P-PLEASE, SAM! MUST THEE FLY SO HIGH-- AND S-SO FAST?!
'MARA DIDN'T USED TO BE SCARED WHEN AH TOOK HER FLYING. HER CHANGE IS A LOT MORE THAN SKIN-DEEP!
PCHAM!
THAT ROAR--AND EXPLOSION -- IT MUST BE SAM!
SHAN--?!?
Oh, NO-- THAT DEMON'S GOT THE DROP ON HER!
SO MUCH FOR FRIENDSHIP, eh, DANI?
ILLYANA--?!!
BY MY ANCESTORS, WHAT HAVE I DONE?!
CONSOLE THYSELF, CHIEF. THE WEAPON DOTH NOT EXIST WHICH CAN DO THIS FORM HARM.
A PITY THAT NEITHER IS THERE ONE ABLE TO SAFEGUARD THEE FROM ME!
WHEREFORE THY PROUD BOAST NOW, KARMA?
BDOOM!

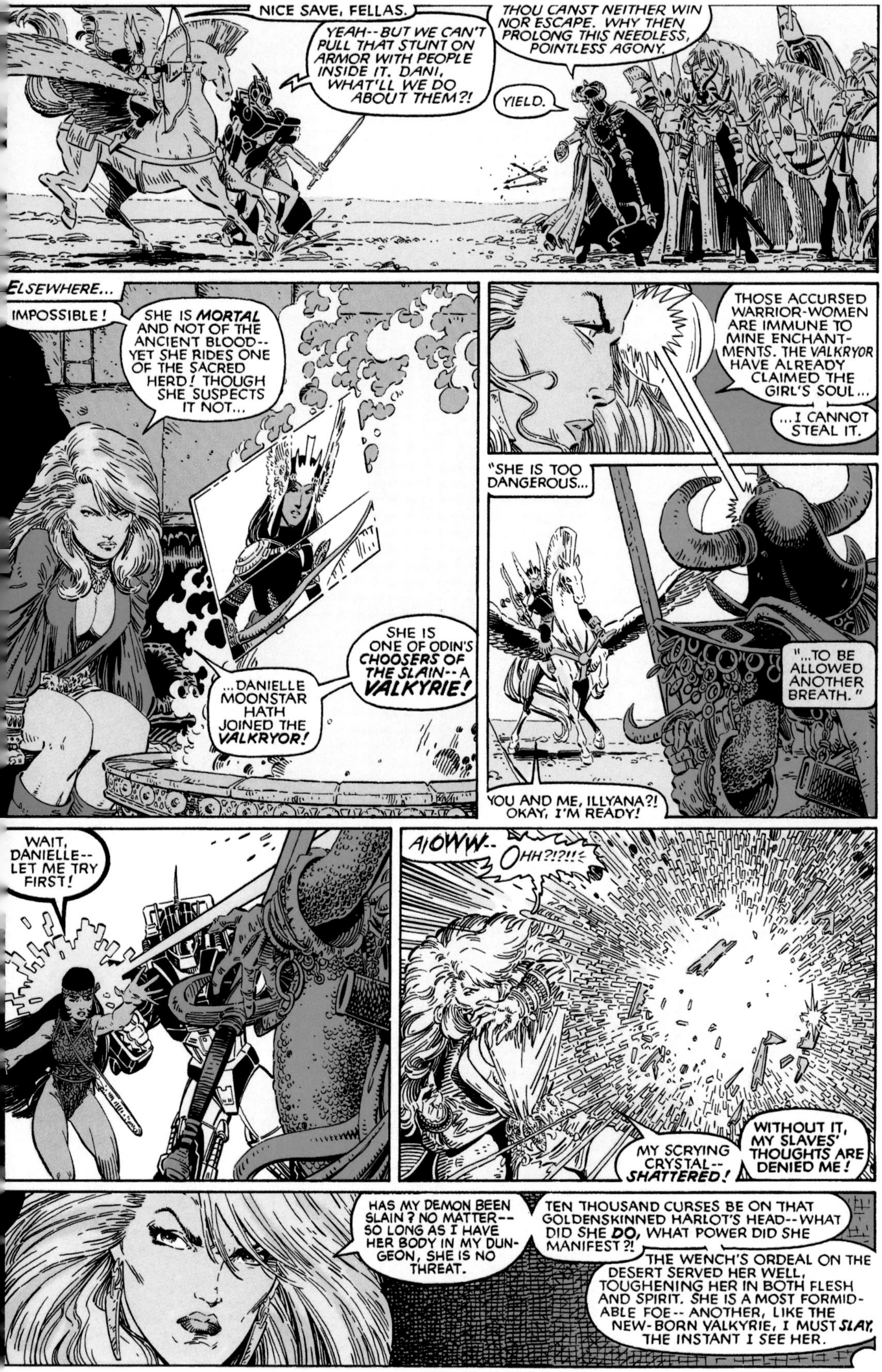
NICE SAVE, FELLAS.
YEAH--BUT WE CAN'T PULL THAT STUNT ON ARMOR WITH PEOPLE INSIDE IT. DANI, WHAT'LL WE DO ABOUT THEM?!
THOU CANST NEITHER WIN NOR ESCAPE. WHY THEN PROLONG THIS NEEDLESS, POINTLESS AGONY.
YIELD.
ELSEWHERE...
IMPOSSIBLE!
SHE IS MORTAL AND NOT OF THE ANCIENT BLOOD-- YET SHE RIDES ONE OF THE SACRED HERD! THOUGH SHE SUSPECTS IT NOT...
...DANIELLE MOONSTAR HATH JOINED THE VALKRYOR!
SHE IS ONE OF ODIN'S CHOOSERS OF THE SLAIN--A VALKYRIE!
THOSE ACCURSED WARRIOR-WOMEN ARE IMMUNE TO MINE ENCHANTMENTS. THE VALKRYOR HAVE ALREADY CLAIMED THE GIRL'S SOUL...
...I CANNOT STEAL IT.
"SHE IS TOO DANGEROUS...
"...TO BE ALLOWED ANOTHER BREATH."
YOU AND ME, ILLYANA?! OKAY, I'M READY!
WAIT, DANIELLE-- LET ME TRY FIRST!
AIOWW-- OHH?!?!!
MY SCRYING CRYSTAL-- SHATTERED!
WITHOUT IT, MY SLAVES' THOUGHTS ARE DENIED ME!
HAS MY DEMON BEEN SLAIN? NO MATTER-- SO LONG AS I HAVE HER BODY IN MY DUNGEON, SHE IS NO THREAT.
TEN THOUSAND CURSES BE ON THAT GOLDENSKINNED HARLOT'S HEAD--WHAT DID SHE DO, WHAT POWER DID SHE MANIFEST?!
THE WENCH'S ORDEAL ON THE DESERT SERVED HER WELL, TOUGHENING HER IN BOTH FLESH AND SPIRIT. SHE IS A MOST FORMIDABLE FOE-- ANOTHER, LIKE THE NEW-BORN VALKYRIE, I MUST SLAY THE INSTANT I SEE HER.

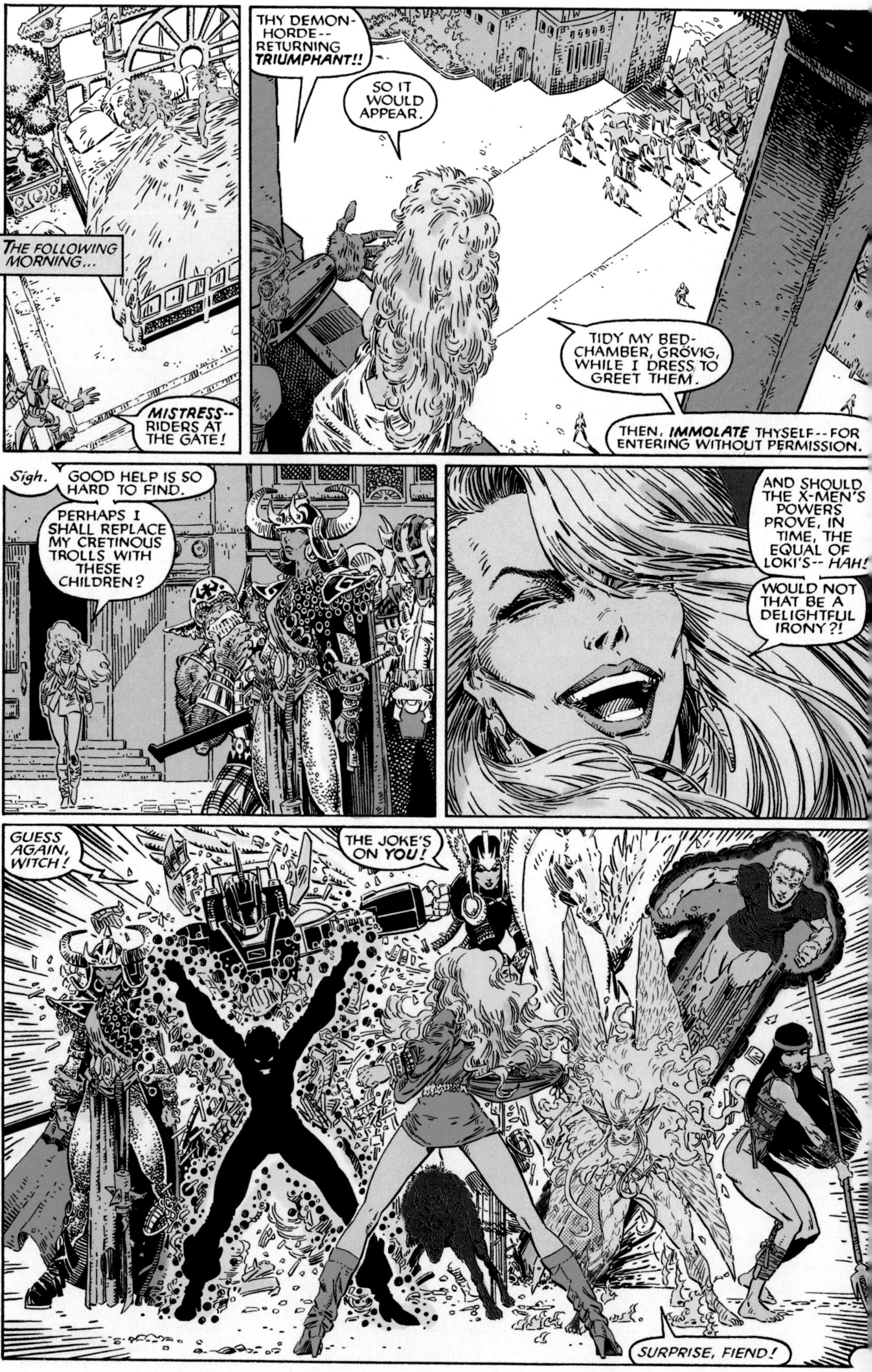
THE FOLLOWING MORNING...
MISTRESS-- RIDERS AT THE GATE!
THY DEMON-HORDE-- RETURNING TRIUMPHANT!!
SO IT WOULD APPEAR.
TIDY MY BED-CHAMBER, GRÖVIG, WHILE I DRESS TO GREET THEM.
THEN, IMMOLATE THYSELF--FOR ENTERING WITHOUT PERMISSION.
Sigh.
GOOD HELP IS SO HARD TO FIND.
PERHAPS I SHALL REPLACE MY CRETINOUS TROLLS WITH THESE CHILDREN?
AND SHOULD THE X-MEN'S POWERS PROVE, IN TIME, THE EQUAL OF LOKI'S-- HAH!
WOULD NOT THAT BE A DELIGHTFUL IRONY?!
GUESS AGAIN, WITCH!
THE JOKE'S ON YOU!
SURPRISE, FIEND!

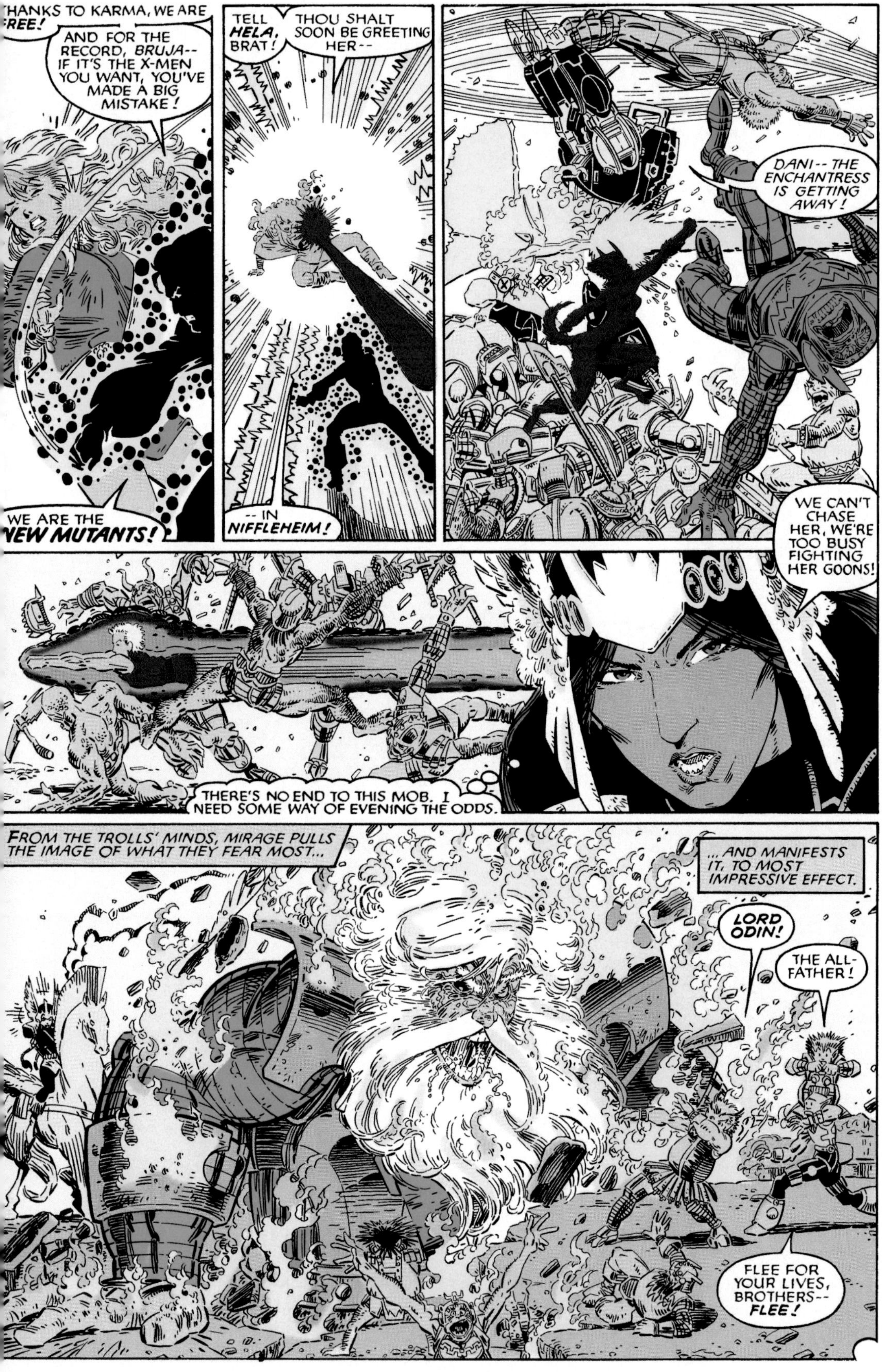
THANKS TO KARMA, WE ARE FREE!
AND FOR THE RECORD, BRUJA-- IF IT'S THE X-MEN YOU WANT, YOU'VE MADE A BIG MISTAKE!
WE ARE THE NEW MUTANTS!
TELL HELA, BRAT!
THOU SHALT SOON BE GREETING HER--
-- IN NIFFLEHEIM!
DANI-- THE ENCHANTRESS IS GETTING AWAY!
WE CAN'T CHASE HER, WE'RE TOO BUSY FIGHTING HER GOONS!
THERE'S NO END TO THIS MOB. I NEED SOME WAY OF EVENING THE ODDS.
FROM THE TROLLS' MINDS, MIRAGE PULLS THE IMAGE OF WHAT THEY FEAR MOST...
...AND MANIFESTS IT, TO MOST IMPRESSIVE EFFECT.
LORD ODIN!
THE ALL-FATHER!
FLEE FOR YOUR LIVES, BROTHERS-- FLEE!

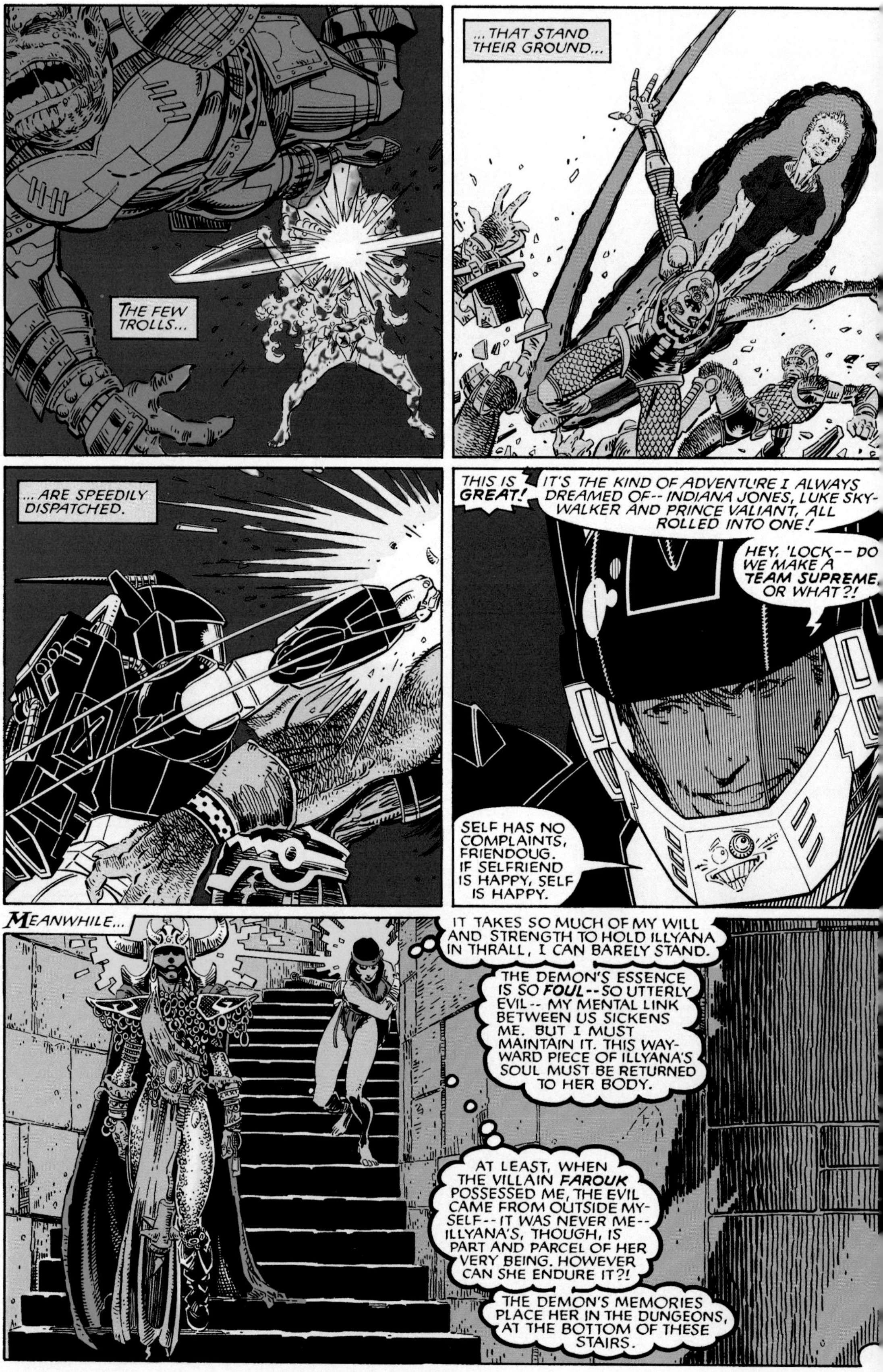
THE FEW TROLLS...
...THAT STAND THEIR GROUND...
...ARE SPEEDILY DISPATCHED.
THIS IS GREAT!
IT'S THE KIND OF ADVENTURE I ALWAYS DREAMED OF-- INDIANA JONES, LUKE SKY-WALKER AND PRINCE VALIANT, ALL ROLLED INTO ONE!
HEY, 'LOCK-- DO WE MAKE A TEAM SUPREME, OR WHAT?!
SELF HAS NO COMPLAINTS, FRIENDOUG. IF SELFRIEND IS HAPPY, SELF IS HAPPY.
MEANWHILE...
IT TAKES SO MUCH OF MY WILL AND STRENGTH TO HOLD ILLYANA IN THRALL, I CAN BARELY STAND.
THE DEMON'S ESSENCE IS SO FOUL-- SO UTTERLY EVIL-- MY MENTAL LINK BETWEEN US SICKENS ME. BUT I MUST MAINTAIN IT. THIS WAY-WARD PIECE OF ILLYANA'S SOUL MUST BE RETURNED TO HER BODY.
AT LEAST, WHEN THE VILLAIN FAROUK POSSESSED ME, THE EVIL CAME FROM OUTSIDE MY-SELF-- IT WAS NEVER ME-- ILLYANA'S, THOUGH, IS PART AND PARCEL OF HER VERY BEING. HOWEVER CAN SHE ENDURE IT?!
THE DEMON'S MEMORIES PLACE HER IN THE DUNGEONS, AT THE BOTTOM OF THESE STAIRS.

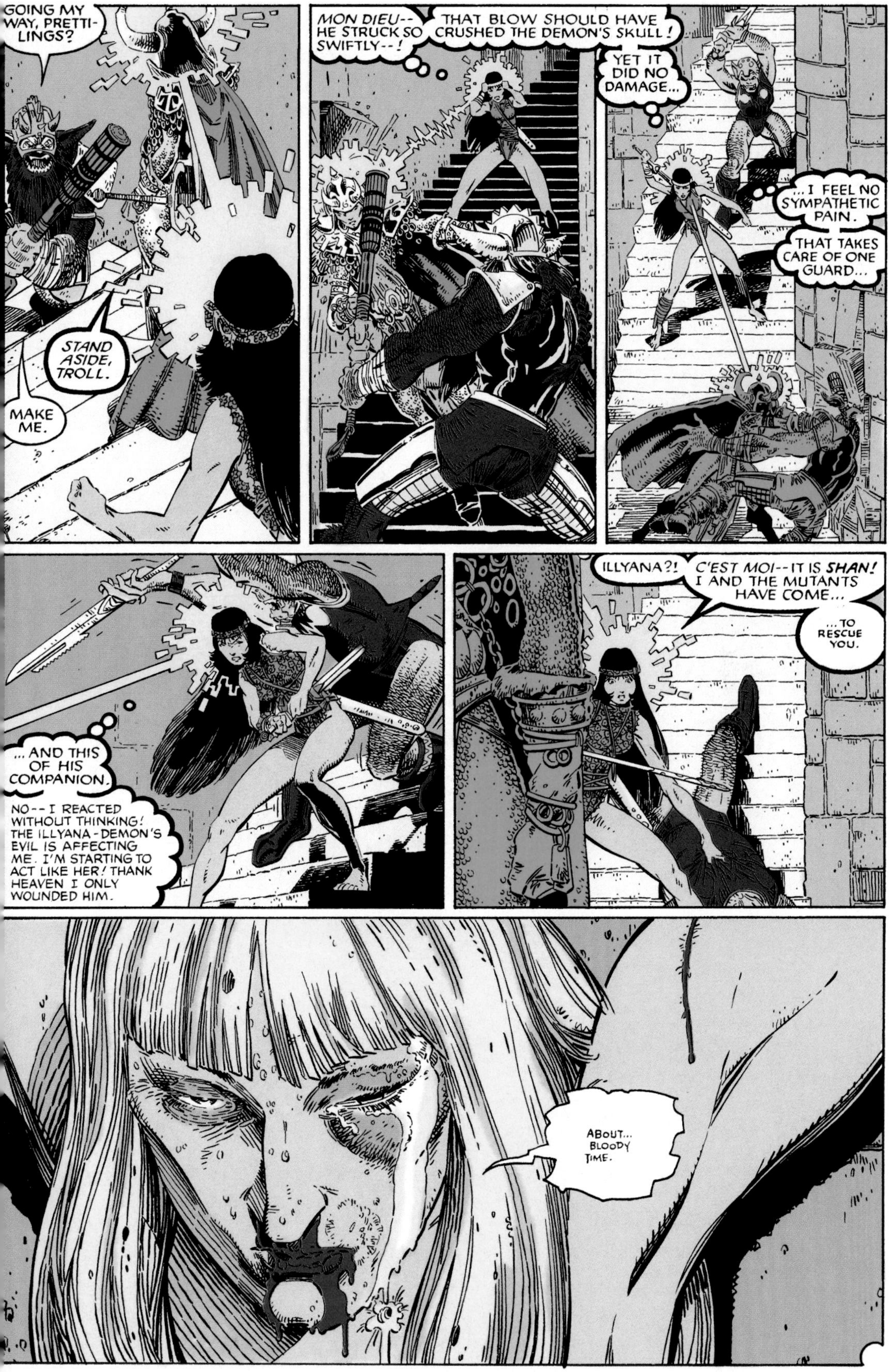
GOING MY WAY, PRETTILINGS?
STAND ASIDE, TROLL.
MAKE ME.
MON DIEU-- HE STRUCK SO SWIFTLY--!
THAT BLOW SHOULD HAVE CRUSHED THE DEMON'S SKULL!
YET IT DID NO DAMAGE...
...I FEEL NO SYMPATHETIC PAIN.
THAT TAKES CARE OF ONE GUARD...
...AND THIS OF HIS COMPANION.
NO-- I REACTED WITHOUT THINKING! THE ILLYANA-DEMON'S EVIL IS AFFECTING ME. I'M STARTING TO ACT LIKE HER! THANK HEAVEN I ONLY WOUNDED HIM.
ILLYANA?!
C'EST MOI--IT IS SHAN! I AND THE MUTANTS HAVE COME...
...TO RESCUE YOU.
ABOUT... BLOODY TIME.

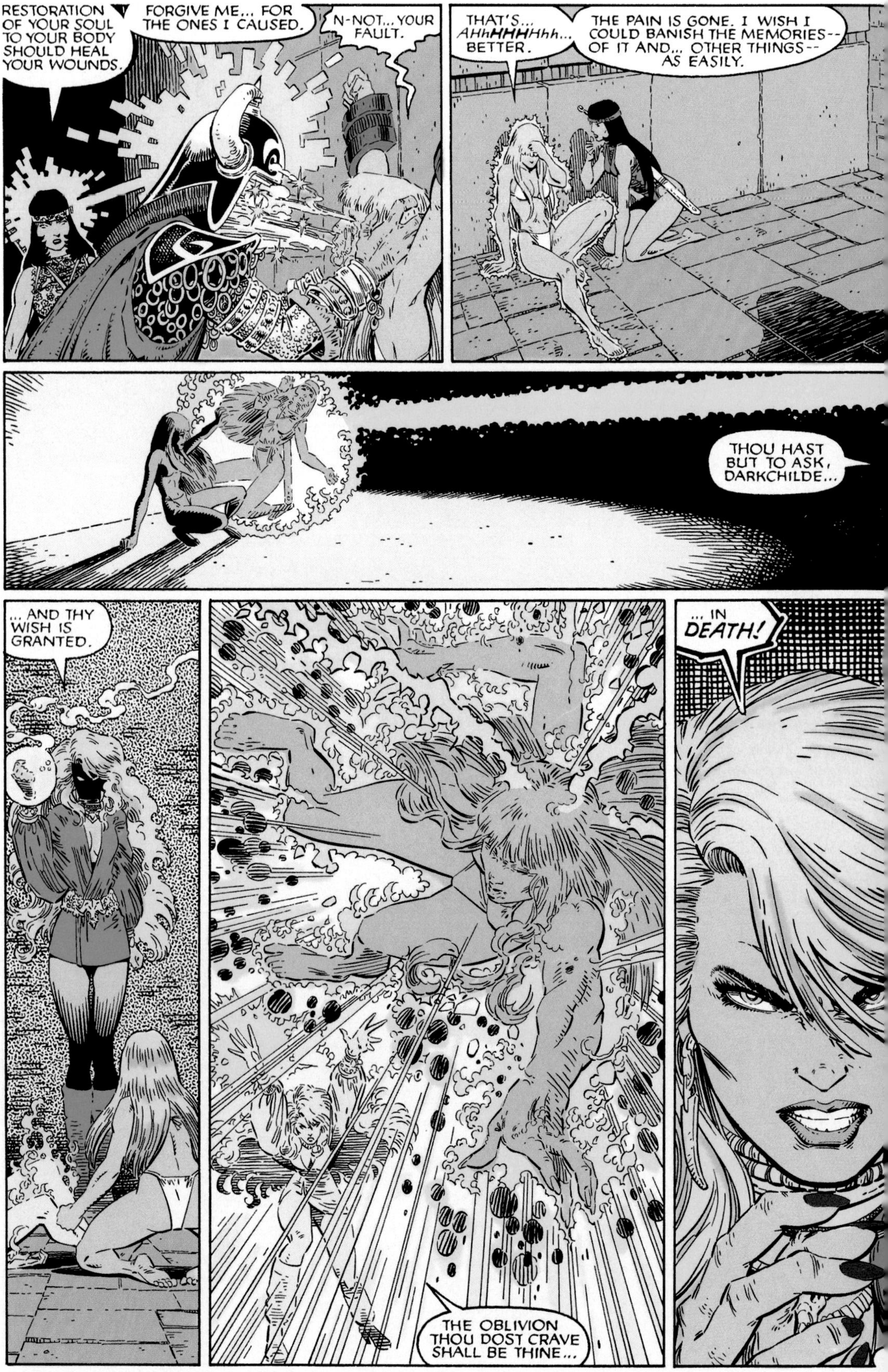
RESTORATION OF YOUR SOUL TO YOUR BODY SHOULD HEAL YOUR WOUNDS.
FORGIVE ME... FOR THE ONES I CAUSED.
N-NOT... YOUR FAULT.
THAT'S... AHhHHHHhh... BETTER.
THE PAIN IS GONE. I WISH I COULD BANISH THE MEMORIES-- OF IT AND... OTHER THINGS-- AS EASILY.
THOU HAST BUT TO ASK, DARKCHILDE...
...AND THY WISH IS GRANTED.
THE OBLIVION THOU DOST CRAVE SHALL BE THINE...
...IN DEATH!

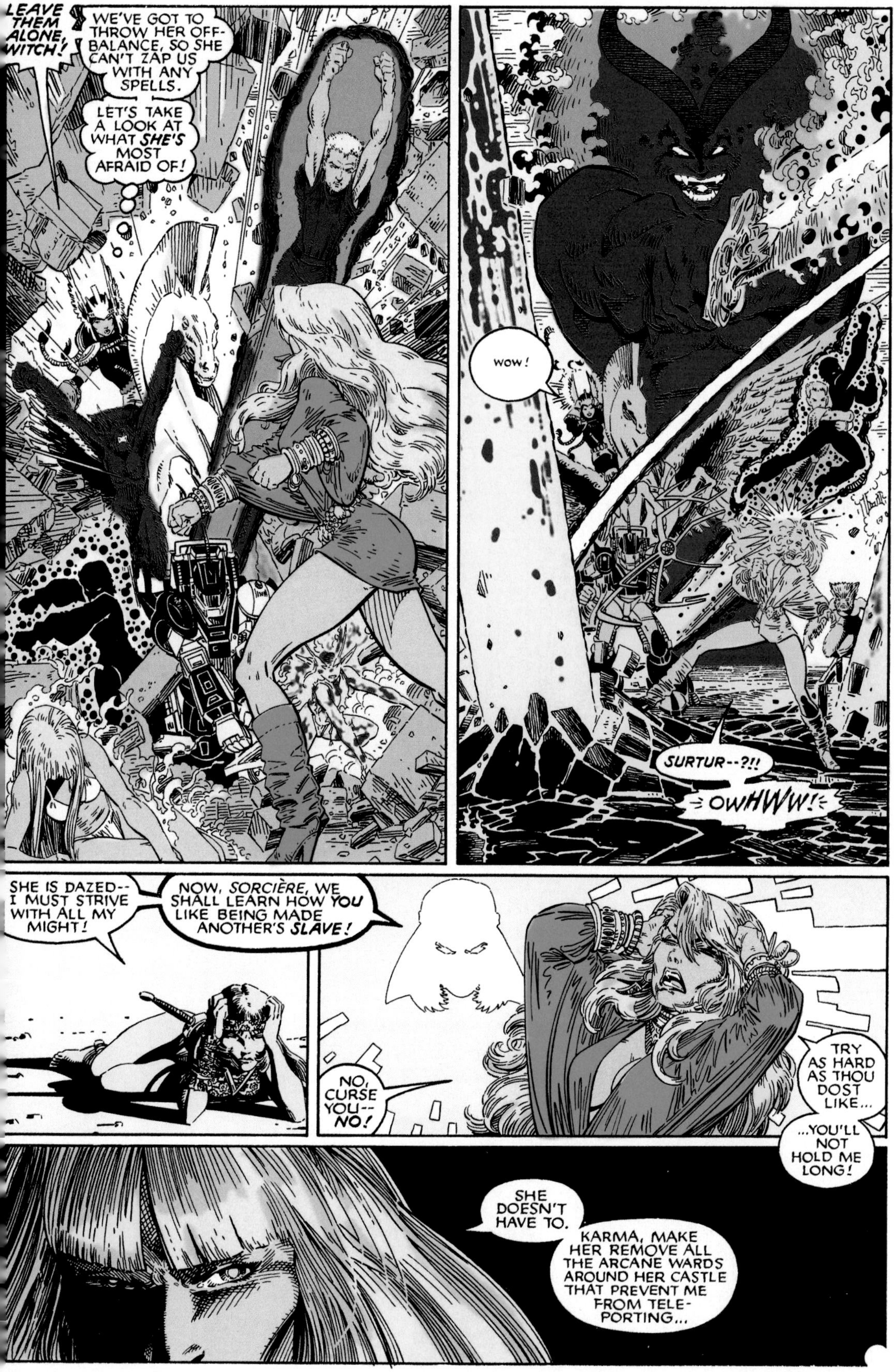
LEAVE THEM ALONE, WITCH!
WE'VE GOT TO THROW HER OFF-BALANCE, SO SHE CAN'T ZAP US WITH ANY SPELLS.
LET'S TAKE A LOOK AT WHAT SHE'S MOST AFRAID OF!
WOW!
SURTUR--?!!
OWHWW!
SHE IS DAZED-- I MUST STRIVE WITH ALL MY MIGHT!
NOW, SORCIÈRE, WE SHALL LEARN HOW YOU LIKE BEING MADE ANOTHER'S SLAVE!
NO, CURSE YOU-- NO!
TRY AS HARD AS THOU DOST LIKE...
...YOU'LL NOT HOLD ME LONG!
SHE DOESN'T HAVE TO.
KARMA, MAKE HER REMOVE ALL THE ARCANE WARDS AROUND HER CASTLE THAT PREVENT ME FROM TELE-PORTING...

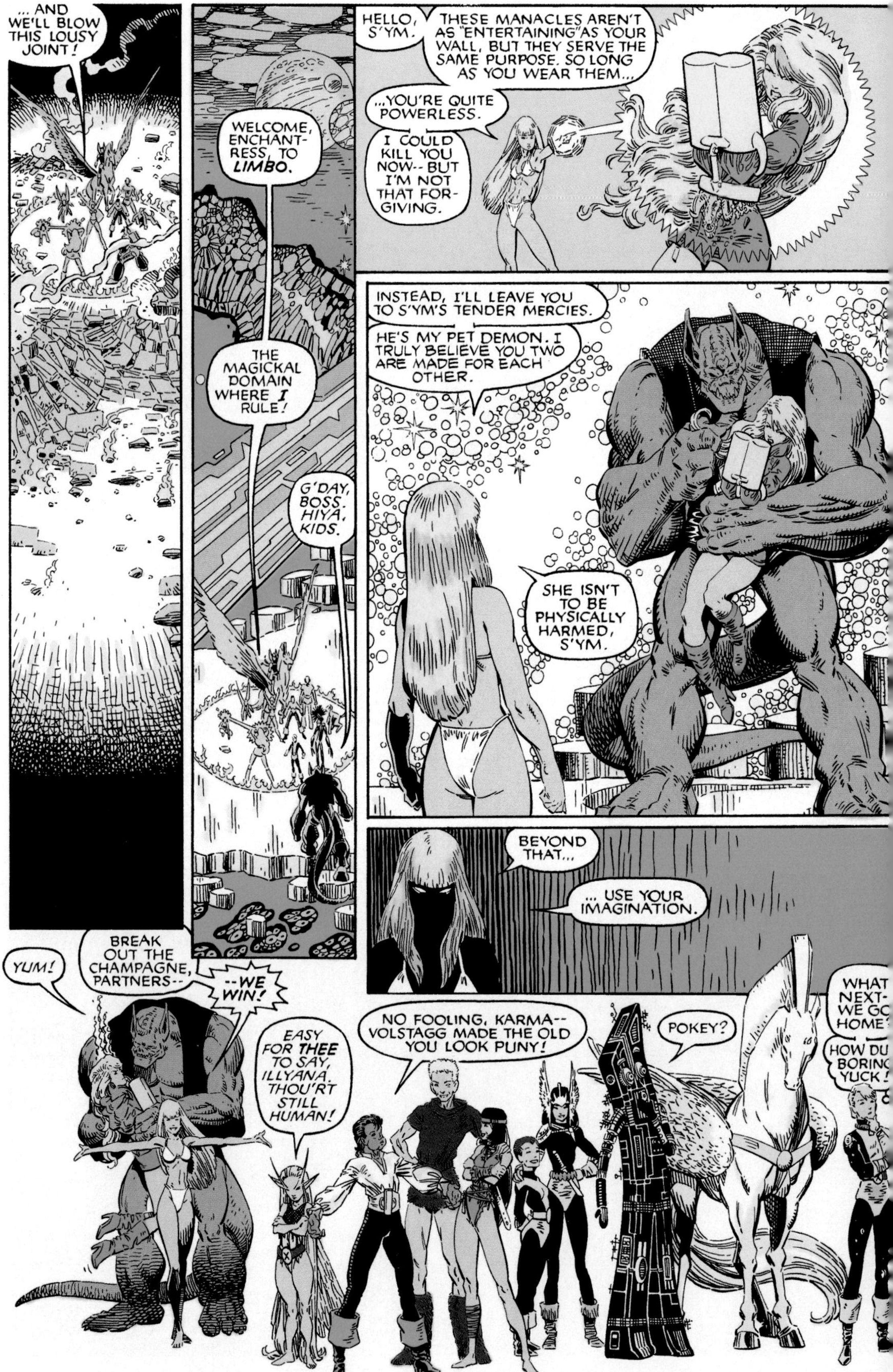
... AND WE'LL BLOW THIS LOUSY JOINT!
WELCOME, ENCHANTRESS, TO LIMBO.
THE MAGICKAL DOMAIN WHERE I RULE!
G'DAY, BOSS. HIYA, KIDS.
HELLO, S'YM.
THESE MANACLES AREN'T AS "ENTERTAINING" AS YOUR WALL, BUT THEY SERVE THE SAME PURPOSE. SO LONG AS YOU WEAR THEM...
...YOU'RE QUITE POWERLESS.
I COULD KILL YOU NOW-- BUT I'M NOT THAT FORGIVING.
INSTEAD, I'LL LEAVE YOU TO S'YM'S TENDER MERCIES.
HE'S MY PET DEMON. I TRULY BELIEVE YOU TWO ARE MADE FOR EACH OTHER.
SHE ISN'T TO BE PHYSICALLY HARMED, S'YM.
BEYOND THAT...
... USE YOUR IMAGINATION.
YUM!
BREAK OUT THE CHAMPAGNE, PARTNERS--
--WE WIN!
EASY FOR THEE TO SAY, ILLYANA. THOU'RT STILL HUMAN!
NO FOOLING, KARMA-- VOLSTAGG MADE THE OLD YOU LOOK PUNY!
POKEY?
WHAT NEXT- WE GO HOME

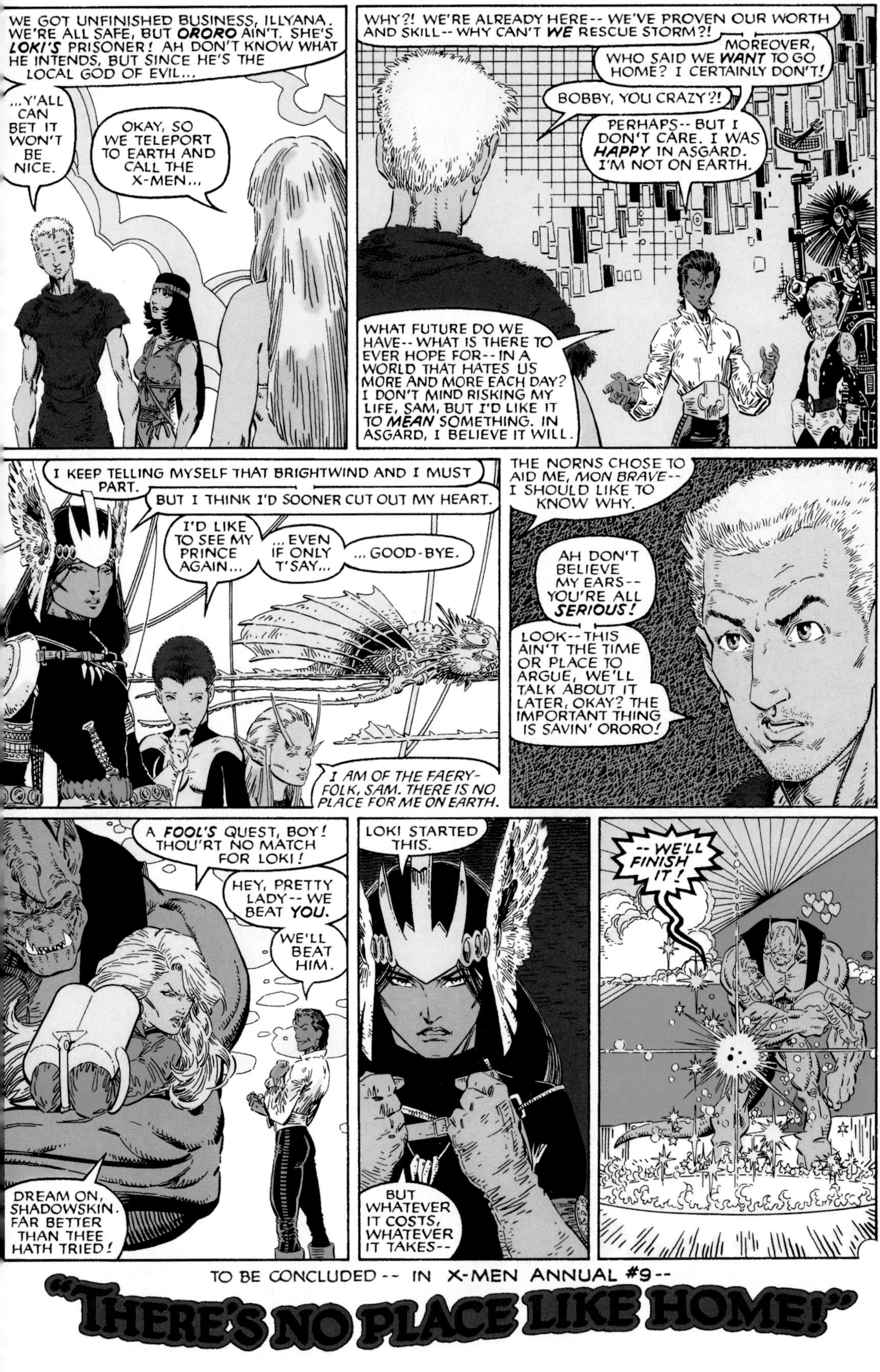
WE GOT UNFINISHED BUSINESS, ILLYANA. WE'RE ALL SAFE, BUT ORORO AIN'T. SHE'S LOKI'S PRISONER! AH DON'T KNOW WHAT HE INTENDS, BUT SINCE HE'S THE LOCAL GOD OF EVIL...
...Y'ALL CAN BET IT WON'T BE NICE.
OKAY, SO WE TELEPORT TO EARTH AND CALL THE X-MEN...
WHY?! WE'RE ALREADY HERE-- WE'VE PROVEN OUR WORTH AND SKILL-- WHY CAN'T WE RESCUE STORM?!
MOREOVER, WHO SAID WE WANT TO GO HOME? I CERTAINLY DON'T!
BOBBY, YOU CRAZY?!
PERHAPS-- BUT I DON'T CARE. I WAS HAPPY IN ASGARD. I'M NOT ON EARTH.
WHAT FUTURE DO WE HAVE-- WHAT IS THERE TO EVER HOPE FOR-- IN A WORLD THAT HATES US MORE AND MORE EACH DAY? I DON'T MIND RISKING MY LIFE, SAM, BUT I'D LIKE IT TO MEAN SOMETHING. IN ASGARD, I BELIEVE IT WILL.
I KEEP TELLING MYSELF THAT BRIGHTWIND AND I MUST PART.
BUT I THINK I'D SOONER CUT OUT MY HEART.
I'D LIKE TO SEE MY PRINCE AGAIN...
... EVEN IF ONLY T'SAY...
... GOOD-BYE.
I AM OF THE FAERY-FOLK, SAM. THERE IS NO PLACE FOR ME ON EARTH.
THE NORNS CHOSE TO AID ME, MON BRAVE-- I SHOULD LIKE TO KNOW WHY.
AH DON'T BELIEVE MY EARS-- YOU'RE ALL SERIOUS!
LOOK-- THIS AIN'T THE TIME OR PLACE TO ARGUE, WE'LL TALK ABOUT IT LATER, OKAY? THE IMPORTANT THING IS SAVIN' ORORO!
A FOOL'S QUEST, BOY! THOU'RT NO MATCH FOR LOKI!
HEY, PRETTY LADY-- WE BEAT YOU.
WE'LL BEAT HIM.
DREAM ON, SHADOWSKIN. FAR BETTER THAN THEE HATH TRIED!
LOKI STARTED THIS.
BUT WHATEVER IT COSTS, WHATEVER IT TAKES--
-- WE'LL FINISH IT!
TO BE CONCLUDED -- IN X-MEN ANNUAL #9 --
"THERE'S NO PLACE LIKE HOME!"

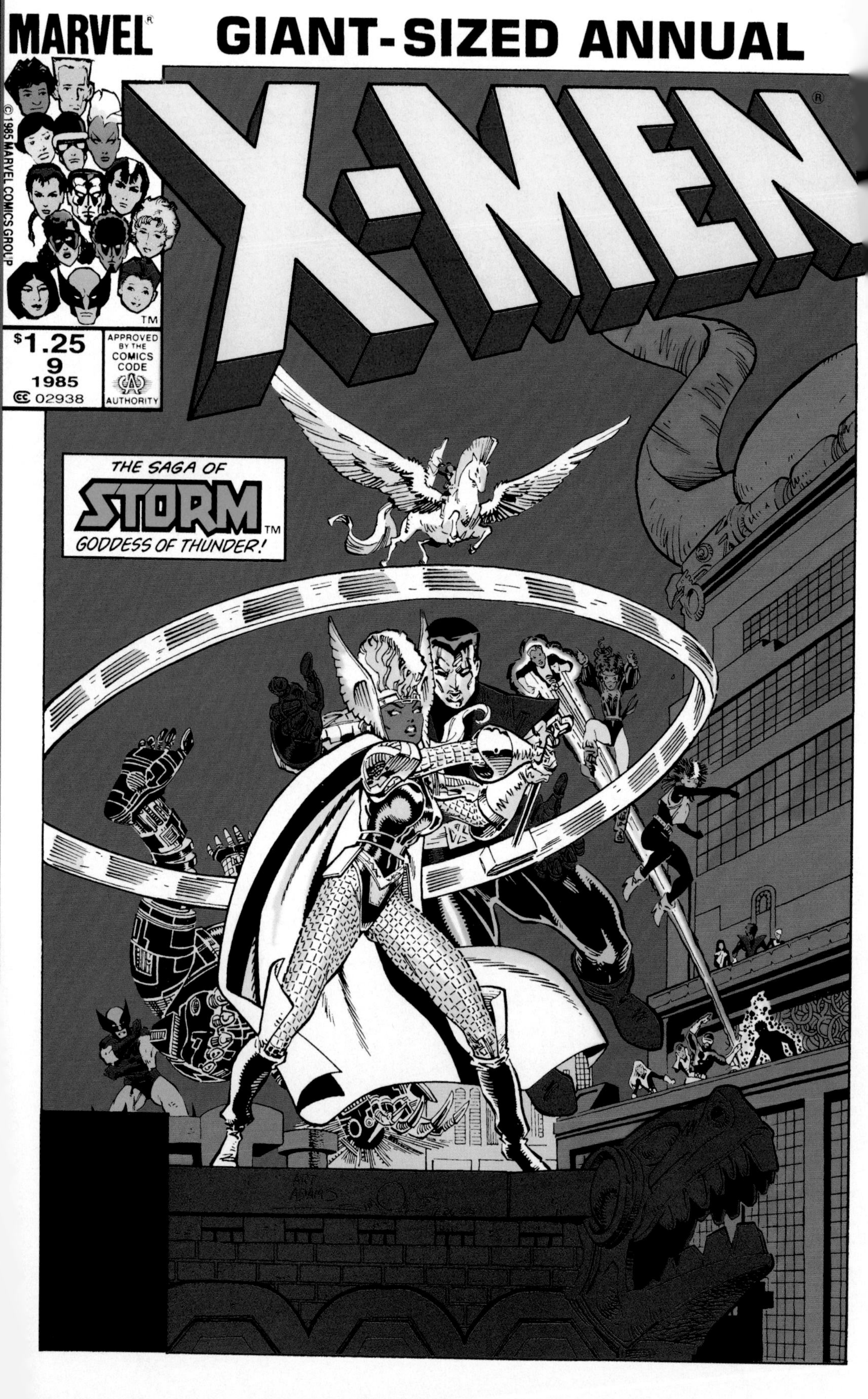

MARVEL®
GIANT-SIZED ANNUAL
X-MEN®
© 1985 MARVEL COMICS GROUP
TM
$1.25
9
1985
02938
APPROVED BY THE COMICS CODE AUTHORITY
THE SAGA OF
STORM™
GODDESS OF THUNDER!

THE UNCANNY X-MEN

PHOENIX | CYCLOPS | STORM | COLOSSUS | WOLVERINE | NIGHTCRAWLER | SHADOWCAT | ROGUE

STAN LEE PRESENTS

There's NO place like HOME

CHRIS CLAREMONT — writer —

ARTHUR ADAMS — penciler —

ALAN GORDON & MIKE MIGNOLA & ART ADAMS — inkers —

TOM ORZECHOWSKI, letterer   PETRA SCOTESE, colorist   ANN NOCENTI, editor   JIM SHOOTER, chief

GUEST-STARRING THE NEW MUTANTS

WARLOCK | MIRAGE | KARMA | MAGIK | WOLFSBANE | MAGMA | CYPHER | CANNONBALL | SUNSPOT

71

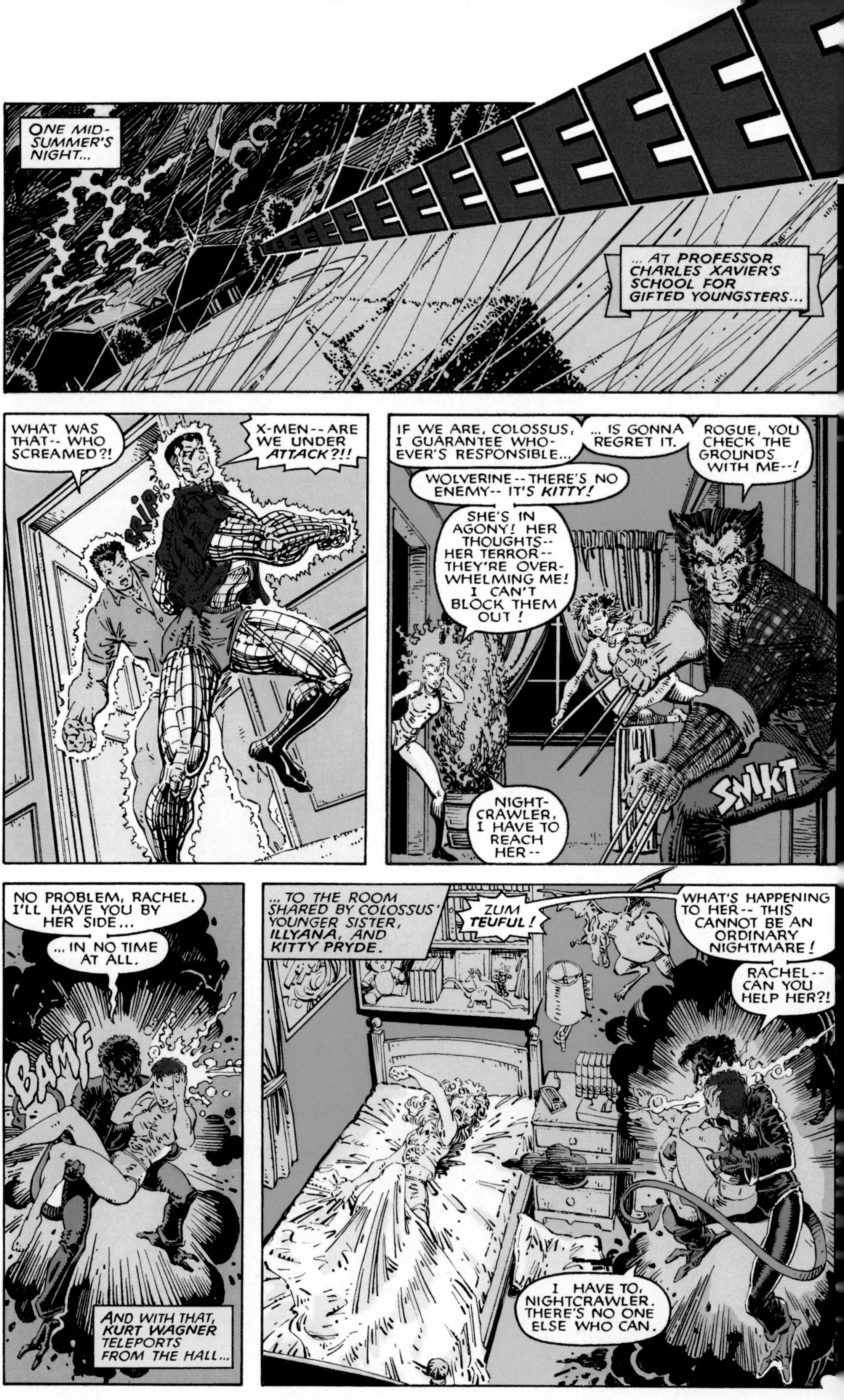
ONE MID-SUMMER'S NIGHT...
EEEEEEEEEEEEEEEEE
...AT PROFESSOR CHARLES XAVIER'S SCHOOL FOR GIFTED YOUNGSTERS...
WHAT WAS THAT-- WHO SCREAMED?!
X-MEN--ARE WE UNDER ATTACK?!!
RRIP
IF WE ARE, COLOSSUS, I GUARANTEE WHO-EVER'S RESPONSIBLE...
...IS GONNA REGRET IT.
ROGUE, YOU CHECK THE GROUNDS WITH ME--!
WOLVERINE--THERE'S NO ENEMY-- IT'S KITTY!
SHE'S IN AGONY! HER THOUGHTS-- HER TERROR-- THEY'RE OVER-WHELMING ME! I CAN'T BLOCK THEM OUT!
NIGHT-CRAWLER, I HAVE TO REACH HER--
SNIKT
NO PROBLEM, RACHEL. I'LL HAVE YOU BY HER SIDE...
...IN NO TIME AT ALL.
BAMF
AND WITH THAT, KURT WAGNER TELEPORTS FROM THE HALL...
...TO THE ROOM SHARED BY COLOSSUS' YOUNGER SISTER, ILLYANA, AND KITTY PRYDE.
ZUM TEUFUL!
WHAT'S HAPPENING TO HER-- THIS CANNOT BE AN ORDINARY NIGHTMARE!
RACHEL-- CAN YOU HELP HER?!
I HAVE TO, NIGHTCRAWLER. THERE'S NO ONE ELSE WHO CAN.

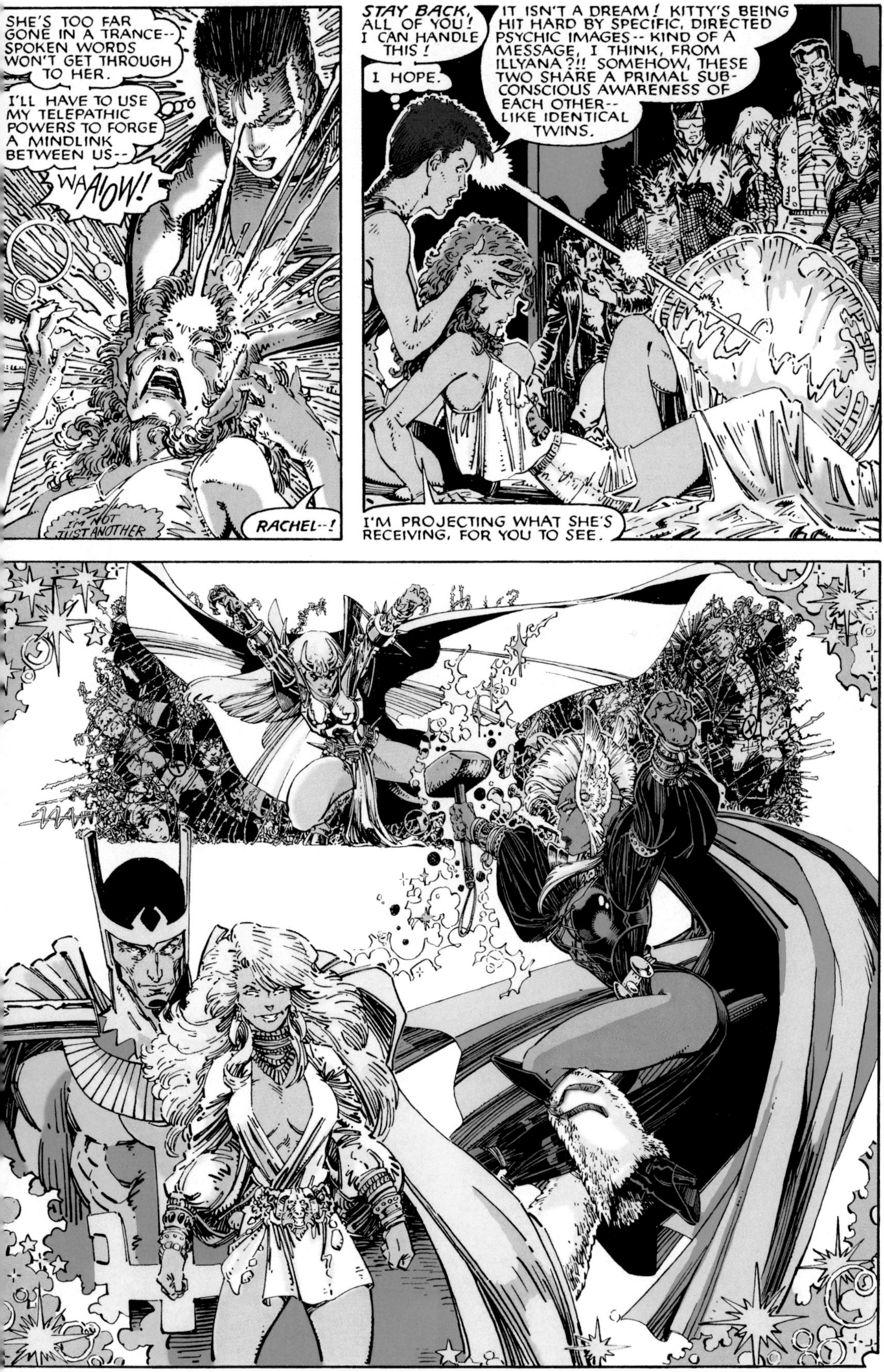
SHE'S TOO FAR GONE IN A TRANCE-- SPOKEN WORDS WON'T GET THROUGH TO HER.
I'LL HAVE TO USE MY TELEPATHIC POWERS TO FORGE A MINDLINK BETWEEN US--
WAAOW!
I'M NOT JUST ANOTHER
RACHEL--!
STAY BACK, ALL OF YOU! I CAN HANDLE THIS!
I HOPE.
IT ISN'T A DREAM! KITTY'S BEING HIT HARD BY SPECIFIC, DIRECTED PSYCHIC IMAGES-- KIND OF A MESSAGE, I THINK, FROM ILLYANA?!! SOMEHOW, THESE TWO SHARE A PRIMAL SUBCONSCIOUS AWARENESS OF EACH OTHER-- LIKE IDENTICAL TWINS.
I'M PROJECTING WHAT SHE'S RECEIVING, FOR YOU TO SEE.

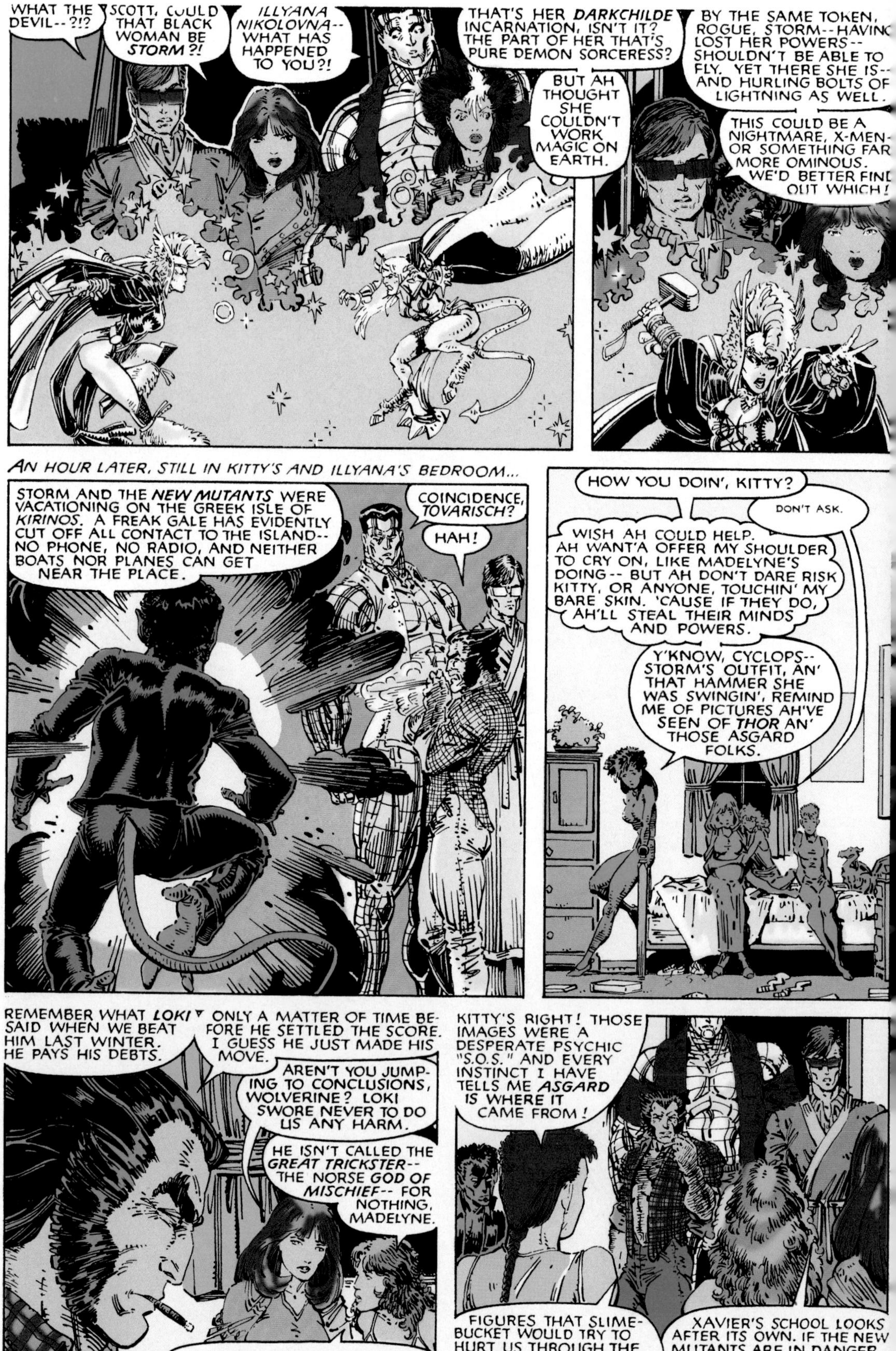

WHAT THE DEVIL--?!?
SCOTT, COULD THAT BLACK WOMAN BE STORM?!
ILLYANA NIKOLOVNA-- WHAT HAS HAPPENED TO YOU?!
THAT'S HER DARKCHILDE INCARNATION, ISN'T IT? THE PART OF HER THAT'S PURE DEMON SORCERESS?
BUT AH THOUGHT SHE COULDN'T WORK MAGIC ON EARTH.
BY THE SAME TOKEN, ROGUE, STORM--HAVING LOST HER POWERS-- SHOULDN'T BE ABLE TO FLY. YET THERE SHE IS-- AND HURLING BOLTS OF LIGHTNING AS WELL.
THIS COULD BE A NIGHTMARE, X-MEN-- OR SOMETHING FAR MORE OMINOUS. WE'D BETTER FIND OUT WHICH!
AN HOUR LATER, STILL IN KITTY'S AND ILLYANA'S BEDROOM...
STORM AND THE NEW MUTANTS WERE VACATIONING ON THE GREEK ISLE OF KIRINOS. A FREAK GALE HAS EVIDENTLY CUT OFF ALL CONTACT TO THE ISLAND-- NO PHONE, NO RADIO, AND NEITHER BOATS NOR PLANES CAN GET NEAR THE PLACE.
COINCIDENCE, TOVARISCH?
HAH!
HOW YOU DOIN', KITTY?
DON'T ASK.
WISH AH COULD HELP. AH WANT'A OFFER MY SHOULDER TO CRY ON, LIKE MADELYNE'S DOING-- BUT AH DON'T DARE RISK KITTY, OR ANYONE, TOUCHIN' MY BARE SKIN. 'CAUSE IF THEY DO, AH'LL STEAL THEIR MINDS AND POWERS.
Y'KNOW, CYCLOPS-- STORM'S OUTFIT, AN' THAT HAMMER SHE WAS SWINGIN', REMIND ME OF PICTURES AH'VE SEEN OF THOR AN' THOSE ASGARD FOLKS.
REMEMBER WHAT LOKI SAID WHEN WE BEAT HIM LAST WINTER. HE PAYS HIS DEBTS.
ONLY A MATTER OF TIME BEFORE HE SETTLED THE SCORE. I GUESS HE JUST MADE HIS MOVE.
AREN'T YOU JUMPING TO CONCLUSIONS, WOLVERINE? LOKI SWORE NEVER TO DO US ANY HARM.
HE ISN'T CALLED THE GREAT TRICKSTER-- THE NORSE GOD OF MISCHIEF-- FOR NOTHING, MADELYNE.
IF ANYONE CAN FIND A LOOPHOLE IN A PROMISE, IT'S HIM.
KITTY'S RIGHT! THOSE IMAGES WERE A DESPERATE PSYCHIC "S.O.S." AND EVERY INSTINCT I HAVE TELLS ME ASGARD IS WHERE IT CAME FROM!
FIGURES THAT SLIMEBUCKET WOULD TRY TO HURT US THROUGH THE MUTANTS. THEY'RE JUST KIDS-- NO MATCH FOR HIM.
XAVIER'S SCHOOL LOOKS AFTER ITS OWN. IF THE NEW MUTANTS ARE IN DANGER, IT'S THE X-MEN'S JOB TO GO TO THE RESCUE!

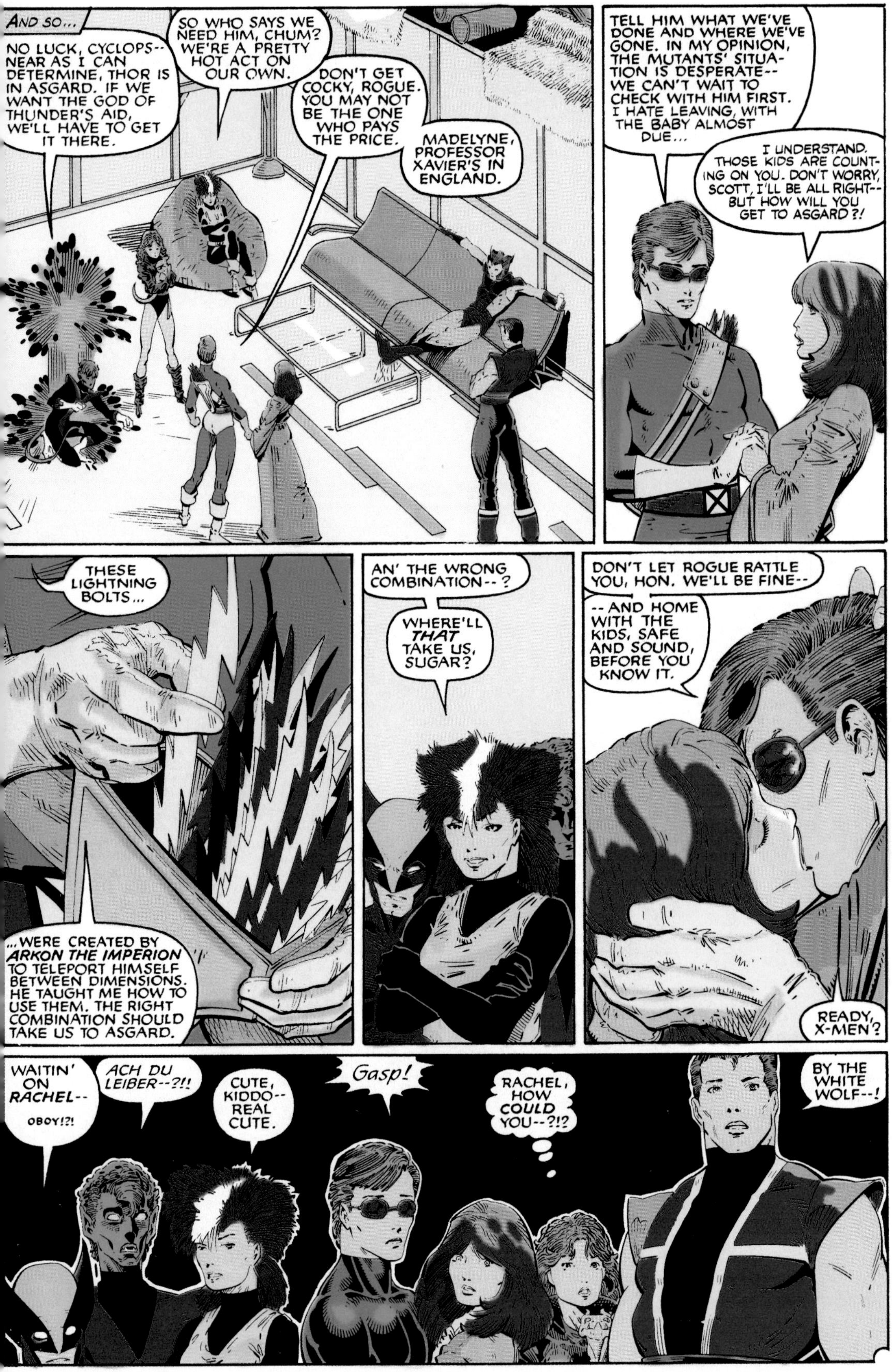
AND SO...
NO LUCK, CYCLOPS--NEAR AS I CAN DETERMINE, THOR IS IN ASGARD. IF WE WANT THE GOD OF THUNDER'S AID, WE'LL HAVE TO GET IT THERE.
SO WHO SAYS WE NEED HIM, CHUM? WE'RE A PRETTY HOT ACT ON OUR OWN.
DON'T GET COCKY, ROGUE. YOU MAY NOT BE THE ONE WHO PAYS THE PRICE.
MADELYNE, PROFESSOR XAVIER'S IN ENGLAND.
TELL HIM WHAT WE'VE DONE AND WHERE WE'VE GONE. IN MY OPINION, THE MUTANTS' SITUATION IS DESPERATE--WE CAN'T WAIT TO CHECK WITH HIM FIRST. I HATE LEAVING, WITH THE BABY ALMOST DUE...
I UNDERSTAND. THOSE KIDS ARE COUNTING ON YOU. DON'T WORRY, SCOTT, I'LL BE ALL RIGHT--BUT HOW WILL YOU GET TO ASGARD?!
THESE LIGHTNING BOLTS...
...WERE CREATED BY ARKON THE IMPERION TO TELEPORT HIMSELF BETWEEN DIMENSIONS. HE TAUGHT ME HOW TO USE THEM. THE RIGHT COMBINATION SHOULD TAKE US TO ASGARD.
AN' THE WRONG COMBINATION--?
WHERE'LL THAT TAKE US, SUGAR?
DON'T LET ROGUE RATTLE YOU, HON. WE'LL BE FINE--
--AND HOME WITH THE KIDS, SAFE AND SOUND, BEFORE YOU KNOW IT.
READY, X-MEN?
WAITIN' ON RACHEL--
OBOY!?!
ACH DU LEIBER--?!!
CUTE, KIDDO--REAL CUTE.
Gasp!
RACHEL, HOW COULD YOU--?!?
BY THE WHITE WOLF--!

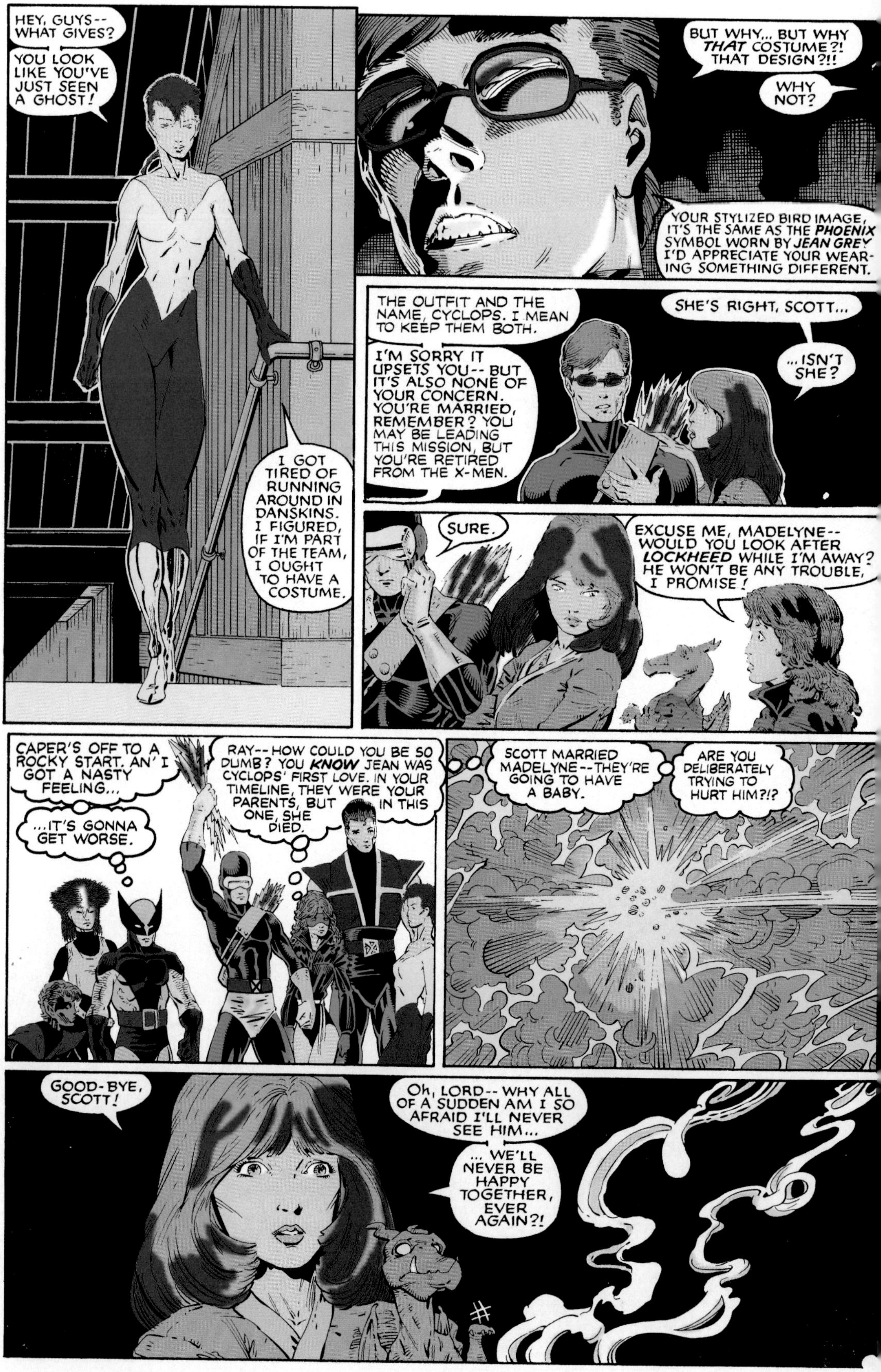

HEY, GUYS-- WHAT GIVES?
YOU LOOK LIKE YOU'VE JUST SEEN A GHOST!
BUT WHY... BUT WHY THAT COSTUME?! THAT DESIGN?!!
WHY NOT?
YOUR STYLIZED BIRD IMAGE, IT'S THE SAME AS THE PHOENIX SYMBOL WORN BY JEAN GREY. I'D APPRECIATE YOUR WEARING SOMETHING DIFFERENT.
THE OUTFIT AND THE NAME, CYCLOPS. I MEAN TO KEEP THEM BOTH.
I'M SORRY IT UPSETS YOU-- BUT IT'S ALSO NONE OF YOUR CONCERN. YOU'RE MARRIED, REMEMBER? YOU MAY BE LEADING THIS MISSION, BUT YOU'RE RETIRED FROM THE X-MEN.
SHE'S RIGHT, SCOTT...
...ISN'T SHE?
I GOT TIRED OF RUNNING AROUND IN DANSKINS. I FIGURED, IF I'M PART OF THE TEAM, I OUGHT TO HAVE A COSTUME.
SURE.
EXCUSE ME, MADELYNE-- WOULD YOU LOOK AFTER LOCKHEED WHILE I'M AWAY? HE WON'T BE ANY TROUBLE, I PROMISE!
CAPER'S OFF TO A ROCKY START. AN' I GOT A NASTY FEELING...
...IT'S GONNA GET WORSE.
RAY-- HOW COULD YOU BE SO DUMB? YOU KNOW JEAN WAS CYCLOPS' FIRST LOVE. IN YOUR TIMELINE, THEY WERE YOUR PARENTS, BUT IN THIS ONE, SHE DIED.
SCOTT MARRIED MADELYNE-- THEY'RE GOING TO HAVE A BABY.
ARE YOU DELIBERATELY TRYING TO HURT HIM?!?
GOOD-BYE, SCOTT!
Oh, LORD-- WHY ALL OF A SUDDEN AM I SO AFRAID I'LL NEVER SEE HIM...
... WE'LL NEVER BE HAPPY TOGETHER, EVER AGAIN?!

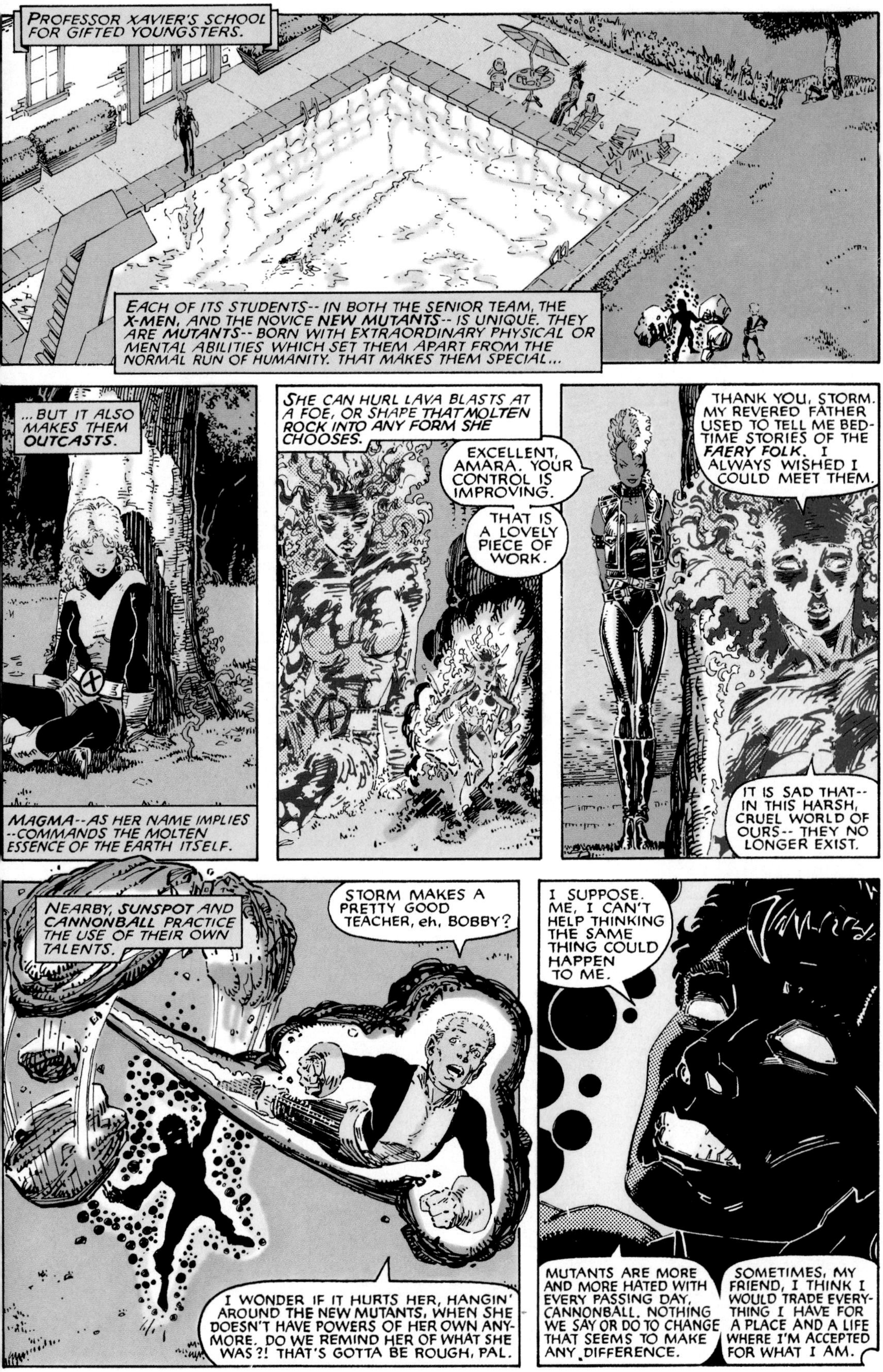

PROFESSOR XAVIER'S SCHOOL FOR GIFTED YOUNGSTERS.
EACH OF ITS STUDENTS-- IN BOTH THE SENIOR TEAM, THE X-MEN, AND THE NOVICE NEW MUTANTS-- IS UNIQUE. THEY ARE MUTANTS-- BORN WITH EXTRAORDINARY PHYSICAL OR MENTAL ABILITIES WHICH SET THEM APART FROM THE NORMAL RUN OF HUMANITY. THAT MAKES THEM SPECIAL...
...BUT IT ALSO MAKES THEM OUTCASTS.
MAGMA--AS HER NAME IMPLIES --COMMANDS THE MOLTEN ESSENCE OF THE EARTH ITSELF.
SHE CAN HURL LAVA BLASTS AT A FOE, OR SHAPE THAT MOLTEN ROCK INTO ANY FORM SHE CHOOSES.
EXCELLENT, AMARA. YOUR CONTROL IS IMPROVING.
THAT IS A LOVELY PIECE OF WORK.
THANK YOU, STORM. MY REVERED FATHER USED TO TELL ME BED-TIME STORIES OF THE FAERY FOLK. I ALWAYS WISHED I COULD MEET THEM.
IT IS SAD THAT-- IN THIS HARSH, CRUEL WORLD OF OURS-- THEY NO LONGER EXIST.
NEARBY, SUNSPOT AND CANNONBALL PRACTICE THE USE OF THEIR OWN TALENTS.
STORM MAKES A PRETTY GOOD TEACHER, eh, BOBBY?
I WONDER IF IT HURTS HER, HANGIN' AROUND THE NEW MUTANTS, WHEN SHE DOESN'T HAVE POWERS OF HER OWN ANY-MORE. DO WE REMIND HER OF WHAT SHE WAS?! THAT'S GOTTA BE ROUGH, PAL.
I SUPPOSE. ME, I CAN'T HELP THINKING THE SAME THING COULD HAPPEN TO ME.
MUTANTS ARE MORE AND MORE HATED WITH EVERY PASSING DAY, CANNONBALL. NOTHING WE SAY OR DO TO CHANGE THAT SEEMS TO MAKE ANY DIFFERENCE.
SOMETIMES, MY FRIEND, I THINK I WOULD TRADE EVERY-THING I HAVE FOR A PLACE AND A LIFE WHERE I'M ACCEPTED FOR WHAT I AM.

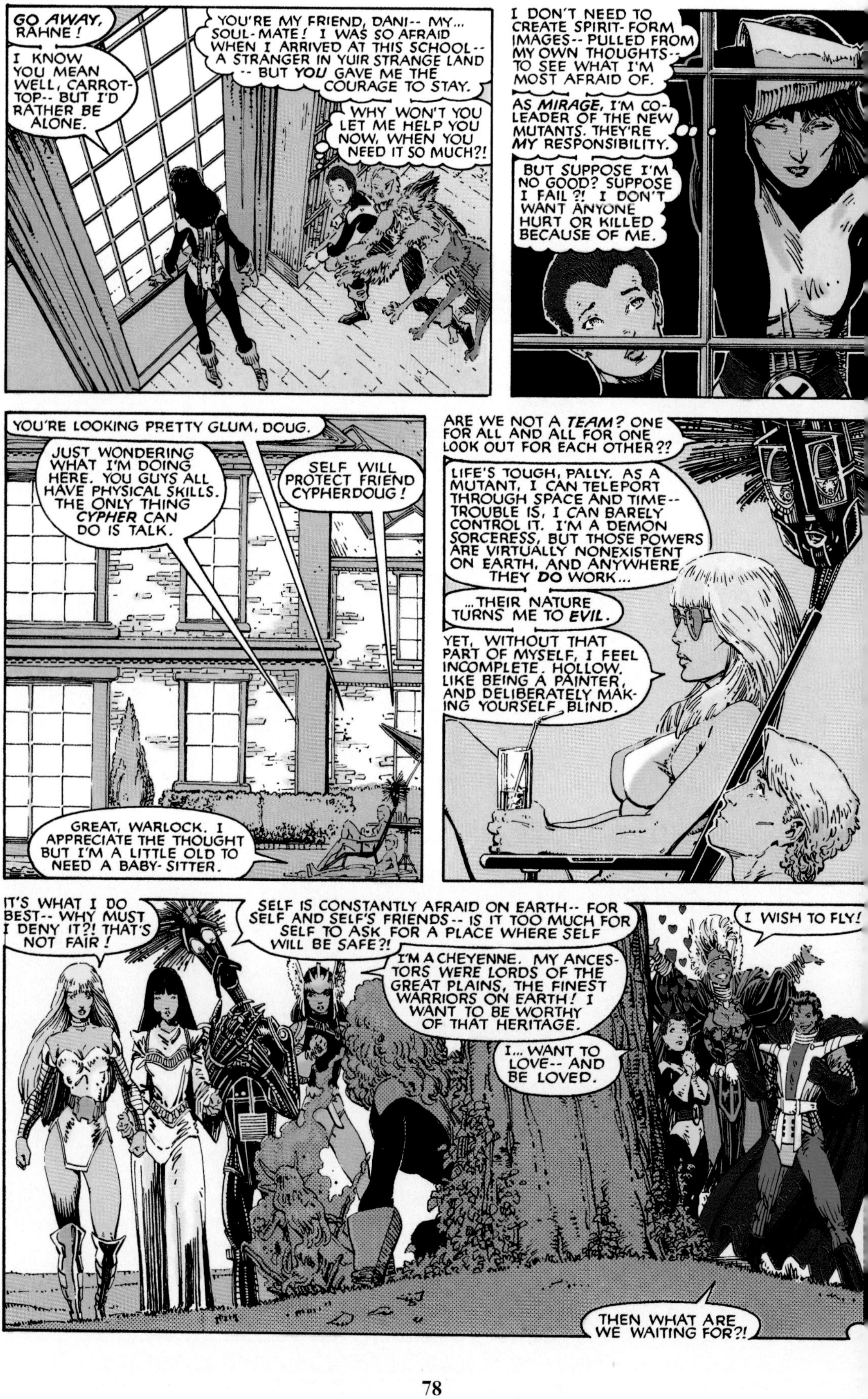
GO AWAY, RAHNE!
I KNOW YOU MEAN WELL, CARROT-TOP-- BUT I'D RATHER BE ALONE.
YOU'RE MY FRIEND, DANI-- MY... SOUL-MATE! I WAS SO AFRAID WHEN I ARRIVED AT THIS SCHOOL-- A STRANGER IN YUIR STRANGE LAND -- BUT YOU GAVE ME THE COURAGE TO STAY.
WHY WON'T YOU LET ME HELP YOU NOW, WHEN YOU NEED IT SO MUCH?!
I DON'T NEED TO CREATE SPIRIT-FORM IMAGES-- PULLED FROM MY OWN THOUGHTS-- TO SEE WHAT I'M MOST AFRAID OF.
AS MIRAGE, I'M CO-LEADER OF THE NEW MUTANTS. THEY'RE MY RESPONSIBILITY.
BUT SUPPOSE I'M NO GOOD? SUPPOSE I FAIL?! I DON'T WANT ANYONE HURT OR KILLED BECAUSE OF ME.
YOU'RE LOOKING PRETTY GLUM, DOUG.
JUST WONDERING WHAT I'M DOING HERE. YOU GUYS ALL HAVE PHYSICAL SKILLS. THE ONLY THING CYPHER CAN DO IS TALK.
SELF WILL PROTECT FRIEND CYPHERDOUG!
GREAT, WARLOCK. I APPRECIATE THE THOUGHT BUT I'M A LITTLE OLD TO NEED A BABY-SITTER.
ARE WE NOT A TEAM? ONE FOR ALL AND ALL FOR ONE LOOK OUT FOR EACH OTHER??
LIFE'S TOUGH, PALLY. AS A MUTANT, I CAN TELEPORT THROUGH SPACE AND TIME-- TROUBLE IS, I CAN BARELY CONTROL IT. I'M A DEMON SORCERESS, BUT THOSE POWERS ARE VIRTUALLY NONEXISTENT ON EARTH, AND ANYWHERE THEY DO WORK...
...THEIR NATURE TURNS ME TO EVIL.
YET, WITHOUT THAT PART OF MYSELF, I FEEL INCOMPLETE. HOLLOW. LIKE BEING A PAINTER, AND DELIBERATELY MAKING YOURSELF BLIND.
IT'S WHAT I DO BEST-- WHY MUST I DENY IT?! THAT'S NOT FAIR!
SELF IS CONSTANTLY AFRAID ON EARTH-- FOR SELF AND SELF'S FRIENDS-- IS IT TOO MUCH FOR SELF TO ASK FOR A PLACE WHERE SELF WILL BE SAFE?!
I'M A CHEYENNE. MY ANCESTORS WERE LORDS OF THE GREAT PLAINS, THE FINEST WARRIORS ON EARTH! I WANT TO BE WORTHY OF THAT HERITAGE.
I... WANT TO LOVE-- AND BE LOVED.
I WISH TO FLY!
THEN WHAT ARE WE WAITING FOR?!

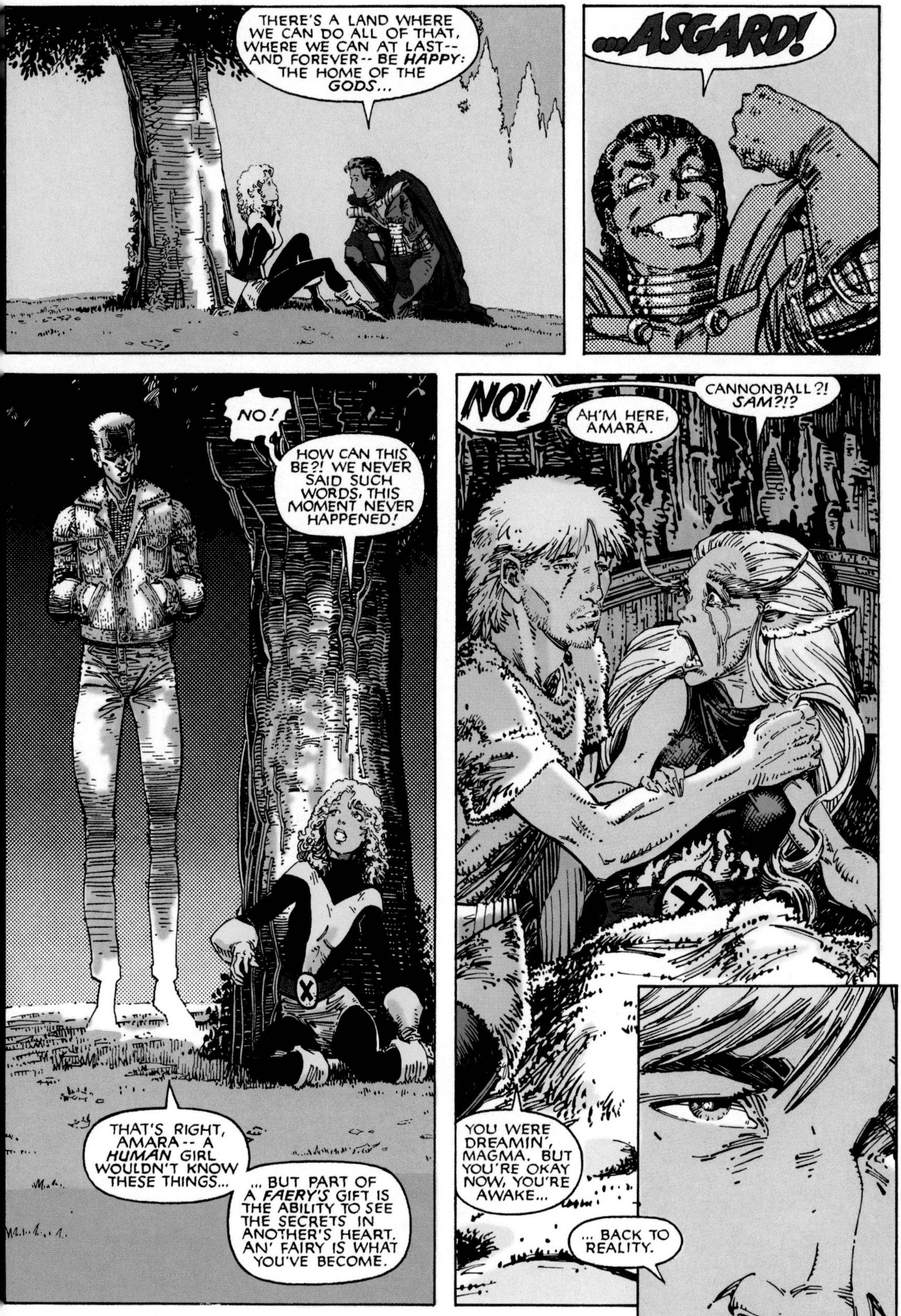
THERE'S A LAND WHERE WE CAN DO ALL OF THAT, WHERE WE CAN AT LAST-- AND FOREVER-- BE HAPPY: THE HOME OF THE GODS...
...ASGARD!
NO!
HOW CAN THIS BE?! WE NEVER SAID SUCH WORDS, THIS MOMENT NEVER HAPPENED!
THAT'S RIGHT, AMARA-- A HUMAN GIRL WOULDN'T KNOW THESE THINGS...
... BUT PART OF A FAERY'S GIFT IS THE ABILITY TO SEE THE SECRETS IN ANOTHER'S HEART. AN' FAIRY IS WHAT YOU'VE BECOME.
NO!
CANNONBALL?! SAM?!?
AH'M HERE, AMARA.
YOU WERE DREAMIN', MAGMA. BUT YOU'RE OKAY NOW, YOU'RE AWAKE...
... BACK TO REALITY.

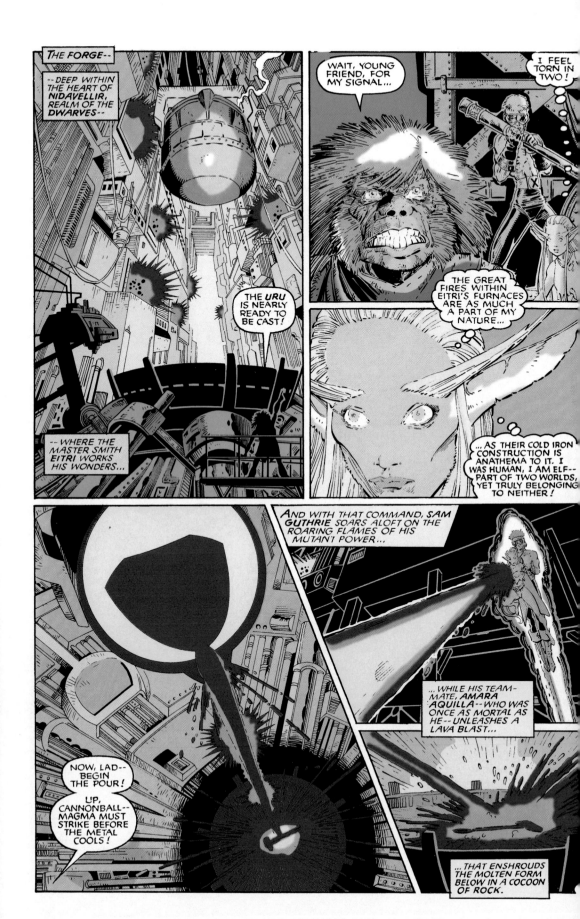

THE FORGE--

--DEEP WITHIN THE HEART OF *NIDAVELLIR,* REALM OF THE DWARVES--

WAIT, YOUNG FRIEND, FOR MY SIGNAL...

I FEEL TORN IN TWO!

THE *URU* IS NEARLY READY TO BE CAST!

THE GREAT FIRES WITHIN EITRI'S FURNACES ARE AS MUCH A PART OF MY NATURE...

--WHERE THE MASTER SMITH *EITRI* WORKS HIS WONDERS...

...AS THEIR COLD IRON CONSTRUCTION IS ANATHEMA TO IT. I WAS HUMAN, I AM ELF-- PART OF TWO WORLDS, YET TRULY BELONGING TO NEITHER!

AND WITH THAT COMMAND, SAM *GUTHRIE* SOARS ALOFT ON THE ROARING FLAMES OF HIS MUTANT POWER...

...WHILE HIS TEAM- MATE, *AMARA AQUILLA--*WHO WAS ONCE AS MORTAL AS HE-- UNLEASHES A LAVA BLAST...

NOW, LAD-- BEGIN THE POUR!

UP, CANNONBALL-- MAGMA MUST STRIKE BEFORE THE METAL COOLS!

...THAT ENSHROUDS THE MOLTEN FORM BELOW IN A COCOON OF ROCK.

PERFECT! I NOW PLACE YON HAMMER IN THY CHARGE, YOUNGLING. THOU MUST BEAR IT TO ASGARD.

LORD EITRI-- *NO!* I AM OF THE *FAERY-FOLK!* THE HAMMER'S SUBSTANCE IS *DEADLY* TO ME!

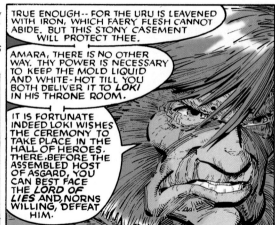

TRUE ENOUGH-- FOR THE URU IS LEAVENED WITH IRON, WHICH FAERY FLESH CANNOT ABIDE. BUT THIS STONY CASEMENT WILL PROTECT THEE.

AMARA, THERE IS NO OTHER WAY. THY POWER IS NECESSARY TO KEEP THE MOLD LIQUID AND WHITE-HOT TILL YOU BOTH DELIVER IT TO *LOKI* IN HIS THRONE ROOM.

IT IS FORTUNATE INDEED LOKI WISHES THE CEREMONY TO TAKE PLACE IN THE HALL OF HEROES. THERE, BEFORE THE ASSEMBLED HOST OF ASGARD, YOU CAN BEST FACE THE *LORD OF LIES* AND, NORNS WILLING, DEFEAT HIM.

THEN-- AND ONLY THEN-- WILT THOU HAVE A CHANCE OF FREEING THY COMPANION, STORM.

WE APPRECIATE THE HELP, SIR.

THOU ART A FRIEND, SAM. THOU HAST SHED BLOOD ON OUR BEHALF. THAT DEBT MUST BE REPAID.

MOREOVER, BY CONFRONTING THE TRICKSTER IN ASGARD, ALL THE GODS CAN BEAR WITNESS TO LOKI'S PERFIDITY.

AN' IF THERE'S A FIGHT-- AN' THERE'S ALWAYS A FIGHT-- IT'LL BE THEIR HOMES THAT GET WRECKED, NOT YOURS.

AYE. AH, SAM, I SHALL MISS THEE.

SAME HERE, SIR. THERE'S A LOT TO LIKE ABOUT THIS PLACE-- AN' YOUR PEOPLE-- BUT IT AIN'T HOME. IT AIN'T WHERE AH BELONG.

WHAT OF AMARA? DOES SHE FEEL THE SAME? DO THY FRIENDS?

AH DUNNO. SOME OF 'EM-- AH THINK THEY REALLY WANT TO STAY.

I'VE SOME FAREWELL GIFTS FOR THEE.

NOT MUCH AGAINST SUCH MIGHT AS LOKI'S...

... BUT BETTER THAN NOTHING.

THE MAIL IS PROOF AGAINST ANY BLOW, ANY WEAPON.

AND THIS BLADE WILL CLEAVE THROUGH ALL...

... SAVE THAT WHICH LIVES.

USE THEM WELL. BRING HONOR-- AND GLORY-- TO THY NAME. MAKE ME PROUD...

... SON OF MY HEART!

AH'LL TRY, SIR. AH'LL DO MY BEST.

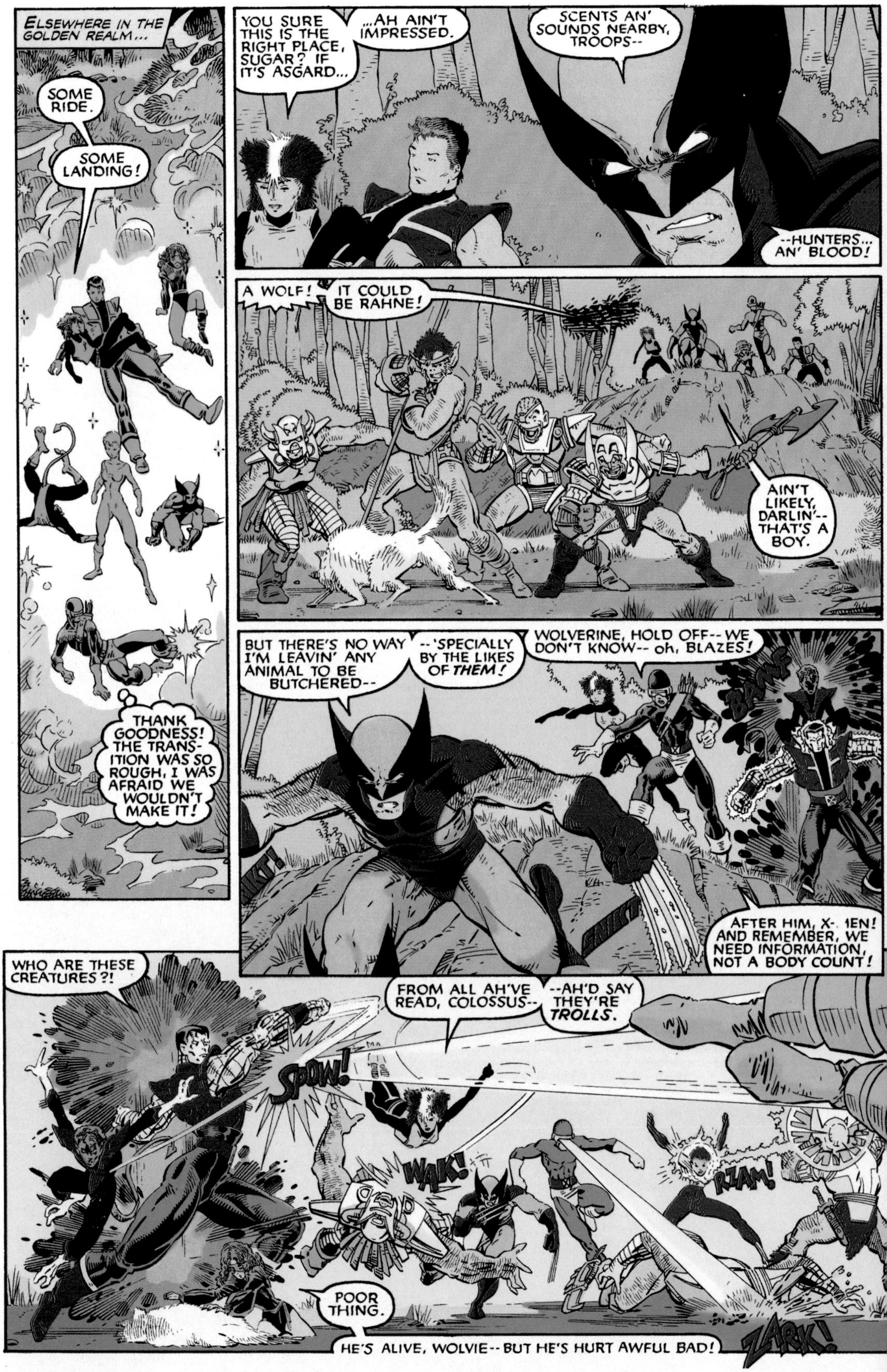

ELSEWHERE IN THE GOLDEN REALM...
SOME RIDE.
SOME LANDING!
THANK GOODNESS! THE TRANSITION WAS SO ROUGH, I WAS AFRAID WE WOULDN'T MAKE IT!
YOU SURE THIS IS THE RIGHT PLACE, SUGAR? IF IT'S ASGARD...
...AH AIN'T IMPRESSED.
SCENTS AN' SOUNDS NEARBY, TROOPS--
--HUNTERS... AN' BLOOD!
A WOLF!
IT COULD BE RAHNE!
AIN'T LIKELY, DARLIN'-- THAT'S A BOY.
BUT THERE'S NO WAY I'M LEAVIN' ANY ANIMAL TO BE BUTCHERED--
--'SPECIALLY BY THE LIKES OF *THEM*!
WOLVERINE, HOLD OFF-- WE DON'T KNOW-- oh, BLAZES!
BAMF
AFTER HIM, X-MEN! AND REMEMBER, WE NEED INFORMATION, NOT A BODY COUNT!
WHO ARE THESE CREATURES?!
FROM ALL AH'VE READ, COLOSSUS--
--AH'D SAY THEY'RE *TROLLS*.
SPOW!
WAK!
RZAM!
POOR THING.
HE'S ALIVE, WOLVIE-- BUT HE'S HURT AWFUL BAD!
ZARK!

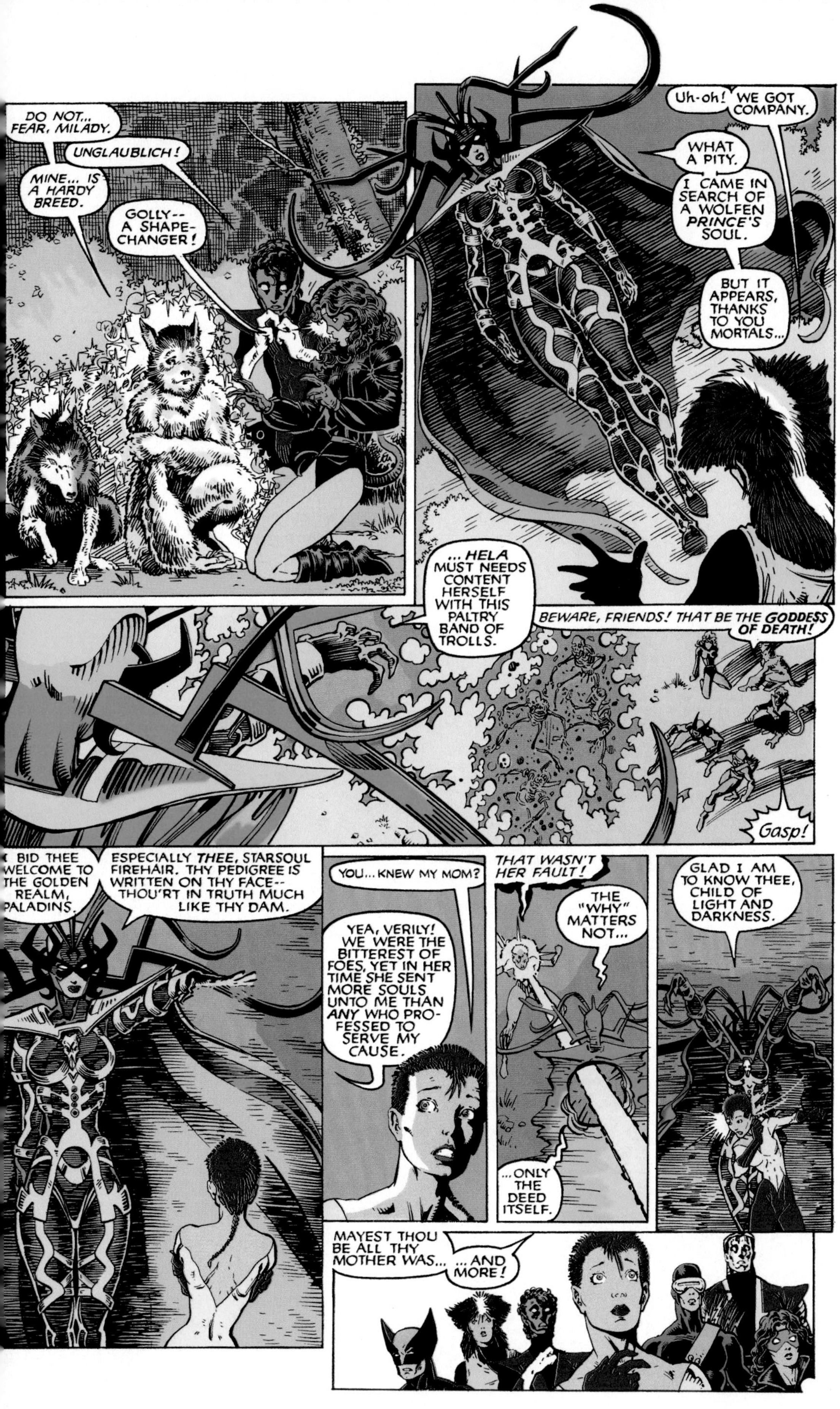
DO NOT... FEAR, MILADY.
UNGLAUBLICH!
MINE... IS A HARDY BREED.
GOLLY-- A SHAPE-CHANGER!
Uh-oh! WE GOT COMPANY.
WHAT A PITY.
I CAME IN SEARCH OF A WOLFEN PRINCE'S SOUL.
BUT IT APPEARS, THANKS TO YOU MORTALS...
...HELA MUST NEEDS CONTENT HERSELF WITH THIS PALTRY BAND OF TROLLS.
BEWARE, FRIENDS! THAT BE THE GODDESS OF DEATH!
Gasp!
BID THEE WELCOME TO THE GOLDEN REALM, PALADINS.
ESPECIALLY THEE, STARSOUL FIREHAIR. THY PEDIGREE IS WRITTEN ON THY FACE-- THOU'RT IN TRUTH MUCH LIKE THY DAM.
YOU... KNEW MY MOM?
YEA, VERILY! WE WERE THE BITTEREST OF FOES, YET IN HER TIME SHE SENT MORE SOULS UNTO ME THAN ANY WHO PROFESSED TO SERVE MY CAUSE.
THAT WASN'T HER FAULT!
THE "WHY" MATTERS NOT...
...ONLY THE DEED ITSELF.
GLAD I AM TO KNOW THEE, CHILD OF LIGHT AND DARKNESS.
MAYEST THOU BE ALL THY MOTHER WAS...
...AND MORE!

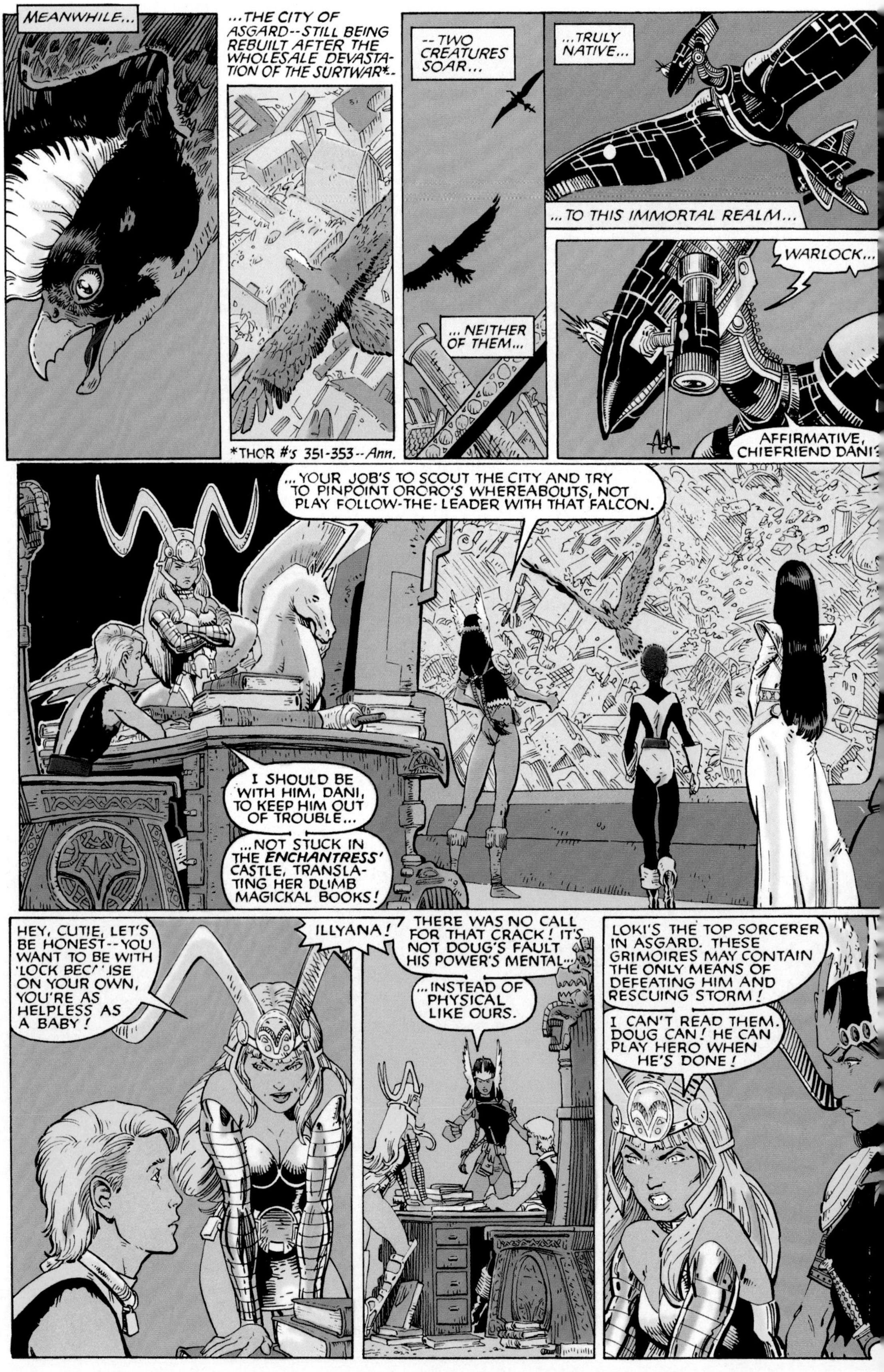

MEANWHILE...
...THE CITY OF ASGARD--STILL BEING REBUILT AFTER THE WHOLESALE DEVASTATION OF THE SURTWAR*-
*THOR #'s 351-353--Ann.
--TWO CREATURES SOAR...
...NEITHER OF THEM...
...TRULY NATIVE...
...TO THIS IMMORTAL REALM...
WARLOCK...
AFFIRMATIVE, CHIEFRIEND DANI?
...YOUR JOB'S TO SCOUT THE CITY AND TRY TO PINPOINT ORORO'S WHEREABOUTS, NOT PLAY FOLLOW-THE-LEADER WITH THAT FALCON.
I SHOULD BE WITH HIM, DANI, TO KEEP HIM OUT OF TROUBLE...
...NOT STUCK IN THE ENCHANTRESS' CASTLE, TRANSLATING HER DUMB MAGICKAL BOOKS!
HEY, CUTIE, LET'S BE HONEST--YOU WANT TO BE WITH 'LOCK BECAUSE ON YOUR OWN, YOU'RE AS HELPLESS AS A BABY!
ILLYANA!
THERE WAS NO CALL FOR THAT CRACK! IT'S NOT DOUG'S FAULT HIS POWER'S MENTAL...
...INSTEAD OF PHYSICAL LIKE OURS.
LOKI'S THE TOP SORCERER IN ASGARD. THESE GRIMOIRES MAY CONTAIN THE ONLY MEANS OF DEFEATING HIM AND RESCUING STORM!
I CAN'T READ THEM. DOUG CAN! HE CAN PLAY HERO WHEN HE'S DONE!

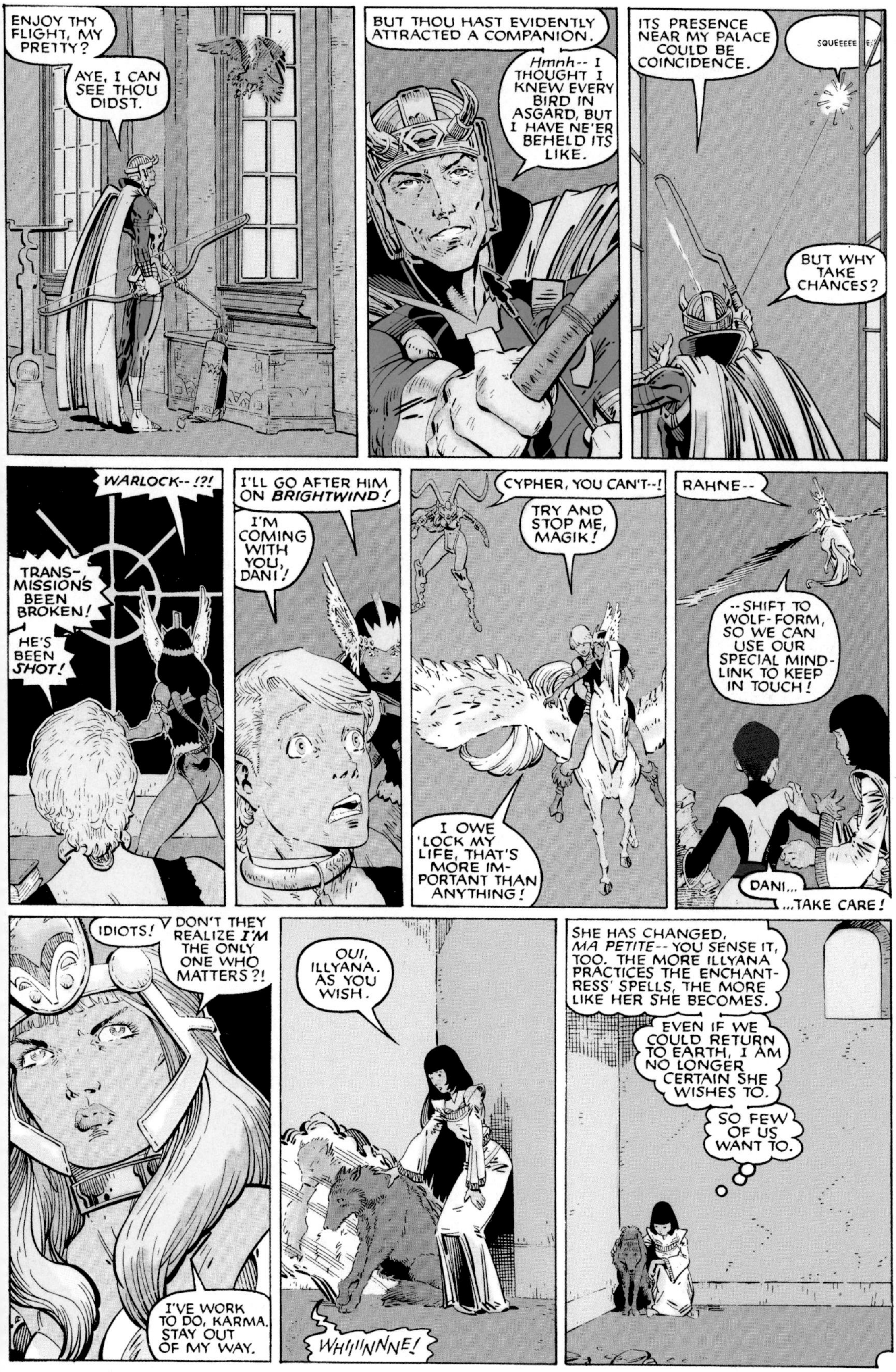
ENJOY THY FLIGHT, MY PRETTY?
AYE, I CAN SEE THOU DIDST.
BUT THOU HAST EVIDENTLY ATTRACTED A COMPANION.
Hmnh-- I THOUGHT I KNEW EVERY BIRD IN ASGARD, BUT I HAVE NE'ER BEHELD ITS LIKE.
ITS PRESENCE NEAR MY PALACE COULD BE COINCIDENCE.
SQUEEEEE EE
BUT WHY TAKE CHANCES?
WARLOCK-- !?!
TRANS-MISSION'S BEEN BROKEN!
HE'S BEEN SHOT!
I'LL GO AFTER HIM ON BRIGHTWIND!
I'M COMING WITH YOU, DANI!
CYPHER, YOU CAN'T--!
TRY AND STOP ME, MAGIK!
I OWE 'LOCK MY LIFE, THAT'S MORE IM-PORTANT THAN ANYTHING!
RAHNE--
--SHIFT TO WOLF-FORM, SO WE CAN USE OUR SPECIAL MIND-LINK TO KEEP IN TOUCH!
DANI...
...TAKE CARE!
IDIOTS!
DON'T THEY REALIZE I'M THE ONLY ONE WHO MATTERS?!
I'VE WORK TO DO, KARMA. STAY OUT OF MY WAY.
OUI, ILLYANA. AS YOU WISH.
WHIIIINNNE!
SHE HAS CHANGED, MA PETITE-- YOU SENSE IT, TOO. THE MORE ILLYANA PRACTICES THE ENCHANT-RESS' SPELLS, THE MORE LIKE HER SHE BECOMES.
EVEN IF WE COULD RETURN TO EARTH, I AM NO LONGER CERTAIN SHE WISHES TO.
SO FEW OF US WANT TO.

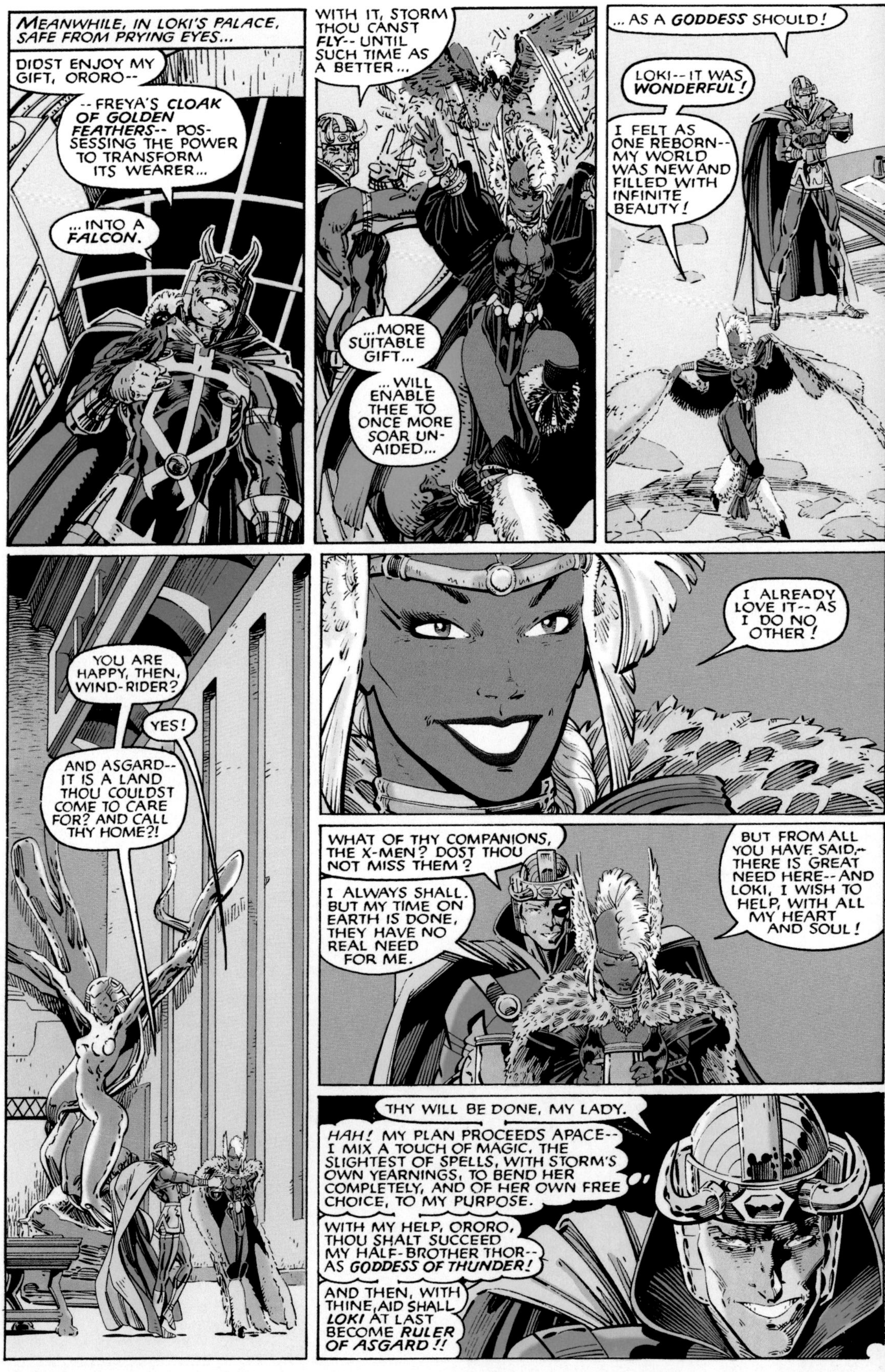
MEANWHILE, IN LOKI'S PALACE, SAFE FROM PRYING EYES...
DIDST ENJOY MY GIFT, ORORO--
--FREYA'S CLOAK OF GOLDEN FEATHERS-- POSSESSING THE POWER TO TRANSFORM ITS WEARER...
...INTO A FALCON.
WITH IT, STORM THOU CANST FLY-- UNTIL SUCH TIME AS A BETTER...
...MORE SUITABLE GIFT...
...WILL ENABLE THEE TO ONCE MORE SOAR UNAIDED...
...AS A GODDESS SHOULD!
LOKI-- IT WAS WONDERFUL!
I FELT AS ONE REBORN-- MY WORLD WAS NEW AND FILLED WITH INFINITE BEAUTY!
YOU ARE HAPPY, THEN, WIND-RIDER?
YES!
AND ASGARD-- IT IS A LAND THOU COULDST COME TO CARE FOR? AND CALL THY HOME?!
I ALREADY LOVE IT-- AS I DO NO OTHER!
WHAT OF THY COMPANIONS, THE X-MEN? DOST THOU NOT MISS THEM?
I ALWAYS SHALL. BUT MY TIME ON EARTH IS DONE. THEY HAVE NO REAL NEED FOR ME.
BUT FROM ALL YOU HAVE SAID,-- THERE IS GREAT NEED HERE-- AND LOKI, I WISH TO HELP, WITH ALL MY HEART AND SOUL!
THY WILL BE DONE, MY LADY.
HAH! MY PLAN PROCEEDS APACE-- I MIX A TOUCH OF MAGIC, THE SLIGHTEST OF SPELLS, WITH STORM'S OWN YEARNINGS, TO BEND HER COMPLETELY, AND OF HER OWN FREE CHOICE, TO MY PURPOSE.
WITH MY HELP, ORORO, THOU SHALT SUCCEED MY HALF-BROTHER THOR-- AS GODDESS OF THUNDER!
AND THEN, WITH THINE AID SHALL LOKI AT LAST BECOME RULER OF ASGARD!!

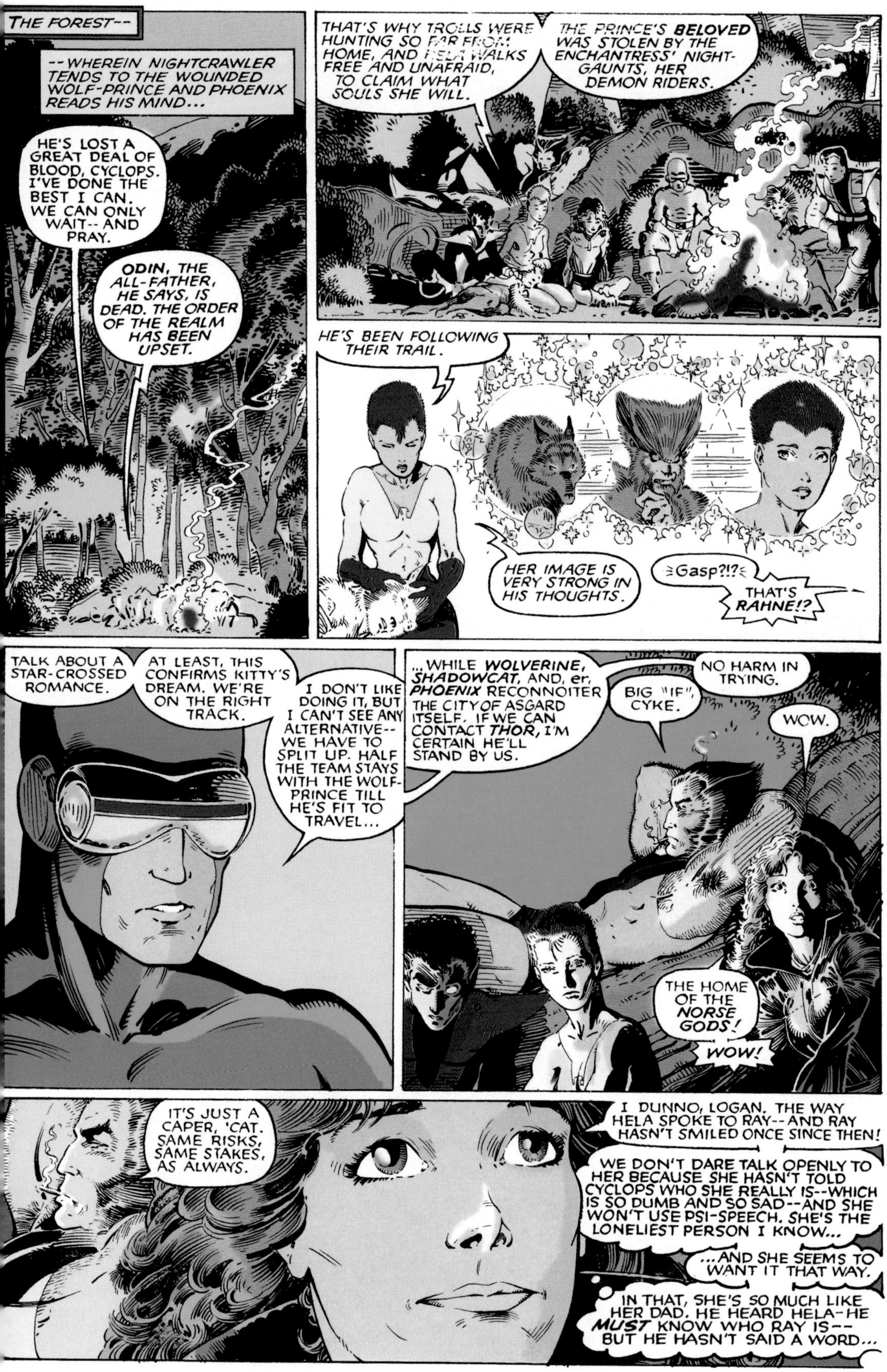
THE FOREST--
--WHEREIN NIGHTCRAWLER TENDS TO THE WOUNDED WOLF-PRINCE AND PHOENIX READS HIS MIND...
HE'S LOST A GREAT DEAL OF BLOOD, CYCLOPS. I'VE DONE THE BEST I CAN. WE CAN ONLY WAIT-- AND PRAY.
ODIN, THE ALL-FATHER, HE SAYS, IS DEAD. THE ORDER OF THE REALM HAS BEEN UPSET.
THAT'S WHY TROLLS WERE HUNTING SO FAR FROM HOME, AND HELA WALKS FREE AND UNAFRAID, TO CLAIM WHAT SOULS SHE WILL.
THE PRINCE'S BELOVED WAS STOLEN BY THE ENCHANTRESS' NIGHT-GAUNTS, HER DEMON RIDERS.
HE'S BEEN FOLLOWING THEIR TRAIL.
HER IMAGE IS VERY STRONG IN HIS THOUGHTS.
Gasp?!?
THAT'S RAHNE!?
TALK ABOUT A STAR-CROSSED ROMANCE.
AT LEAST, THIS CONFIRMS KITTY'S DREAM. WE'RE ON THE RIGHT TRACK.
I DON'T LIKE DOING IT, BUT I CAN'T SEE ANY ALTERNATIVE-- WE HAVE TO SPLIT UP. HALF THE TEAM STAYS WITH THE WOLF-PRINCE TILL HE'S FIT TO TRAVEL...
...WHILE WOLVERINE, SHADOWCAT, AND, er, PHOENIX RECONNOITER THE CITY OF ASGARD ITSELF. IF WE CAN CONTACT THOR, I'M CERTAIN HE'LL STAND BY US.
NO HARM IN TRYING.
BIG "IF", CYKE.
WOW.
THE HOME OF THE NORSE GODS!
WOW!
IT'S JUST A CAPER, 'CAT. SAME RISKS, SAME STAKES, AS ALWAYS.
I DUNNO, LOGAN. THE WAY HELA SPOKE TO RAY-- AND RAY HASN'T SMILED ONCE SINCE THEN!
WE DON'T DARE TALK OPENLY TO HER BECAUSE SHE HASN'T TOLD CYCLOPS WHO SHE REALLY IS--WHICH IS SO DUMB AND SO SAD--AND SHE WON'T USE PSI-SPEECH. SHE'S THE LONELIEST PERSON I KNOW...
...AND SHE SEEMS TO WANT IT THAT WAY.
IN THAT, SHE'S SO MUCH LIKE HER DAD. HE HEARD HELA-HE MUST KNOW WHO RAY IS-- BUT HE HASN'T SAID A WORD...

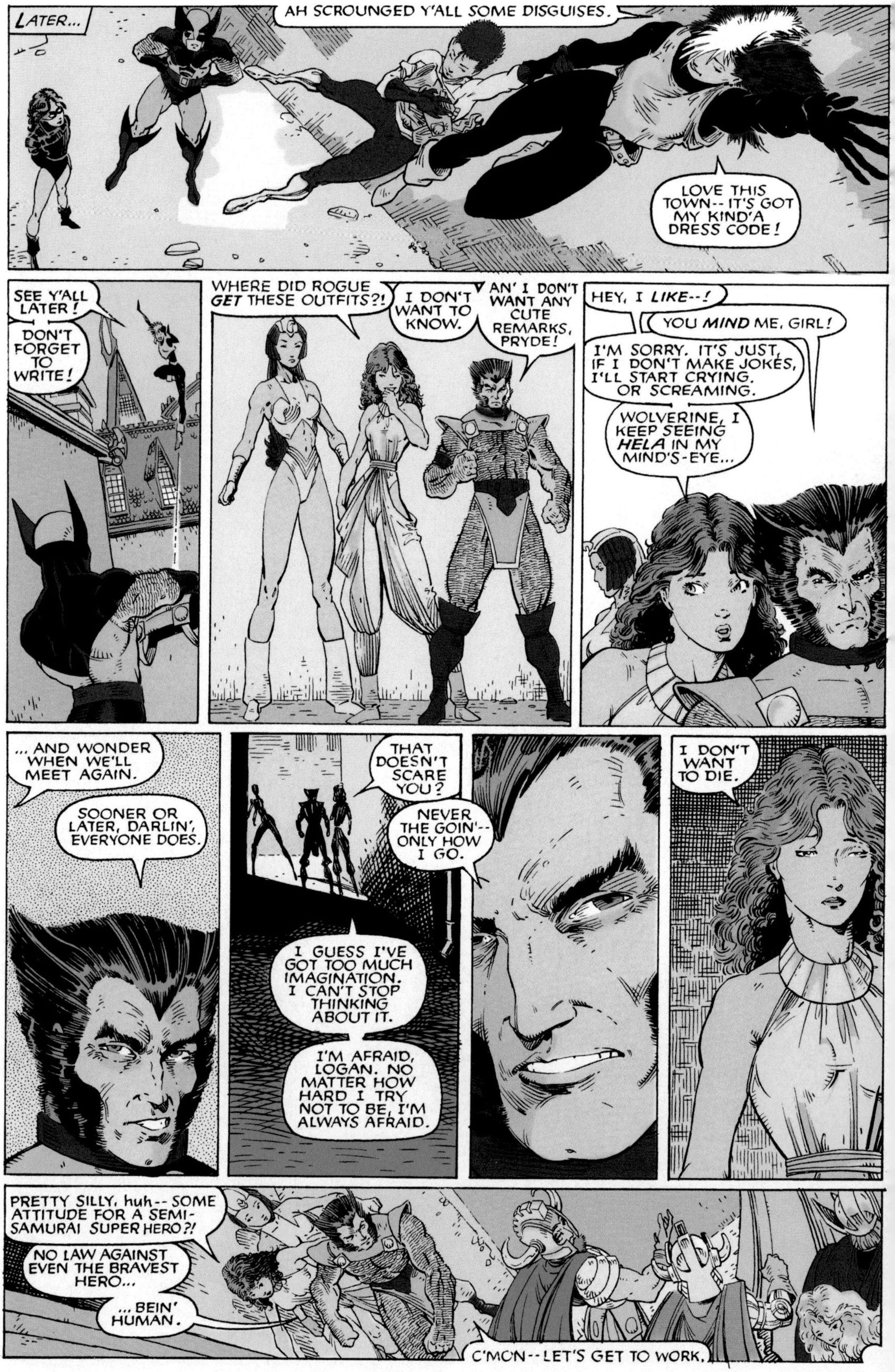
LATER...
AH SCROUNGED Y'ALL SOME DISGUISES.
LOVE THIS TOWN-- IT'S GOT MY KIND'A DRESS CODE!
SEE Y'ALL LATER!
DON'T FORGET TO WRITE!
WHERE DID ROGUE GET THESE OUTFITS?!
I DON'T WANT TO KNOW.
AN' I DON'T WANT ANY CUTE REMARKS, PRYDE!
HEY, I LIKE--!
YOU MIND ME, GIRL!
I'M SORRY. IT'S JUST, IF I DON'T MAKE JOKES, I'LL START CRYING. OR SCREAMING.
WOLVERINE, I KEEP SEEING HELA IN MY MIND'S-EYE...
... AND WONDER WHEN WE'LL MEET AGAIN.
SOONER OR LATER, DARLIN', EVERYONE DOES.
THAT DOESN'T SCARE YOU?
NEVER THE GOIN'-- ONLY HOW I GO.
I GUESS I'VE GOT TOO MUCH IMAGINATION. I CAN'T STOP THINKING ABOUT IT.
I'M AFRAID, LOGAN. NO MATTER HOW HARD I TRY NOT TO BE, I'M ALWAYS AFRAID.
I DON'T WANT TO DIE.
PRETTY SILLY, huh-- SOME ATTITUDE FOR A SEMI-SAMURAI SUPER HERO?!
NO LAW AGAINST EVEN THE BRAVEST HERO...
... BEIN' HUMAN.
C'MON-- LET'S GET TO WORK.

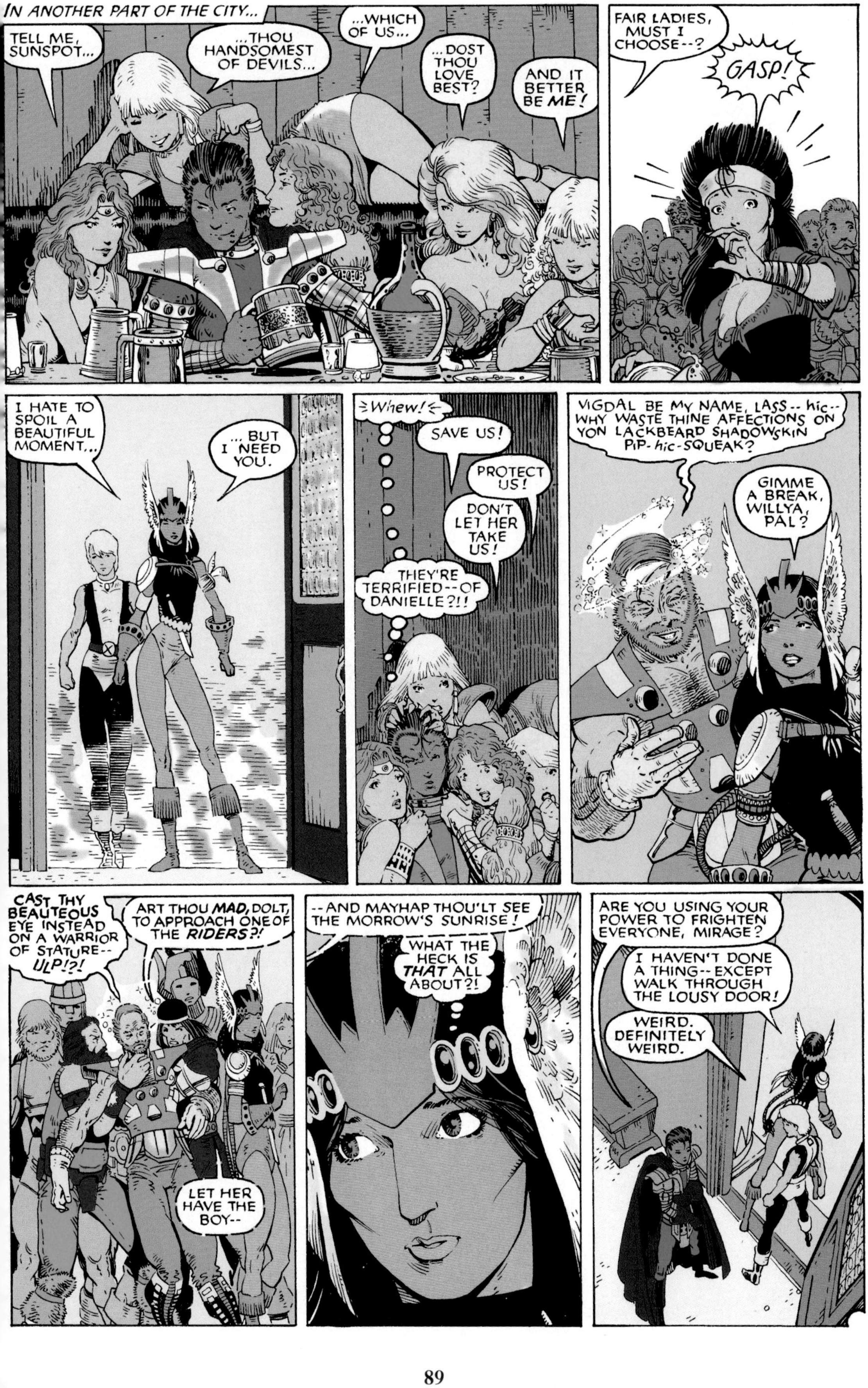
IN ANOTHER PART OF THE CITY...
TELL ME, SUNSPOT...
...THOU HANDSOMEST OF DEVILS...
...WHICH OF US...
...DOST THOU LOVE BEST?
AND IT BETTER BE ME!
FAIR LADIES, MUST I CHOOSE--?
GASP!
I HATE TO SPOIL A BEAUTIFUL MOMENT...
...BUT I NEED YOU.
Whew!
SAVE US!
PROTECT US!
DON'T LET HER TAKE US!
THEY'RE TERRIFIED--OF DANIELLE?!!
VIGDAL BE MY NAME, LASS--hic--WHY WASTE THINE AFFECTIONS ON YON LACKBEARD SHADOWSKIN PIP-hic-SQUEAK?
GIMME A BREAK, WILLYA, PAL?
CAST THY BEAUTEOUS EYE INSTEAD ON A WARRIOR OF STATURE--ULP!?!
ART THOU MAD, DOLT, TO APPROACH ONE OF THE RIDERS?!
LET HER HAVE THE BOY--
--AND MAYHAP THOU'LT SEE THE MORROW'S SUNRISE!
WHAT THE HECK IS THAT ALL ABOUT?!
ARE YOU USING YOUR POWER TO FRIGHTEN EVERYONE, MIRAGE?
I HAVEN'T DONE A THING--EXCEPT WALK THROUGH THE LOUSY DOOR!
WEIRD. DEFINITELY WEIRD.

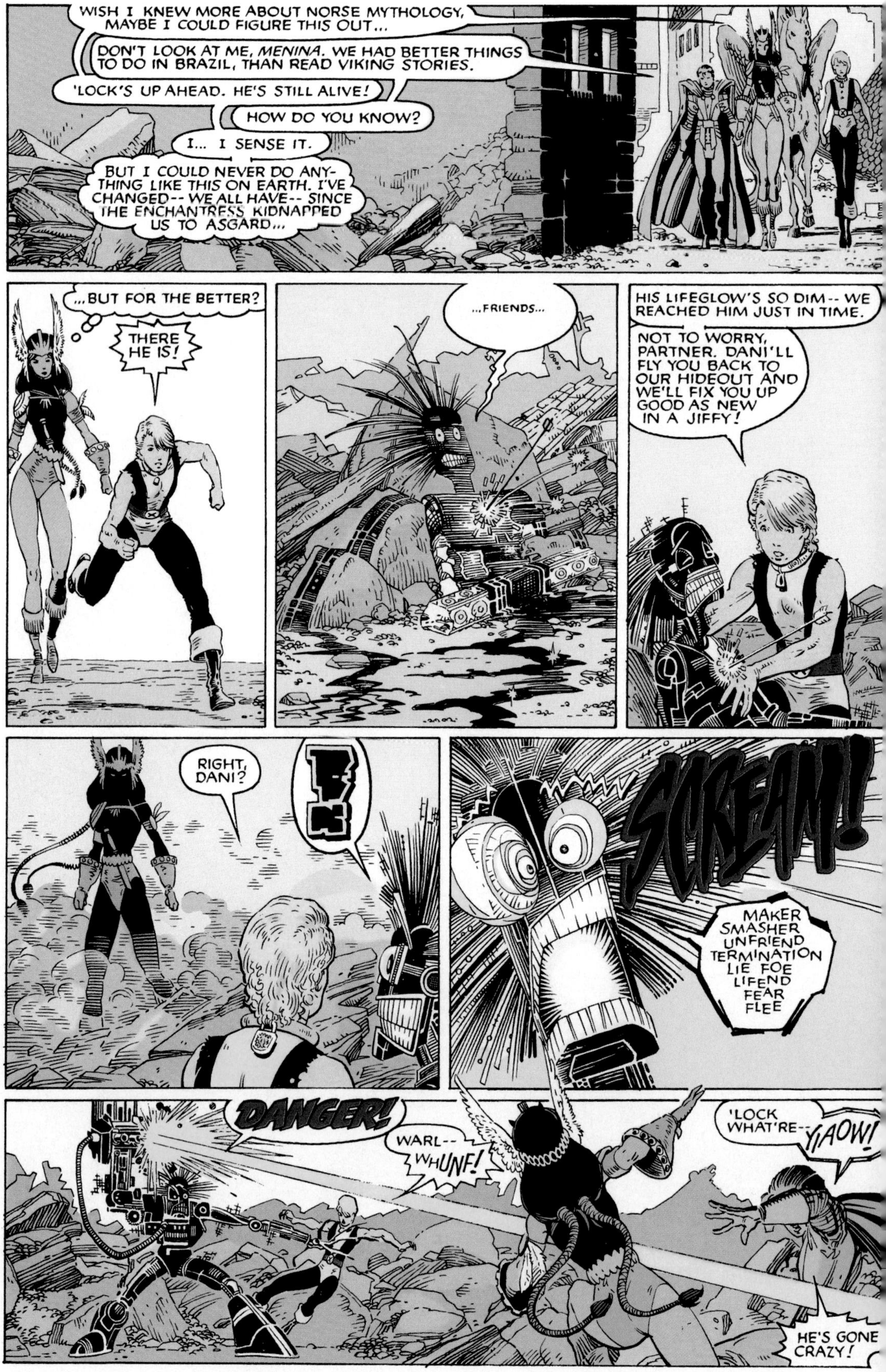

WISH I KNEW MORE ABOUT NORSE MYTHOLOGY, MAYBE I COULD FIGURE THIS OUT...
DON'T LOOK AT ME, MENINA. WE HAD BETTER THINGS TO DO IN BRAZIL, THAN READ VIKING STORIES.
'LOCK'S UP AHEAD. HE'S STILL ALIVE!
HOW DO YOU KNOW?
I... I SENSE IT.
BUT I COULD NEVER DO ANYTHING LIKE THIS ON EARTH. I'VE CHANGED-- WE ALL HAVE-- SINCE THE ENCHANTRESS KIDNAPPED US TO ASGARD...
...BUT FOR THE BETTER?
THERE HE IS!
...FRIENDS...
HIS LIFEGLOW'S SO DIM-- WE REACHED HIM JUST IN TIME.
NOT TO WORRY, PARTNER. DANI'LL FLY YOU BACK TO OUR HIDEOUT AND WE'LL FIX YOU UP GOOD AS NEW IN A JIFFY!
RIGHT, DANI?
SCREAM!
MAKER SMASHER UNFRIEND TERMINATION LIE FOE LIFEND FEAR FLEE
DANGER!
WARL-- WHUNF!
'LOCK WHAT'RE-- YIAOW!
HE'S GONE CRAZY!

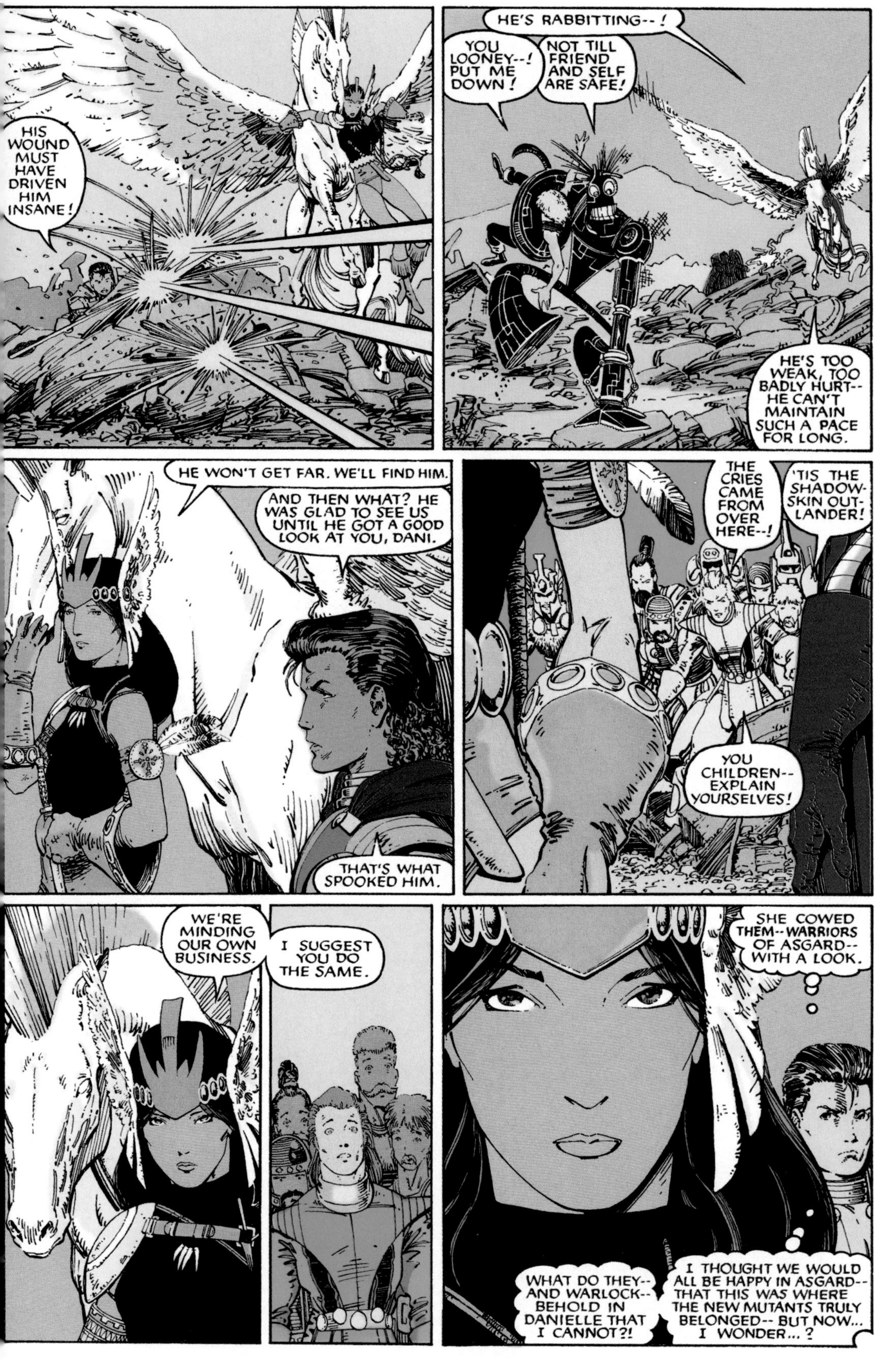
HIS WOUND MUST HAVE DRIVEN HIM INSANE!
HE'S RABBITTING--!
YOU LOONEY--! PUT ME DOWN!
NOT TILL FRIEND AND SELF ARE SAFE!
HE'S TOO WEAK, TOO BADLY HURT-- HE CAN'T MAINTAIN SUCH A PACE FOR LONG.
HE WON'T GET FAR. WE'LL FIND HIM.
AND THEN WHAT? HE WAS GLAD TO SEE US UNTIL HE GOT A GOOD LOOK AT YOU, DANI.
THAT'S WHAT SPOOKED HIM.
THE CRIES CAME FROM OVER HERE--!
'TIS THE SHADOW-SKIN OUT-LANDER!
YOU CHILDREN-- EXPLAIN YOURSELVES!
WE'RE MINDING OUR OWN BUSINESS.
I SUGGEST YOU DO THE SAME.
SHE COWED THEM--WARRIORS OF ASGARD-- WITH A LOOK.
WHAT DO THEY-- AND WARLOCK-- BEHOLD IN DANIELLE THAT I CANNOT?!
I THOUGHT WE WOULD ALL BE HAPPY IN ASGARD-- THAT THIS WAS WHERE THE NEW MUTANTS TRULY BELONGED-- BUT NOW... I WONDER...?

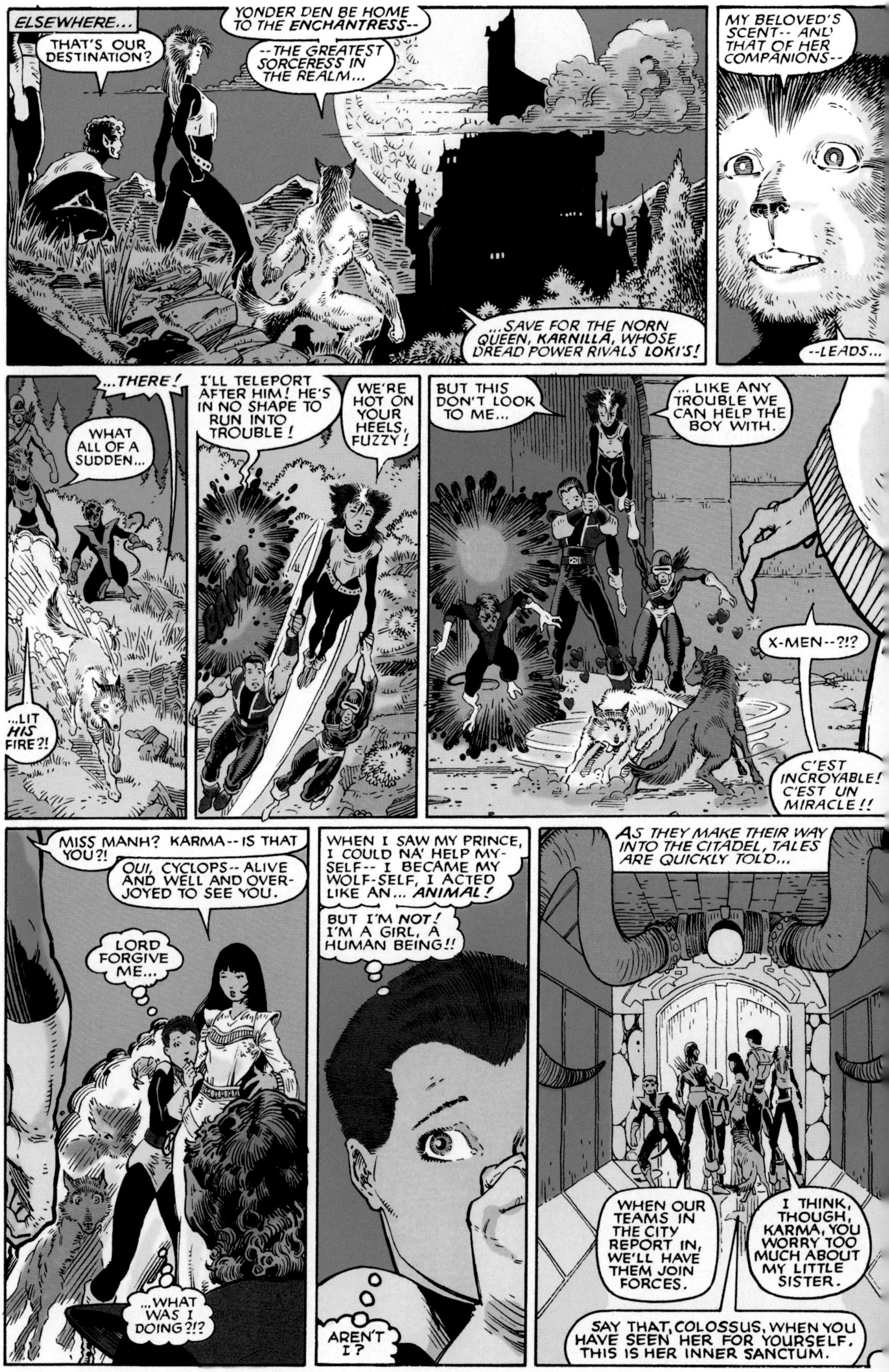
ELSEWHERE...
THAT'S OUR DESTINATION?
YONDER DEN BE HOME TO THE ENCHANTRESS--
--THE GREATEST SORCERESS IN THE REALM...
...SAVE FOR THE NORN QUEEN, KARNILLA, WHOSE DREAD POWER RIVALS LOKI'S!
MY BELOVED'S SCENT-- AND THAT OF HER COMPANIONS--
--LEADS...
...THERE!
WHAT ALL OF A SUDDEN...
...LIT HIS FIRE?!
I'LL TELEPORT AFTER HIM! HE'S IN NO SHAPE TO RUN INTO TROUBLE!
WE'RE HOT ON YOUR HEELS, FUZZY!
BAMF
BUT THIS DON'T LOOK TO ME...
...LIKE ANY TROUBLE WE CAN HELP THE BOY WITH.
X-MEN--?!?
C'EST INCROYABLE! C'EST UN MIRACLE!!
MISS MANH? KARMA-- IS THAT YOU?!
OUI, CYCLOPS-- ALIVE AND WELL AND OVERJOYED TO SEE YOU.
LORD FORGIVE ME...
...WHAT WAS I DOING?!?
WHEN I SAW MY PRINCE, I COULD NA' HELP MYSELF-- I BECAME MY WOLF-SELF, I ACTED LIKE AN... ANIMAL!
BUT I'M NOT! I'M A GIRL, A HUMAN BEING!!
AREN'T I?
AS THEY MAKE THEIR WAY INTO THE CITADEL, TALES ARE QUICKLY TOLD...
WHEN OUR TEAMS IN THE CITY REPORT IN, WE'LL HAVE THEM JOIN FORCES.
I THINK, THOUGH, KARMA, YOU WORRY TOO MUCH ABOUT MY LITTLE SISTER.
SAY THAT, COLOSSUS, WHEN YOU HAVE SEEN HER FOR YOURSELF. THIS IS HER INNER SANCTUM.

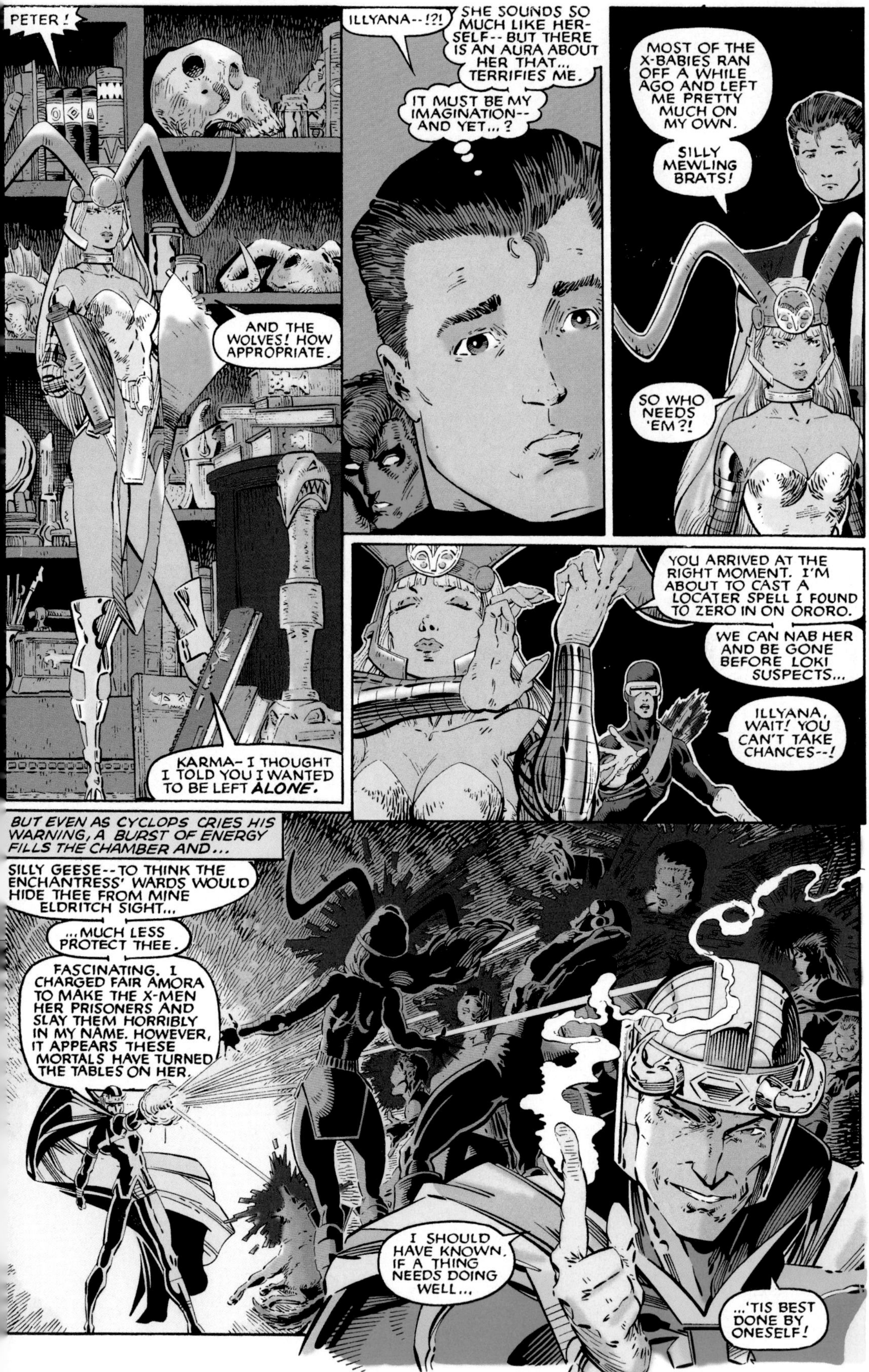
PETER!
AND THE WOLVES! HOW APPROPRIATE.
KARMA- I THOUGHT I TOLD YOU I WANTED TO BE LEFT ALONE.
ILLYANA--!?!
SHE SOUNDS SO MUCH LIKE HER-SELF-- BUT THERE IS AN AURA ABOUT HER THAT... TERRIFIES ME.
IT MUST BE MY IMAGINATION-- AND YET...?
MOST OF THE X-BABIES RAN OFF A WHILE AGO AND LEFT ME PRETTY MUCH ON MY OWN.
SILLY MEWLING BRATS!
SO WHO NEEDS 'EM?!
YOU ARRIVED AT THE RIGHT MOMENT. I'M ABOUT TO CAST A LOCATER SPELL I FOUND TO ZERO IN ON ORORO.
WE CAN NAB HER AND BE GONE BEFORE LOKI SUSPECTS...
ILLYANA, WAIT! YOU CAN'T TAKE CHANCES--!
BUT EVEN AS CYCLOPS CRIES HIS WARNING, A BURST OF ENERGY FILLS THE CHAMBER AND...
SILLY GEESE--TO THINK THE ENCHANTRESS' WARDS WOULD HIDE THEE FROM MINE ELDRITCH SIGHT...
...MUCH LESS PROTECT THEE.
FASCINATING. I CHARGED FAIR AMORA TO MAKE THE X-MEN HER PRISONERS AND SLAY THEM HORRIBLY IN MY NAME. HOWEVER, IT APPEARS THESE MORTALS HAVE TURNED THE TABLES ON HER.
I SHOULD HAVE KNOWN. IF A THING NEEDS DOING WELL...
...'TIS BEST DONE BY ONESELF!

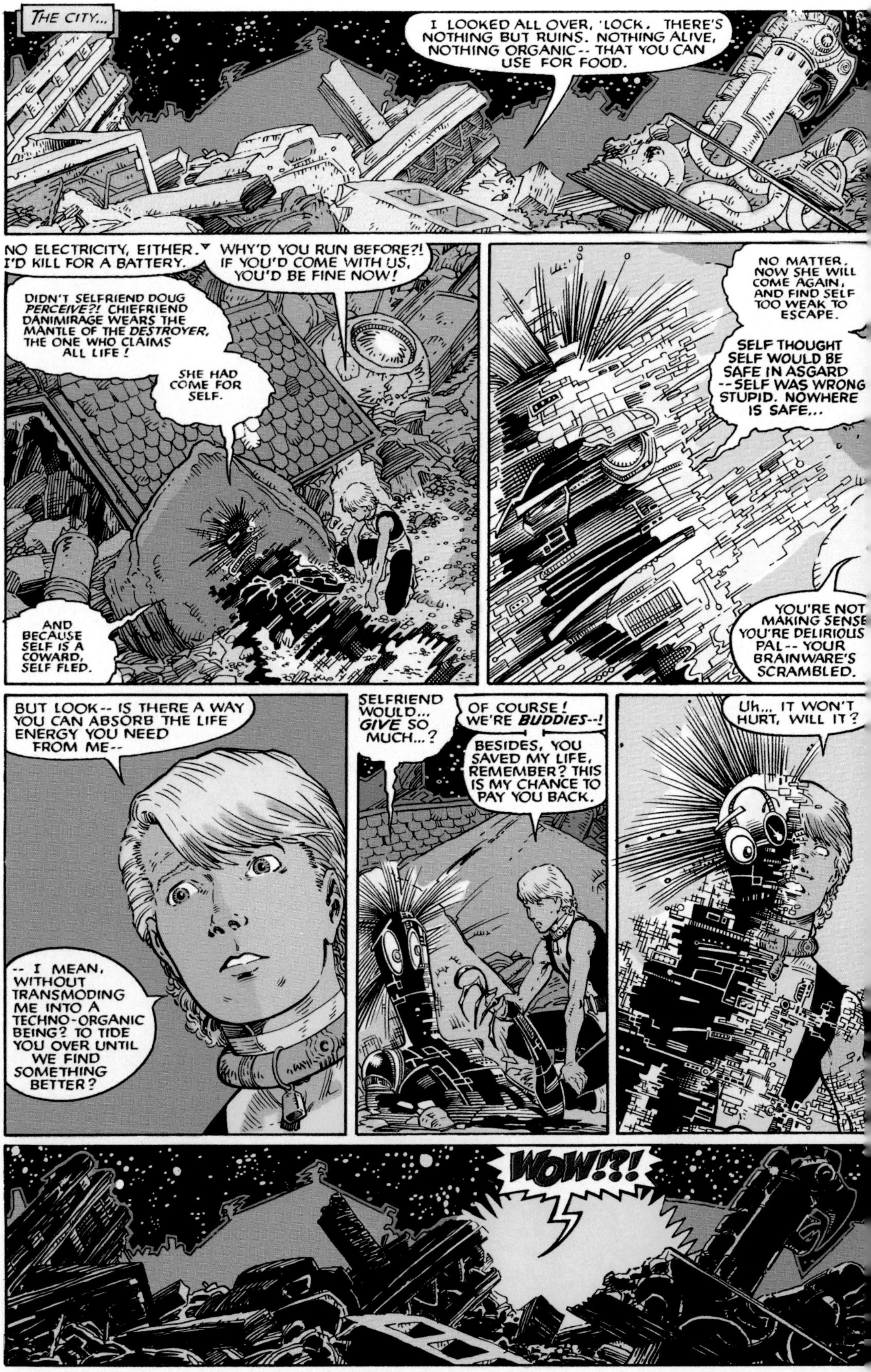
THE CITY...
I LOOKED ALL OVER, 'LOCK. THERE'S NOTHING BUT RUINS. NOTHING ALIVE, NOTHING ORGANIC-- THAT YOU CAN USE FOR FOOD.
NO ELECTRICITY, EITHER. I'D KILL FOR A BATTERY.
WHY'D YOU RUN BEFORE?! IF YOU'D COME WITH US, YOU'D BE FINE NOW!
DIDN'T SELFRIEND DOUG PERCEIVE?! CHIEFRIEND DANIMIRAGE WEARS THE MANTLE OF THE DESTROYER, THE ONE WHO CLAIMS ALL LIFE!
SHE HAD COME FOR SELF.
AND BECAUSE SELF IS A COWARD, SELF FLED.
NO MATTER. NOW SHE WILL COME AGAIN, AND FIND SELF TOO WEAK TO ESCAPE.
SELF THOUGHT SELF WOULD BE SAFE IN ASGARD --SELF WAS WRONG STUPID. NOWHERE IS SAFE...
YOU'RE NOT MAKING SENSE YOU'RE DELIRIOUS PAL-- YOUR BRAINWARE'S SCRAMBLED.
BUT LOOK-- IS THERE A WAY YOU CAN ABSORB THE LIFE ENERGY YOU NEED FROM ME--
-- I MEAN, WITHOUT TRANSMODING ME INTO A TECHNO-ORGANIC BEING? TO TIDE YOU OVER UNTIL WE FIND SOMETHING BETTER?
SELFRIEND WOULD... GIVE SO MUCH...?
OF COURSE! WE'RE BUDDIES--!
BESIDES, YOU SAVED MY LIFE, REMEMBER? THIS IS MY CHANCE TO PAY YOU BACK.
Uh... IT WON'T HURT, WILL IT?
WOW!?!

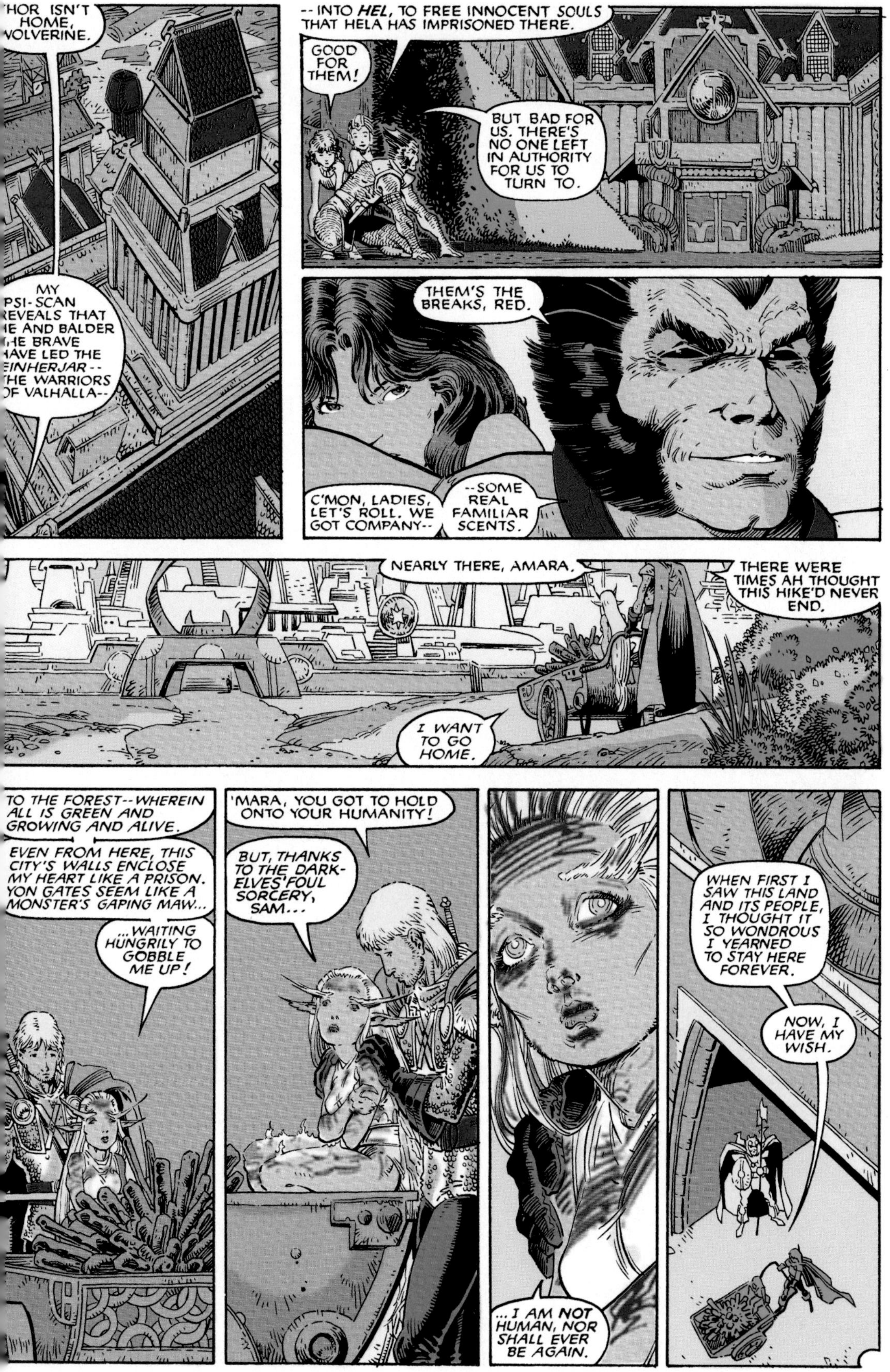
THOR ISN'T HOME, WOLVERINE.
MY PSI-SCAN REVEALS THAT HE AND BALDER THE BRAVE HAVE LED THE EINHERJAR -- THE WARRIORS OF VALHALLA--
-- INTO HEL, TO FREE INNOCENT SOULS THAT HELA HAS IMPRISONED THERE.
GOOD FOR THEM!
BUT BAD FOR US. THERE'S NO ONE LEFT IN AUTHORITY FOR US TO TURN TO.
THEM'S THE BREAKS, RED.
C'MON, LADIES, LET'S ROLL. WE GOT COMPANY--
--SOME REAL FAMILIAR SCENTS.
NEARLY THERE, AMARA.
THERE WERE TIMES AH THOUGHT THIS HIKE'D NEVER END.
I WANT TO GO HOME.
TO THE FOREST--WHEREIN ALL IS GREEN AND GROWING AND ALIVE.
EVEN FROM HERE, THIS CITY'S WALLS ENCLOSE MY HEART LIKE A PRISON. YON GATES SEEM LIKE A MONSTER'S GAPING MAW...
...WAITING HUNGRILY TO GOBBLE ME UP!
'MARA, YOU GOT TO HOLD ONTO YOUR HUMANITY!
BUT, THANKS TO THE DARK-ELVES' FOUL SORCERY, SAM...
...I AM NOT HUMAN, NOR SHALL EVER BE AGAIN.
WHEN FIRST I SAW THIS LAND AND ITS PEOPLE, I THOUGHT IT SO WONDROUS I YEARNED TO STAY HERE FOREVER.
NOW, I HAVE MY WISH.

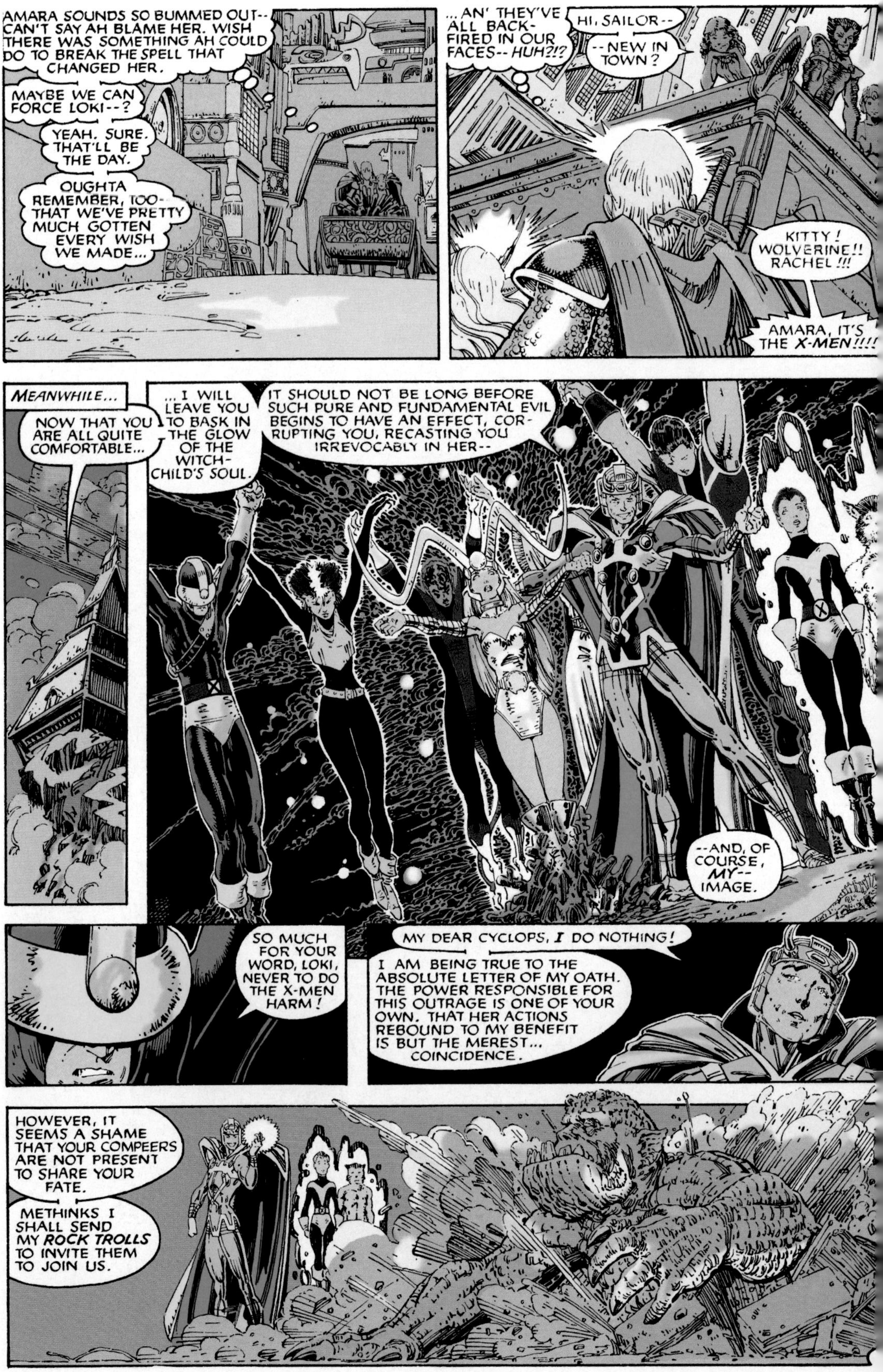

AMARA SOUNDS SO BUMMED OUT-- CAN'T SAY AH BLAME HER. WISH THERE WAS SOMETHING AH COULD DO TO BREAK THE SPELL THAT CHANGED HER.
MAYBE WE CAN FORCE LOKI--?
YEAH. SURE. THAT'LL BE THE DAY.
OUGHTA REMEMBER, TOO-- THAT WE'VE PRETTY MUCH GOTTEN EVERY WISH WE MADE...
...AN' THEY'VE ALL BACK-FIRED IN OUR FACES-- HUH?!?
HI, SAILOR--
--NEW IN TOWN?
KITTY! WOLVERINE!! RACHEL!!!
AMARA, IT'S THE X-MEN!!!!
MEANWHILE...
NOW THAT YOU ARE ALL QUITE COMFORTABLE...
...I WILL LEAVE YOU TO BASK IN THE GLOW OF THE WITCH-CHILD'S SOUL.
IT SHOULD NOT BE LONG BEFORE SUCH PURE AND FUNDAMENTAL EVIL BEGINS TO HAVE AN EFFECT, COR-RUPTING YOU, RECASTING YOU IRREVOCABLY IN HER--
--AND, OF COURSE, MY-- IMAGE.
SO MUCH FOR YOUR WORD, LOKI, NEVER TO DO THE X-MEN HARM!
MY DEAR CYCLOPS, I DO NOTHING!
I AM BEING TRUE TO THE ABSOLUTE LETTER OF MY OATH. THE POWER RESPONSIBLE FOR THIS OUTRAGE IS ONE OF YOUR OWN. THAT HER ACTIONS REBOUND TO MY BENEFIT IS BUT THE MEREST... COINCIDENCE.
HOWEVER, IT SEEMS A SHAME THAT YOUR COMPEERS ARE NOT PRESENT TO SHARE YOUR FATE.
METHINKS I SHALL SEND MY ROCK TROLLS TO INVITE THEM TO JOIN US.

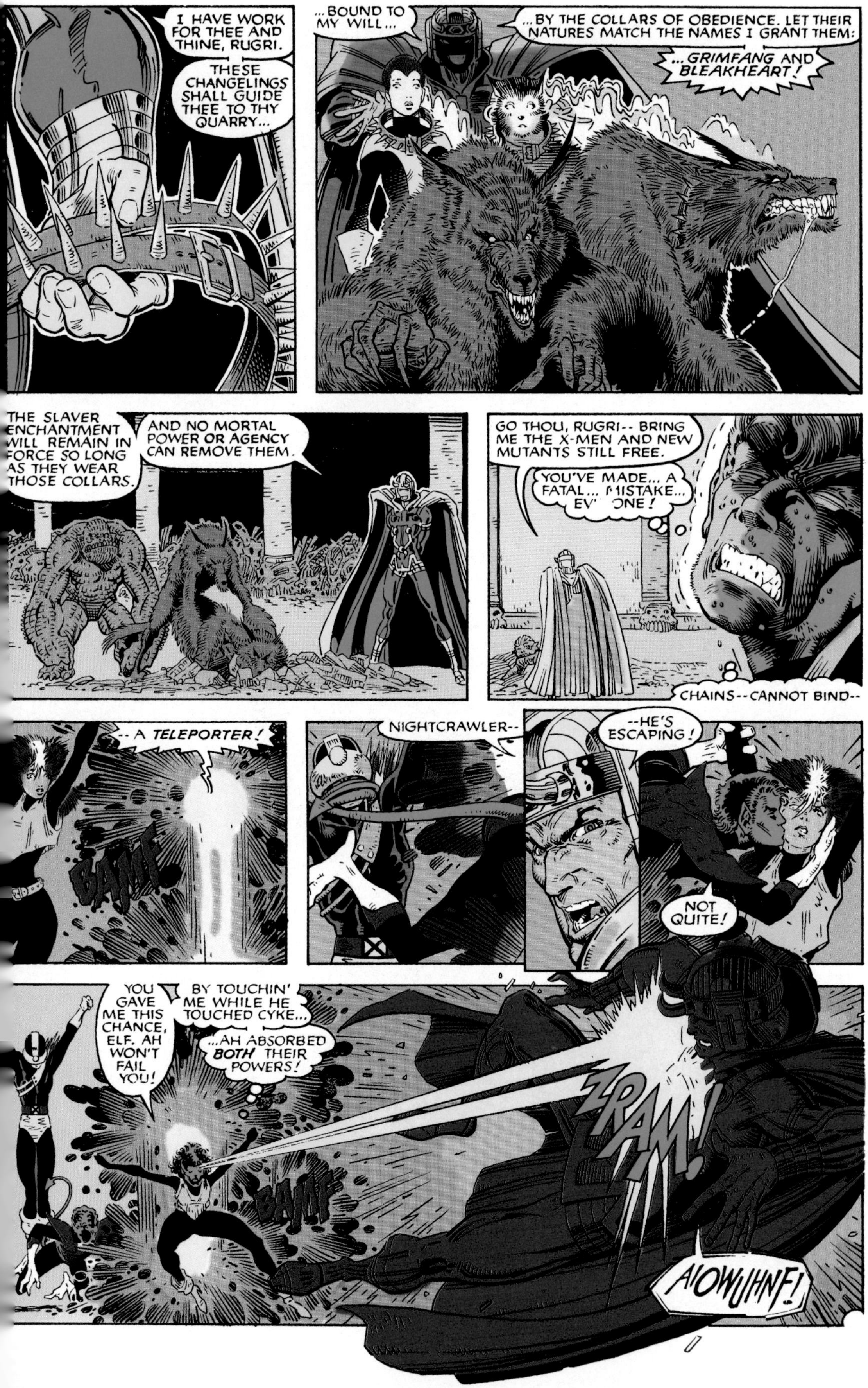
I HAVE WORK FOR THEE AND THINE, RUGRI.
THESE CHANGELINGS SHALL GUIDE THEE TO THY QUARRY...
...BOUND TO MY WILL...
...BY THE COLLARS OF OBEDIENCE. LET THEIR NATURES MATCH THE NAMES I GRANT THEM:
...GRIMFANG AND BLEAKHEART!
THE SLAVER ENCHANTMENT WILL REMAIN IN FORCE SO LONG AS THEY WEAR THOSE COLLARS.
AND NO MORTAL POWER OR AGENCY CAN REMOVE THEM.
GO THOU, RUGRI-- BRING ME THE X-MEN AND NEW MUTANTS STILL FREE.
CHAINS--CANNOT BIND--
-- A TELEPORTER!
BAMF
NIGHTCRAWLER--
--HE'S ESCAPING!
NOT QUITE!
YOU GAVE ME THIS CHANCE, ELF. AH WON'T FAIL YOU!
BY TOUCHIN' ME WHILE HE TOUCHED CYKE...
...AH ABSORBED BOTH THEIR POWERS!
BAMF
ZRAM!
AIOWUHNF!

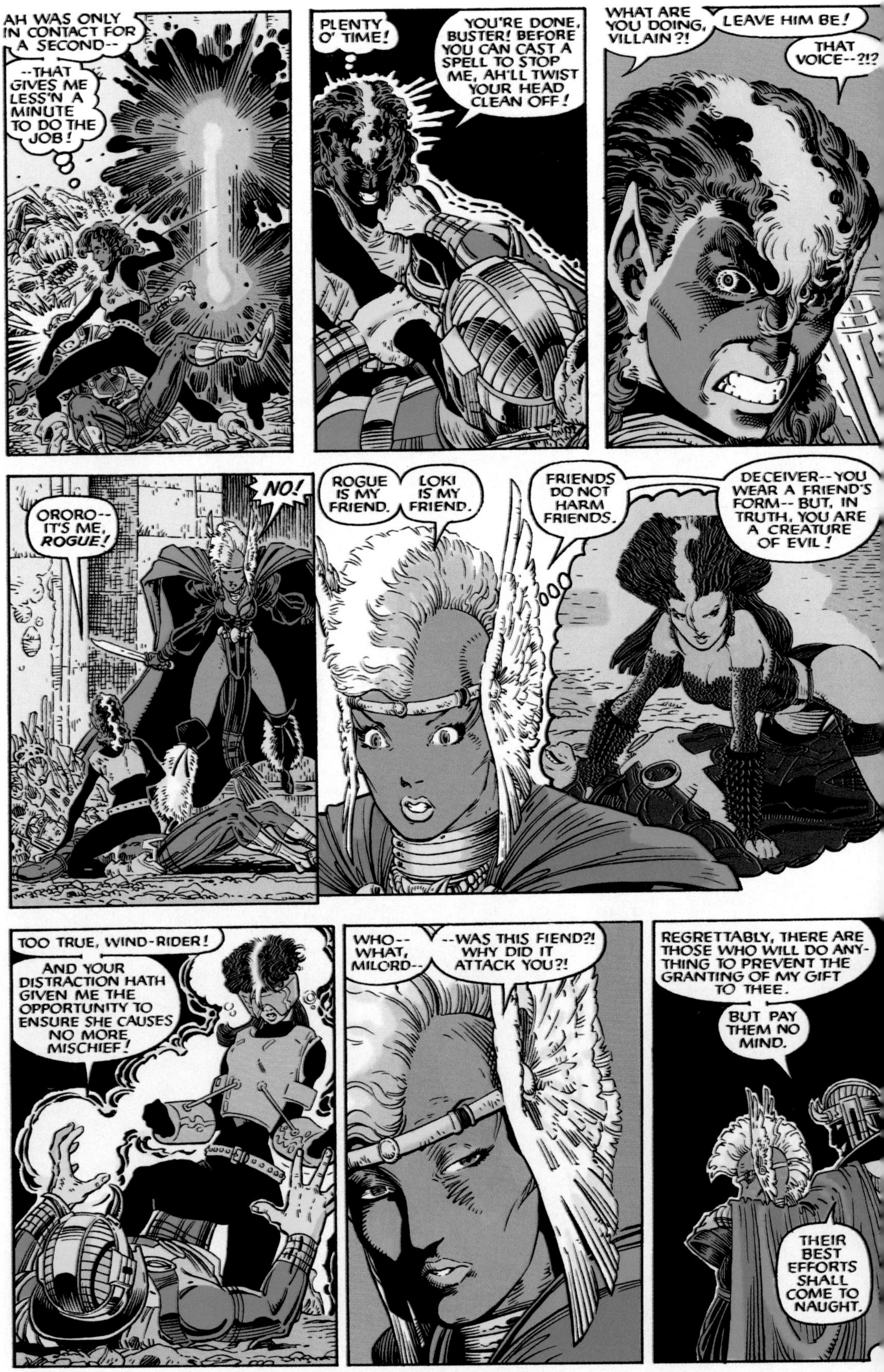
AH WAS ONLY IN CONTACT FOR A SECOND--
--THAT GIVES ME LESS'N A MINUTE TO DO THE JOB!
PLENTY O' TIME!
YOU'RE DONE, BUSTER! BEFORE YOU CAN CAST A SPELL TO STOP ME, AH'LL TWIST YOUR HEAD CLEAN OFF!
WHAT ARE YOU DOING, VILLAIN?!
LEAVE HIM BE!
THAT VOICE--?!?
NO!
ORORO-- IT'S ME, ROGUE!
ROGUE IS MY FRIEND.
LOKI IS MY FRIEND.
FRIENDS DO NOT HARM FRIENDS.
DECEIVER--YOU WEAR A FRIEND'S FORM--BUT, IN TRUTH, YOU ARE A CREATURE OF EVIL!
TOO TRUE, WIND-RIDER!
AND YOUR DISTRACTION HATH GIVEN ME THE OPPORTUNITY TO ENSURE SHE CAUSES NO MORE MISCHIEF!
WHO-- WHAT, MILORD--
--WAS THIS FIEND?! WHY DID IT ATTACK YOU?!
REGRETTABLY, THERE ARE THOSE WHO WILL DO ANYTHING TO PREVENT THE GRANTING OF MY GIFT TO THEE.
BUT PAY THEM NO MIND.
THEIR BEST EFFORTS SHALL COME TO NAUGHT.

HOW CAN ANY CITY ON EARTH-- EVEN MY HOME, RIO de JANIERO-- COMPARE TO THIS?

HOW CAN OUR LIVES THERE...

... EVEN HOPE TO RIVAL WHAT WE CAN DO-- AND HAVE-- HERE?

WHO ARE YOU TRYING TO CONVINCE, BOBBY?

ME... ...OR YOURSELF?

HI, GUYS!

RACHEL--?!

CARE TO JOIN US?

IT'S SO GREAT TO SEE YOU!

NOW LOKI'S REALLY IN TROUBLE!

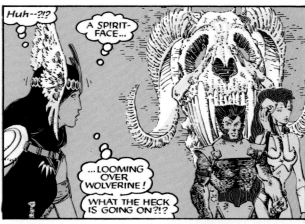

Huh--?!?

A SPIRIT-FACE...

...LOOMING OVER WOLVERINE!

WHAT THE HECK IS GOING ON?!?

NONE OF THE OTHERS SAW ANYTHING, ONLY ME. I FEEL SO COLD INSIDE, TOO, AS IF MY HEART JUST TURNED TO ICE. SOMETHING AWFUL'S GOING TO HAPPEN, I KNOW IT-- BUT HOW?! WHAT?!!

CAN I STOP IT? AM I PART OF IT?!!

EVERY TIME I TURN AROUND, I COME FACE-TO-FACE WITH A NEW MYSTERY-- AND I DON'T LIKE IT ONE BIT! I HAVEN'T EVEN A CLUE EEIYAIOW!

THE GROUND--?!

WHAT THE FLAMIN'--!?!

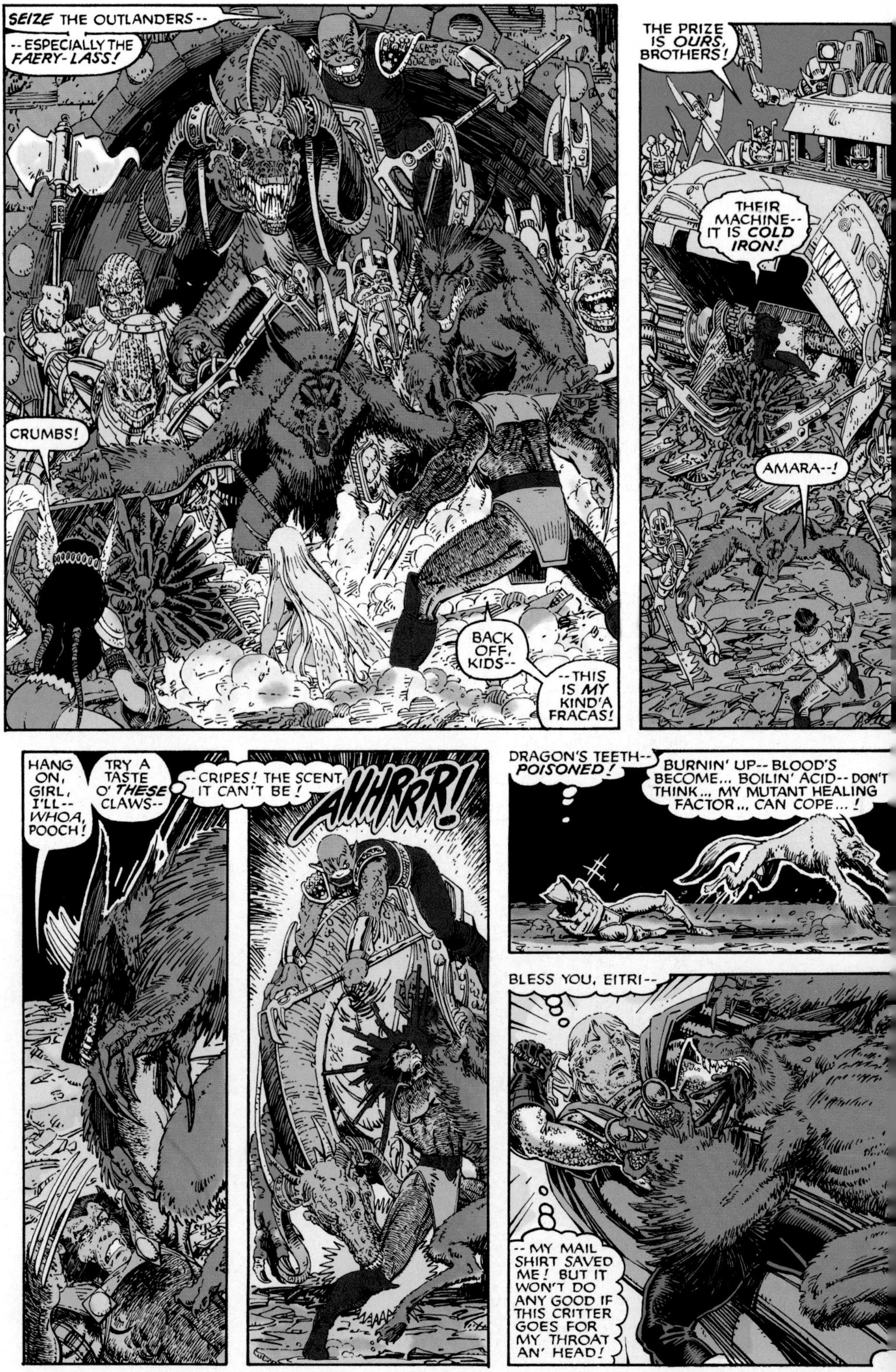
SEIZE THE OUTLANDERS--
--ESPECIALLY THE FAERY-LASS!
CRUMBS!
BACK OFF, KIDS--
--THIS IS MY KIND'A FRACAS!
THE PRIZE IS OURS, BROTHERS!
THEIR MACHINE-- IT IS COLD IRON!
AMARA--!
HANG ON, GIRL, I'LL-- WHOA, POOCH!
TRY A TASTE O' THESE CLAWS--
--CRIPES! THE SCENT, IT CAN'T BE!
AHHRRR!
DRAGON'S TEETH-- POISONED!
BURNIN' UP-- BLOOD'S BECOME... BOILIN' ACID-- DON'T THINK... MY MUTANT HEALING FACTOR... CAN COPE...!
BLESS YOU, EITRI--
--MY MAIL SHIRT SAVED ME! BUT IT WON'T DO ANY GOOD IF THIS CRITTER GOES FOR MY THROAT AN' HEAD!

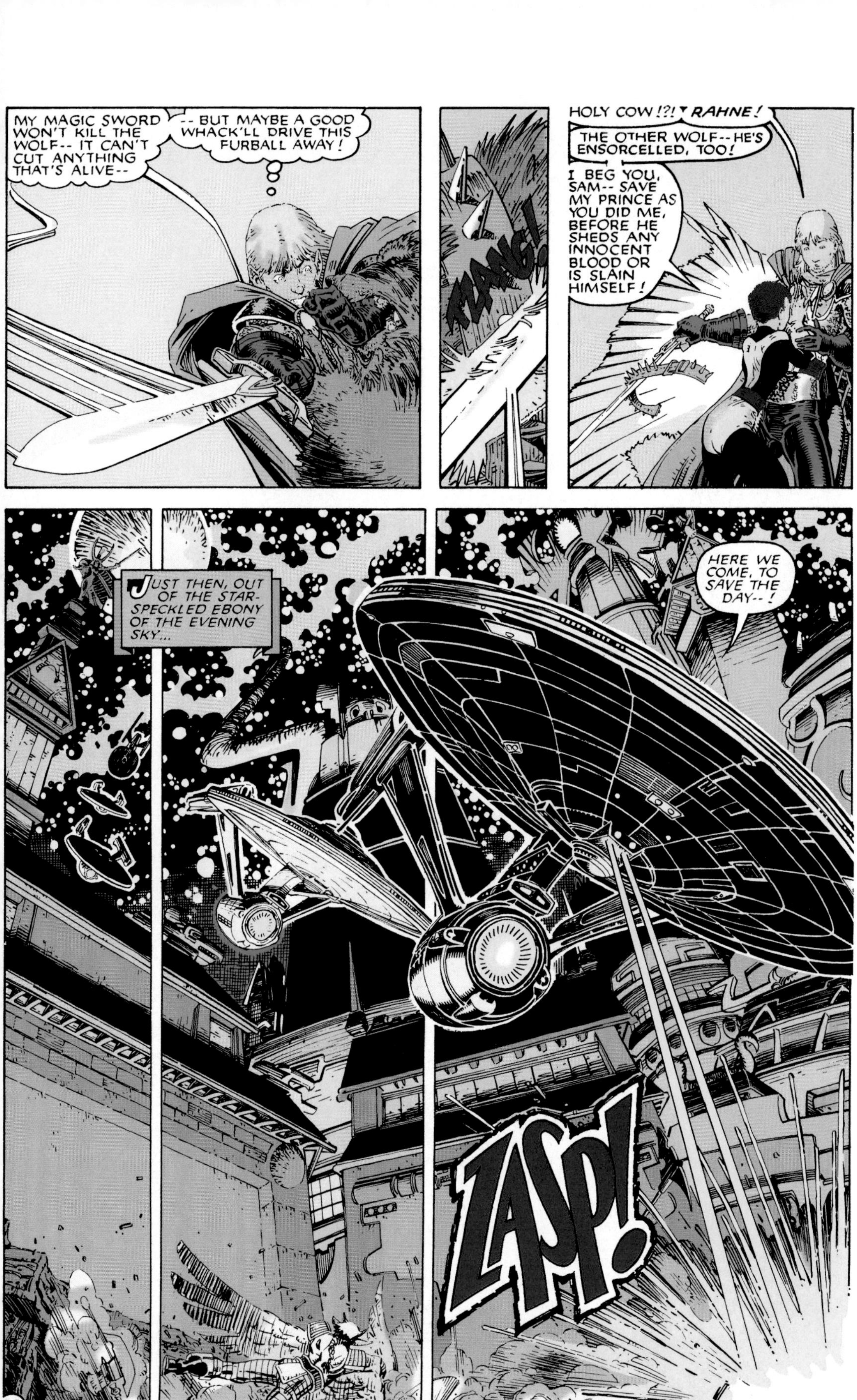
MY MAGIC SWORD WON'T KILL THE WOLF-- IT CAN'T CUT ANYTHING THAT'S ALIVE--
-- BUT MAYBE A GOOD WHACK'LL DRIVE THIS FURBALL AWAY!
TZANG!
HOLY COW!?!
RAHNE!
THE OTHER WOLF-- HE'S ENSORCELLED, TOO!
I BEG YOU, SAM-- SAVE MY PRINCE AS YOU DID ME, BEFORE HE SHEDS ANY INNOCENT BLOOD OR IS SLAIN HIMSELF!
JUST THEN, OUT OF THE STAR-SPECKLED EBONY OF THE EVENING SKY...
HERE WE COME, TO SAVE THE DAY-- !
ZASP!
26

FLEE, BROTHERS-- WE HAVE THE PRIZE MOST CRAVED BY LOKI!

WE'LL FINISH THESE MORTALS ANOTHER TIME!

SPRONG!

BTANG!

FRIENDOUG--

--SHALL WE ENGAGE IN HOT PURSUIT?

LEMME CHECK WITH THE OTHERS, PARTNER.

THEY TOOK AMARA-- WE GOTTA GO AFTER 'EM!

THAT'S WHAT THEY WANT, BOY-- TO TRY TO TACKLE 'EM ON THEIR OWN TURF.

WOLVERINE'S RIGHT, SAM--

--BUT IS HE OKAY?! HIS VOICE SOUNDS SO ROUGH-- WAS HE WOUNDED?! NO SIGN OF ANY INJURIES-- HIS HEALING FACTOR MUST BE HANDLING THINGS JUST FINE.

FROM WHAT RAHNE SAYS, WE'RE THE ONLY ONES LEFT. LOKI'S EVIDENTLY CALLED SOME BIG MEETING TONIGHT. WHATEVER HE HAS PLANNED FOR ORORO, THAT LOOKS LIKE WHERE IT'S GOING TO HAPPEN.

WE'LL HAVE TO SPLIT UP AGAIN. WOLVERINE, YOU TAKE RAY, 'BERTO, DOUG, DANI AND WARLOCK TO THE CEREMONY...

...WHILE RAHNE, SAM AND I TRY TO FREE LOKI'S PRISONERS.

NO-- PLEASE, KITTY, NOT THERE!

I CANNA--

--HE'LL CAPTURE ME!

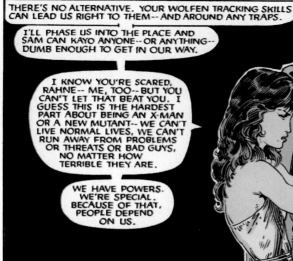

THERE'S NO ALTERNATIVE. YOUR WOLFEN TRACKING SKILLS CAN LEAD US RIGHT TO THEM-- AND AROUND ANY TRAPS.

I'LL PHASE US INTO THE PLACE AND SAM CAN KAYO ANYONE-- OR ANYTHING-- DUMB ENOUGH TO GET IN OUR WAY.

I KNOW YOU'RE SCARED, RAHNE-- ME, TOO-- BUT YOU CAN'T LET THAT BEAT YOU. I GUESS THIS IS THE HARDEST PART ABOUT BEING AN X-MAN OR A NEW MUTANT-- WE CAN'T LIVE NORMAL LIVES, WE CAN'T RUN AWAY FROM PROBLEMS OR THREATS OR BAD GUYS, NO MATTER HOW TERRIBLE THEY ARE.

WE HAVE POWERS. WE'RE SPECIAL. BECAUSE OF THAT, PEOPLE DEPEND ON US.

WE CAN'T FAIL THEM, RAHNE.

WE WON'T.

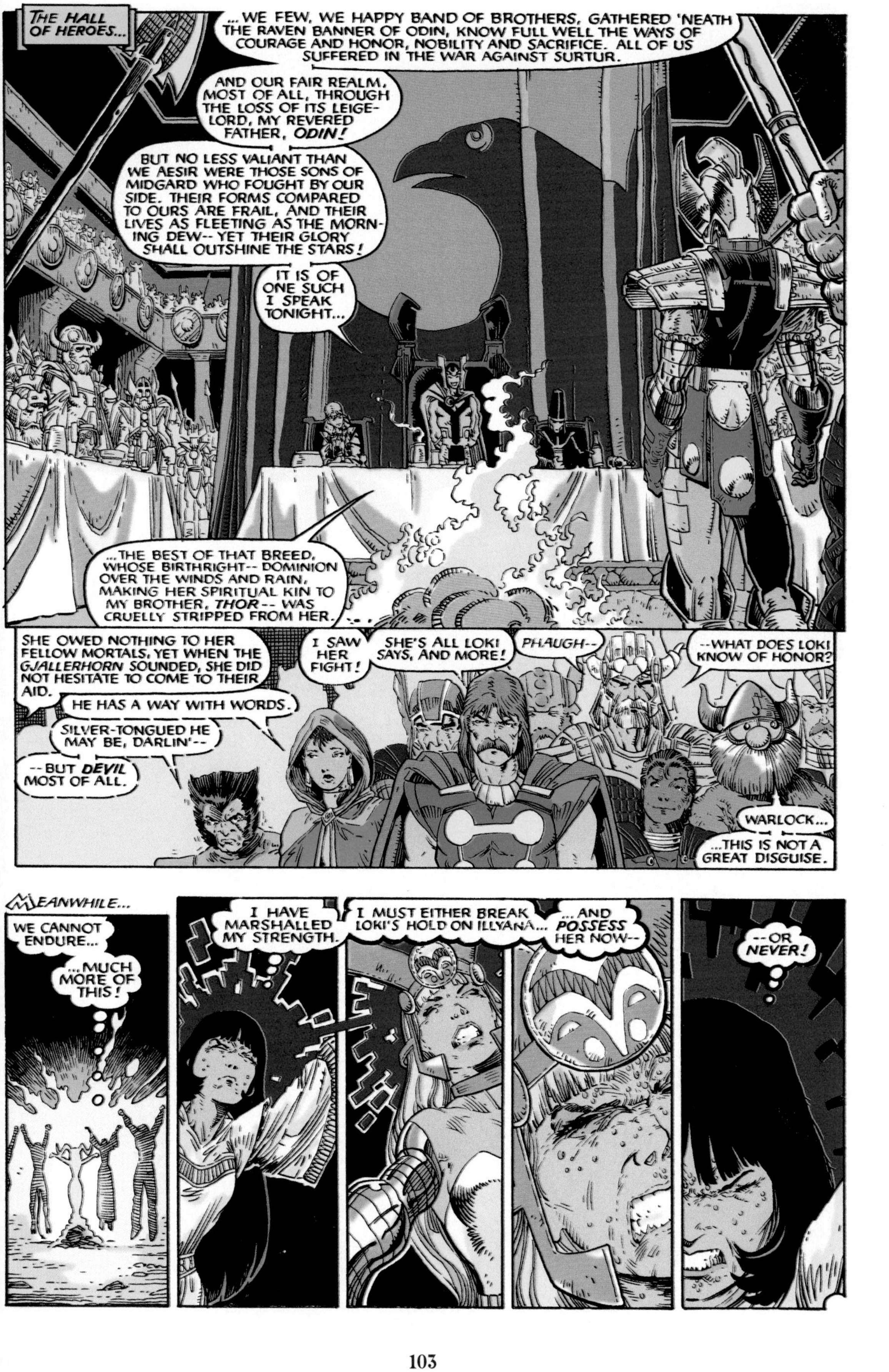
THE HALL OF HEROES...
...WE FEW, WE HAPPY BAND OF BROTHERS, GATHERED 'NEATH THE RAVEN BANNER OF ODIN, KNOW FULL WELL THE WAYS OF COURAGE AND HONOR, NOBILITY AND SACRIFICE. ALL OF US SUFFERED IN THE WAR AGAINST SURTUR.
AND OUR FAIR REALM, MOST OF ALL, THROUGH THE LOSS OF ITS LEIGE-LORD, MY REVERED FATHER, ODIN!
BUT NO LESS VALIANT THAN WE AESIR WERE THOSE SONS OF MIDGARD WHO FOUGHT BY OUR SIDE. THEIR FORMS COMPARED TO OURS ARE FRAIL, AND THEIR LIVES AS FLEETING AS THE MORNING DEW-- YET THEIR GLORY SHALL OUTSHINE THE STARS!
IT IS OF ONE SUCH I SPEAK TONIGHT...
...THE BEST OF THAT BREED, WHOSE BIRTHRIGHT-- DOMINION OVER THE WINDS AND RAIN, MAKING HER SPIRITUAL KIN TO MY BROTHER, THOR-- WAS CRUELLY STRIPPED FROM HER.
SHE OWED NOTHING TO HER FELLOW MORTALS, YET WHEN THE GJALLERHORN SOUNDED, SHE DID NOT HESITATE TO COME TO THEIR AID.
HE HAS A WAY WITH WORDS.
SILVER-TONGUED HE MAY BE, DARLIN'--
--BUT DEVIL MOST OF ALL.
I SAW HER FIGHT!
SHE'S ALL LOKI SAYS, AND MORE!
PHAUGH--
--WHAT DOES LOKI KNOW OF HONOR?
WARLOCK...
...THIS IS NOT A GREAT DISGUISE.
MEANWHILE...
WE CANNOT ENDURE...
...MUCH MORE OF THIS!
I HAVE MARSHALLED MY STRENGTH.
I MUST EITHER BREAK LOKI'S HOLD ON ILLYANA...
...AND POSSESS HER NOW--
--OR NEVER!

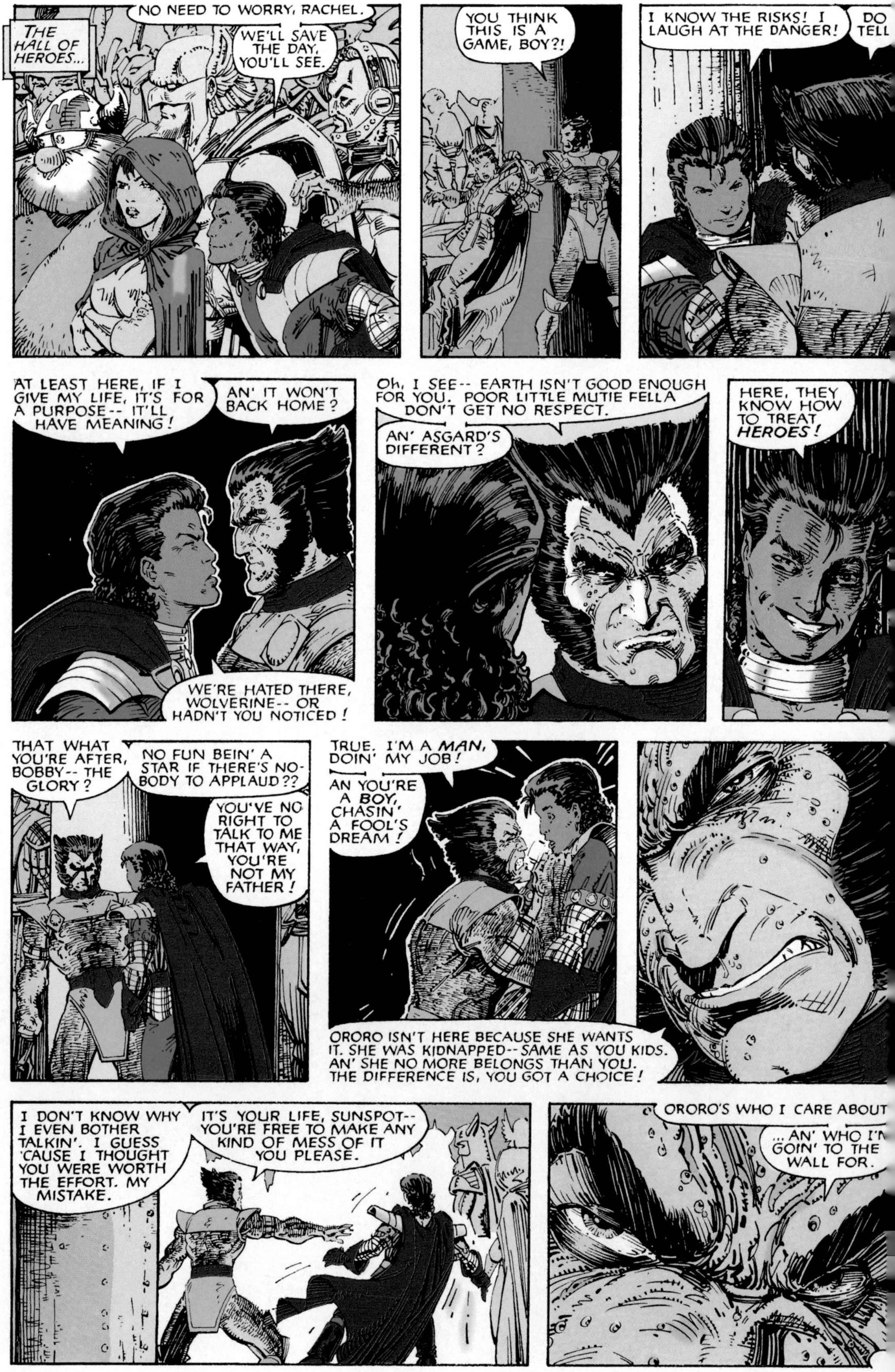
THE HALL OF HEROES...
NO NEED TO WORRY, RACHEL.
WE'LL SAVE THE DAY, YOU'LL SEE.
YOU THINK THIS IS A GAME, BOY?!
I KNOW THE RISKS! I LAUGH AT THE DANGER!
DO TELL
AT LEAST HERE, IF I GIVE MY LIFE, IT'S FOR A PURPOSE-- IT'LL HAVE MEANING!
AN' IT WON'T BACK HOME?
WE'RE HATED THERE, WOLVERINE-- OR HADN'T YOU NOTICED!
Oh, I SEE-- EARTH ISN'T GOOD ENOUGH FOR YOU. POOR LITTLE MUTIE FELLA DON'T GET NO RESPECT.
AN' ASGARD'S DIFFERENT?
HERE, THEY KNOW HOW TO TREAT HEROES!
THAT WHAT YOU'RE AFTER, BOBBY-- THE GLORY?
NO FUN BEIN' A STAR IF THERE'S NOBODY TO APPLAUD??
YOU'VE NO RIGHT TO TALK TO ME THAT WAY, YOU'RE NOT MY FATHER!
TRUE. I'M A MAN, DOIN' MY JOB!
AN YOU'RE A BOY, CHASIN' A FOOL'S DREAM!
ORORO ISN'T HERE BECAUSE SHE WANTS IT. SHE WAS KIDNAPPED-- SAME AS YOU KIDS. AN' SHE NO MORE BELONGS THAN YOU. THE DIFFERENCE IS, YOU GOT A CHOICE!
I DON'T KNOW WHY I EVEN BOTHER TALKIN'. I GUESS 'CAUSE I THOUGHT YOU WERE WORTH THE EFFORT. MY MISTAKE.
IT'S YOUR LIFE, SUNSPOT-- YOU'RE FREE TO MAKE ANY KIND OF MESS OF IT YOU PLEASE.
ORORO'S WHO I CARE ABOUT
...AN' WHO I'M GOIN' TO THE WALL FOR.

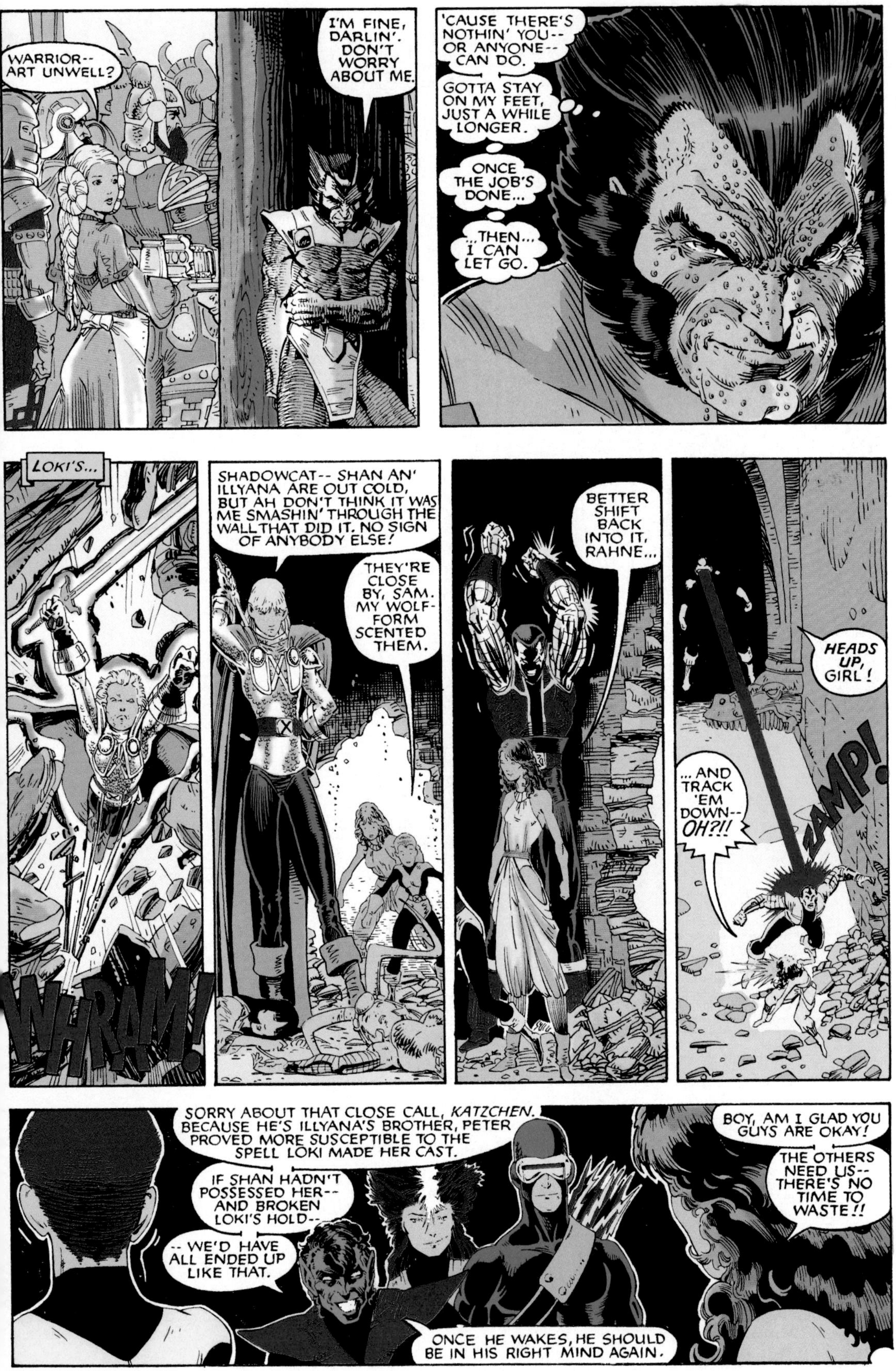
WARRIOR-- ART UNWELL?
I'M FINE, DARLIN'. DON'T WORRY ABOUT ME.
'CAUSE THERE'S NOTHIN' YOU-- OR ANYONE-- CAN DO.
GOTTA STAY ON MY FEET, JUST A WHILE LONGER.
ONCE THE JOB'S DONE...
...THEN... I CAN LET GO.
LOKI'S...
WHRAM!
SHADOWCAT-- SHAN AN' ILLYANA ARE OUT COLD, BUT AH DON'T THINK IT WAS ME SMASHIN' THROUGH THE WALL THAT DID IT. NO SIGN OF ANYBODY ELSE!
THEY'RE CLOSE BY, SAM. MY WOLF-FORM SCENTED THEM.
BETTER SHIFT BACK INTO IT, RAHNE...
...AND TRACK 'EM DOWN-- OH?!!
HEADS UP, GIRL!
ZAMP!
SORRY ABOUT THAT CLOSE CALL, KATZCHEN. BECAUSE HE'S ILLYANA'S BROTHER, PETER PROVED MORE SUSCEPTIBLE TO THE SPELL LOKI MADE HER CAST.
IF SHAN HADN'T POSSESSED HER-- AND BROKEN LOKI'S HOLD--
-- WE'D HAVE ALL ENDED UP LIKE THAT.
ONCE HE WAKES, HE SHOULD BE IN HIS RIGHT MIND AGAIN.
BOY, AM I GLAD YOU GUYS ARE OKAY!
THE OTHERS NEED US-- THERE'S NO TIME TO WASTE!!

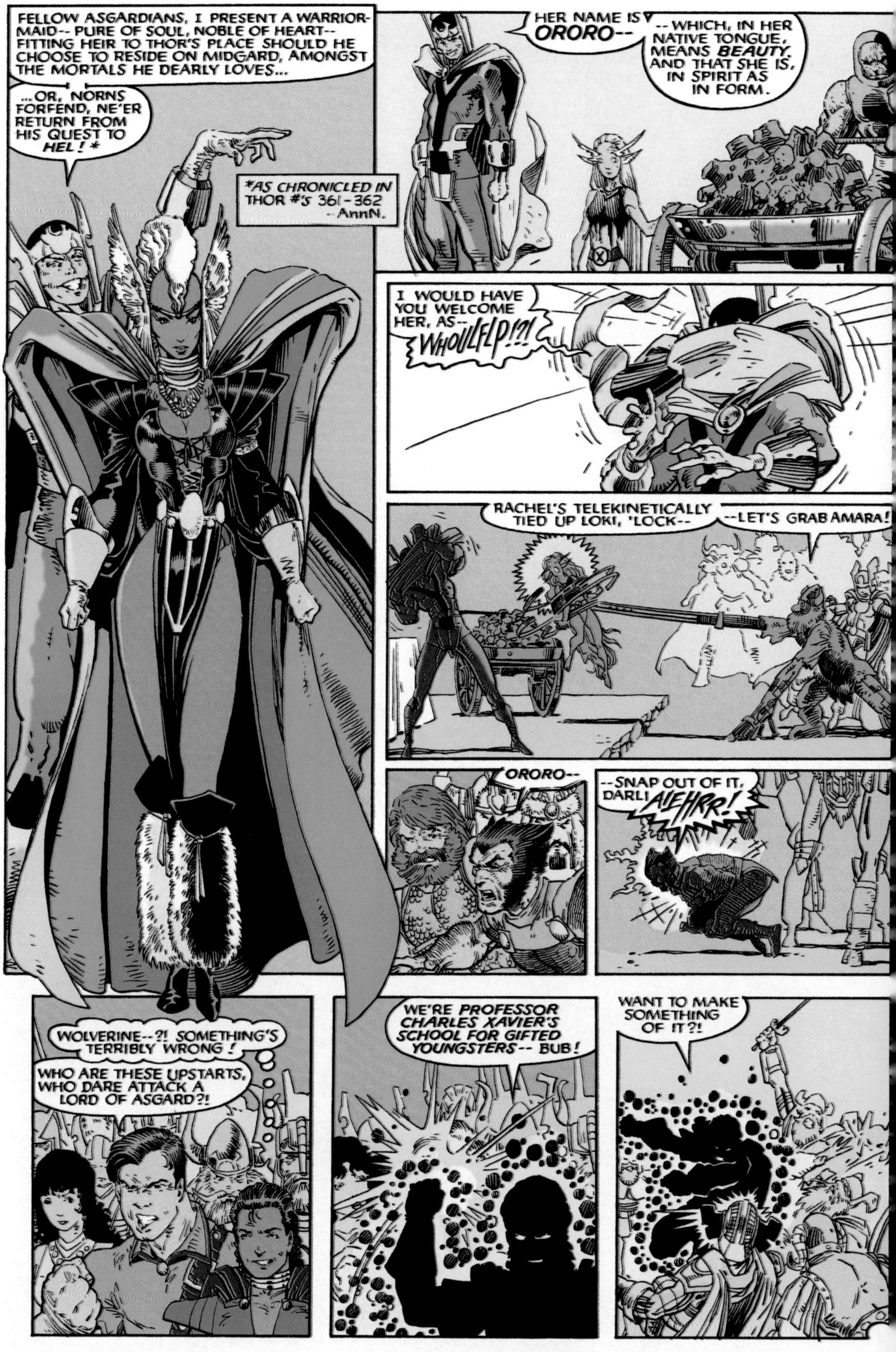
FELLOW ASGARDIANS, I PRESENT A WARRIOR-MAID-- PURE OF SOUL, NOBLE OF HEART-- FITTING HEIR TO THOR'S PLACE SHOULD HE CHOOSE TO RESIDE ON MIDGARD, AMONGST THE MORTALS HE DEARLY LOVES...
...OR, NORNS FORFEND, NE'ER RETURN FROM HIS QUEST TO HEL! *
*AS CHRONICLED IN THOR #'S 361-362 --AnnN.
HER NAME IS ORORO--
--WHICH, IN HER NATIVE TONGUE, MEANS BEAUTY. AND THAT SHE IS, IN SPIRIT AS IN FORM.
I WOULD HAVE YOU WELCOME HER, AS--
WHOULFLP!?!
RACHEL'S TELEKINETICALLY TIED UP LOKI, 'LOCK--
--LET'S GRAB AMARA!
ORORO--
--SNAP OUT OF IT, DARLI
AIEHRR!
WOLVERINE--?! SOMETHING'S TERRIBLY WRONG!
WHO ARE THESE UPSTARTS, WHO DARE ATTACK A LORD OF ASGARD?!
WE'RE PROFESSOR CHARLES XAVIER'S SCHOOL FOR GIFTED YOUNGSTERS-- BUB!
WANT TO MAKE SOMETHING OF IT?!

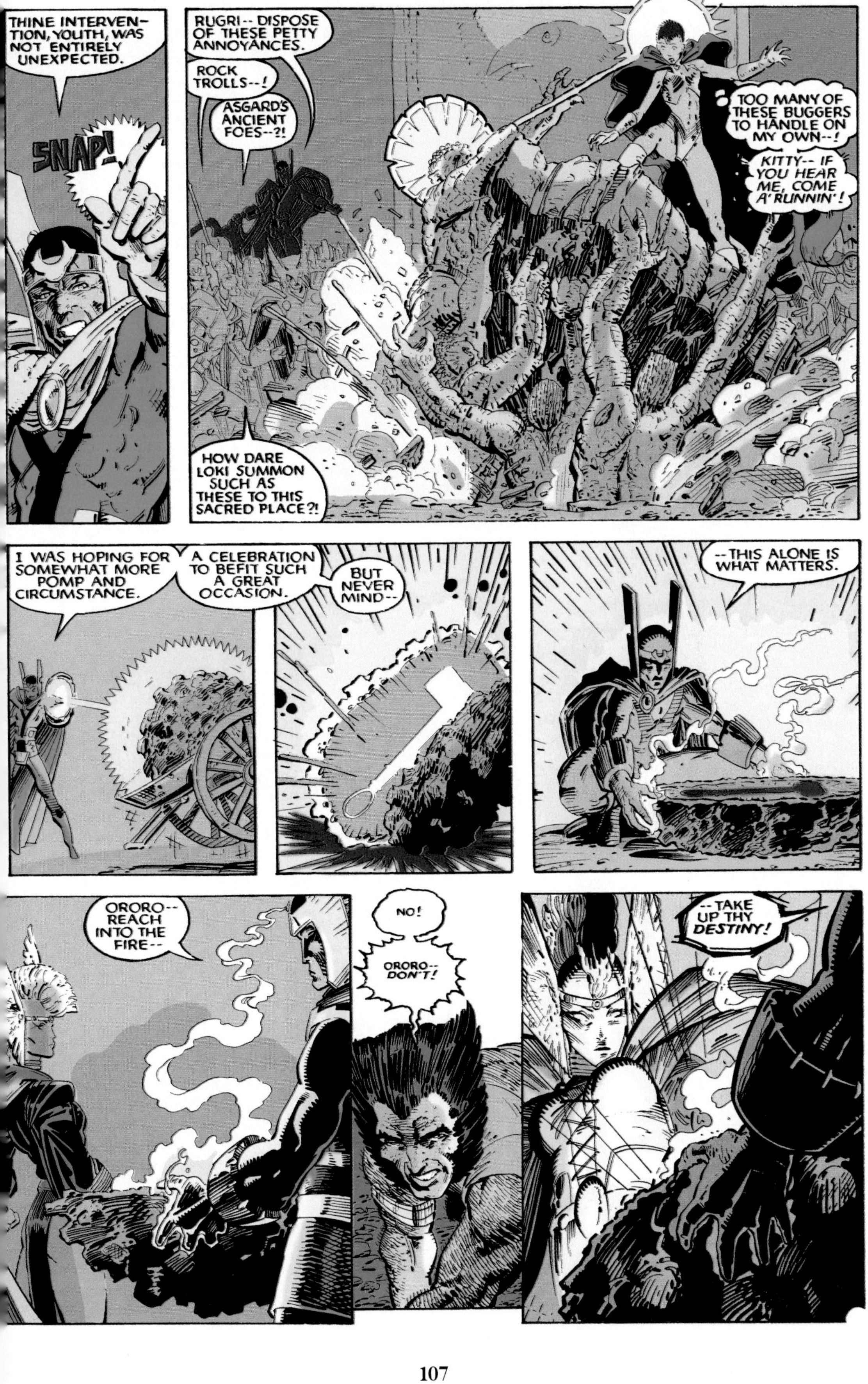
THINE INTERVENTION, YOUTH, WAS NOT ENTIRELY UNEXPECTED.
SNAP!
RUGRI-- DISPOSE OF THESE PETTY ANNOYANCES.
ROCK TROLLS--!
ASGARD'S ANCIENT FOES--?!
TOO MANY OF THESE BUGGERS TO HANDLE ON MY OWN--!
KITTY-- IF YOU HEAR ME, COME A'RUNNIN'!
HOW DARE LOKI SUMMON SUCH AS THESE TO THIS SACRED PLACE?!
I WAS HOPING FOR SOMEWHAT MORE POMP AND CIRCUMSTANCE.
A CELEBRATION TO BEFIT SUCH A GREAT OCCASION.
BUT NEVER MIND--
--THIS ALONE IS WHAT MATTERS.
ORORO-- REACH INTO THE FIRE--
NO!
ORORO-- DON'T!
--TAKE UP THY DESTINY!

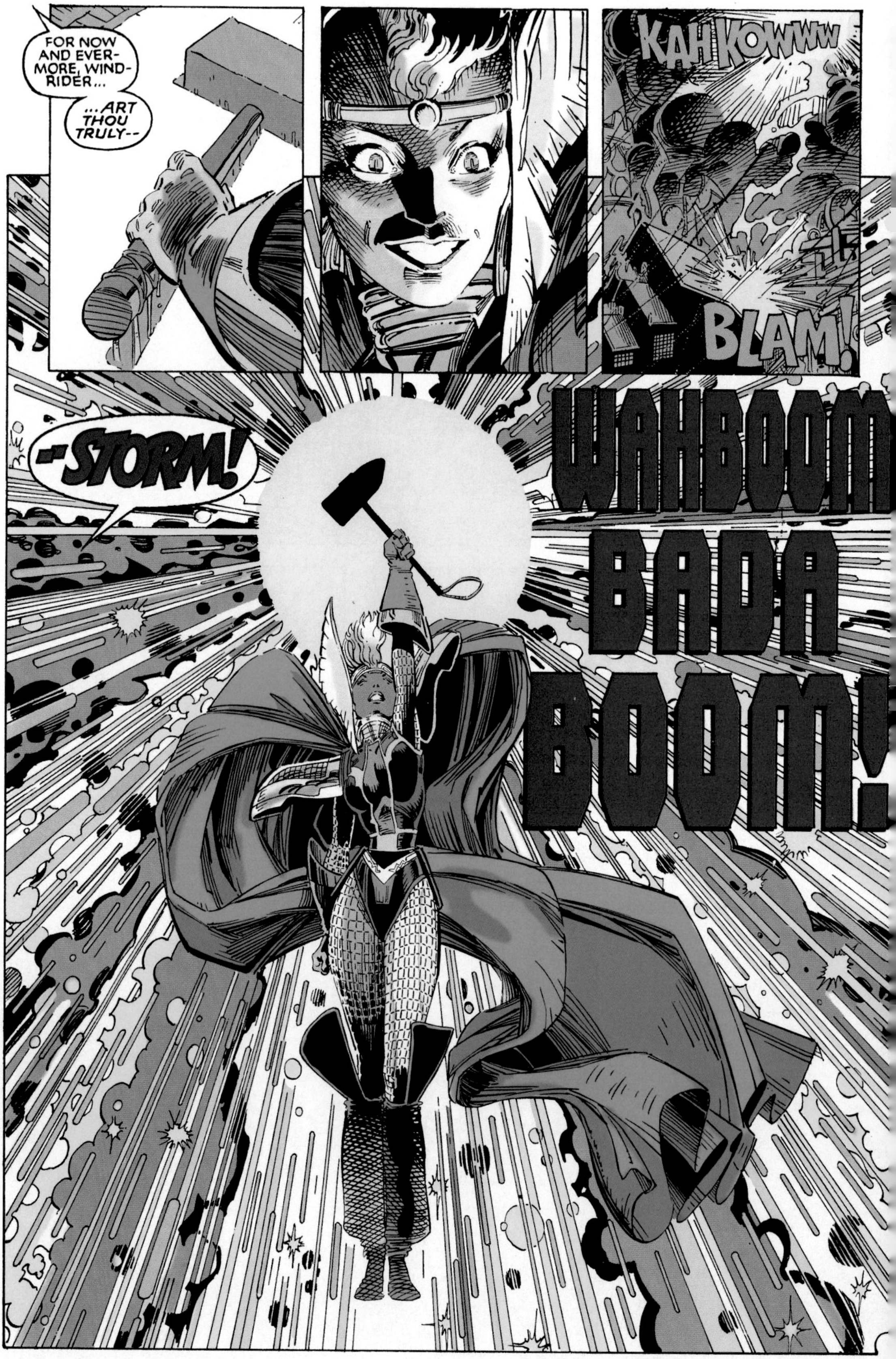
FOR NOW AND EVER-MORE, WIND-RIDER...
...ART THOU TRULY--
KAH KOWWW
BLAM!
--STORM!
WAHBOOM BADA BOOM!

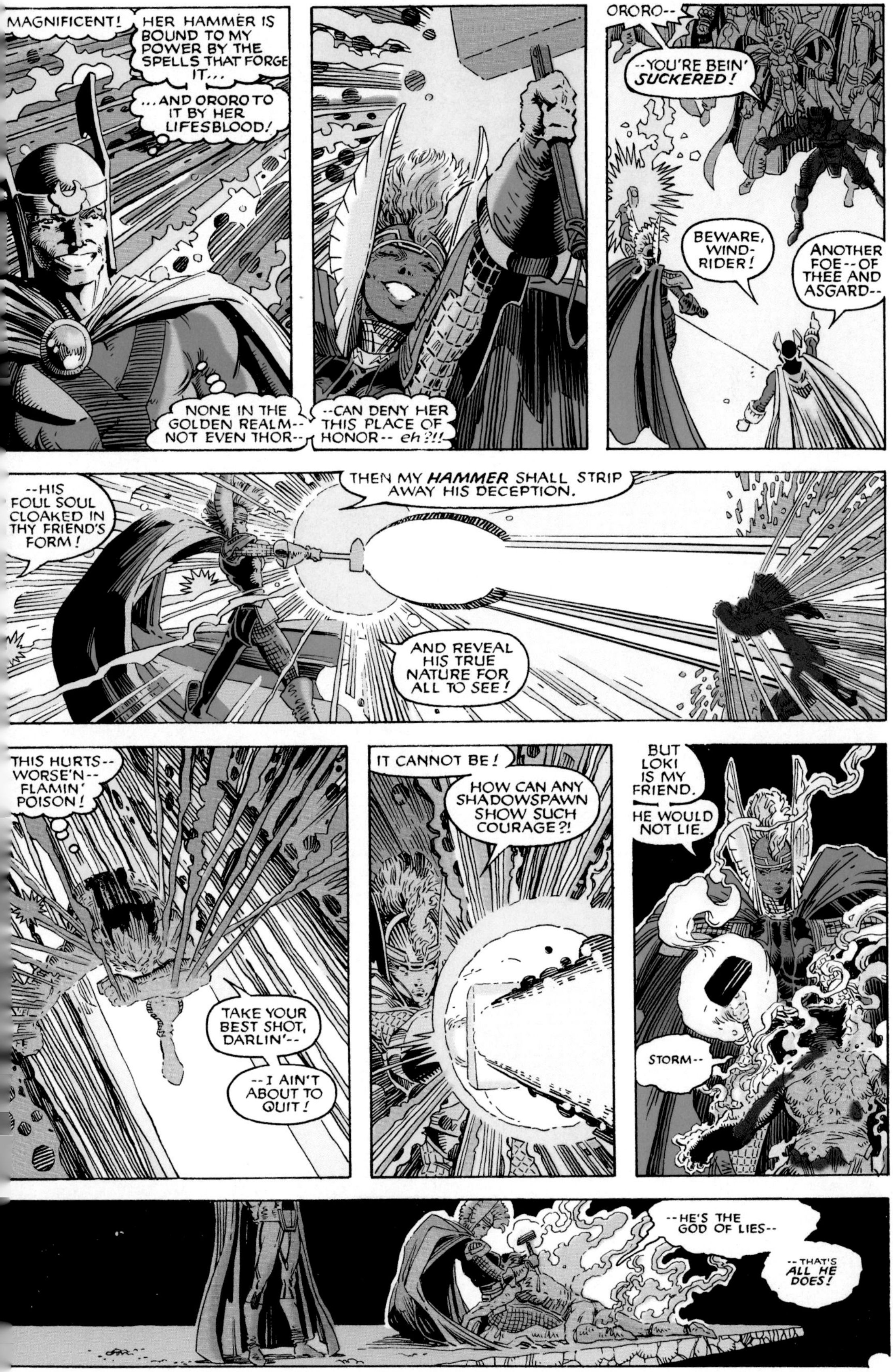

MAGNIFICENT!
HER HAMMER IS BOUND TO MY POWER BY THE SPELLS THAT FORGE IT...
...AND ORORO TO IT BY HER LIFESBLOOD!
NONE IN THE GOLDEN REALM--NOT EVEN THOR--
--CAN DENY HER THIS PLACE OF HONOR-- eh?!!
ORORO--
--YOU'RE BEIN' SUCKERED!
BEWARE, WIND-RIDER!
ANOTHER FOE--OF THEE AND ASGARD--
--HIS FOUL SOUL CLOAKED IN THY FRIEND'S FORM!
THEN MY HAMMER SHALL STRIP AWAY HIS DECEPTION.
AND REVEAL HIS TRUE NATURE FOR ALL TO SEE!
THIS HURTS--WORSE'N--FLAMIN' POISON!
TAKE YOUR BEST SHOT, DARLIN'--
--I AIN'T ABOUT TO QUIT!
IT CANNOT BE!
HOW CAN ANY SHADOWSPAWN SHOW SUCH COURAGE?!
BUT LOKI IS MY FRIEND.
HE WOULD NOT LIE.
STORM--
--HE'S THE GOD OF LIES--
--THAT'S ALL HE DOES!

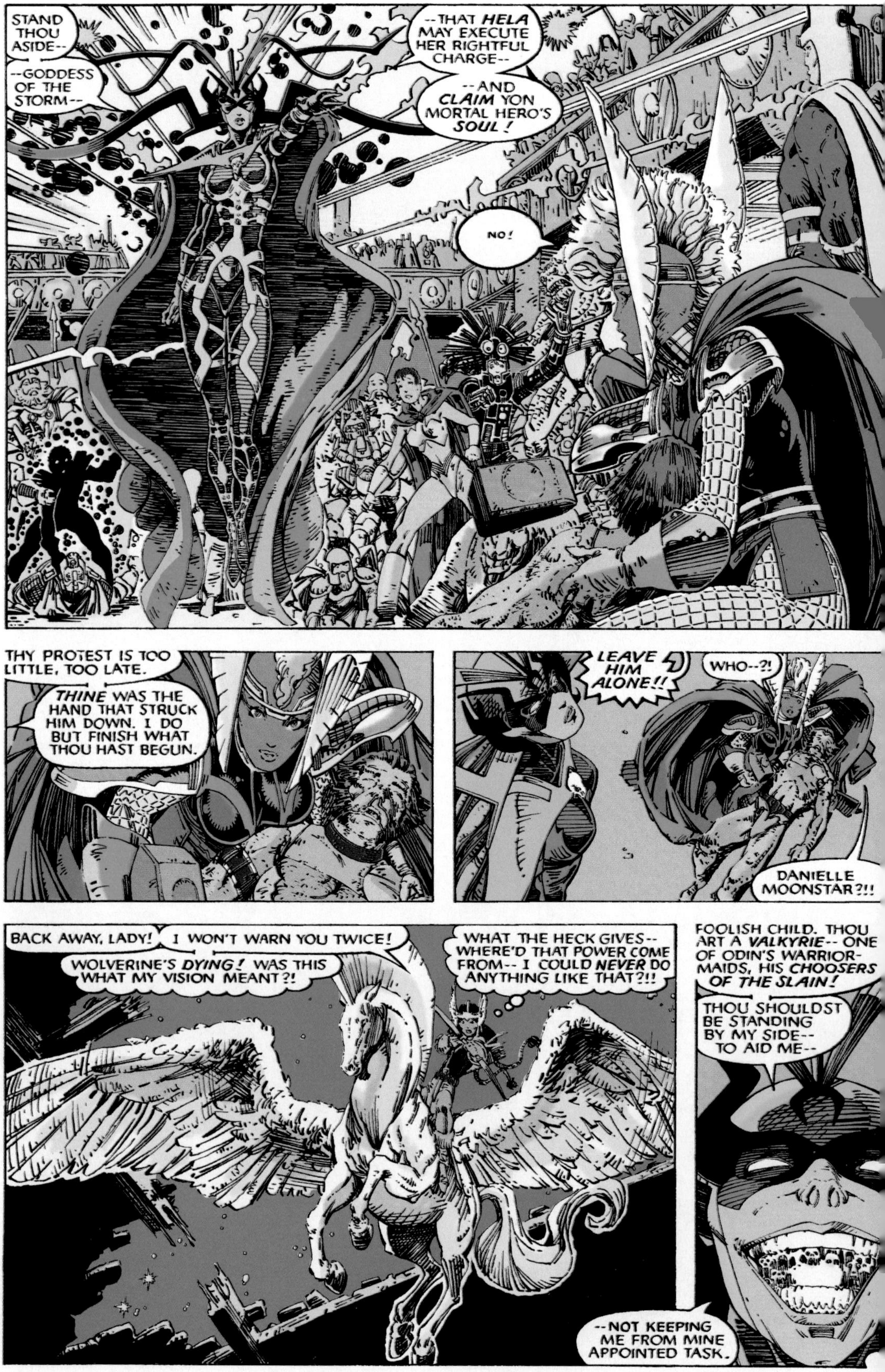
STAND THOU ASIDE--
--GODDESS OF THE STORM--
--THAT HELA MAY EXECUTE HER RIGHTFUL CHARGE--
--AND CLAIM YON MORTAL HERO'S SOUL!
NO!
THY PROTEST IS TOO LITTLE, TOO LATE.
THINE WAS THE HAND THAT STRUCK HIM DOWN. I DO BUT FINISH WHAT THOU HAST BEGUN.
LEAVE HIM ALONE!!
WHO--?!
DANIELLE MOONSTAR?!!
BACK AWAY, LADY!
I WON'T WARN YOU TWICE!
WOLVERINE'S DYING! WAS THIS WHAT MY VISION MEANT?!
WHAT THE HECK GIVES-- WHERE'D THAT POWER COME FROM-- I COULD NEVER DO ANYTHING LIKE THAT?!!
FOOLISH CHILD. THOU ART A VALKYRIE-- ONE OF ODIN'S WARRIOR-MAIDS, HIS CHOOSERS OF THE SLAIN!
THOU SHOULDST BE STANDING BY MY SIDE-- TO AID ME--
--NOT KEEPING ME FROM MINE APPOINTED TASK.

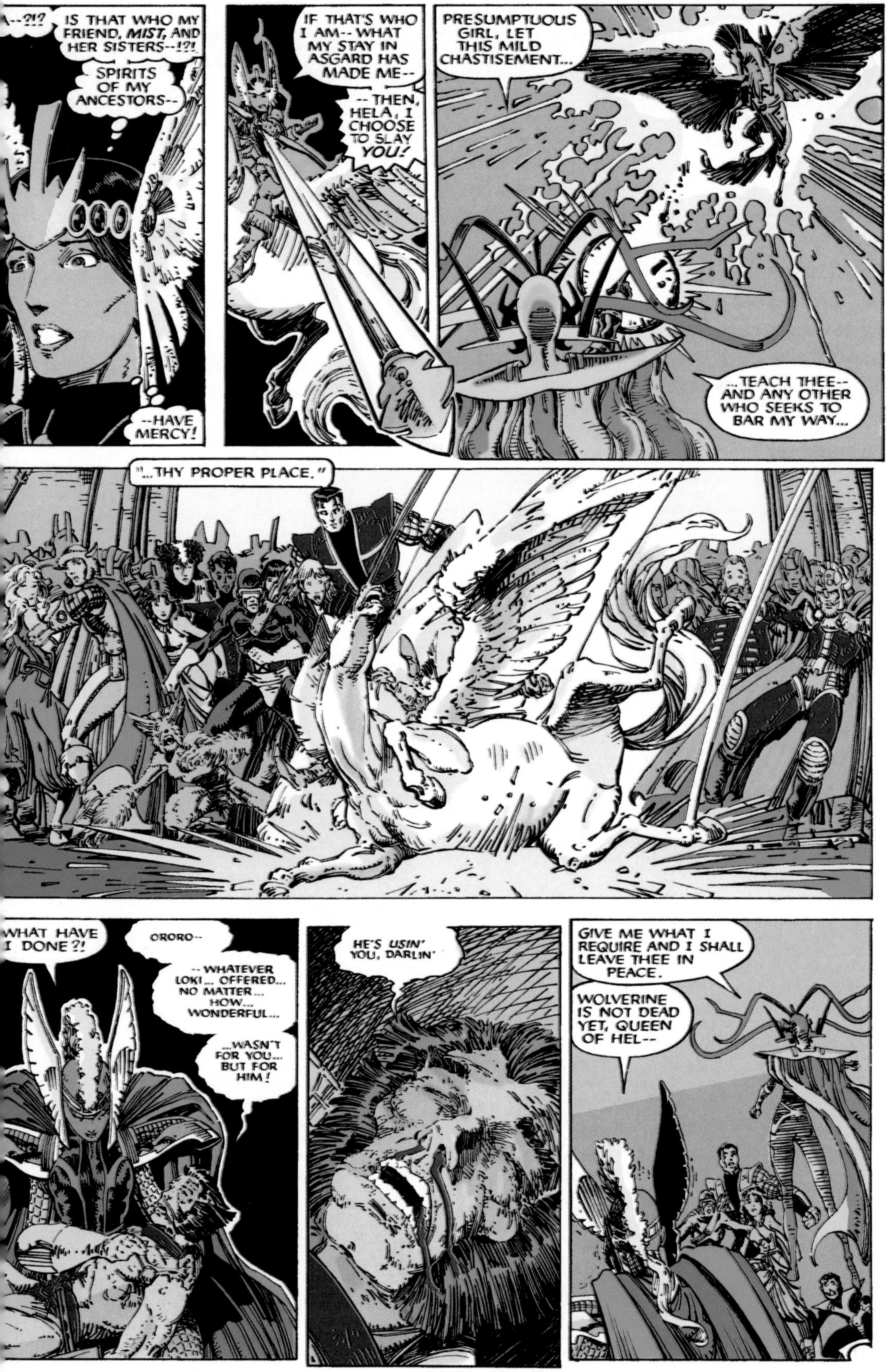
--?!?
IS THAT WHO MY FRIEND, MIST, AND HER SISTERS--!?!
SPIRITS OF MY ANCESTORS--
--HAVE MERCY!
IF THAT'S WHO I AM-- WHAT MY STAY IN ASGARD HAS MADE ME--
--THEN, HELA, I CHOOSE TO SLAY YOU!
PRESUMPTUOUS GIRL, LET THIS MILD CHASTISEMENT...
...TEACH THEE-- AND ANY OTHER WHO SEEKS TO BAR MY WAY...
"...THY PROPER PLACE."
WHAT HAVE I DONE?!
ORORO--
--WHATEVER LOKI... OFFERED... NO MATTER... HOW... WONDERFUL...
...WASN'T FOR YOU... BUT FOR HIM!
HE'S USIN' YOU, DARLIN'
GIVE ME WHAT I REQUIRE AND I SHALL LEAVE THEE IN PEACE.
WOLVERINE IS NOT DEAD YET, QUEEN OF HEL--

-- AND YOU SHALL *NEVER* HAVE HIM...

...WHILE *STORM* HAS BREATH AND POWER TO *DEFY* YOU!

ORORO'S EVERYTHING SHE EVER *WAS*-- AND *MORE*!

BUT EVEN THAT MAY NOT BE ENOUGH!

SO LET'S YOU AND I, YOUNG PHOENIX, LEND A HAND!

WITH YOUR *MINDBLASTS* AND MY *OPTIC BEAMS*!

MY CURSE UPON THEE, MORTALS! I'LL *FLAY* THE SKIN FROM THY BONES!

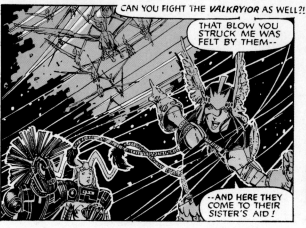

CAN YOU FIGHT THE *VALKYRIOR* AS WELL?!

THAT BLOW YOU STRUCK ME WAS *FELT* BY THEM--

--AND HERE THEY COME TO THEIR *SISTER'S* AID!

*SEE *THOR* #'s 361-362.*

THE *EINHERJAR* ARE AT MY GATES! I MUST HUSBAND MY STRENGH TO MATCH IT AGAINST THAT OF *THOR**--

--AND THEREFORE *CANNOT* DEAL WITH THESE UPSTARTS AS THEY *DESERVE*! BUT, I SWEAR, WE SHALL *MEET AGAIN*!

THE LAST *LAUGH* SHALL BE MINE!

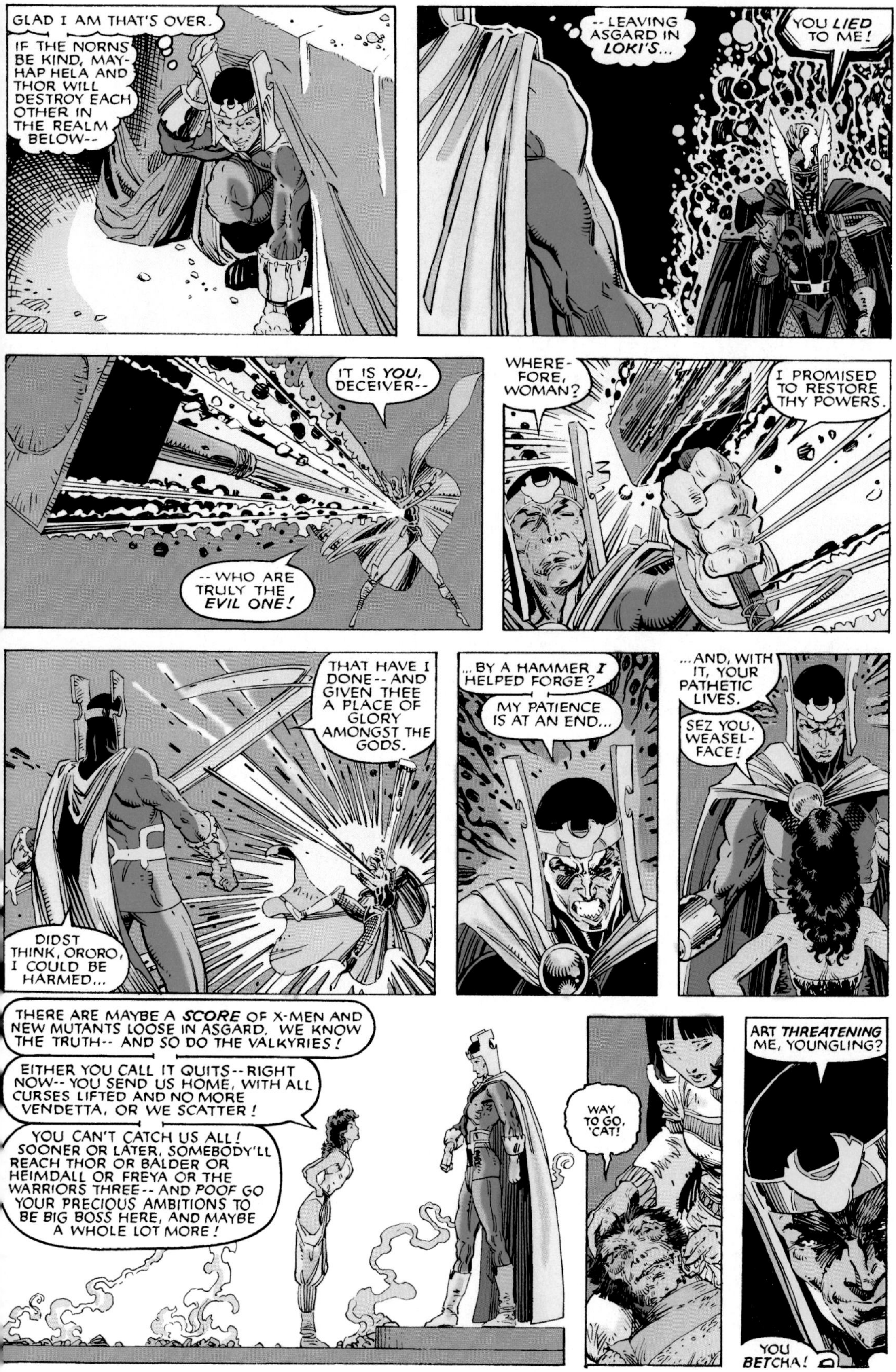
GLAD I AM THAT'S OVER.
IF THE NORNS BE KIND, MAY-HAP HELA AND THOR WILL DESTROY EACH OTHER IN THE REALM BELOW--
--LEAVING ASGARD IN LOKI'S...
YOU LIED TO ME!
IT IS YOU, DECEIVER--
--WHO ARE TRULY THE EVIL ONE!
WHEREFORE, WOMAN?
I PROMISED TO RESTORE THY POWERS.
THAT HAVE I DONE-- AND GIVEN THEE A PLACE OF GLORY AMONGST THE GODS.
DIDST THINK, ORORO, I COULD BE HARMED...
...BY A HAMMER I HELPED FORGE?
MY PATIENCE IS AT AN END...
...AND, WITH IT, YOUR PATHETIC LIVES.
SEZ YOU, WEASEL-FACE!
THERE ARE MAYBE A SCORE OF X-MEN AND NEW MUTANTS LOOSE IN ASGARD. WE KNOW THE TRUTH-- AND SO DO THE VALKYRIES!
EITHER YOU CALL IT QUITS-- RIGHT NOW-- YOU SEND US HOME, WITH ALL CURSES LIFTED AND NO MORE VENDETTA, OR WE SCATTER!
YOU CAN'T CATCH US ALL! SOONER OR LATER, SOMEBODY'LL REACH THOR OR BALDER OR HEIMDALL OR FREYA OR THE WARRIORS THREE-- AND POOF GO YOUR PRECIOUS AMBITIONS TO BE BIG BOSS HERE, AND MAYBE A WHOLE LOT MORE!
WAY TO GO, 'CAT!
ART THREATENING ME, YOUNGLING?
YOU BETCHA!

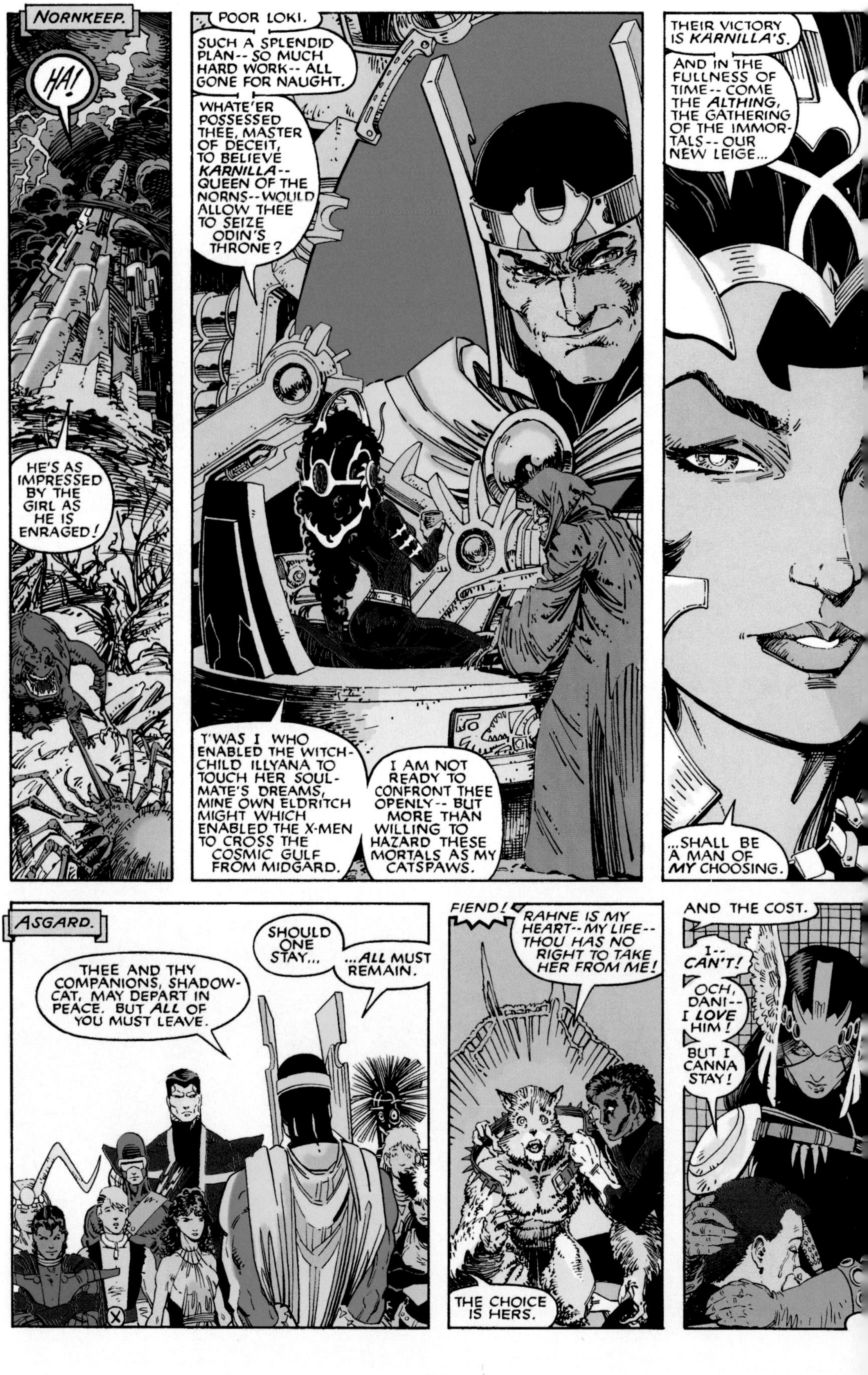
NORNKEEP.
HA!
HE'S AS IMPRESSED BY THE GIRL AS HE IS ENRAGED!
POOR LOKI.
SUCH A SPLENDID PLAN-- SO MUCH HARD WORK-- ALL GONE FOR NAUGHT.
WHATE'ER POSSESSED THEE, MASTER OF DECEIT, TO BELIEVE KARNILLA-- QUEEN OF THE NORNS--WOULD ALLOW THEE TO SEIZE ODIN'S THRONE?
T'WAS I WHO ENABLED THE WITCH-CHILD ILLYANA TO TOUCH HER SOUL-MATE'S DREAMS, MINE OWN ELDRITCH MIGHT WHICH ENABLED THE X-MEN TO CROSS THE COSMIC GULF FROM MIDGARD.
I AM NOT READY TO CONFRONT THEE OPENLY-- BUT MORE THAN WILLING TO HAZARD THESE MORTALS AS MY CATSPAWS.
THEIR VICTORY IS KARNILLA'S.
AND IN THE FULLNESS OF TIME-- COME THE ALTHING, THE GATHERING OF THE IMMORTALS-- OUR NEW LEIGE...
...SHALL BE A MAN OF MY CHOOSING.
ASGARD.
THEE AND THY COMPANIONS, SHADOWCAT, MAY DEPART IN PEACE. BUT ALL OF YOU MUST LEAVE.
SHOULD ONE STAY...
...ALL MUST REMAIN.
FIEND!
RAHNE IS MY HEART--MY LIFE-- THOU HAS NO RIGHT TO TAKE HER FROM ME!
THE CHOICE IS HERS.
AND THE COST.
I-- CAN'T!
OCH, DANI-- I LOVE HIM!
BUT I CANNA STAY!

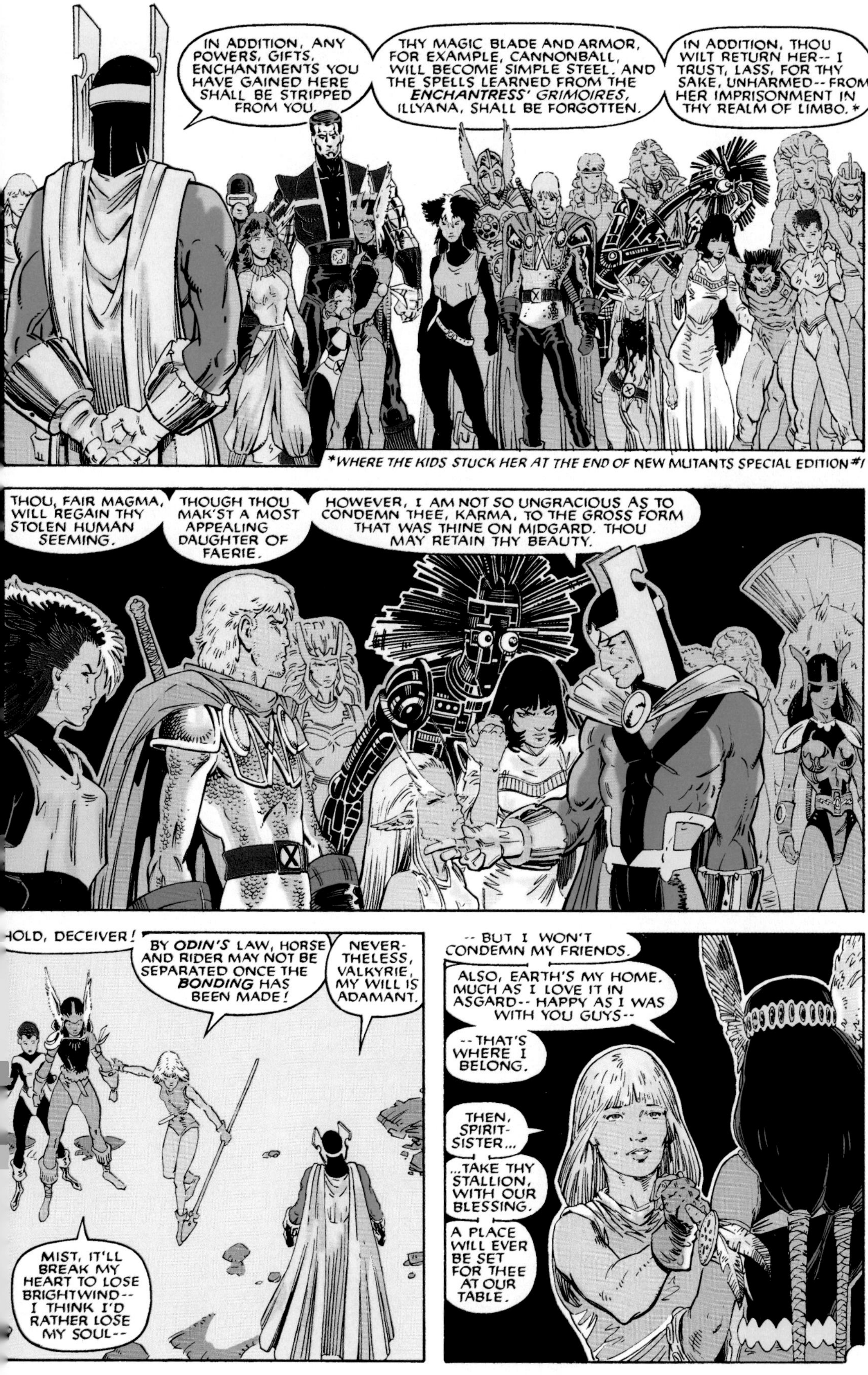
IN ADDITION, ANY POWERS, GIFTS, ENCHANTMENTS YOU HAVE GAINED HERE SHALL BE STRIPPED FROM YOU.
THY MAGIC BLADE AND ARMOR, FOR EXAMPLE, CANNONBALL, WILL BECOME SIMPLE STEEL. AND THE SPELLS LEARNED FROM THE ENCHANTRESS' GRIMOIRES, ILLYANA, SHALL BE FORGOTTEN.
IN ADDITION, THOU WILT RETURN HER-- I TRUST, LASS, FOR THY SAKE, UNHARMED-- FROM HER IMPRISONMENT IN THY REALM OF LIMBO.*
*WHERE THE KIDS STUCK HER AT THE END OF NEW MUTANTS SPECIAL EDITION #1
THOU, FAIR MAGMA, WILL REGAIN THY STOLEN HUMAN SEEMING.
THOUGH THOU MAK'ST A MOST APPEALING DAUGHTER OF FAERIE.
HOWEVER, I AM NOT SO UNGRACIOUS AS TO CONDEMN THEE, KARMA, TO THE GROSS FORM THAT WAS THINE ON MIDGARD. THOU MAY RETAIN THY BEAUTY.
HOLD, DECEIVER!
BY ODIN'S LAW, HORSE AND RIDER MAY NOT BE SEPARATED ONCE THE BONDING HAS BEEN MADE!
NEVERTHELESS, VALKYRIE, MY WILL IS ADAMANT.
MIST, IT'LL BREAK MY HEART TO LOSE BRIGHTWIND-- I THINK I'D RATHER LOSE MY SOUL--
-- BUT I WON'T CONDEMN MY FRIENDS.
ALSO, EARTH'S MY HOME. MUCH AS I LOVE IT IN ASGARD-- HAPPY AS I WAS WITH YOU GUYS--
-- THAT'S WHERE I BELONG.
THEN, SPIRIT-SISTER...
...TAKE THY STALLION, WITH OUR BLESSING.
A PLACE WILL EVER BE SET FOR THEE AT OUR TABLE.

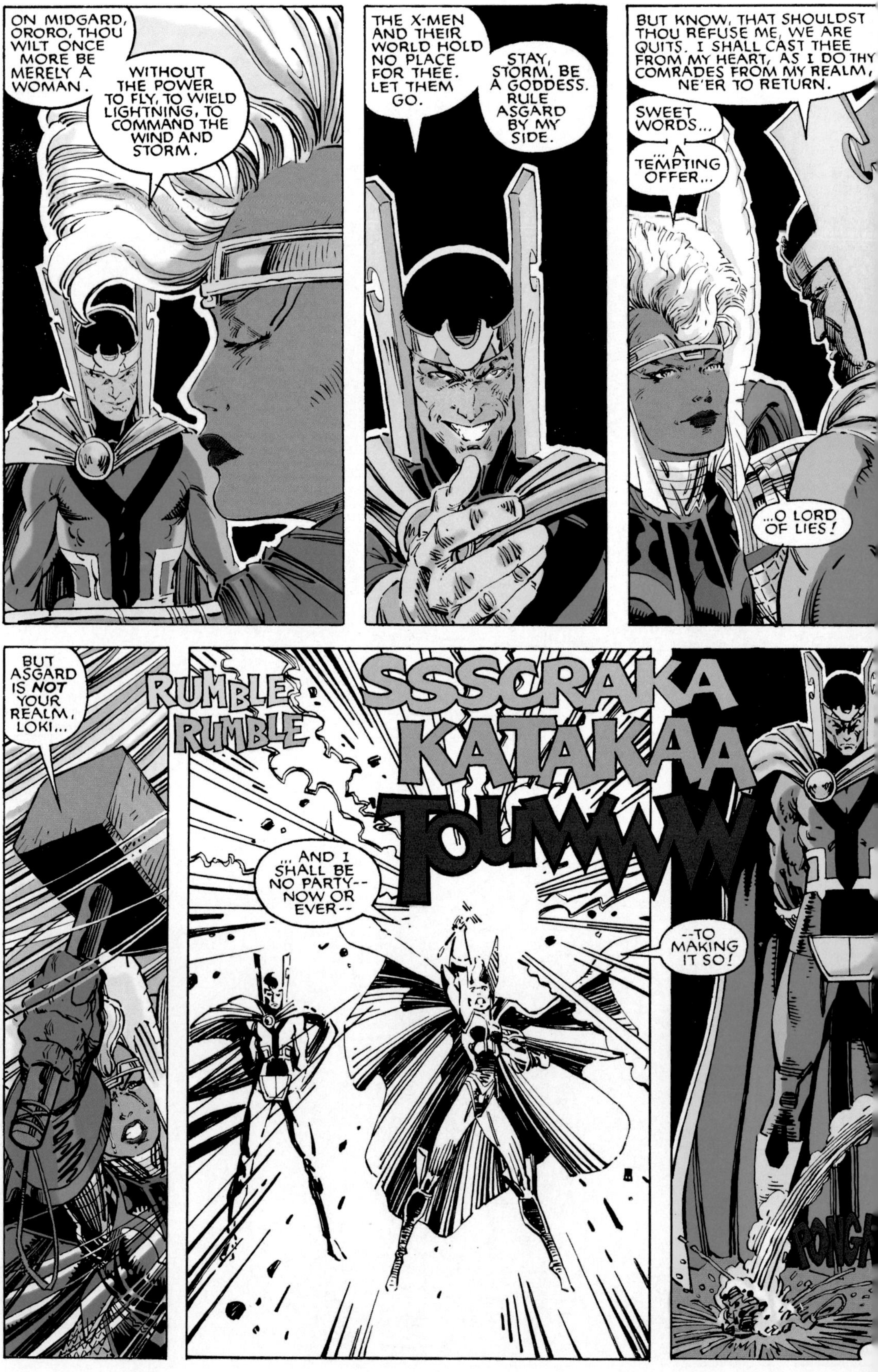
ON MIDGARD, ORORO, THOU WILT ONCE MORE BE MERELY A WOMAN.
WITHOUT THE POWER TO FLY, TO WIELD LIGHTNING, TO COMMAND THE WIND AND STORM.
THE X-MEN AND THEIR WORLD HOLD NO PLACE FOR THEE. LET THEM GO.
STAY, STORM. BE A GODDESS. RULE ASGARD BY MY SIDE.
BUT KNOW, THAT SHOULDST THOU REFUSE ME, WE ARE QUITS. I SHALL CAST THEE FROM MY HEART, AS I DO THY COMRADES FROM MY REALM, NE'ER TO RETURN.
SWEET WORDS...
...A TEMPTING OFFER...
...O LORD OF LIES!
BUT ASGARD IS NOT YOUR REALM, LOKI...
RUMBLE RUMBLE
SSSCRAKA KATAKAA TOUMMMM
...AND I SHALL BE NO PARTY-- NOW OR EVER--
--TO MAKING IT SO!

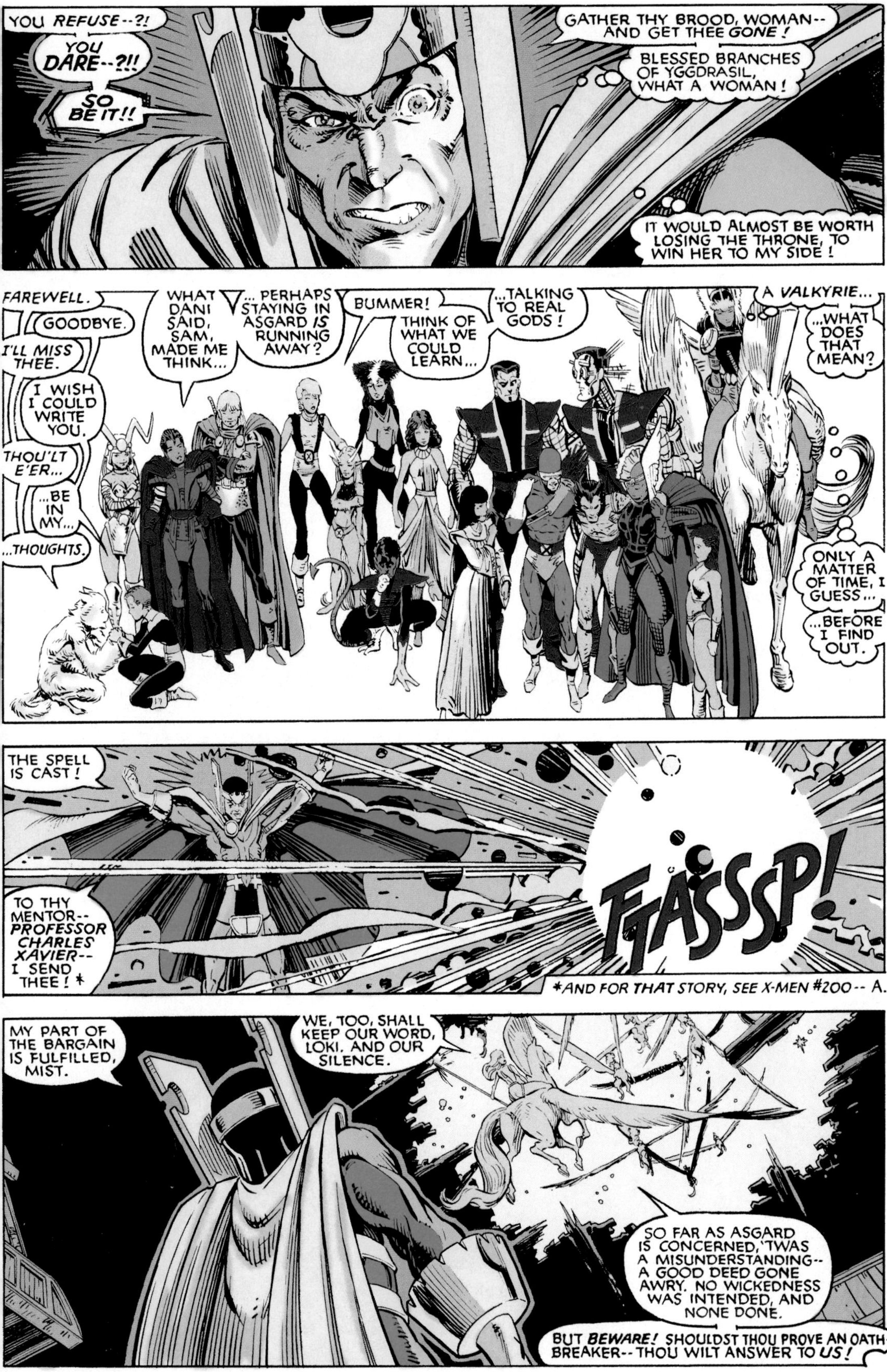
YOU REFUSE--?!
YOU DARE--?!!
SO BE IT!!
GATHER THY BROOD, WOMAN-- AND GET THEE GONE!
BLESSED BRANCHES OF YGGDRASIL, WHAT A WOMAN!
IT WOULD ALMOST BE WORTH LOSING THE THRONE, TO WIN HER TO MY SIDE!
FAREWELL.
GOODBYE.
I'LL MISS THEE.
I WISH I COULD WRITE YOU.
THOU'LT E'ER...
...BE IN MY...
...THOUGHTS.
WHAT DANI SAID, SAM, MADE ME THINK...
...PERHAPS STAYING IN ASGARD IS RUNNING AWAY?
BUMMER!
THINK OF WHAT WE COULD LEARN...
...TALKING TO REAL GODS!
A VALKYRIE...
...WHAT DOES THAT MEAN?
ONLY A MATTER OF TIME, I GUESS...
...BEFORE I FIND OUT.
THE SPELL IS CAST!
TO THY MENTOR-- PROFESSOR CHARLES XAVIER-- I SEND THEE! *
FTASSSP!
*AND FOR THAT STORY, SEE X-MEN #200-- A.
MY PART OF THE BARGAIN IS FULFILLED, MIST.
WE, TOO, SHALL KEEP OUR WORD, LOKI. AND OUR SILENCE.
SO FAR AS ASGARD IS CONCERNED, 'TWAS A MISUNDERSTANDING-- A GOOD DEED GONE AWRY. NO WICKEDNESS WAS INTENDED, AND NONE DONE.
BUT BEWARE! SHOULDST THOU PROVE AN OATH-BREAKER-- THOU WILT ANSWER TO US!

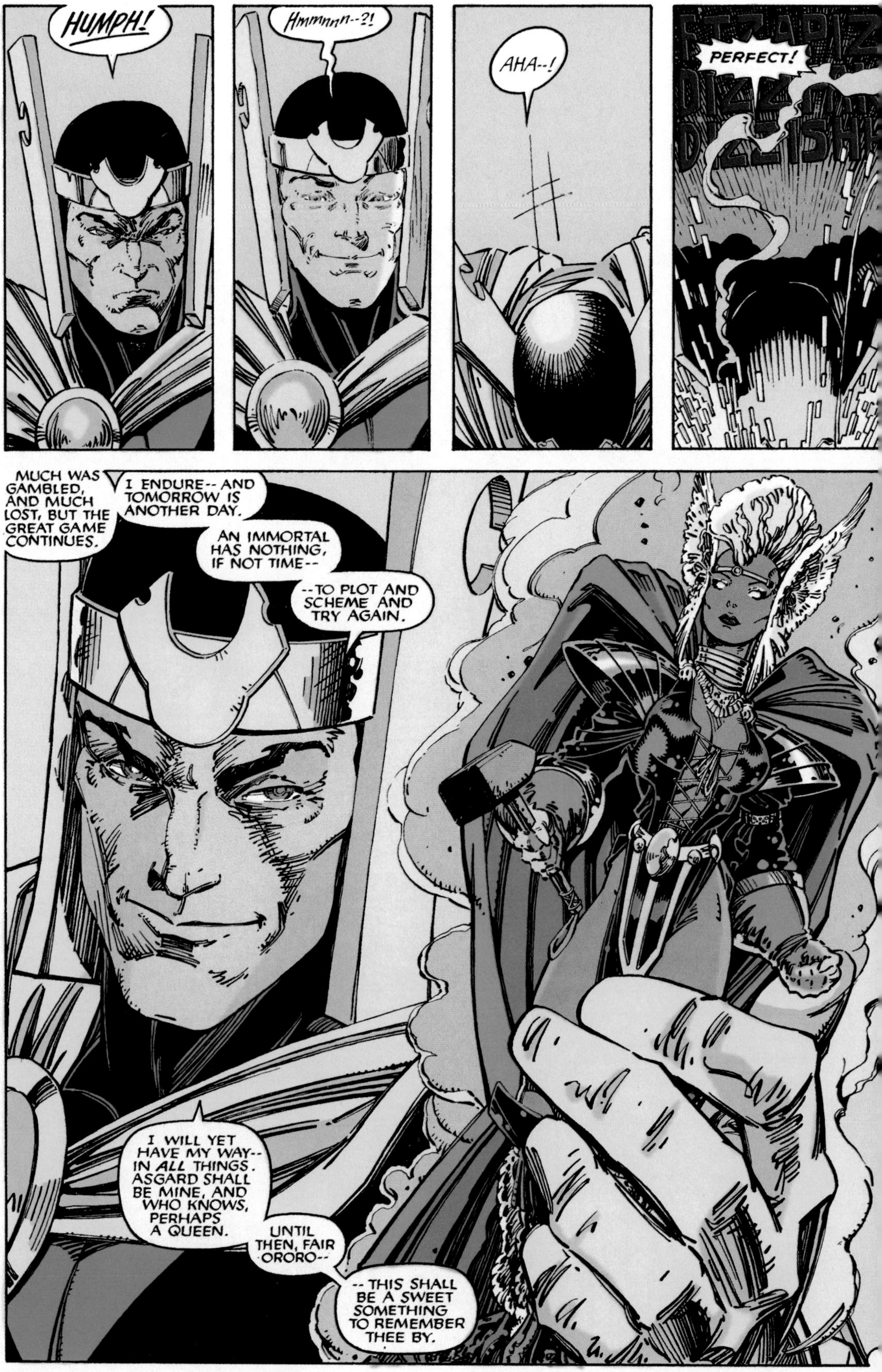

HUMPH!
Hmmnnn--?!
AHA--!
PERFECT!
MUCH WAS GAMBLED, AND MUCH LOST, BUT THE GREAT GAME CONTINUES.
I ENDURE-- AND TOMORROW IS ANOTHER DAY.
AN IMMORTAL HAS NOTHING, IF NOT TIME--
--TO PLOT AND SCHEME AND TRY AGAIN.
I WILL YET HAVE MY WAY-- IN ALL THINGS. ASGARD SHALL BE MINE, AND WHO KNOWS, PERHAPS A QUEEN.
UNTIL THEN, FAIR ORORO--
-- THIS SHALL BE A SWEET SOMETHING TO REMEMBER THEE BY.

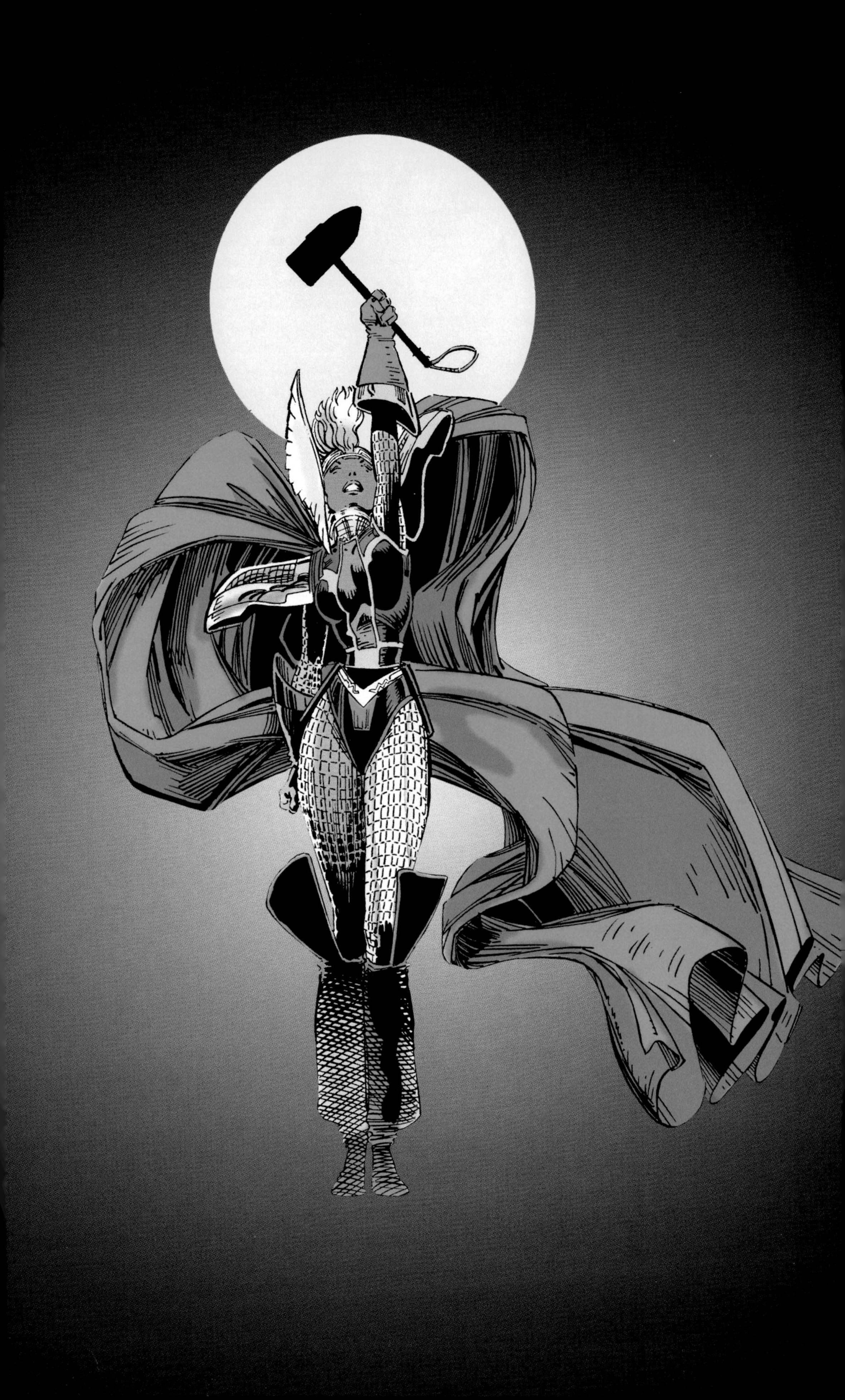

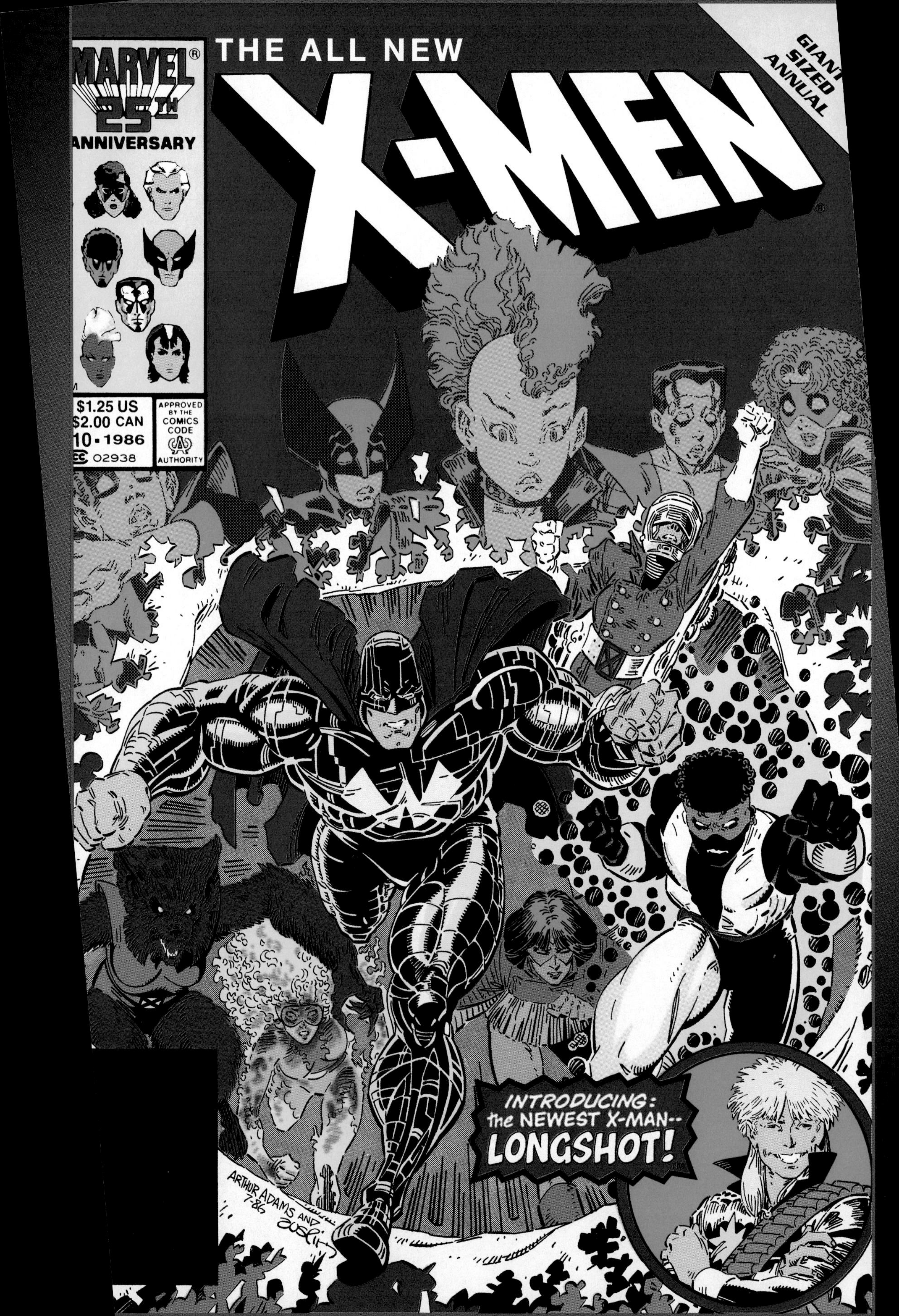
MARVEL®
25TH
ANNIVERSARY
THE ALL NEW
X-MEN®
GIANT SIZED ANNUAL
$1.25 US
$2.00 CAN
10 • 1986
02938
APPROVED BY THE COMICS CODE AUTHORITY
INTRODUCING: the NEWEST X-MAN-- LONGSHOT!
ARTHUR ADAMS AND
7-86

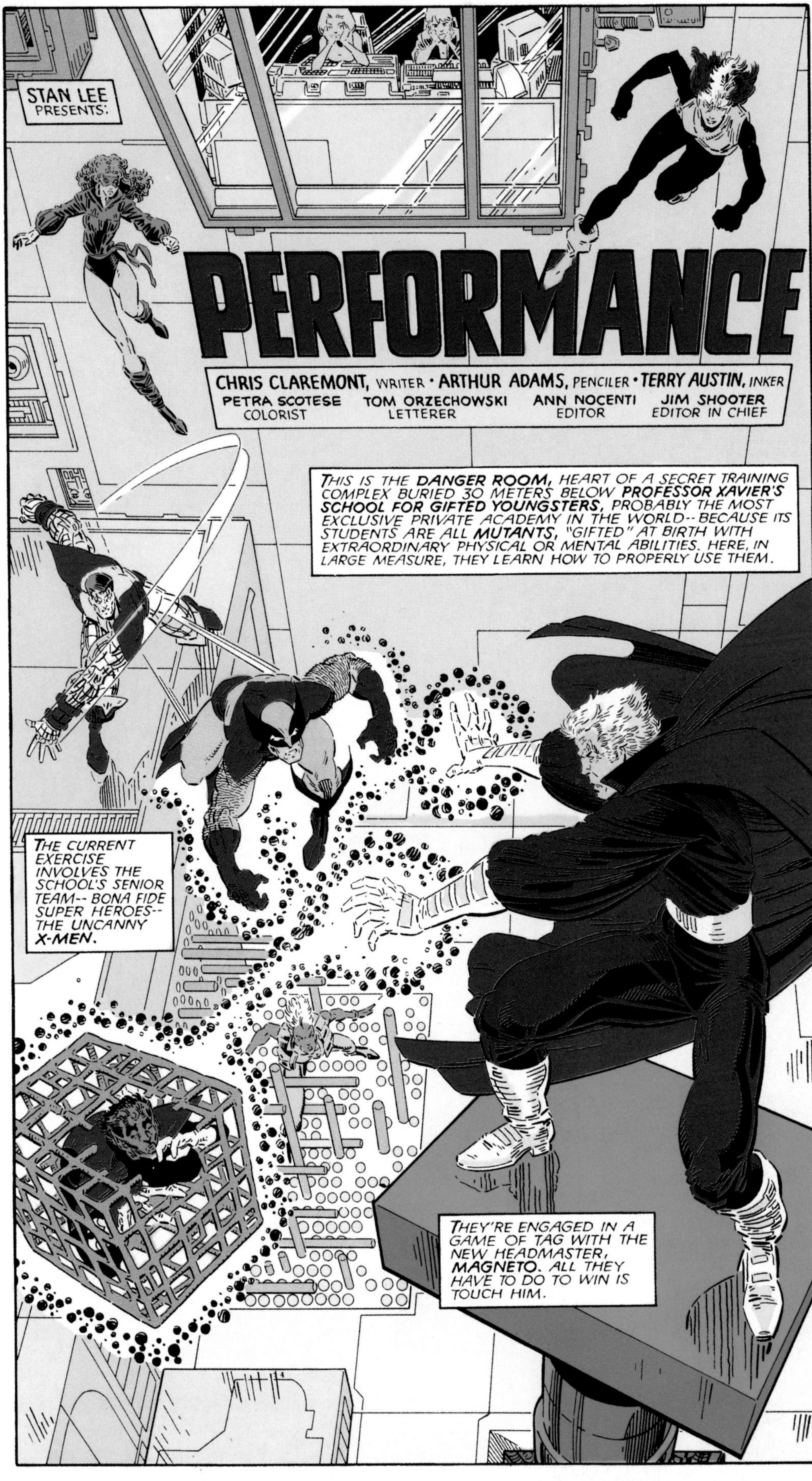

STAN LEE PRESENTS:
PERFORMANCE
CHRIS CLAREMONT, WRITER • ARTHUR ADAMS, PENCILER • TERRY AUSTIN, INKER
PETRA SCOTESE COLORIST TOM ORZECHOWSKI LETTERER ANN NOCENTI EDITOR JIM SHOOTER EDITOR IN CHIEF
THIS IS THE DANGER ROOM, HEART OF A SECRET TRAINING COMPLEX BURIED 30 METERS BELOW PROFESSOR XAVIER'S SCHOOL FOR GIFTED YOUNGSTERS, PROBABLY THE MOST EXCLUSIVE PRIVATE ACADEMY IN THE WORLD-- BECAUSE ITS STUDENTS ARE ALL MUTANTS, "GIFTED" AT BIRTH WITH EXTRAORDINARY PHYSICAL OR MENTAL ABILITIES. HERE, IN LARGE MEASURE, THEY LEARN HOW TO PROPERLY USE THEM.
THE CURRENT EXERCISE INVOLVES THE SCHOOL'S SENIOR TEAM-- BONA FIDE SUPER HEROES-- THE UNCANNY X-MEN.
THEY'RE ENGAGED IN A GAME OF TAG WITH THE NEW HEADMASTER, MAGNETO. ALL THEY HAVE TO DO TO WIN IS TOUCH HIM.

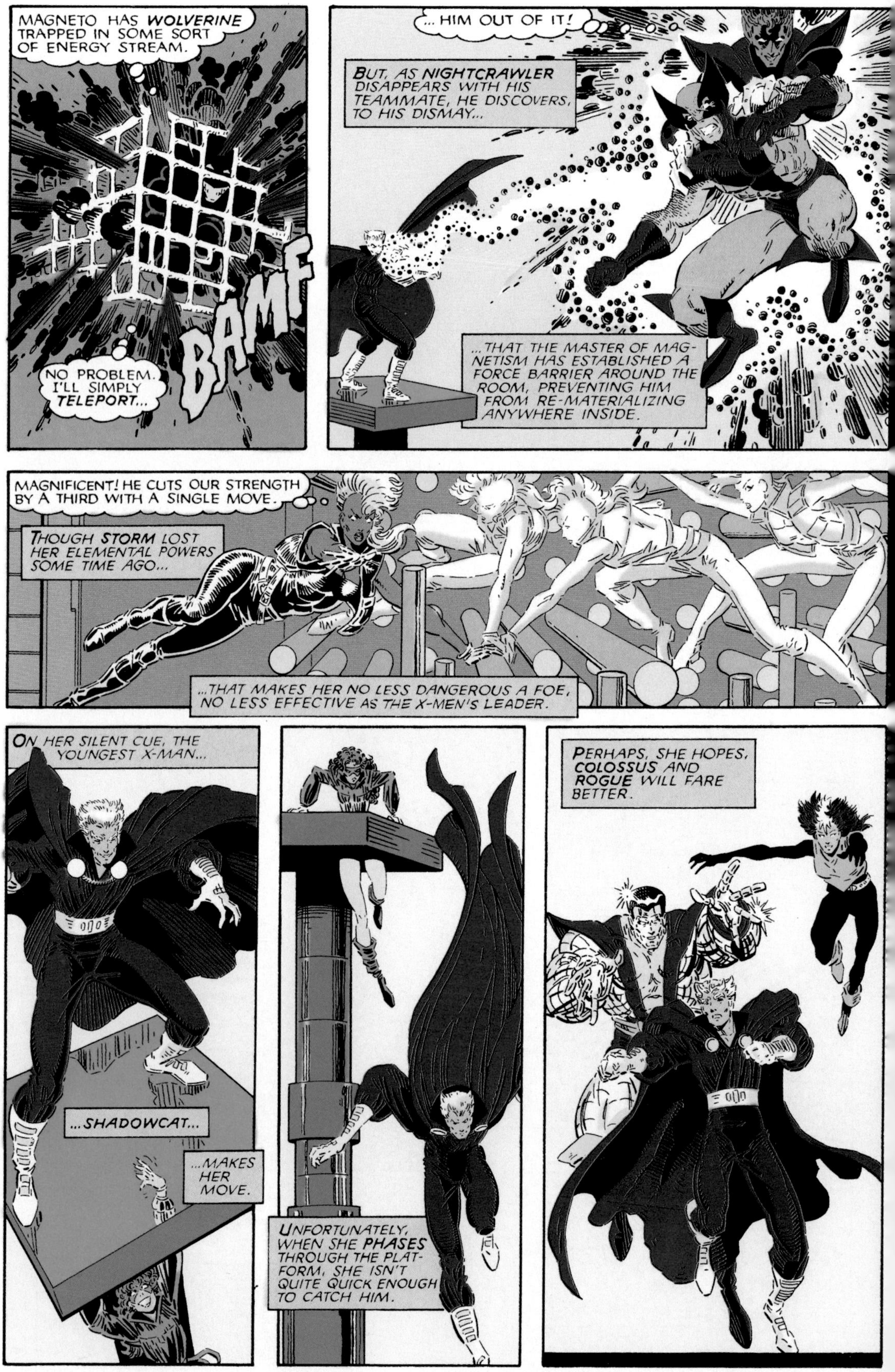

MAGNETO HAS WOLVERINE TRAPPED IN SOME SORT OF ENERGY STREAM.
NO PROBLEM. I'LL SIMPLY TELEPORT...
BAMF
... HIM OUT OF IT!
BUT, AS NIGHTCRAWLER DISAPPEARS WITH HIS TEAMMATE, HE DISCOVERS, TO HIS DISMAY...
...THAT THE MASTER OF MAGNETISM HAS ESTABLISHED A FORCE BARRIER AROUND THE ROOM, PREVENTING HIM FROM RE-MATERIALIZING ANYWHERE INSIDE.
MAGNIFICENT! HE CUTS OUR STRENGTH BY A THIRD WITH A SINGLE MOVE.
THOUGH STORM LOST HER ELEMENTAL POWERS SOME TIME AGO...
...THAT MAKES HER NO LESS DANGEROUS A FOE, NO LESS EFFECTIVE AS THE X-MEN'S LEADER.
ON HER SILENT CUE, THE YOUNGEST X-MAN...
...SHADOWCAT...
...MAKES HER MOVE.
UNFORTUNATELY, WHEN SHE PHASES THROUGH THE PLATFORM, SHE ISN'T QUITE QUICK ENOUGH TO CATCH HIM.
PERHAPS, SHE HOPES, COLOSSUS AND ROGUE WILL FARE BETTER.

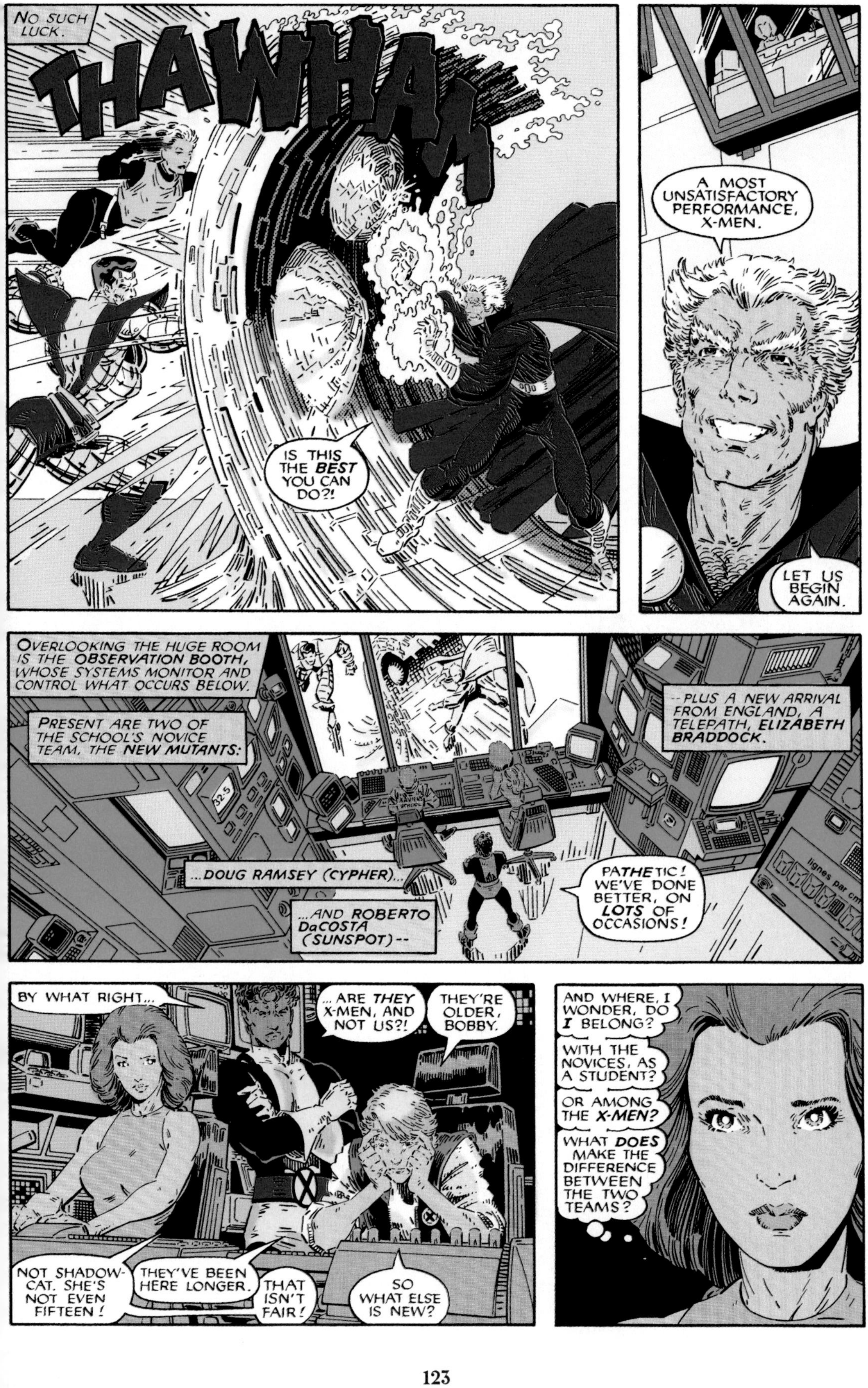
NO SUCH LUCK.
THAWHAM
IS THIS THE BEST YOU CAN DO?!
A MOST UNSATISFACTORY PERFORMANCE, X-MEN.
LET US BEGIN AGAIN.
OVERLOOKING THE HUGE ROOM IS THE OBSERVATION BOOTH, WHOSE SYSTEMS MONITOR AND CONTROL WHAT OCCURS BELOW.
PRESENT ARE TWO OF THE SCHOOL'S NOVICE TEAM, THE NEW MUTANTS:
...DOUG RAMSEY (CYPHER)...
...AND ROBERTO DaCOSTA (SUNSPOT)--
--PLUS A NEW ARRIVAL FROM ENGLAND, A TELEPATH, ELIZABETH BRADDOCK.
PATHETIC! WE'VE DONE BETTER, ON LOTS OF OCCASIONS!
BY WHAT RIGHT...
...ARE THEY X-MEN, AND NOT US?!
THEY'RE OLDER, BOBBY.
NOT SHADOWCAT. SHE'S NOT EVEN FIFTEEN!
THEY'VE BEEN HERE LONGER.
THAT ISN'T FAIR!
SO WHAT ELSE IS NEW?
AND WHERE, I WONDER, DO I BELONG?
WITH THE NOVICES, AS A STUDENT?
OR AMONG THE X-MEN?
WHAT DOES MAKE THE DIFFERENCE BETWEEN THE TWO TEAMS?

THE CROWD *ROARS*-- CHEERING EVERY SHOT, EVERY WORD, EVERY THOUGHT.

THIS IS ANOTHER WORLD, WHERE *HUMANITY* IS A DIRTY WORD, RESERVED FOR THE DIRTIEST OF PEOPLE. TO WALK UPRIGHT, TO HAVE A SPINE, IS TO BE A *SLAVE*.

TO RULE, ONE MUST BE *SPINELESS*.

BEFORE SHE CAME TO *XAVIER'S* SCHOOL, BETSY WAS THE PET OF THE LORD OF THE WILDWAY, THE LIFE-BRINGER *MOJO*. SHE WAS ALSO *BLIND*. MOJO GAVE HER THE GIFT OF SIGHT-- BUT, LIKE ALL HIS PRESENTS, IT POSSESSED A WICKED LITTLE WRINKLE.

BETSY'S EYES ARE *CAMERAS*, TRANSMITTING EVERYTHING SHE SEES, HEARS, THINKS, FEELS BACK TO MOJO. HE'S MARKETED HER MASTERFULLY, AND MADE HER A *STAR*.

IN RETURN, UN-WITTINGLY, SHE'S MAKING HIM...

RICH!

SPIRAL-- *MAJOR DOMO*-- LISTEN TO THOSE COCKLE-PATED CRETINS, THEY *LOVE* MY EPIC! MY PET *PSYLOCKE* IS A *SENSATION*, THEY CAN'T GET ENOUGH OF HER!

NO AC-COUNTING FOR TASTE.

VERY POPULAR

ADVISE MERCHAN-DISING

ATINGS HIGHER

ACTUALLY, DARLING, REVENUES TO DATE ON THIS LATEST PRODUCTION...

... ARE ONLY JUST BEGINNING TO BALANCE THE COST OF THE *WILDWAYS* DEBACLE.*

*FOR *THA* STORY, SEE THE CURRE NEW MUTA ANNUAL--An

124

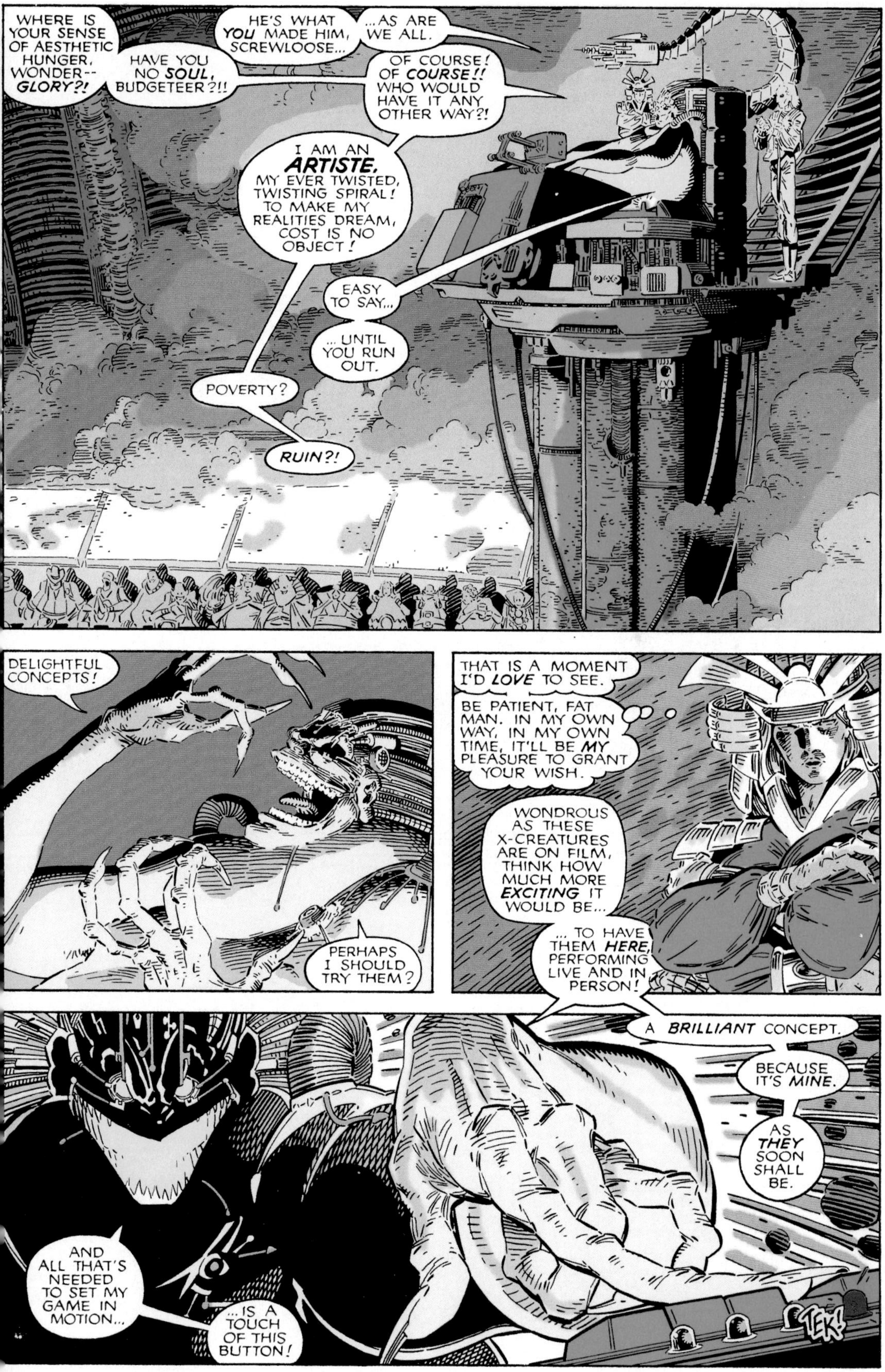
WHERE IS YOUR SENSE OF AESTHETIC HUNGER, WONDER-- GLORY?!
HAVE YOU NO SOUL, BUDGETEER?!!
HE'S WHAT YOU MADE HIM, SCREWLOOSE...
...AS ARE WE ALL.
OF COURSE! OF COURSE!! WHO WOULD HAVE IT ANY OTHER WAY?!
I AM AN ARTISTE. MY EVER TWISTED, TWISTING SPIRAL! TO MAKE MY REALITIES DREAM, COST IS NO OBJECT!
EASY TO SAY...
... UNTIL YOU RUN OUT.
POVERTY?
RUIN?!
DELIGHTFUL CONCEPTS!
PERHAPS I SHOULD TRY THEM?
THAT IS A MOMENT I'D LOVE TO SEE.
BE PATIENT, FAT MAN. IN MY OWN WAY, IN MY OWN TIME, IT'LL BE MY PLEASURE TO GRANT YOUR WISH.
WONDROUS AS THESE X-CREATURES ARE ON FILM, THINK HOW MUCH MORE EXCITING IT WOULD BE...
... TO HAVE THEM HERE, PERFORMING LIVE AND IN PERSON!
A BRILLIANT CONCEPT.
BECAUSE IT'S MINE.
AS THEY SOON SHALL BE.
AND ALL THAT'S NEEDED TO SET MY GAME IN MOTION...
...IS A TOUCH OF THIS BUTTON!
TEK!

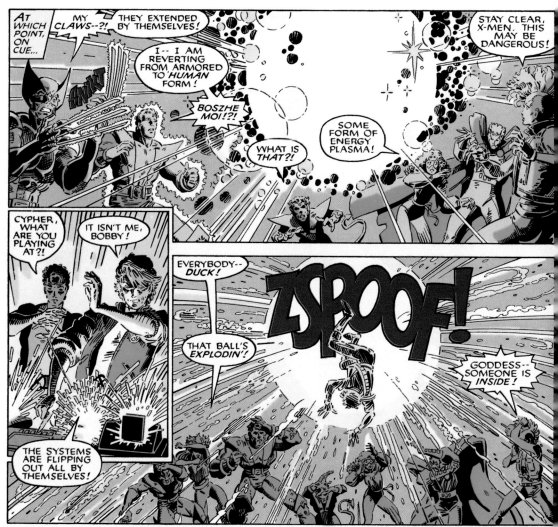

AT WHICH POINT, ON CUE...

MY CLAWS--?! THEY EXTENDED BY THEMSELVES!

SNIKT

I-- I AM REVERTING FROM ARMORED TO 'HUMAN' FORM!

BOSZHE MOI!?!

WHAT IS THAT?!

STAY CLEAR, X-MEN. THIS MAY BE DANGEROUS!

SOME FORM OF ENERGY PLASMA!

CYPHER, WHAT ARE YOU PLAYING AT?!

IT ISN'T ME, BOBBY!

THE SYSTEMS ARE FLIPPING OUT ALL BY THEMSELVES!

EVERYBODY-- DUCK!

THAT BALL'S EXPLODIN'!

ZSPOOF!

GODDESS-- SOMEONE IS INSIDE!

THE SPHERE MUST HAVE BEEN A SORT OF MATTER TRANSFER WARP.

Poit

STORM, IT'S A *GUY!*

WHUMMF!

HE BREATHIN', ELF?

WEIRD SCENT ON THIS GOOP. MAKES ME EDGY.

WHAT A *MESS!*

I HAVE THE *MEDICAL KIT!*

DANKË, FRAULEIN BRADDOCK.

GOOD NEWS. I'VE FOUND HIS PULSE.

BOTH OF THEM

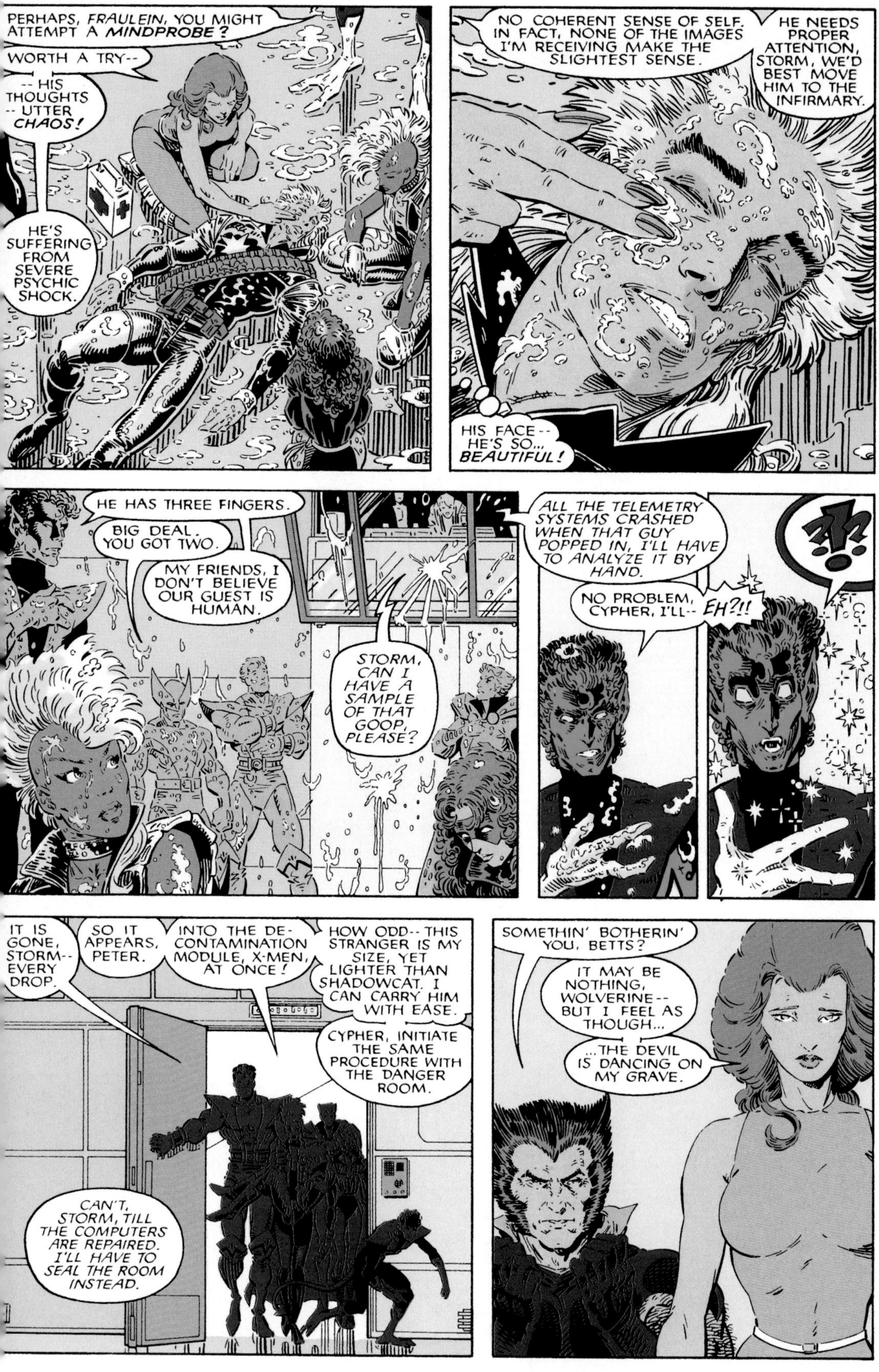

PERHAPS, FRAULEIN, YOU MIGHT ATTEMPT A MINDPROBE?
WORTH A TRY--
-- HIS THOUGHTS -- UTTER CHAOS!
HE'S SUFFERING FROM SEVERE PSYCHIC SHOCK.
NO COHERENT SENSE OF SELF. IN FACT, NONE OF THE IMAGES I'M RECEIVING MAKE THE SLIGHTEST SENSE.
HE NEEDS PROPER ATTENTION, STORM, WE'D BEST MOVE HIM TO THE INFIRMARY.
HIS FACE -- HE'S SO... BEAUTIFUL!
HE HAS THREE FINGERS.
BIG DEAL. YOU GOT TWO.
MY FRIENDS, I DON'T BELIEVE OUR GUEST IS HUMAN.
STORM, CAN I HAVE A SAMPLE OF THAT GOOP, PLEASE?
ALL THE TELEMETRY SYSTEMS CRASHED WHEN THAT GUY POPPED IN, I'LL HAVE TO ANALYZE IT BY HAND.
NO PROBLEM, CYPHER, I'LL-- EH?!!
?!
IT IS GONE, STORM-- EVERY DROP.
SO IT APPEARS, PETER.
INTO THE DE-CONTAMINATION MODULE, X-MEN, AT ONCE!
HOW ODD-- THIS STRANGER IS MY SIZE, YET LIGHTER THAN SHADOWCAT. I CAN CARRY HIM WITH EASE.
CYPHER, INITIATE THE SAME PROCEDURE WITH THE DANGER ROOM.
CAN'T, STORM, TILL THE COMPUTERS ARE REPAIRED. I'LL HAVE TO SEAL THE ROOM INSTEAD.
SOMETHIN' BOTHERIN' YOU, BETTS?
IT MAY BE NOTHING, WOLVERINE -- BUT I FEEL AS THOUGH...
...THE DEVIL IS DANCING ON MY GRAVE.

THE WORLD TURNS.

A NEW DAY DAWNS.

WARM ROASTY TOASTY SNUGGLEBUN...

...WANNA SLEEP YOUR LIFE AWAY?

LOVE TO.

BETTER NOT.

BODY LIKE CEREAL--

--GOES SNAP-CRACKLE-POP!

OLD SO OLD BEFORE MY TIME!

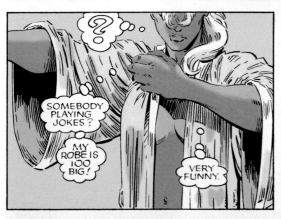

?

SOMEBODY PLAYING JOKES?

MY ROBE IS TOO BIG!

VERY FUNNY.

HIYA, PLANTS!

A LOVELIEST OF MORNINGS TO YOU, MY PRETTIEST OF PRETTIES!

WISH I STILL HAD MY POWERS...

...I WOULD CREATE A RAIN SHOWER FOR YOU-- eh?!!

YAOW!

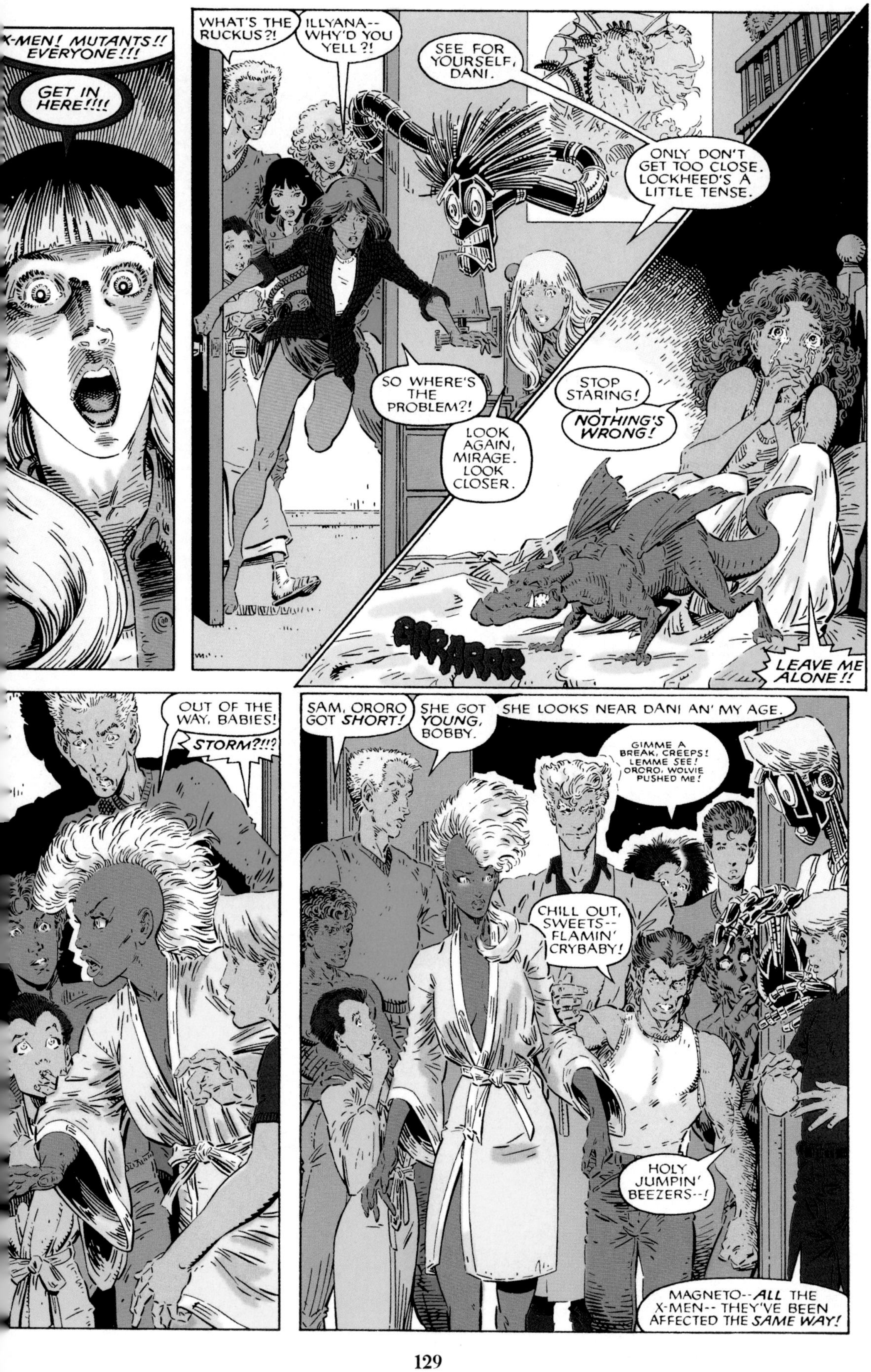
X-MEN! MUTANTS!! EVERYONE!!!
GET IN HERE!!!!
WHAT'S THE RUCKUS?!
ILLYANA-- WHY'D YOU YELL?!
SEE FOR YOURSELF, DANI.
ONLY DON'T GET TOO CLOSE. LOCKHEED'S A LITTLE TENSE.
SO WHERE'S THE PROBLEM?!
LOOK AGAIN, MIRAGE. LOOK CLOSER.
STOP STARING! NOTHING'S WRONG!
BRRARRR
LEAVE ME ALONE!!
OUT OF THE WAY, BABIES!
STORM?!!?
SAM, ORORO GOT SHORT!
SHE GOT YOUNG, BOBBY.
SHE LOOKS NEAR DANI AN' MY AGE.
GIMME A BREAK, CREEPS! LEMME SEE! ORORO, WOLVIE PUSHED ME!
CHILL OUT, SWEETS-- FLAMIN' CRYBABY!
HOLY JUMPIN' BEEZERS--!
MAGNETO--ALL THE X-MEN-- THEY'VE BEEN AFFECTED THE SAME WAY!

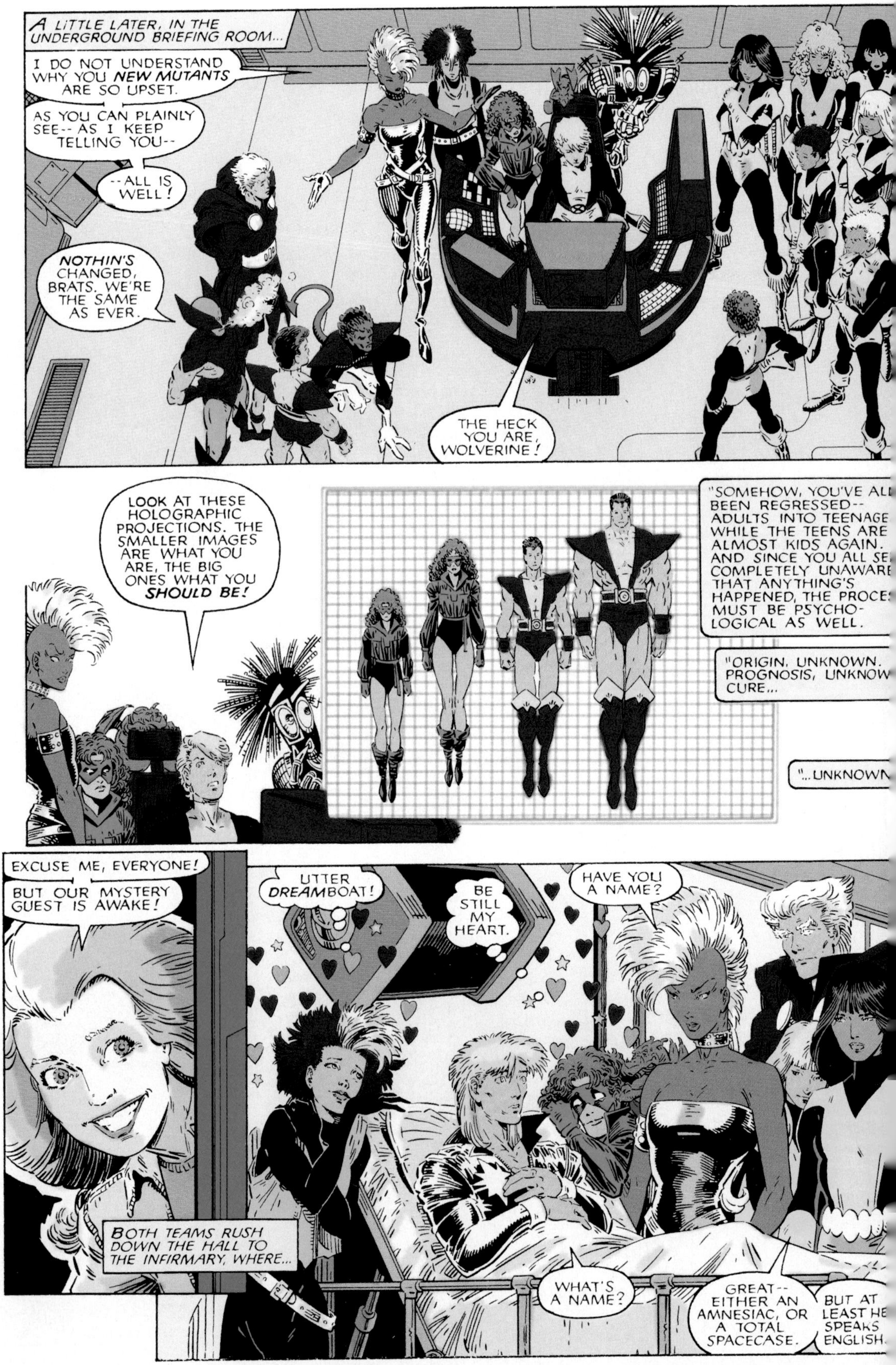

A LITTLE LATER, IN THE UNDERGROUND BRIEFING ROOM...
I DO NOT UNDERSTAND WHY YOU NEW MUTANTS ARE SO UPSET.
AS YOU CAN PLAINLY SEE-- AS I KEEP TELLING YOU--
--ALL IS WELL!
NOTHIN'S CHANGED, BRATS. WE'RE THE SAME AS EVER.
THE HECK YOU ARE, WOLVERINE!
LOOK AT THESE HOLOGRAPHIC PROJECTIONS. THE SMALLER IMAGES ARE WHAT YOU ARE, THE BIG ONES WHAT YOU SHOULD BE!
"SOMEHOW, YOU'VE ALL BEEN REGRESSED-- ADULTS INTO TEENAGE WHILE THE TEENS ARE ALMOST KIDS AGAIN. AND SINCE YOU ALL SE COMPLETELY UNAWARE THAT ANYTHING'S HAPPENED, THE PROCES MUST BE PSYCHO-LOGICAL AS WELL.
"ORIGIN, UNKNOWN. PROGNOSIS, UNKNOW CURE...
"...UNKNOWN
EXCUSE ME, EVERYONE!
BUT OUR MYSTERY GUEST IS AWAKE!
BOTH TEAMS RUSH DOWN THE HALL TO THE INFIRMARY, WHERE...
UTTER DREAMBOAT!
BE STILL MY HEART.
HAVE YOU A NAME?
WHAT'S A NAME?
GREAT-- EITHER AN AMNESIAC, OR A TOTAL SPACECASE.
BUT AT LEAST HE SPEAKS ENGLISH.

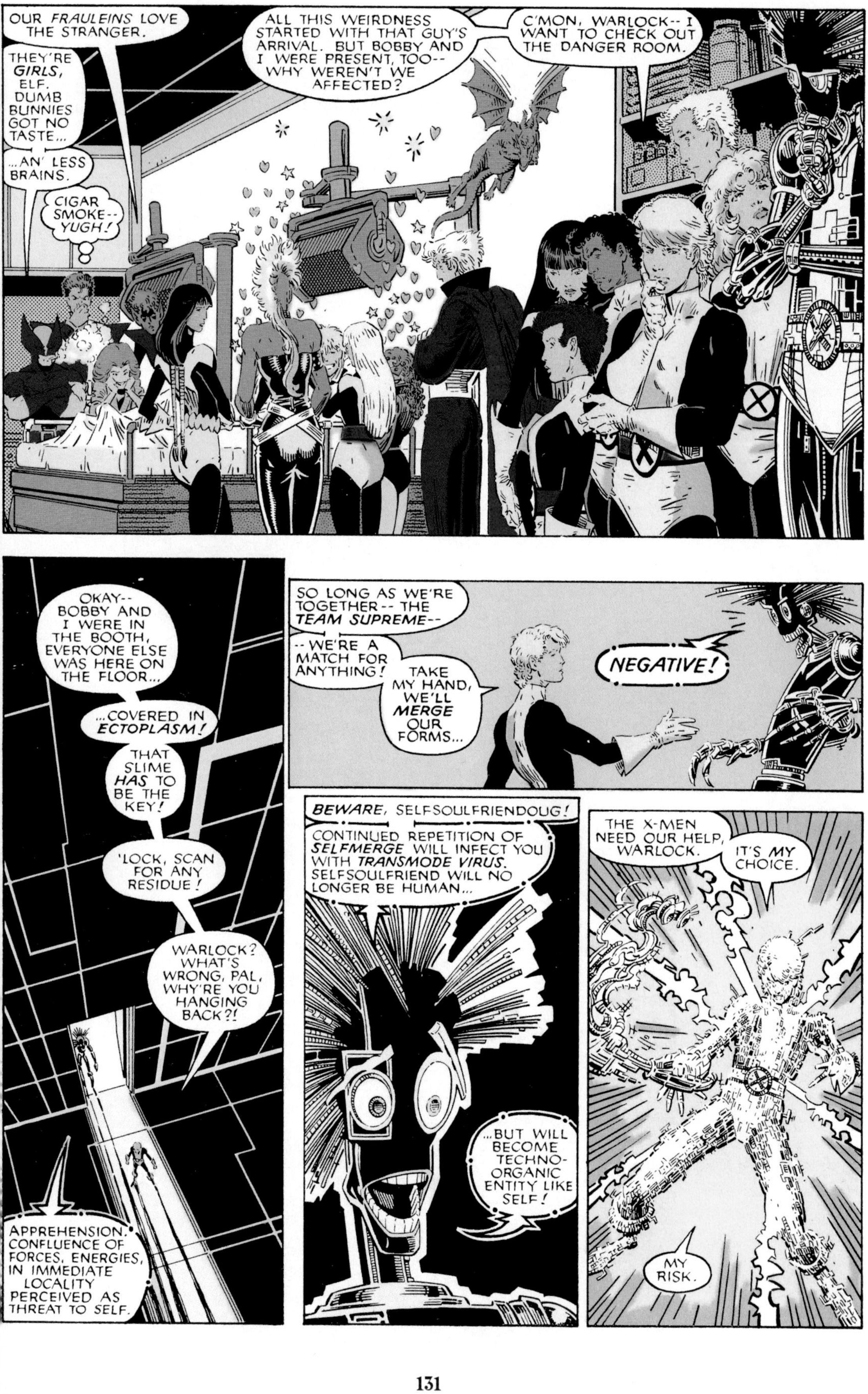
OUR FRAULEINS LOVE THE STRANGER.
THEY'RE GIRLS, ELF. DUMB BUNNIES GOT NO TASTE...
...AN' LESS BRAINS.
CIGAR SMOKE-- YUGH!
ALL THIS WEIRDNESS STARTED WITH THAT GUY'S ARRIVAL. BUT BOBBY AND I WERE PRESENT, TOO-- WHY WEREN'T WE AFFECTED?
C'MON, WARLOCK-- I WANT TO CHECK OUT THE DANGER ROOM.
OKAY-- BOBBY AND I WERE IN THE BOOTH, EVERYONE ELSE WAS HERE ON THE FLOOR...
...COVERED IN ECTOPLASM!
THAT SLIME HAS TO BE THE KEY!
'LOCK, SCAN FOR ANY RESIDUE!
WARLOCK? WHAT'S WRONG, PAL, WHY'RE YOU HANGING BACK?!
APPREHENSION. CONFLUENCE OF FORCES, ENERGIES, IN IMMEDIATE LOCALITY PERCEIVED AS THREAT TO SELF.
SO LONG AS WE'RE TOGETHER -- THE TEAM SUPREME--
-- WE'RE A MATCH FOR ANYTHING!
TAKE MY HAND, WE'LL MERGE OUR FORMS...
NEGATIVE!
BEWARE, SELFSOULFRIENDOUG!
CONTINUED REPETITION OF SELFMERGE WILL INFECT YOU WITH TRANSMODE VIRUS. SELFSOULFRIEND WILL NO LONGER BE HUMAN...
...BUT WILL BECOME TECHNO-ORGANIC ENTITY LIKE SELF!
THE X-MEN NEED OUR HELP, WARLOCK.
IT'S MY CHOICE.
MY RISK.

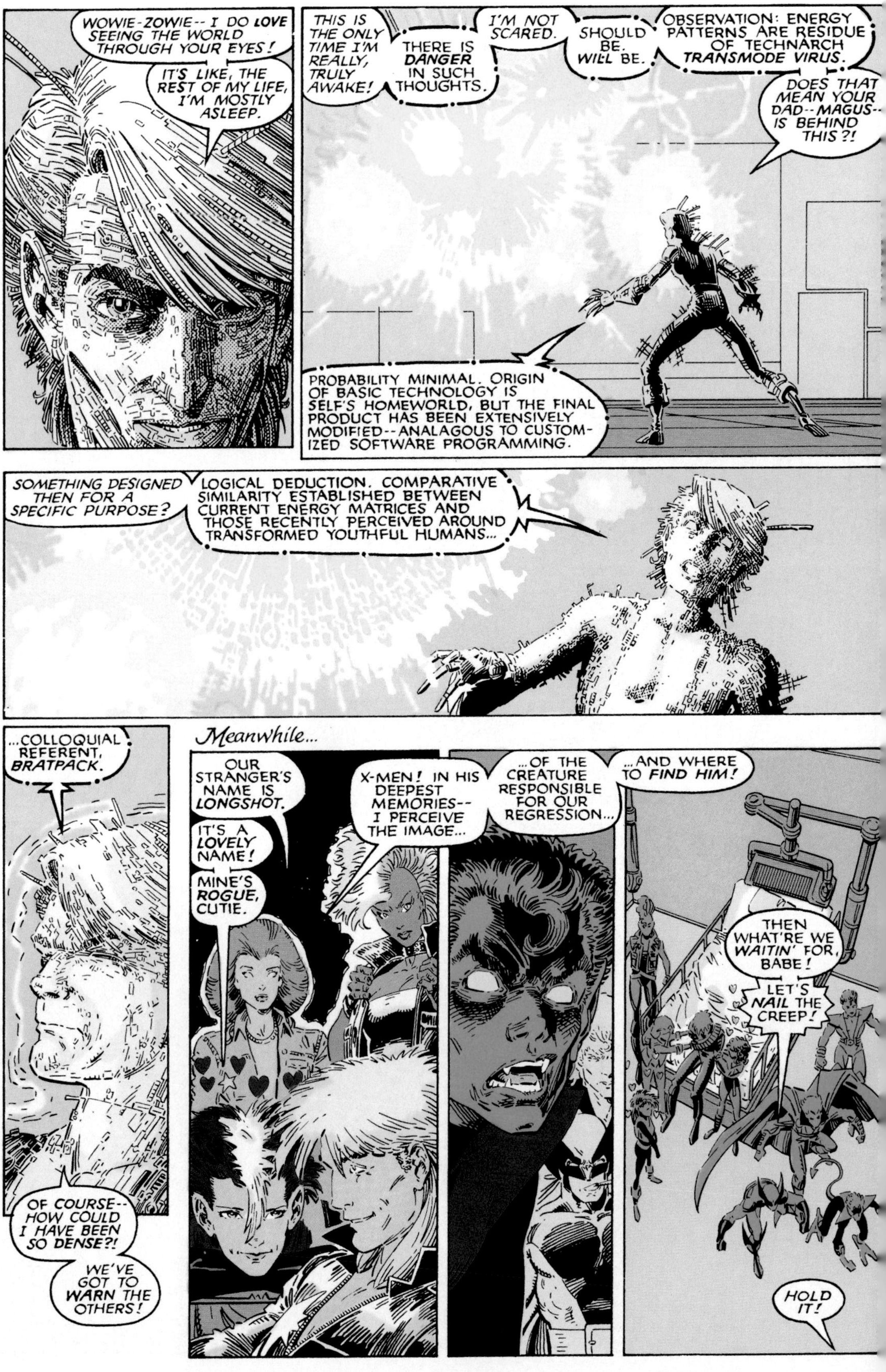

WOWIE-ZOWIE-- I DO LOVE SEEING THE WORLD THROUGH YOUR EYES!
IT'S LIKE, THE REST OF MY LIFE, I'M MOSTLY ASLEEP.
THIS IS THE ONLY TIME I'M REALLY, TRULY AWAKE!
THERE IS DANGER IN SUCH THOUGHTS.
I'M NOT SCARED.
SHOULD BE. WILL BE.
OBSERVATION: ENERGY PATTERNS ARE RESIDUE OF TECHNARCH TRANSMODE VIRUS.
DOES THAT MEAN YOUR DAD--MAGUS--IS BEHIND THIS?!
PROBABILITY MINIMAL. ORIGIN OF BASIC TECHNOLOGY IS SELF'S HOMEWORLD, BUT THE FINAL PRODUCT HAS BEEN EXTENSIVELY MODIFIED--ANALAGOUS TO CUSTOMIZED SOFTWARE PROGRAMMING.
SOMETHING DESIGNED THEN FOR A SPECIFIC PURPOSE?
LOGICAL DEDUCTION. COMPARATIVE SIMILARITY ESTABLISHED BETWEEN CURRENT ENERGY MATRICES AND THOSE RECENTLY PERCEIVED AROUND TRANSFORMED YOUTHFUL HUMANS...
...COLLOQUIAL REFERENT, BRATPACK.
OF COURSE--HOW COULD I HAVE BEEN SO DENSE?!
WE'VE GOT TO WARN THE OTHERS!
Meanwhile...
OUR STRANGER'S NAME IS LONGSHOT.
IT'S A LOVELY NAME!
MINE'S ROGUE, CUTIE.
X-MEN! IN HIS DEEPEST MEMORIES-- I PERCEIVE THE IMAGE...
...OF THE CREATURE RESPONSIBLE FOR OUR REGRESSION...
...AND WHERE TO FIND HIM!
THEN WHAT'RE WE WAITIN' FOR, BABE!
LET'S NAIL THE CREEP!
HOLD IT!

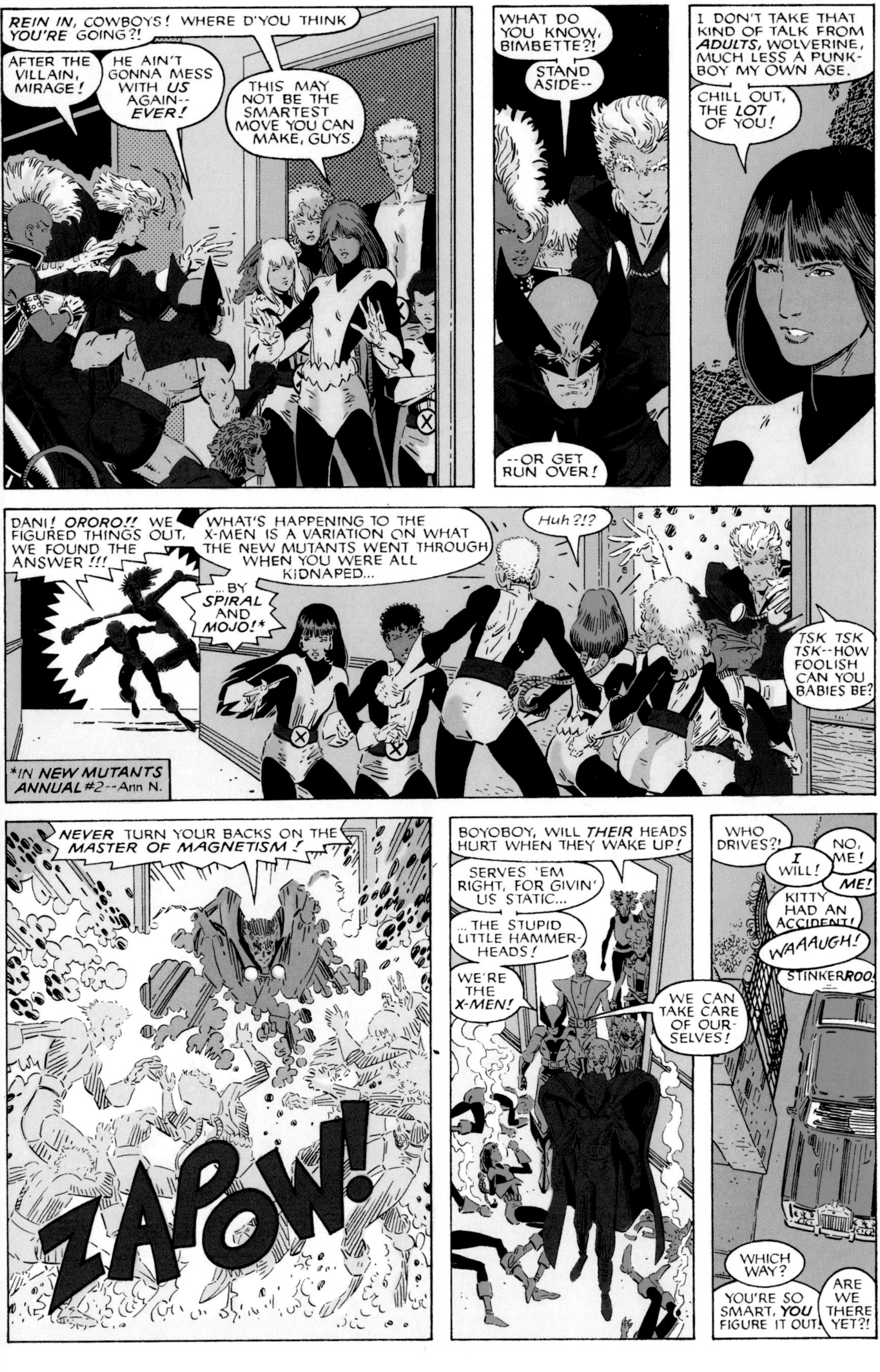
REIN IN, COWBOYS! WHERE D'YOU THINK YOU'RE GOING?!
AFTER THE VILLAIN, MIRAGE!
HE AIN'T GONNA MESS WITH US AGAIN-- EVER!
THIS MAY NOT BE THE SMARTEST MOVE YOU CAN MAKE, GUYS.
WHAT DO YOU KNOW, BIMBETTE?!
STAND ASIDE--
--OR GET RUN OVER!
I DON'T TAKE THAT KIND OF TALK FROM ADULTS, WOLVERINE, MUCH LESS A PUNK-BOY MY OWN AGE.
CHILL OUT, THE LOT OF YOU!
DANI! ORORO!! WE FIGURED THINGS OUT, WE FOUND THE ANSWER!!!
WHAT'S HAPPENING TO THE X-MEN IS A VARIATION ON WHAT THE NEW MUTANTS WENT THROUGH WHEN YOU WERE ALL KIDNAPED...
...BY SPIRAL AND MOJO!*
Huh?!?
TSK TSK TSK--HOW FOOLISH CAN YOU BABIES BE?
*IN NEW MUTANTS ANNUAL #2--Ann N.
NEVER TURN YOUR BACKS ON THE MASTER OF MAGNETISM!
ZAPOW!
BOYOBOY, WILL THEIR HEADS HURT WHEN THEY WAKE UP!
SERVES 'EM RIGHT, FOR GIVIN' US STATIC...
...THE STUPID LITTLE HAMMER-HEADS!
WE'RE THE X-MEN!
WE CAN TAKE CARE OF OUR-SELVES!
WHO DRIVES?!
I WILL!
NO, ME!
ME!
KITTY HAD AN ACCIDENT!
WAAAUGH!
STINKERROO!
WHICH WAY?
YOU'RE SO SMART, YOU FIGURE IT OUT!
ARE WE THERE YET?!

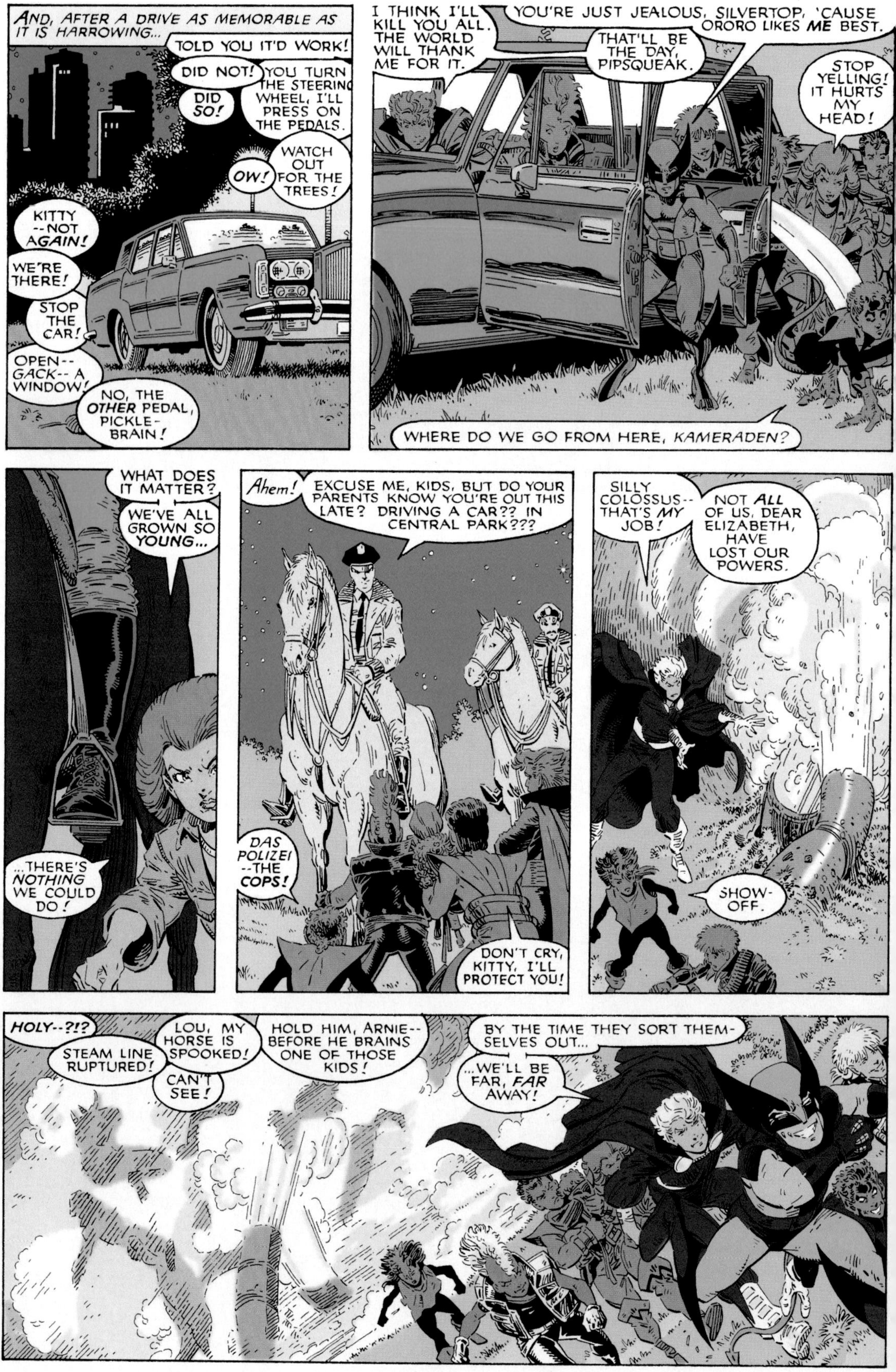
AND, AFTER A DRIVE AS MEMORABLE AS IT IS HARROWING...
TOLD YOU IT'D WORK!
DID NOT!
DID SO!
YOU TURN THE STEERING WHEEL, I'LL PRESS ON THE PEDALS.
WATCH OUT FOR THE TREES!
OW!
KITTY --NOT AGAIN!
WE'RE THERE!
STOP THE CAR!
OPEN-- GACK-- A WINDOW!
NO, THE OTHER PEDAL, PICKLE-BRAIN!
I THINK I'LL KILL YOU ALL. THE WORLD WILL THANK ME FOR IT.
YOU'RE JUST JEALOUS, SILVERTOP, 'CAUSE ORORO LIKES ME BEST.
THAT'LL BE THE DAY, PIPSQUEAK.
STOP YELLING! IT HURTS MY HEAD!
WHERE DO WE GO FROM HERE, KAMERADEN?
WHAT DOES IT MATTER?
WE'VE ALL GROWN SO YOUNG...
...THERE'S NOTHING WE COULD DO!
Ahem!
EXCUSE ME, KIDS, BUT DO YOUR PARENTS KNOW YOU'RE OUT THIS LATE? DRIVING A CAR?? IN CENTRAL PARK???
DAS POLIZEI --THE COPS!
DON'T CRY, KITTY, I'LL PROTECT YOU!
SILLY COLOSSUS-- THAT'S MY JOB!
NOT ALL OF US, DEAR ELIZABETH, HAVE LOST OUR POWERS.
SHOW-OFF.
HOLY--?!?
STEAM LINE RUPTURED!
LOU, MY HORSE IS SPOOKED!
CAN'T SEE!
HOLD HIM, ARNIE-- BEFORE HE BRAINS ONE OF THOSE KIDS!
BY THE TIME THEY SORT THEMSELVES OUT...
...WE'LL BE FAR, FAR AWAY!

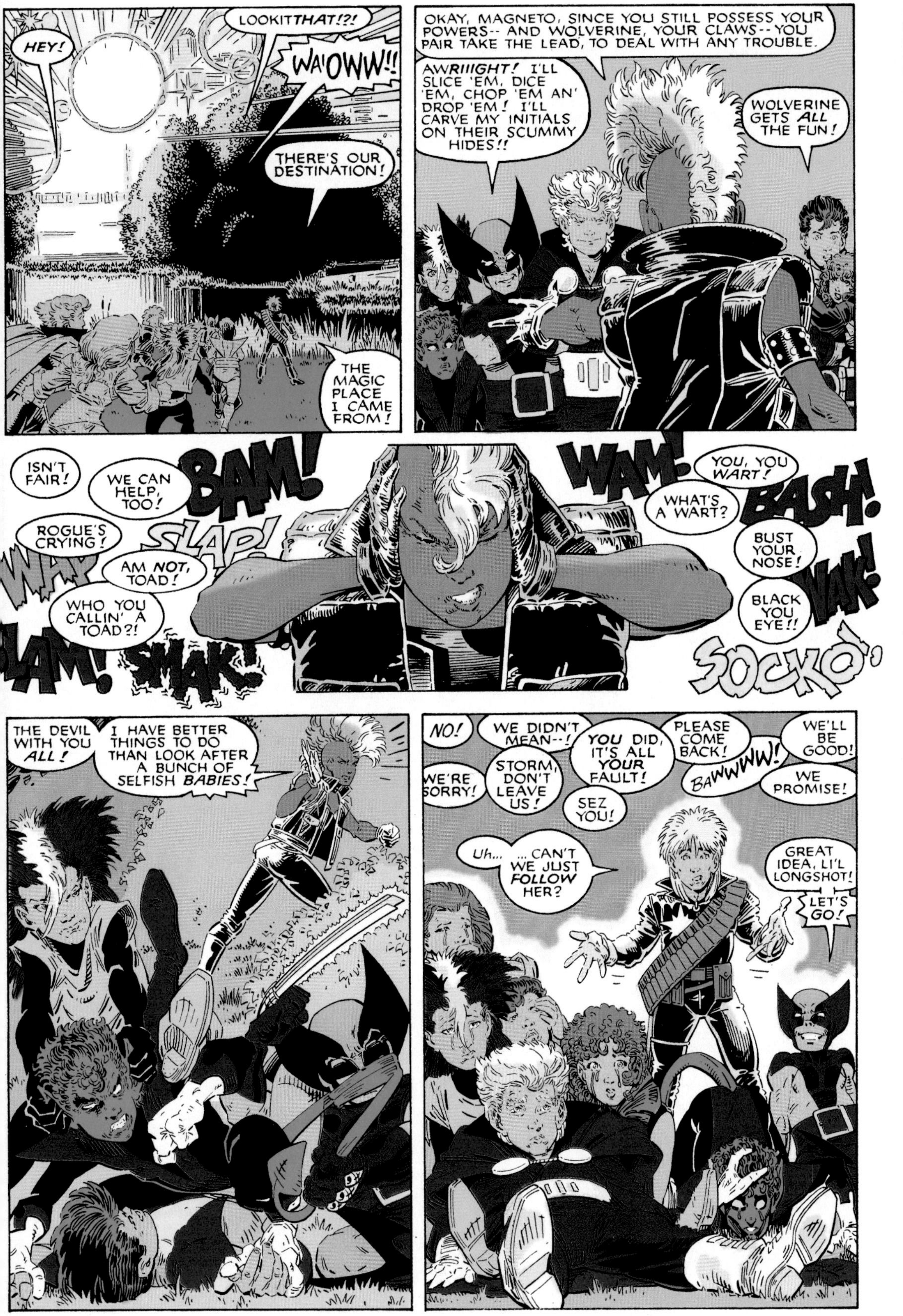
HEY!
LOOKITTHAT!?!
WA'OWW!!
THERE'S OUR DESTINATION!
THE MAGIC PLACE I CAME FROM!
OKAY, MAGNETO, SINCE YOU STILL POSSESS YOUR POWERS-- AND WOLVERINE, YOUR CLAWS-- YOU PAIR TAKE THE LEAD, TO DEAL WITH ANY TROUBLE.
AWRIIIGHT! I'LL SLICE 'EM, DICE 'EM, CHOP 'EM AN' DROP 'EM! I'LL CARVE MY INITIALS ON THEIR SCUMMY HIDES!!
WOLVERINE GETS ALL THE FUN!
ISN'T FAIR!
WE CAN HELP, TOO!
BAM!
ROGUE'S CRYING!
SLAP!
AM NOT, TOAD!
WHO YOU CALLIN' A TOAD?!
LAM!
SHAK!
WAM!
YOU, YOU WART!
WHAT'S A WART?
BASH!
BUST YOUR NOSE!
WAK!
BLACK YOU EYE!!
SOCKO!
THE DEVIL WITH YOU ALL!
I HAVE BETTER THINGS TO DO THAN LOOK AFTER A BUNCH OF SELFISH BABIES!
NO!
WE DIDN'T MEAN--!
YOU DID, IT'S ALL YOUR FAULT!
PLEASE COME BACK!
WE'LL BE GOOD!
WE'RE SORRY!
STORM, DON'T LEAVE US!
SEZ YOU!
BAWWWW!
WE PROMISE!
Uh... ...CAN'T WE JUST FOLLOW HER?
GREAT IDEA, LI'L LONGSHOT!
LET'S GO!

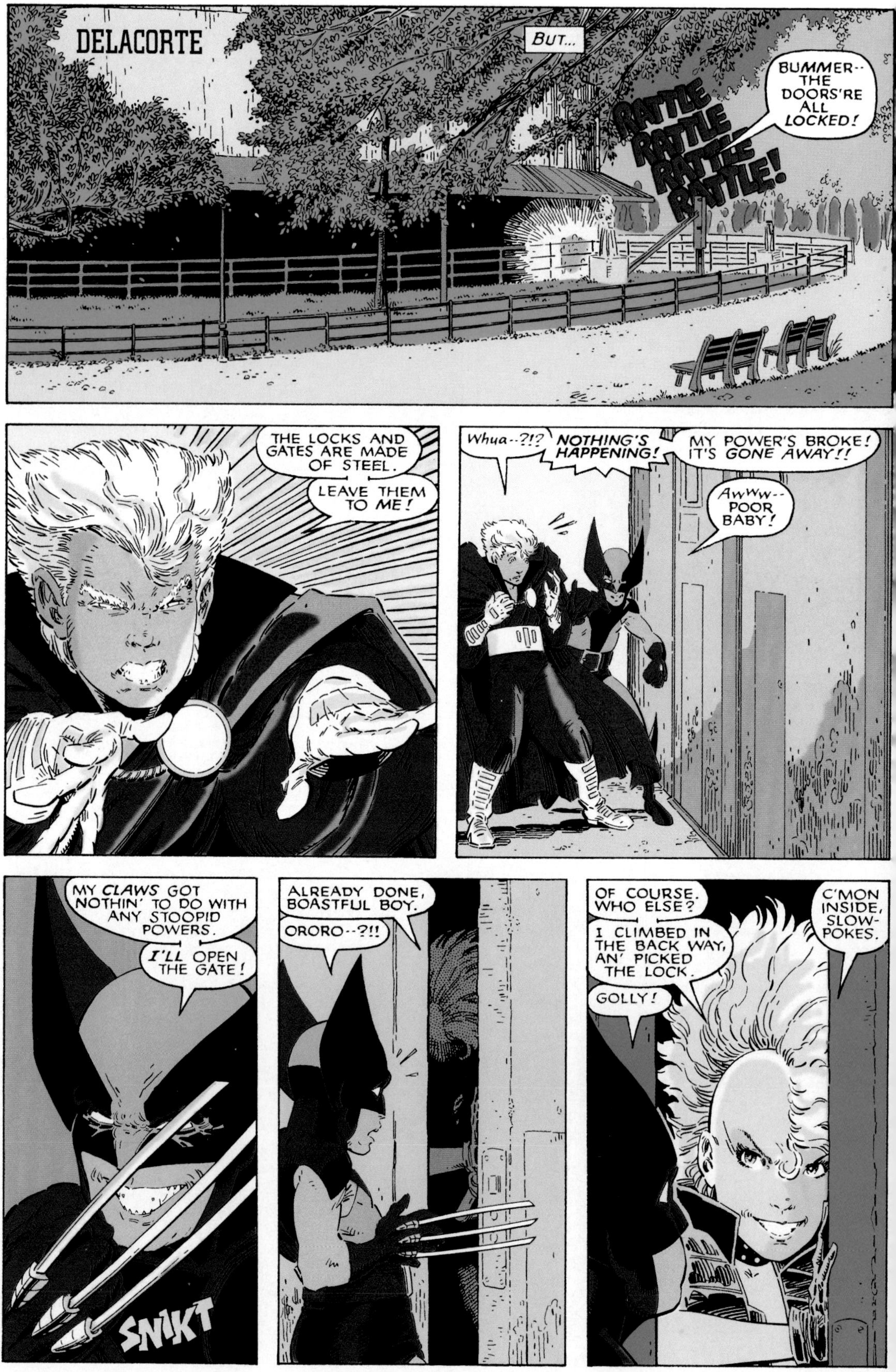
DELACORTE
BUT...
RATTLE RATTLE RATTLE RATTLE!
BUMMER-- THE DOORS'RE ALL LOCKED!
THE LOCKS AND GATES ARE MADE OF STEEL.
LEAVE THEM TO ME!
Whua--?!?
NOTHING'S HAPPENING!
MY POWER'S BROKE! IT'S GONE AWAY!!
Awww-- POOR BABY!
MY CLAWS GOT NOTHIN' TO DO WITH ANY STOOPID POWERS.
I'LL OPEN THE GATE!
SNIKT
ALREADY DONE, BOASTFUL BOY.
ORORO--?!!
OF COURSE. WHO ELSE?
I CLIMBED IN THE BACK WAY, AN' PICKED THE LOCK.
GOLLY!
C'MON INSIDE, SLOW-POKES.

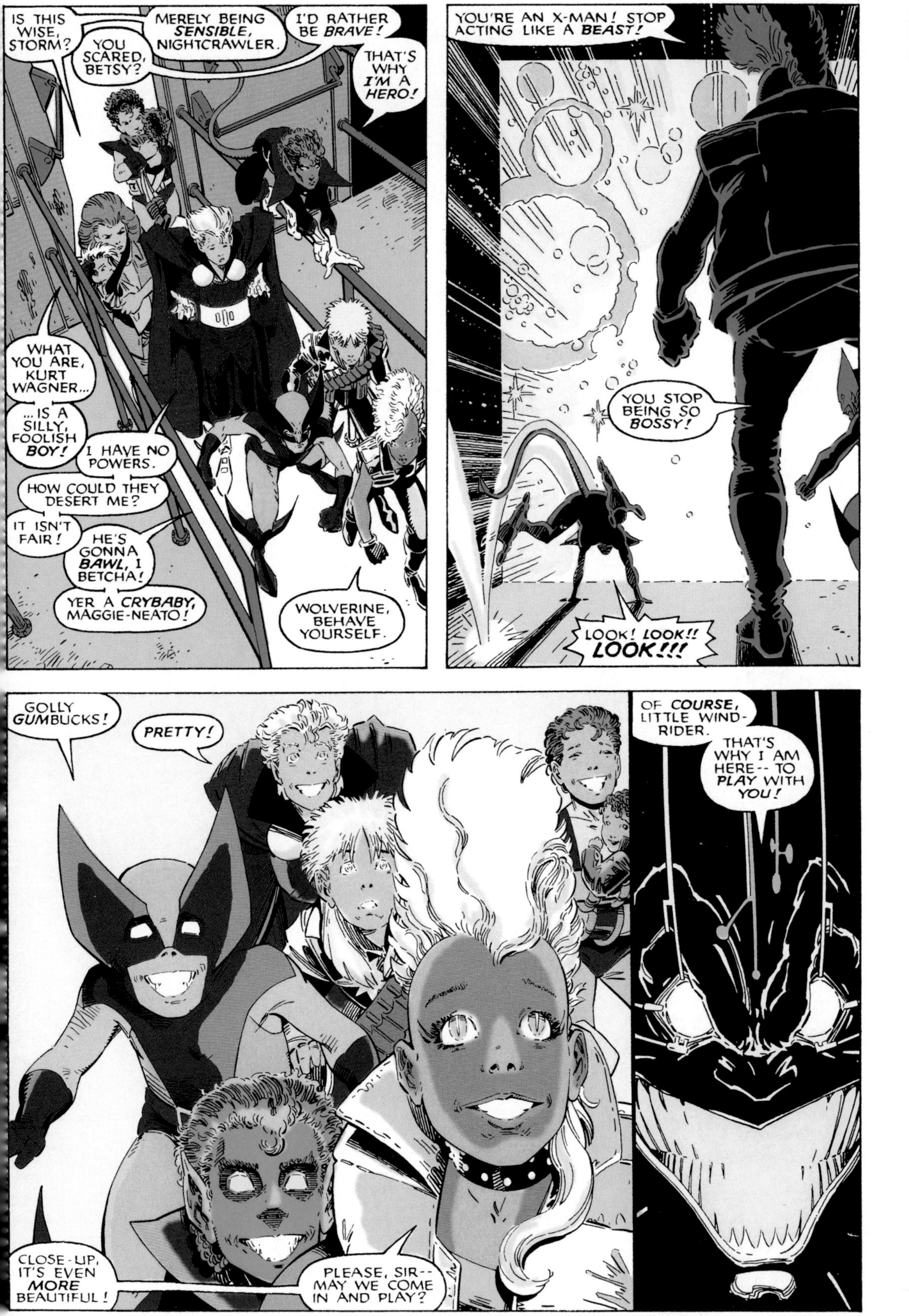
IS THIS WISE, STORM?
MERELY BEING SENSIBLE, NIGHTCRAWLER.
YOU SCARED, BETSY?
I'D RATHER BE BRAVE!
THAT'S WHY I'M A HERO!
WHAT YOU ARE, KURT WAGNER...
...IS A SILLY, FOOLISH BOY!
I HAVE NO POWERS.
HOW COULD THEY DESERT ME?
IT ISN'T FAIR!
HE'S GONNA BAWL, I BETCHA!
YER A CRYBABY, MAGGIE-NEATO!
WOLVERINE, BEHAVE YOURSELF.
YOU'RE AN X-MAN! STOP ACTING LIKE A BEAST!
YOU STOP BEING SO BOSSY!
LOOK! LOOK!! LOOK!!!
GOLLY GUMBUCKS!
PRETTY!
OF COURSE, LITTLE WIND-RIDER.
THAT'S WHY I AM HERE-- TO PLAY WITH YOU!
CLOSE-UP, IT'S EVEN MORE BEAUTIFUL!
PLEASE, SIR-- MAY WE COME IN AND PLAY?

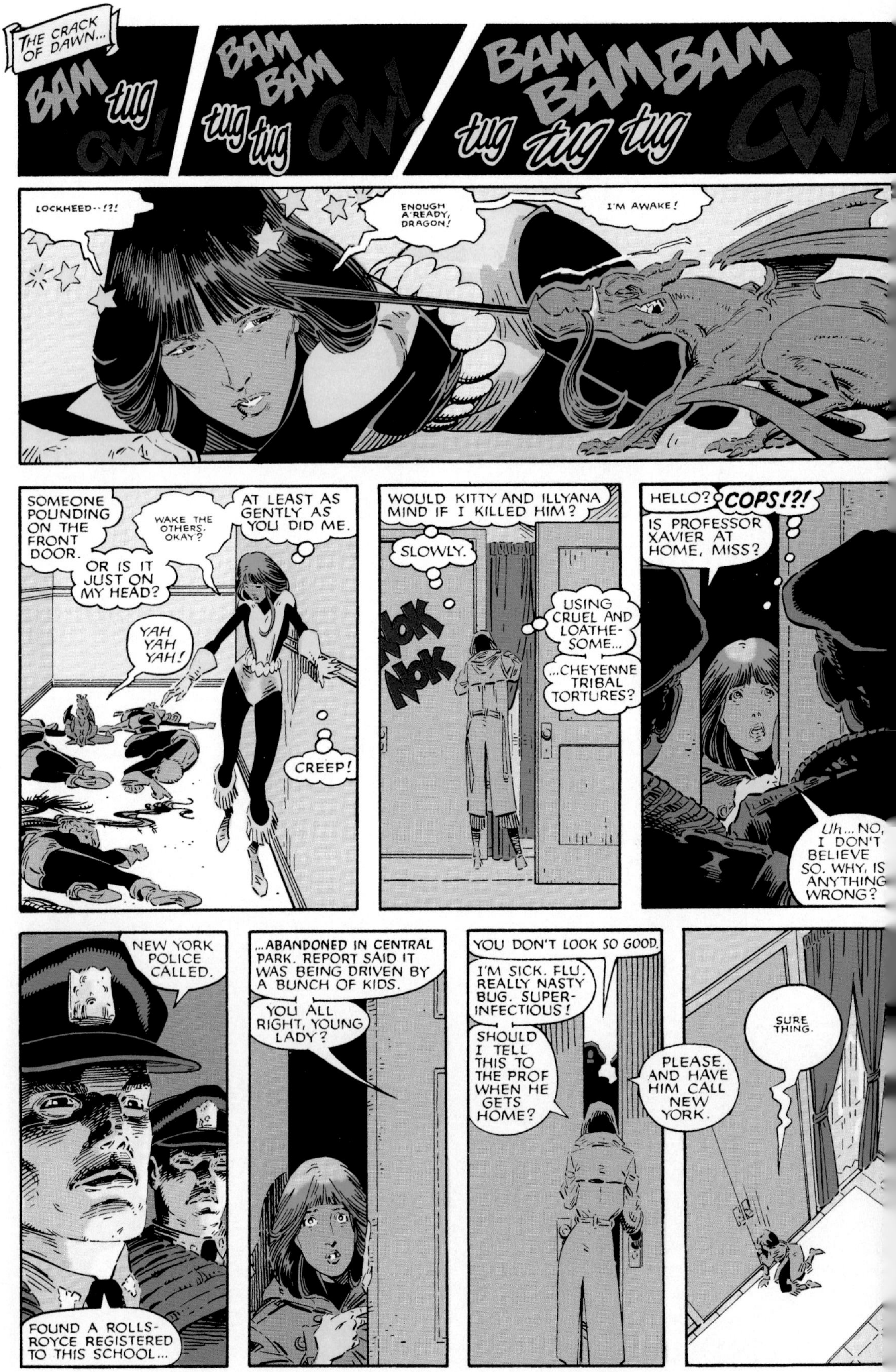
THE CRACK OF DAWN...
BAM tug OW!
BAM BAM tug tug OW!
BAM BAMBAM tug tug tug OW!
LOCKHEED--!?!
ENOUGH A'READY, DRAGON!
I'M AWAKE!
SOMEONE POUNDING ON THE FRONT DOOR.
OR IS IT JUST ON MY HEAD?
WAKE THE OTHERS, OKAY?
AT LEAST AS GENTLY AS YOU DID ME.
YAH YAH YAH!
CREEP!
WOULD KITTY AND ILLYANA MIND IF I KILLED HIM?
SLOWLY.
NOK NOK
USING CRUEL AND LOATHE-SOME...
...CHEYENNE TRIBAL TORTURES?
HELLO?
COPS!?!
IS PROFESSOR XAVIER AT HOME, MISS?
Uh... NO, I DON'T BELIEVE SO. WHY, IS ANYTHING WRONG?
NEW YORK POLICE CALLED.
FOUND A ROLLS-ROYCE REGISTERED TO THIS SCHOOL...
...ABANDONED IN CENTRAL PARK. REPORT SAID IT WAS BEING DRIVEN BY A BUNCH OF KIDS.
YOU ALL RIGHT, YOUNG LADY?
YOU DON'T LOOK SO GOOD.
I'M SICK. FLU. REALLY NASTY BUG. SUPER-INFECTIOUS!
SHOULD I TELL THIS TO THE PROF WHEN HE GETS HOME?
PLEASE. AND HAVE HIM CALL NEW YORK.
SURE THING.

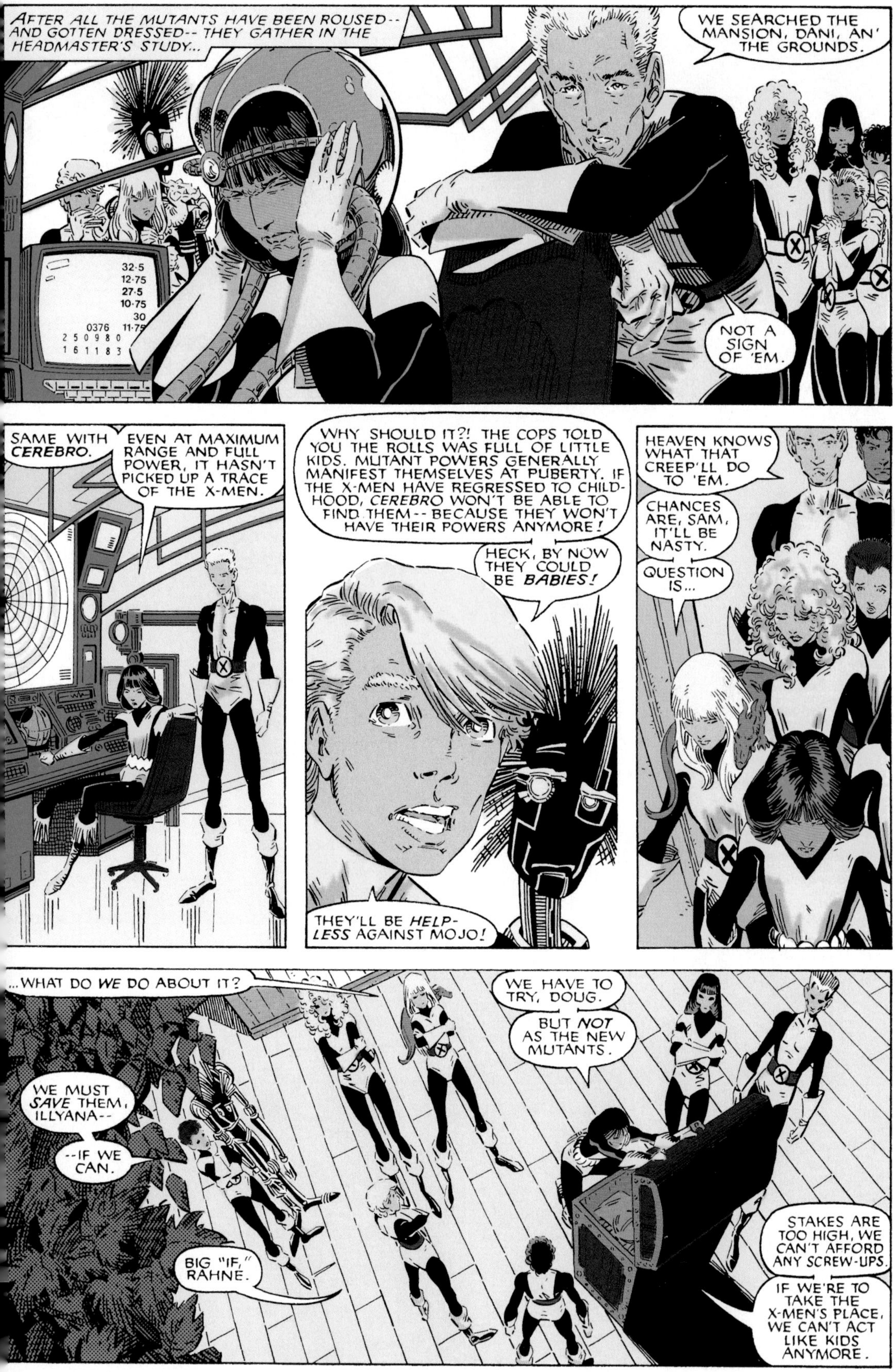

AFTER ALL THE MUTANTS HAVE BEEN ROUSED-- AND GOTTEN DRESSED-- THEY GATHER IN THE HEADMASTER'S STUDY...
WE SEARCHED THE MANSION, DANI, AN' THE GROUNDS.
NOT A SIGN OF 'EM.
SAME WITH CEREBRO.
EVEN AT MAXIMUM RANGE AND FULL POWER, IT HASN'T PICKED UP A TRACE OF THE X-MEN.
WHY SHOULD IT?! THE COPS TOLD YOU THE ROLLS WAS FULL OF LITTLE KIDS. MUTANT POWERS GENERALLY MANIFEST THEMSELVES AT PUBERTY. IF THE X-MEN HAVE REGRESSED TO CHILDHOOD, CEREBRO WON'T BE ABLE TO FIND THEM-- BECAUSE THEY WON'T HAVE THEIR POWERS ANYMORE!
HECK, BY NOW THEY COULD BE BABIES!
THEY'LL BE HELPLESS AGAINST MOJO!
HEAVEN KNOWS WHAT THAT CREEP'LL DO TO 'EM.
CHANCES ARE, SAM, IT'LL BE NASTY.
QUESTION IS...
...WHAT DO WE DO ABOUT IT?
WE HAVE TO TRY, DOUG.
BUT NOT AS THE NEW MUTANTS.
WE MUST SAVE THEM, ILLYANA--
--IF WE CAN.
BIG "IF," RAHNE.
STAKES ARE TOO HIGH, WE CAN'T AFFORD ANY SCREW-UPS.
IF WE'RE TO TAKE THE X-MEN'S PLACE, WE CAN'T ACT LIKE KIDS ANYMORE.

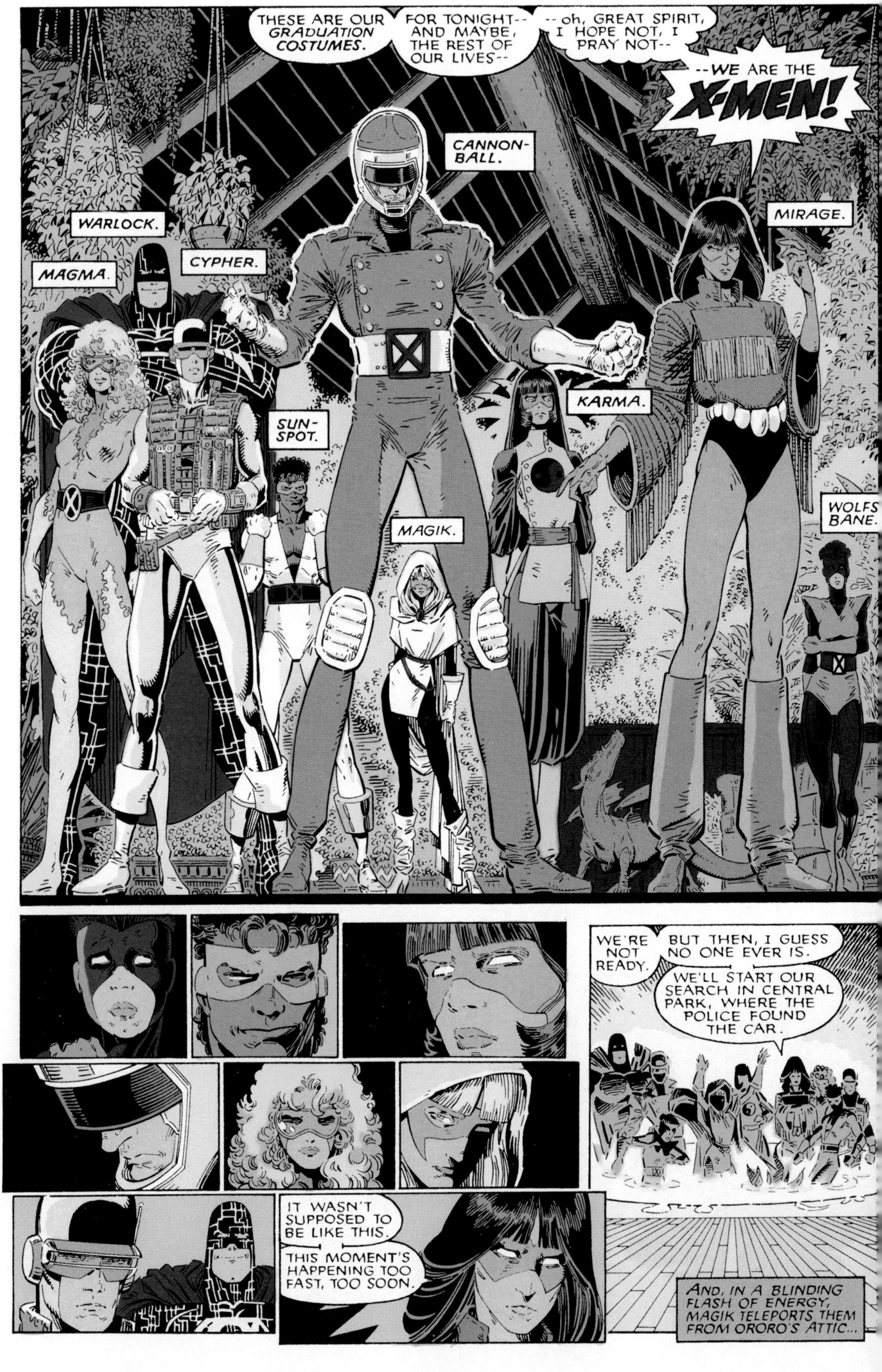
THESE ARE OUR GRADUATION COSTUMES.
FOR TONIGHT-- AND MAYBE, THE REST OF OUR LIVES--
--oh, GREAT SPIRIT, I HOPE NOT, I PRAY NOT--
--WE ARE THE X-MEN!
CANNON-BALL.
WARLOCK.
MAGMA.
CYPHER.
MIRAGE.
KARMA.
SUN-SPOT.
MAGIK.
WOLFS BANE.
WE'RE NOT READY.
BUT THEN, I GUESS NO ONE EVER IS.
WE'LL START OUR SEARCH IN CENTRAL PARK, WHERE THE POLICE FOUND THE CAR.
IT WASN'T SUPPOSED TO BE LIKE THIS.
THIS MOMENT'S HAPPENING TOO FAST, TOO SOON.
AND, IN A BLINDING FLASH OF ENERGY, MAGIK TELEPORTS THEM FROM ORORO'S ATTIC...

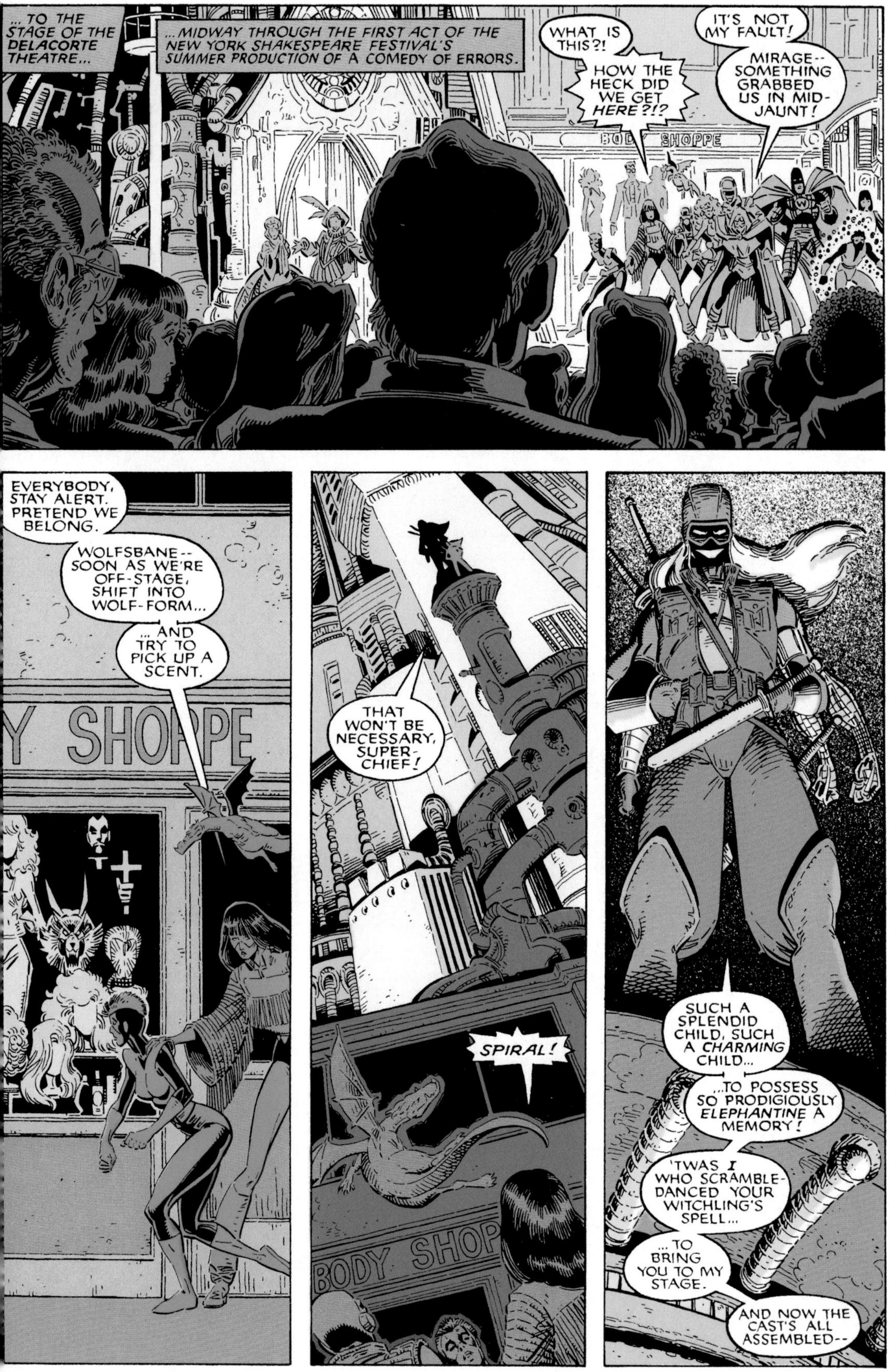
...TO THE STAGE OF THE DELACORTE THEATRE...
...MIDWAY THROUGH THE FIRST ACT OF THE NEW YORK SHAKESPEARE FESTIVAL'S SUMMER PRODUCTION OF A COMEDY OF ERRORS.
WHAT IS THIS?!
HOW THE HECK DID WE GET HERE?!?
IT'S NOT MY FAULT!
MIRAGE--SOMETHING GRABBED US IN MID-JAUNT!
BODY SHOPPE
EVERYBODY, STAY ALERT. PRETEND WE BELONG.
WOLFSBANE--SOON AS WE'RE OFF-STAGE, SHIFT INTO WOLF-FORM...
...AND TRY TO PICK UP A SCENT.
Y SHOPPE
THAT WON'T BE NECESSARY, SUPER-CHIEF!
SPIRAL!
BODY SHOP
SUCH A SPLENDID CHILD, SUCH A CHARMING CHILD...
...TO POSSESS SO PRODIGIOUSLY ELEPHANTINE A MEMORY!
'TWAS I WHO SCRAMBLE-DANCED YOUR WITCHLING'S SPELL...
...TO BRING YOU TO MY STAGE.
AND NOW THE CAST'S ALL ASSEMBLED--

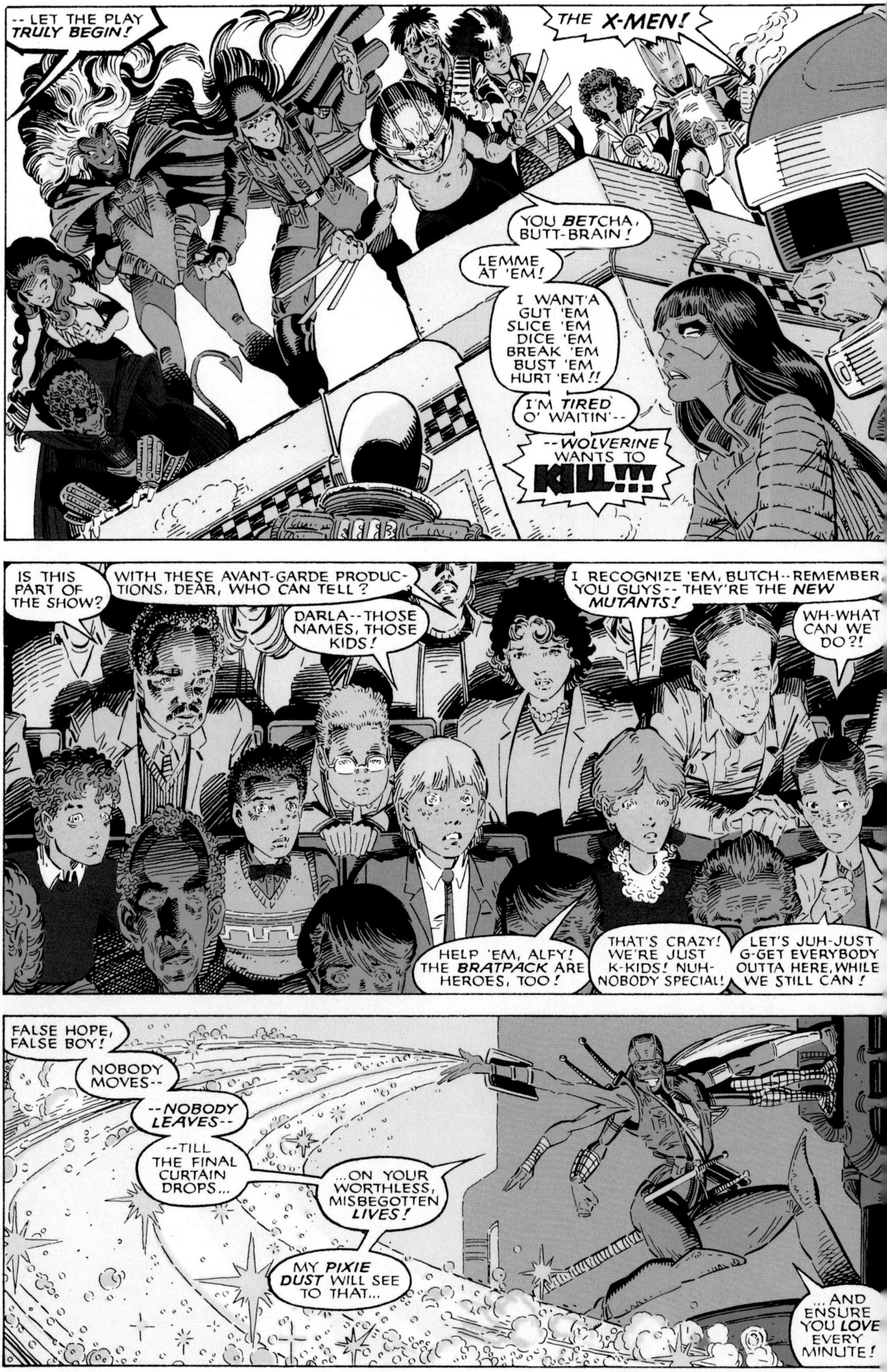

--LET THE PLAY TRULY BEGIN!
THE X-MEN!
YOU BETCHA, BUTT-BRAIN!
LEMME AT 'EM!
I WANT'A GUT 'EM SLICE 'EM DICE 'EM BREAK 'EM BUST 'EM HURT 'EM!!
I'M TIRED O' WAITIN'--
--WOLVERINE WANTS TO KILL!!!
IS THIS PART OF THE SHOW?
WITH THESE AVANT-GARDE PRODUCTIONS, DEAR, WHO CAN TELL?
DARLA--THOSE NAMES, THOSE KIDS!
I RECOGNIZE 'EM, BUTCH--REMEMBER YOU GUYS--THEY'RE THE NEW MUTANTS!
WH-WHAT CAN WE DO?!
HELP 'EM, ALFY! THE BRATPACK ARE HEROES, TOO!
THAT'S CRAZY! WE'RE JUST K-KIDS! NUH-NOBODY SPECIAL!
LET'S JUH-JUST G-GET EVERYBODY OUTTA HERE, WHILE WE STILL CAN!
FALSE HOPE, FALSE BOY!
NOBODY MOVES--
--NOBODY LEAVES--
--TILL THE FINAL CURTAIN DROPS...
...ON YOUR WORTHLESS, MISBEGOTTEN LIVES!
MY PIXIE DUST WILL SEE TO THAT...
...AND ENSURE YOU LOVE EVERY MINUTE!

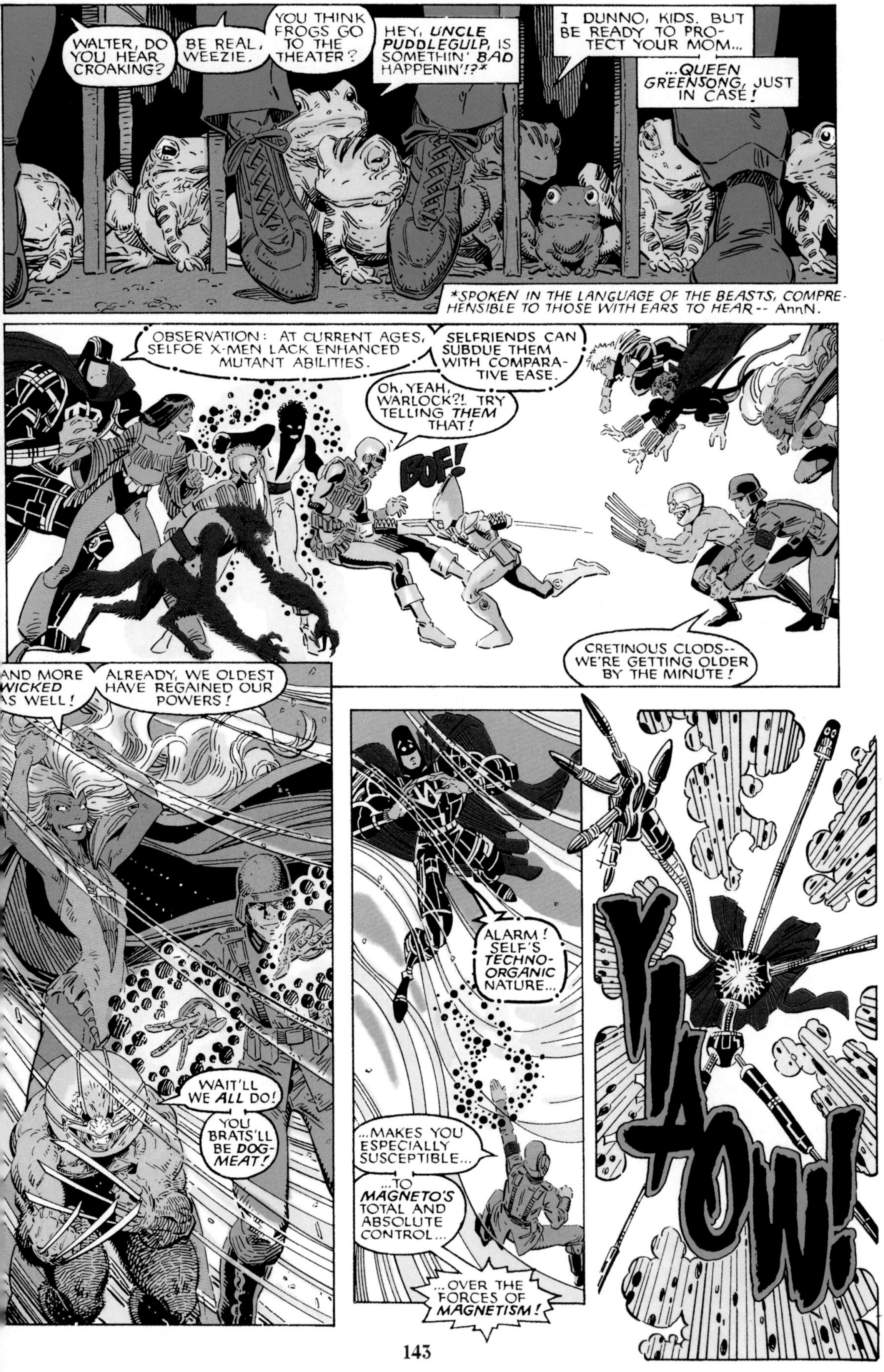
WALTER, DO YOU HEAR CROAKING?
BE REAL, WEEZIE.
YOU THINK FROGS GO TO THE THEATER?
HEY, UNCLE PUDDLEGULP, IS SOMETHIN' BAD HAPPENIN'!?*
I DUNNO, KIDS. BUT BE READY TO PROTECT YOUR MOM...
...QUEEN GREENSONG, JUST IN CASE!
*SPOKEN IN THE LANGUAGE OF THE BEASTS, COMPREHENSIBLE TO THOSE WITH EARS TO HEAR -- AnnN.
OBSERVATION: AT CURRENT AGES, SELFOE X-MEN LACK ENHANCED MUTANT ABILITIES.
SELFRIENDS CAN SUBDUE THEM WITH COMPARATIVE EASE.
Oh, YEAH, WARLOCK?! TRY TELLING THEM THAT!
BOF!
CRETINOUS CLODS-- WE'RE GETTING OLDER BY THE MINUTE!
AND MORE WICKED AS WELL!
ALREADY, WE OLDEST HAVE REGAINED OUR POWERS!
WAIT'LL WE ALL DO!
YOU BRATS'LL BE DOG-MEAT!
ALARM! SELF'S TECHNO-ORGANIC NATURE...
...MAKES YOU ESPECIALLY SUSCEPTIBLE...
...TO MAGNETO'S TOTAL AND ABSOLUTE CONTROL...
...OVER THE FORCES OF MAGNETISM!
YAHOW!

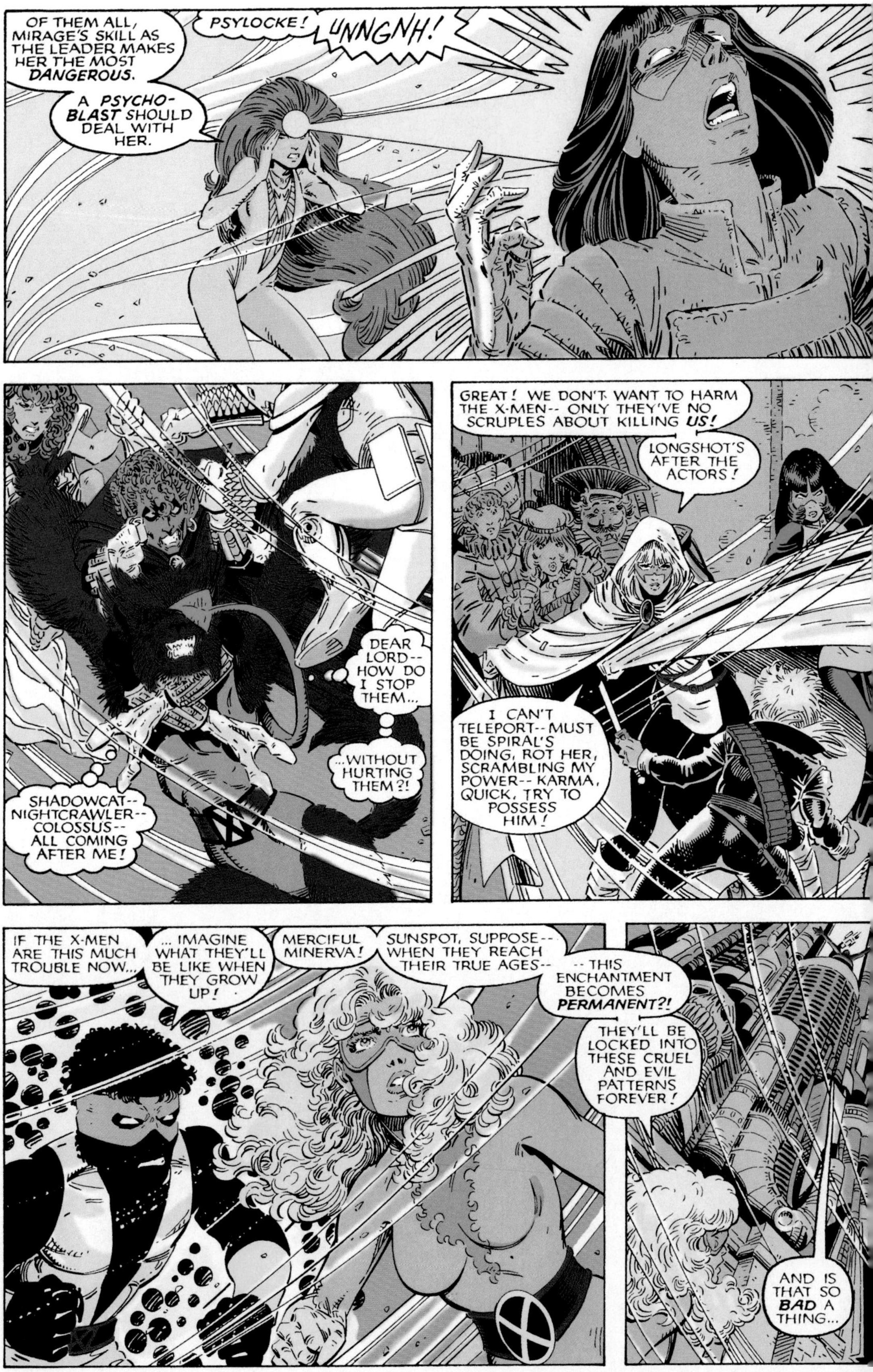
OF THEM ALL, MIRAGE'S SKILL AS THE LEADER MAKES HER THE MOST DANGEROUS.
A PSYCHO-BLAST SHOULD DEAL WITH HER.
PSYLOCKE!
UNNGNH!
SHADOWCAT-- NIGHTCRAWLER-- COLOSSUS-- ALL COMING AFTER ME!
DEAR LORD-- HOW DO I STOP THEM...
...WITHOUT HURTING THEM?!
GREAT! WE DON'T WANT TO HARM THE X-MEN-- ONLY THEY'VE NO SCRUPLES ABOUT KILLING US!
LONGSHOT'S AFTER THE ACTORS!
I CAN'T TELEPORT-- MUST BE SPIRAL'S DOING, ROT HER, SCRAMBLING MY POWER-- KARMA, QUICK, TRY TO POSSESS HIM!
IF THE X-MEN ARE THIS MUCH TROUBLE NOW...
... IMAGINE WHAT THEY'LL BE LIKE WHEN THEY GROW UP!
MERCIFUL MINERVA!
SUNSPOT, SUPPOSE-- WHEN THEY REACH THEIR TRUE AGES--
-- THIS ENCHANTMENT BECOMES PERMANENT?!
THEY'LL BE LOCKED INTO THESE CRUEL AND EVIL PATTERNS FOREVER!
AND IS THAT SO BAD A THING...

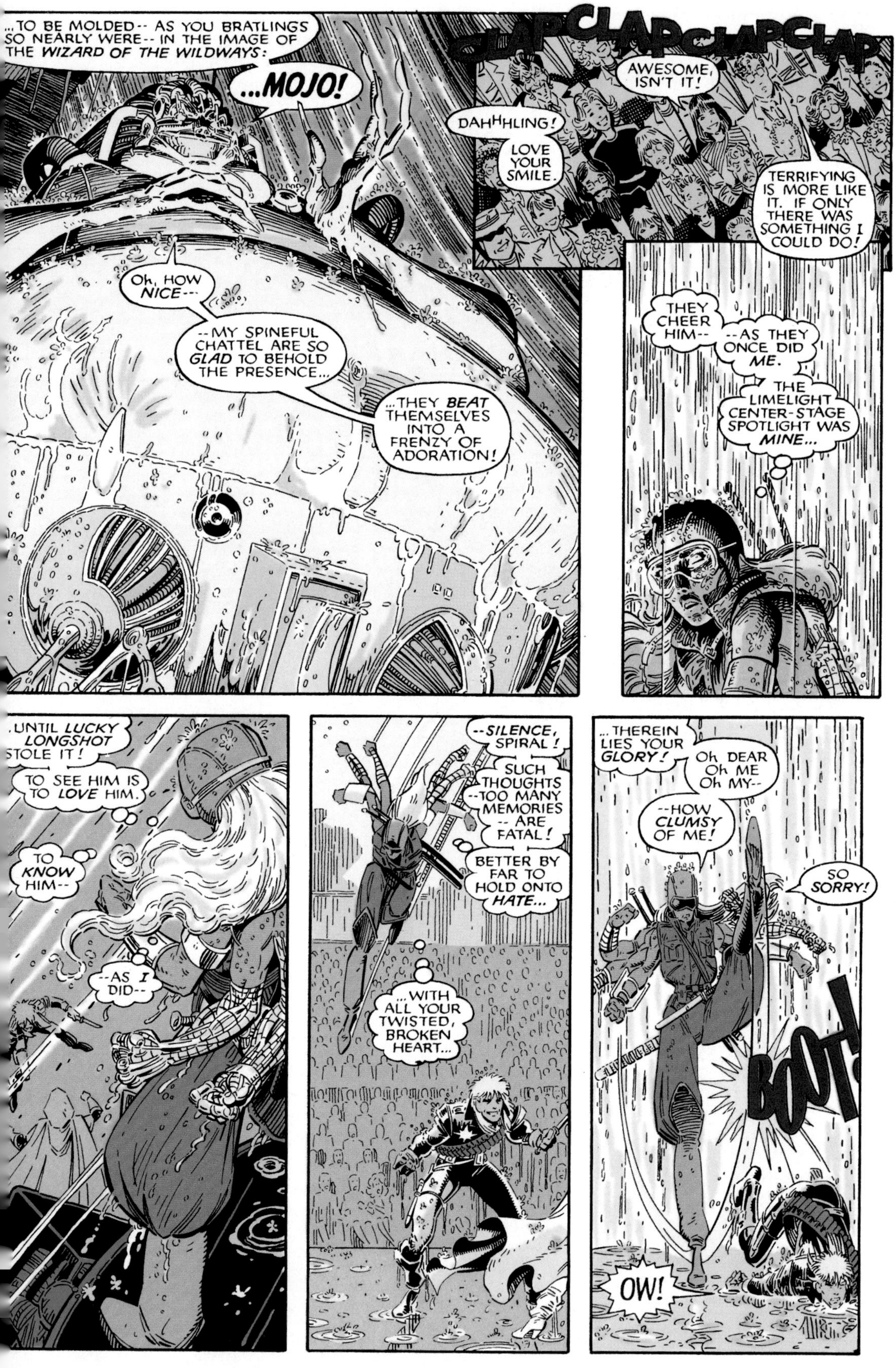

...TO BE MOLDED-- AS YOU BRATLINGS SO NEARLY WERE-- IN THE IMAGE OF THE WIZARD OF THE WILDWAYS:
...MOJO!
Oh, HOW NICE---
--MY SPINEFUL CHATTEL ARE SO GLAD TO BEHOLD THE PRESENCE...
...THEY BEAT THEMSELVES INTO A FRENZY OF ADORATION!
CLAPCLAPCLAPCLAP
AWESOME, ISN'T IT!
DAHHHLING!
LOVE YOUR SMILE.
TERRIFYING IS MORE LIKE IT. IF ONLY THERE WAS SOMETHING I COULD DO!
THEY CHEER HIM--
--AS THEY ONCE DID ME.
THE LIMELIGHT CENTER-STAGE SPOTLIGHT WAS MINE...
...UNTIL LUCKY LONGSHOT STOLE IT!
TO SEE HIM IS TO LOVE HIM.
TO KNOW HIM--
--AS I DID--
--SILENCE, SPIRAL!
SUCH THOUGHTS --TOO MANY MEMORIES -- ARE FATAL!
BETTER BY FAR TO HOLD ONTO HATE...
...WITH ALL YOUR TWISTED, BROKEN HEART...
...THEREIN LIES YOUR GLORY!
Oh DEAR Oh ME Oh MY--
--HOW CLUMSY OF ME!
SO SORRY!
BOOT!
OW!

NAUGHTY DANCER!

SNAP

PLINK

I DON'T REMEMBER...

...PUTTING *THAT* IN THE CHOREOGRAPHY.

COULD YOU HAVE FORGOTTEN...

...YOU'RE ONLY AS *FREE* AN AGENT...

...AS *I* ALLOW?

PLINK

THAT'S BETTER. NOW YOU LOOK HAPPILY PLEASED--

--AS WELL YOU SHOULD--

--TO DISCOVER HOW *ABSOLUTE* MY CONTROL IS...

...OVER YOUR POWERS AND YOUR LIFE!

SOARED TO THE *HEIGHTS* YOU HAVE, LITTLE SCHEMING SCREAMER.

BUT NEVER FORGET WHO CAST YOU UP...

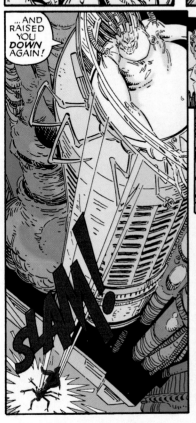

...AND RAISED YOU *DOWN* AGAIN!

SLAM!

RIP CITY!

OH, MY!

MAXIMUM SLASH AN' *BURN!*

CARRIE, THIS ISN'T FUN ANYMORE.

WHO *SAID THAT?!!*

HOW *DARE* YOU TURN YOUR HEARTS AGAINST ME?!

MY PETS, BRING THEM TO ME--*EACH AND EVERY ONE!*

JUST THE *HEARTS,* MIND YOU.

LEAVE THE SHELLS BEHIND.

HE *MEANS* IT!

MOJO WANTS THE X-MEN TO *SLAUGHTER* THE WHOLE AUDIENCE--

--AND, ENTRANCED AS THEY ARE, THEY *WILL!*

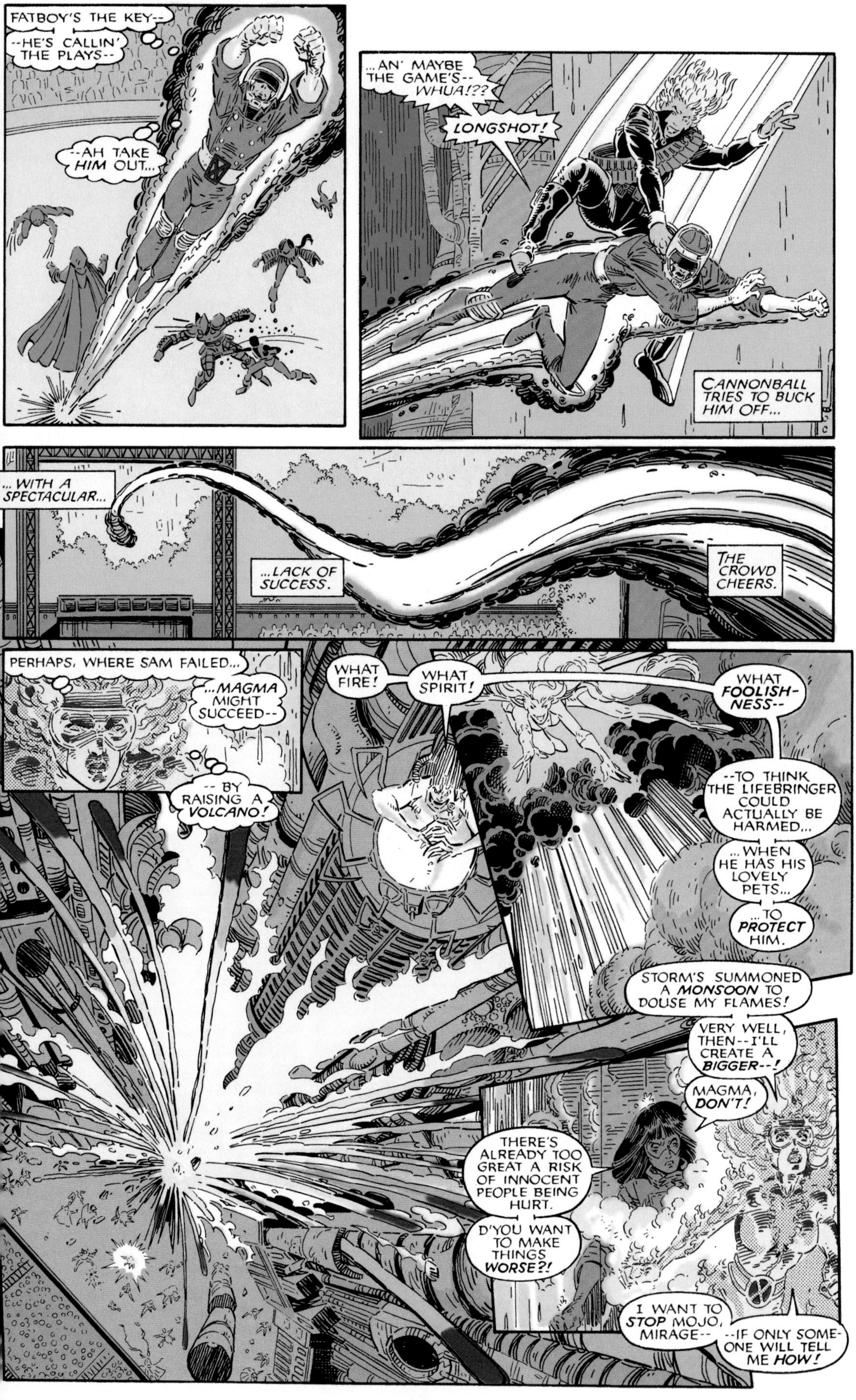
FATBOY'S THE KEY--
--HE'S CALLIN' THE PLAYS--
--AH TAKE HIM OUT...
...AN' MAYBE THE GAME'S-- WHUA!??
LONGSHOT!
CANNONBALL TRIES TO BUCK HIM OFF...
...WITH A SPECTACULAR...
...LACK OF SUCCESS.
THE CROWD CHEERS.
PERHAPS, WHERE SAM FAILED...
...MAGMA MIGHT SUCCEED--
-- BY RAISING A VOLCANO!
WHAT FIRE!
WHAT SPIRIT!
WHAT FOOLISHNESS--
--TO THINK THE LIFEBRINGER COULD ACTUALLY BE HARMED...
...WHEN HE HAS HIS LOVELY PETS...
...TO PROTECT HIM.
STORM'S SUMMONED A MONSOON TO DOUSE MY FLAMES!
VERY WELL, THEN--I'LL CREATE A BIGGER--!
MAGMA, DON'T!
THERE'S ALREADY TOO GREAT A RISK OF INNOCENT PEOPLE BEING HURT.
D'YOU WANT TO MAKE THINGS WORSE?!
I WANT TO STOP MOJO, MIRAGE--
--IF ONLY SOMEONE WILL TELL ME HOW!

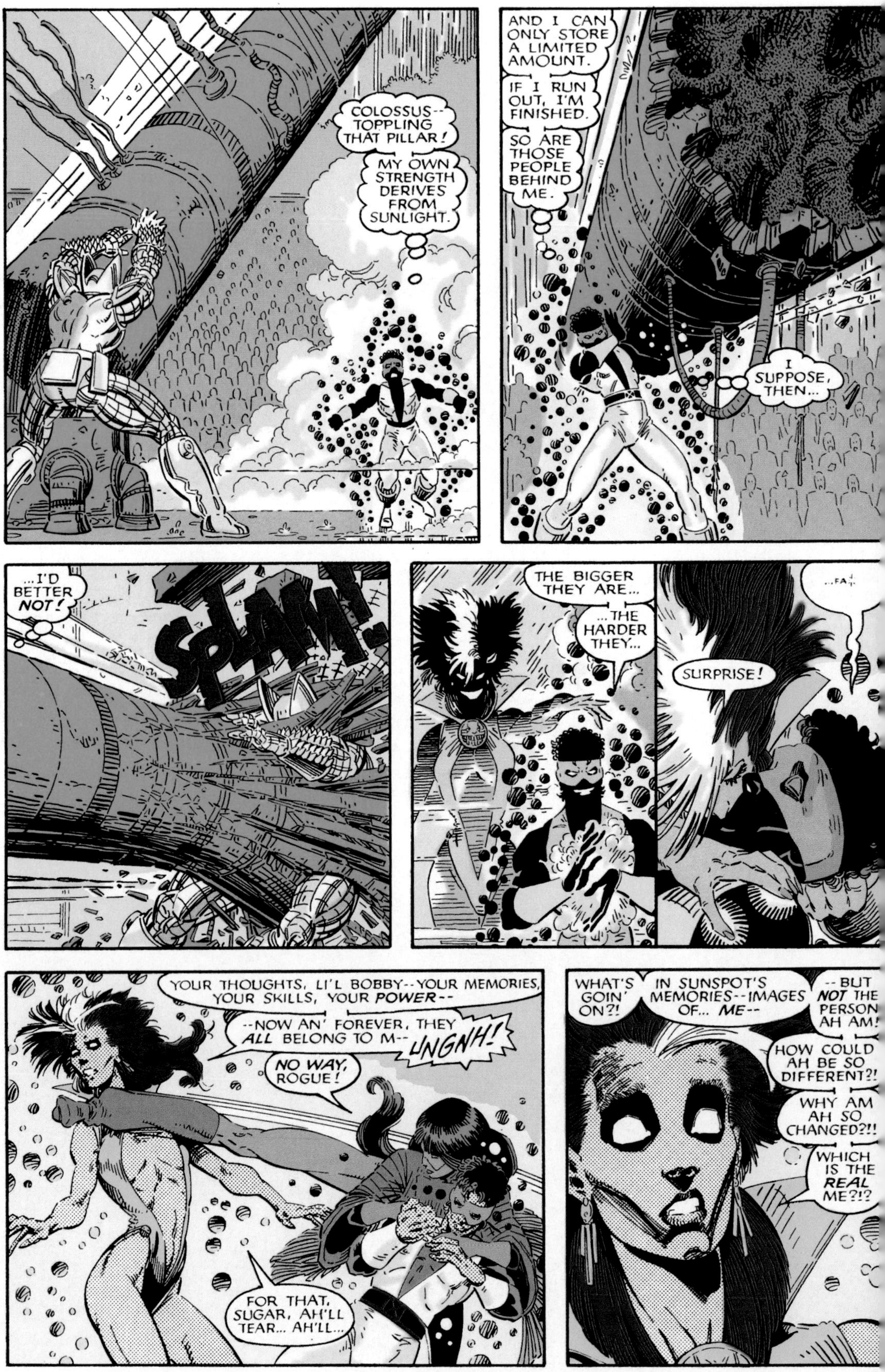

COLOSSUS-- TOPPLING THAT PILLAR!
MY OWN STRENGTH DERIVES FROM SUNLIGHT.
AND I CAN ONLY STORE A LIMITED AMOUNT.
IF I RUN OUT, I'M FINISHED.
SO ARE THOSE PEOPLE BEHIND ME.
I SUPPOSE, THEN...
...I'D BETTER NOT!
SPLAM!
THE BIGGER THEY ARE...
...THE HARDER THEY...
SURPRISE!
YOUR THOUGHTS, LI'L BOBBY--YOUR MEMORIES, YOUR SKILLS, YOUR POWER--
--NOW AN' FOREVER, THEY ALL BELONG TO M-- UNGNH!
NO WAY, ROGUE!
FOR THAT, SUGAR, AH'LL TEAR... AH'LL...
WHAT'S GOIN' ON?!
IN SUNSPOT'S MEMORIES--IMAGES OF... ME--
--BUT NOT THE PERSON AH AM!
HOW COULD AH BE SO DIFFERENT?!
WHY AM AH SO CHANGED?!!
WHICH IS THE REAL ME?!?

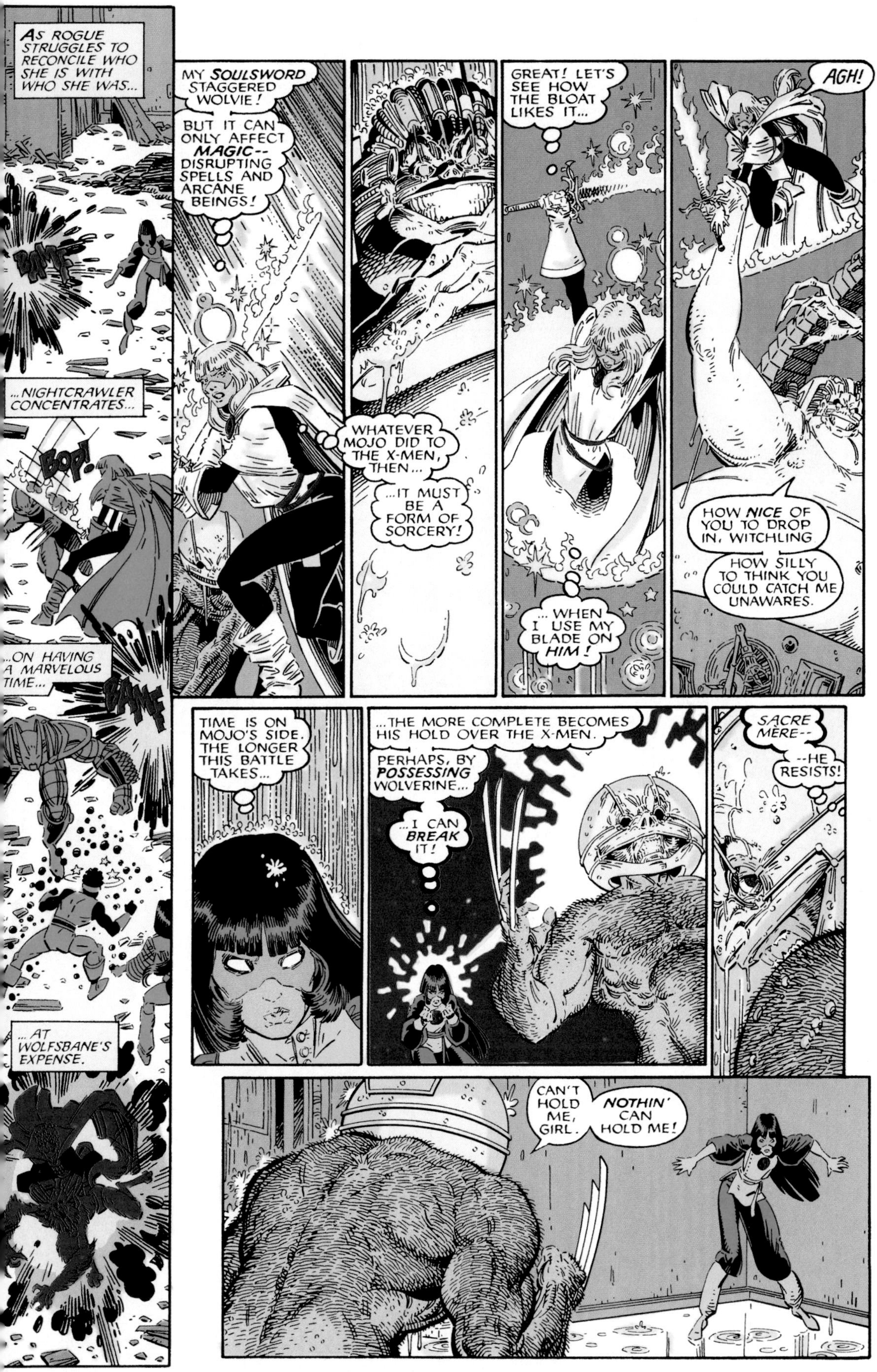
AS ROGUE STRUGGLES TO RECONCILE WHO SHE IS WITH WHO SHE WAS...
BAMF
...NIGHTCRAWLER CONCENTRATES...
BOP!
...ON HAVING A MARVELOUS TIME...
BAMF
...AT WOLFSBANE'S EXPENSE.
MY SOULSWORD STAGGERED WOLVIE!
BUT IT CAN ONLY AFFECT MAGIC--DISRUPTING SPELLS AND ARCANE BEINGS!
WHATEVER MOJO DID TO THE X-MEN, THEN...
...IT MUST BE A FORM OF SORCERY!
GREAT! LET'S SEE HOW THE BLOAT LIKES IT...
...WHEN I USE MY BLADE ON HIM!
AGH!
HOW NICE OF YOU TO DROP IN, WITCHLING
HOW SILLY TO THINK YOU COULD CATCH ME UNAWARES.
TIME IS ON MOJO'S SIDE. THE LONGER THIS BATTLE TAKES...
...THE MORE COMPLETE BECOMES HIS HOLD OVER THE X-MEN.
PERHAPS, BY POSSESSING WOLVERINE...
...I CAN BREAK IT!
SACRE MÈRE--
--HE RESISTS!
CAN'T HOLD ME, GIRL.
NOTHIN' CAN HOLD ME!

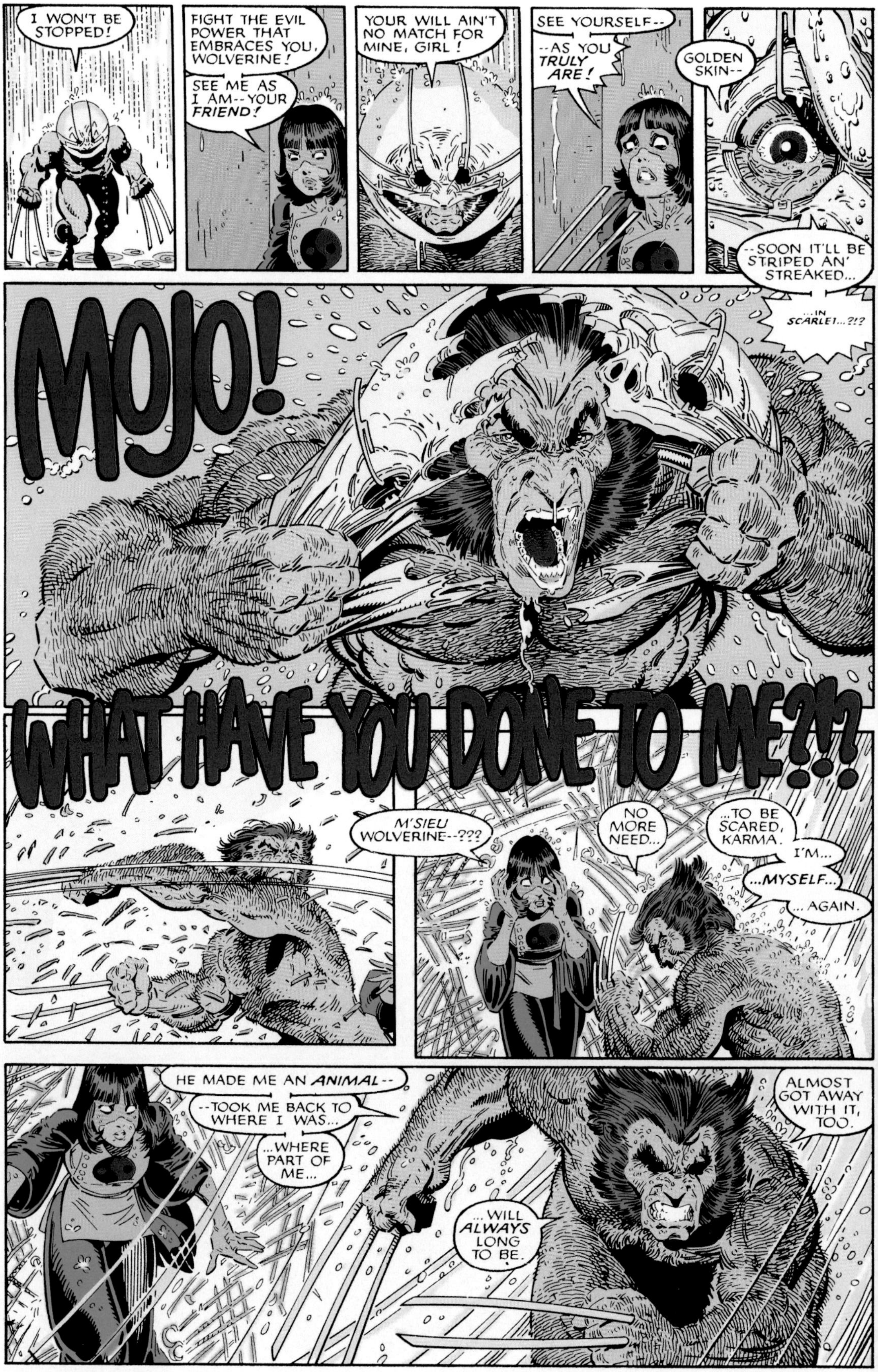

I WON'T BE STOPPED!
FIGHT THE EVIL POWER THAT EMBRACES YOU, WOLVERINE!
SEE ME AS I AM--YOUR FRIEND!
YOUR WILL AIN'T NO MATCH FOR MINE, GIRL!
SEE YOURSELF--
--AS YOU TRULY ARE!
GOLDEN SKIN--
--SOON IT'LL BE STRIPED AN' STREAKED...
...IN SCARLET...?!?
MOJO!
WHAT HAVE YOU DONE TO ME?!?
M'SIEU WOLVERINE--???
NO MORE NEED...
...TO BE SCARED, KARMA.
I'M...
...MYSELF...
...AGAIN.
HE MADE ME AN ANIMAL--
--TOOK ME BACK TO WHERE I WAS...
...WHERE PART OF ME...
...WILL ALWAYS LONG TO BE.
ALMOST GOT AWAY WITH IT, TOO.

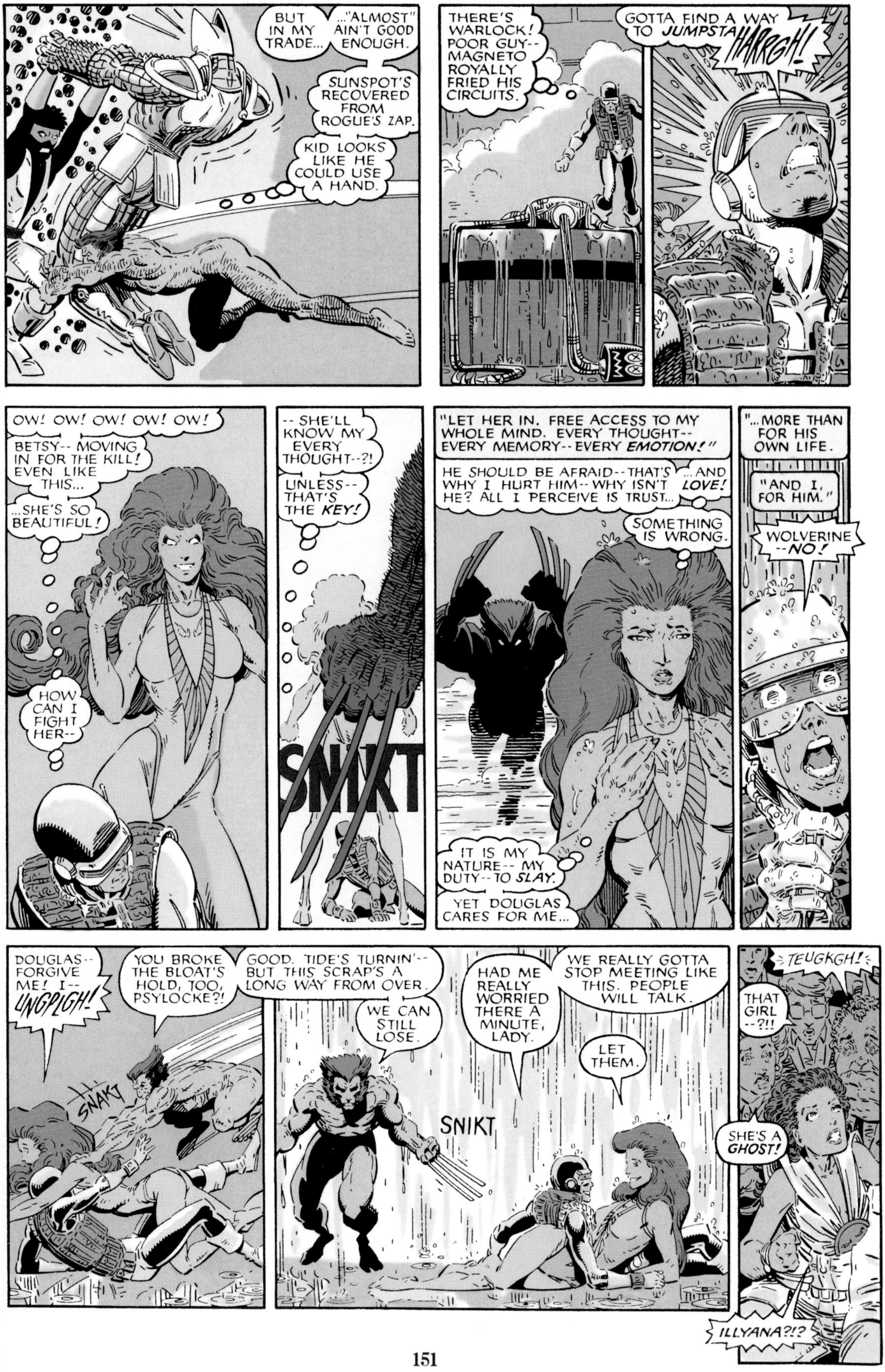
BUT IN MY TRADE...
..."ALMOST" AIN'T GOOD ENOUGH.
SUNSPOT'S RECOVERED FROM ROGUE'S ZAP.
KID LOOKS LIKE HE COULD USE A HAND.
THERE'S WARLOCK! POOR GUY-- MAGNETO ROYALLY FRIED HIS CIRCUITS.
GOTTA FIND A WAY TO JUMPSTA
HARRGH!
OW! OW! OW! OW! OW!
BETSY-- MOVING IN FOR THE KILL! EVEN LIKE THIS...
...SHE'S SO BEAUTIFUL!
HOW CAN I FIGHT HER--
-- SHE'LL KNOW MY EVERY THOUGHT--?!
UNLESS-- THAT'S THE KEY!
SNIKT
"LET HER IN. FREE ACCESS TO MY WHOLE MIND. EVERY THOUGHT-- EVERY MEMORY-- EVERY EMOTION!"
HE SHOULD BE AFRAID--THAT'S WHY I HURT HIM--WHY ISN'T HE? ALL I PERCEIVE IS TRUST...
...AND LOVE!
SOMETHING IS WRONG.
IT IS MY NATURE-- MY DUTY-- TO SLAY.
YET DOUGLAS CARES FOR ME...
"...MORE THAN FOR HIS OWN LIFE.
"AND I, FOR HIM."
WOLVERINE --NO!
DOUGLAS-- FORGIVE ME! I-- UNGPLGH!
YOU BROKE THE BLOAT'S HOLD, TOO, PSYLOCKE?!
SNAKT
GOOD. TIDE'S TURNIN'-- BUT THIS SCRAP'S A LONG WAY FROM OVER.
WE CAN STILL LOSE.
HAD ME REALLY WORRIED THERE A MINUTE, LADY.
WE REALLY GOTTA STOP MEETING LIKE THIS. PEOPLE WILL TALK.
LET THEM.
SNIKT
TEUGKGH!
THAT GIRL --?!!
SHE'S A GHOST!
ILLYANA?!?

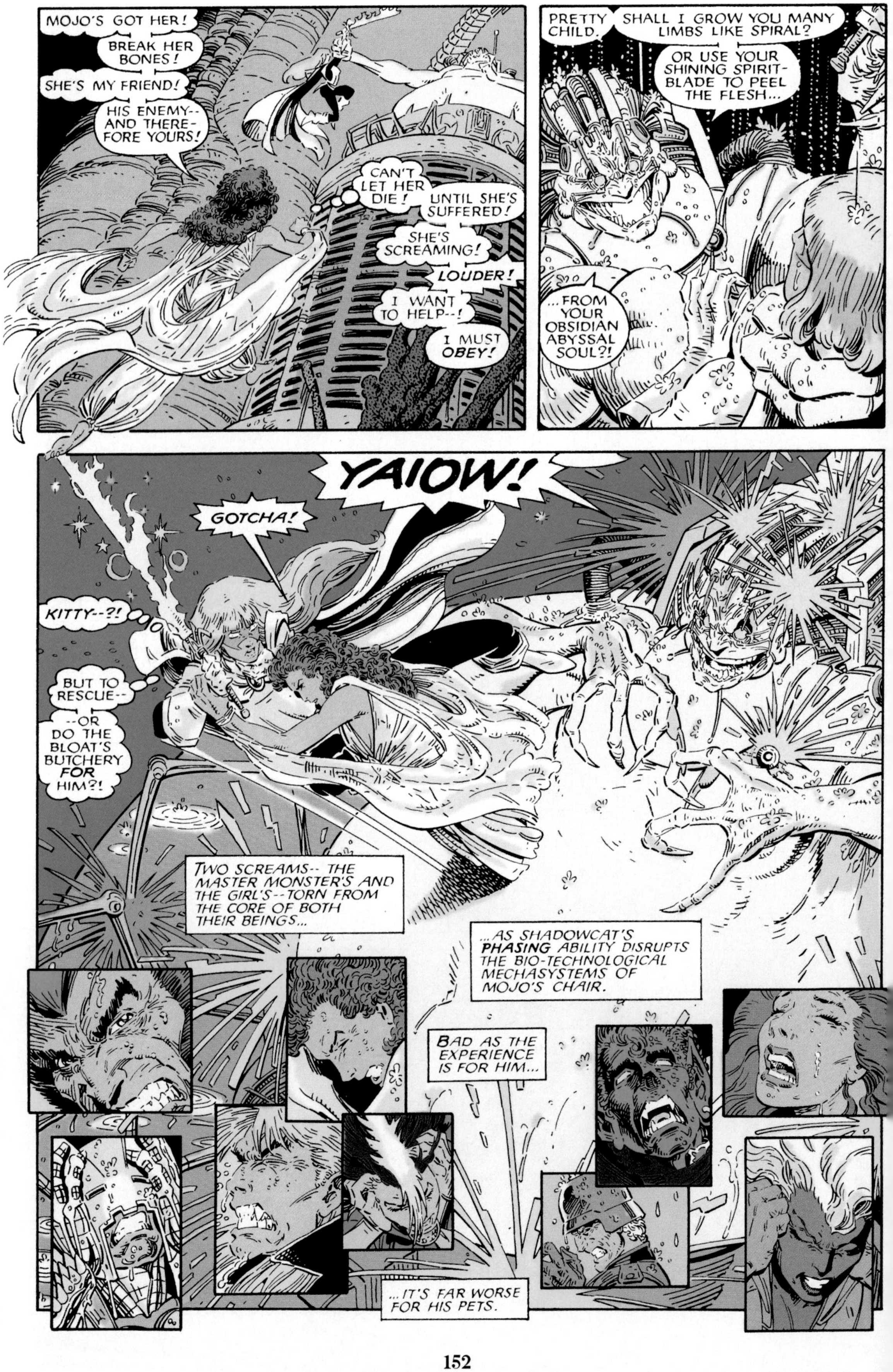
MOJO'S GOT HER!
BREAK HER BONES!
SHE'S MY FRIEND!
HIS ENEMY-- AND THERE-FORE YOURS!
CAN'T LET HER DIE!
UNTIL SHE'S SUFFERED!
SHE'S SCREAMING!
LOUDER!
I WANT TO HELP--!
I MUST OBEY!
PRETTY CHILD.
SHALL I GROW YOU MANY LIMBS LIKE SPIRAL?
OR USE YOUR SHINING SPIRIT-BLADE TO PEEL THE FLESH...
...FROM YOUR OBSIDIAN ABYSSAL SOUL?!
YAIOW!
GOTCHA!
KITTY--?!
BUT TO RESCUE--
--OR DO THE BLOAT'S BUTCHERY FOR HIM?!
TWO SCREAMS-- THE MASTER MONSTER'S AND THE GIRL'S--TORN FROM THE CORE OF BOTH THEIR BEINGS...
...AS SHADOWCAT'S PHASING ABILITY DISRUPTS THE BIO-TECHNOLOGICAL MECHASYSTEMS OF MOJO'S CHAIR.
BAD AS THE EXPERIENCE IS FOR HIM...
...IT'S FAR WORSE FOR HIS PETS.

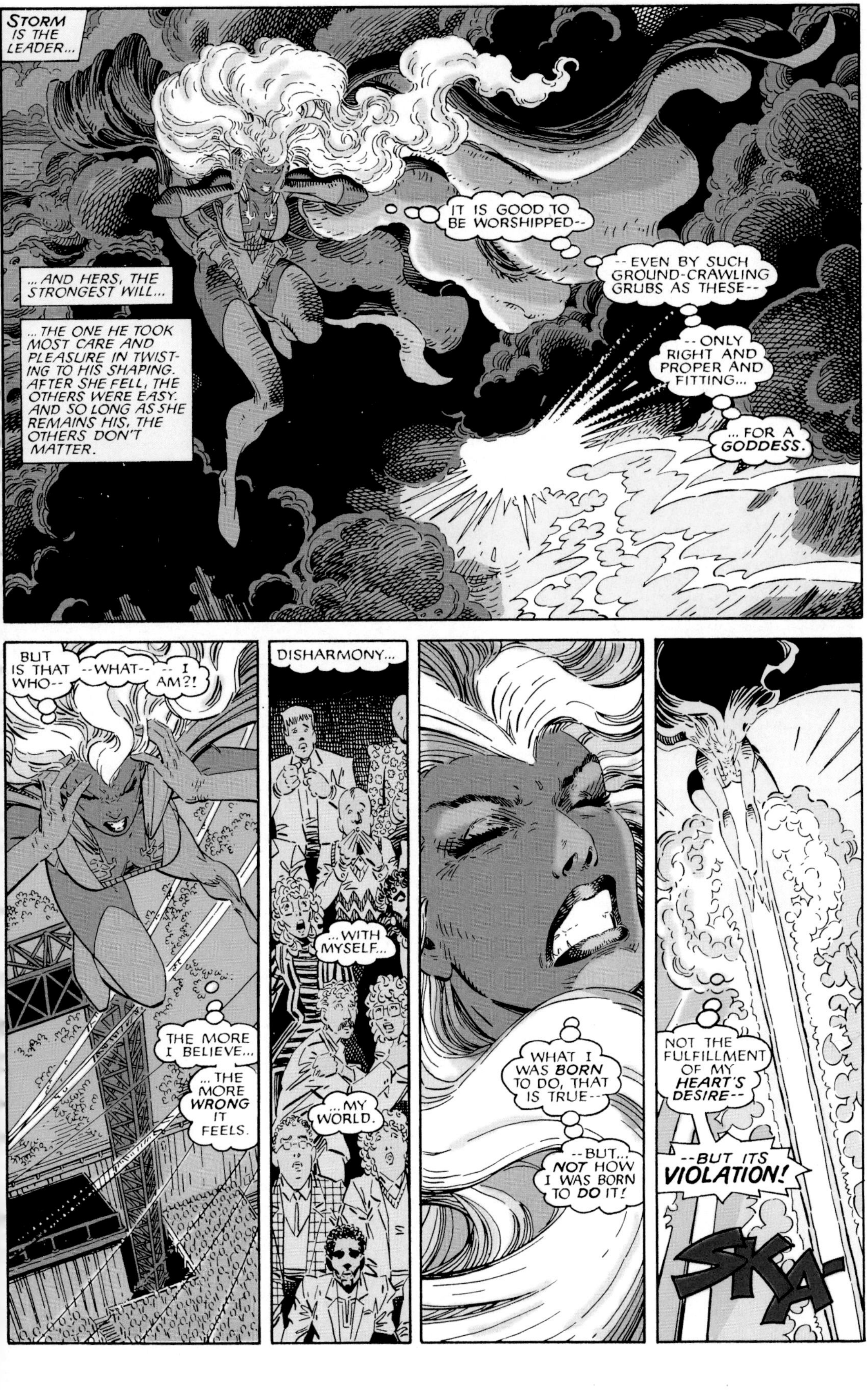
STORM IS THE LEADER...
...AND HERS, THE STRONGEST WILL...
...THE ONE HE TOOK MOST CARE AND PLEASURE IN TWISTING TO HIS SHAPING. AFTER SHE FELL, THE OTHERS WERE EASY. AND SO LONG AS SHE REMAINS HIS, THE OTHERS DON'T MATTER.
IT IS GOOD TO BE WORSHIPPED--
--EVEN BY SUCH GROUND-CRAWLING GRUBS AS THESE--
--ONLY RIGHT AND PROPER AND FITTING...
...FOR A GODDESS.
BUT IS THAT WHO--
--WHAT--
--I AM?!
THE MORE I BELIEVE...
...THE MORE WRONG IT FEELS.
DISHARMONY...
...WITH MYSELF...
...MY WORLD.
WHAT I WAS BORN TO DO, THAT IS TRUE--
--BUT... NOT HOW I WAS BORN TO DO IT!
NOT THE FULFILLMENT OF MY HEART'S DESIRE--
--BUT ITS VIOLATION!
SKA-

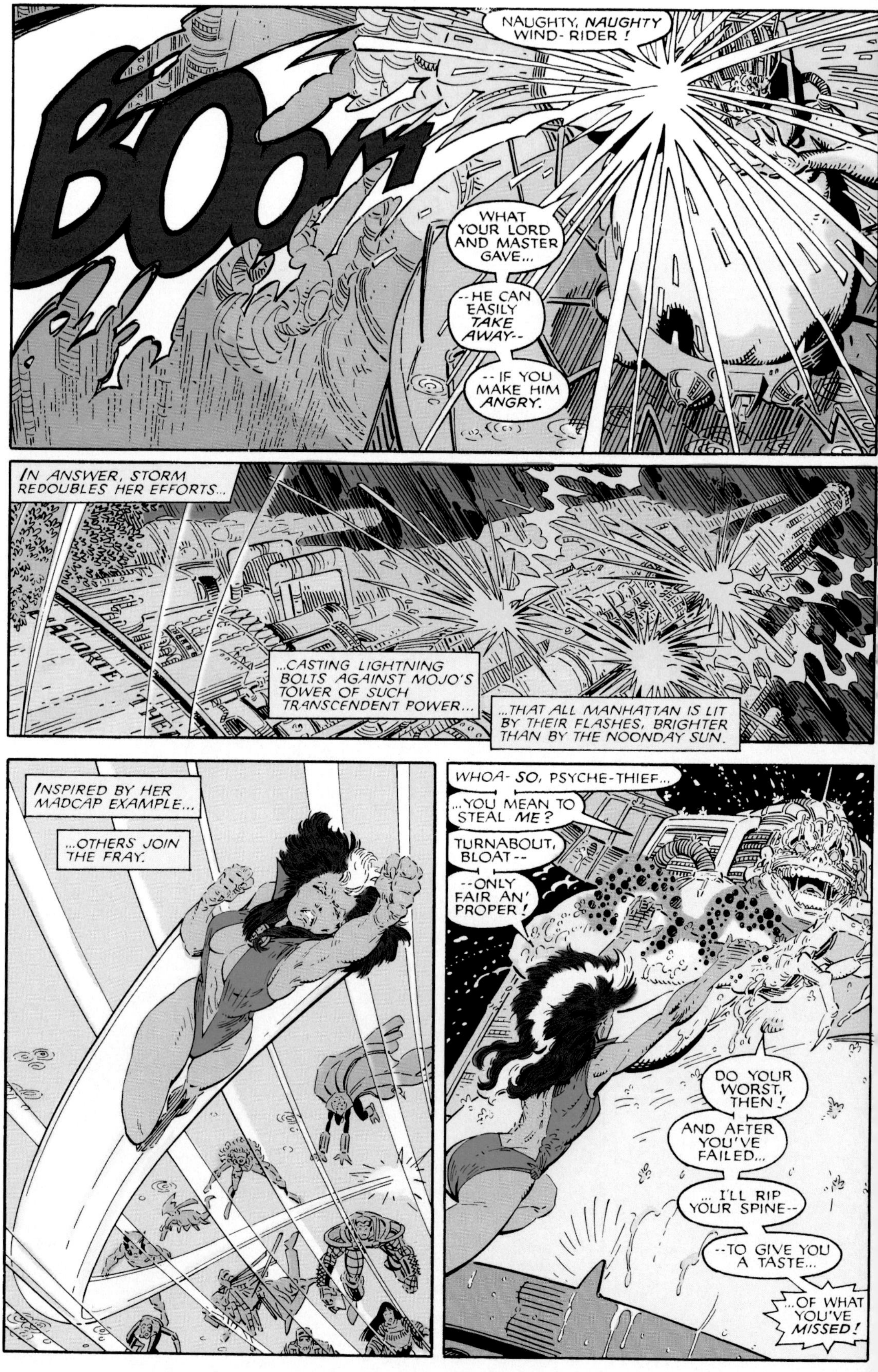
NAUGHTY, NAUGHTY WIND-RIDER!
BOOM
WHAT YOUR LORD AND MASTER GAVE...
--HE CAN EASILY TAKE AWAY--
--IF YOU MAKE HIM ANGRY.
IN ANSWER, STORM REDOUBLES HER EFFORTS...
...CASTING LIGHTNING BOLTS AGAINST MOJO'S TOWER OF SUCH TRANSCENDENT POWER...
...THAT ALL MANHATTAN IS LIT BY THEIR FLASHES, BRIGHTER THAN BY THE NOONDAY SUN.
INSPIRED BY HER MADCAP EXAMPLE...
...OTHERS JOIN THE FRAY.
WHOA-SO, PSYCHE-THIEF...
...YOU MEAN TO STEAL ME?
TURNABOUT, BLOAT--
--ONLY FAIR AN' PROPER!
DO YOUR WORST, THEN!
AND AFTER YOU'VE FAILED...
...I'LL RIP YOUR SPINE--
--TO GIVE YOU A TASTE...
...OF WHAT YOU'VE MISSED!

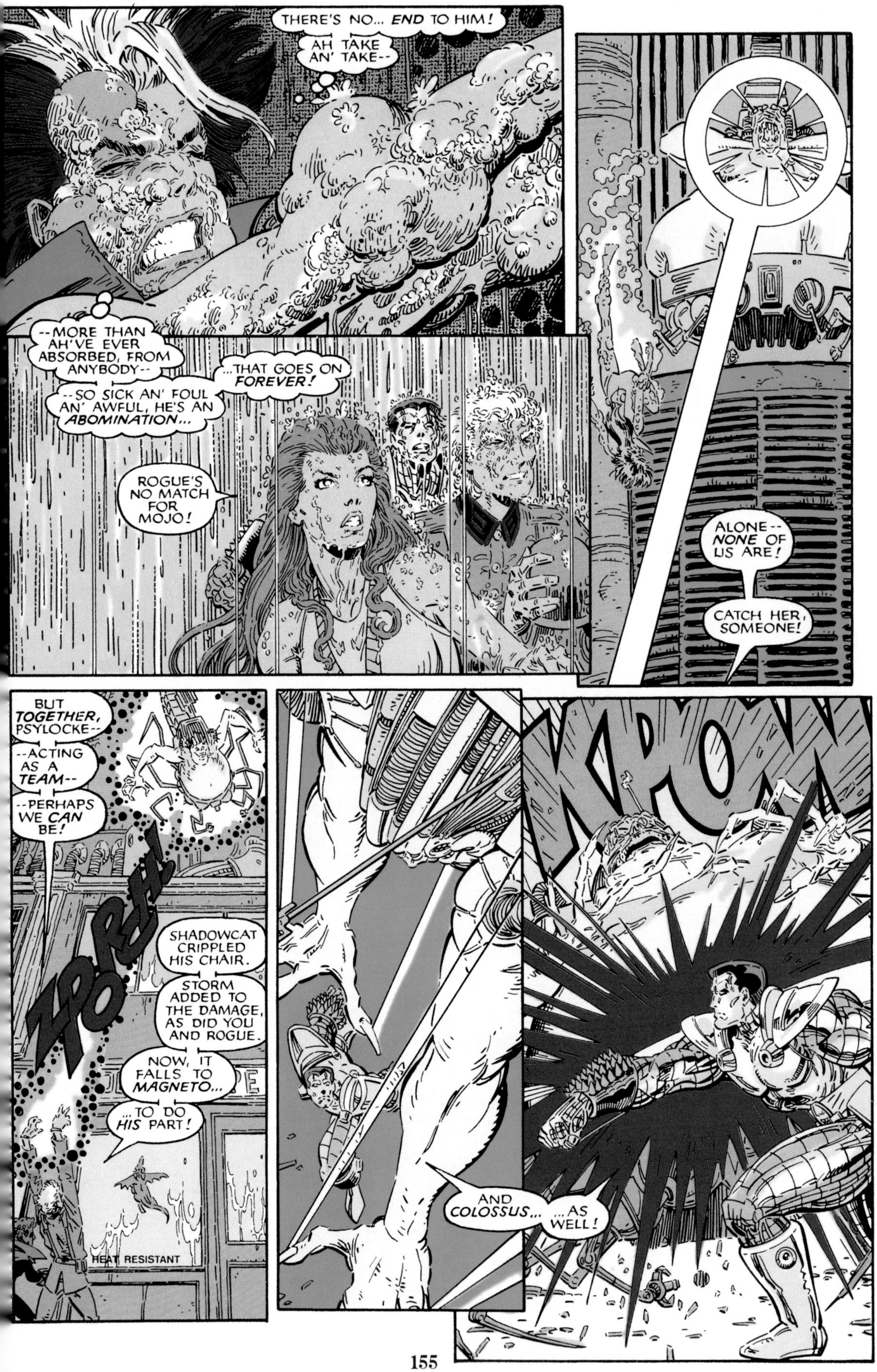
THERE'S NO... END TO HIM!
AH TAKE AN' TAKE--
--MORE THAN AH'VE EVER ABSORBED, FROM ANYBODY--
--SO SICK AN' FOUL AN' AWFUL, HE'S AN ABOMINATION...
...THAT GOES ON FOREVER!
ROGUE'S NO MATCH FOR MOJO!
ALONE-- NONE OF US ARE!
CATCH HER, SOMEONE!
BUT TOGETHER, PSYLOCKE--
--ACTING AS A TEAM--
--PERHAPS WE CAN BE!
ZPORCH!
SHADOWCAT CRIPPLED HIS CHAIR.
STORM ADDED TO THE DAMAGE, AS DID YOU AND ROGUE.
NOW, IT FALLS TO MAGNETO...
...TO DO HIS PART!
HEAT RESISTANT
KPOW
AND COLOSSUS...
...AS WELL!

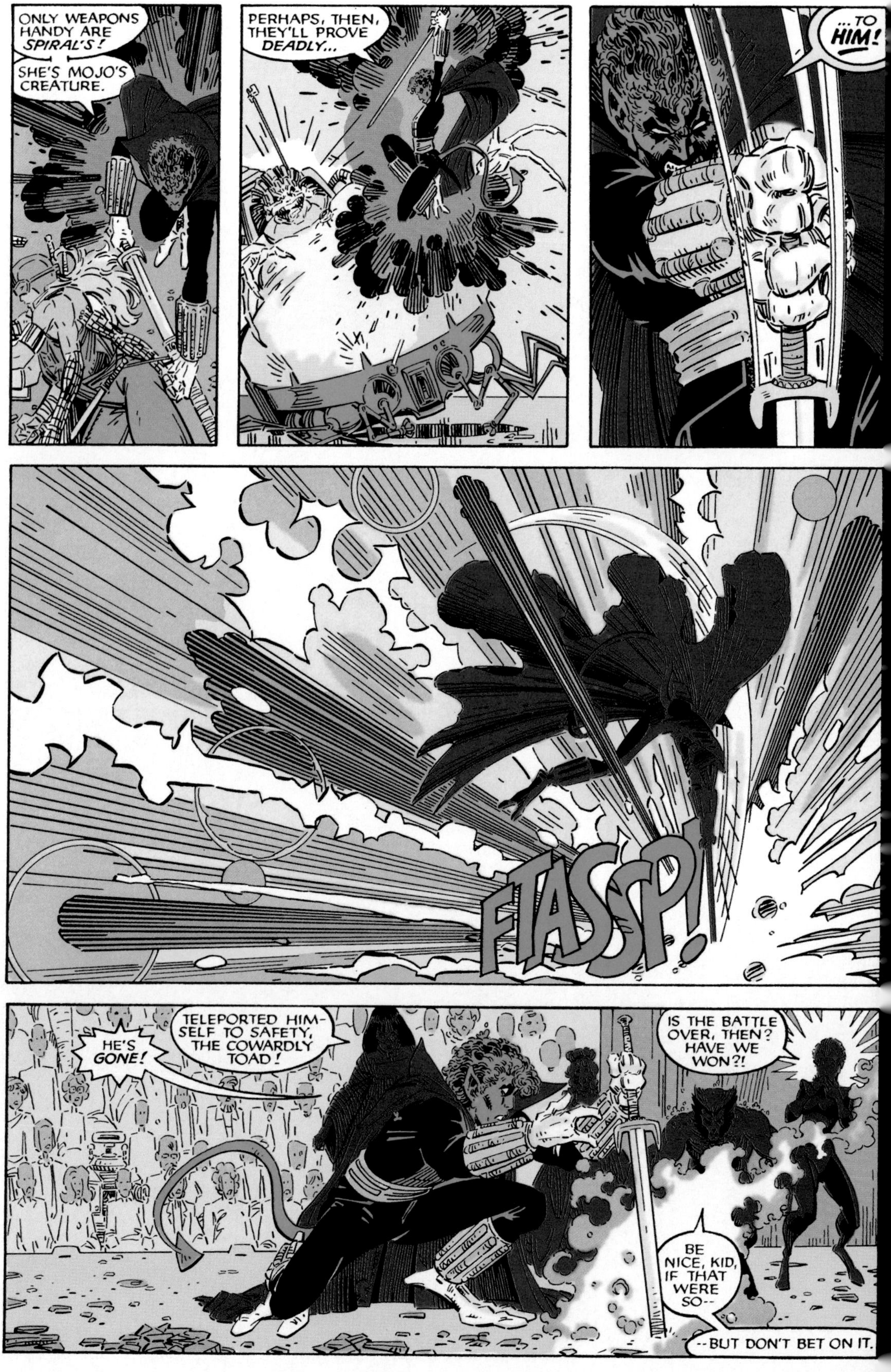
ONLY WEAPONS HANDY ARE SPIRAL'S!
SHE'S MOJO'S CREATURE.
PERHAPS, THEN, THEY'LL PROVE DEADLY...
...TO HIM!
FTASP!
HE'S GONE!
TELEPORTED HIMSELF TO SAFETY, THE COWARDLY TOAD!
IS THE BATTLE OVER, THEN? HAVE WE WON?!
BE NICE, KID, IF THAT WERE SO--
--BUT DON'T BET ON IT.

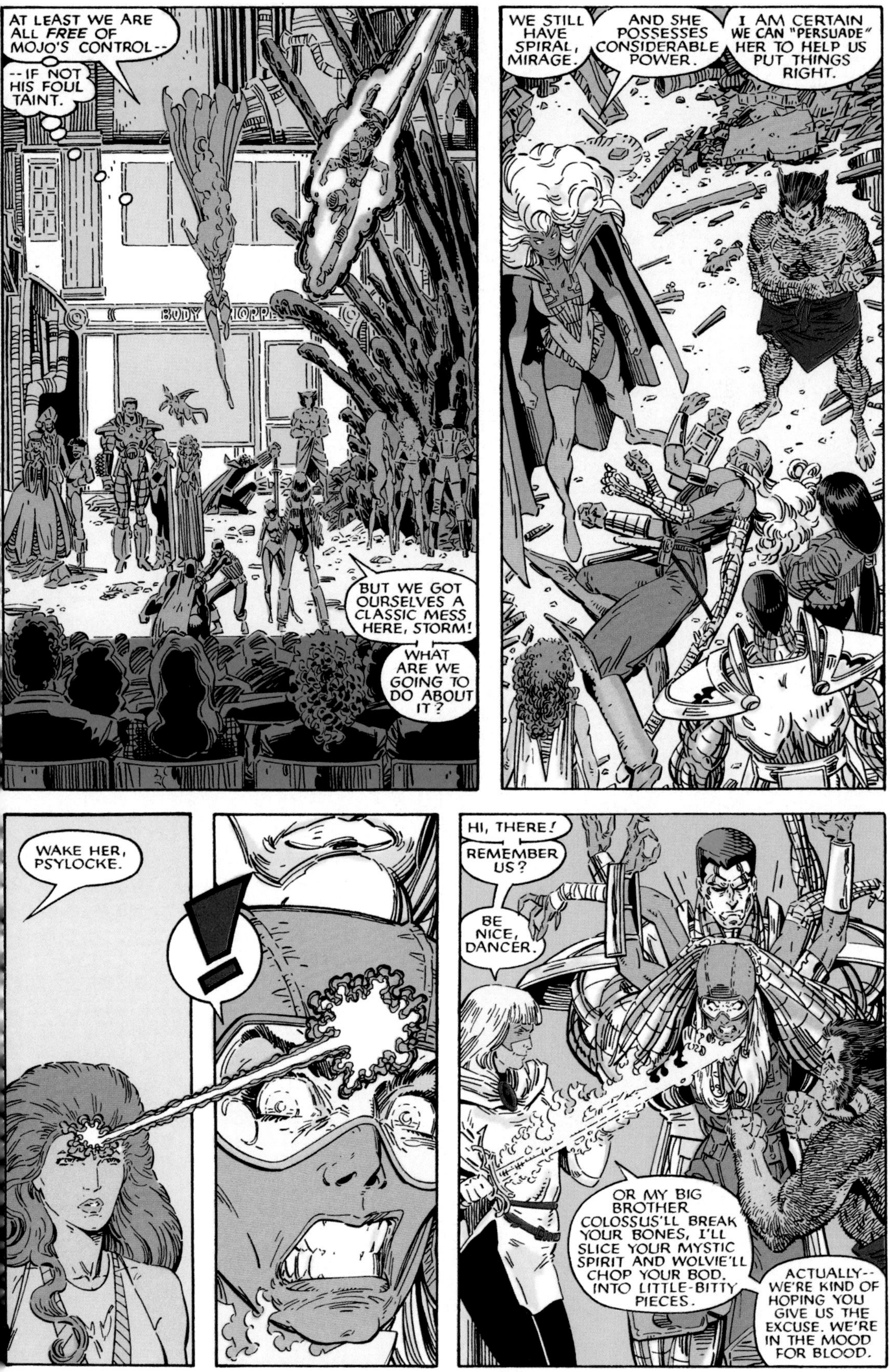
AT LEAST WE ARE ALL FREE OF MOJO'S CONTROL--
--IF NOT HIS FOUL TAINT.
BODY SHOPPE
BUT WE GOT OURSELVES A CLASSIC MESS HERE, STORM!
WHAT ARE WE GOING TO DO ABOUT IT?
WE STILL HAVE SPIRAL, MIRAGE.
AND SHE POSSESSES CONSIDERABLE POWER.
I AM CERTAIN WE CAN "PERSUADE" HER TO HELP US PUT THINGS RIGHT.
WAKE HER, PSYLOCKE.
!
HI, THERE!
REMEMBER US?
BE NICE, DANCER.
OR MY BIG BROTHER COLOSSUS'LL BREAK YOUR BONES, I'LL SLICE YOUR MYSTIC SPIRIT AND WOLVIE'LL CHOP YOUR BOD. INTO LITTLE-BITTY PIECES.
ACTUALLY-- WE'RE KIND OF HOPING YOU GIVE US THE EXCUSE. WE'RE IN THE MOOD FOR BLOOD.

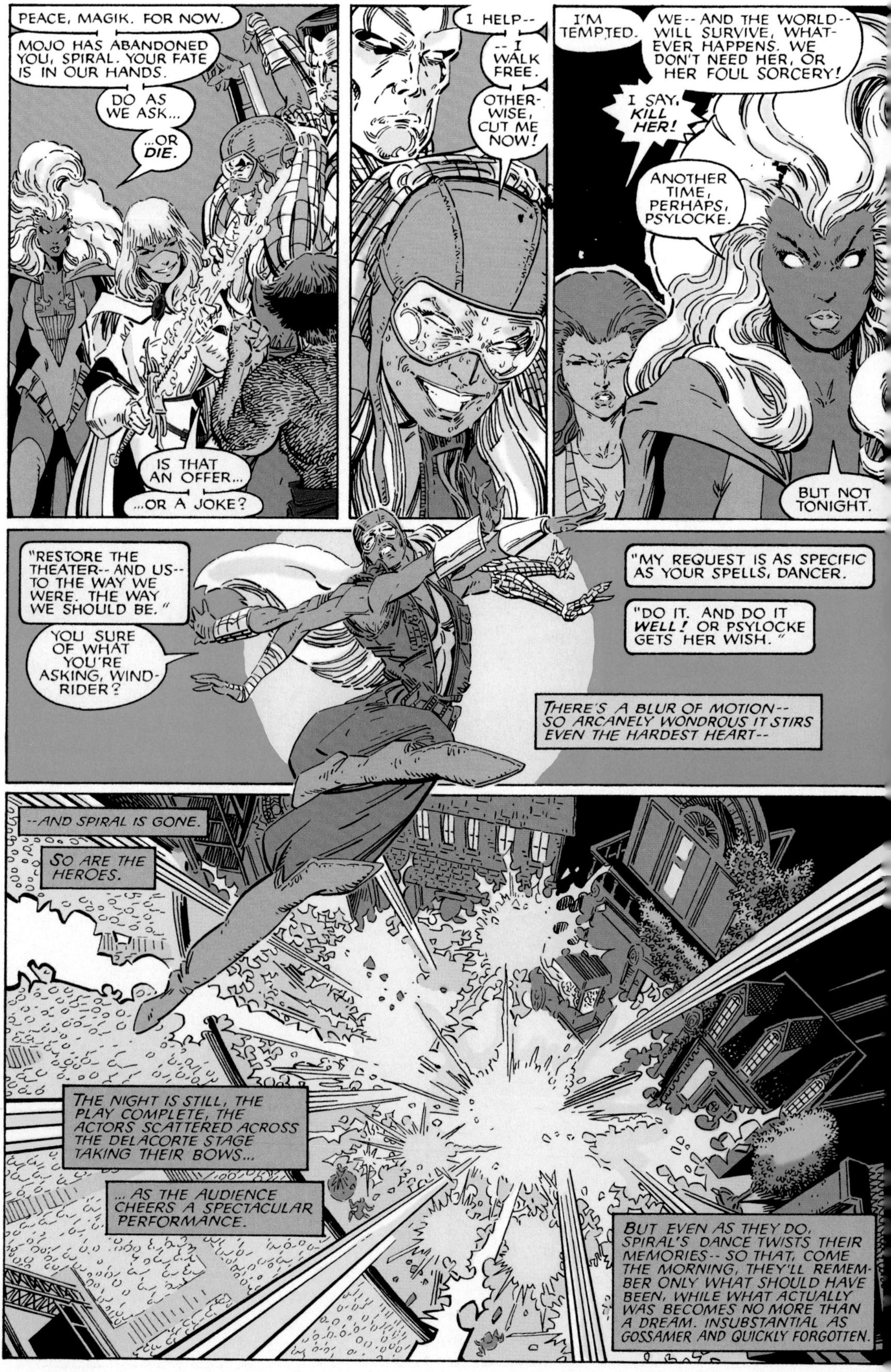
PEACE, MAGIK. FOR NOW.
MOJO HAS ABANDONED YOU, SPIRAL. YOUR FATE IS IN OUR HANDS.
DO AS WE ASK...
...OR DIE.
IS THAT AN OFFER...
...OR A JOKE?
I HELP--
--I WALK FREE.
OTHERWISE, CUT ME NOW!
I'M TEMPTED.
WE--AND THE WORLD--WILL SURVIVE, WHATEVER HAPPENS. WE DON'T NEED HER, OR HER FOUL SORCERY!
I SAY, KILL HER!
ANOTHER TIME, PERHAPS, PSYLOCKE.
BUT NOT TONIGHT.
"RESTORE THE THEATER-- AND US-- TO THE WAY WE WERE. THE WAY WE SHOULD BE."
YOU SURE OF WHAT YOU'RE ASKING, WINDRIDER?
"MY REQUEST IS AS SPECIFIC AS YOUR SPELLS, DANCER.
"DO IT. AND DO IT WELL! OR PSYLOCKE GETS HER WISH."
THERE'S A BLUR OF MOTION-- SO ARCANELY WONDROUS IT STIRS EVEN THE HARDEST HEART--
--AND SPIRAL IS GONE.
SO ARE THE HEROES.
THE NIGHT IS STILL, THE PLAY COMPLETE, THE ACTORS SCATTERED ACROSS THE DELACORTE STAGE TAKING THEIR BOWS...
...AS THE AUDIENCE CHEERS A SPECTACULAR PERFORMANCE.
BUT EVEN AS THEY DO, SPIRAL'S DANCE TWISTS THEIR MEMORIES-- SO THAT, COME THE MORNING, THEY'LL REMEMBER ONLY WHAT SHOULD HAVE BEEN, WHILE WHAT ACTUALLY WAS BECOMES NO MORE THAN A DREAM. INSUBSTANTIAL AS GOSSAMER AND QUICKLY FORGOTTEN.

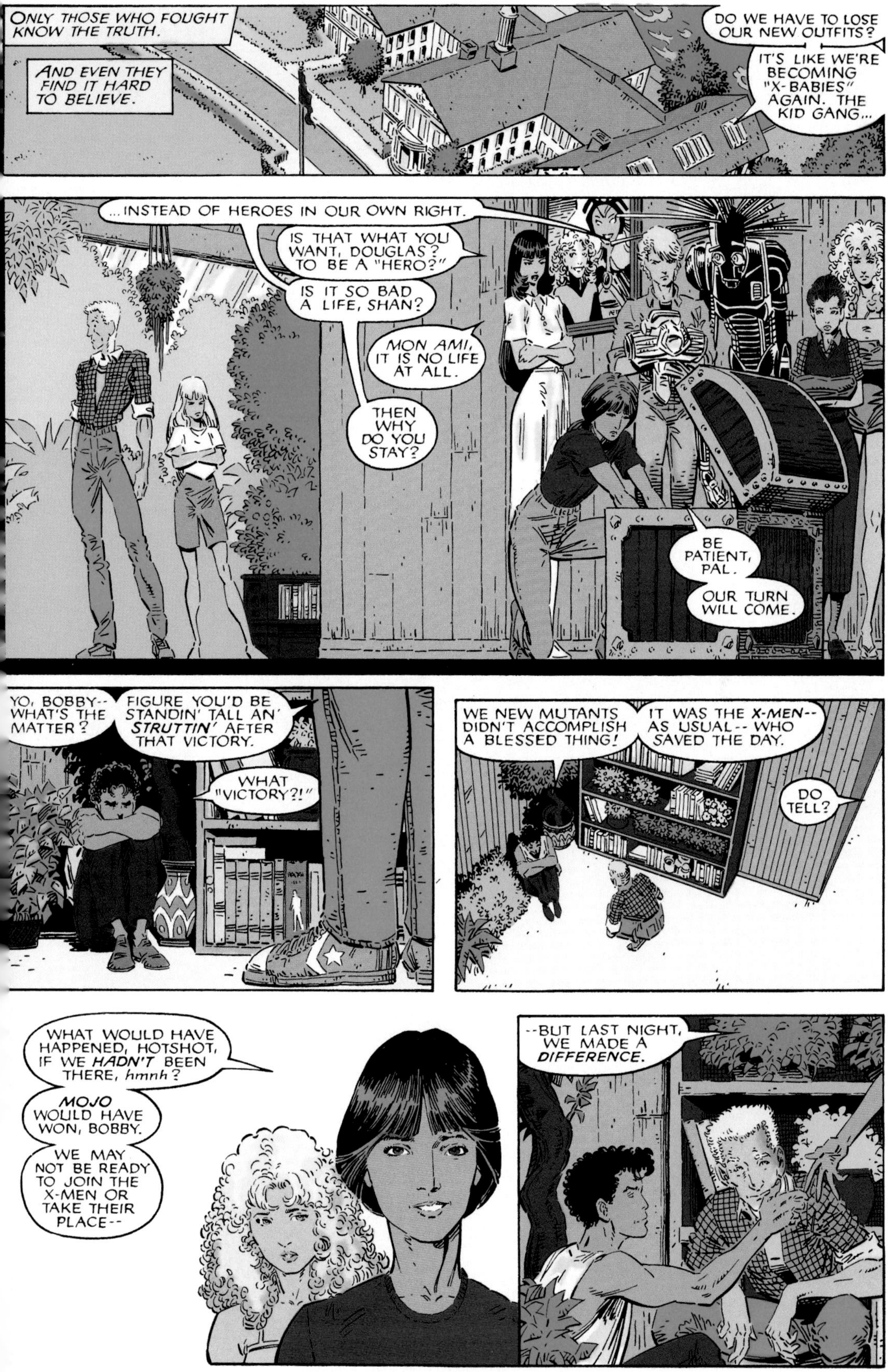

ONLY THOSE WHO FOUGHT KNOW THE TRUTH.
AND EVEN THEY FIND IT HARD TO BELIEVE.
DO WE HAVE TO LOSE OUR NEW OUTFITS?
IT'S LIKE WE'RE BECOMING "X-BABIES" AGAIN. THE KID GANG...
...INSTEAD OF HEROES IN OUR OWN RIGHT.
IS THAT WHAT YOU WANT, DOUGLAS? TO BE A "HERO?"
IS IT SO BAD A LIFE, SHAN?
MON AMI, IT IS NO LIFE AT ALL.
THEN WHY DO YOU STAY?
BE PATIENT, PAL.
OUR TURN WILL COME.
YO, BOBBY-- WHAT'S THE MATTER?
FIGURE YOU'D BE STANDIN' TALL AN' STRUTTIN' AFTER THAT VICTORY.
WHAT "VICTORY?!"
WE NEW MUTANTS DIDN'T ACCOMPLISH A BLESSED THING!
IT WAS THE X-MEN-- AS USUAL-- WHO SAVED THE DAY.
DO TELL?
WHAT WOULD HAVE HAPPENED, HOTSHOT, IF WE HADN'T BEEN THERE, hmnh?
MOJO WOULD HAVE WON, BOBBY.
WE MAY NOT BE READY TO JOIN THE X-MEN OR TAKE THEIR PLACE--
--BUT LAST NIGHT, WE MADE A DIFFERENCE.

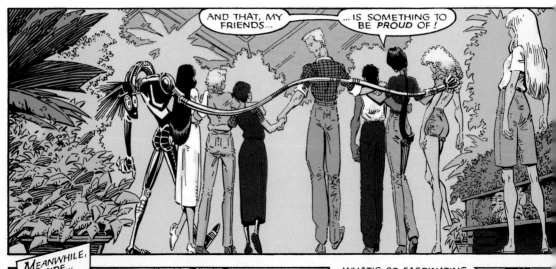

AND THAT, MY FRIENDS...

...IS SOMETHING TO BE *PROUD* OF!

MEANWHILE, OUTSIDE...

LOOK OUT BELOW!

GL/AEOULPP!

MUNCHIES HERE, *KAMERADEN,* IF ANYONE'S INTERESTED!

BAMF!

WHAT'S SO FASCINATING, LONGSHOT?

THE FLOOR... ...MOVES.

THAT'S BECAUSE IT'S *WATER.*

TRANSITIONAL STATE BETWEEN GAS AND SOLID.

CARE FOR A *CLOSER* LOOK?

BOOT!

SPLASH!

A LOVELY TIME IS BEING HAD BY ALL.

NORMAL HORSE-PLAY, ON A NORMAL AFTERNOON--

--AS IF NOTHING UNTOWARD HAD HAPPENED TO US.

DOES THAT BETOKEN RESILIENCE, I WONDER--

--OR CALLOUSNESS?

HULLO, STORM.

HI, DARLIN'!

I CAN SEE WHY WOLVERINE SAYS THIS IS YOUR FAVORITE SPOT-- THE VIEW IS MAGNIFICENT!

WHY, ORORO-- YOU'VE CUT YOUR HAIR!?!

THE STYLE SUITS ME.

AND IF I GROW IT BACK, IT SHALL BE BY *MY* CHOICE, NOT MOJO'S.

SO EVERYTHING'S BACK THE WAY IT WAS, THEN?

EVERYTHING. WHEN SPIRAL WOVE HER MAGIC DANCE...

...SHE STRIPPED ME OF MY ELEMENTAL POWERS.

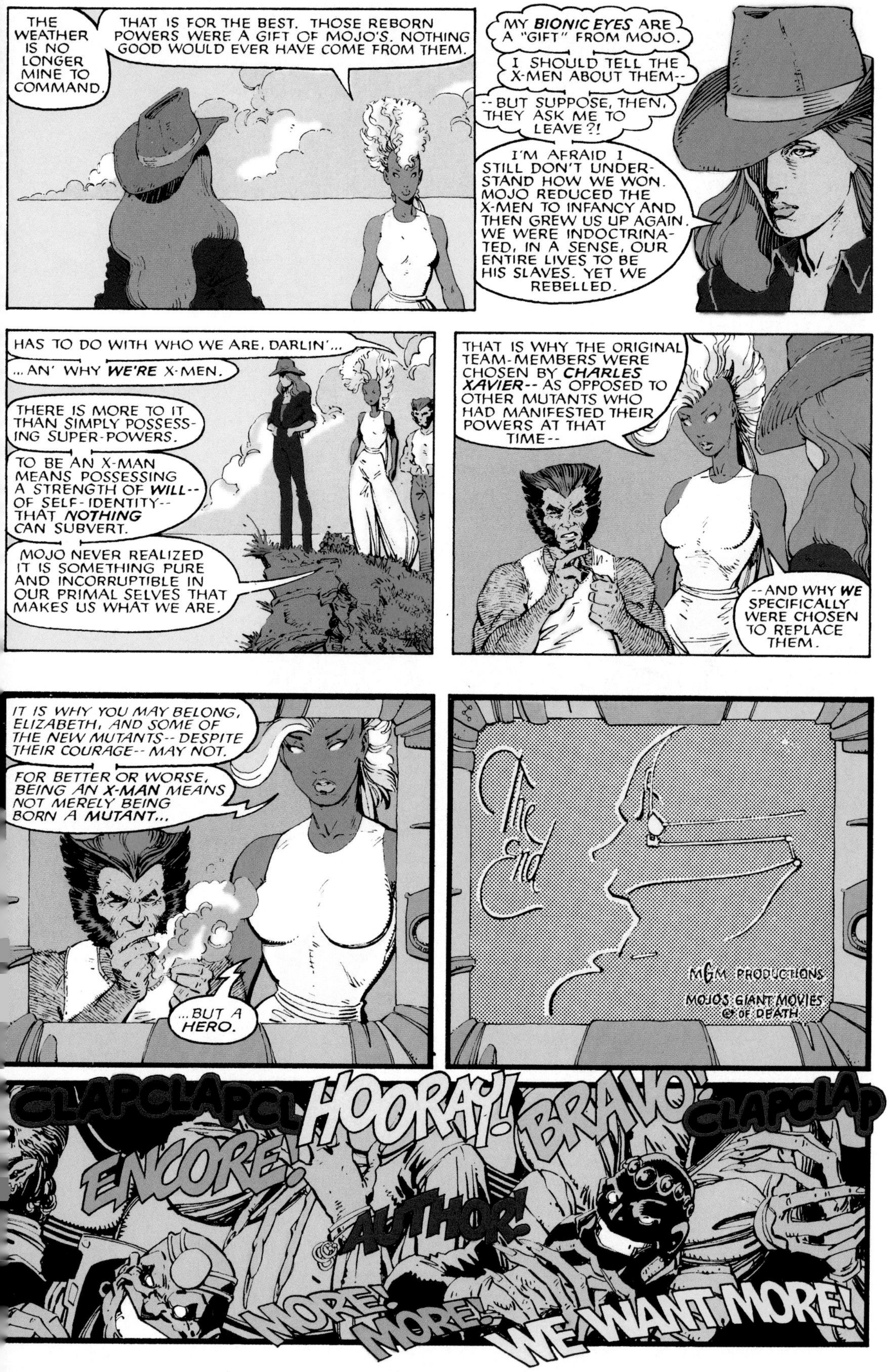
THE WEATHER IS NO LONGER MINE TO COMMAND.
THAT IS FOR THE BEST. THOSE REBORN POWERS WERE A GIFT OF MOJO'S. NOTHING GOOD WOULD EVER HAVE COME FROM THEM.
MY BIONIC EYES ARE A "GIFT" FROM MOJO.
I SHOULD TELL THE X-MEN ABOUT THEM--
--BUT SUPPOSE, THEN, THEY ASK ME TO LEAVE?!
I'M AFRAID I STILL DON'T UNDERSTAND HOW WE WON. MOJO REDUCED THE X-MEN TO INFANCY AND THEN GREW US UP AGAIN. WE WERE INDOCTRINATED, IN A SENSE, OUR ENTIRE LIVES TO BE HIS SLAVES. YET WE REBELLED.
HAS TO DO WITH WHO WE ARE, DARLIN'...
...AN' WHY WE'RE X-MEN.
THERE IS MORE TO IT THAN SIMPLY POSSESSING SUPER-POWERS.
TO BE AN X-MAN MEANS POSSESSING A STRENGTH OF WILL-- OF SELF-IDENTITY-- THAT NOTHING CAN SUBVERT.
MOJO NEVER REALIZED IT IS SOMETHING PURE AND INCORRUPTIBLE IN OUR PRIMAL SELVES THAT MAKES US WHAT WE ARE.
THAT IS WHY THE ORIGINAL TEAM-MEMBERS WERE CHOSEN BY CHARLES XAVIER-- AS OPPOSED TO OTHER MUTANTS WHO HAD MANIFESTED THEIR POWERS AT THAT TIME--
--AND WHY WE SPECIFICALLY WERE CHOSEN TO REPLACE THEM.
IT IS WHY YOU MAY BELONG, ELIZABETH, AND SOME OF THE NEW MUTANTS-- DESPITE THEIR COURAGE-- MAY NOT.
FOR BETTER OR WORSE, BEING AN X-MAN MEANS NOT MERELY BEING BORN A MUTANT...
...BUT A HERO.
The End
MGM PRODUCTIONS
MOJO'S GIANT MOVIES OF DEATH
CLAPCLAPCL
HOORAY!
BRAVO!
CLAPCLAP
ENCORE!
AUTHOR!
MORE!
MORE!
WE WANT MORE!

WELL, MAJOR-DOMO-- *WELL?!*

MUTTER-MUTTER-MUTTER-GRUMBLE-GRUMBLE-GRUMBLE-COST-COST-COST--
--*sigh!*

PRELIMINARY INDICATIONS ARE THAT THIS WILL BE YOUR HIGHEST GROSSING SUCCESS. WHICH MEANS, I SUPPOSE...

...YOU'LL WANT TO DO IT AGAIN NEXT YEAR.

NEVER!

OH, DOMO, MY DOMO, MY DEAR PHILISTINE-- HAVE YOU NO *SOUL?*

OF COURSE YOU DON'T, I DIDN'T DESIGN ONE INTO YOU, WHY SHOULD I SHARE THAT MOST UNIQUE PART OF MYSELF?

SILLY BOY, IF ONLY YOUR POWER COULD BE HARNESSED FOR GOOD!

I CAN'T WAIT.

USE YOUR INSIGHT FOR SOMETHING MORE THAN NUMBER MUNCHIE-CRUNCHING!

THEY'RE *HEROES,* DOMO! BUT WHERE WOULD ALL THAT HEROISM BE WITHOUT SOMEONE TRULY NASTY TO PROPERLY TEST THEM?! THANKS TO ME, THEIR EXISTENCE HAS *PURPOSE.* THAT'S WHY *I'M* THE LIFE-BRINGER.

A TRUE *ARTISTE* NEVER REPEATS HIMSELF! *THAT'S* WHY I'M LEAVING THE LUCKY *LONGSHOT* WITH THE X-MEN. HE'LL WIN THEIR HEARTS, AND THEN I'LL *BREAK* THEM.

HIS PRESENCE ON EARTH WILL INFURIATE SPIRAL DE*LIGHT*FULLY. TEACH HER A LESSON.

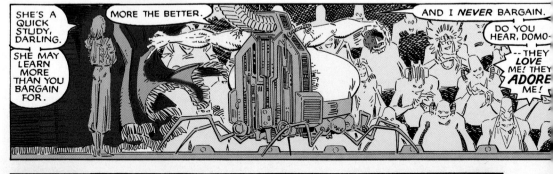

SHE'S A QUICK STUDY, DARLING.

MORE THE BETTER.

SHE MAY LEARN MORE THAN YOU BARGAIN FOR.

AND I *NEVER* BARGAIN.

DO YOU HEAR, DOMO--

--THEY *LOVE* ME! THEY *ADORE* ME!

AND I MAKE THEM *PAY* FOR IT!

Bedee-bedee-bedee--

--th-th-that's *ALL,* folks!

BUT I'LL BE BACK!

THE END

162

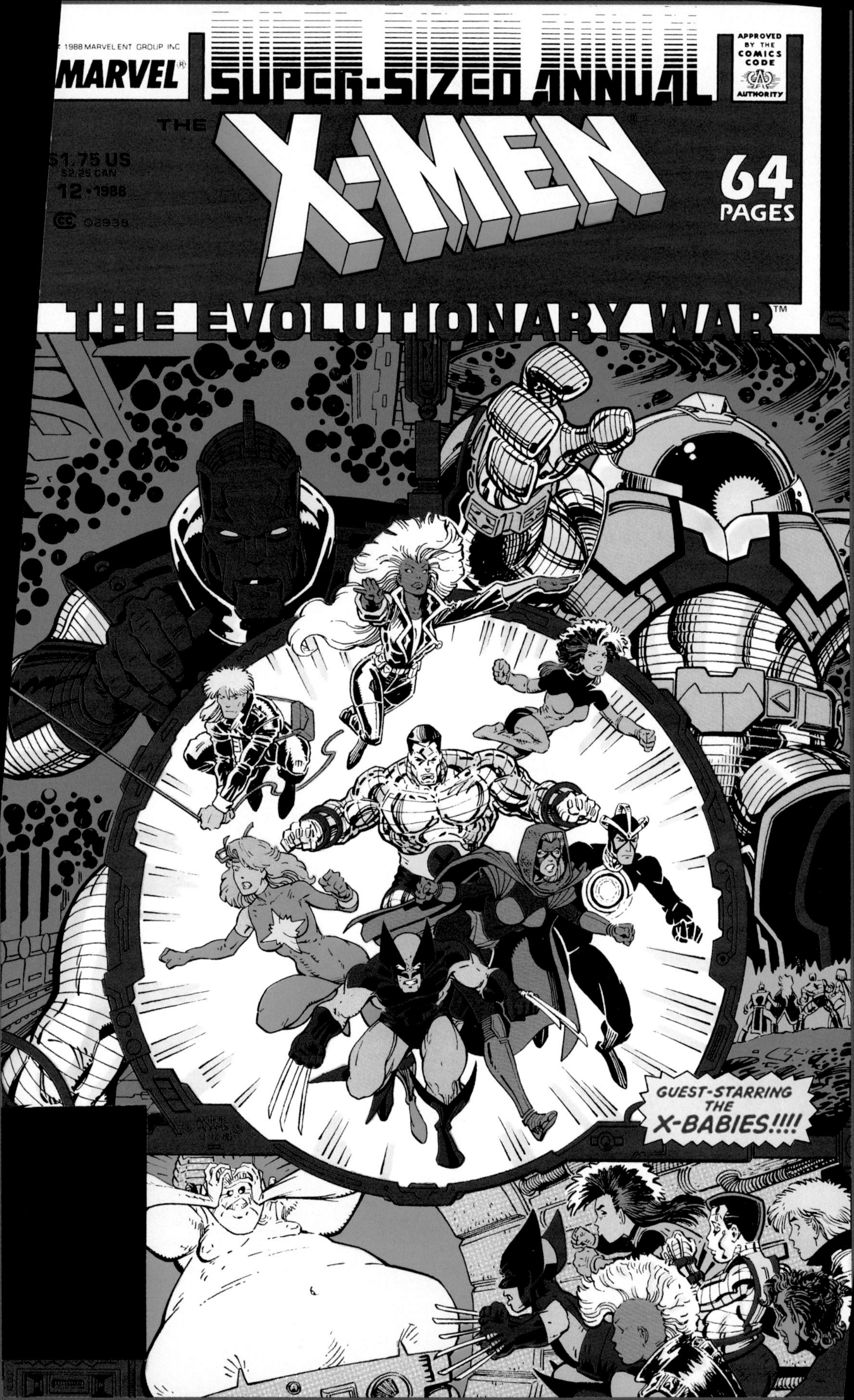

© 1988 MARVEL ENT. GROUP INC
MARVEL
SUPER-SIZED ANNUAL
APPROVED BY THE COMICS CODE AUTHORITY
THE X-MEN
$1.75 US
$2.25 CAN
12 • 1988
64 PAGES
THE EVOLUTIONARY WAR
GUEST-STARRING THE X-BABIES!!!!

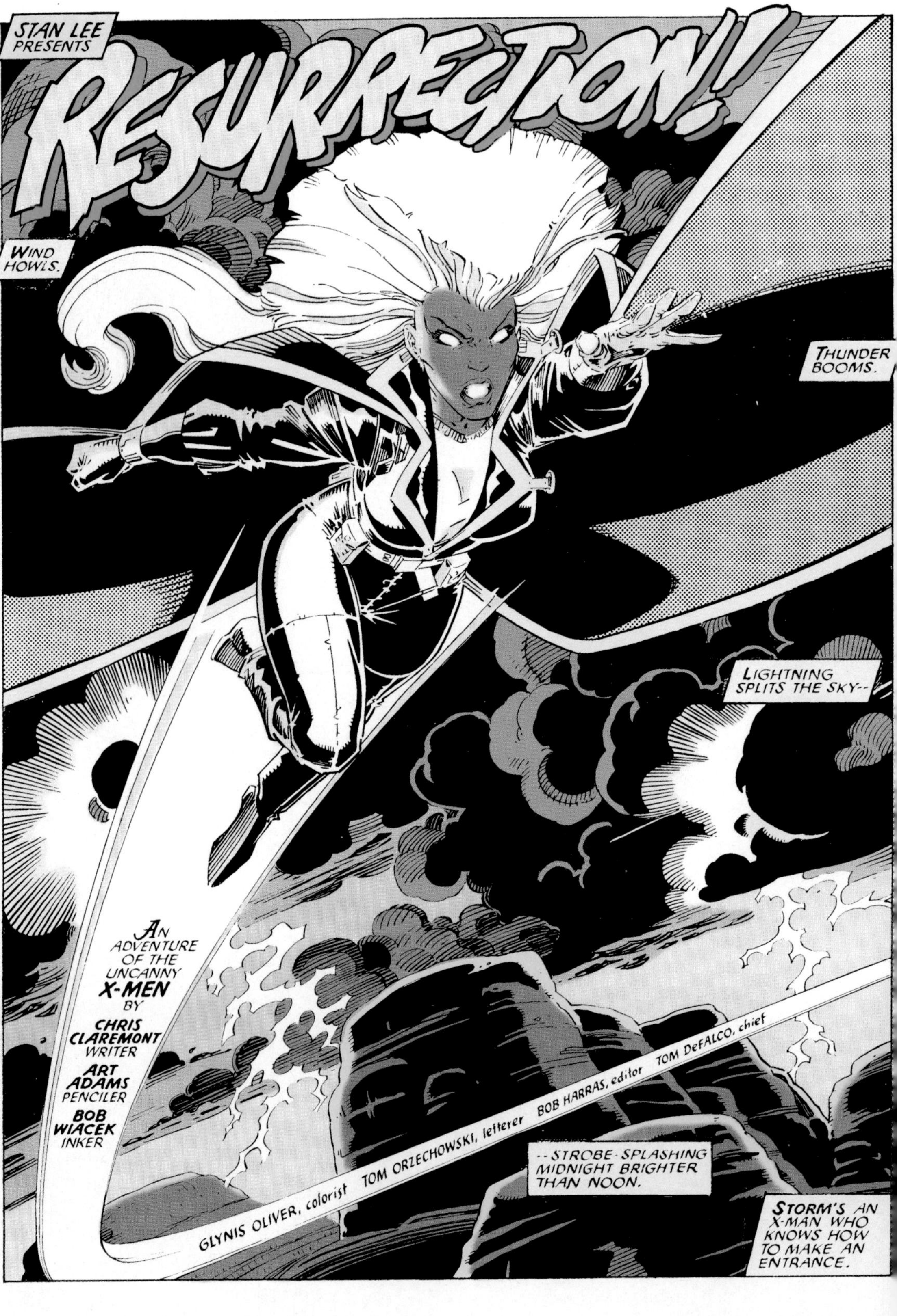

STAN LEE PRESENTS
RESURRECTION!!
WIND HOWLS.
THUNDER BOOMS.
LIGHTNING SPLITS THE SKY--
--STROBE-SPLASHING MIDNIGHT BRIGHTER THAN NOON.
STORM'S AN X-MAN WHO KNOWS HOW TO MAKE AN ENTRANCE.
AN ADVENTURE OF THE UNCANNY X-MEN BY
CHRIS CLAREMONT WRITER
ART ADAMS PENCILER
BOB WIACEK INKER
GLYNIS OLIVER, colorist TOM ORZECHOWSKI, letterer BOB HARRAS, editor TOM DeFALCO, chief

AND AN EXIT.

IN A HEARTBEAT, SHE'S GONE...

...THROUGH THE ABANDONED OUT-BACK TOWN SHE AND HER TEAM-MATES HAVE ADOPTED AS THEIR HOME...

...AND OFF TOWARDS THE HEAVENS.

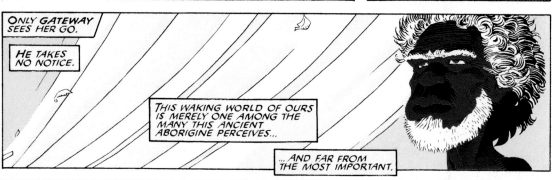

ONLY GATEWAY SEES HER GO.

HE TAKES NO NOTICE.

THIS WAKING WORLD OF OURS IS MERELY ONE AMONG THE MANY THIS ANCIENT ABORIGINE PERCEIVES...

...AND FAR FROM THE MOST IMPORTANT.

OTHERS, HOWEVER...

WHERE ARE YOU GO--

STORM, WHAT'S WRONG?!

--whiaOhWHH!

LONGSHOT!

THE WIND--

--HURRICANE FORCE--

--HIS HOLLOW-BONED BODY COULDN'T STAND AGAINST IT...

...IT'S SWEEPING HIM AWAY!

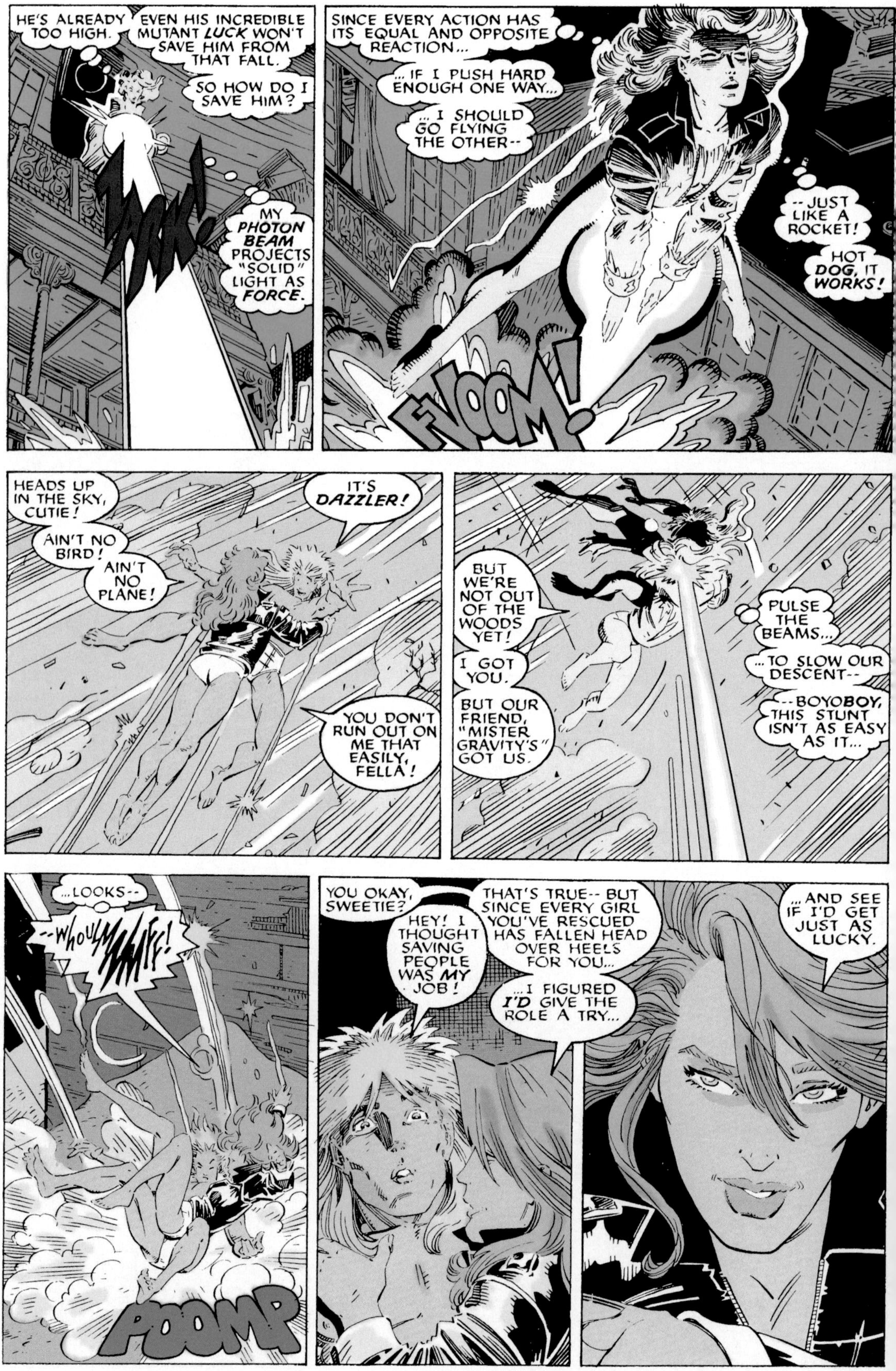
HE'S ALREADY TOO HIGH.
EVEN HIS INCREDIBLE MUTANT LUCK WON'T SAVE HIM FROM THAT FALL.
SO HOW DO I SAVE HIM?
MY PHOTON BEAM PROJECTS "SOLID" LIGHT AS FORCE.
SINCE EVERY ACTION HAS ITS EQUAL AND OPPOSITE REACTION...
... IF I PUSH HARD ENOUGH ONE WAY...
... I SHOULD GO FLYING THE OTHER--
--JUST LIKE A ROCKET!
HOT DOG, IT WORKS!
FVOOM!
HEADS UP IN THE SKY, CUTIE!
AIN'T NO BIRD!
AIN'T NO PLANE!
IT'S DAZZLER!
YOU DON'T RUN OUT ON ME THAT EASILY, FELLA!
BUT WE'RE NOT OUT OF THE WOODS YET!
I GOT YOU.
BUT OUR FRIEND, "MISTER GRAVITY'S" GOT US.
PULSE THE BEAMS...
...TO SLOW OUR DESCENT--
--BOYOBOY, THIS STUNT ISN'T AS EASY AS IT...
...LOOKS--
POOMP
YOU OKAY, SWEETIE?
HEY! I THOUGHT SAVING PEOPLE WAS MY JOB!
THAT'S TRUE-- BUT SINCE EVERY GIRL YOU'VE RESCUED HAS FALLEN HEAD OVER HEELS FOR YOU...
...I FIGURED I'D GIVE THE ROLE A TRY...
...AND SEE IF I'D GET JUST AS LUCKY.

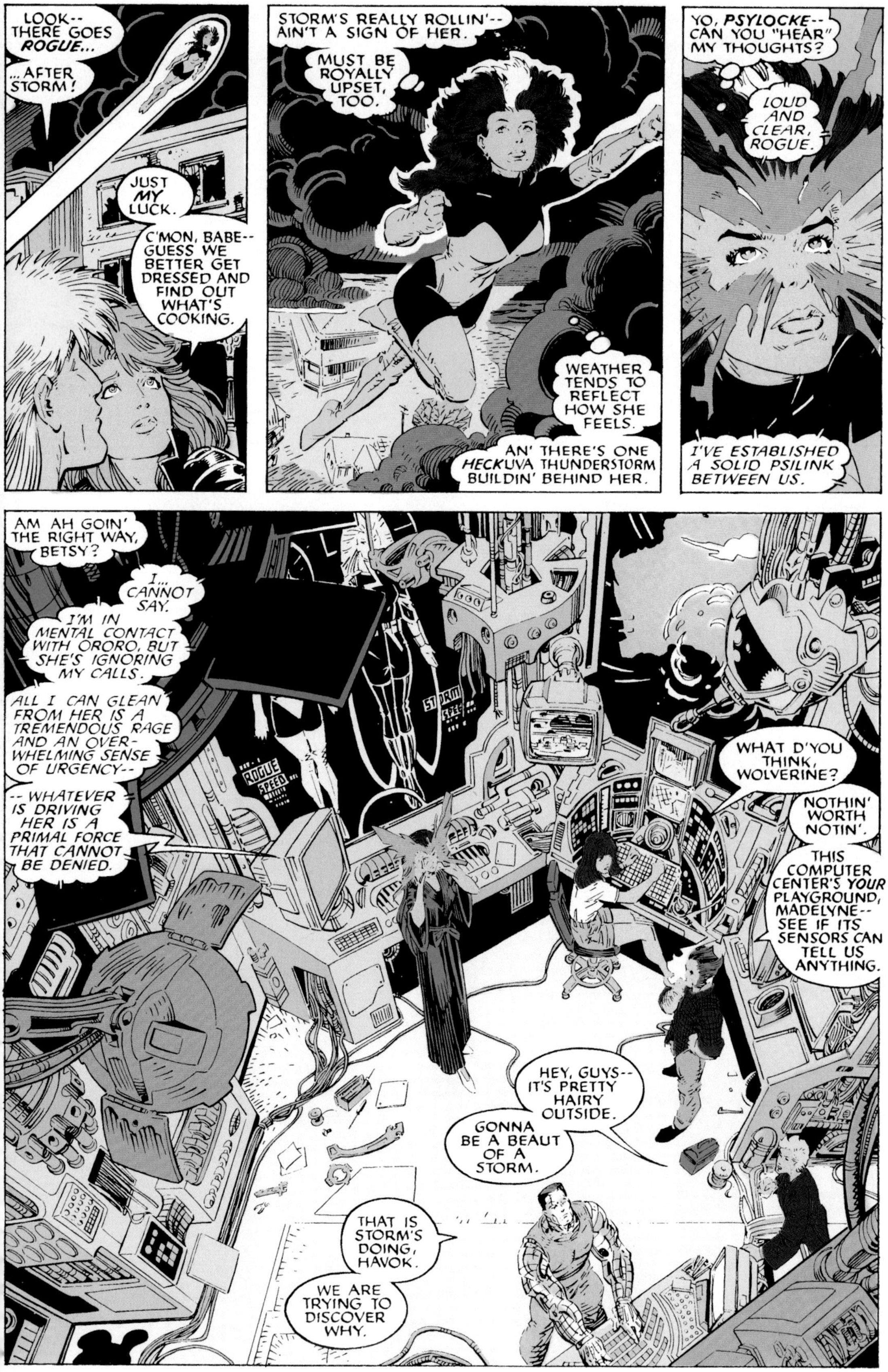

LOOK-- THERE GOES ROGUE...
...AFTER STORM!
JUST MY LUCK.
C'MON, BABE-- GUESS WE BETTER GET DRESSED AND FIND OUT WHAT'S COOKING.
STORM'S REALLY ROLLIN'-- AIN'T A SIGN OF HER.
MUST BE ROYALLY UPSET, TOO.
WEATHER TENDS TO REFLECT HOW SHE FEELS.
AN' THERE'S ONE HECKUVA THUNDERSTORM BUILDIN' BEHIND HER.
YO, PSYLOCKE-- CAN YOU "HEAR" MY THOUGHTS?
LOUD AND CLEAR, ROGUE.
I'VE ESTABLISHED A SOLID PSILINK BETWEEN US.
AM AH GOIN' THE RIGHT WAY, BETSY?
I... CANNOT SAY.
I'M IN MENTAL CONTACT WITH ORORO, BUT SHE'S IGNORING MY CALLS.
ALL I CAN GLEAN FROM HER IS A TREMENDOUS RAGE AND AN OVER-WHELMING SENSE OF URGENCY--
--WHATEVER IS DRIVING HER IS A PRIMAL FORCE THAT CANNOT BE DENIED.
STORM SPEED
ROGUE SPEED
WHAT D'YOU THINK, WOLVERINE?
NOTHIN' WORTH NOTIN'.
THIS COMPUTER CENTER'S YOUR PLAYGROUND, MADELYNE-- SEE IF ITS SENSORS CAN TELL US ANYTHING.
HEY, GUYS-- IT'S PRETTY HAIRY OUTSIDE.
GONNA BE A BEAUT OF A STORM.
THAT IS STORM'S DOING, HAVOK.
WE ARE TRYING TO DISCOVER WHY.

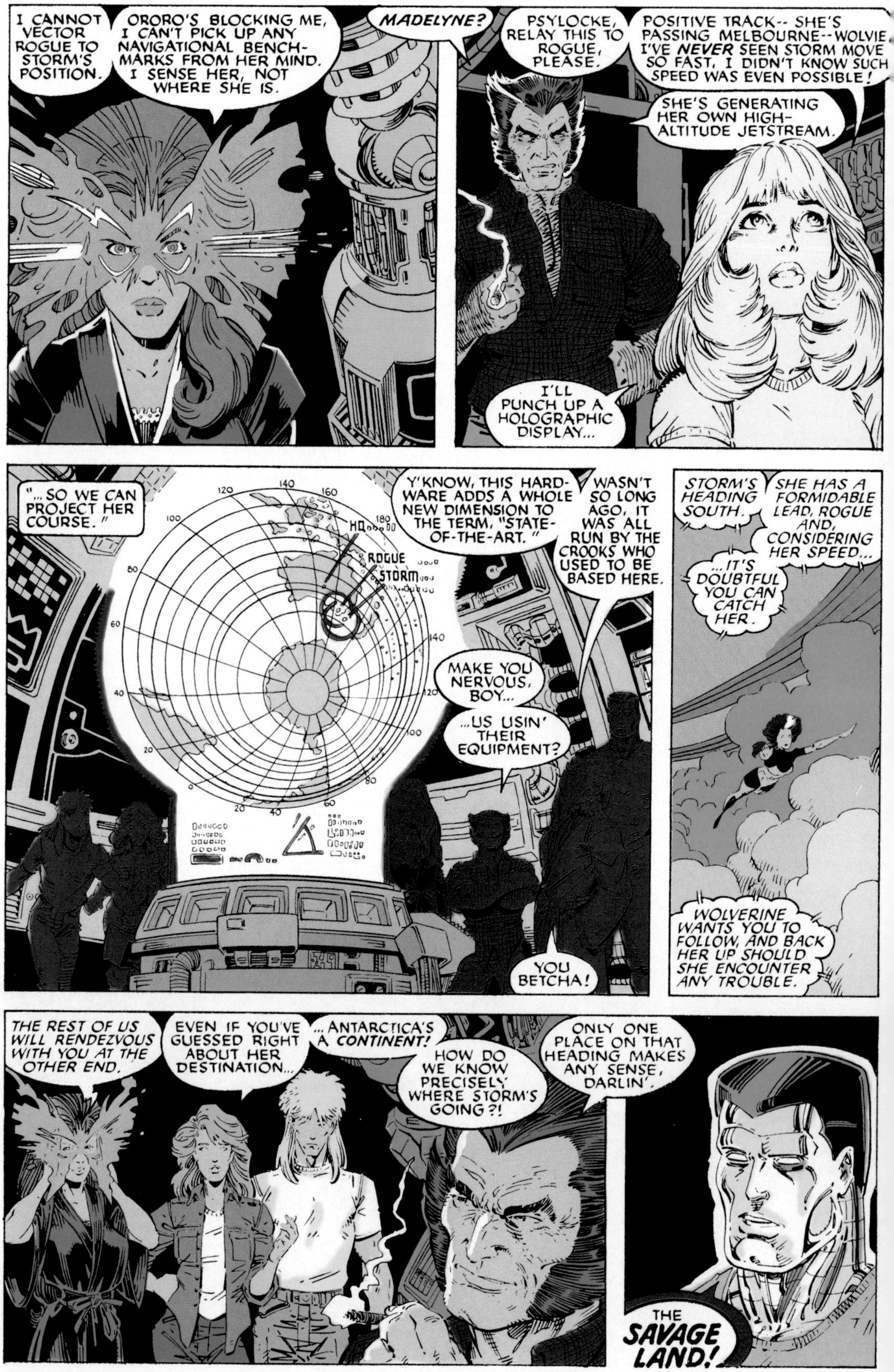

I CANNOT VECTOR ROGUE TO STORM'S POSITION.
ORORO'S BLOCKING ME, I CAN'T PICK UP ANY NAVIGATIONAL BENCH-MARKS FROM HER MIND. I SENSE HER, NOT WHERE SHE IS.
MADELYNE?
PSYLOCKE, RELAY THIS TO ROGUE, PLEASE.
POSITIVE TRACK-- SHE'S PASSING MELBOURNE--WOLVIE I'VE NEVER SEEN STORM MOVE SO FAST, I DIDN'T KNOW SUCH SPEED WAS EVEN POSSIBLE!
SHE'S GENERATING HER OWN HIGH-ALTITUDE JETSTREAM.
I'LL PUNCH UP A HOLOGRAPHIC DISPLAY...
"...SO WE CAN PROJECT HER COURSE."
HQ
ROGUE
STORM
Y'KNOW, THIS HARD-WARE ADDS A WHOLE NEW DIMENSION TO THE TERM, "STATE-OF-THE-ART."
WASN'T SO LONG AGO, IT WAS ALL RUN BY THE CROOKS WHO USED TO BE BASED HERE.
MAKE YOU NERVOUS, BOY...
...US USIN' THEIR EQUIPMENT?
YOU BETCHA!
STORM'S HEADING SOUTH.
SHE HAS A FORMIDABLE LEAD, ROGUE AND, CONSIDERING HER SPEED...
...IT'S DOUBTFUL YOU CAN CATCH HER.
WOLVERINE WANTS YOU TO FOLLOW, AND BACK HER UP SHOULD SHE ENCOUNTER ANY TROUBLE.
THE REST OF US WILL RENDEZVOUS WITH YOU AT THE OTHER END.
EVEN IF YOU'VE GUESSED RIGHT ABOUT HER DESTINATION...
...ANTARCTICA'S A CONTINENT!
HOW DO WE KNOW PRECISELY WHERE STORM'S GOING?!
ONLY ONE PLACE ON THAT HEADING MAKES ANY SENSE, DARLIN'.
THE SAVAGE LAND!

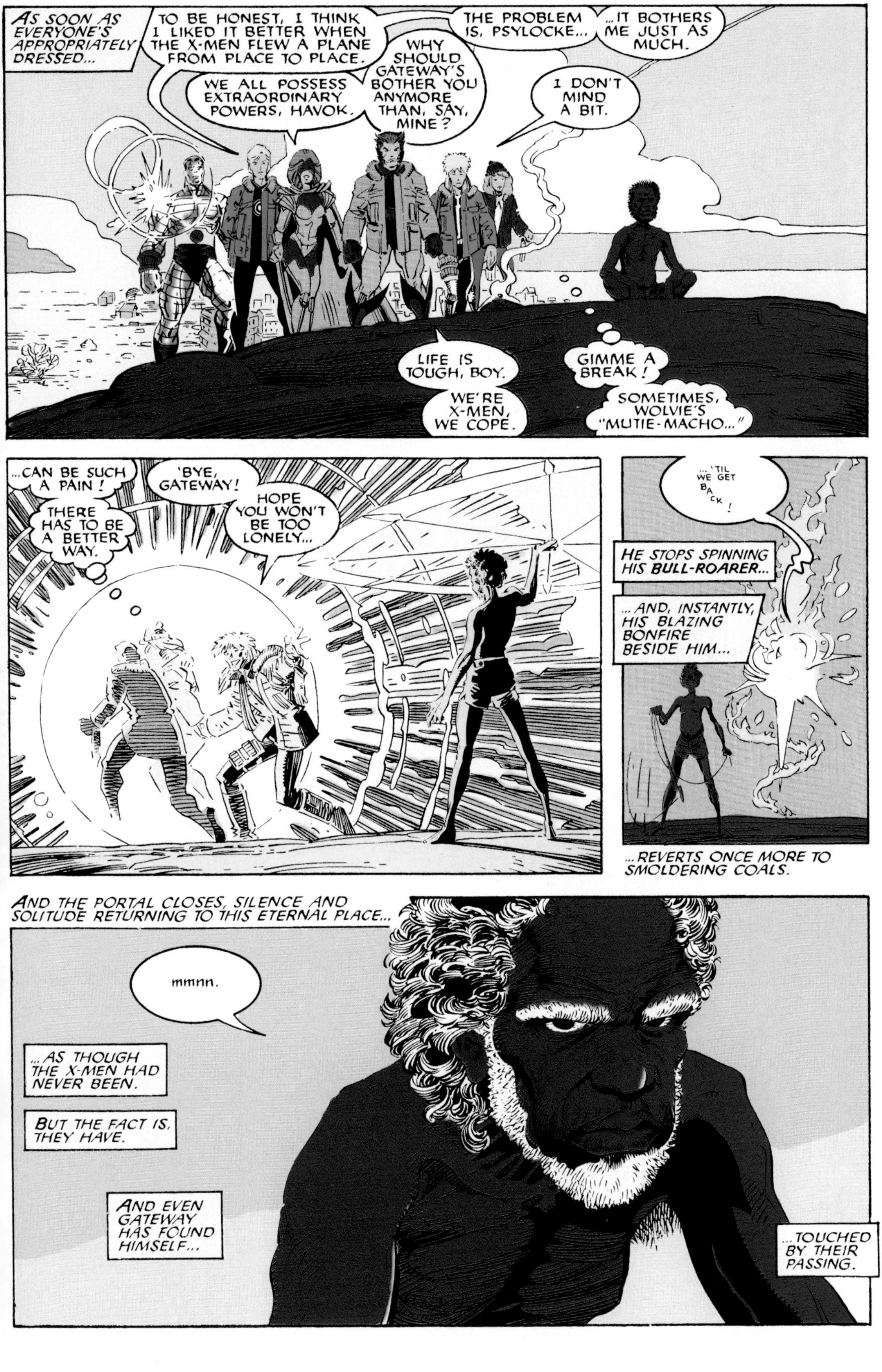
AS SOON AS EVERYONE'S APPROPRIATELY DRESSED...
TO BE HONEST, I THINK I LIKED IT BETTER WHEN THE X-MEN FLEW A PLANE FROM PLACE TO PLACE.
WE ALL POSSESS EXTRAORDINARY POWERS, HAVOK.
WHY SHOULD GATEWAY'S BOTHER YOU ANYMORE THAN, SAY, MINE?
THE PROBLEM IS, PSYLOCKE...
...IT BOTHERS ME JUST AS MUCH.
I DON'T MIND A BIT.
LIFE IS TOUGH, BOY.
WE'RE X-MEN, WE COPE.
GIMME A BREAK!
SOMETIMES, WOLVIE'S "MUTIE-MACHO..."
...CAN BE SUCH A PAIN!
THERE HAS TO BE A BETTER WAY.
'BYE, GATEWAY!
HOPE YOU WON'T BE TOO LONELY...
...'TIL WE GET BACK!
HE STOPS SPINNING HIS BULL-ROARER...
...AND, INSTANTLY, HIS BLAZING BONFIRE BESIDE HIM...
...REVERTS ONCE MORE TO SMOLDERING COALS.
AND THE PORTAL CLOSES, SILENCE AND SOLITUDE RETURNING TO THIS ETERNAL PLACE...
mmnn.
...AS THOUGH THE X-MEN HAD NEVER BEEN.
BUT THE FACT IS, THEY HAVE.
AND EVEN GATEWAY HAS FOUND HIMSELF...
...TOUCHED BY THEIR PASSING.

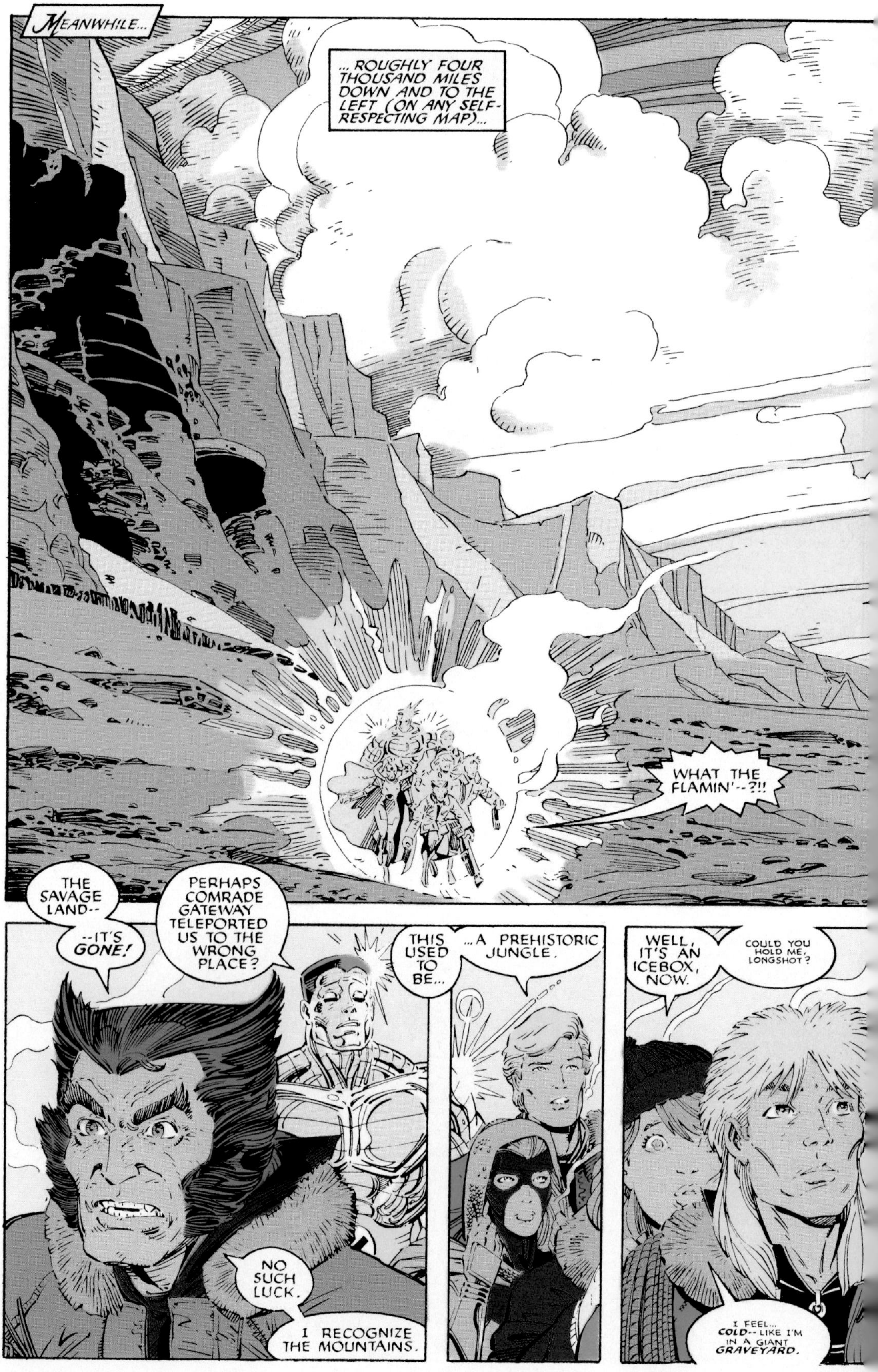
MEANWHILE...
...ROUGHLY FOUR THOUSAND MILES DOWN AND TO THE LEFT (ON ANY SELF-RESPECTING MAP)...
WHAT THE FLAMIN'--?!!
THE SAVAGE LAND--
--IT'S GONE!
PERHAPS COMRADE GATEWAY TELEPORTED US TO THE WRONG PLACE?
NO SUCH LUCK.
I RECOGNIZE THE MOUNTAINS.
THIS USED TO BE...
...A PREHISTORIC JUNGLE.
WELL, IT'S AN ICEBOX, NOW.
COULD YOU HOLD ME, LONGSHOT?
I FEEL... COLD--LIKE I'M IN A GIANT GRAVEYARD.

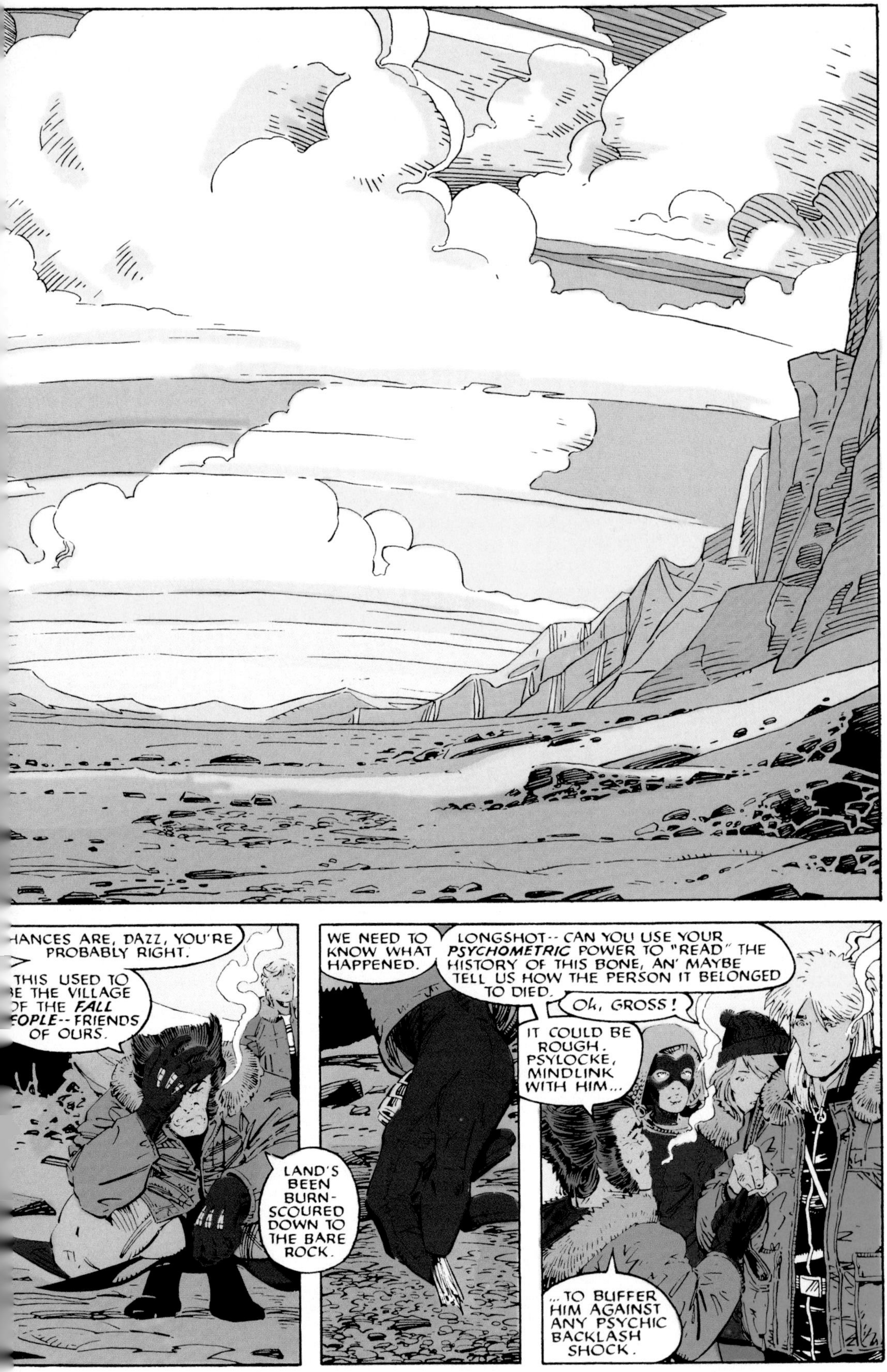

HANCES ARE, DAZZ, YOU'RE PROBABLY RIGHT.
THIS USED TO
E THE VILLAGE
F THE FALL
EOPLE-- FRIENDS OF OURS.
LAND'S BEEN BURN-SCOURED DOWN TO THE BARE ROCK.
WE NEED TO KNOW WHAT HAPPENED.
LONGSHOT-- CAN YOU USE YOUR PSYCHOMETRIC POWER TO "READ" THE HISTORY OF THIS BONE, AN' MAYBE TELL US HOW THE PERSON IT BELONGED TO DIED.
Oh, GROSS!
IT COULD BE ROUGH. PSYLOCKE, MINDLINK WITH HIM...
...TO BUFFER HIM AGAINST ANY PSYCHIC BACKLASH SHOCK.

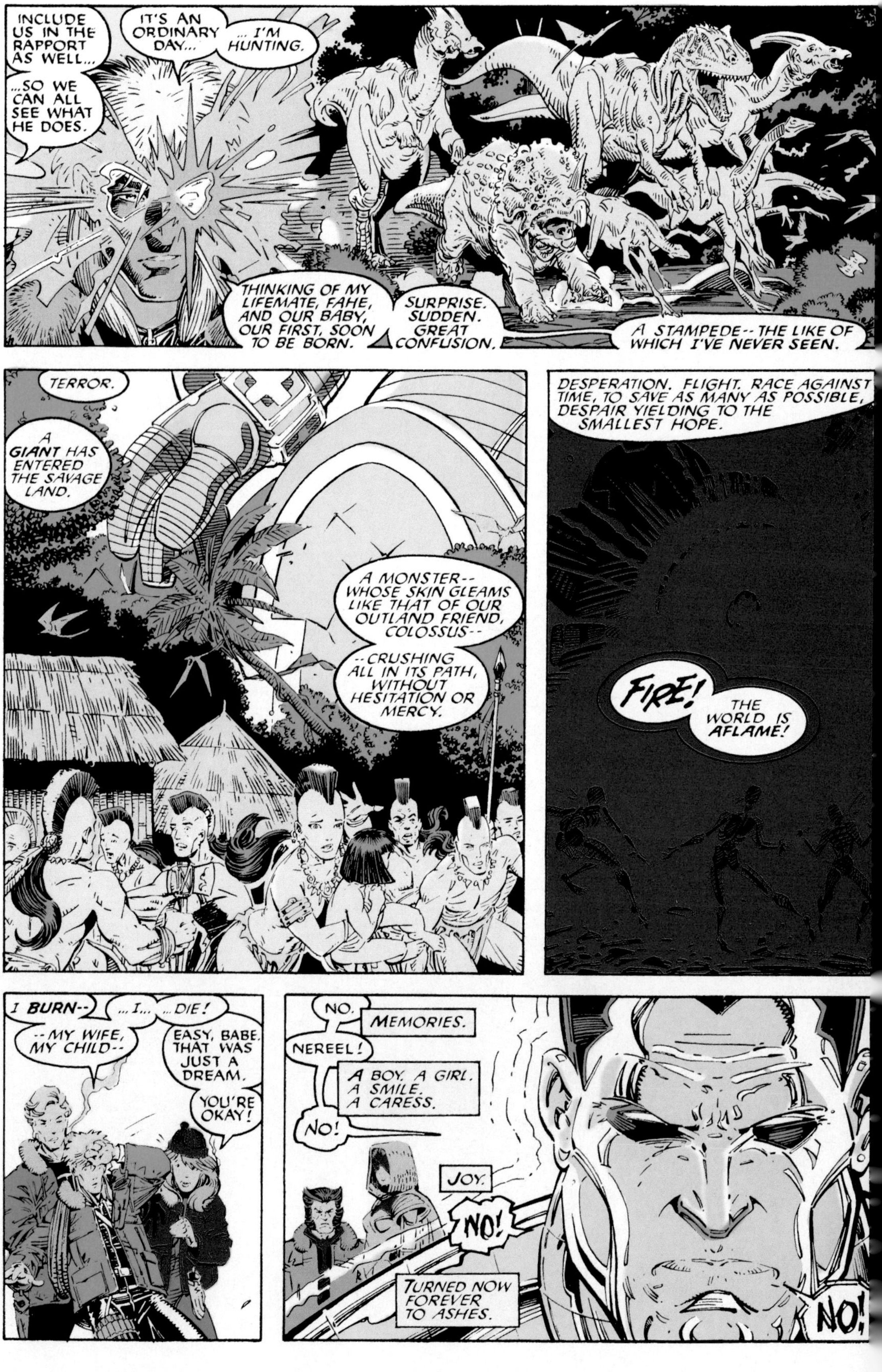
INCLUDE US IN THE RAPPORT AS WELL...
...SO WE CAN ALL SEE WHAT HE DOES.
IT'S AN ORDINARY DAY...
...I'M HUNTING.
THINKING OF MY LIFEMATE, FAHE, AND OUR BABY, OUR FIRST, SOON TO BE BORN.
SURPRISE. SUDDEN. GREAT CONFUSION.
A STAMPEDE--THE LIKE OF WHICH I'VE NEVER SEEN.
TERROR.
A GIANT HAS ENTERED THE SAVAGE LAND.
A MONSTER--WHOSE SKIN GLEAMS LIKE THAT OF OUR OUTLAND FRIEND, COLOSSUS--
--CRUSHING ALL IN ITS PATH, WITHOUT HESITATION OR MERCY.
DESPERATION. FLIGHT. RACE AGAINST TIME, TO SAVE AS MANY AS POSSIBLE, DESPAIR YIELDING TO THE SMALLEST HOPE.
FIRE!
THE WORLD IS AFLAME!
I BURN--
...I...
...DIE!
--MY WIFE, MY CHILD--
EASY, BABE. THAT WAS JUST A DREAM.
YOU'RE OKAY!
NO.
MEMORIES.
NEREEL!
A BOY. A GIRL. A SMILE. A CARESS.
NO!
JOY.
NO!
TURNED NOW FOREVER TO ASHES.
NO!

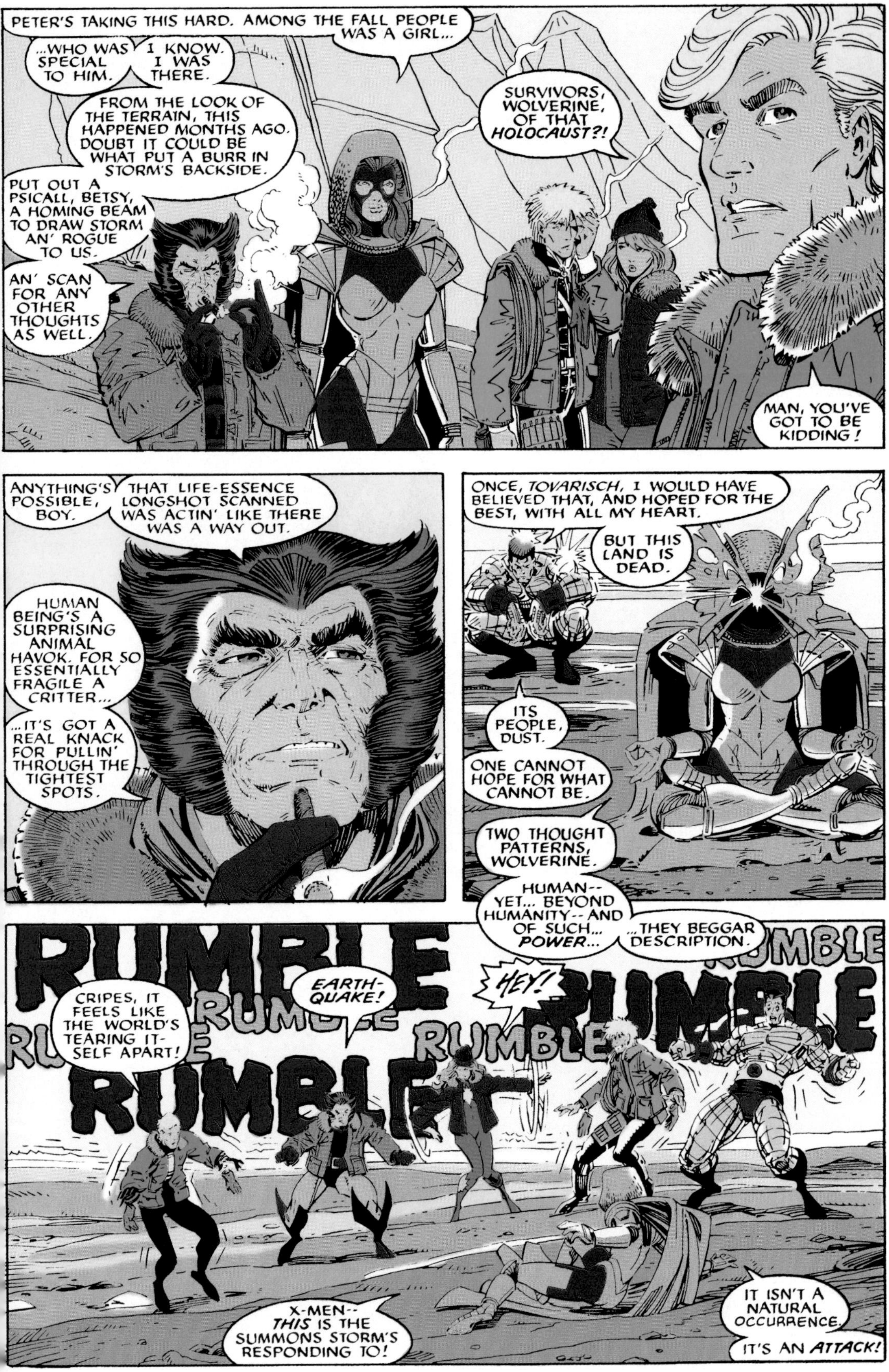
PETER'S TAKING THIS HARD. AMONG THE FALL PEOPLE WAS A GIRL...
...WHO WAS SPECIAL TO HIM.
I KNOW. I WAS THERE.
FROM THE LOOK OF THE TERRAIN, THIS HAPPENED MONTHS AGO. DOUBT IT COULD BE WHAT PUT A BURR IN STORM'S BACKSIDE.
PUT OUT A PSICALL, BETSY, A HOMING BEAM TO DRAW STORM AN' ROGUE TO US.
AN' SCAN FOR ANY OTHER THOUGHTS AS WELL.
SURVIVORS, WOLVERINE, OF THAT *HOLOCAUST?!*
MAN, YOU'VE GOT TO BE KIDDING!
ANYTHING'S POSSIBLE, BOY.
THAT LIFE-ESSENCE LONGSHOT SCANNED WAS ACTIN' LIKE THERE WAS A WAY OUT.
HUMAN BEING'S A SURPRISING ANIMAL HAVOK. FOR SO ESSENTIALLY FRAGILE A CRITTER...
...IT'S GOT A REAL KNACK FOR PULLIN' THROUGH THE TIGHTEST SPOTS.
ONCE, *TOVARISCH*, I WOULD HAVE BELIEVED THAT, AND HOPED FOR THE BEST, WITH ALL MY HEART.
BUT THIS LAND IS DEAD.
ITS PEOPLE, DUST.
ONE CANNOT HOPE FOR WHAT CANNOT BE.
TWO THOUGHT PATTERNS, WOLVERINE.
HUMAN-- YET... BEYOND HUMANITY-- AND OF SUCH... *POWER*...
...THEY BEGGAR DESCRIPTION.
RUMBLE RUMBLE RUMBLE RUMBLE RUMBLE RUMBLE RUMBLE
CRIPES, IT FEELS LIKE THE WORLD'S TEARING IT-SELF APART!
EARTH-QUAKE!
HEY!
X-MEN-- *THIS* IS THE SUMMONS STORM'S RESPONDING TO!
IT ISN'T A NATURAL OCCURRENCE.
IT'S AN *ATTACK!*

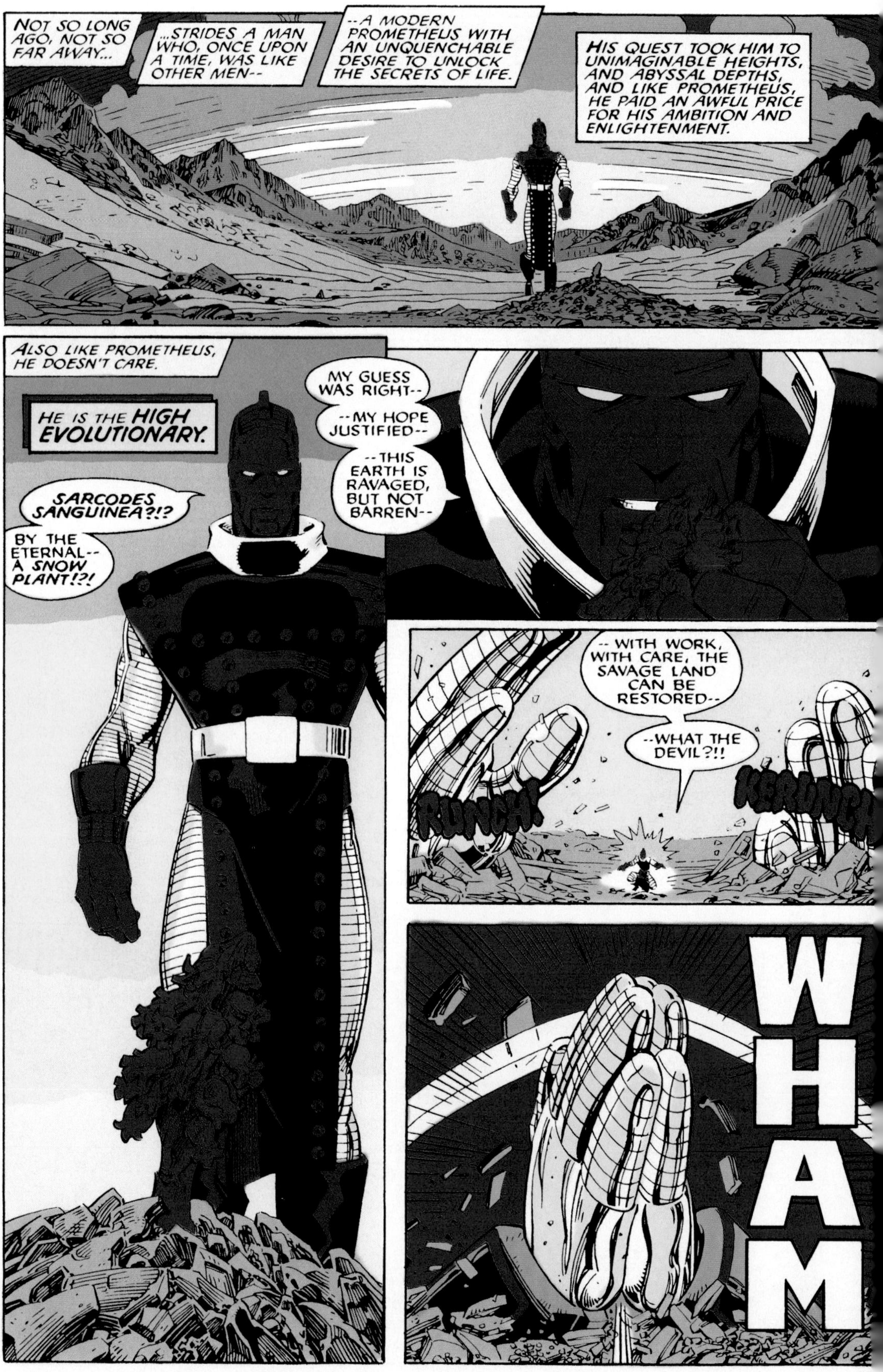
NOT SO LONG AGO, NOT SO FAR AWAY...
...STRIDES A MAN WHO, ONCE UPON A TIME, WAS LIKE OTHER MEN--
--A MODERN PROMETHEUS WITH AN UNQUENCHABLE DESIRE TO UNLOCK THE SECRETS OF LIFE.
HIS QUEST TOOK HIM TO UNIMAGINABLE HEIGHTS, AND ABYSSAL DEPTHS, AND LIKE PROMETHEUS, HE PAID AN AWFUL PRICE FOR HIS AMBITION AND ENLIGHTENMENT.
ALSO LIKE PROMETHEUS, HE DOESN'T CARE.
HE IS THE HIGH EVOLUTIONARY.
SARCODES SANGUINEA?!?
BY THE ETERNAL-- A SNOW PLANT!?!
MY GUESS WAS RIGHT--
--MY HOPE JUSTIFIED--
--THIS EARTH IS RAVAGED, BUT NOT BARREN--
-- WITH WORK, WITH CARE, THE SAVAGE LAND CAN BE RESTORED--
RUNCH!
--WHAT THE DEVIL?!!
KERUNCH
WHAM

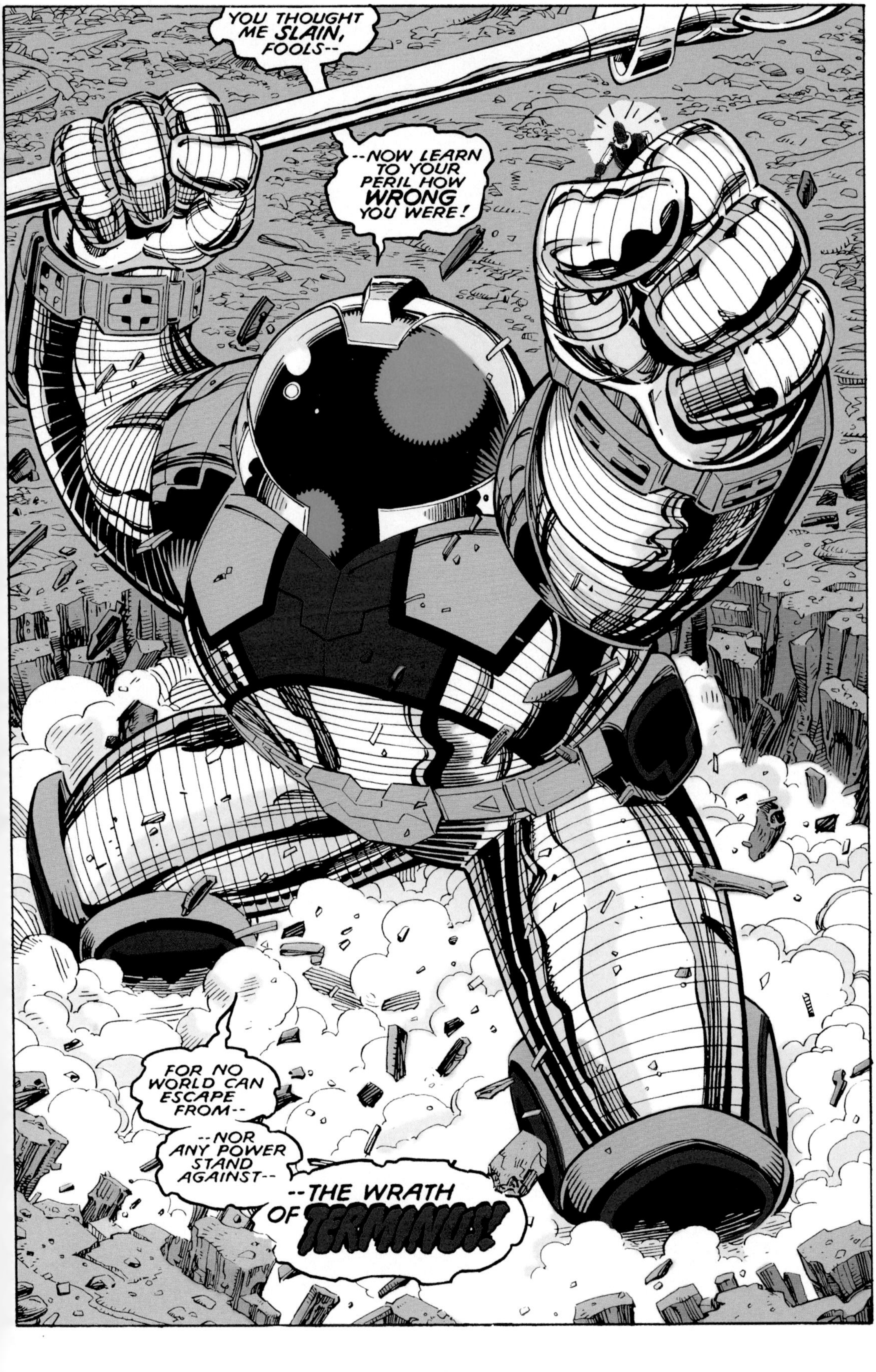
YOU THOUGHT ME SLAIN, FOOLS--
--NOW LEARN TO YOUR PERIL HOW WRONG YOU WERE!
FOR NO WORLD CAN ESCAPE FROM--
--NOR ANY POWER STAND AGAINST--
--THE WRATH OF TERMINUS!

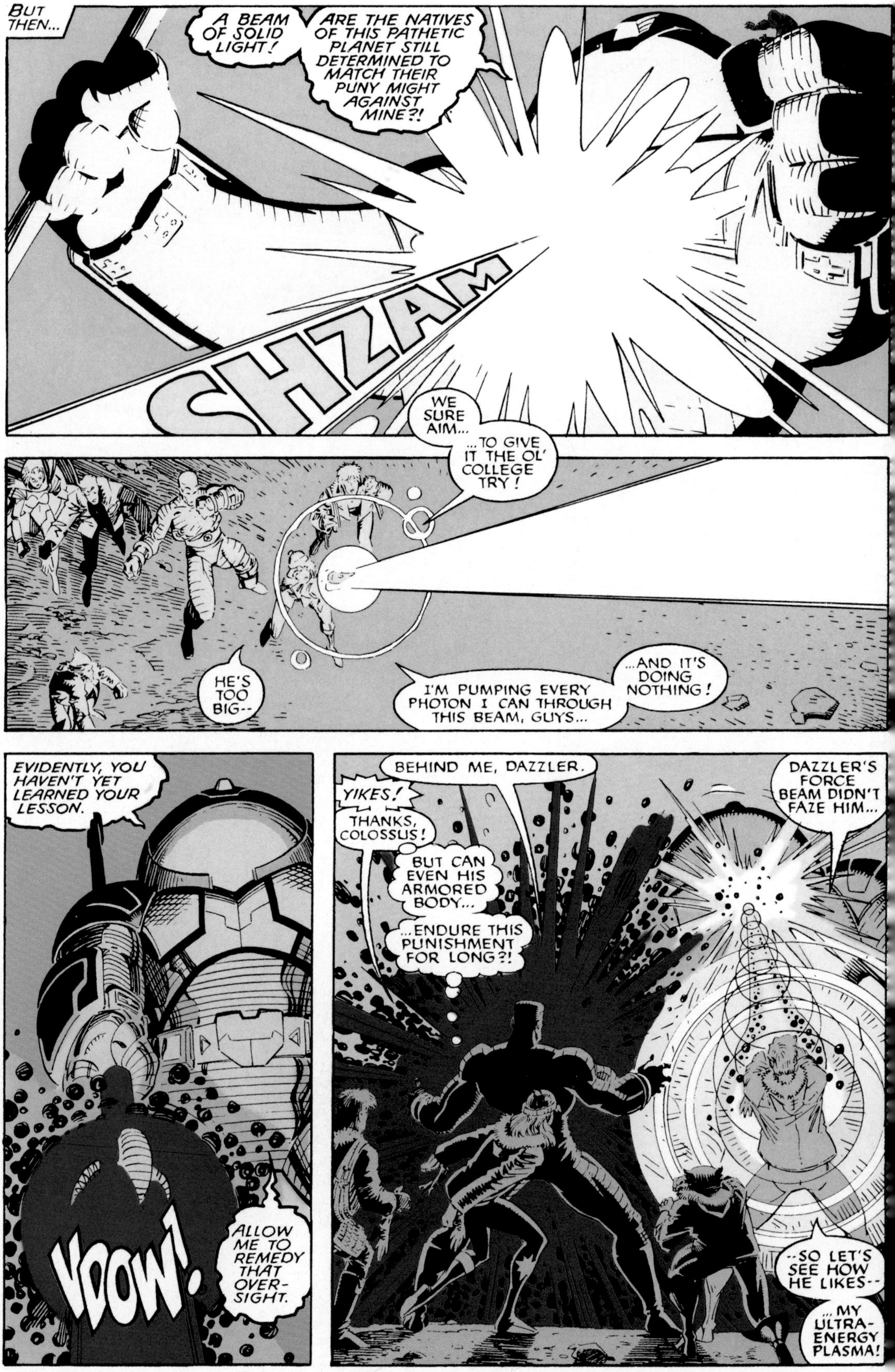

BUT THEN...
A BEAM OF SOLID LIGHT!
ARE THE NATIVES OF THIS PATHETIC PLANET STILL DETERMINED TO MATCH THEIR PUNY MIGHT AGAINST MINE?!
SHZAM
WE SURE AIM...
...TO GIVE IT THE OL' COLLEGE TRY!
HE'S TOO BIG--
I'M PUMPING EVERY PHOTON I CAN THROUGH THIS BEAM, GUYS...
...AND IT'S DOING NOTHING!
EVIDENTLY, YOU HAVEN'T YET LEARNED YOUR LESSON.
VDOOM!
ALLOW ME TO REMEDY THAT OVER-SIGHT.
BEHIND ME, DAZZLER.
YIKES!
THANKS, COLOSSUS!
BUT CAN EVEN HIS ARMORED BODY...
...ENDURE THIS PUNISHMENT FOR LONG?!
DAZZLER'S FORCE BEAM DIDN'T FAZE HIM...
--SO LET'S SEE HOW HE LIKES--
...MY ULTRA-ENERGY PLASMA!

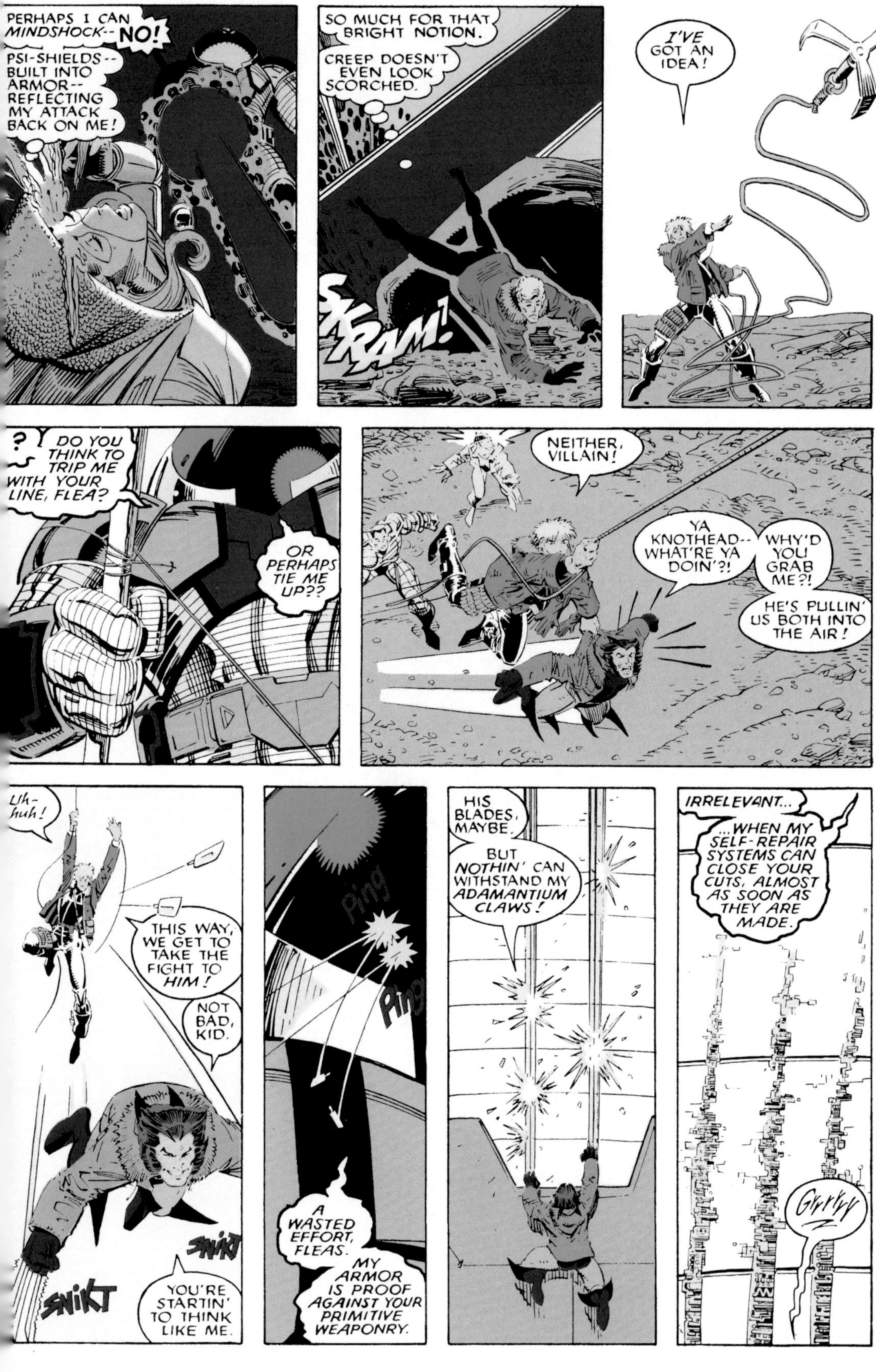
PERHAPS I CAN MINDSHOCK-- NO!
PSI-SHIELDS-- BUILT INTO ARMOR-- REFLECTING MY ATTACK BACK ON ME!
SO MUCH FOR THAT BRIGHT NOTION.
CREEP DOESN'T EVEN LOOK SCORCHED.
SKRAM!
I'VE GOT AN IDEA!
?
DO YOU THINK TO TRIP ME WITH YOUR LINE, FLEA?
OR PERHAPS TIE ME UP??
NEITHER, VILLAIN!
YA KNOTHEAD-- WHAT'RE YA DOIN'?!
WHY'D YOU GRAB ME?!
HE'S PULLIN' US BOTH INTO THE AIR!
Uh-huh!
THIS WAY, WE GET TO TAKE THE FIGHT TO HIM!
NOT BAD, KID.
SNIKT
SNIKT
YOU'RE STARTIN' TO THINK LIKE ME.
Ping
Ping
A WASTED EFFORT, FLEAS.
MY ARMOR IS PROOF AGAINST YOUR PRIMITIVE WEAPONRY.
HIS BLADES, MAYBE.
BUT NOTHIN' CAN WITHSTAND MY ADAMANTIUM CLAWS!
IRRELEVANT...
...WHEN MY SELF-REPAIR SYSTEMS CAN CLOSE YOUR CUTS, ALMOST AS SOON AS THEY ARE MADE.
Grrrlyy

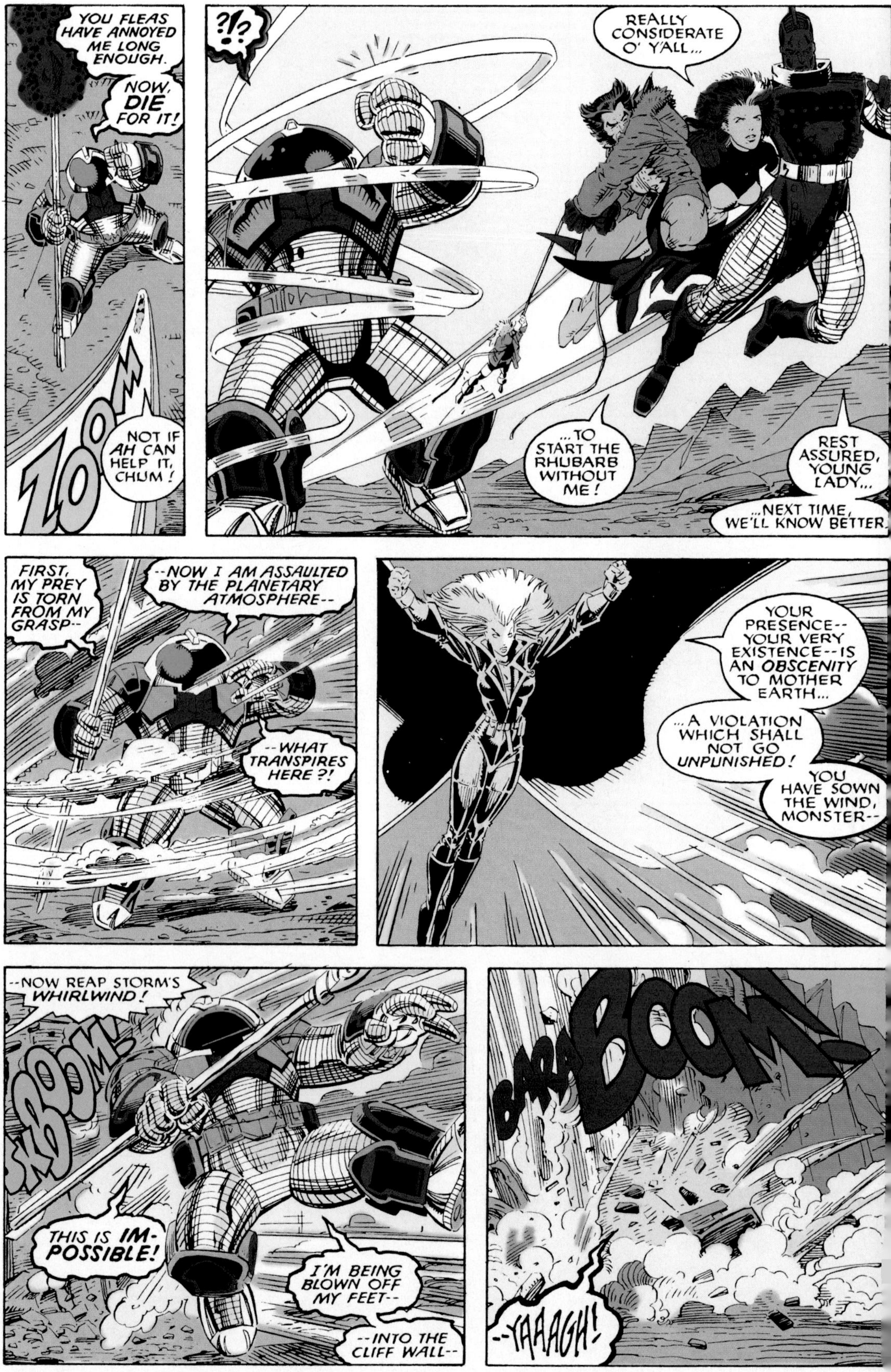
YOU FLEAS HAVE ANNOYED ME LONG ENOUGH.
NOW, DIE FOR IT!
ZOOOM
NOT IF AH CAN HELP IT, CHUM!
?!?
REALLY CONSIDERATE O' Y'ALL...
...TO START THE RHUBARB WITHOUT ME!
REST ASSURED, YOUNG LADY...
...NEXT TIME, WE'LL KNOW BETTER.
FIRST, MY PREY IS TORN FROM MY GRASP--
--NOW I AM ASSAULTED BY THE PLANETARY ATMOSPHERE--
--WHAT TRANSPIRES HERE?!
YOUR PRESENCE-- YOUR VERY EXISTENCE--IS AN OBSCENITY TO MOTHER EARTH...
...A VIOLATION WHICH SHALL NOT GO UNPUNISHED!
YOU HAVE SOWN THE WIND, MONSTER--
--NOW REAP STORM'S WHIRLWIND!
KBOOM!
THIS IS IM-POSSIBLE!
I'M BEING BLOWN OFF MY FEET--
--INTO THE CLIFF WALL--
BARABOOM!
--YAAAGH!

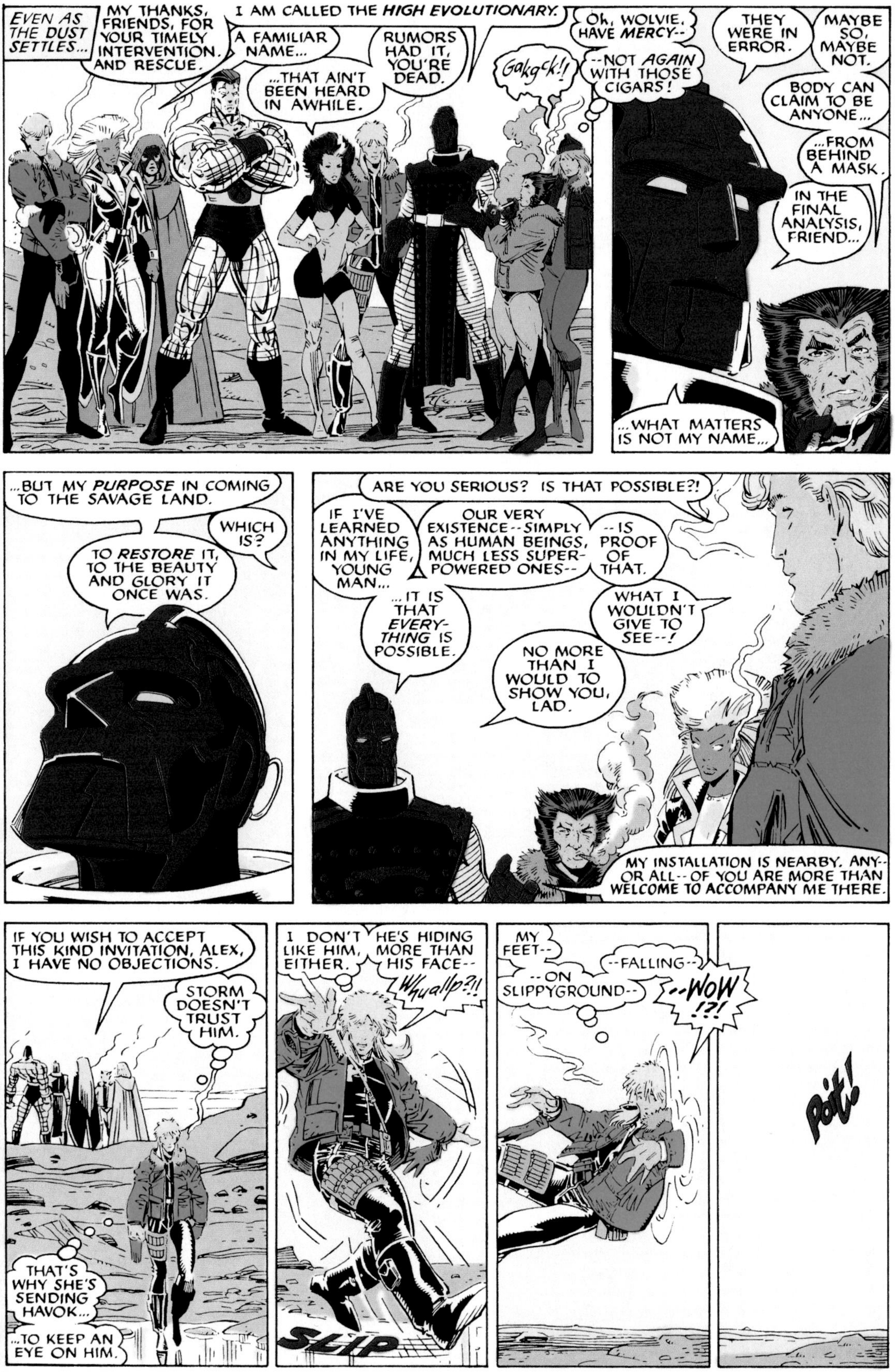
EVEN AS THE DUST SETTLES...
MY THANKS, FRIENDS, FOR YOUR TIMELY INTERVENTION, AND RESCUE.
I AM CALLED THE HIGH EVOLUTIONARY.
A FAMILIAR NAME...
...THAT AIN'T BEEN HEARD IN AWHILE.
RUMORS HAD IT, YOU'RE DEAD.
Oh, WOLVIE, HAVE MERCY--
Gakgck!!
--NOT AGAIN WITH THOSE CIGARS!
THEY WERE IN ERROR.
MAYBE SO, MAYBE NOT.
BODY CAN CLAIM TO BE ANYONE...
...FROM BEHIND A MASK.
IN THE FINAL ANALYSIS, FRIEND...
...WHAT MATTERS IS NOT MY NAME...
...BUT MY PURPOSE IN COMING TO THE SAVAGE LAND.
WHICH IS?
TO RESTORE IT, TO THE BEAUTY AND GLORY IT ONCE WAS.
ARE YOU SERIOUS? IS THAT POSSIBLE?!
IF I'VE LEARNED ANYTHING IN MY LIFE, YOUNG MAN...
...IT IS THAT EVERYTHING IS POSSIBLE.
OUR VERY EXISTENCE--SIMPLY AS HUMAN BEINGS, MUCH LESS SUPER-POWERED ONES--
--IS PROOF OF THAT.
WHAT I WOULDN'T GIVE TO SEE--!
NO MORE THAN I WOULD TO SHOW YOU, LAD.
MY INSTALLATION IS NEARBY. ANY--OR ALL--OF YOU ARE MORE THAN WELCOME TO ACCOMPANY ME THERE.
IF YOU WISH TO ACCEPT THIS KIND INVITATION, ALEX, I HAVE NO OBJECTIONS.
STORM DOESN'T TRUST HIM.
THAT'S WHY SHE'S SENDING HAVOK...
...TO KEEP AN EYE ON HIM.
I DON'T LIKE HIM, EITHER.
HE'S HIDING MORE THAN HIS FACE--
Whuallp?!!
SLIP
MY FEET--
--ON SLIPPYGROUND--
--FALLING--
--WOW !?!
Poit!

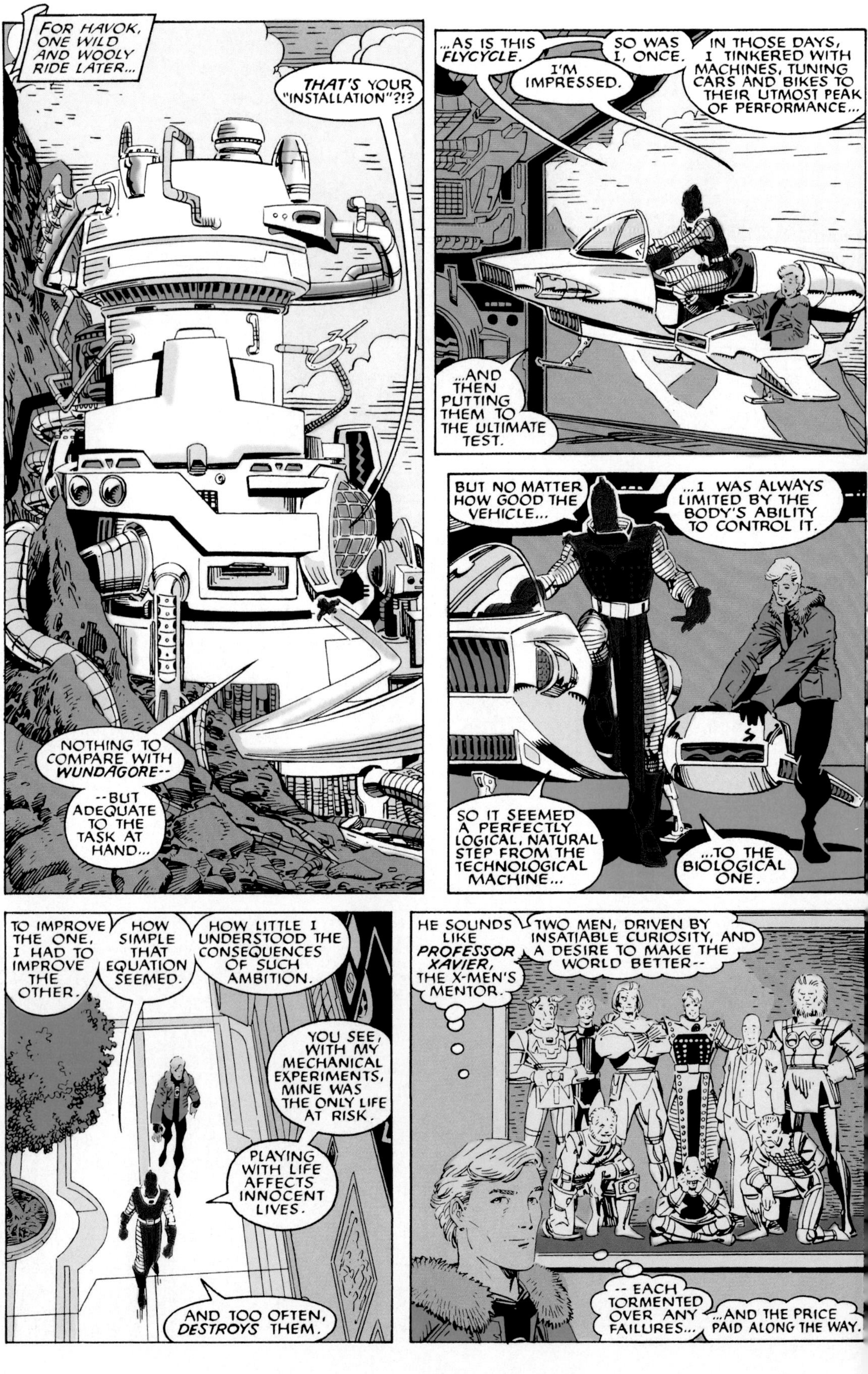

FOR HAVOK, ONE WILD AND WOOLY RIDE LATER...
THAT'S YOUR "INSTALLATION"?!?
NOTHING TO COMPARE WITH WUNDAGORE--
--BUT ADEQUATE TO THE TASK AT HAND...
...AS IS THIS FLYCYCLE.
I'M IMPRESSED.
SO WAS I, ONCE.
IN THOSE DAYS, I TINKERED WITH MACHINES, TUNING CARS AND BIKES TO THEIR UTMOST PEAK OF PERFORMANCE...
...AND THEN PUTTING THEM TO THE ULTIMATE TEST.
BUT NO MATTER HOW GOOD THE VEHICLE...
...I WAS ALWAYS LIMITED BY THE BODY'S ABILITY TO CONTROL IT.
SO IT SEEMED A PERFECTLY LOGICAL, NATURAL STEP FROM THE TECHNOLOGICAL MACHINE...
...TO THE BIOLOGICAL ONE.
TO IMPROVE THE ONE, I HAD TO IMPROVE THE OTHER.
HOW SIMPLE THAT EQUATION SEEMED.
HOW LITTLE I UNDERSTOOD THE CONSEQUENCES OF SUCH AMBITION.
YOU SEE, WITH MY MECHANICAL EXPERIMENTS, MINE WAS THE ONLY LIFE AT RISK.
PLAYING WITH LIFE AFFECTS INNOCENT LIVES.
AND TOO OFTEN, DESTROYS THEM.
HE SOUNDS LIKE PROFESSOR XAVIER, THE X-MEN'S MENTOR.
TWO MEN, DRIVEN BY INSATIABLE CURIOSITY, AND A DESIRE TO MAKE THE WORLD BETTER--
-- EACH TORMENTED OVER ANY FAILURES...
...AND THE PRICE PAID ALONG THE WAY.

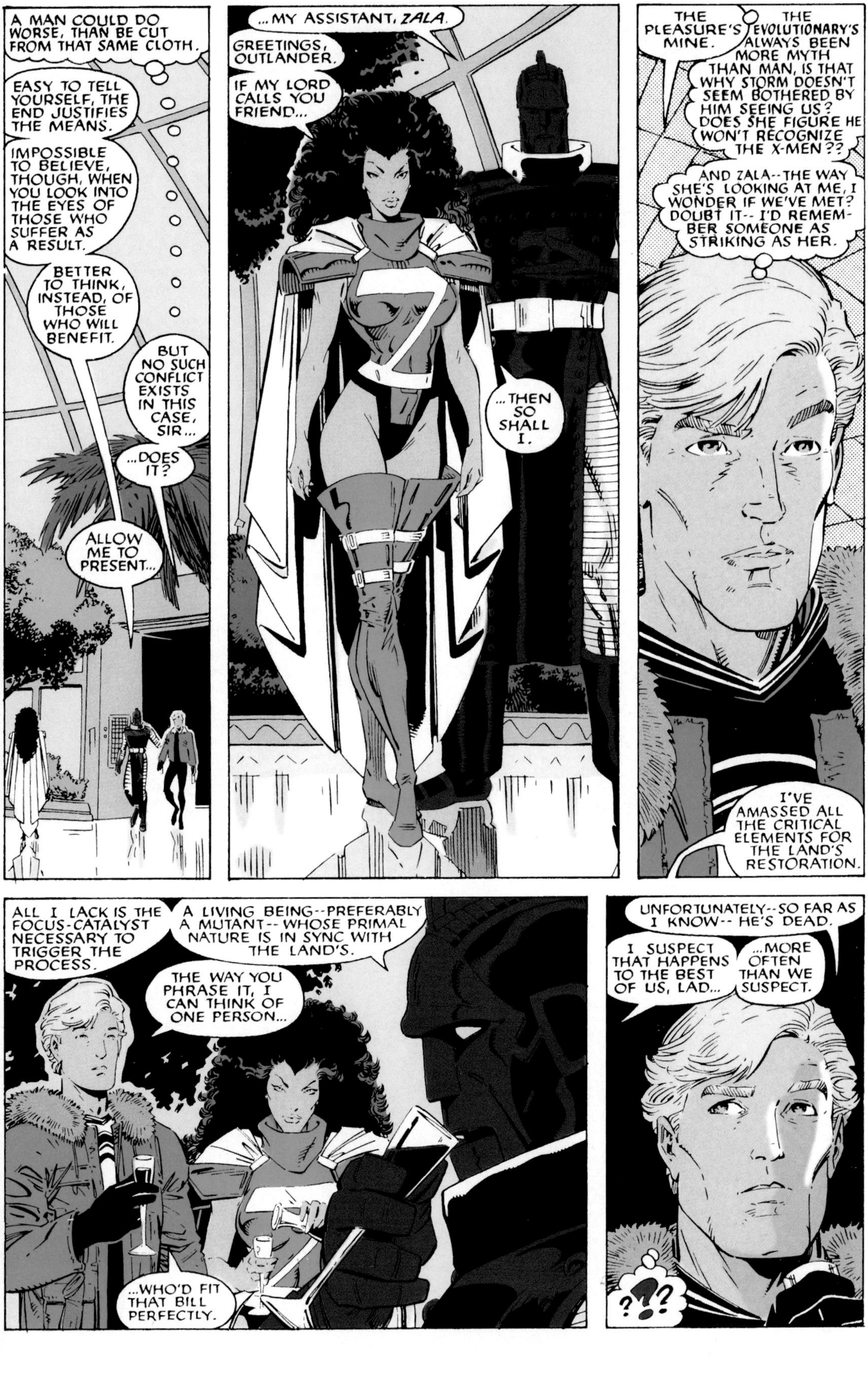
A MAN COULD DO WORSE, THAN BE CUT FROM THAT SAME CLOTH.
EASY TO TELL YOURSELF, THE END JUSTIFIES THE MEANS.
IMPOSSIBLE TO BELIEVE, THOUGH, WHEN YOU LOOK INTO THE EYES OF THOSE WHO SUFFER AS A RESULT.
BETTER TO THINK, INSTEAD, OF THOSE WHO WILL BENEFIT.
BUT NO SUCH CONFLICT EXISTS IN THIS CASE, SIR...
...DOES IT?
ALLOW ME TO PRESENT...
...MY ASSISTANT, ZALA.
GREETINGS, OUTLANDER.
IF MY LORD CALLS YOU FRIEND...
...THEN SO SHALL I.
THE PLEASURE'S MINE.
THE EVOLUTIONARY'S ALWAYS BEEN MORE MYTH THAN MAN, IS THAT WHY STORM DOESN'T SEEM BOTHERED BY HIM SEEING US? DOES SHE FIGURE HE WON'T RECOGNIZE THE X-MEN??
AND ZALA--THE WAY SHE'S LOOKING AT ME, I WONDER IF WE'VE MET? DOUBT IT-- I'D REMEMBER SOMEONE AS STRIKING AS HER.
I'VE AMASSED ALL THE CRITICAL ELEMENTS FOR THE LAND'S RESTORATION.
ALL I LACK IS THE FOCUS-CATALYST NECESSARY TO TRIGGER THE PROCESS.
A LIVING BEING--PREFERABLY A MUTANT-- WHOSE PRIMAL NATURE IS IN SYNC WITH THE LAND'S.
THE WAY YOU PHRASE IT, I CAN THINK OF ONE PERSON...
...WHO'D FIT THAT BILL PERFECTLY.
UNFORTUNATELY--SO FAR AS I KNOW-- HE'S DEAD.
I SUSPECT THAT HAPPENS TO THE BEST OF US, LAD...
...MORE OFTEN THAN WE SUSPECT.
???

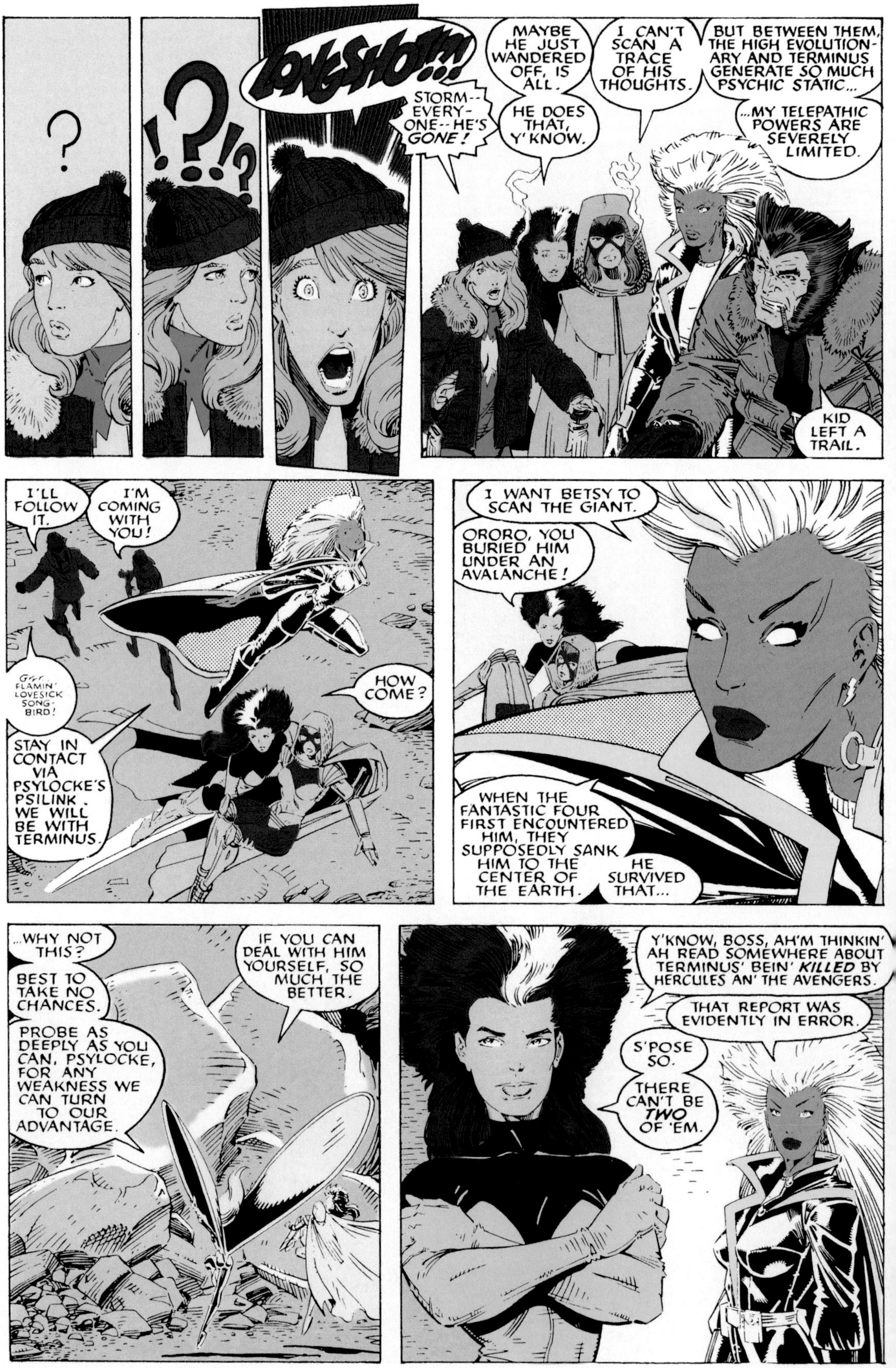
?
!?!?
LONGSHOT!!
STORM-- EVERYONE--HE'S GONE!
MAYBE HE JUST WANDERED OFF, IS ALL.
HE DOES THAT, Y'KNOW.
I CAN'T SCAN A TRACE OF HIS THOUGHTS.
BUT BETWEEN THEM, THE HIGH EVOLUTIONARY AND TERMINUS GENERATE SO MUCH PSYCHIC STATIC...
...MY TELEPATHIC POWERS ARE SEVERELY LIMITED.
KID LEFT A TRAIL.
I'LL FOLLOW IT.
I'M COMING WITH YOU!
Grrr.. FLAMIN' LOVESICK SONG-BIRD!
HOW COME?
STAY IN CONTACT VIA PSYLOCKE'S PSILINK. WE WILL BE WITH TERMINUS.
I WANT BETSY TO SCAN THE GIANT.
ORORO, YOU BURIED HIM UNDER AN AVALANCHE!
WHEN THE FANTASTIC FOUR FIRST ENCOUNTERED HIM, THEY SUPPOSEDLY SANK HIM TO THE CENTER OF THE EARTH.
HE SURVIVED THAT...
...WHY NOT THIS?
BEST TO TAKE NO CHANCES.
PROBE AS DEEPLY AS YOU CAN, PSYLOCKE, FOR ANY WEAKNESS WE CAN TURN TO OUR ADVANTAGE.
IF YOU CAN DEAL WITH HIM YOURSELF, SO MUCH THE BETTER.
Y'KNOW, BOSS, AH'M THINKIN' AH READ SOMEWHERE ABOUT TERMINUS' BEIN' KILLED BY HERCULES AN' THE AVENGERS.
THAT REPORT WAS EVIDENTLY IN ERROR.
S'POSE SO.
THERE CAN'T BE TWO OF 'EM.

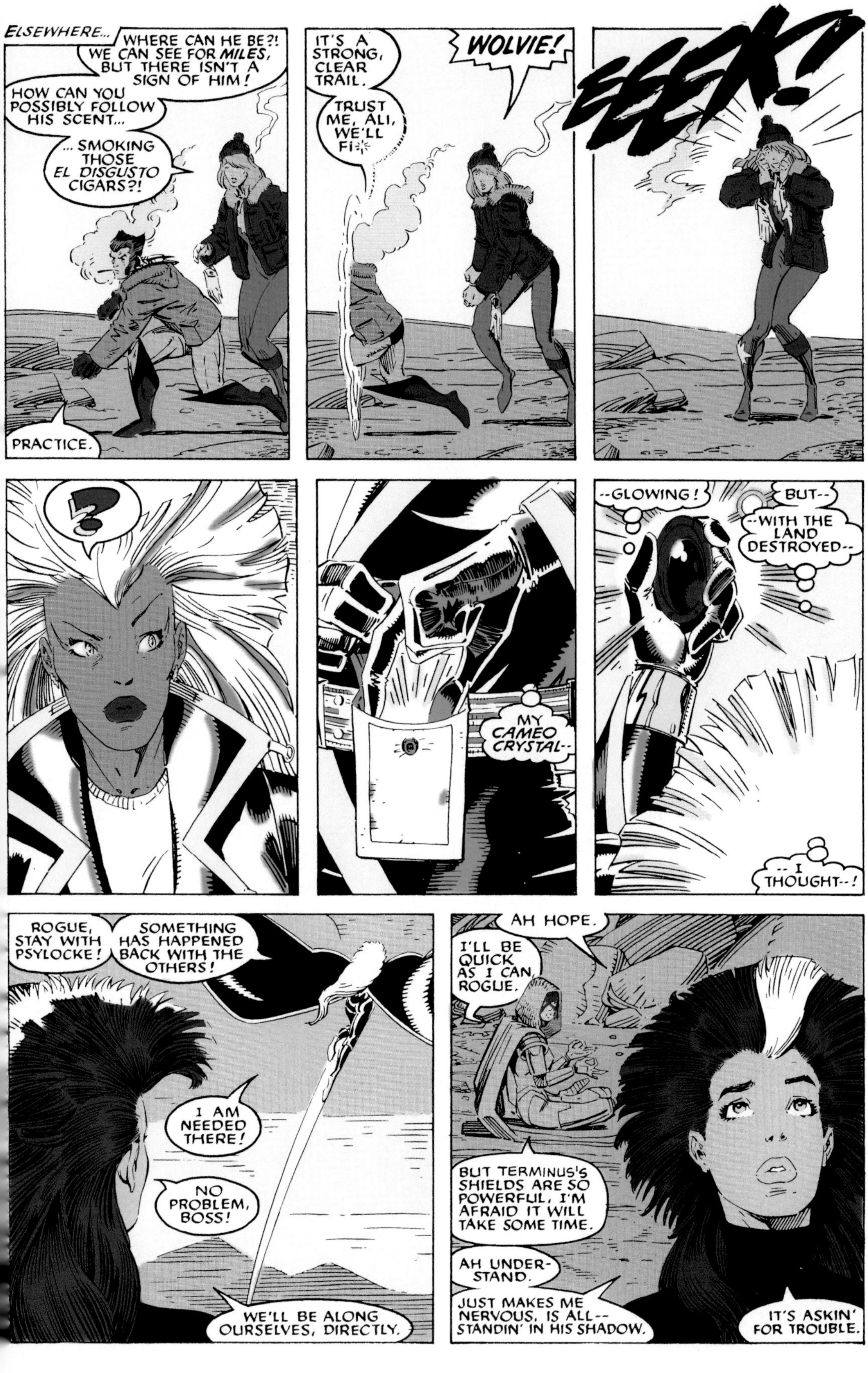

ELSEWHERE...
WHERE CAN HE BE?! WE CAN SEE FOR MILES, BUT THERE ISN'T A SIGN OF HIM!
HOW CAN YOU POSSIBLY FOLLOW HIS SCENT...
... SMOKING THOSE EL DISGUSTO CIGARS?!
PRACTICE.
IT'S A STRONG, CLEAR TRAIL.
TRUST ME, ALI, WE'LL FI
WOLVIE!
EEEK!
?
MY CAMEO CRYSTAL--
--GLOWING!
BUT--
--WITH THE LAND DESTROYED--
-- I THOUGHT--!
ROGUE, STAY WITH PSYLOCKE!
SOMETHING HAS HAPPENED BACK WITH THE OTHERS!
I AM NEEDED THERE!
NO PROBLEM, BOSS!
WE'LL BE ALONG OURSELVES, DIRECTLY.
AH HOPE.
I'LL BE QUICK AS I CAN, ROGUE.
BUT TERMINUS'S SHIELDS ARE SO POWERFUL, I'M AFRAID IT WILL TAKE SOME TIME.
AH UNDERSTAND.
JUST MAKES ME NERVOUS, IS ALL-- STANDIN' IN HIS SHADOW.
IT'S ASKIN' FOR TROUBLE.

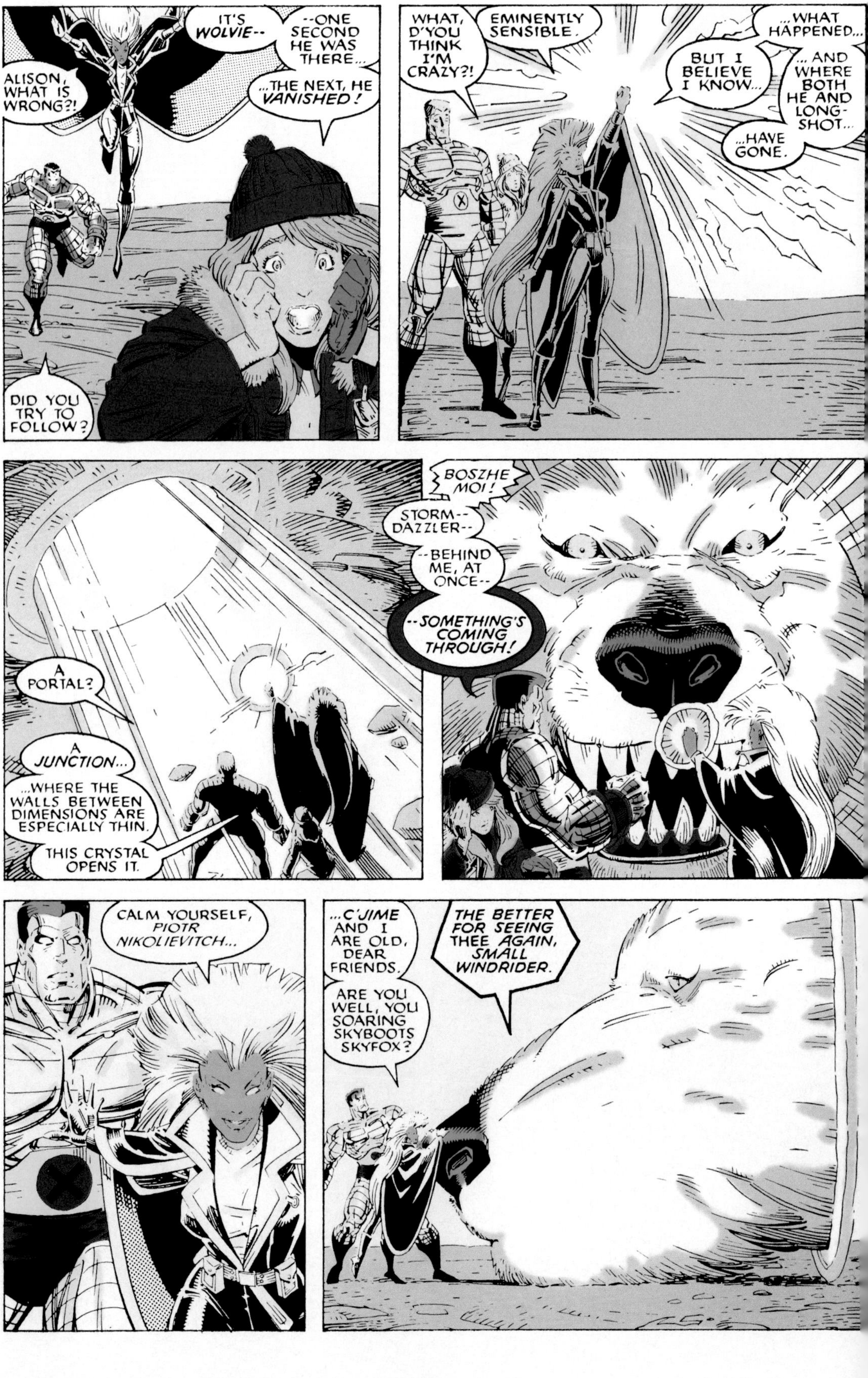
ALISON, WHAT IS WRONG?!
IT'S WOLVIE--
--ONE SECOND HE WAS THERE...
...THE NEXT, HE VANISHED!
DID YOU TRY TO FOLLOW?
WHAT, D'YOU THINK I'M CRAZY?!
EMINENTLY SENSIBLE.
BUT I BELIEVE I KNOW...
...WHAT HAPPENED...
...AND WHERE BOTH HE AND LONGSHOT...
...HAVE GONE.
A PORTAL?
A JUNCTION...
...WHERE THE WALLS BETWEEN DIMENSIONS ARE ESPECIALLY THIN.
THIS CRYSTAL OPENS IT.
BOSZHE MOI!
STORM--DAZZLER--
--BEHIND ME, AT ONCE--
--SOMETHING'S COMING THROUGH!
CALM YOURSELF, PIOTR NIKOLIEVITCH...
...C'JIME AND I ARE OLD, DEAR FRIENDS.
ARE YOU WELL, YOU SOARING SKYBOOTS SKYFOX?
THE BETTER FOR SEEING THEE AGAIN, SMALL WINDRIDER.

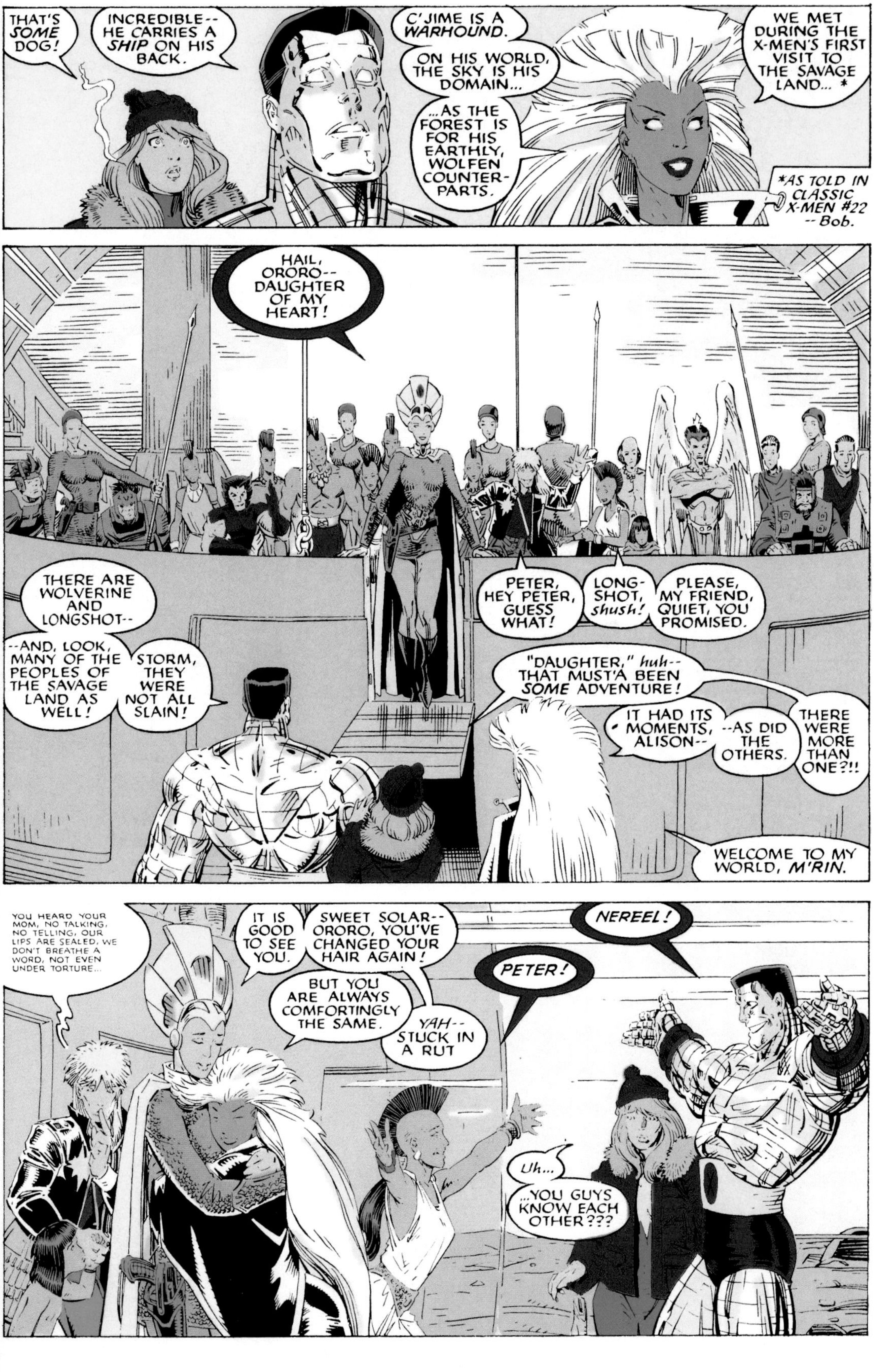
THAT'S SOME DOG!
INCREDIBLE-- HE CARRIES A SHIP ON HIS BACK.
C'JIME IS A WARHOUND.
ON HIS WORLD, THE SKY IS HIS DOMAIN...
...AS THE FOREST IS FOR HIS EARTHLY, WOLFEN COUNTER-PARTS.
WE MET DURING THE X-MEN'S FIRST VISIT TO THE SAVAGE LAND... *
*AS TOLD IN CLASSIC X-MEN #22 -- Bob.
HAIL, ORORO-- DAUGHTER OF MY HEART!
THERE ARE WOLVERINE AND LONGSHOT--
--AND, LOOK, MANY OF THE PEOPLES OF THE SAVAGE LAND AS WELL!
STORM, THEY WERE NOT ALL SLAIN!
PETER, HEY PETER, GUESS WHAT!
LONG-SHOT, shush!
PLEASE, MY FRIEND, QUIET, YOU PROMISED.
"DAUGHTER," huh-- THAT MUST'A BEEN SOME ADVENTURE!
IT HAD ITS MOMENTS, ALISON--
--AS DID THE OTHERS.
THERE WERE MORE THAN ONE?!!
WELCOME TO MY WORLD, M'RIN.
YOU HEARD YOUR MOM, NO TALKING, NO TELLING, OUR LIPS ARE SEALED, WE DON'T BREATHE A WORD, NOT EVEN UNDER TORTURE...
IT IS GOOD TO SEE YOU.
SWEET SOLAR-- ORORO, YOU'VE CHANGED YOUR HAIR AGAIN!
BUT YOU ARE ALWAYS COMFORTINGLY THE SAME.
YAH-- STUCK IN A RUT
PETER!
NEREEL!
Uh...
...YOU GUYS KNOW EACH OTHER???

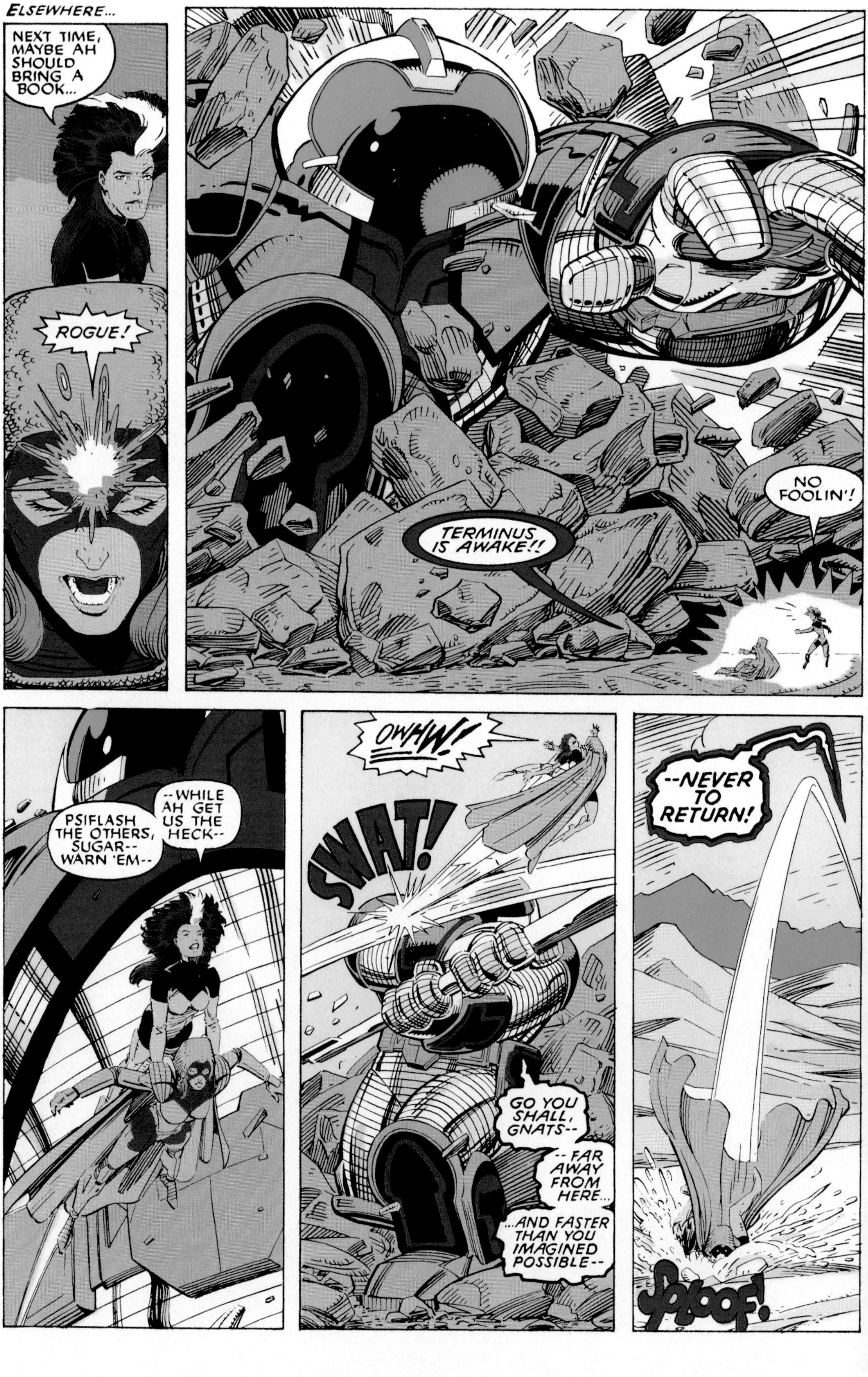
ELSEWHERE...
NEXT TIME, MAYBE AH SHOULD BRING A BOOK...
ROGUE!
TERMINUS IS AWAKE!!
NO FOOLIN'!
PSIFLASH THE OTHERS, SUGAR-- WARN 'EM--
--WHILE AH GET US THE HECK--
OWHW!
SWAT!
GO YOU SHALL, GNATS--
--FAR AWAY FROM HERE...
...AND FASTER THAN YOU IMAGINED POSSIBLE--
--NEVER TO RETURN!
SPLOOF!

THAT IS YOUR FOE?!

A SELF-STYLED...

...RAVAGER OF WORLDS--

--WHO, IN THE X-MEN...

...HAS MET HIS MATCH!

ZERAK!

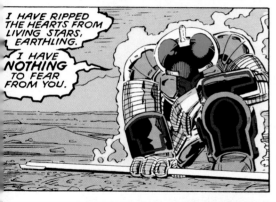

I HAVE RIPPED THE HEARTS FROM LIVING STARS, EARTHLING. I HAVE NOTHING TO FEAR FROM YOU.

THAT, VILLAIN, REMAINS TO BE SEEN.

EVERYONE ABOARD--

--FIRST OFFICER, SOUND THE CALL TO ARMS.

BARE YOUR FANGS, MY BRAVE WARHOUND--

--AND ATTACK!

M'RIN'S WARRIORS UNLEASH A BARRAGE THAT WOULD DO A STARFLEET PROUD...

...AND TO THEIR CREDIT...

...TERMINUS IS ACTUALLY STAGGERED.

SKARR

KRAM

BRAM

KROW

BOOM

BOOOM

BUT HE DOESN'T FALL.

AND ONLY C'JIME'S PRETERNATURAL AGILITY...

...SAVES THE WARHOUND FROM HIS RETURN FIRE.

SO MUCH FOR MY PROUD BOAST.

ORORO, IF WE CANNOT BREACH THAT TITAN'S ARMOR--

--STORM?!!

BE... NOT ALARMED, M'RIN.

IT IS PSYLOCKE-- OUR TELEPATH-- CONTACTING ME!

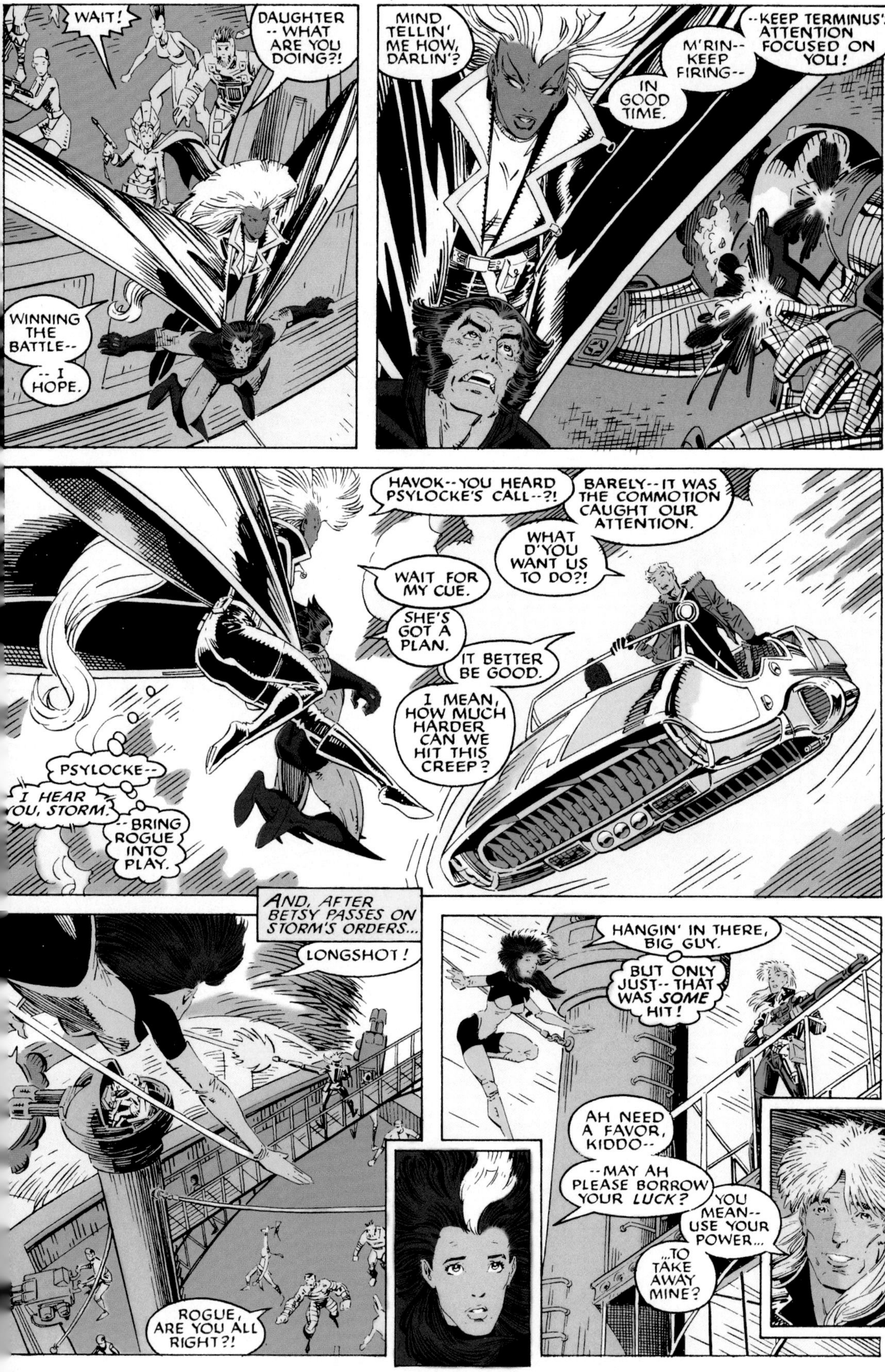
WAIT!
DAUGHTER -- WHAT ARE YOU DOING?!
WINNING THE BATTLE--
-- I HOPE.
MIND TELLIN' ME HOW, DARLIN'?
IN GOOD TIME.
M'RIN-- KEEP FIRING--
--KEEP TERMINUS'S ATTENTION FOCUSED ON YOU!
HAVOK--YOU HEARD PSYLOCKE'S CALL--?!
BARELY--IT WAS THE COMMOTION CAUGHT OUR ATTENTION.
WHAT D'YOU WANT US TO DO?!
WAIT FOR MY CUE.
SHE'S GOT A PLAN.
IT BETTER BE GOOD.
I MEAN, HOW MUCH HARDER CAN WE HIT THIS CREEP?
PSYLOCKE--
I HEAR YOU, STORM.
--BRING ROGUE INTO PLAY.
AND, AFTER BETSY PASSES ON STORM'S ORDERS...
LONGSHOT!
ROGUE, ARE YOU ALL RIGHT?!
HANGIN' IN THERE, BIG GUY.
BUT ONLY JUST-- THAT WAS SOME HIT!
AH NEED A FAVOR, KIDDO--
--MAY AH PLEASE BORROW YOUR LUCK?
YOU MEAN-- USE YOUR POWER...
...TO TAKE AWAY MINE?

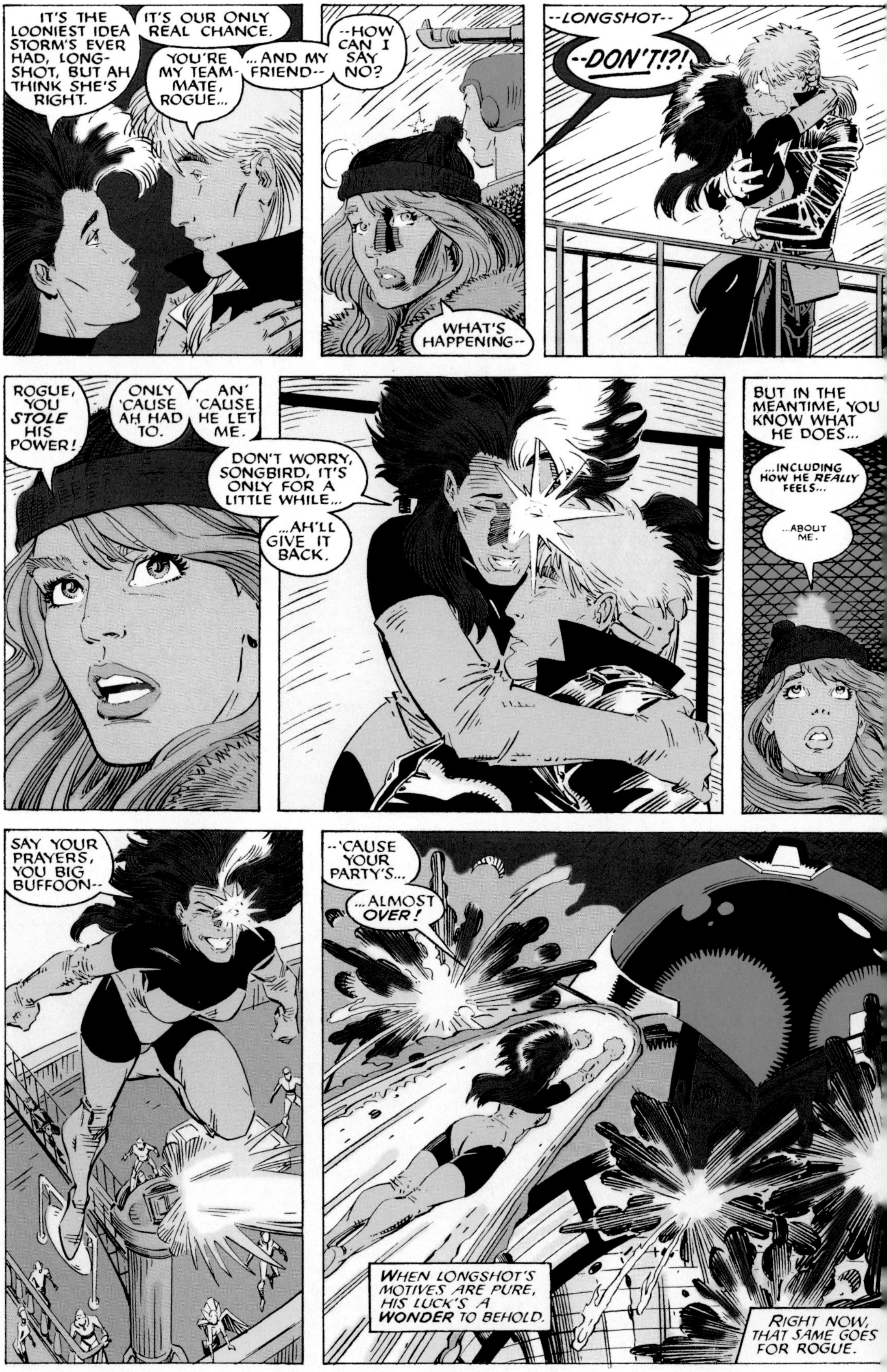
IT'S THE LOONIEST IDEA STORM'S EVER HAD, LONGSHOT, BUT AH THINK SHE'S RIGHT.
IT'S OUR ONLY REAL CHANCE.
YOU'RE MY TEAMMATE, ROGUE...
...AND MY FRIEND--
--HOW CAN I SAY NO?
WHAT'S HAPPENING--
--LONGSHOT--
--DON'T!?!
ROGUE, YOU STOLE HIS POWER!
ONLY 'CAUSE AH HAD TO.
AN' 'CAUSE HE LET ME.
DON'T WORRY, SONGBIRD, IT'S ONLY FOR A LITTLE WHILE...
...AH'LL GIVE IT BACK.
BUT IN THE MEANTIME, YOU KNOW WHAT HE DOES...
...INCLUDING HOW HE REALLY FEELS...
...ABOUT ME.
SAY YOUR PRAYERS, YOU BIG BUFFOON--
--'CAUSE YOUR PARTY'S...
...ALMOST OVER!
WHEN LONGSHOT'S MOTIVES ARE PURE, HIS LUCK'S A WONDER TO BEHOLD.
RIGHT NOW, THAT SAME GOES FOR ROGUE.

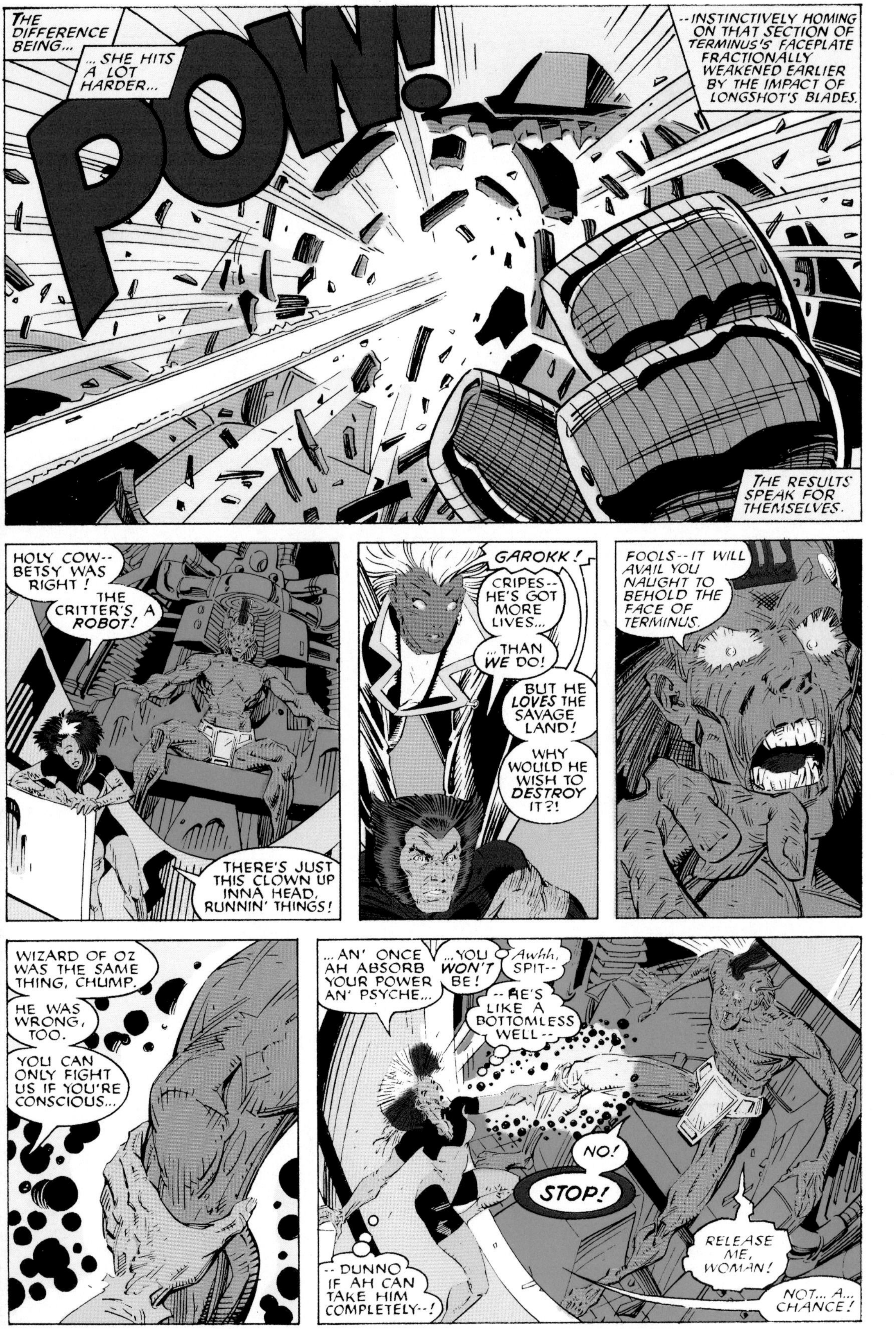
THE DIFFERENCE BEING...
... SHE HITS A LOT HARDER...
POW!
--INSTINCTIVELY HOMING ON THAT SECTION OF TERMINUS'S FACEPLATE FRACTIONALLY WEAKENED EARLIER BY THE IMPACT OF LONGSHOT'S BLADES.
THE RESULTS SPEAK FOR THEMSELVES.
HOLY COW-- BETSY WAS RIGHT!
THE CRITTER'S A ROBOT!
THERE'S JUST THIS CLOWN UP INNA HEAD, RUNNIN' THINGS!
GAROKK!
CRIPES-- HE'S GOT MORE LIVES...
... THAN WE DO!
BUT HE LOVES THE SAVAGE LAND!
WHY WOULD HE WISH TO DESTROY IT?!
FOOLS-- IT WILL AVAIL YOU NAUGHT TO BEHOLD THE FACE OF TERMINUS.
WIZARD OF OZ WAS THE SAME THING, CHUMP.
HE WAS WRONG, TOO.
YOU CAN ONLY FIGHT US IF YOU'RE CONSCIOUS...
... AN' ONCE AH ABSORB YOUR POWER AN' PSYCHE...
... YOU WON'T BE!
Awhh, SPIT--
-- HE'S LIKE A BOTTOMLESS WELL--
NO!
STOP!
-- DUNNO IF AH CAN TAKE HIM COMPLETELY--!
RELEASE ME, WOMAN!
NOT... A... CHANCE!

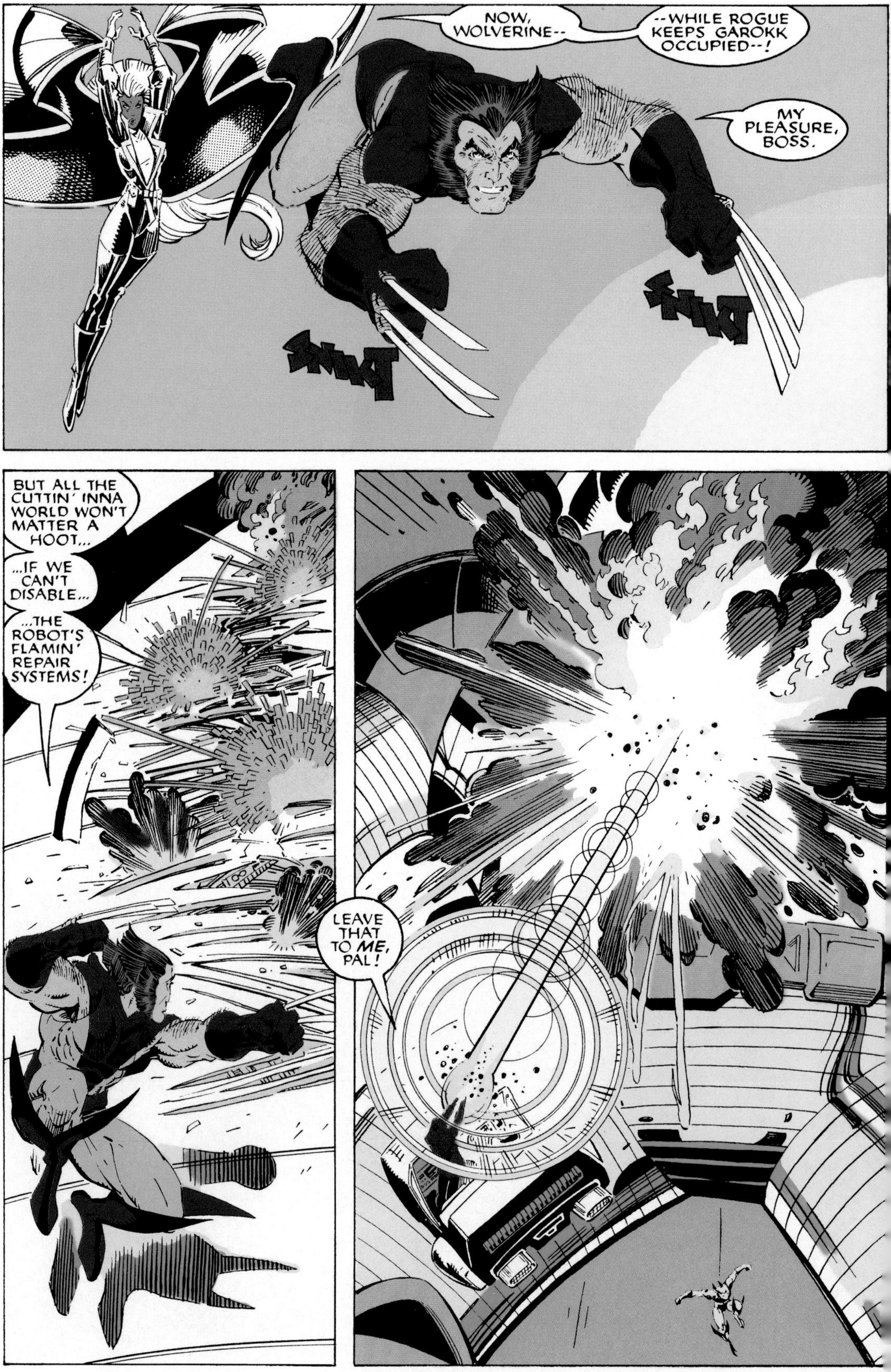
NOW, WOLVERINE--
--WHILE ROGUE KEEPS GAROKK OCCUPIED--!
MY PLEASURE, BOSS.
SNIKT
SNIKT
BUT ALL THE CUTTIN' INNA WORLD WON'T MATTER A HOOT...
...IF WE CAN'T DISABLE...
...THE ROBOT'S FLAMIN' REPAIR SYSTEMS!
LEAVE THAT TO *ME*, PAL!

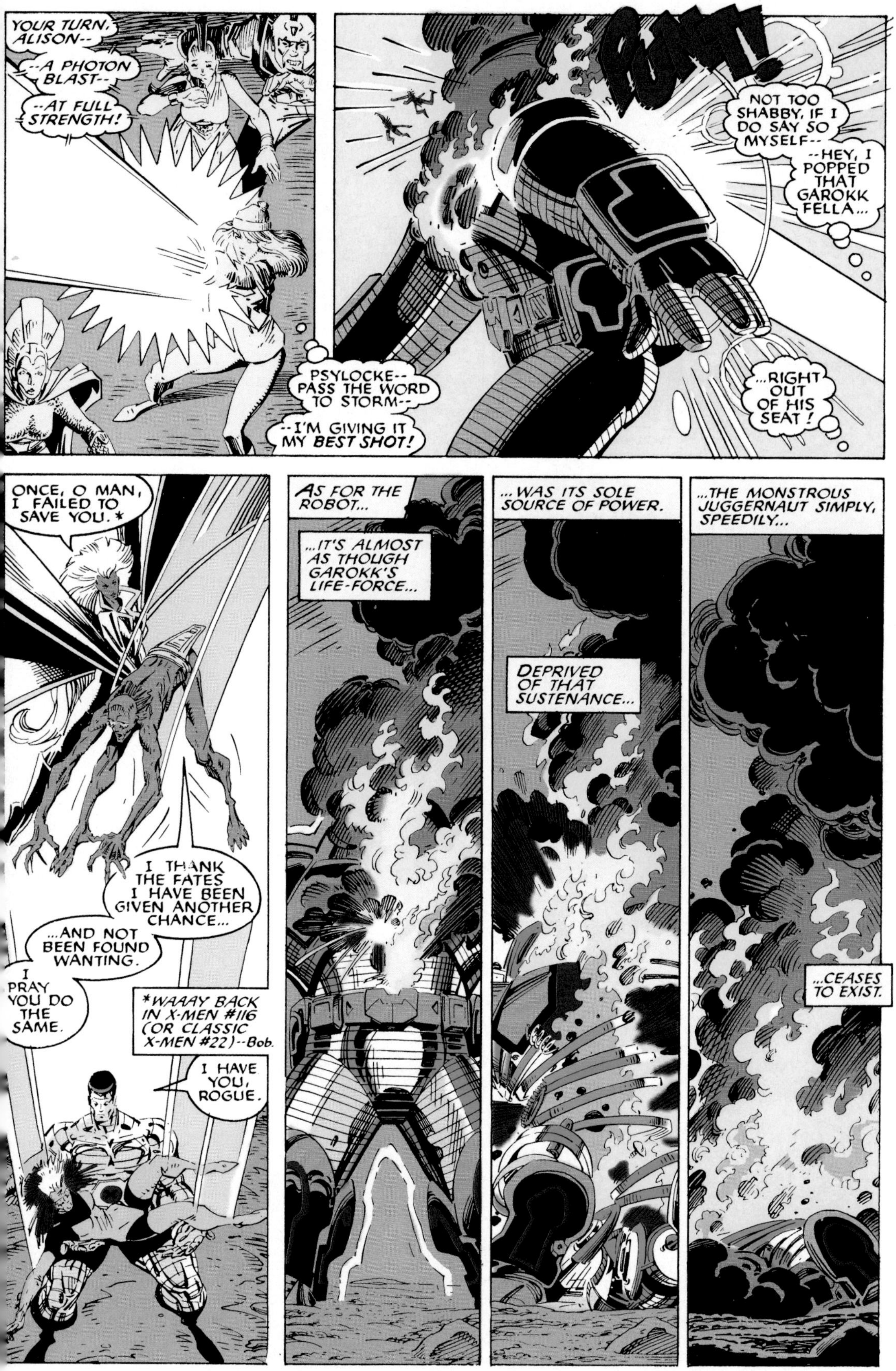

YOUR TURN, ALISON--
--A PHOTON BLAST--
--AT FULL STRENGTH!
PSYLOCKE-- PASS THE WORD TO STORM--
--I'M GIVING IT MY BEST SHOT!
POOM!
NOT TOO SHABBY, IF I DO SAY SO MYSELF--
--HEY, I POPPED THAT GAROKK FELLA...
...RIGHT OUT OF HIS SEAT!
ONCE, O MAN, I FAILED TO SAVE YOU.*
I THANK THE FATES I HAVE BEEN GIVEN ANOTHER CHANCE...
...AND NOT BEEN FOUND WANTING.
I PRAY YOU DO THE SAME.
*WAAAY BACK IN X-MEN #116 (OR CLASSIC X-MEN #22)--Bob.
I HAVE YOU, ROGUE.
AS FOR THE ROBOT...
...IT'S ALMOST AS THOUGH GAROKK'S LIFE-FORCE...
...WAS ITS SOLE SOURCE OF POWER.
DEPRIVED OF THAT SUSTENANCE...
...THE MONSTROUS JUGGERNAUT SIMPLY, SPEEDILY...
...CEASES TO EXIST.

AND WHEN THE EFFECTS OF ROGUE'S ATTACK HAVE WORN OFF AND GAROKK IS ONCE MORE HIMSELF...

I'M SORRY. I REMEMBER...

...NOTHING.

FROM THE END OF MY LAST ENCOUNTER WITH THE X-MEN...

...TO THE MOMENT I AWOKE HERE-- NOTHING.

BY ALL THE GODS--

--THE LAND, MY BELOVED LAND--

--WHAT HAS HAPPENED TO THE SAVAGE LAND?!!

AND THE TALE IS TOLD AGAIN, OF HOW TERMINUS LAID WASTE TO IT.

TERMINUS-- --BUT I... WAS IT NOT...

...COULD THAT DESTROYER HAVE BEEN...

...ME?

NO, MY FRIEND, NOT YOU-- --BUT ANOTHER WHO WORE THAT ACCURSED ARMOR.

EVOLUTIONARY, HAVE YOU CONSIDERED THE IMPLICATIONS?

IF THE LAST GUY WASN'T TERMINUS, AND GAROKK ISN'T...

...THEN THE REAL ONE MUST STILL BE ON THE LOOSE.

PRECISELY, YOUNG ALEX.

AND WHEN HE STRIKES AGAIN, YOU AND YOUR COMRADES MUST STAND READY TO STOP HIM.

IT'S WHAT WE'RE HERE FOR, SIR.

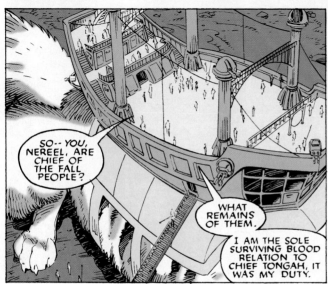

SO-- YOU, NEREEL, ARE CHIEF OF THE FALL PEOPLE?

WHAT REMAINS OF THEM.

I AM THE SOLE SURVIVING BLOOD RELATION TO CHIEF TONGAH, IT WAS MY DUTY.

AND WHO IS THIS WRIGGLER?

I MUST BE CAREFUL WITH THE BOY-- WITH EVERYONE. I AM SO STRONG, I COULD SNAP HIS BONES WITHOUT THINKING.

MY SON.

I LIKE HIM.

THE FEELING APPEARS MUTUAL

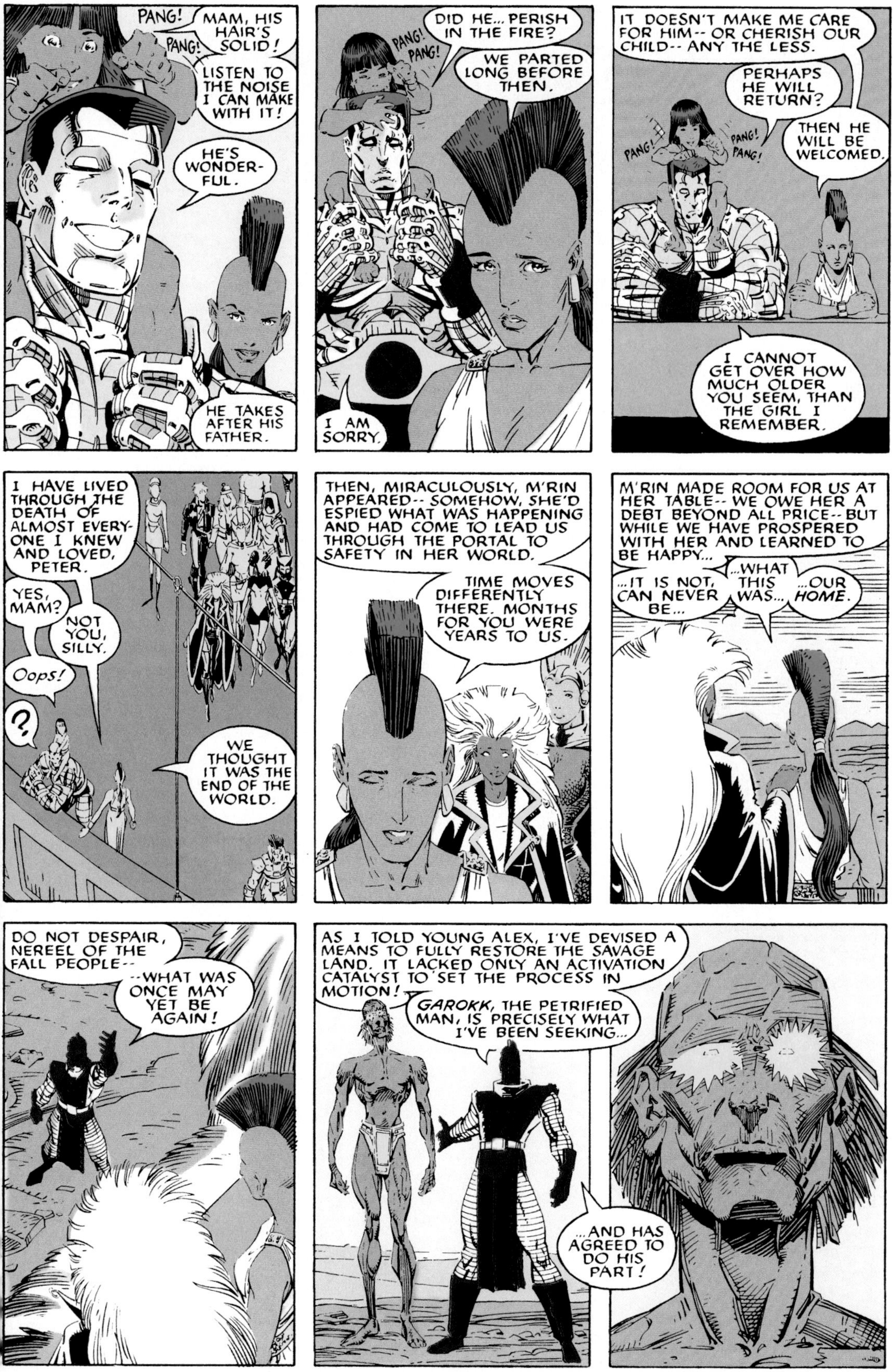
PANG!
MAM, HIS HAIR'S SOLID!
PANG!
LISTEN TO THE NOISE I CAN MAKE WITH IT!
HE'S WONDERFUL.
HE TAKES AFTER HIS FATHER.
DID HE... PERISH IN THE FIRE?
PANG! PANG!
WE PARTED LONG BEFORE THEN.
I AM SORRY.
IT DOESN'T MAKE ME CARE FOR HIM-- OR CHERISH OUR CHILD-- ANY THE LESS.
PERHAPS HE WILL RETURN?
PANG! PANG! PANG!
THEN HE WILL BE WELCOMED.
I CANNOT GET OVER HOW MUCH OLDER YOU SEEM, THAN THE GIRL I REMEMBER.
I HAVE LIVED THROUGH THE DEATH OF ALMOST EVERYONE I KNEW AND LOVED, PETER.
YES, MAM?
NOT YOU, SILLY.
Oops!
?
WE THOUGHT IT WAS THE END OF THE WORLD.
THEN, MIRACULOUSLY, M'RIN APPEARED-- SOMEHOW, SHE'D ESPIED WHAT WAS HAPPENING AND HAD COME TO LEAD US THROUGH THE PORTAL TO SAFETY IN HER WORLD.
TIME MOVES DIFFERENTLY THERE. MONTHS FOR YOU WERE YEARS TO US.
M'RIN MADE ROOM FOR US AT HER TABLE-- WE OWE HER A DEBT BEYOND ALL PRICE-- BUT WHILE WE HAVE PROSPERED WITH HER AND LEARNED TO BE HAPPY...
...IT IS NOT, CAN NEVER BE...
...WHAT THIS WAS...
...OUR HOME.
DO NOT DESPAIR, NEREEL OF THE FALL PEOPLE--
--WHAT WAS ONCE MAY YET BE AGAIN!
AS I TOLD YOUNG ALEX, I'VE DEVISED A MEANS TO FULLY RESTORE THE SAVAGE LAND. IT LACKED ONLY AN ACTIVATION CATALYST TO SET THE PROCESS IN MOTION!
GAROKK, THE PETRIFIED MAN, IS PRECISELY WHAT I'VE BEEN SEEKING...
...AND HAS AGREED TO DO HIS PART!

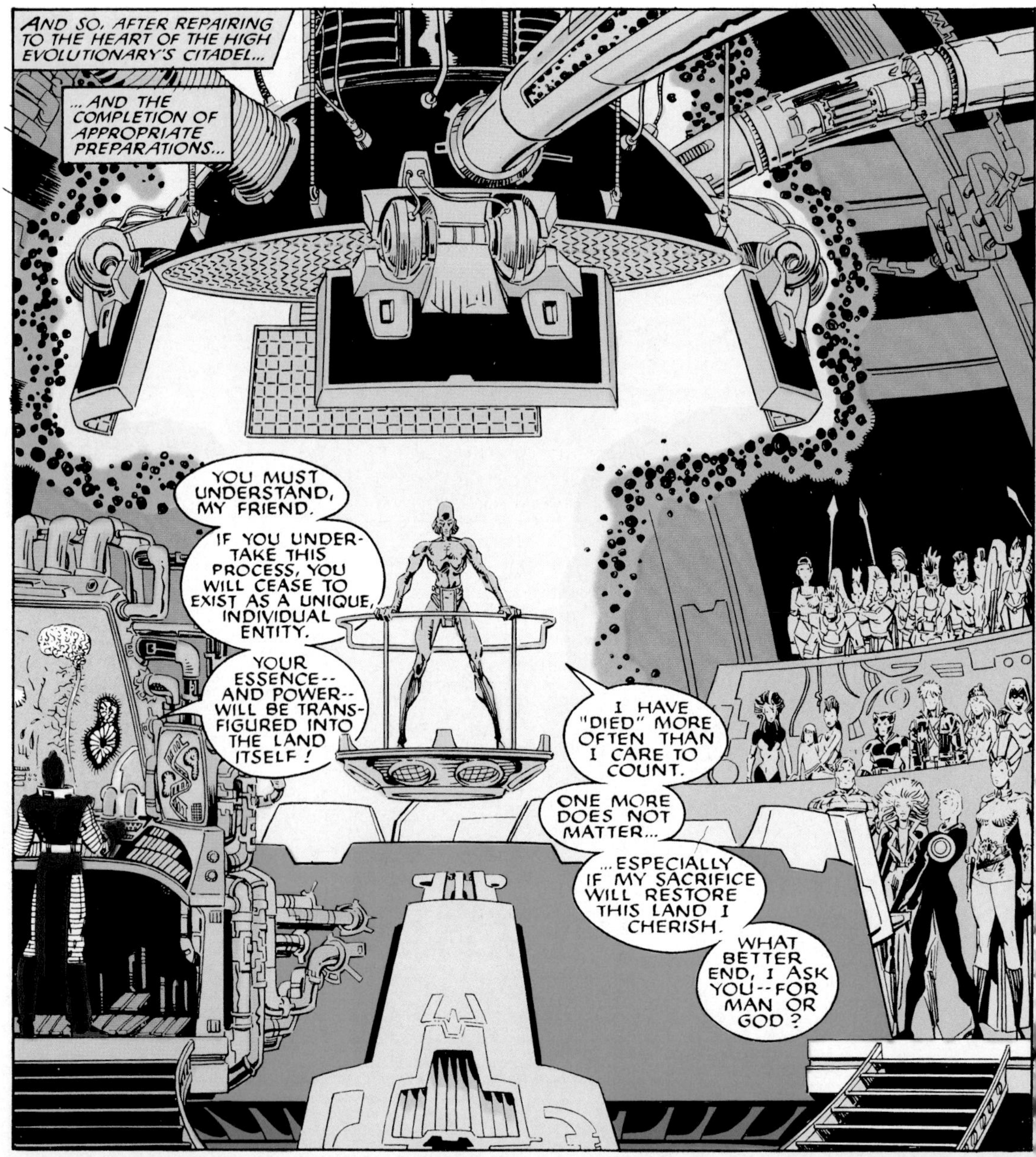
AND SO, AFTER REPAIRING TO THE HEART OF THE HIGH EVOLUTIONARY'S CITADEL...
...AND THE COMPLETION OF APPROPRIATE PREPARATIONS...
YOU MUST UNDERSTAND, MY FRIEND.
IF YOU UNDERTAKE THIS PROCESS, YOU WILL CEASE TO EXIST AS A UNIQUE, INDIVIDUAL ENTITY.
YOUR ESSENCE--AND POWER--WILL BE TRANSFIGURED INTO THE LAND ITSELF!
I HAVE "DIED" MORE OFTEN THAN I CARE TO COUNT.
ONE MORE DOES NOT MATTER...
...ESPECIALLY IF MY SACRIFICE WILL RESTORE THIS LAND I CHERISH.
WHAT BETTER END, I ASK YOU--FOR MAN OR GOD?

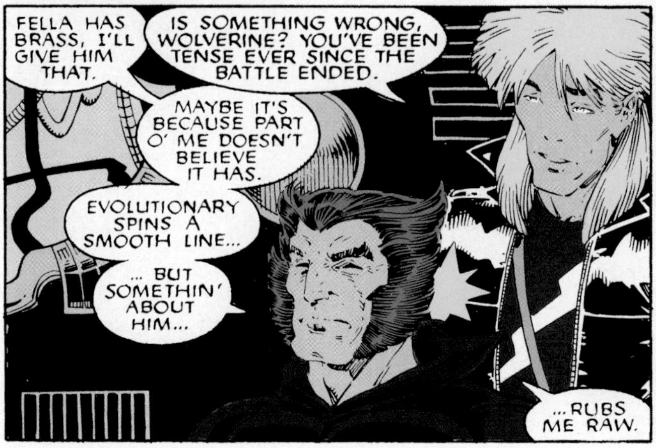
FELLA HAS BRASS, I'LL GIVE HIM THAT.
IS SOMETHING WRONG, WOLVERINE? YOU'VE BEEN TENSE EVER SINCE THE BATTLE ENDED.
MAYBE IT'S BECAUSE PART O' ME DOESN'T BELIEVE IT HAS.
EVOLUTIONARY SPINS A SMOOTH LINE...
...BUT SOMETHIN' ABOUT HIM...
...RUBS ME RAW.

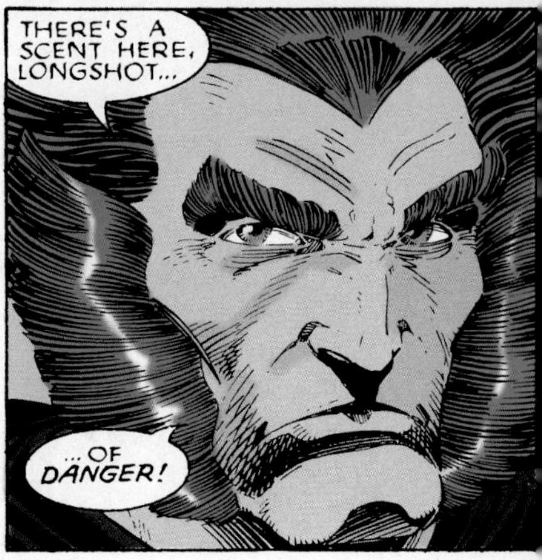
THERE'S A SCENT HERE, LONGSHOT...
...OF DANGER!

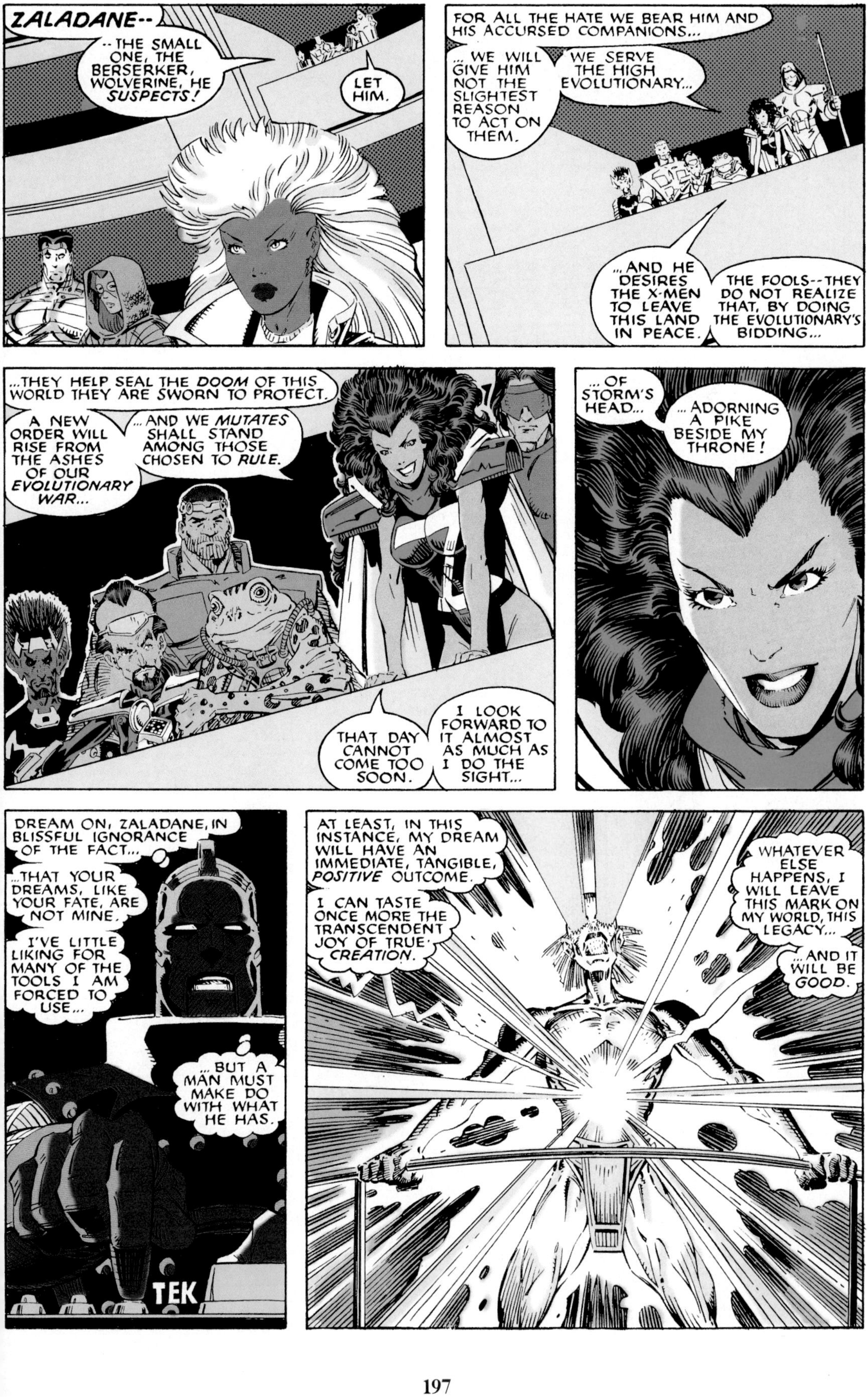

ZALADANE--
--THE SMALL ONE, THE BERSERKER, WOLVERINE, HE SUSPECTS!
LET HIM.
FOR ALL THE HATE WE BEAR HIM AND HIS ACCURSED COMPANIONS...
...WE WILL GIVE HIM NOT THE SLIGHTEST REASON TO ACT ON THEM.
WE SERVE THE HIGH EVOLUTIONARY...
...AND HE DESIRES THE X-MEN TO LEAVE THIS LAND IN PEACE.
THE FOOLS--THEY DO NOT REALIZE THAT, BY DOING THE EVOLUTIONARY'S BIDDING...
...THEY HELP SEAL THE DOOM OF THIS WORLD THEY ARE SWORN TO PROTECT.
A NEW ORDER WILL RISE FROM THE ASHES OF OUR EVOLUTIONARY WAR...
...AND WE MUTATES SHALL STAND AMONG THOSE CHOSEN TO RULE.
THAT DAY CANNOT COME TOO SOON.
I LOOK FORWARD TO IT ALMOST AS MUCH AS I DO THE SIGHT...
...OF STORM'S HEAD...
...ADORNING A PIKE BESIDE MY THRONE!
DREAM ON, ZALADANE, IN BLISSFUL IGNORANCE OF THE FACT...
...THAT YOUR DREAMS, LIKE YOUR FATE, ARE NOT MINE.
I'VE LITTLE LIKING FOR MANY OF THE TOOLS I AM FORCED TO USE...
...BUT A MAN MUST MAKE DO WITH WHAT HE HAS.
TEK
AT LEAST, IN THIS INSTANCE, MY DREAM WILL HAVE AN IMMEDIATE, TANGIBLE, POSITIVE OUTCOME.
I CAN TASTE ONCE MORE THE TRANSCENDENT JOY OF TRUE CREATION.
WHATEVER ELSE HAPPENS, I WILL LEAVE THIS MARK ON MY WORLD, THIS LEGACY...
...AND IT WILL BE GOOD.

AND IT WAS--

--MORE QUICKLY, MORE COMPLETELY, THAN ANY IMAGINED.

MAGNIFICENT--

--THE LAND TRULY *IS* REBORN...

...MORE BEAUTIFUL THAN BEFORE!

AT LAST, I THINK, GAROKK HAS FOUND THE PURPOSE AND PEACE HE SOUGHT FOR SO LONG.

AND YOU, CHILD OF MY HEART...

...CAN YOU SAY THE SAME?

I PRAY SO. I DO MY BEST.

ORORO-- I MUST GO.

EACH TIME WE PART, DAUGHTER, I WISH YOU WOULD COME WITH ME--

--NO LONGER TO VISIT, BUT TO *STAY!*

PERHAPS, SOMEDAY...

...I SHALL.

YOU MEAN THAT?

YES-- BUT I AM BOUND, LIKE NEREEL, LIKE M'RIN HER-SELF, BY PRIOR RESPONSI-BILITIES.

THE HIGH EVOLUTIONARY'S GONE. HIS ASSISTANT SAID HE LEFT AS SOON AS HE WAS SURE HIS PROCESS WAS A SUCCESS.

THAT, I SUSPECT IS FOR THE BEST.

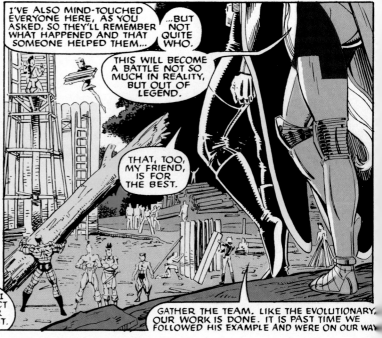

I'VE ALSO MIND-TOUCHED EVERYONE HERE, AS YOU ASKED, SO THEY'LL REMEMBER WHAT HAPPENED AND THAT SOMEONE HELPED THEM...

...BUT NOT QUITE WHO.

THIS WILL BECOME A BATTLE NOT SO MUCH IN REALITY, BUT OUT OF LEGEND.

THAT, TOO, MY FRIEND, IS FOR THE BEST.

GATHER THE TEAM. LIKE THE EVOLUTIONARY, OUR WORK IS DONE. IT IS PAST TIME WE FOLLOWED HIS EXAMPLE AND WERE ON OUR WAY.

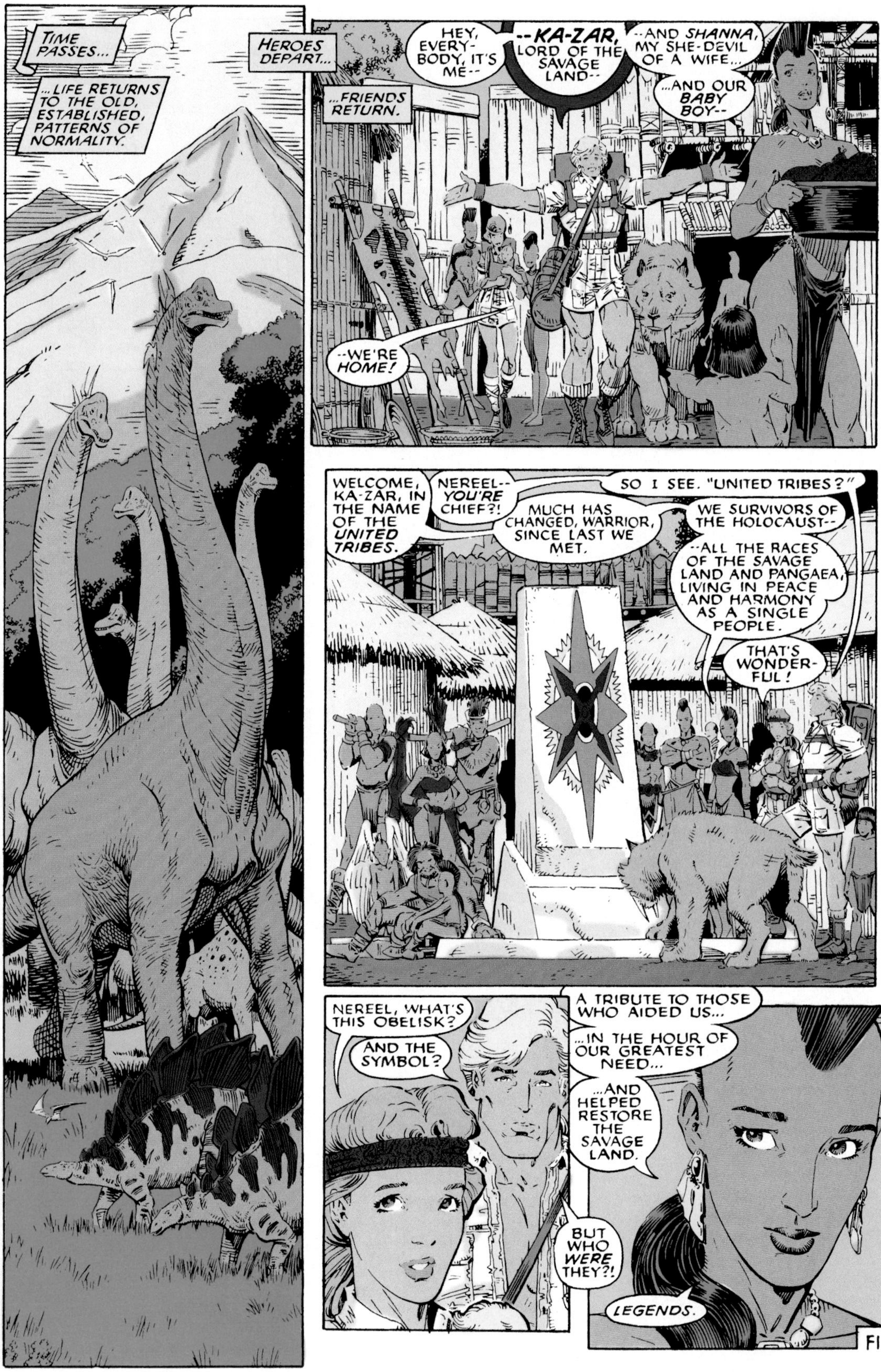
TIME PASSES...
...LIFE RETURNS TO THE OLD, ESTABLISHED, PATTERNS OF NORMALITY.
HEROES DEPART...
...FRIENDS RETURN.
HEY, EVERY-BODY, IT'S ME--
--KA-ZAR, LORD OF THE SAVAGE LAND--
--AND SHANNA, MY SHE-DEVIL OF A WIFE...
...AND OUR BABY BOY--
--WE'RE HOME!
WELCOME, KA-ZAR, IN THE NAME OF THE UNITED TRIBES.
NEREEL-- YOU'RE CHIEF?!
MUCH HAS CHANGED, WARRIOR, SINCE LAST WE MET.
SO I SEE. "UNITED TRIBES?"
WE SURVIVORS OF THE HOLOCAUST--
--ALL THE RACES OF THE SAVAGE LAND AND PANGAEA, LIVING IN PEACE AND HARMONY AS A SINGLE PEOPLE.
THAT'S WONDER-FUL!
NEREEL, WHAT'S THIS OBELISK?
AND THE SYMBOL?
A TRIBUTE TO THOSE WHO AIDED US...
...IN THE HOUR OF OUR GREATEST NEED...
...AND HELPED RESTORE THE SAVAGE LAND.
BUT WHO WERE THEY?!
LEGENDS.
FIN.

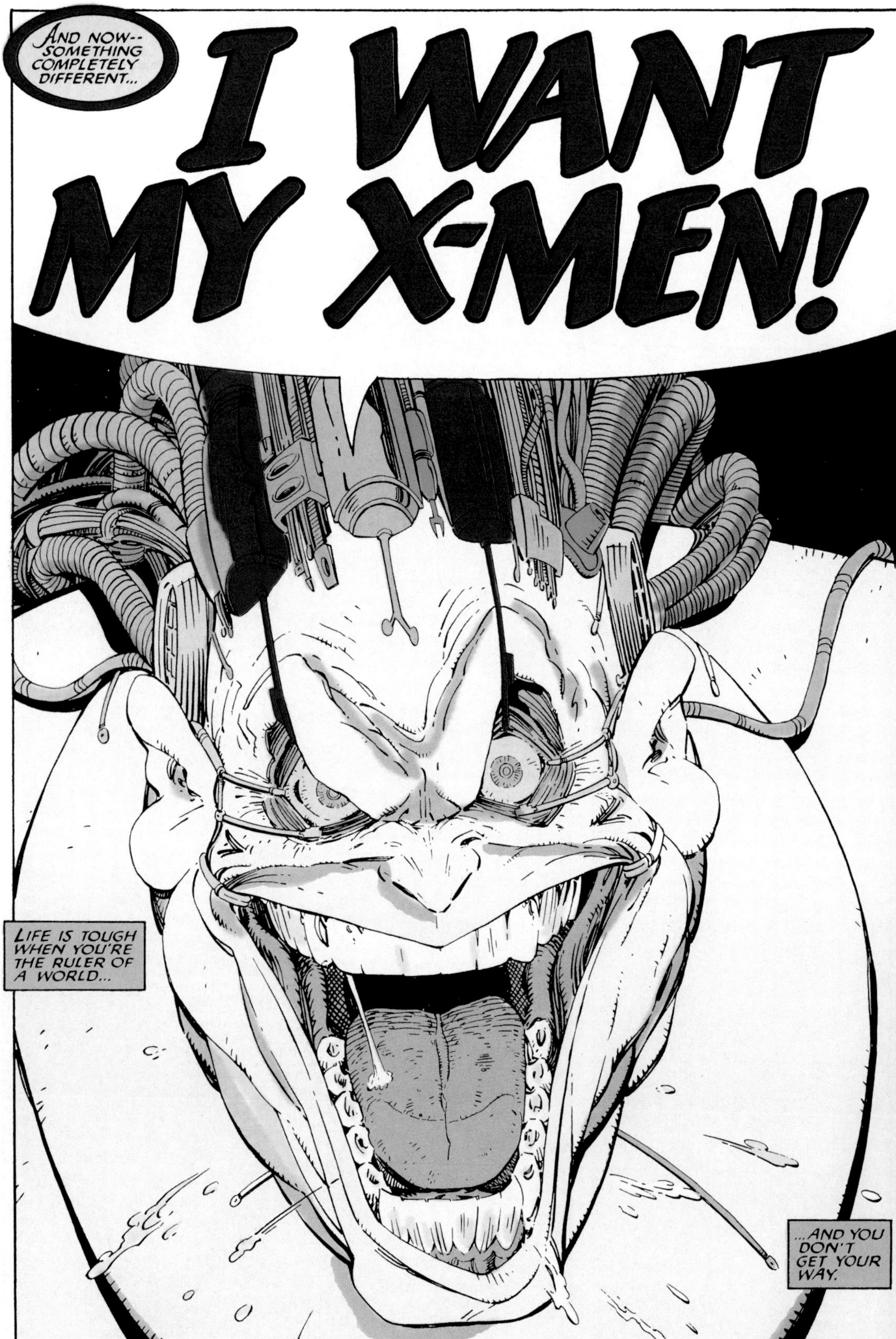
AND NOW--SOMETHING COMPLETELY DIFFERENT...
I WANT MY X-MEN!
LIFE IS TOUGH WHEN YOU'RE THE RULER OF A WORLD...
...AND YOU DON'T GET YOUR WAY.

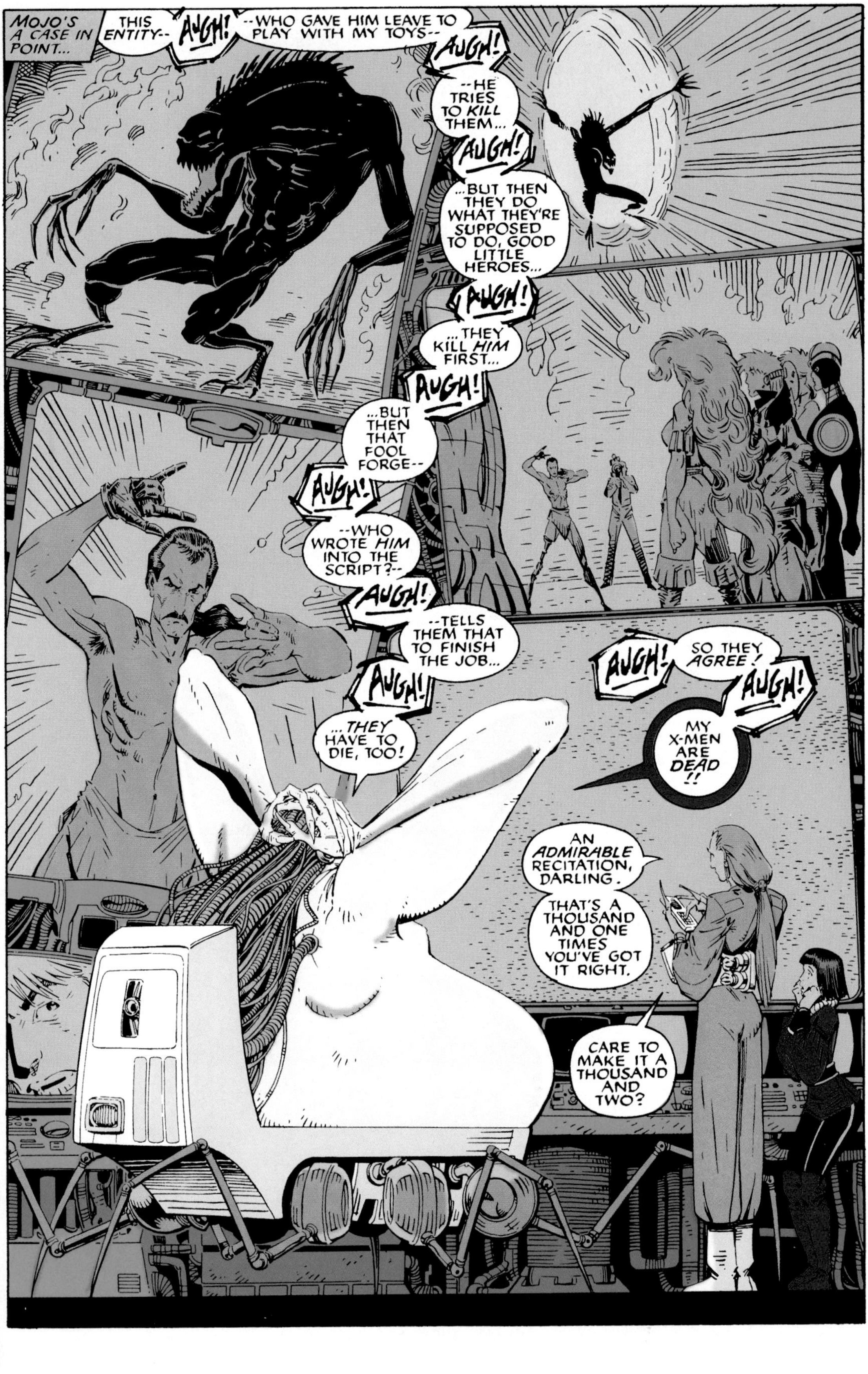
MOJO'S A CASE IN POINT...
THIS ENTITY--
AUGH!
--WHO GAVE HIM LEAVE TO PLAY WITH MY TOYS--
AUGH!
--HE TRIES TO KILL THEM...
AUGH!
...BUT THEN THEY DO WHAT THEY'RE SUPPOSED TO DO, GOOD LITTLE HEROES...
AUGH!
...THEY KILL HIM FIRST...
AUGH!
...BUT THEN THAT FOOL FORGE--
AUGH!
--WHO WROTE HIM INTO THE SCRIPT?--
AUGH!
--TELLS THEM THAT TO FINISH THE JOB...
AUGH!
...THEY HAVE TO DIE, TOO!
AUGH!
SO THEY AGREE!
AUGH!
MY X-MEN ARE DEAD!!
AN ADMIRABLE RECITATION, DARLING.
THAT'S A THOUSAND AND ONE TIMES YOU'VE GOT IT RIGHT.
CARE TO MAKE IT A THOUSAND AND TWO?

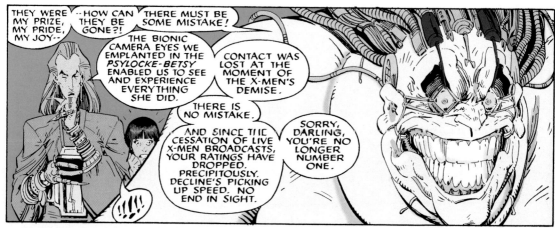

THEY WERE MY PRIZE, MY PRIDE, MY JOY--

--HOW CAN THEY BE GONE?!

THERE MUST BE SOME MISTAKE!

THE BIONIC CAMERA EYES WE EMPLANTED IN THE *PSYLOCKE-BETSY* ENABLED US TO SEE AND EXPERIENCE EVERYTHING SHE DID.

CONTACT WAS LOST AT THE MOMENT OF THE X-MEN'S DEMISE.

THERE IS NO MISTAKE.

AND SINCE THE CESSATION OF LIVE X-MEN BROADCASTS, YOUR RATINGS HAVE DROPPED. PRECIPITOUSLY. DECLINE'S PICKING UP SPEED. NO END IN SIGHT.

SORRY, DARLING, YOU'RE NO LONGER NUMBER ONE.

!!!!

AAAUGH!!!!

HE'S MAD MAD MAD!

LEMME-OUTTAHERE!

SCATTER!

HIDE!

RUN AWAY RUN AWAY!

BEAT IT!

FEETS, DO YOUR STUFF!

OHMIGOSH **OH** MIGOSH HE'S LOSING IT WE'RE DOOMED IT'S A DISASTER WE'LL NEVER RECOVER HE'LL BLOW OUR CIRCUITS BLAST HIS MIND CAST US ON THE TRASH PILE NO JOB NO PAY NO HOME NO FUN THINK OF THE SHAME THE DISGRACE BEGGING STARVING FILTHY STINKING RAGS TATTERS EVERY HAND AGAINST US TILL WE...

SLAP
SLAP
SLAP
SLAP

?

DIEEEK!
OOK!
GACK!
Sputter!

Sigh!

MINOR-DOMO, MUST YOU?

THIS IS NOT THE TIME.

WHUMP!

WHAT'S THAT WHAT'S THAT?!

HOW DARE *ANYONE* DIE WITHOUT PERMISSION?!!

FIRST THE X-MEN, NOW THIS, WHAT'S LIFE *COMING* TO?!!!

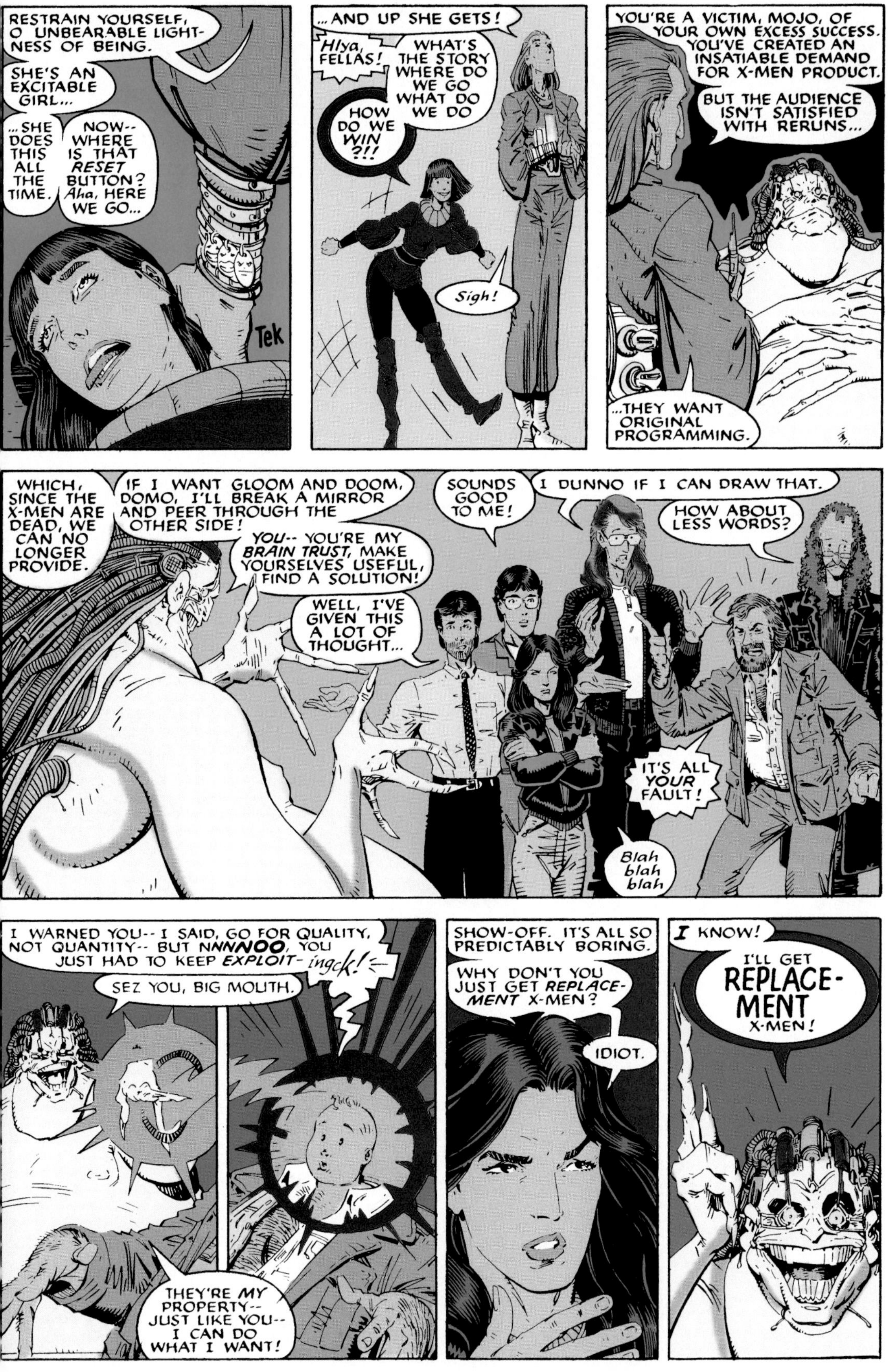
RESTRAIN YOURSELF, O UNBEARABLE LIGHTNESS OF BEING.
SHE'S AN EXCITABLE GIRL...
...SHE DOES THIS ALL THE TIME.
NOW-- WHERE IS THAT RESET BUTTON? Aha, HERE WE GO...
Tek
...AND UP SHE GETS!
HIya, FELLAS!
WHAT'S THE STORY WHERE DO WE GO WHAT DO WE DO
HOW DO WE WIN ?!!
Sigh!
YOU'RE A VICTIM, MOJO, OF YOUR OWN EXCESS SUCCESS. YOU'VE CREATED AN INSATIABLE DEMAND FOR X-MEN PRODUCT.
BUT THE AUDIENCE ISN'T SATISFIED WITH RERUNS...
...THEY WANT ORIGINAL PROGRAMMING.
WHICH, SINCE THE X-MEN ARE DEAD, WE CAN NO LONGER PROVIDE.
IF I WANT GLOOM AND DOOM, DOMO, I'LL BREAK A MIRROR AND PEER THROUGH THE OTHER SIDE!
YOU-- YOU'RE MY BRAIN TRUST, MAKE YOURSELVES USEFUL, FIND A SOLUTION!
SOUNDS GOOD TO ME!
I DUNNO IF I CAN DRAW THAT.
HOW ABOUT LESS WORDS?
WELL, I'VE GIVEN THIS A LOT OF THOUGHT...
IT'S ALL YOUR FAULT!
Blah blah blah
I WARNED YOU-- I SAID, GO FOR QUALITY, NOT QUANTITY-- BUT NNNNOO, YOU JUST HAD TO KEEP EXPLOIT- ingck!
SEZ YOU, BIG MOUTH.
THEY'RE MY PROPERTY-- JUST LIKE YOU-- I CAN DO WHAT I WANT!
SHOW-OFF. IT'S ALL SO PREDICTABLY BORING.
WHY DON'T YOU JUST GET REPLACEMENT X-MEN?
IDIOT.
I KNOW!
I'LL GET REPLACEMENT X-MEN!

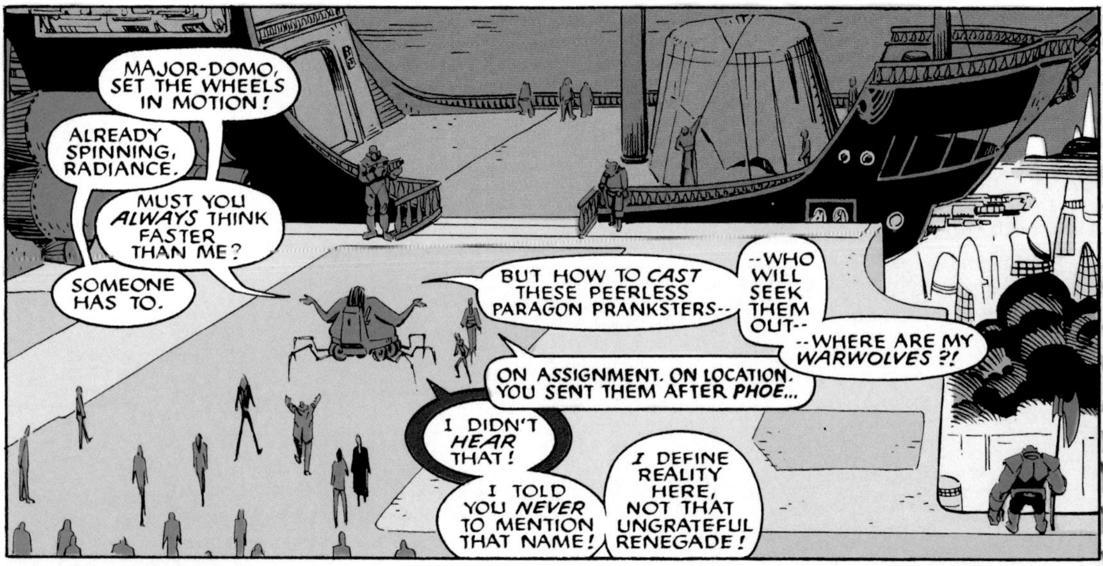
MAJOR-DOMO, SET THE WHEELS IN MOTION!
ALREADY SPINNING, RADIANCE.
MUST YOU ALWAYS THINK FASTER THAN ME?
SOMEONE HAS TO.
BUT HOW TO CAST THESE PEERLESS PARAGON PRANKSTERS--
--WHO WILL SEEK THEM OUT--
--WHERE ARE MY WARWOLVES ?!
ON ASSIGNMENT. ON LOCATION. YOU SENT THEM AFTER PHOE...
I DIDN'T HEAR THAT!
I TOLD YOU NEVER TO MENTION THAT NAME!
I DEFINE REALITY HERE, NOT THAT UNGRATEFUL RENEGADE!

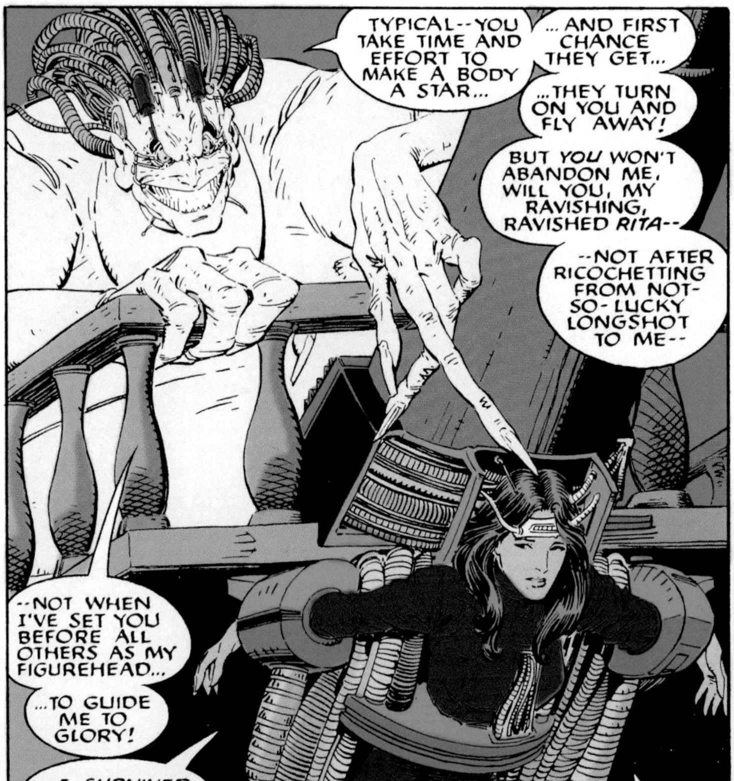
TYPICAL--YOU TAKE TIME AND EFFORT TO MAKE A BODY A STAR...
...AND FIRST CHANCE THEY GET...
...THEY TURN ON YOU AND FLY AWAY!
BUT YOU WON'T ABANDON ME, WILL YOU, MY RAVISHING, RAVISHED RITA--
--NOT AFTER RICOCHETTING FROM NOT-SO-LUCKY LONGSHOT TO ME--
--NOT WHEN I'VE SET YOU BEFORE ALL OTHERS AS MY FIGUREHEAD...
...TO GUIDE ME TO GLORY!
I SURVIVED MY LAST JAUNT UP HERE, FATS, REMEMBER?*
THESE ARE WILD RIDES YOU SEND ME ON.
I'M STARTING TO ENJOY 'EM!
*IN LONGSHOT #'s 5 & 6--Bob. (AND WASN'T THAT SO GROSS, WHAT JUST HAPPENED TO CHRIS--guffaw! :-)

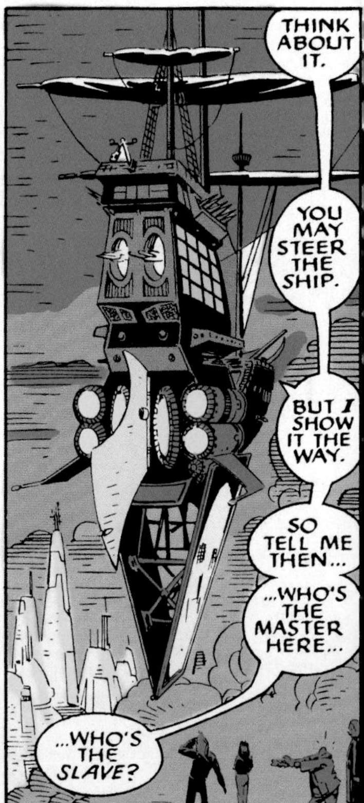
THINK ABOUT IT.
YOU MAY STEER THE SHIP.
BUT I SHOW IT THE WAY.
SO TELL ME THEN...
...WHO'S THE MASTER HERE...
...WHO'S THE SLAVE?

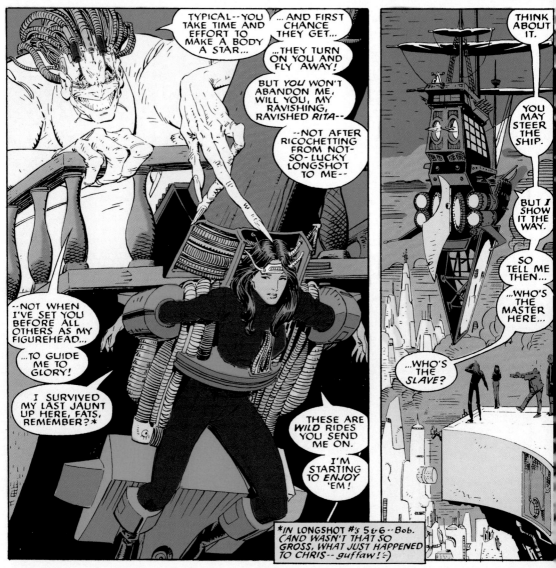

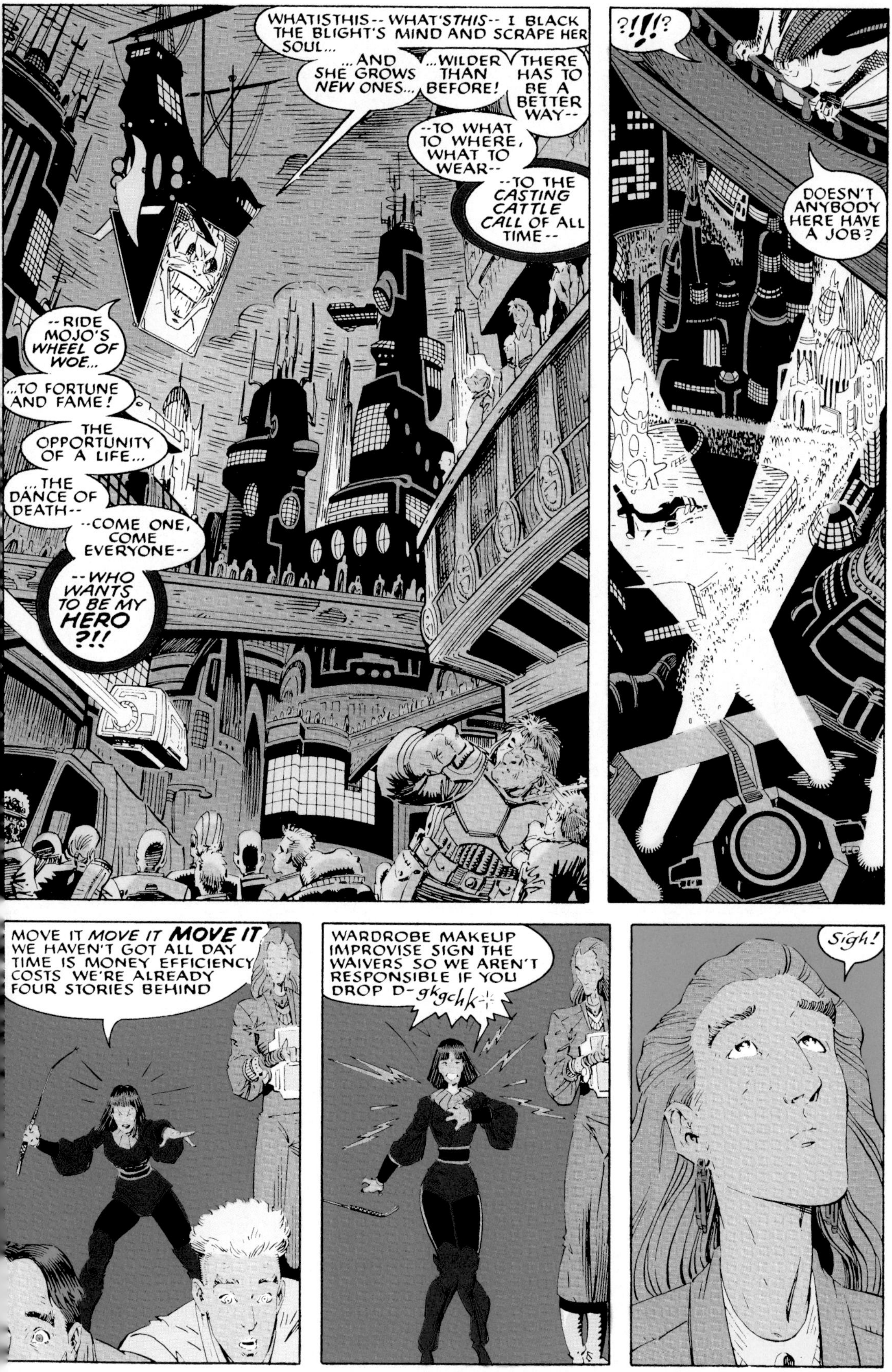
WHATISTHIS-- WHAT'S THIS-- I BLACK THE BLIGHT'S MIND AND SCRAPE HER SOUL...
...AND SHE GROWS NEW ONES...
...WILDER THAN BEFORE!
THERE HAS TO BE A BETTER WAY--
--TO WHAT TO WHERE, WHAT TO WEAR--
--TO THE CASTING CATTLE CALL OF ALL TIME--
--RIDE MOJO'S WHEEL OF WOE...
...TO FORTUNE AND FAME!
THE OPPORTUNITY OF A LIFE...
...THE DANCE OF DEATH--
--COME ONE, COME EVERYONE--
--WHO WANTS TO BE MY HERO ?!!
?!!!?
DOESN'T ANYBODY HERE HAVE A JOB?
MOVE IT MOVE IT MOVE IT WE HAVEN'T GOT ALL DAY TIME IS MONEY EFFICIENCY COSTS WE'RE ALREADY FOUR STORIES BEHIND
WARDROBE MAKEUP IMPROVISE SIGN THE WAIVERS SO WE AREN'T RESPONSIBLE IF YOU DROP D-gkgchk
Sigh!

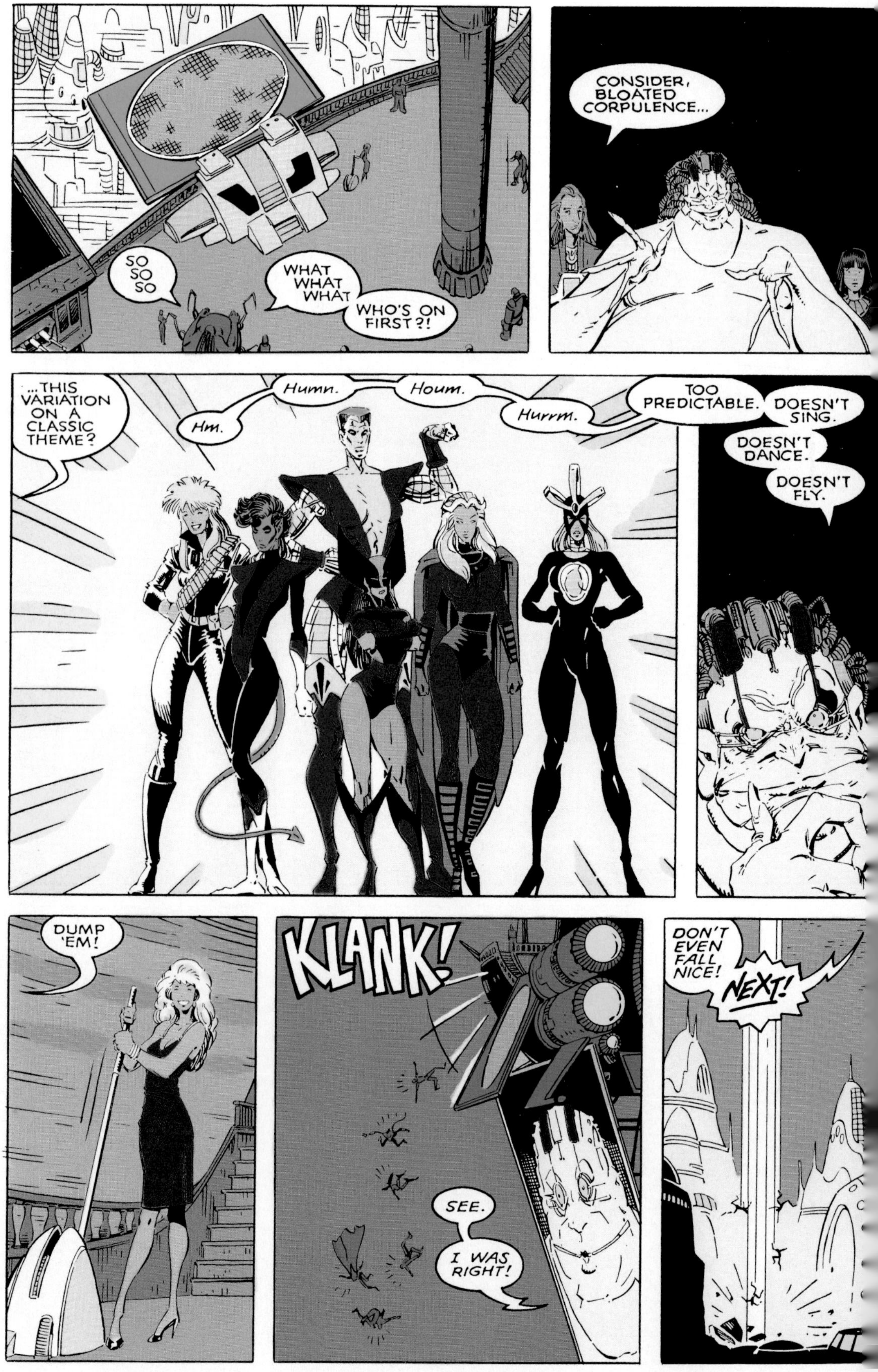
SO SO SO
WHAT WHAT WHAT
WHO'S ON FIRST?!
CONSIDER, BLOATED CORPULENCE...
...THIS VARIATION ON A CLASSIC THEME?
Hm.
Humn.
Houm.
Hurrm.
TOO PREDICTABLE.
DOESN'T SING.
DOESN'T DANCE.
DOESN'T FLY.
DUMP 'EM!
KLANK!
SEE.
I WAS RIGHT!
DON'T EVEN FALL NICE!
NEXT!

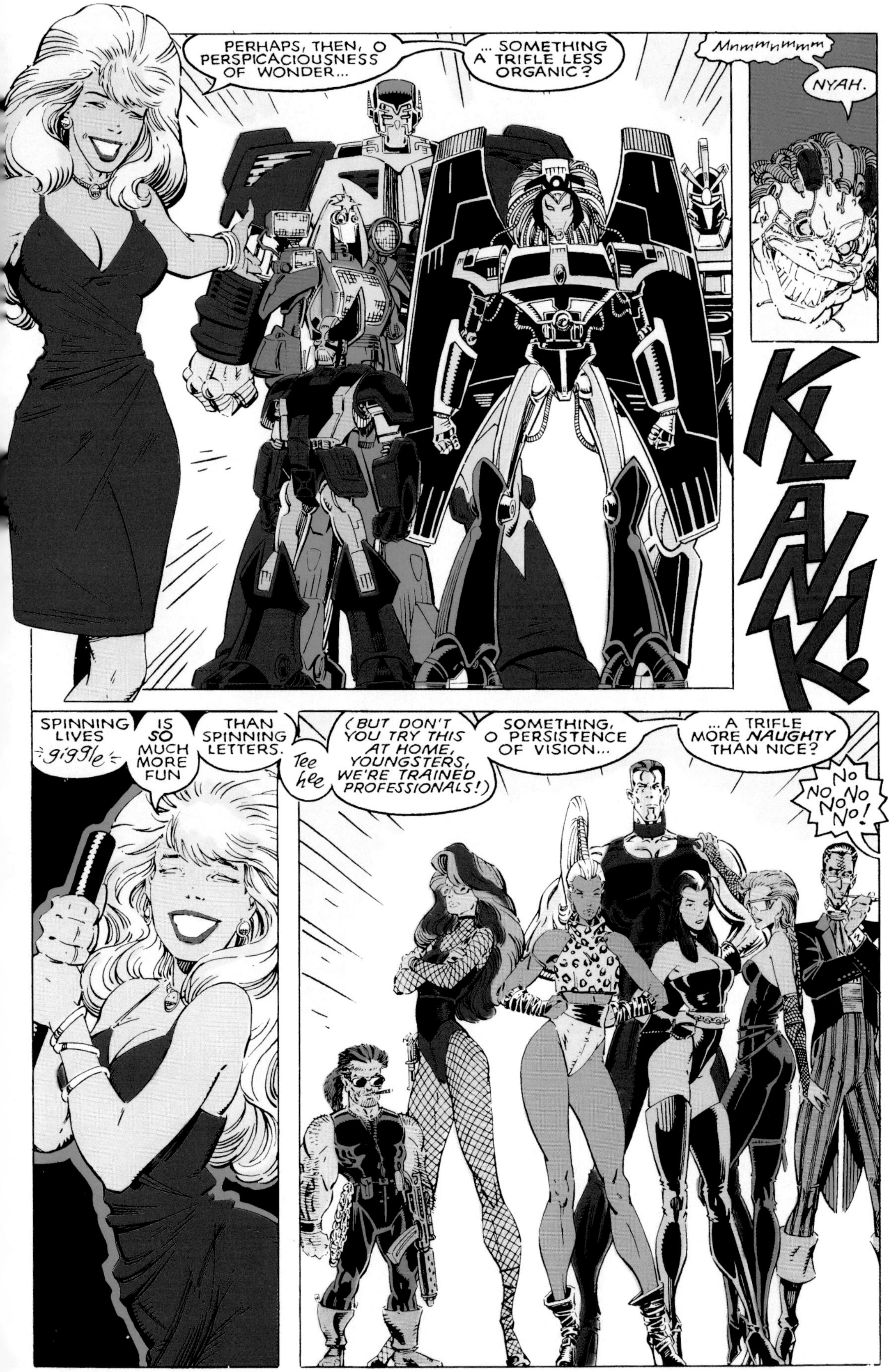
PERHAPS, THEN, O PERSPICACIOUSNESS OF WONDER...
... SOMETHING A TRIFLE LESS ORGANIC?
Mnmmnmmm
NYAH.
KLANK!
SPINNING LIVES
giggle
IS SO MUCH MORE FUN
THAN SPINNING LETTERS.
Tee hee
(BUT DON'T YOU TRY THIS AT HOME, YOUNGSTERS, WE'RE TRAINED PROFESSIONALS!)
SOMETHING, O PERSISTENCE OF VISION...
... A TRIFLE MORE NAUGHTY THAN NICE?
No No No No No!

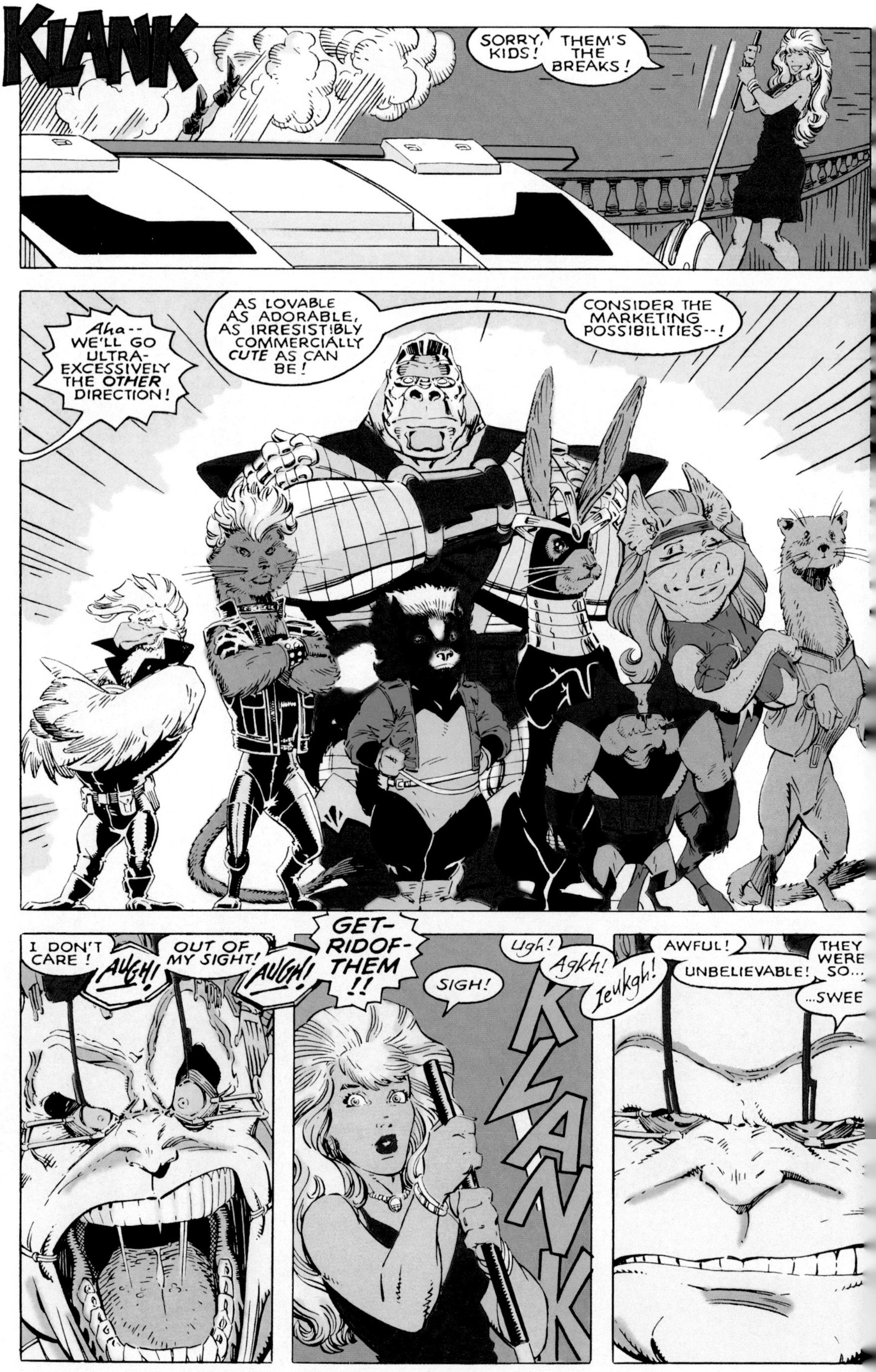
KLANK
SORRY, KIDS!
THEM'S THE BREAKS!
Aha-- WE'LL GO ULTRA-EXCESSIVELY THE OTHER DIRECTION!
AS LOVABLE AS ADORABLE, AS IRRESISTIBLY COMMERCIALLY CUTE AS CAN BE!
CONSIDER THE MARKETING POSSIBILITIES--!
I DON'T CARE!
AUGH!
OUT OF MY SIGHT!
AUGH!
GET-RIDOF-THEM !!
SIGH!
Ugh!
Agkh!
Ieukgh!
KLANK
AWFUL!
UNBELIEVABLE!
THEY WERE SO...
...SWEE

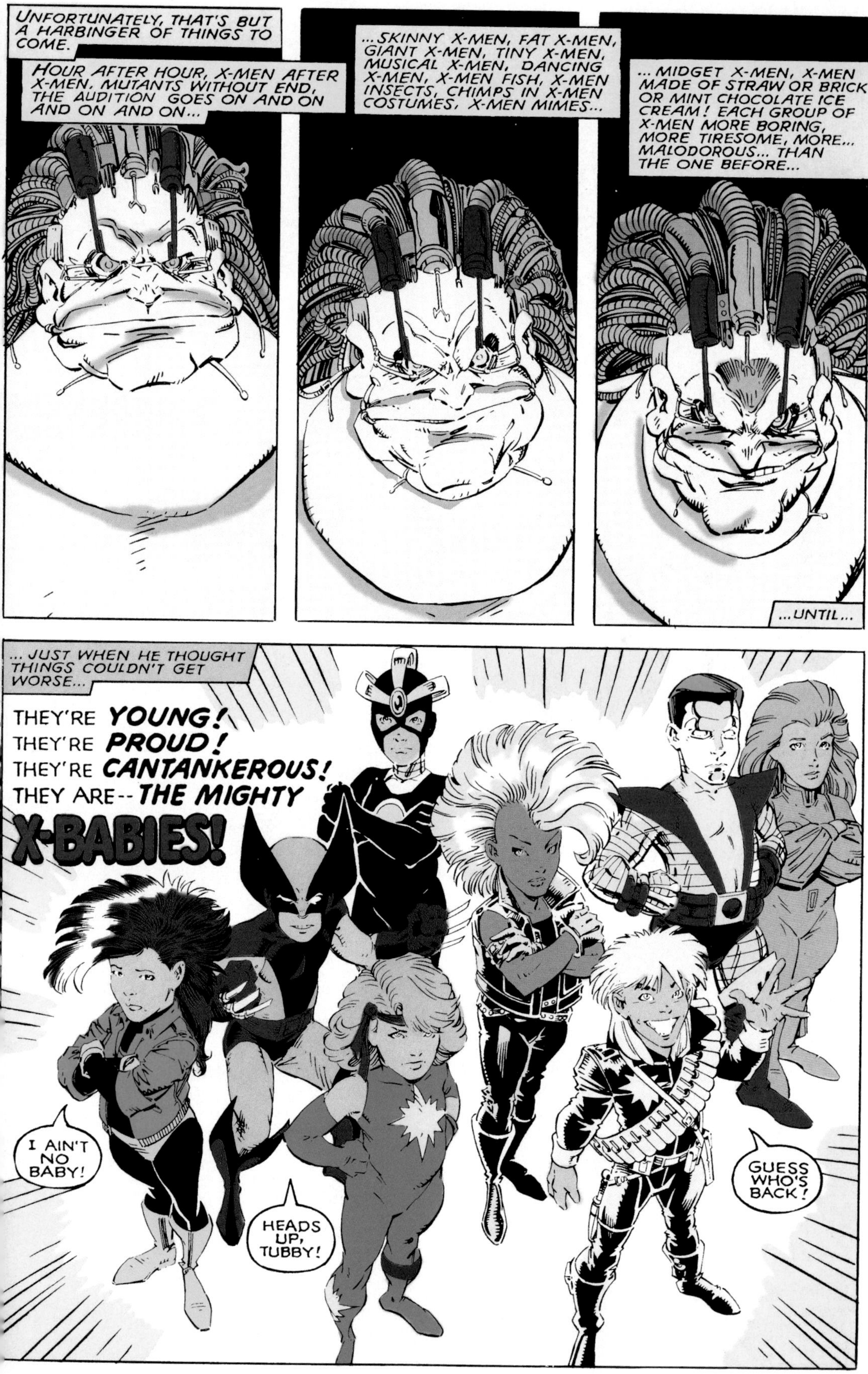

UNFORTUNATELY, THAT'S BUT A HARBINGER OF THINGS TO COME.
HOUR AFTER HOUR, X-MEN AFTER X-MEN. MUTANTS WITHOUT END, THE AUDITION GOES ON AND ON AND ON AND ON...
...SKINNY X-MEN, FAT X-MEN, GIANT X-MEN, TINY X-MEN, MUSICAL X-MEN, DANCING X-MEN, X-MEN FISH, X-MEN INSECTS, CHIMPS IN X-MEN COSTUMES, X-MEN MIMES...
...MIDGET X-MEN, X-MEN MADE OF STRAW OR BRICK OR MINT CHOCOLATE ICE CREAM! EACH GROUP OF X-MEN MORE BORING, MORE TIRESOME, MORE... MALODOROUS... THAN THE ONE BEFORE...
...UNTIL...
...JUST WHEN HE THOUGHT THINGS COULDN'T GET WORSE...
THEY'RE YOUNG! THEY'RE PROUD! THEY'RE CANTANKEROUS! THEY ARE--THE MIGHTY X-BABIES!
I AIN'T NO BABY!
HEADS UP, TUBBY!
GUESS WHO'S BACK!

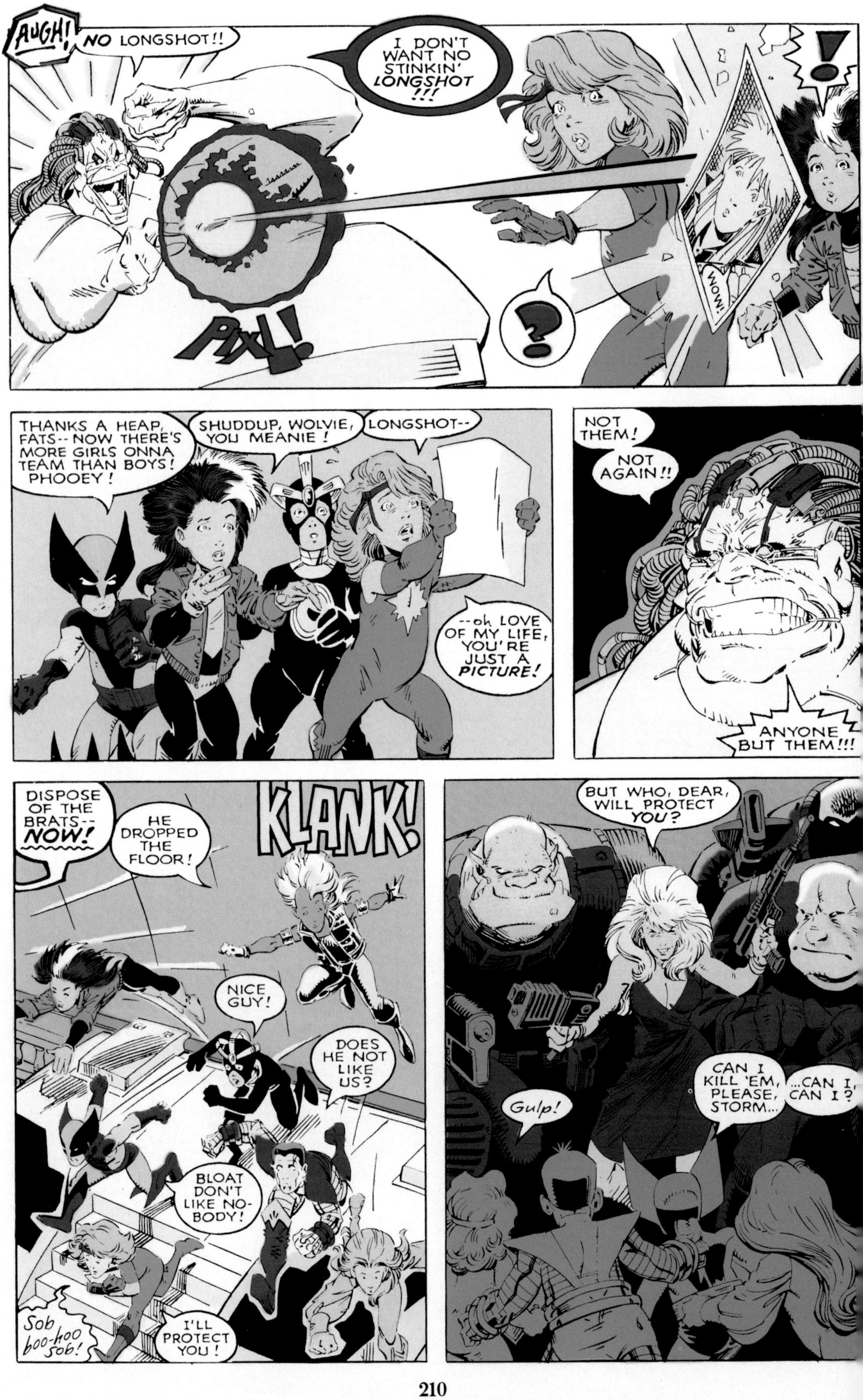
AUGH!
NO LONGSHOT!!
I DON'T WANT NO STINKIN' LONGSHOT!!!
!
WOW!
?
PIXL!
THANKS A HEAP, FATS-- NOW THERE'S MORE GIRLS ONNA TEAM THAN BOYS! PHOOEY!
SHUDDUP, WOLVIE, YOU MEANIE!
LONGSHOT--
--oh LOVE OF MY LIFE, YOU'RE JUST A PICTURE!
NOT THEM!
NOT AGAIN!!
ANYONE BUT THEM!!!
DISPOSE OF THE BRATS-- NOW!
HE DROPPED THE FLOOR!
KLANK!
NICE GUY!
DOES HE NOT LIKE US?
BLOAT DON'T LIKE NO-BODY!
Sob boo-hoo sob!
I'LL PROTECT YOU!
BUT WHO, DEAR, WILL PROTECT YOU?
Gulp!
CAN I KILL 'EM, PLEASE, STORM...
...CAN I, CAN I?

AT THAT VERY (CONVENIENT) MOMENT, BACK ON EARTH, GATEWAY (REMEMBER HIM) FLASHES THE X-MEN (THE *REAL* ONES, WHO WE KNOW AREN'T DEAD) FROM PLACE TO PLACE (SEE THEIR STORY FOR DETAILS, WE AIN'T GOT ROOM HERE!)

AND IN THE PROCESS, THEIR MCMENTARY TRANSIT OF THE OMNI-DIMENSIONAL TETHER...

?!?

... PROVOKES AN IMMEDIATE RESPONSE...

IT CAN'T BE -- I *SENSE* HIM-- BUT HE'S *DEAD!*

QUICK AS I CAN, I'VE GOT TO --NO!

OK, NO -- HE'S *GONE!*

LONG-SHOT?!?

SCUURRREEEEENK

... AS DOES RITA'S SUDDEN, VIOLENT SWERVE IN DIRECTION...

YIKES!

OOPS!

OH DEAR!

ENOUGH OF THIS FOOLISHNESS! TRADEMARK *POLICE,* FRONT AND CENTER!

CAN'T HAVE YOU LITTLE MUNCHKINOIDS RUNNING ABOUT WITHOUT A PROPER ™.

WHY THEN, *ANYBODY* COULD USE YOU, ANYTIME THEY PLEASED, WITHOUT HAVING TO PAY A DIME IN LICENSE FEES!

HUP HOP HUP HOP

MT

MT

BRAND 'EM, BOYS!

HUP HOP HUPHOP HUP HOP

MT MT MT MT

LOOKS LIKE TROUBLE, COMRADES!

GIMME THAT PICTURE!

YEAH-- FOR *THEM!*

HE'S *MY* SWEETIE!

AAG!

WHAP!

ZAP! ZAP!

SMEK!

NK!

GIMME GIMME GIMME!

MINE MINE MINE!

SPAT!

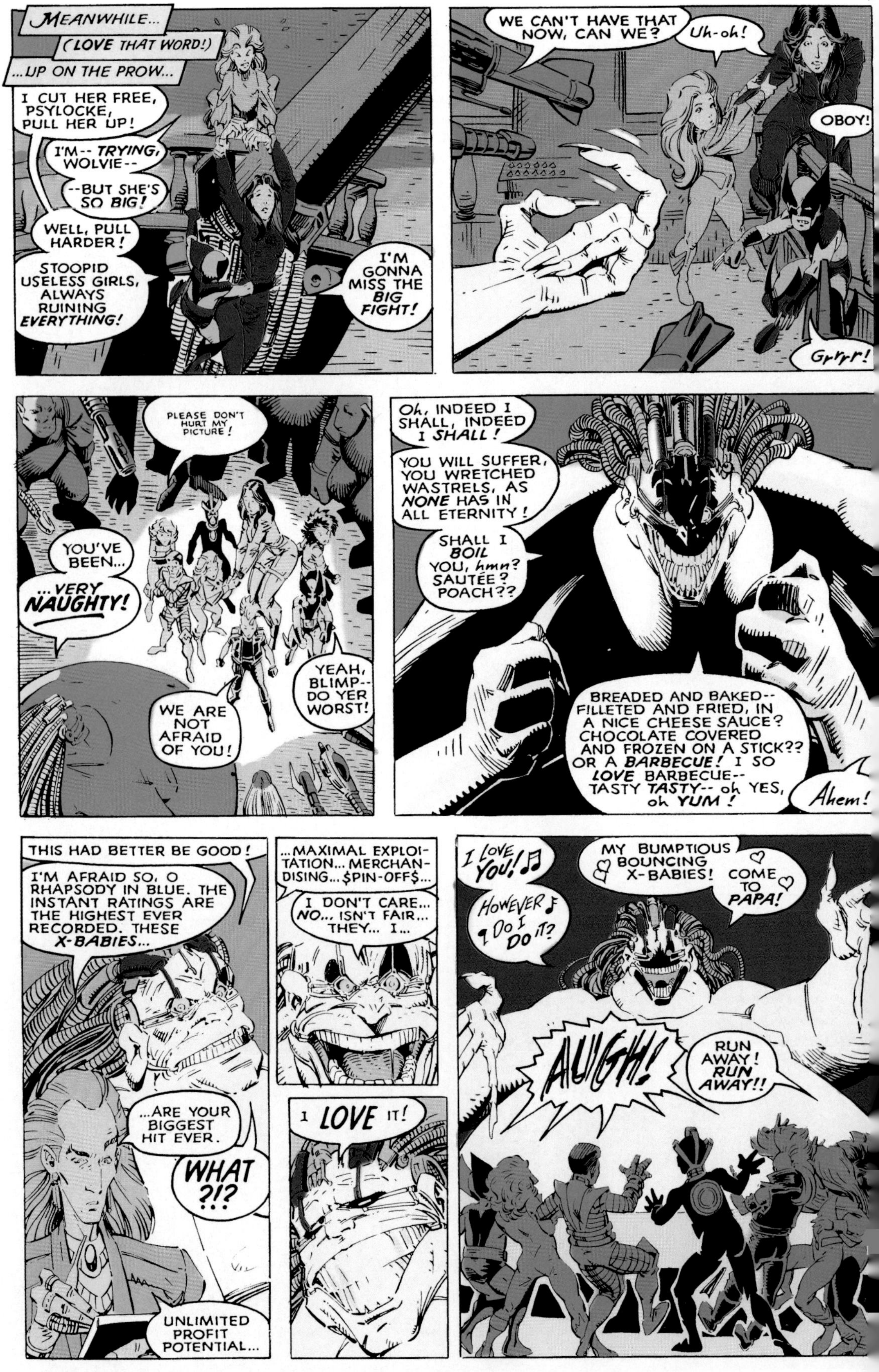
MEANWHILE...
(LOVE THAT WORD!)
...UP ON THE PROW...
I CUT HER FREE, PSYLOCKE, PULL HER UP!
I'M-- TRYING, WOLVIE--
--BUT SHE'S SO BIG!
WELL, PULL HARDER!
STOOPID USELESS GIRLS, ALWAYS RUINING EVERYTHING!
I'M GONNA MISS THE BIG FIGHT!
WE CAN'T HAVE THAT NOW, CAN WE?
Uh-oh!
OBOY!
Grrrr!
PLEASE DON'T HURT MY PICTURE!
YOU'VE BEEN...
...VERY NAUGHTY!
WE ARE NOT AFRAID OF YOU!
YEAH, BLIMP-- DO YER WORST!
Oh, INDEED I SHALL, INDEED I SHALL!
YOU WILL SUFFER, YOU WRETCHED WASTRELS, AS NONE HAS IN ALL ETERNITY!
SHALL I BOIL YOU, hmn? SAUTÉE? POACH??
BREADED AND BAKED-- FILLETED AND FRIED, IN A NICE CHEESE SAUCE? CHOCOLATE COVERED AND FROZEN ON A STICK?? OR A BARBECUE! I SO LOVE BARBECUE-- TASTY TASTY-- oh YES, oh YUM!
Ahem!
THIS HAD BETTER BE GOOD!
I'M AFRAID SO, O RHAPSODY IN BLUE. THE INSTANT RATINGS ARE THE HIGHEST EVER RECORDED. THESE X-BABIES...
...ARE YOUR BIGGEST HIT EVER.
WHAT ?!?
UNLIMITED PROFIT POTENTIAL...
...MAXIMAL EXPLOITATION... MERCHANDISING... $PIN-OFF$...
I DON'T CARE... NO... ISN'T FAIR... THEY... I...
I LOVE IT!
I LOVE YOU!
HOWEVER DO I DO IT?
MY BUMPTIOUS BOUNCING X-BABIES!
COME TO PAPA!
AUGH!
RUN AWAY! RUN AWAY!!

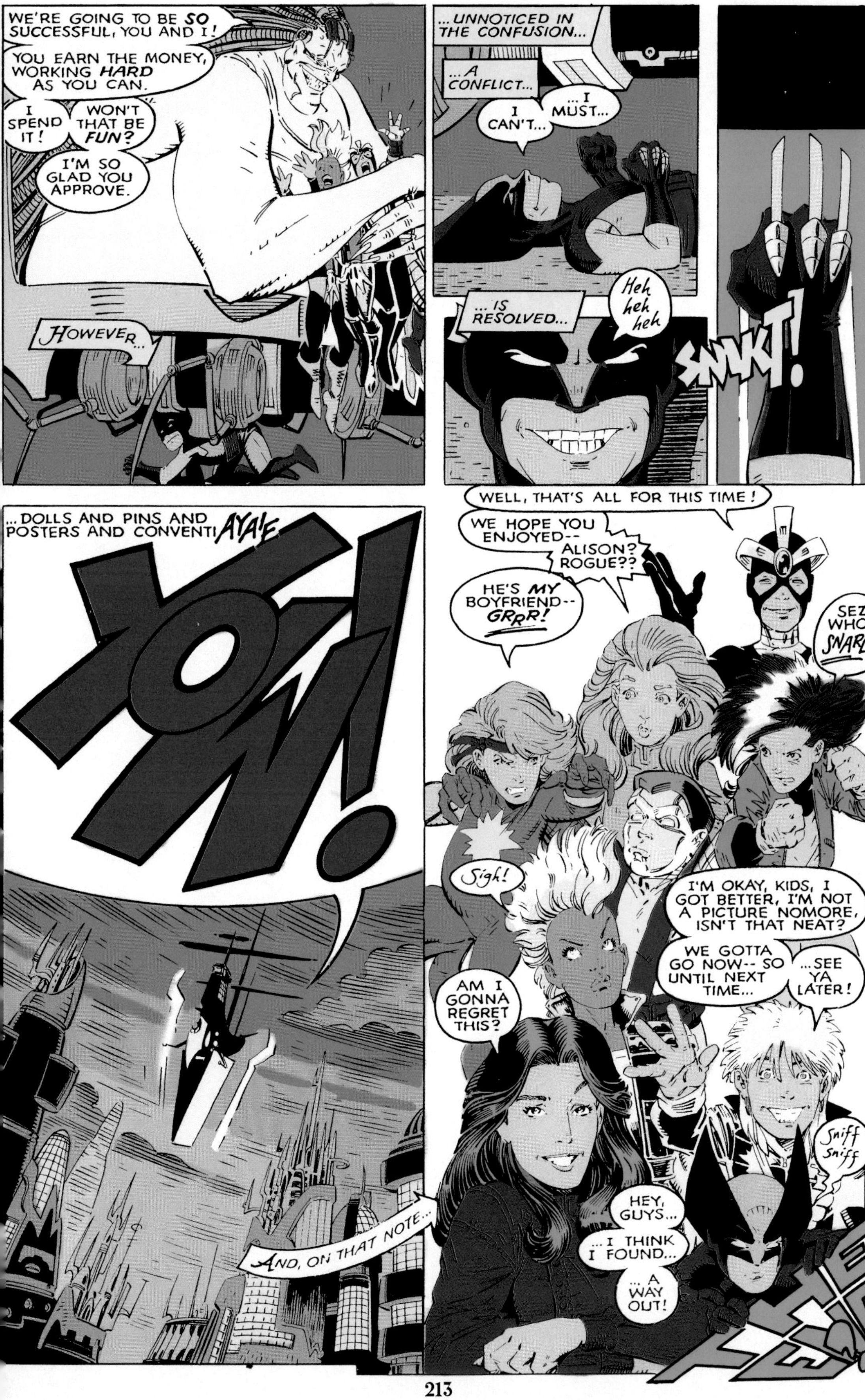

WE'RE GOING TO BE SO SUCCESSFUL, YOU AND I!
YOU EARN THE MONEY, WORKING HARD AS YOU CAN.
I SPEND IT!
WON'T THAT BE FUN?
I'M SO GLAD YOU APPROVE.
HOWEVER...
...UNNOTICED IN THE CONFUSION...
...A CONFLICT...
I CAN'T...
...I MUST...
...IS RESOLVED...
Heh heh heh
SNIKT!
...DOLLS AND PINS AND POSTERS AND CONVENTI AYAIE
YOW!
AND, ON THAT NOTE...
WELL, THAT'S ALL FOR THIS TIME!
WE HOPE YOU ENJOYED--
ALISON? ROGUE??
HE'S MY BOYFRIEND-- GRRR!
SEZ WHO-- SNARL!
Sigh!
I'M OKAY, KIDS, I GOT BETTER, I'M NOT A PICTURE NOMORE, ISN'T THAT NEAT?
WE GOTTA GO NOW-- SO UNTIL NEXT TIME...
...SEE YA LATER!
AM I GONNA REGRET THIS?
Sniff Sniff
HEY, GUYS...
...I THINK I FOUND...
...A WAY OUT!
THE END

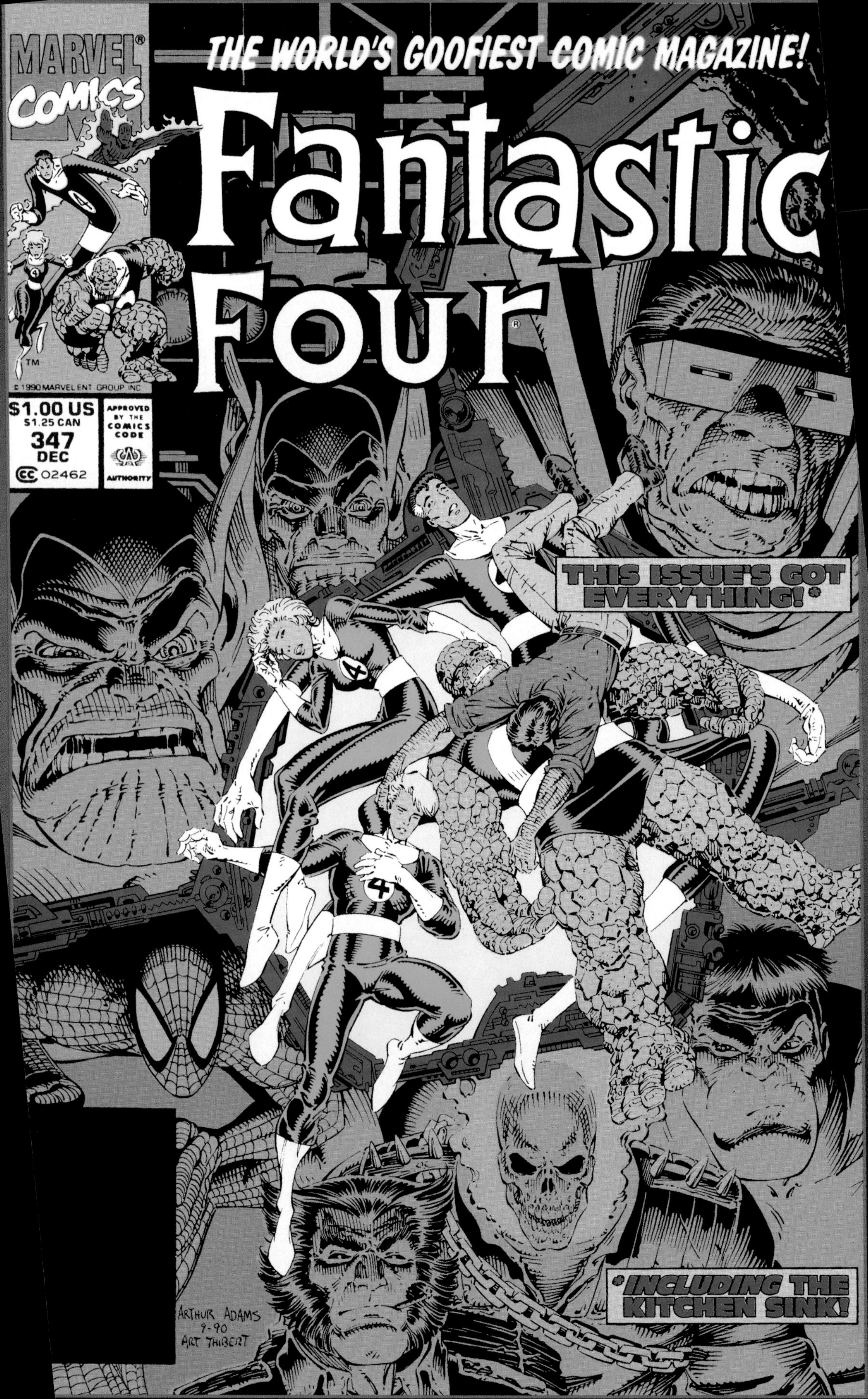
MARVEL COMICS
THE WORLD'S GOOFIEST COMIC MAGAZINE!
Fantastic Four
© 1990 MARVEL ENT GROUP INC
$1.00 US
$1.25 CAN
347
DEC
CC 02462
APPROVED BY THE COMICS CODE AUTHORITY
THIS ISSUE'S GOT EVERYTHING!*
*INCLUDING THE KITCHEN SINK!
ARTHUR ADAMS
9-90
ART THIBERT

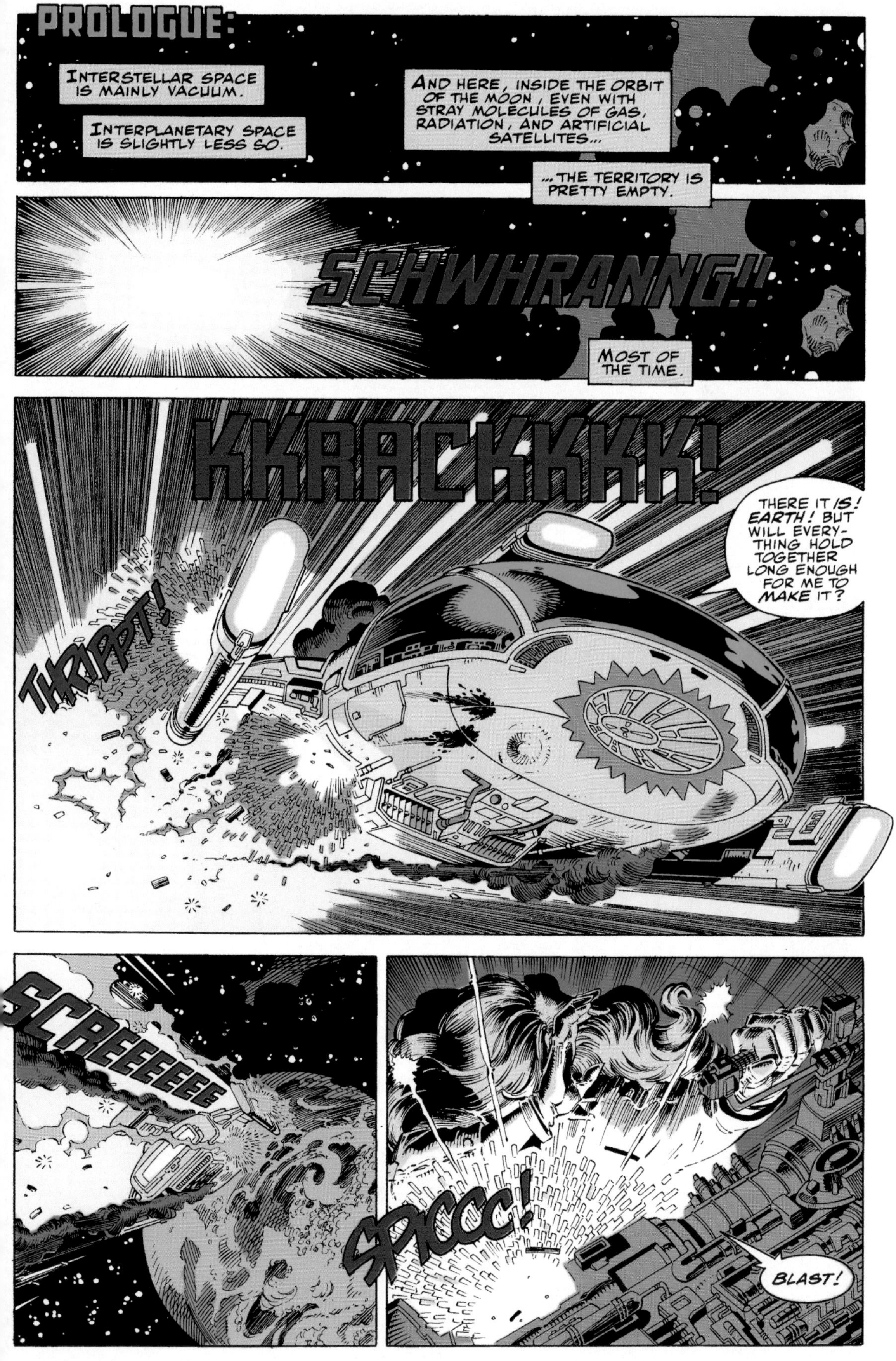
PROLOGUE:
INTERSTELLAR SPACE IS MAINLY VACUUM.
INTERPLANETARY SPACE IS SLIGHTLY LESS SO.
AND HERE, INSIDE THE ORBIT OF THE MOON, EVEN WITH STRAY MOLECULES OF GAS, RADIATION, AND ARTIFICIAL SATELLITES...
...THE TERRITORY IS PRETTY EMPTY.
SCHWHRANNG!!
MOST OF THE TIME.
KKRACKKKK!
THRIPPT!
THERE IT IS! EARTH! BUT WILL EVERYTHING HOLD TOGETHER LONG ENOUGH FOR ME TO MAKE IT?
SCREEEEEEE
SPICCC!
BLAST!

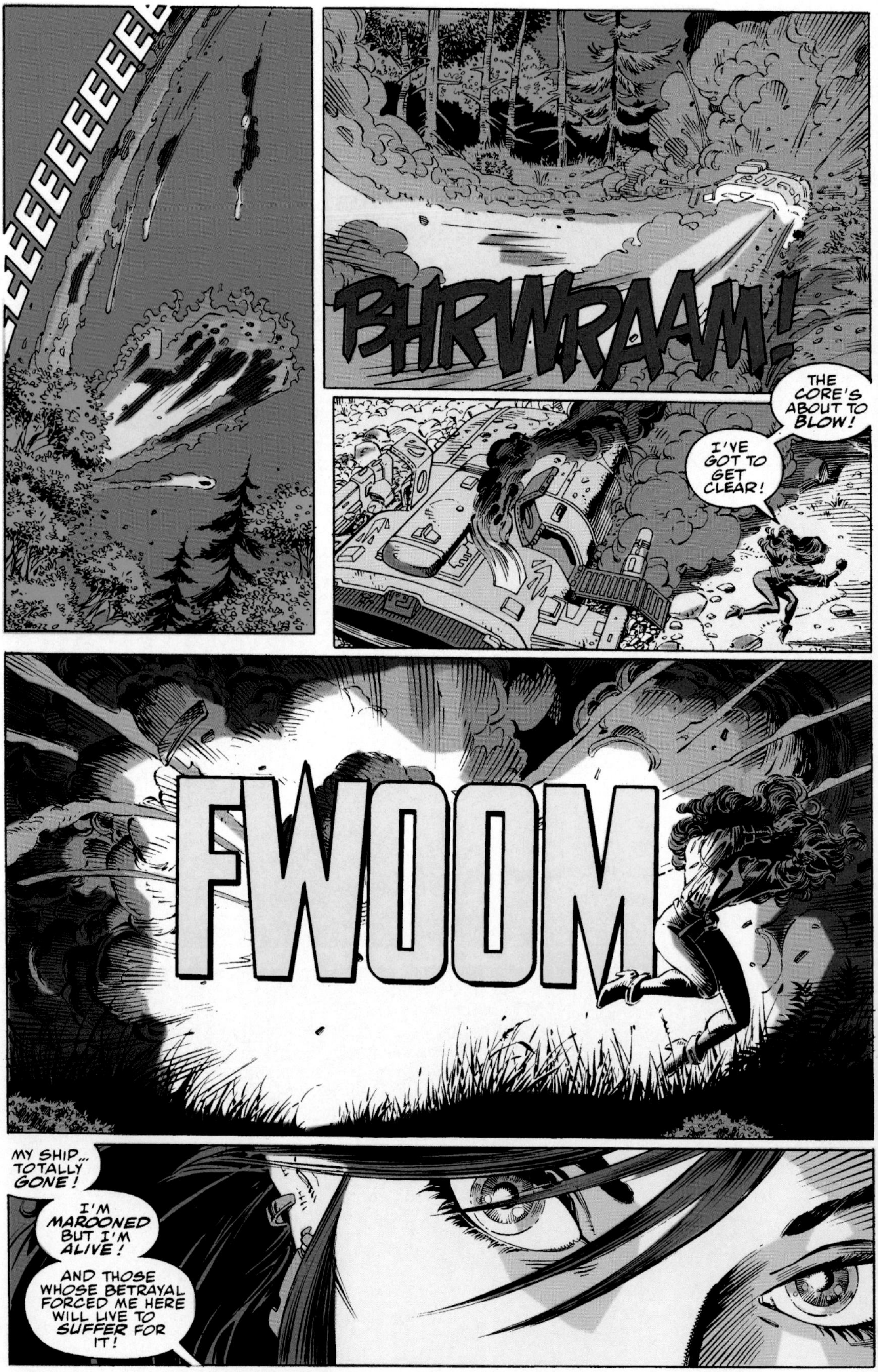
EEEEEEEEEEE
BHRWRAAM!
THE CORE'S ABOUT TO BLOW!
I'VE GOT TO GET CLEAR!
FWOOM
MY SHIP... TOTALLY GONE!
I'M MAROONED BUT I'M ALIVE!
AND THOSE WHOSE BETRAYAL FORCED ME HERE WILL LIVE TO SUFFER FOR IT!

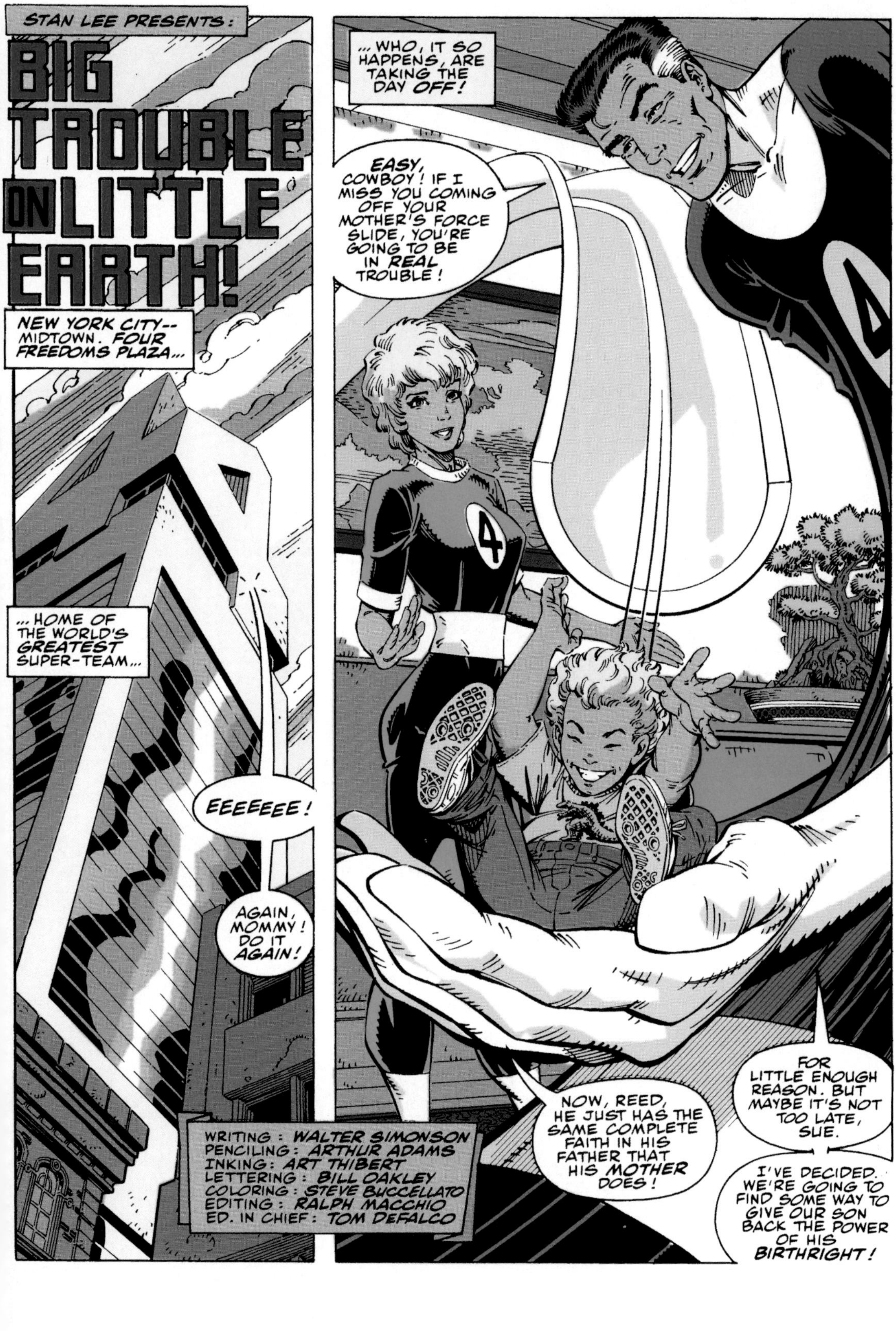
STAN LEE PRESENTS:
BIG TROUBLE ON LITTLE EARTH!
NEW YORK CITY-- MIDTOWN. FOUR FREEDOMS PLAZA...
...HOME OF THE WORLD'S GREATEST SUPER-TEAM...
EEEEEEE!
AGAIN, MOMMY! DO IT AGAIN!
...WHO, IT SO HAPPENS, ARE TAKING THE DAY OFF!
EASY, COWBOY! IF I MISS YOU COMING OFF YOUR MOTHER'S FORCE SLIDE, YOU'RE GOING TO BE IN REAL TROUBLE!
NOW, REED, HE JUST HAS THE SAME COMPLETE FAITH IN HIS FATHER THAT HIS MOTHER DOES!
FOR LITTLE ENOUGH REASON. BUT MAYBE IT'S NOT TOO LATE, SUE.
I'VE DECIDED. WE'RE GOING TO FIND SOME WAY TO GIVE OUR SON BACK THE POWER OF HIS BIRTHRIGHT!
WRITING: WALTER SIMONSON
PENCILING: ARTHUR ADAMS
INKING: ART THIBERT
LETTERING: BILL OAKLEY
COLORING: STEVE BUCCELLATO
EDITING: RALPH MACCHIO
ED. IN CHIEF: TOM DEFALCO

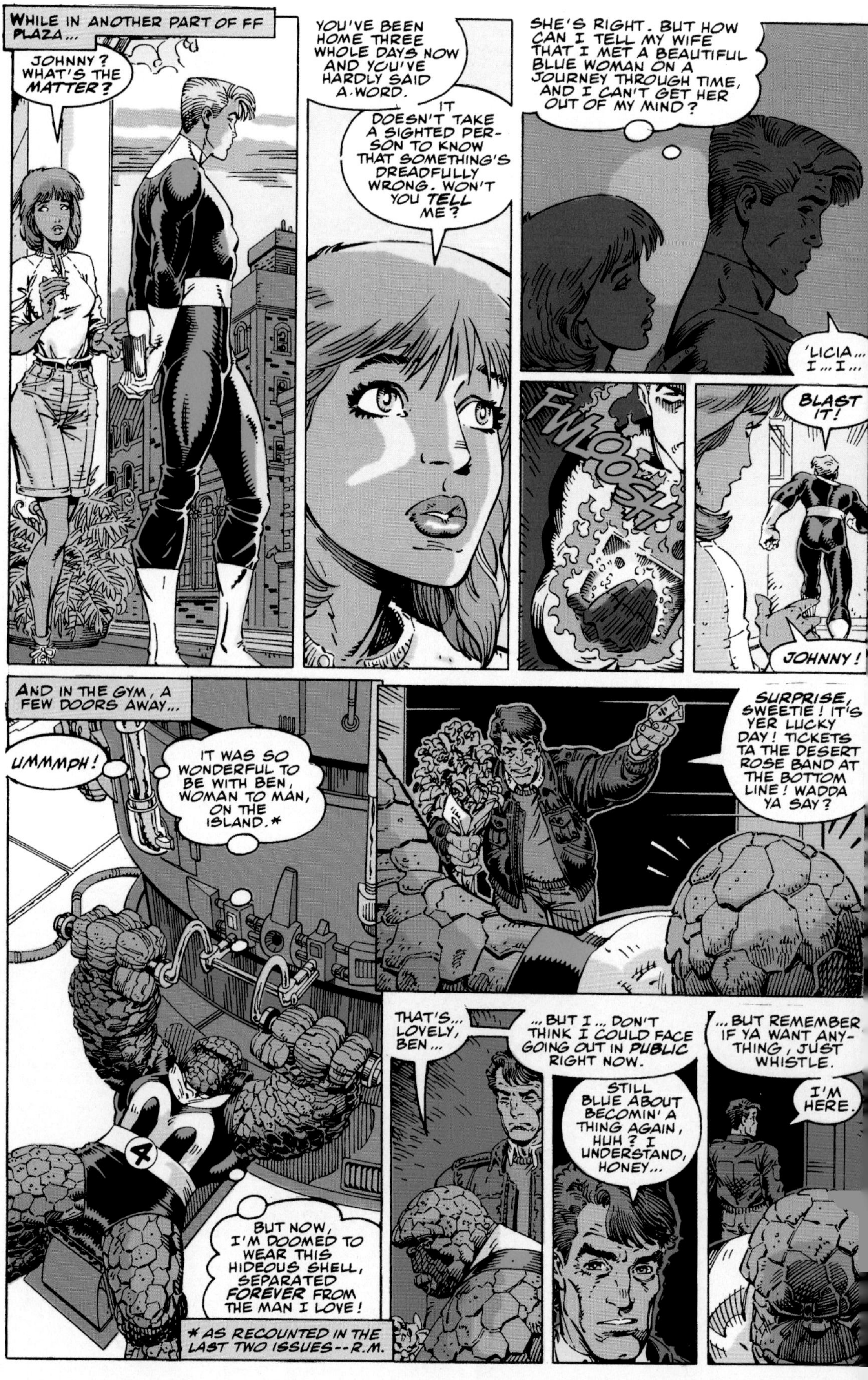

WHILE IN ANOTHER PART OF FF PLAZA...
JOHNNY? WHAT'S THE MATTER?
YOU'VE BEEN HOME THREE WHOLE DAYS NOW AND YOU'VE HARDLY SAID A WORD.
IT DOESN'T TAKE A SIGHTED PERSON TO KNOW THAT SOMETHING'S DREADFULLY WRONG. WON'T YOU TELL ME?
SHE'S RIGHT. BUT HOW CAN I TELL MY WIFE THAT I MET A BEAUTIFUL BLUE WOMAN ON A JOURNEY THROUGH TIME, AND I CAN'T GET HER OUT OF MY MIND?
'LICIA... I... I...
FWOOSH
BLAST IT!
JOHNNY!
AND IN THE GYM, A FEW DOORS AWAY...
UMMMPH!
IT WAS SO WONDERFUL TO BE WITH BEN, WOMAN TO MAN, ON THE ISLAND.*
BUT NOW, I'M DOOMED TO WEAR THIS HIDEOUS SHELL, SEPARATED FOREVER FROM THE MAN I LOVE!
*AS RECOUNTED IN THE LAST TWO ISSUES--R.M.
SURPRISE, SWEETIE! IT'S YER LUCKY DAY! TICKETS TA THE DESERT ROSE BAND AT THE BOTTOM LINE! WADDA YA SAY?
THAT'S... LOVELY, BEN...
...BUT I... DON'T THINK I COULD FACE GOING OUT IN PUBLIC RIGHT NOW.
STILL BLUE ABOUT BECOMIN' A THING AGAIN, HUH? I UNDERSTAND, HONEY...
...BUT REMEMBER IF YA WANT ANYTHING, JUST WHISTLE.
I'M HERE.

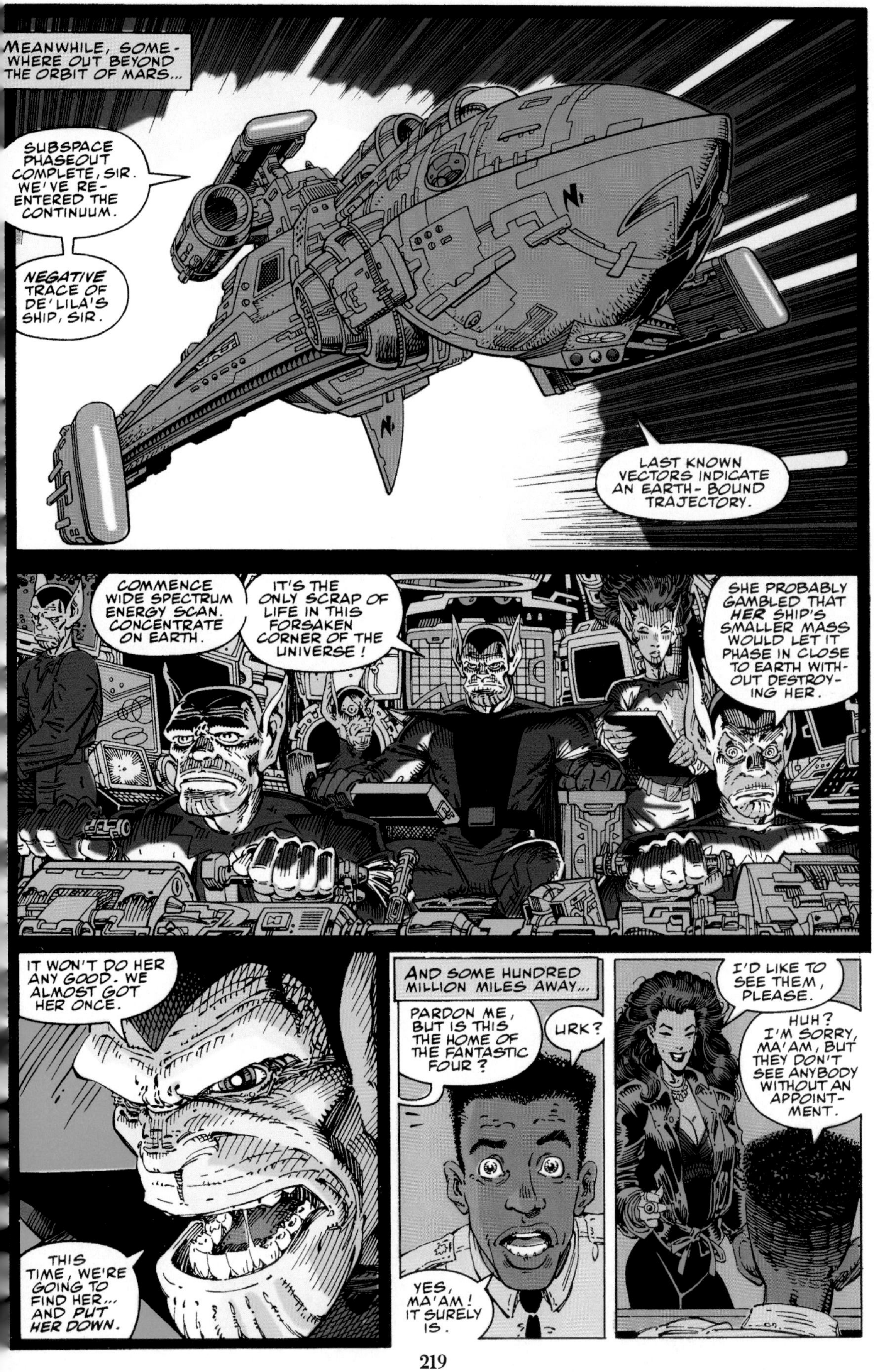
MEANWHILE, SOMEWHERE OUT BEYOND THE ORBIT OF MARS...
SUBSPACE PHASEOUT COMPLETE, SIR. WE'VE RE-ENTERED THE CONTINUUM.
NEGATIVE TRACE OF DE'LILA'S SHIP, SIR.
LAST KNOWN VECTORS INDICATE AN EARTH-BOUND TRAJECTORY.
COMMENCE WIDE SPECTRUM ENERGY SCAN. CONCENTRATE ON EARTH.
IT'S THE ONLY SCRAP OF LIFE IN THIS FORSAKEN CORNER OF THE UNIVERSE!
SHE PROBABLY GAMBLED THAT HER SHIP'S SMALLER MASS WOULD LET IT PHASE IN CLOSE TO EARTH WITHOUT DESTROYING HER.
IT WON'T DO HER ANY GOOD. WE ALMOST GOT HER ONCE.
THIS TIME, WE'RE GOING TO FIND HER... AND PUT HER DOWN.
AND SOME HUNDRED MILLION MILES AWAY...
PARDON ME, BUT IS THIS THE HOME OF THE FANTASTIC FOUR?
URK?
YES, MA'AM! IT SURELY IS.
I'D LIKE TO SEE THEM, PLEASE.
HUH? I'M SORRY, MA'AM, BUT THEY DON'T SEE ANYBODY WITHOUT AN APPOINTMENT.

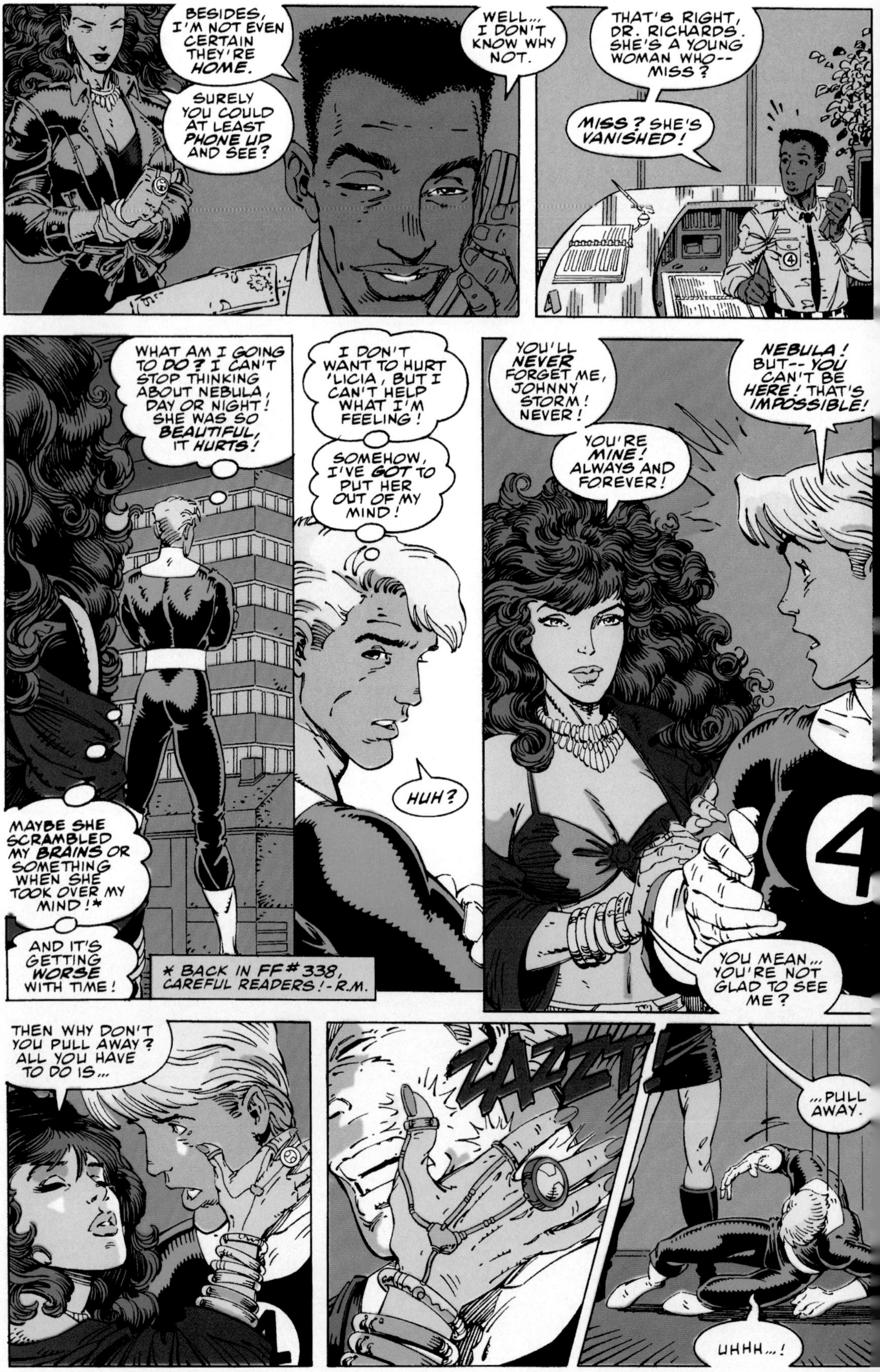
BESIDES, I'M NOT EVEN CERTAIN THEY'RE HOME.
SURELY YOU COULD AT LEAST PHONE UP AND SEE?
WELL... I DON'T KNOW WHY NOT.
THAT'S RIGHT, DR. RICHARDS. SHE'S A YOUNG WOMAN WHO-- MISS?
MISS? SHE'S VANISHED!
WHAT AM I GOING TO DO? I CAN'T STOP THINKING ABOUT NEBULA, DAY OR NIGHT! SHE WAS SO BEAUTIFUL, IT HURTS!
MAYBE SHE SCRAMBLED MY BRAINS OR SOMETHING WHEN SHE TOOK OVER MY MIND!*
AND IT'S GETTING WORSE WITH TIME!
* BACK IN FF #338, CAREFUL READERS! -R.M.
I DON'T WANT TO HURT 'LICIA, BUT I CAN'T HELP WHAT I'M FEELING!
SOMEHOW, I'VE GOT TO PUT HER OUT OF MY MIND!
HUH?
YOU'LL NEVER FORGET ME, JOHNNY STORM! NEVER!
YOU'RE MINE! ALWAYS AND FOREVER!
NEBULA! BUT-- YOU CAN'T BE HERE! THAT'S IMPOSSIBLE!
YOU MEAN... YOU'RE NOT GLAD TO SEE ME?
THEN WHY DON'T YOU PULL AWAY? ALL YOU HAVE TO DO IS...
ZAZZT!
...PULL AWAY.
UHHH...!

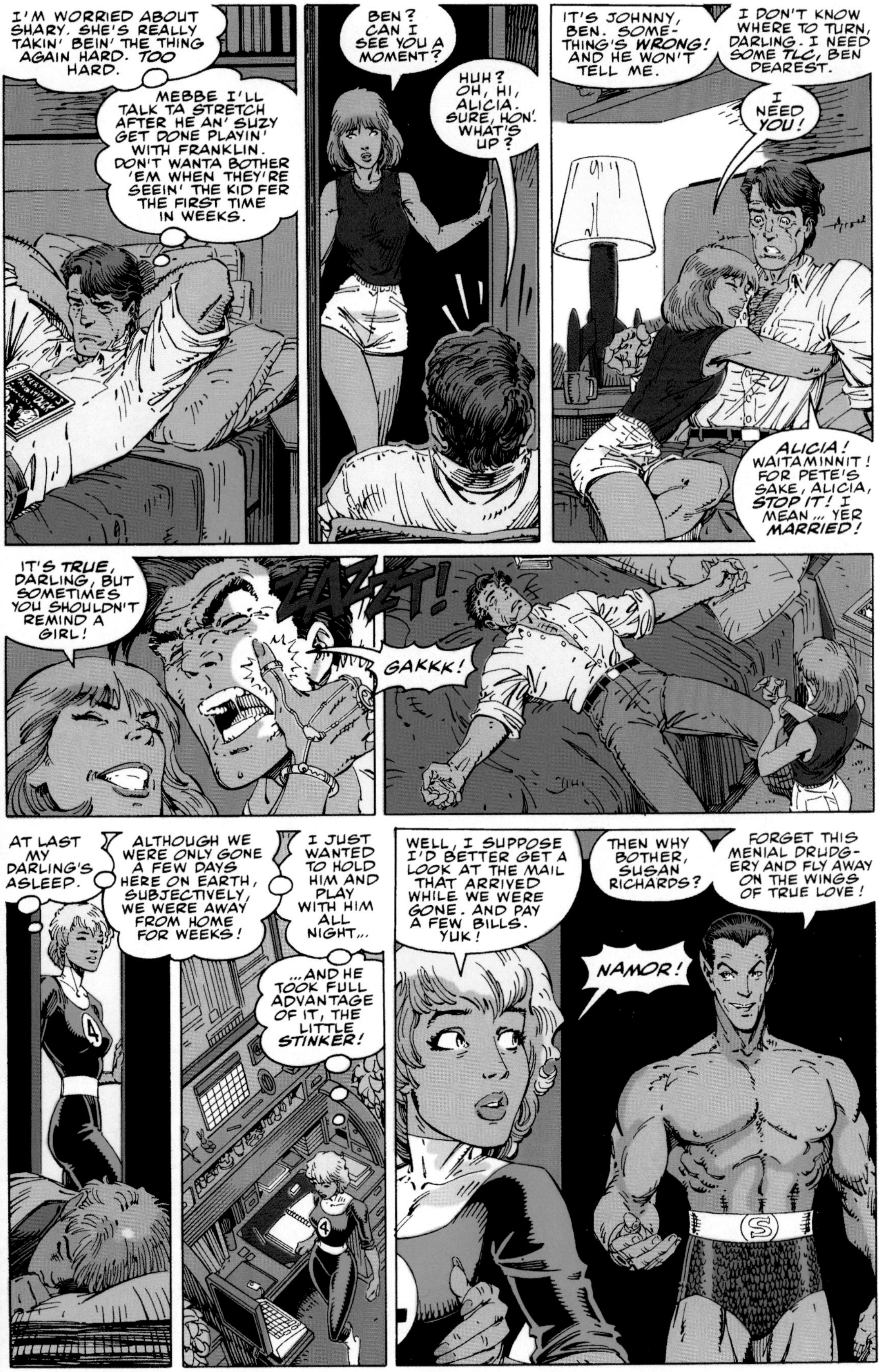
I'M WORRIED ABOUT SHARY. SHE'S REALLY TAKIN' BEIN' THE THING AGAIN HARD. TOO HARD.
MEBBE I'LL TALK TA STRETCH AFTER HE AN' SUZY GET DONE PLAYIN' WITH FRANKLIN. DON'T WANTA BOTHER 'EM WHEN THEY'RE SEEIN' THE KID FER THE FIRST TIME IN WEEKS.
BEN? CAN I SEE YOU A MOMENT?
HUH? OH, HI, ALICIA. SURE, HON'. WHAT'S UP?
IT'S JOHNNY, BEN. SOME-THING'S WRONG! AND HE WON'T TELL ME.
I DON'T KNOW WHERE TO TURN, DARLING. I NEED SOME TLC, BEN DEAREST.
I NEED YOU!
ALICIA! WAITAMINNIT! FOR PETE'S SAKE, ALICIA, STOP IT! I MEAN... YER MARRIED!
IT'S TRUE, DARLING, BUT SOMETIMES YOU SHOULDN'T REMIND A GIRL!
ZAZZT!
GAKKK!
AT LAST MY DARLING'S ASLEEP.
ALTHOUGH WE WERE ONLY GONE A FEW DAYS HERE ON EARTH, SUBJECTIVELY, WE WERE AWAY FROM HOME FOR WEEKS!
I JUST WANTED TO HOLD HIM AND PLAY WITH HIM ALL NIGHT...
...AND HE TOOK FULL ADVANTAGE OF IT, THE LITTLE STINKER!
WELL, I SUPPOSE I'D BETTER GET A LOOK AT THE MAIL THAT ARRIVED WHILE WE WERE GONE. AND PAY A FEW BILLS. YUK!
THEN WHY BOTHER, SUSAN RICHARDS?
FORGET THIS MENIAL DRUDG-ERY AND FLY AWAY ON THE WINGS OF TRUE LOVE!
NAMOR!

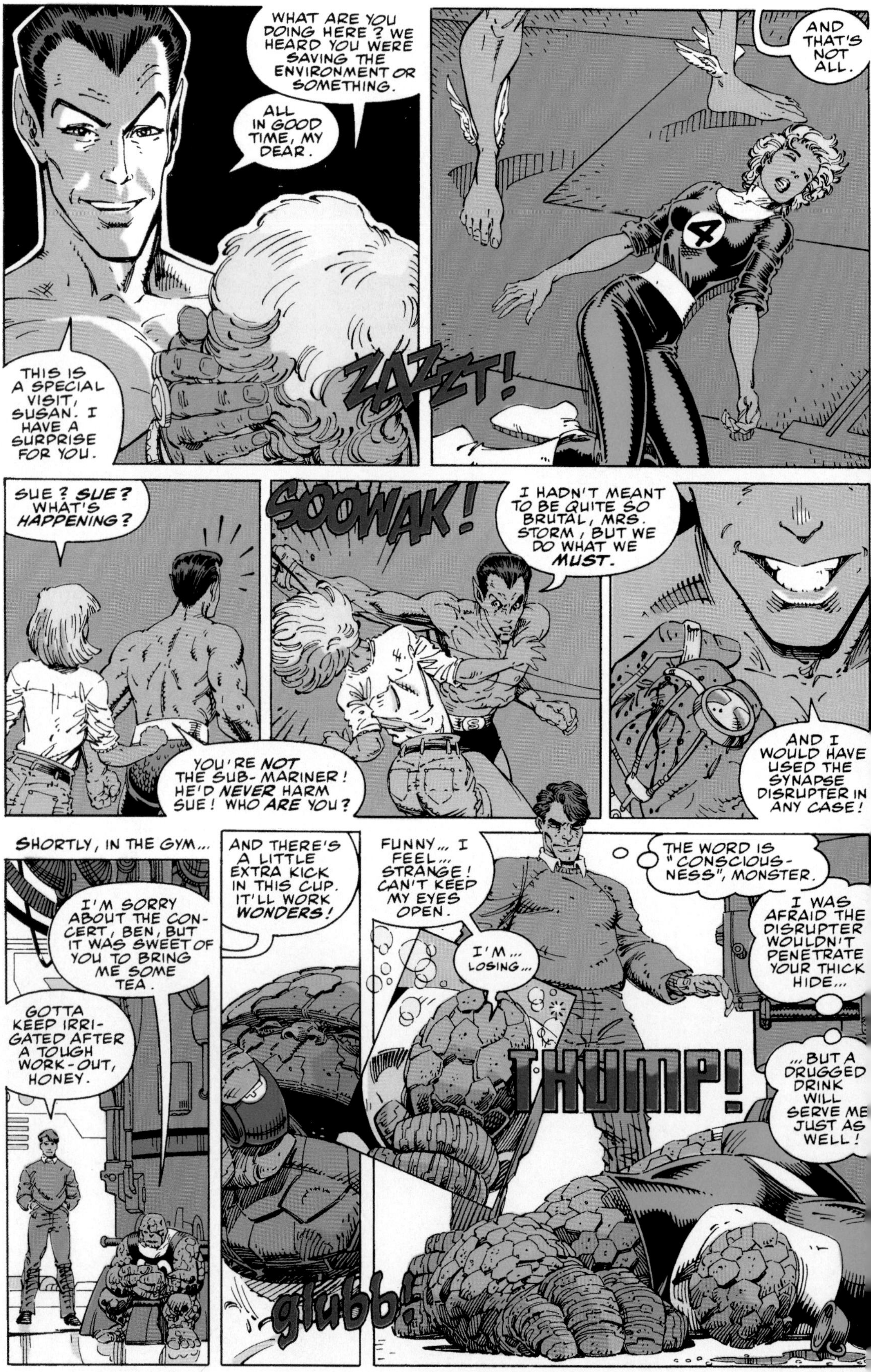
WHAT ARE YOU DOING HERE? WE HEARD YOU WERE SAVING THE ENVIRONMENT OR SOMETHING.
ALL IN GOOD TIME, MY DEAR.
THIS IS A SPECIAL VISIT, SUSAN. I HAVE A SURPRISE FOR YOU.
ZAZZZT!
AND THAT'S NOT ALL.
SUE? SUE? WHAT'S HAPPENING?
YOU'RE NOT THE SUB-MARINER! HE'D NEVER HARM SUE! WHO ARE YOU?
SOOWAK!
I HADN'T MEANT TO BE QUITE SO BRUTAL, MRS. STORM, BUT WE DO WHAT WE MUST.
AND I WOULD HAVE USED THE SYNAPSE DISRUPTER IN ANY CASE!
SHORTLY, IN THE GYM...
I'M SORRY ABOUT THE CONCERT, BEN, BUT IT WAS SWEET OF YOU TO BRING ME SOME TEA.
GOTTA KEEP IRRIGATED AFTER A TOUGH WORK-OUT, HONEY.
AND THERE'S A LITTLE EXTRA KICK IN THIS CUP. IT'LL WORK WONDERS!
FUNNY... I FEEL... STRANGE! CAN'T KEEP MY EYES OPEN.
I'M... LOSING...
THE WORD IS "CONSCIOUSNESS", MONSTER.
I WAS AFRAID THE DISRUPTER WOULDN'T PENETRATE YOUR THICK HIDE...
...BUT A DRUGGED DRINK WILL SERVE ME JUST AS WELL!
THUMP!
glubb!

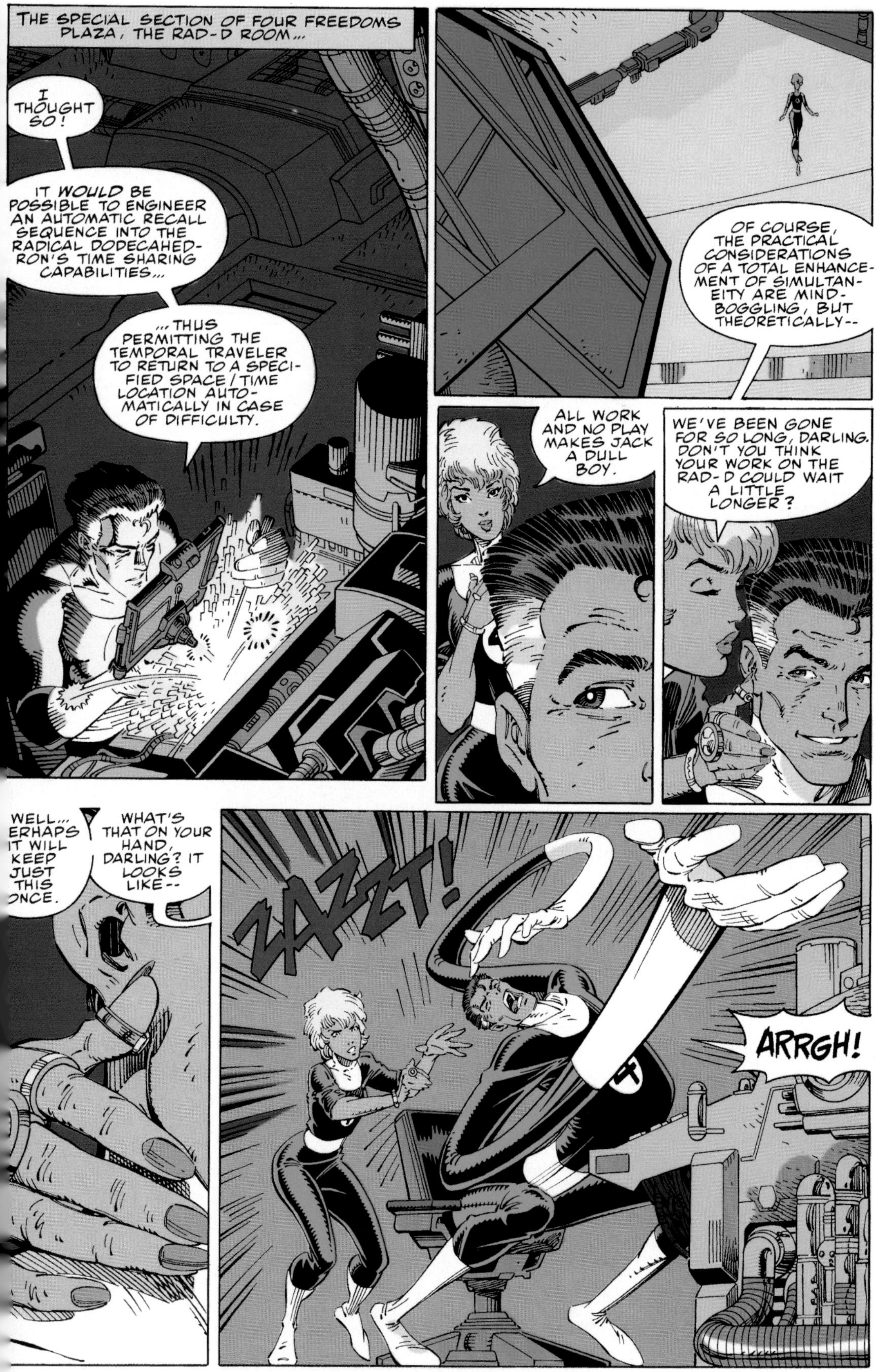
THE SPECIAL SECTION OF FOUR FREEDOMS PLAZA, THE RAD-D ROOM...
I THOUGHT SO!
IT WOULD BE POSSIBLE TO ENGINEER AN AUTOMATIC RECALL SEQUENCE INTO THE RADICAL DODECAHEDRON'S TIME SHARING CAPABILITIES...
...THUS PERMITTING THE TEMPORAL TRAVELER TO RETURN TO A SPECIFIED SPACE/TIME LOCATION AUTOMATICALLY IN CASE OF DIFFICULTY.
OF COURSE, THE PRACTICAL CONSIDERATIONS OF A TOTAL ENHANCEMENT OF SIMULTANEITY ARE MIND-BOGGLING, BUT THEORETICALLY--
ALL WORK AND NO PLAY MAKES JACK A DULL BOY.
WE'VE BEEN GONE FOR SO LONG, DARLING. DON'T YOU THINK YOUR WORK ON THE RAD-D COULD WAIT A LITTLE LONGER?
WELL... ERHAPS IT WILL KEEP JUST THIS ONCE.
WHAT'S THAT ON YOUR HAND, DARLING? IT LOOKS LIKE--
ZAZZT!
ARRGH!

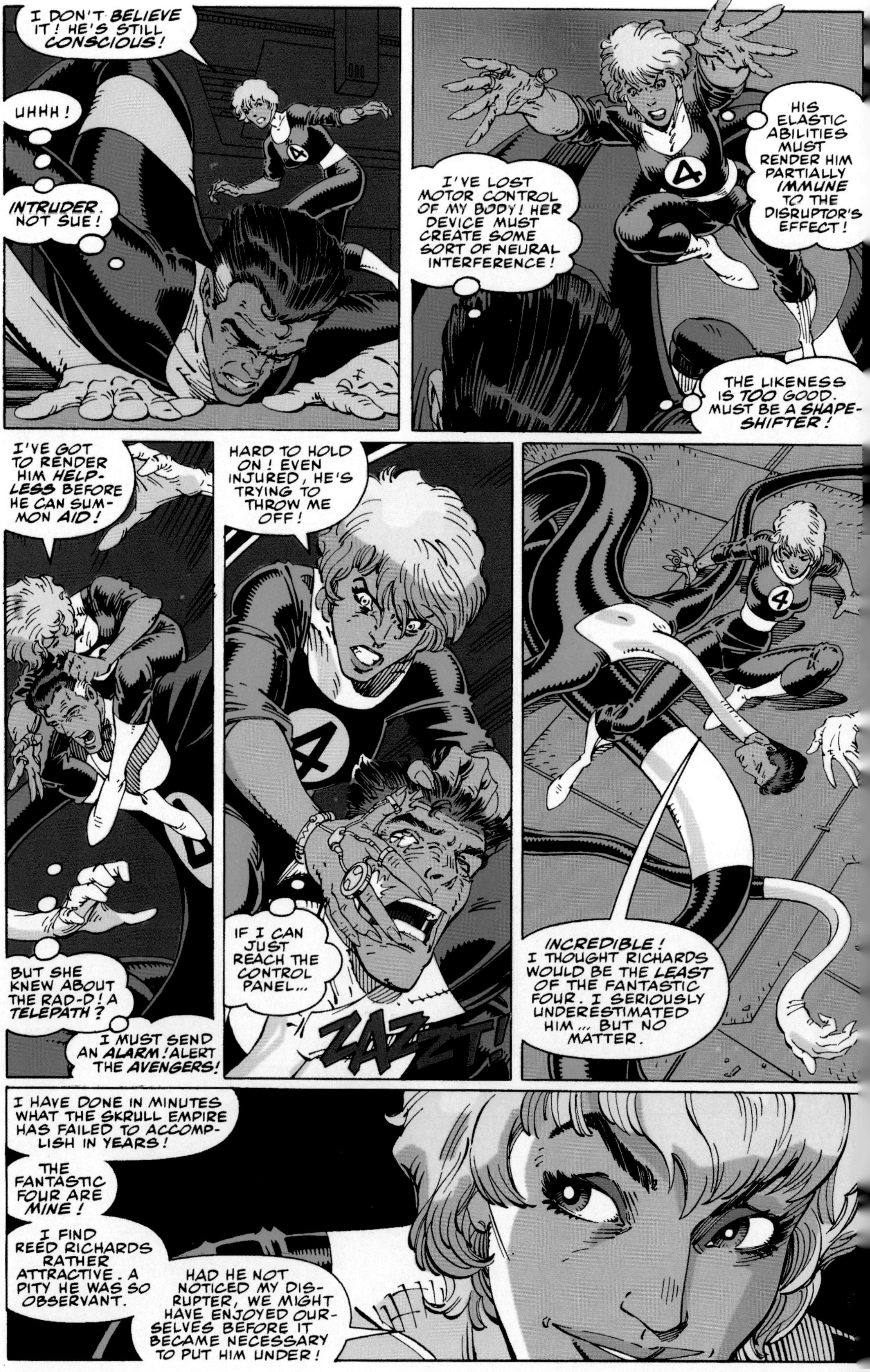

I DON'T BELIEVE IT! HE'S STILL CONSCIOUS!
UHHH!
INTRUDER. NOT SUE!
I'VE LOST MOTOR CONTROL OF MY BODY! HER DEVICE MUST CREATE SOME SORT OF NEURAL INTERFERENCE!
HIS ELASTIC ABILITIES MUST RENDER HIM PARTIALLY IMMUNE TO THE DISRUPTOR'S EFFECT!
THE LIKENESS IS TOO GOOD. MUST BE A SHAPE-SHIFTER!
I'VE GOT TO RENDER HIM HELP-LESS BEFORE HE CAN SUM-MON AID!
BUT SHE KNEW ABOUT THE RAD-D! A TELEPATH?
I MUST SEND AN ALARM! ALERT THE AVENGERS!
HARD TO HOLD ON! EVEN INJURED, HE'S TRYING TO THROW ME OFF!
IF I CAN JUST REACH THE CONTROL PANEL...
ZAZZT!
INCREDIBLE! I THOUGHT RICHARDS WOULD BE THE LEAST OF THE FANTASTIC FOUR. I SERIOUSLY UNDERESTIMATED HIM... BUT NO MATTER.
I HAVE DONE IN MINUTES WHAT THE SKRULL EMPIRE HAS FAILED TO ACCOMP-LISH IN YEARS!
THE FANTASTIC FOUR ARE MINE!
I FIND REED RICHARDS RATHER ATTRACTIVE. A PITY HE WAS SO OBSERVANT.
HAD HE NOT NOTICED MY DIS-RUPTER, WE MIGHT HAVE ENJOYED OUR-SELVES BEFORE IT BECAME NECESSARY TO PUT HIM UNDER!

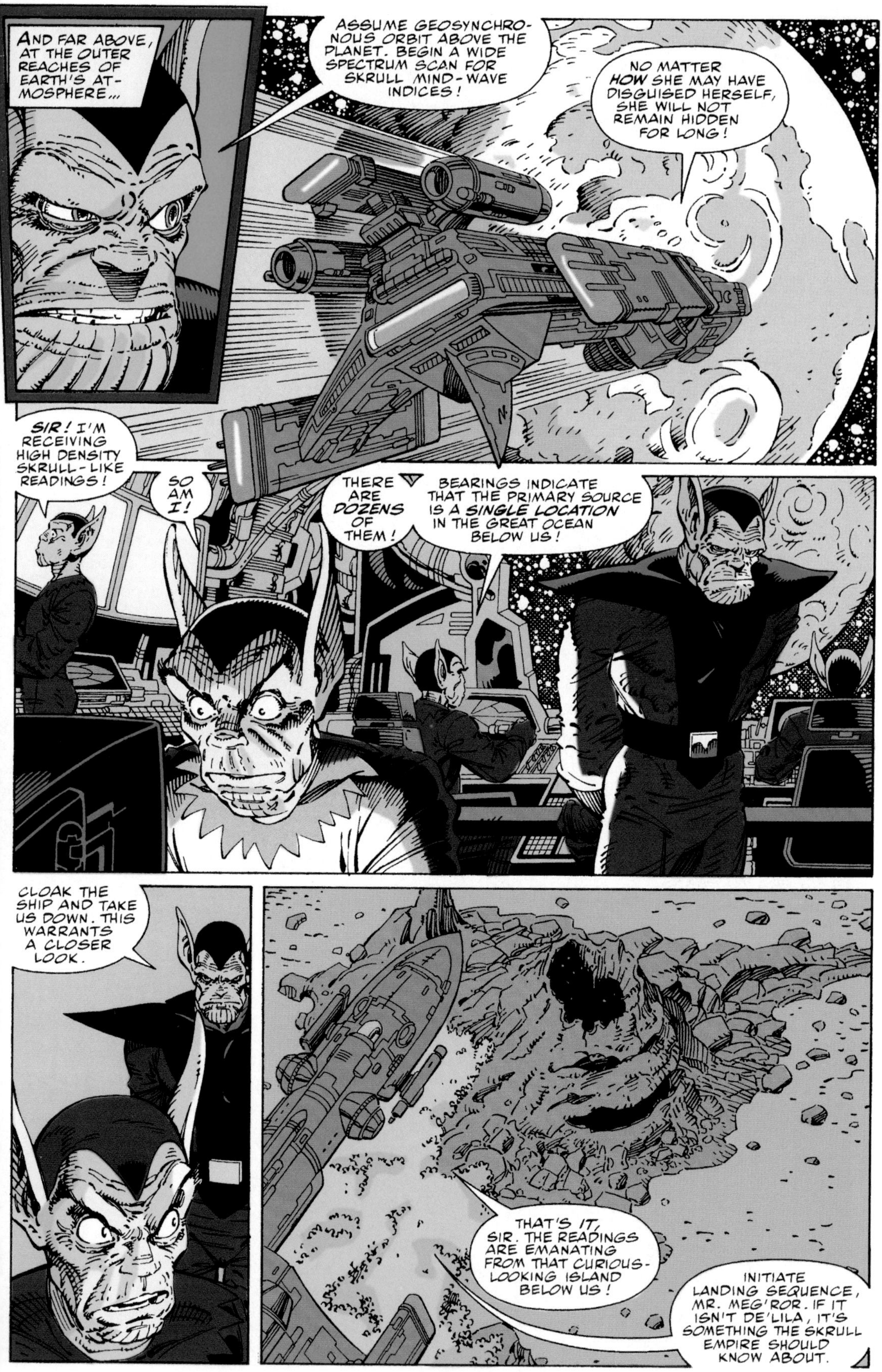
AND FAR ABOVE, AT THE OUTER REACHES OF EARTH'S ATMOSPHERE...
ASSUME GEOSYNCHRONOUS ORBIT ABOVE THE PLANET. BEGIN A WIDE SPECTRUM SCAN FOR SKRULL MIND-WAVE INDICES!
NO MATTER HOW SHE MAY HAVE DISGUISED HERSELF, SHE WILL NOT REMAIN HIDDEN FOR LONG!
SIR! I'M RECEIVING HIGH DENSITY SKRULL-LIKE READINGS!
SO AM I!
THERE ARE DOZENS OF THEM!
BEARINGS INDICATE THAT THE PRIMARY SOURCE IS A SINGLE LOCATION IN THE GREAT OCEAN BELOW US!
CLOAK THE SHIP AND TAKE US DOWN. THIS WARRANTS A CLOSER LOOK.
THAT'S IT, SIR. THE READINGS ARE EMANATING FROM THAT CURIOUS-LOOKING ISLAND BELOW US!
INITIATE LANDING SEQUENCE, MR. MEG'ROR. IF IT ISN'T DE'LILA, IT'S SOMETHING THE SKRULL EMPIRE SHOULD KNOW ABOUT.

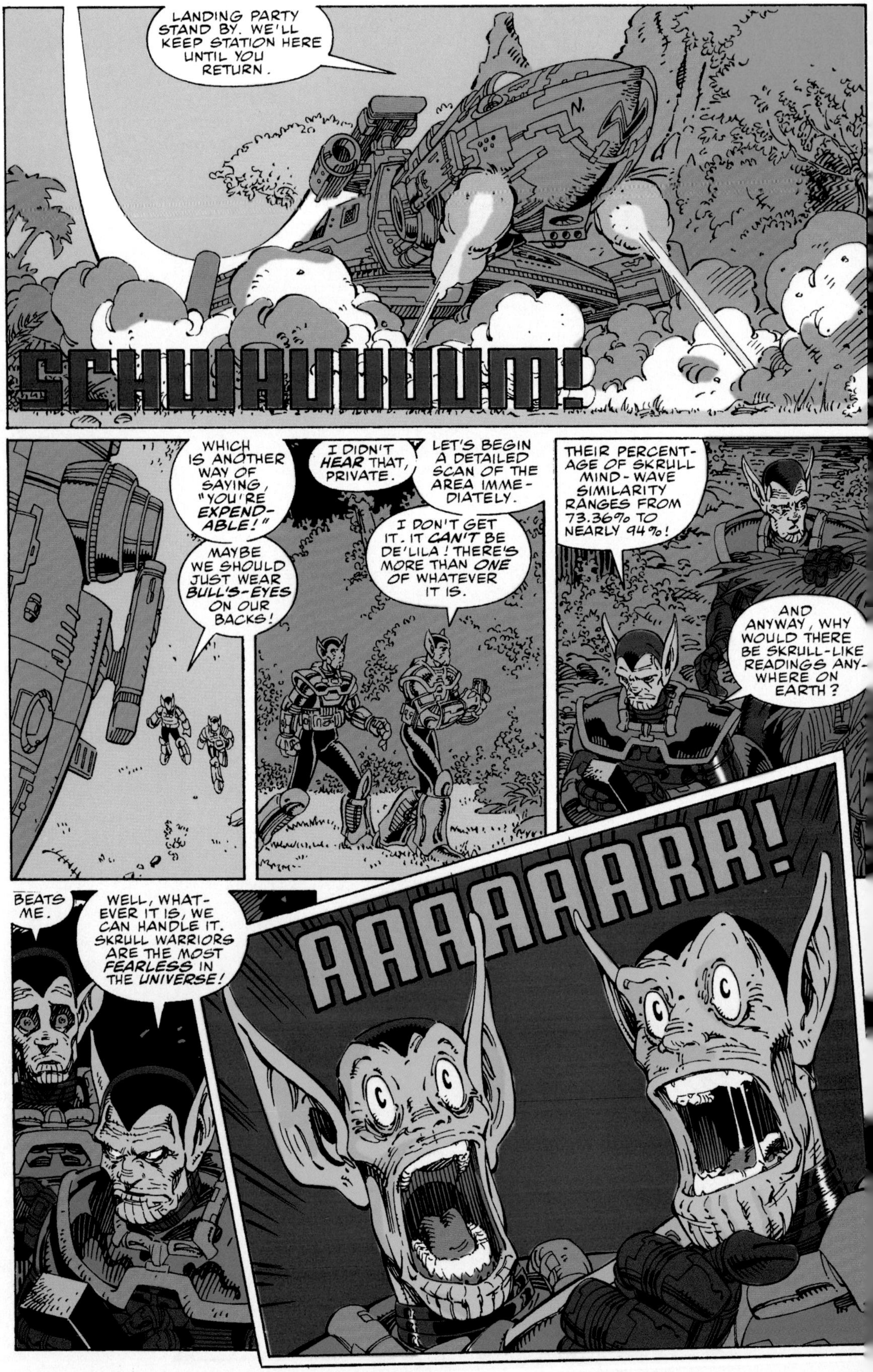
LANDING PARTY STAND BY. WE'LL KEEP STATION HERE UNTIL YOU RETURN.
SCHWHUUUUM!
WHICH IS ANOTHER WAY OF SAYING, "YOU'RE EXPENDABLE!"
MAYBE WE SHOULD JUST WEAR BULL'S-EYES ON OUR BACKS!
I DIDN'T HEAR THAT, PRIVATE.
LET'S BEGIN A DETAILED SCAN OF THE AREA IMMEDIATELY.
I DON'T GET IT. IT CAN'T BE DE'LILA! THERE'S MORE THAN ONE OF WHATEVER IT IS.
THEIR PERCENTAGE OF SKRULL MIND-WAVE SIMILARITY RANGES FROM 73.36% TO NEARLY 94%!
AND ANYWAY, WHY WOULD THERE BE SKRULL-LIKE READINGS ANYWHERE ON EARTH?
BEATS ME.
WELL, WHATEVER IT IS, WE CAN HANDLE IT. SKRULL WARRIORS ARE THE MOST FEARLESS IN THE UNIVERSE!
AAAAAAARR!

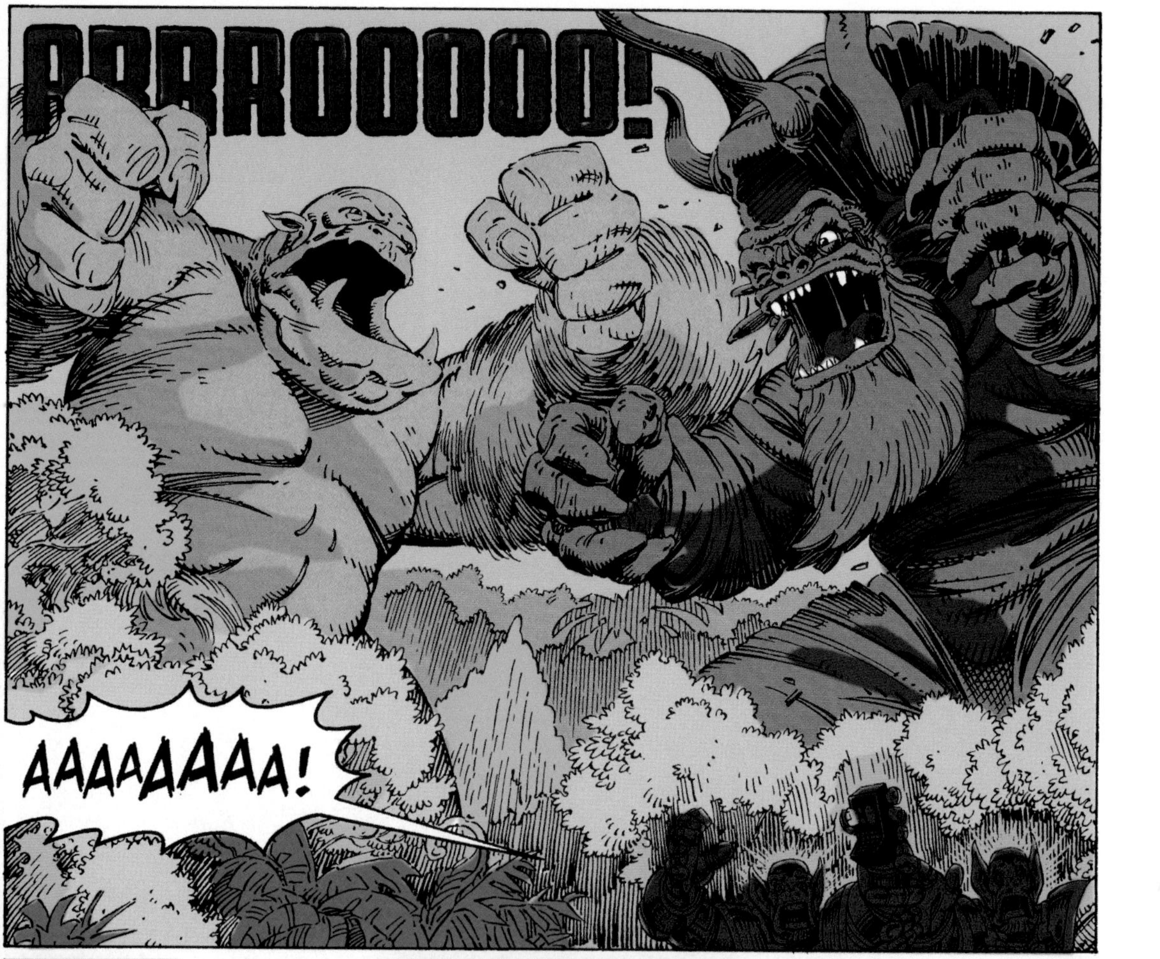
ARRRROOOOOO!
AAAAAAAA!

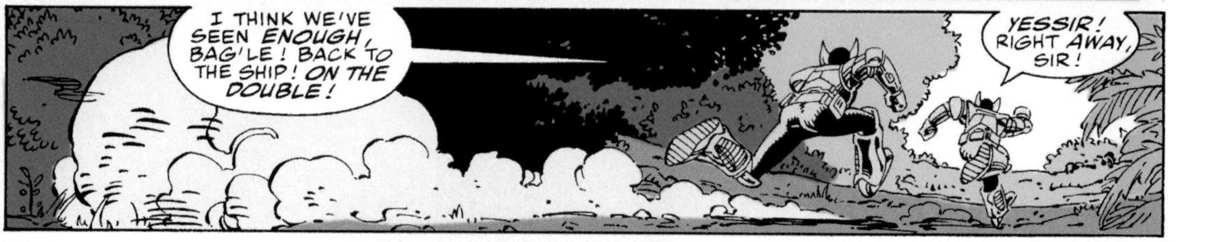
I THINK WE'VE SEEN ENOUGH, BAG'LE! BACK TO THE SHIP! ON THE DOUBLE!
YESSIR! RIGHT AWAY, SIR!

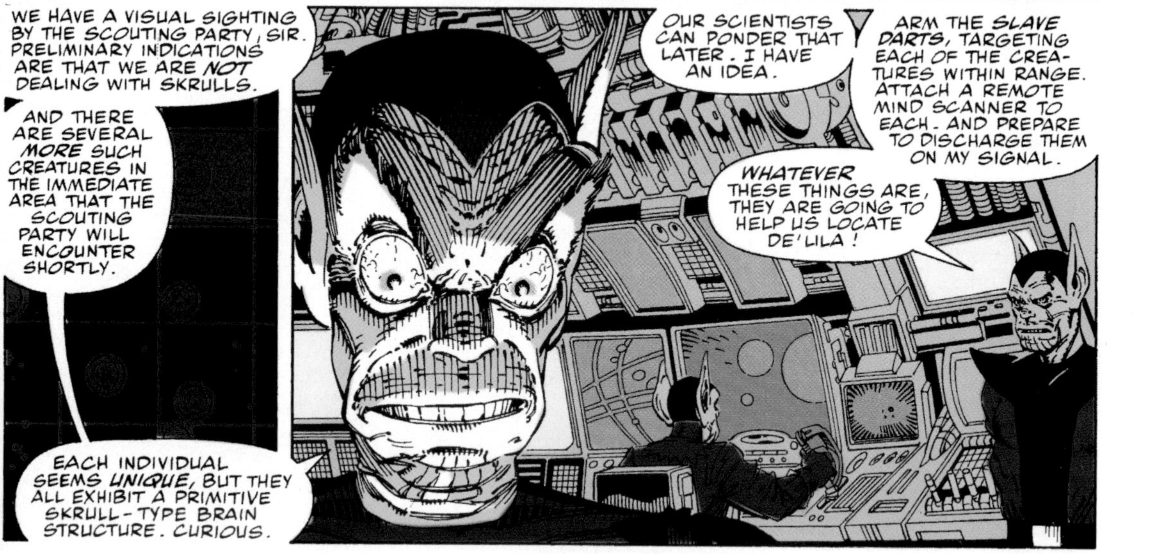
WE HAVE A VISUAL SIGHTING BY THE SCOUTING PARTY, SIR. PRELIMINARY INDICATIONS ARE THAT WE ARE NOT DEALING WITH SKRULLS.
AND THERE ARE SEVERAL MORE SUCH CREATURES IN THE IMMEDIATE AREA THAT THE SCOUTING PARTY WILL ENCOUNTER SHORTLY.
EACH INDIVIDUAL SEEMS UNIQUE, BUT THEY ALL EXHIBIT A PRIMITIVE SKRULL-TYPE BRAIN STRUCTURE. CURIOUS.
OUR SCIENTISTS CAN PONDER THAT LATER. I HAVE AN IDEA.
ARM THE SLAVE DARTS, TARGETING EACH OF THE CREATURES WITHIN RANGE. ATTACH A REMOTE MIND SCANNER TO EACH. AND PREPARE TO DISCHARGE THEM ON MY SIGNAL.
WHATEVER THESE THINGS ARE, THEY ARE GOING TO HELP US LOCATE DE'LILA!

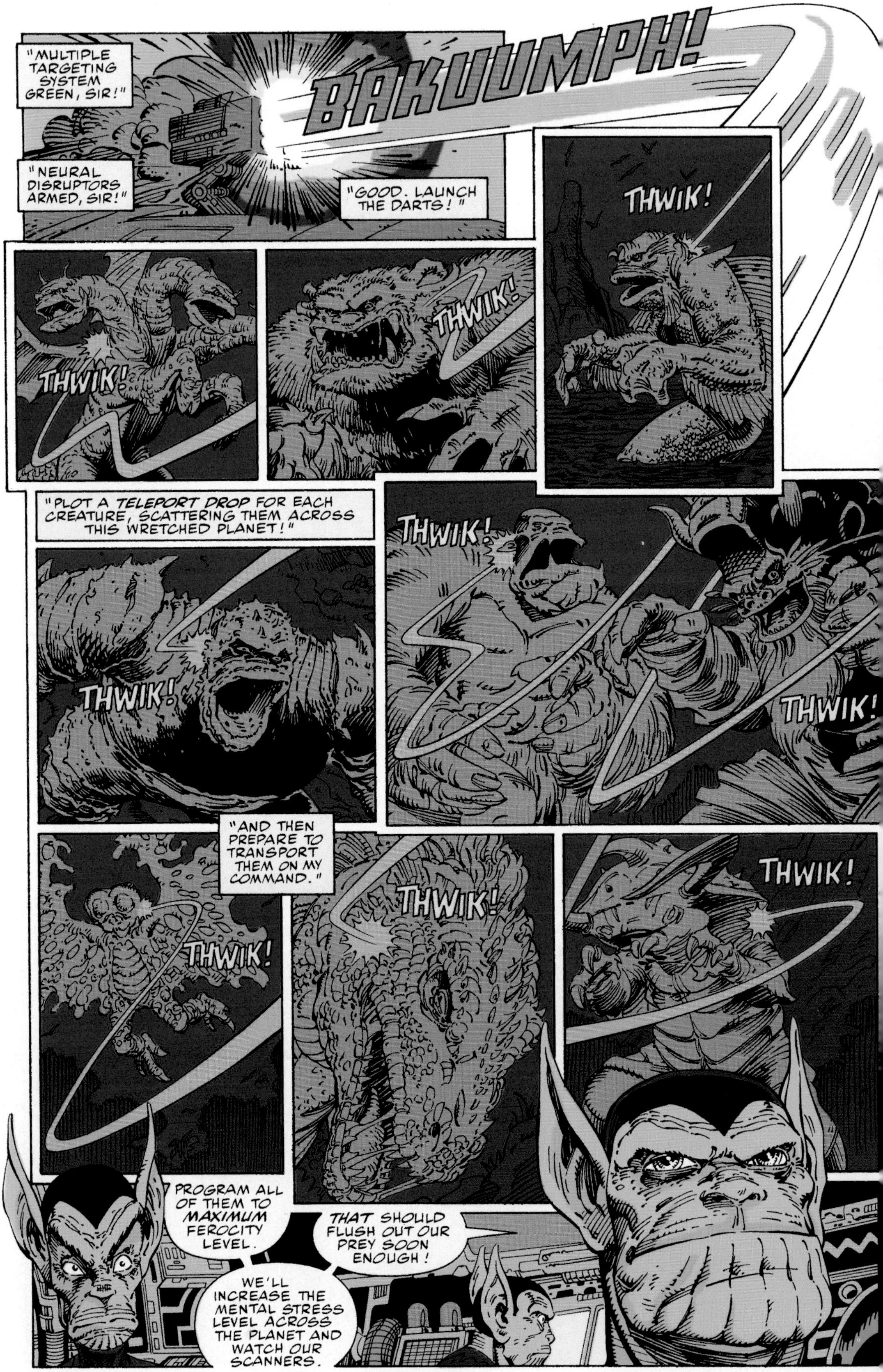
"MULTIPLE TARGETING SYSTEM GREEN, SIR!"
BAKUUMPH!
"NEURAL DISRUPTORS ARMED, SIR!"
"GOOD. LAUNCH THE DARTS!"
THWIK!
THWIK!
THWIK!
"PLOT A TELEPORT DROP FOR EACH CREATURE, SCATTERING THEM ACROSS THIS WRETCHED PLANET!"
THWIK!
THWIK!
THWIK!
"AND THEN PREPARE TO TRANSPORT THEM ON MY COMMAND."
THWIK!
THWIK!
THWIK!
PROGRAM ALL OF THEM TO MAXIMUM FEROCITY LEVEL.
THAT SHOULD FLUSH OUT OUR PREY SOON ENOUGH!
WE'LL INCREASE THE MENTAL STRESS LEVEL ACROSS THE PLANET AND WATCH OUR SCANNERS.

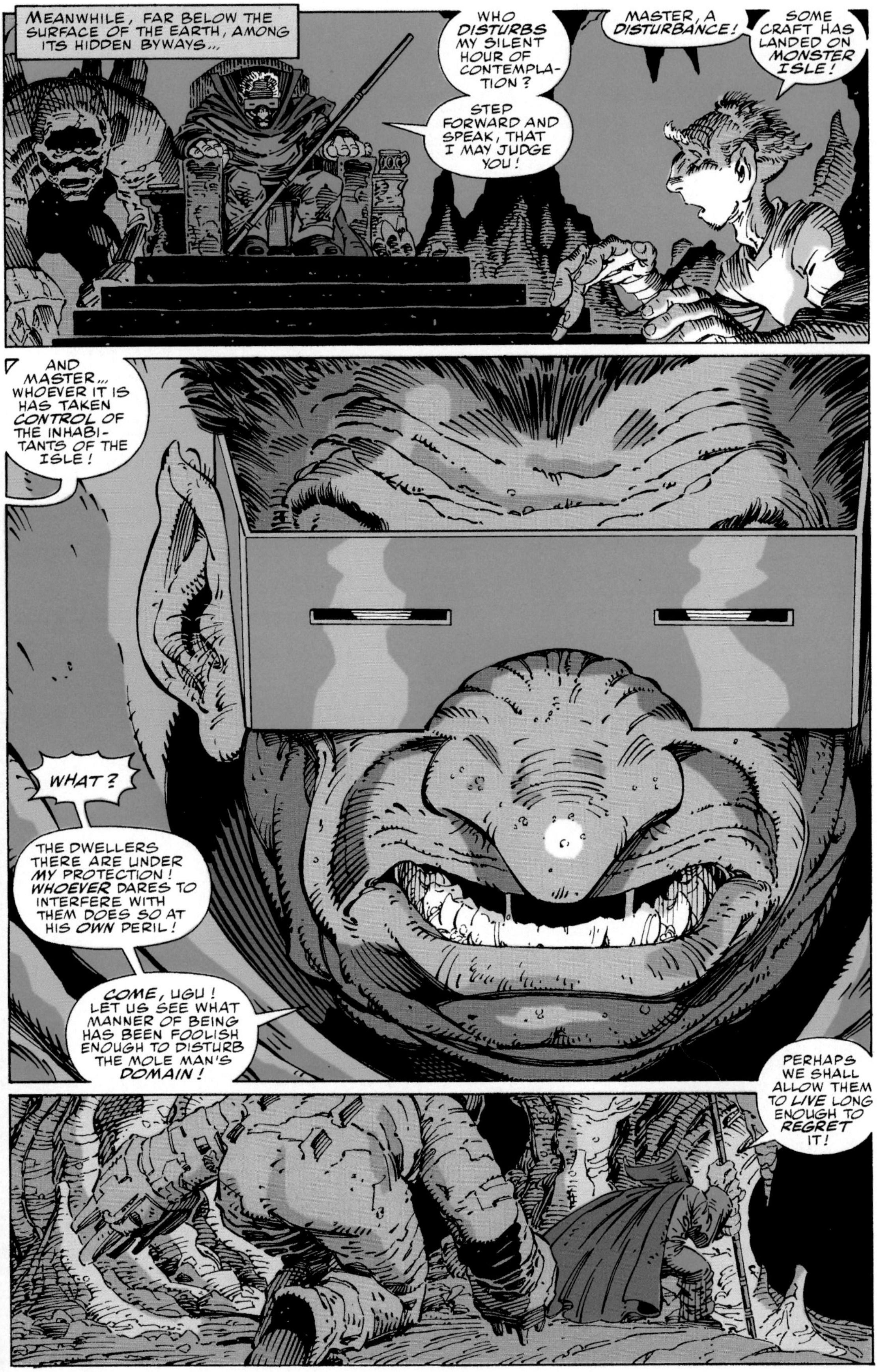
MEANWHILE, FAR BELOW THE SURFACE OF THE EARTH, AMONG ITS HIDDEN BYWAYS...
WHO DISTURBS MY SILENT HOUR OF CONTEMPLATION?
STEP FORWARD AND SPEAK, THAT I MAY JUDGE YOU!
MASTER, A DISTURBANCE!
SOME CRAFT HAS LANDED ON MONSTER ISLE!
AND MASTER... WHOEVER IT IS HAS TAKEN CONTROL OF THE INHABITANTS OF THE ISLE!
WHAT?
THE DWELLERS THERE ARE UNDER MY PROTECTION! WHOEVER DARES TO INTERFERE WITH THEM DOES SO AT HIS OWN PERIL!
COME, UGU! LET US SEE WHAT MANNER OF BEING HAS BEEN FOOLISH ENOUGH TO DISTURB THE MOLE MAN'S DOMAIN!
PERHAPS WE SHALL ALLOW THEM TO LIVE LONG ENOUGH TO REGRET IT!

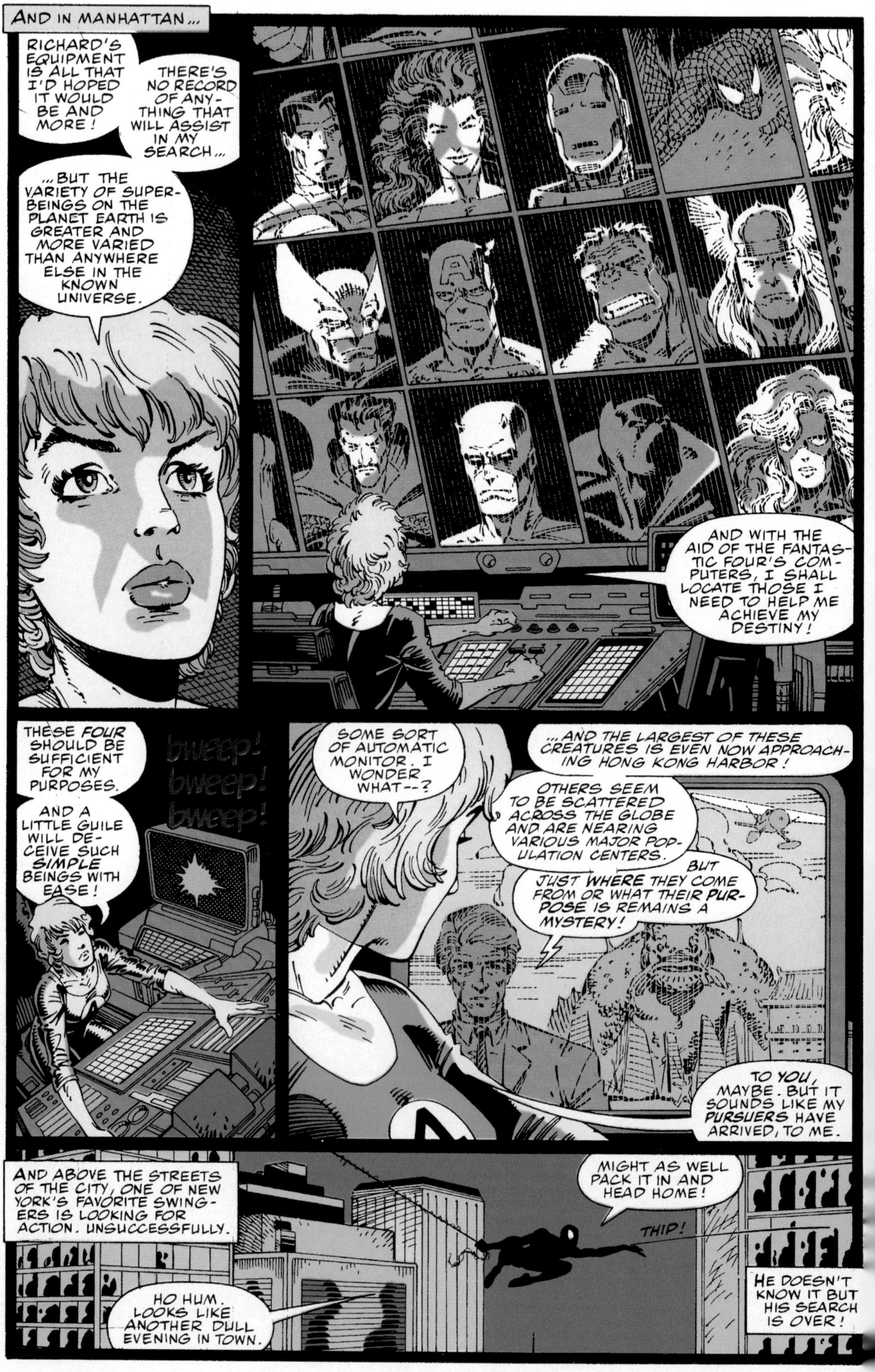
AND IN MANHATTAN...
RICHARD'S EQUIPMENT IS ALL THAT I'D HOPED IT WOULD BE AND MORE!
THERE'S NO RECORD OF ANYTHING THAT WILL ASSIST IN MY SEARCH...
...BUT THE VARIETY OF SUPER-BEINGS ON THE PLANET EARTH IS GREATER AND MORE VARIED THAN ANYWHERE ELSE IN THE KNOWN UNIVERSE.
AND WITH THE AID OF THE FANTASTIC FOUR'S COMPUTERS, I SHALL LOCATE THOSE I NEED TO HELP ME ACHIEVE MY DESTINY!
THESE FOUR SHOULD BE SUFFICIENT FOR MY PURPOSES.
AND A LITTLE GUILE WILL DECEIVE SUCH SIMPLE BEINGS WITH EASE!
bweep! bweep! bweep!
SOME SORT OF AUTOMATIC MONITOR. I WONDER WHAT--?
...AND THE LARGEST OF THESE CREATURES IS EVEN NOW APPROACHING HONG KONG HARBOR!
OTHERS SEEM TO BE SCATTERED ACROSS THE GLOBE AND ARE NEARING VARIOUS MAJOR POPULATION CENTERS.
BUT JUST WHERE THEY COME FROM OR WHAT THEIR PURPOSE IS REMAINS A MYSTERY!
TO YOU, MAYBE. BUT IT SOUNDS LIKE MY PURSUERS HAVE ARRIVED, TO ME.
AND ABOVE THE STREETS OF THE CITY, ONE OF NEW YORK'S FAVORITE SWINGERS IS LOOKING FOR ACTION. UNSUCCESSFULLY.
MIGHT AS WELL PACK IT IN AND HEAD HOME!
THIP!
HO HUM. LOOKS LIKE ANOTHER DULL EVENING IN TOWN.
HE DOESN'T KNOW IT BUT HIS SEARCH IS OVER!

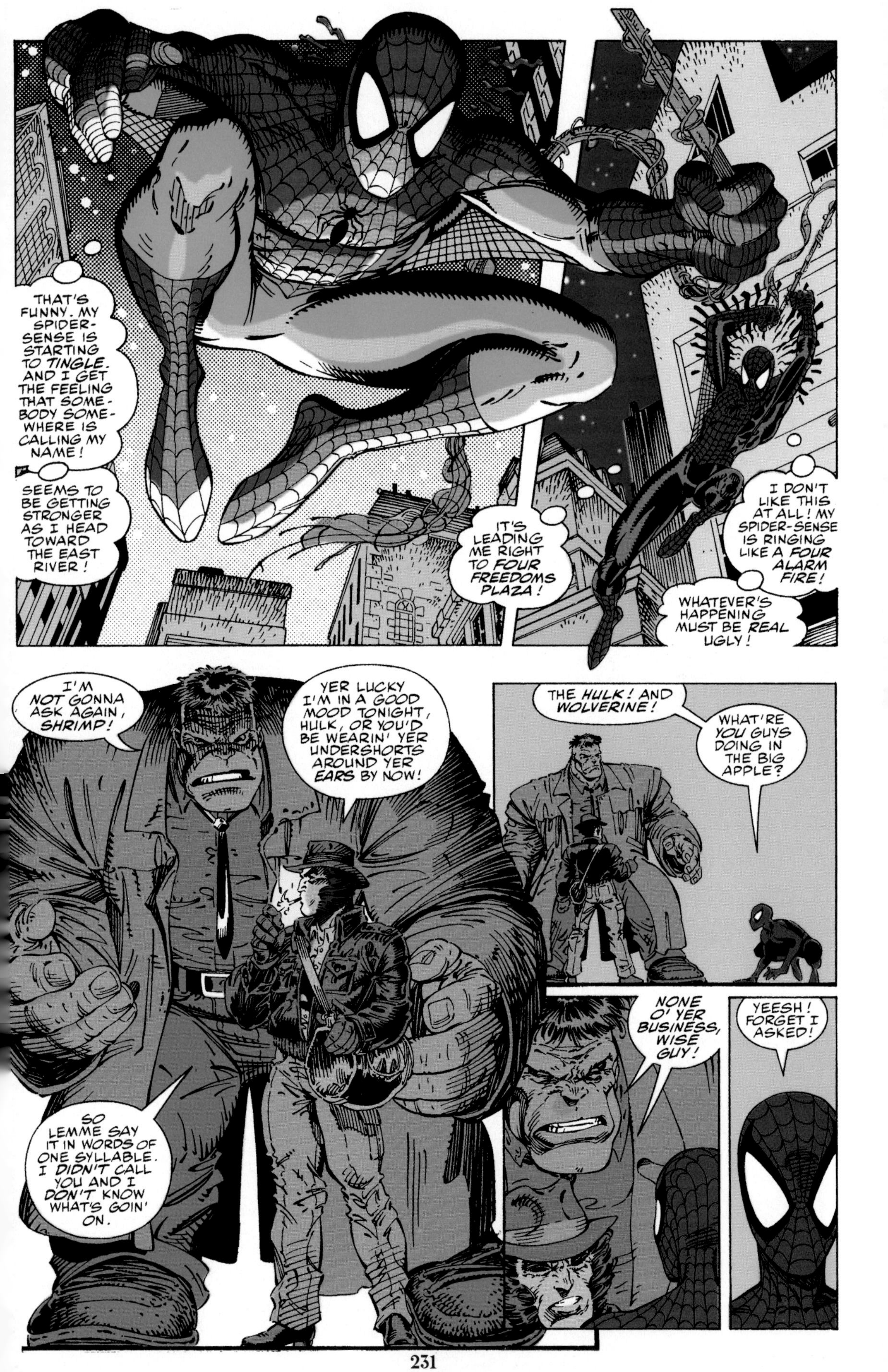
THAT'S FUNNY. MY SPIDER-SENSE IS STARTING TO TINGLE. AND I GET THE FEELING THAT SOMEBODY SOMEWHERE IS CALLING MY NAME!
SEEMS TO BE GETTING STRONGER AS I HEAD TOWARD THE EAST RIVER!
IT'S LEADING ME RIGHT TO FOUR FREEDOMS PLAZA!
I DON'T LIKE THIS AT ALL! MY SPIDER-SENSE IS RINGING LIKE A FOUR ALARM FIRE!
WHATEVER'S HAPPENING MUST BE REAL UGLY!
I'M NOT GONNA ASK AGAIN, SHRIMP!
YER LUCKY I'M IN A GOOD MOOD TONIGHT, HULK, OR YOU'D BE WEARIN' YER UNDERSHORTS AROUND YER EARS BY NOW!
SO LEMME SAY IT IN WORDS OF ONE SYLLABLE. I DIDN'T CALL YOU AND I DON'T KNOW WHAT'S GOIN' ON.
THE HULK! AND WOLVERINE!
WHAT'RE YOU GUYS DOING IN THE BIG APPLE?
NONE O' YER BUSINESS, WISE GUY!
YEESH! FORGET I ASKED!

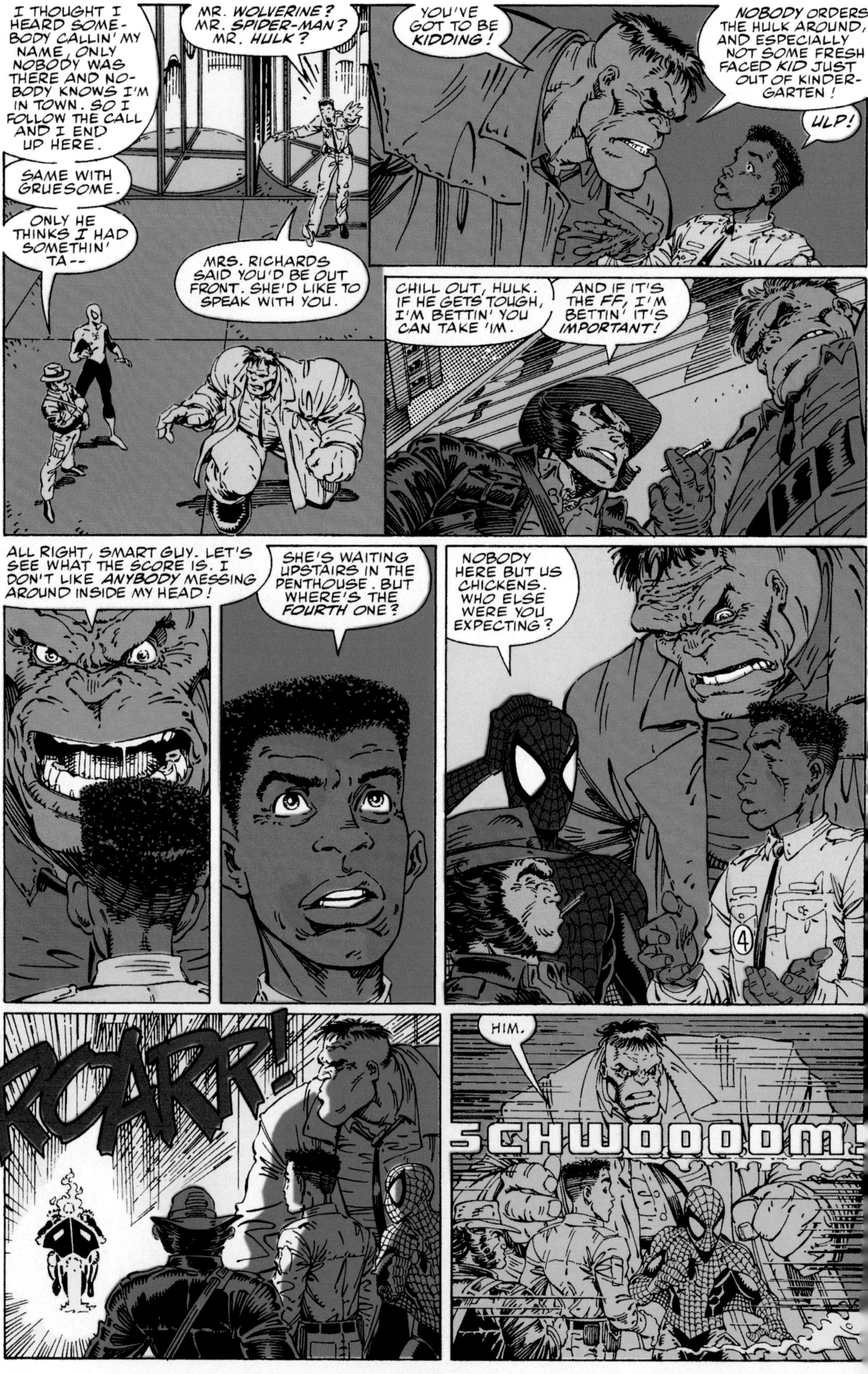
I THOUGHT I HEARD SOME-BODY CALLIN' MY NAME, ONLY NOBODY WAS THERE AND NO-BODY KNOWS I'M IN TOWN. SO I FOLLOW THE CALL AND I END UP HERE.
SAME WITH GRUESOME.
ONLY HE THINKS *I* HAD SOMETHIN' TA--
MR. *WOLVERINE*? MR. *SPIDER-MAN*? MR. *HULK*?
MRS. RICHARDS SAID YOU'D BE OUT FRONT. SHE'D LIKE TO SPEAK WITH YOU.
YOU'VE GOT TO BE *KIDDING*!
NOBODY ORDERS THE HULK AROUND, AND ESPECIALLY NOT SOME FRESH FACED *KID* JUST OUT OF KINDER-GARTEN!
ULP!
CHILL OUT, HULK. IF HE GETS TOUGH, I'M BETTIN' YOU CAN TAKE 'IM.
AND IF IT'S THE *FF*, I'M BETTIN' IT'S *IMPORTANT*!
ALL RIGHT, SMART GUY. LET'S SEE WHAT THE SCORE IS. I DON'T LIKE *ANYBODY* MESSING AROUND INSIDE MY HEAD!
SHE'S WAITING UPSTAIRS IN THE PENTHOUSE. BUT WHERE'S THE *FOURTH* ONE?
NOBODY HERE BUT US CHICKENS. WHO ELSE WERE YOU EXPECTING?
4
ROARR!
HIM.
SCHWOOOOOM!

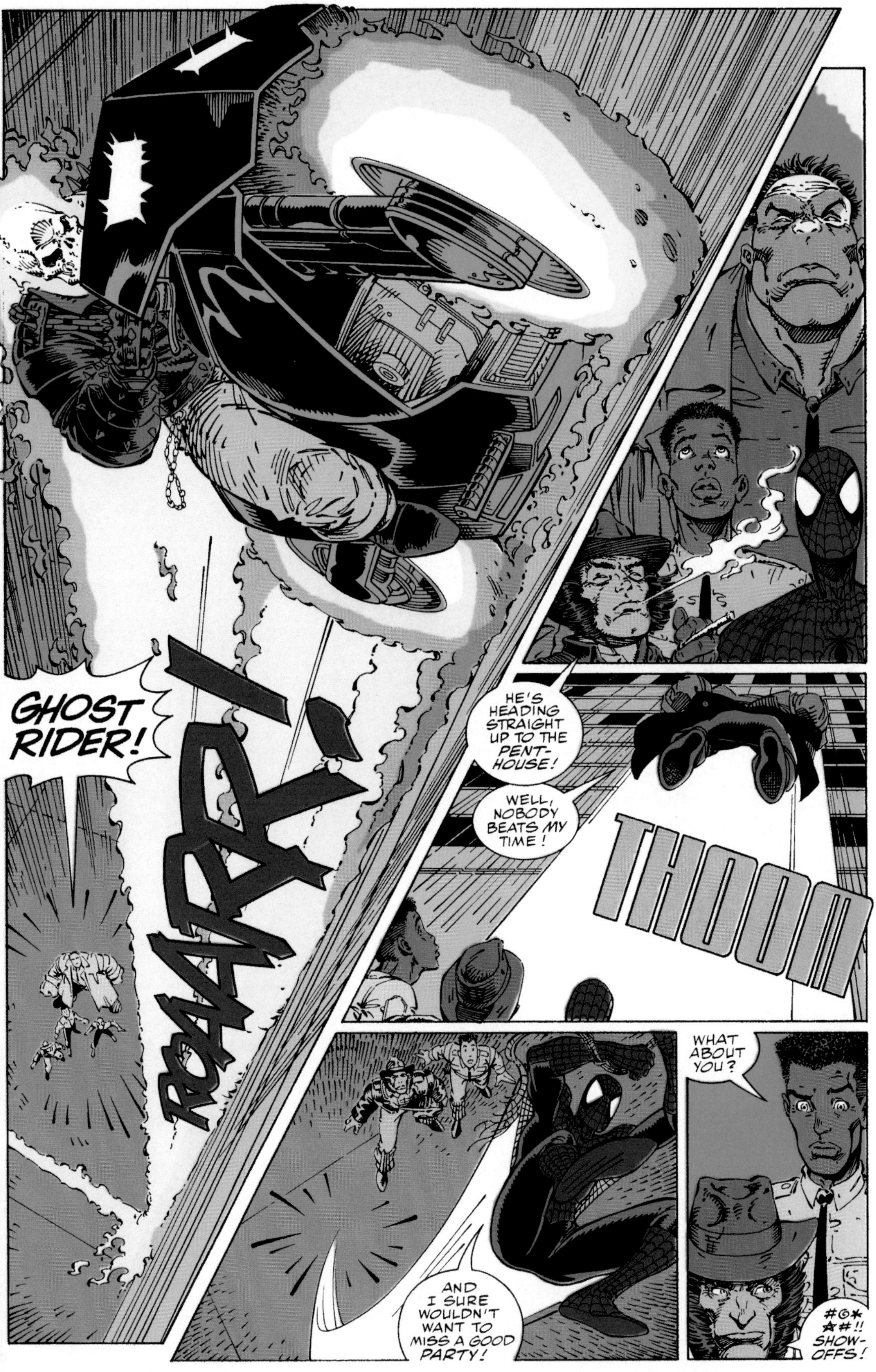
GHOST RIDER!
ROAAARR!
HE'S HEADING STRAIGHT UP TO THE PENT-HOUSE!
WELL, NOBODY BEATS MY TIME!
THOOM
WHAT ABOUT YOU?
AND I SURE WOULDN'T WANT TO MISS A GOOD PARTY!
#@*☆#!! SHOW-OFFS!

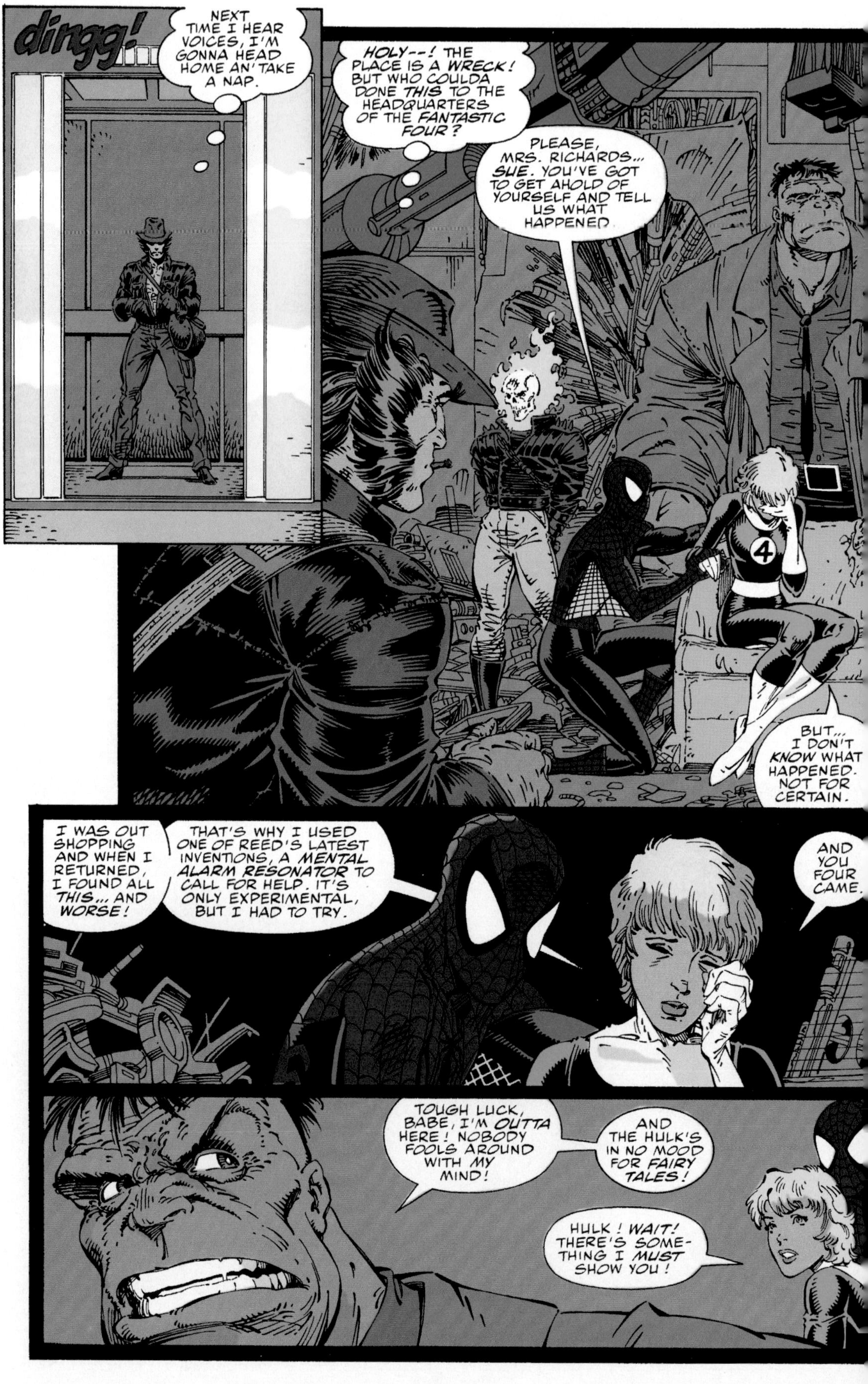
dingg!
NEXT TIME I HEAR VOICES, I'M GONNA HEAD HOME AN' TAKE A NAP.
HOLY--! THE PLACE IS A WRECK! BUT WHO COULDA DONE THIS TO THE HEADQUARTERS OF THE FANTASTIC FOUR?
PLEASE, MRS. RICHARDS... SUE. YOU'VE GOT TO GET AHOLD OF YOURSELF AND TELL US WHAT HAPPENED.
BUT... I DON'T KNOW WHAT HAPPENED. NOT FOR CERTAIN.
I WAS OUT SHOPPING AND WHEN I RETURNED, I FOUND ALL THIS... AND WORSE!
THAT'S WHY I USED ONE OF REED'S LATEST INVENTIONS, A MENTAL ALARM RESONATOR TO CALL FOR HELP. IT'S ONLY EXPERIMENTAL, BUT I HAD TO TRY.
AND YOU FOUR CAME.
TOUGH LUCK, BABE, I'M OUTTA HERE! NOBODY FOOLS AROUND WITH MY MIND!
AND THE HULK'S IN NO MOOD FOR FAIRY TALES!
HULK! WAIT! THERE'S SOMETHING I MUST SHOW YOU!

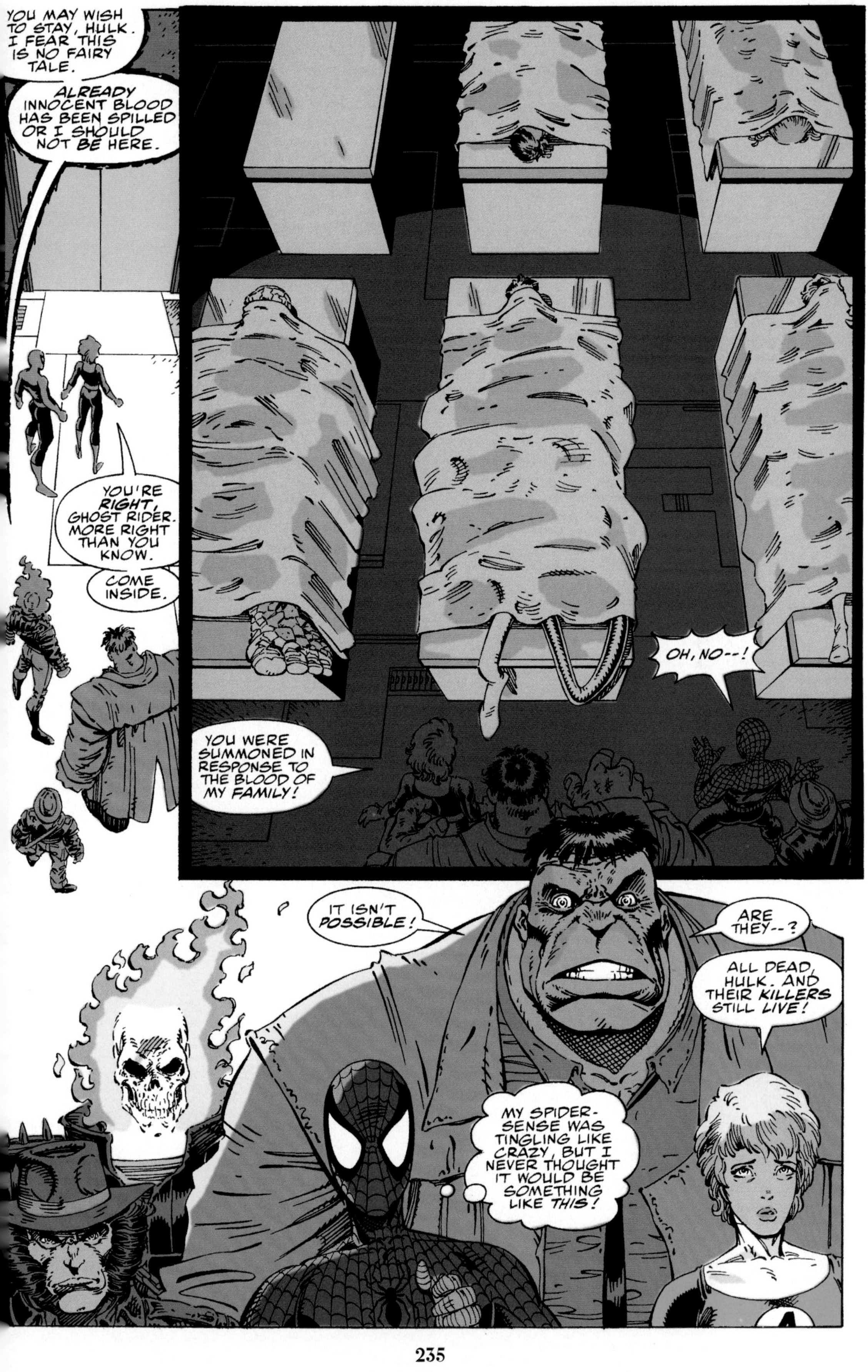

YOU MAY WISH TO STAY, HULK. I FEAR THIS IS NO FAIRY TALE.
ALREADY INNOCENT BLOOD HAS BEEN SPILLED OR I SHOULD NOT BE HERE.
YOU'RE RIGHT, GHOST RIDER. MORE RIGHT THAN YOU KNOW.
COME INSIDE.
OH, NO--!
YOU WERE SUMMONED IN RESPONSE TO THE BLOOD OF MY FAMILY!
IT ISN'T POSSIBLE!
ARE THEY--?
ALL DEAD, HULK. AND THEIR KILLERS STILL LIVE!
MY SPIDER-SENSE WAS TINGLING LIKE CRAZY, BUT I NEVER THOUGHT IT WOULD BE SOMETHING LIKE THIS!

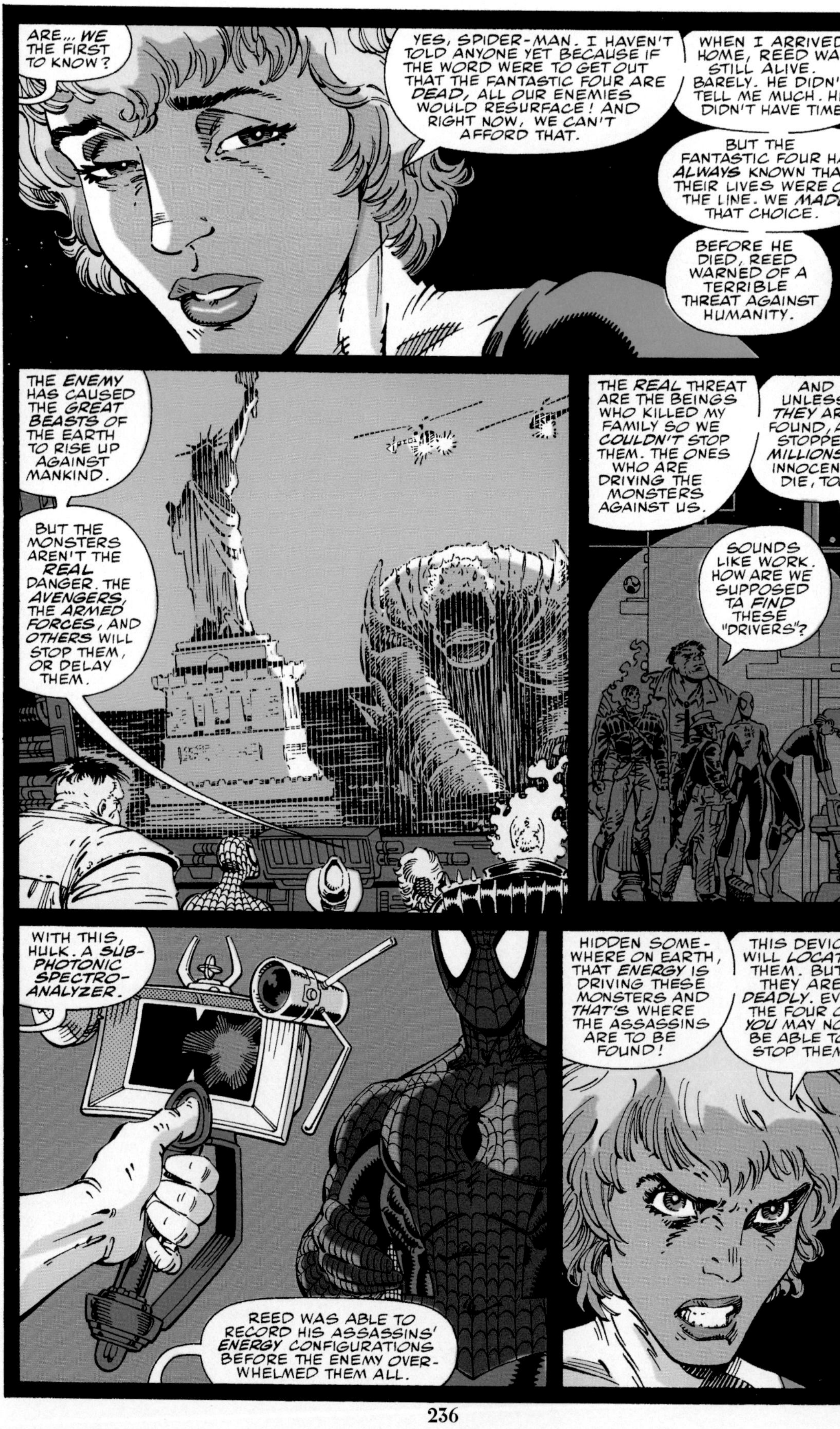

ARE... WE THE FIRST TO KNOW?
YES, SPIDER-MAN. I HAVEN'T TOLD ANYONE YET BECAUSE IF THE WORD WERE TO GET OUT THAT THE FANTASTIC FOUR ARE DEAD, ALL OUR ENEMIES WOULD RESURFACE! AND RIGHT NOW, WE CAN'T AFFORD THAT.
WHEN I ARRIVED HOME, REED WAS STILL ALIVE. BARELY. HE DIDN'T TELL ME MUCH. HE DIDN'T HAVE TIME.
BUT THE FANTASTIC FOUR HAVE ALWAYS KNOWN THAT THEIR LIVES WERE ON THE LINE. WE MADE THAT CHOICE.
BEFORE HE DIED, REED WARNED OF A TERRIBLE THREAT AGAINST HUMANITY.
THE ENEMY HAS CAUSED THE GREAT BEASTS OF THE EARTH TO RISE UP AGAINST MANKIND.
BUT THE MONSTERS AREN'T THE REAL DANGER. THE AVENGERS, THE ARMED FORCES, AND OTHERS WILL STOP THEM, OR DELAY THEM.
THE REAL THREAT ARE THE BEINGS WHO KILLED MY FAMILY SO WE COULDN'T STOP THEM. THE ONES WHO ARE DRIVING THE MONSTERS AGAINST US.
AND UNLESS THEY ARE FOUND, AND STOPPED, MILLIONS OF INNOCENTS DIE, TOO!
SOUNDS LIKE WORK. HOW ARE WE SUPPOSED TA FIND THESE "DRIVERS"?
WITH THIS, HULK. A SUB-PHOTONIC SPECTRO-ANALYZER.
REED WAS ABLE TO RECORD HIS ASSASSINS' ENERGY CONFIGURATIONS BEFORE THE ENEMY OVER-WHELMED THEM ALL.
HIDDEN SOME-WHERE ON EARTH, THAT ENERGY IS DRIVING THESE MONSTERS AND THAT'S WHERE THE ASSASSINS ARE TO BE FOUND!
THIS DEVICE WILL LOCATE THEM. BUT THEY ARE DEADLY. EVEN THE FOUR OF YOU MAY NOT BE ABLE TO STOP THEM.

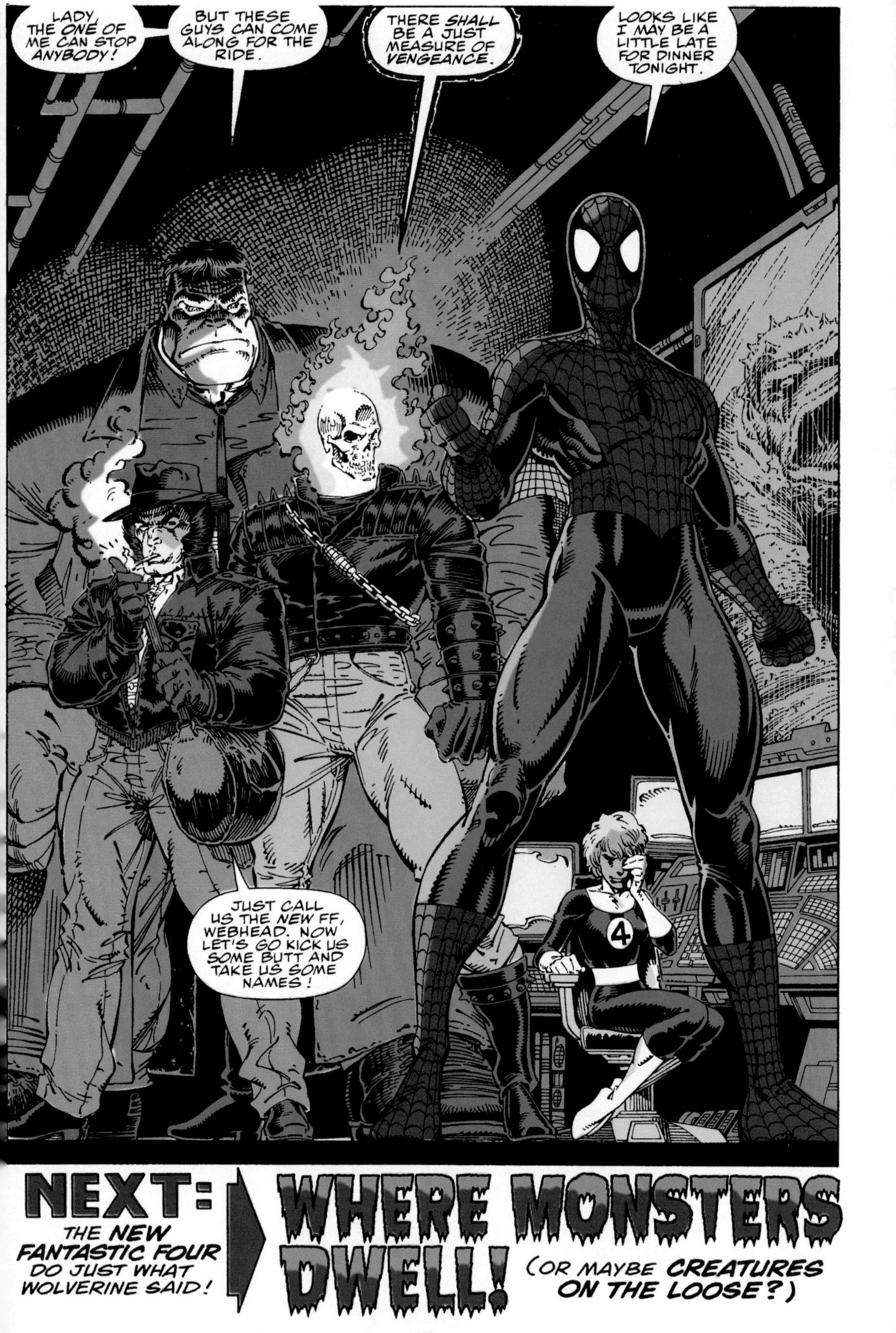
LADY, THE ONE OF ME CAN STOP ANYBODY!
BUT THESE GUYS CAN COME ALONG FOR THE RIDE.
THERE SHALL BE A JUST MEASURE OF VENGEANCE.
LOOKS LIKE I MAY BE A LITTLE LATE FOR DINNER TONIGHT.
JUST CALL US THE NEW FF, WEBHEAD. NOW LET'S GO KICK US SOME BUTT AND TAKE US SOME NAMES!
4
NEXT:
THE NEW FANTASTIC FOUR DO JUST WHAT WOLVERINE SAID!
WHERE MONSTERS DWELL!
(OR MAYBE CREATURES ON THE LOOSE?)

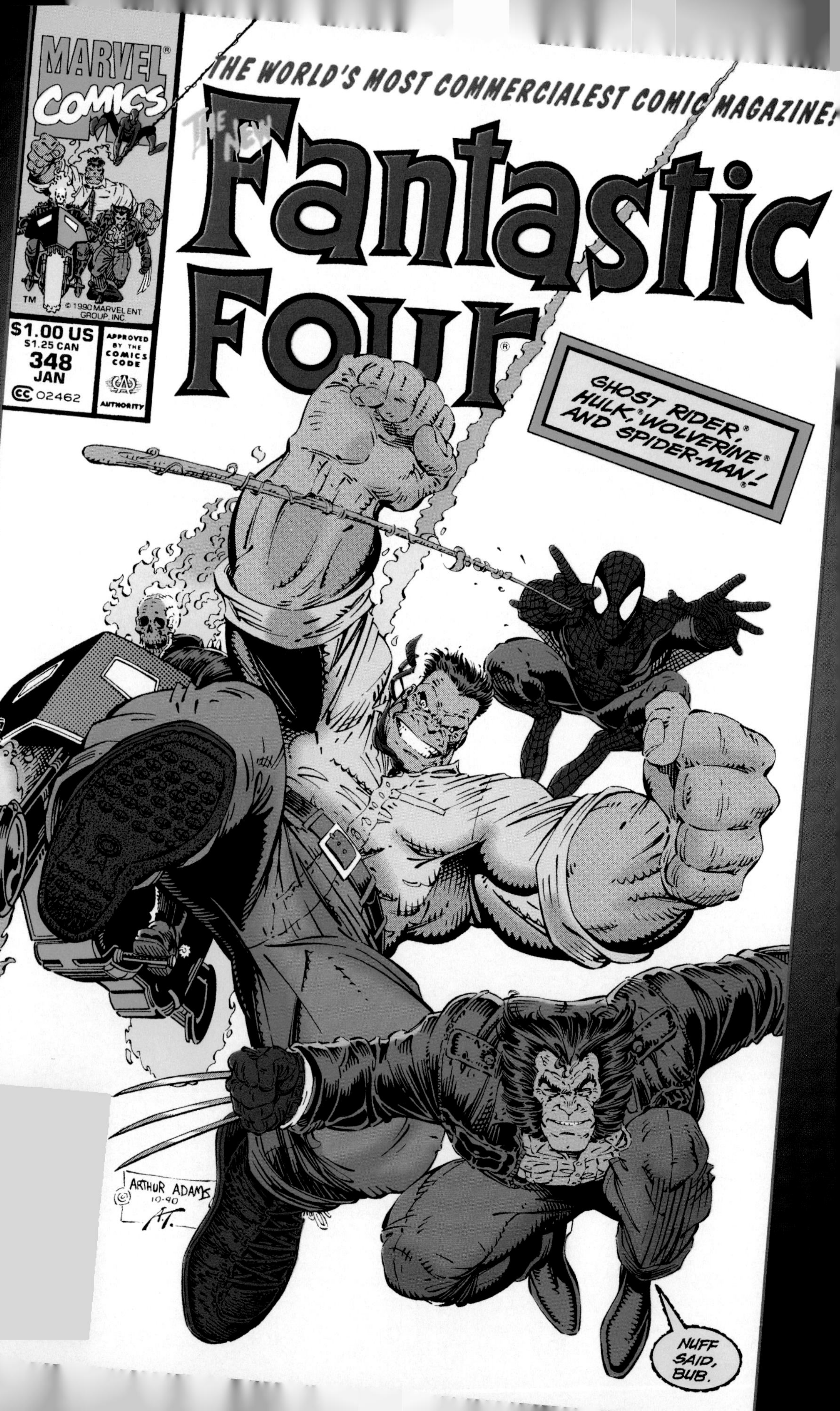
MARVEL COMICS
THE WORLD'S MOST COMMERCIALEST COMIC MAGAZINE!
THE NEW Fantastic Four
TM © 1990 MARVEL ENT. GROUP, INC.
$1.00 US $1.25 CAN 348 JAN
02462
APPROVED BY THE COMICS CODE AUTHORITY
GHOST RIDER, HULK, WOLVERINE AND SPIDER-MAN!
ARTHUR ADAMS 10-90
NUFF SAID, BUB.

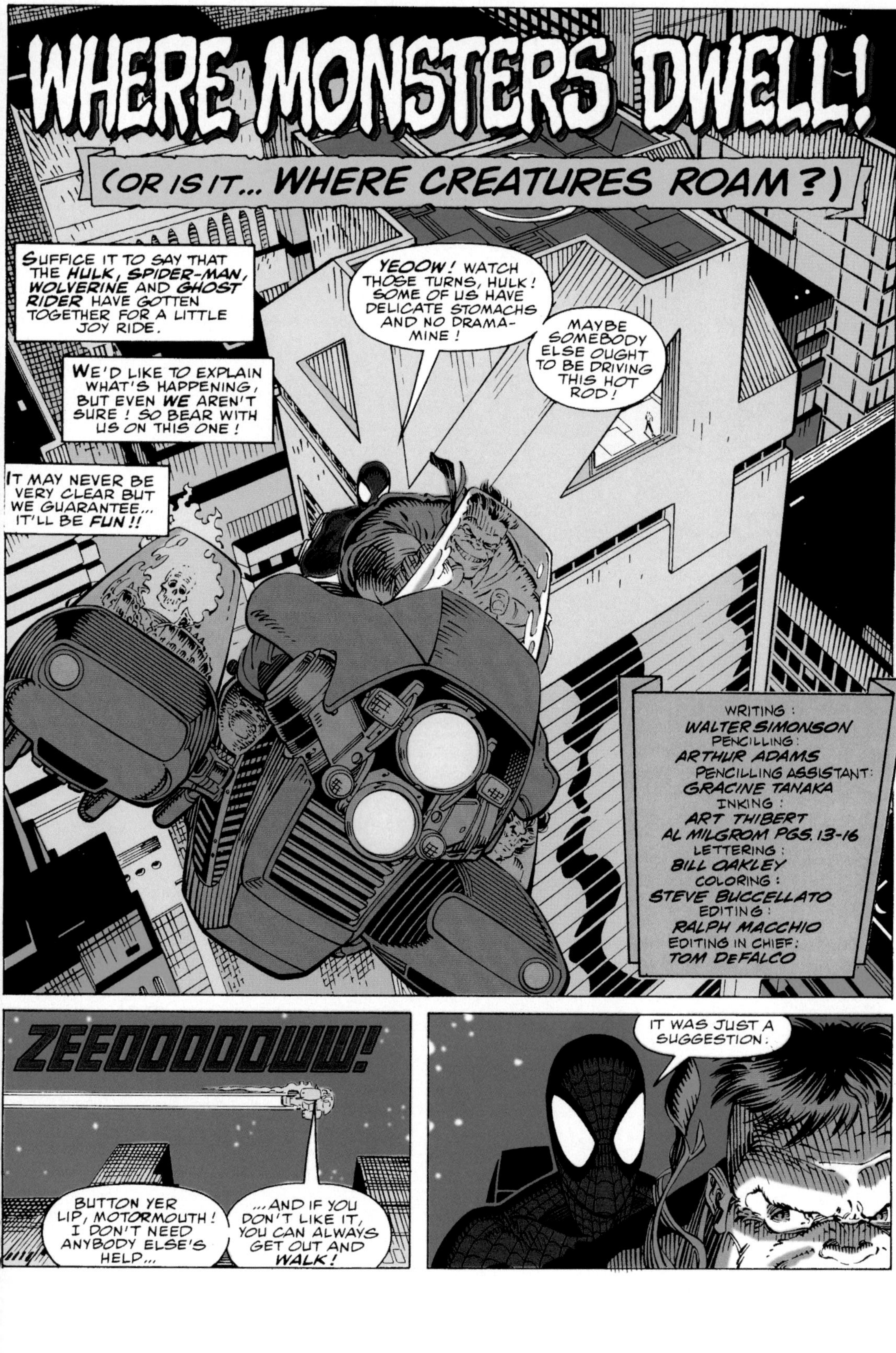
WHERE MONSTERS DWELL!
(OR IS IT... WHERE CREATURES ROAM?)
SUFFICE IT TO SAY THAT THE HULK, SPIDER-MAN, WOLVERINE AND GHOST RIDER HAVE GOTTEN TOGETHER FOR A LITTLE JOY RIDE.
WE'D LIKE TO EXPLAIN WHAT'S HAPPENING, BUT EVEN WE AREN'T SURE! SO BEAR WITH US ON THIS ONE!
IT MAY NEVER BE VERY CLEAR BUT WE GUARANTEE... IT'LL BE FUN!!
YEOOW! WATCH THOSE TURNS, HULK! SOME OF US HAVE DELICATE STOMACHS AND NO DRAMA-MINE!
MAYBE SOMEBODY ELSE OUGHT TO BE DRIVING THIS HOT ROD!
WRITING: WALTER SIMONSON
PENCILLING: ARTHUR ADAMS
PENCILLING ASSISTANT: GRACINE TANAKA
INKING: ART THIBERT
AL MILGROM PGS. 13-16
LETTERING: BILL OAKLEY
COLORING: STEVE BUCCELLATO
EDITING: RALPH MACCHIO
EDITING IN CHIEF: TOM DEFALCO
ZEEOOOOOOWW!
BUTTON YER LIP, MOTORMOUTH! I DON'T NEED ANYBODY ELSE'S HELP...
...AND IF YOU DON'T LIKE IT, YOU CAN ALWAYS GET OUT AND WALK!
IT WAS JUST A SUGGESTION.

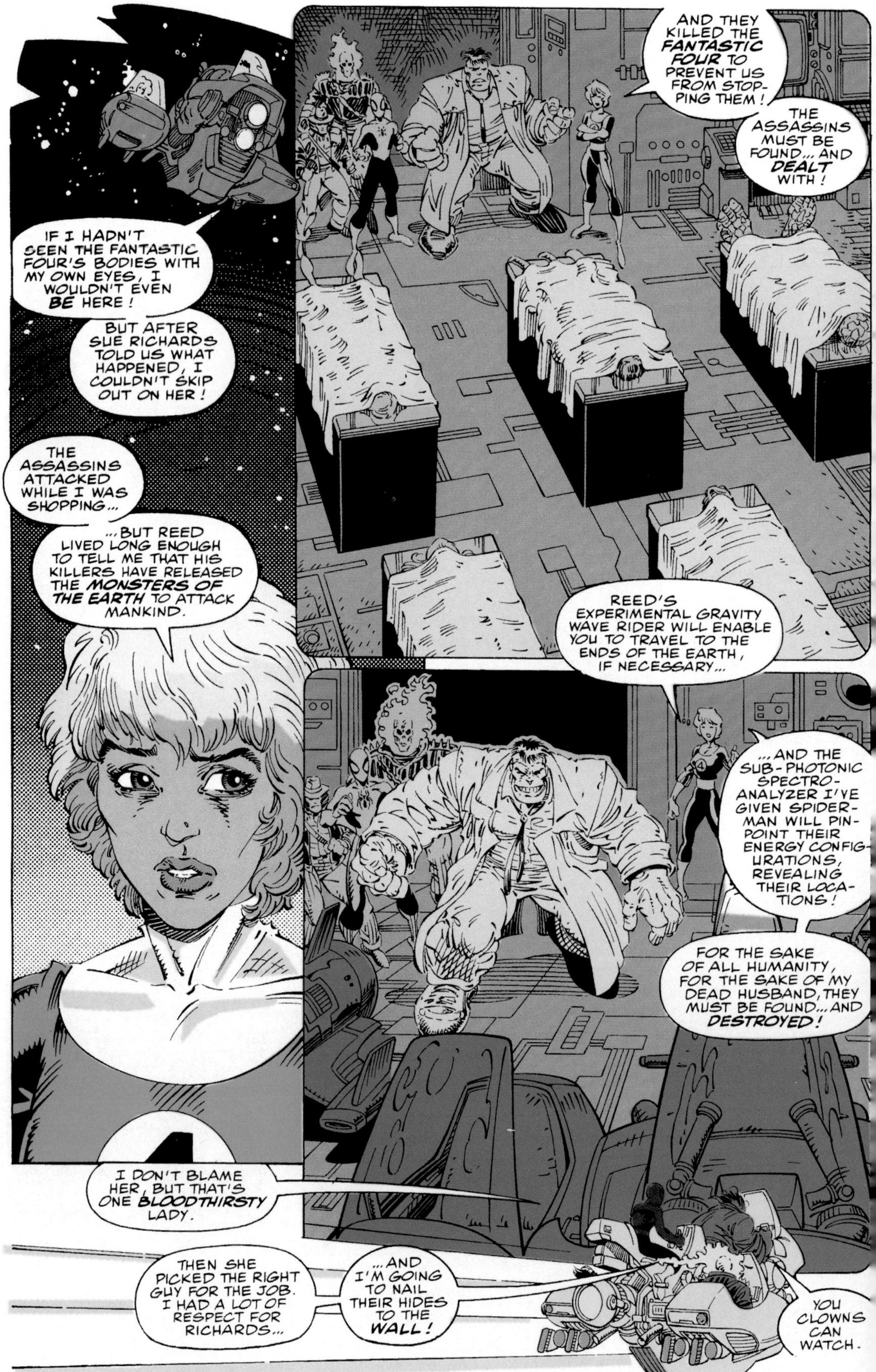
IF I HADN'T SEEN THE FANTASTIC FOUR'S BODIES WITH MY OWN EYES, I WOULDN'T EVEN BE HERE!
BUT AFTER SUE RICHARDS TOLD US WHAT HAPPENED, I COULDN'T SKIP OUT ON HER!
THE ASSASSINS ATTACKED WHILE I WAS SHOPPING...
...BUT REED LIVED LONG ENOUGH TO TELL ME THAT HIS KILLERS HAVE RELEASED THE MONSTERS OF THE EARTH TO ATTACK MANKIND.
AND THEY KILLED THE FANTASTIC FOUR TO PREVENT US FROM STOPPING THEM!
THE ASSASSINS MUST BE FOUND... AND DEALT WITH!
REED'S EXPERIMENTAL GRAVITY WAVE RIDER WILL ENABLE YOU TO TRAVEL TO THE ENDS OF THE EARTH, IF NECESSARY...
...AND THE SUB-PHOTONIC SPECTRO-ANALYZER I'VE GIVEN SPIDER-MAN WILL PIN-POINT THEIR ENERGY CONFIGURATIONS, REVEALING THEIR LOCATIONS!
FOR THE SAKE OF ALL HUMANITY, FOR THE SAKE OF MY DEAD HUSBAND, THEY MUST BE FOUND... AND DESTROYED!
I DON'T BLAME HER, BUT THAT'S ONE BLOODTHIRSTY LADY.
THEN SHE PICKED THE RIGHT GUY FOR THE JOB. I HAD A LOT OF RESPECT FOR RICHARDS...
...AND I'M GOING TO NAIL THEIR HIDES TO THE WALL!
YOU CLOWNS CAN WATCH.

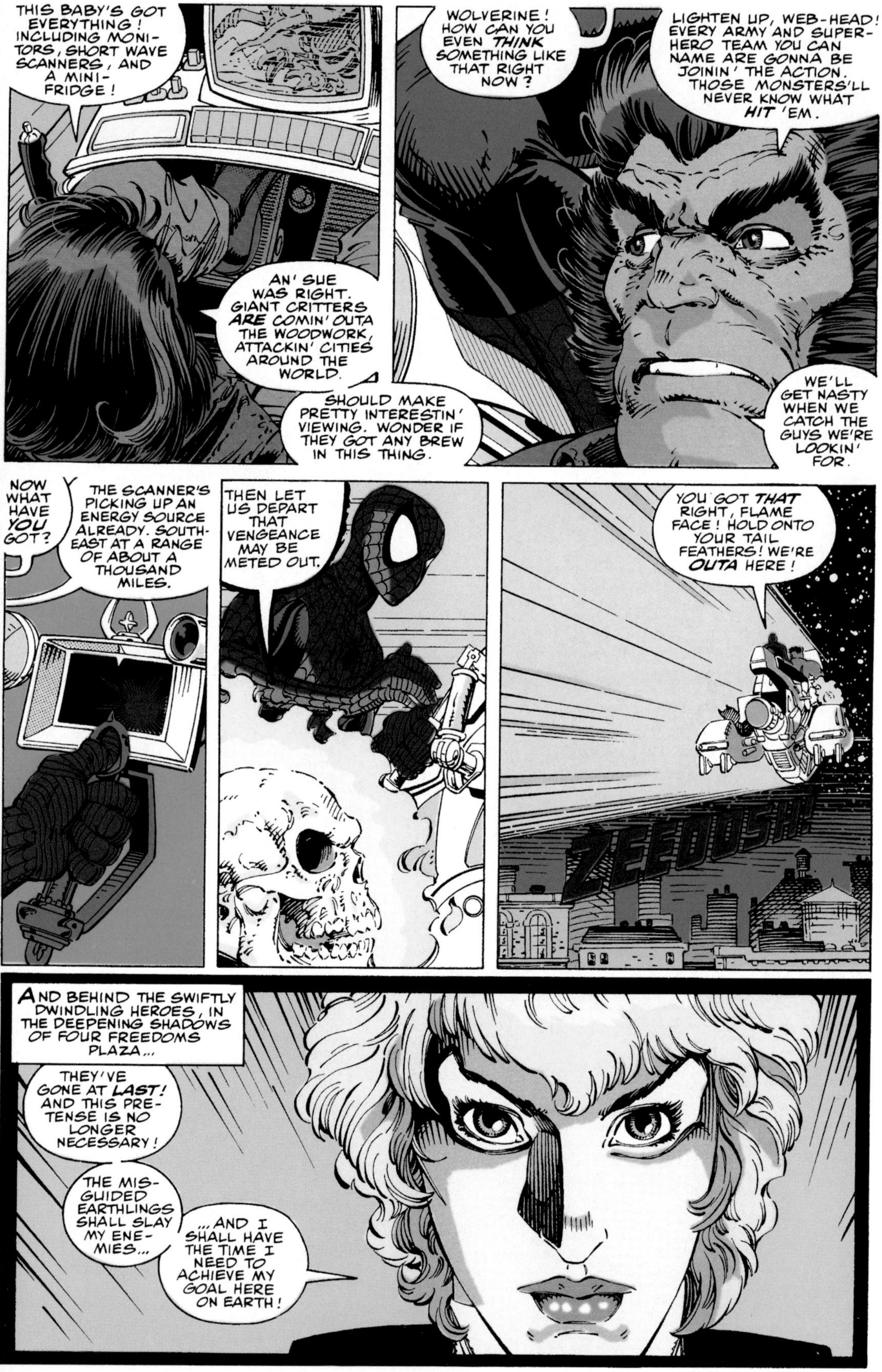
THIS BABY'S GOT EVERYTHING! INCLUDING MONITORS, SHORT WAVE SCANNERS, AND A MINI-FRIDGE!
AN' SUE WAS RIGHT. GIANT CRITTERS ARE COMIN' OUTA THE WOODWORK, ATTACKIN' CITIES AROUND THE WORLD.
SHOULD MAKE PRETTY INTERESTIN' VIEWING. WONDER IF THEY GOT ANY BREW IN THIS THING.
WOLVERINE! HOW CAN YOU EVEN THINK SOMETHING LIKE THAT RIGHT NOW?
LIGHTEN UP, WEB-HEAD! EVERY ARMY AND SUPER-HERO TEAM YOU CAN NAME ARE GONNA BE JOININ' THE ACTION. THOSE MONSTERS'LL NEVER KNOW WHAT HIT 'EM.
WE'LL GET NASTY WHEN WE CATCH THE GUYS WE'RE LOOKIN' FOR.
NOW WHAT HAVE YOU GOT?
THE SCANNER'S PICKING UP AN ENERGY SOURCE ALREADY. SOUTH-EAST AT A RANGE OF ABOUT A THOUSAND MILES.
THEN LET US DEPART THAT VENGEANCE MAY BE METED OUT.
YOU GOT THAT RIGHT, FLAME FACE! HOLD ONTO YOUR TAIL FEATHERS! WE'RE OUTA HERE!
ZEEDOOSH!
AND BEHIND THE SWIFTLY DWINDLING HEROES, IN THE DEEPENING SHADOWS OF FOUR FREEDOMS PLAZA...
THEY'VE GONE AT LAST! AND THIS PRETENSE IS NO LONGER NECESSARY!
THE MISGUIDED EARTHLINGS SHALL SLAY MY ENEMIES...
...AND I SHALL HAVE THE TIME I NEED TO ACHIEVE MY GOAL HERE ON EARTH!

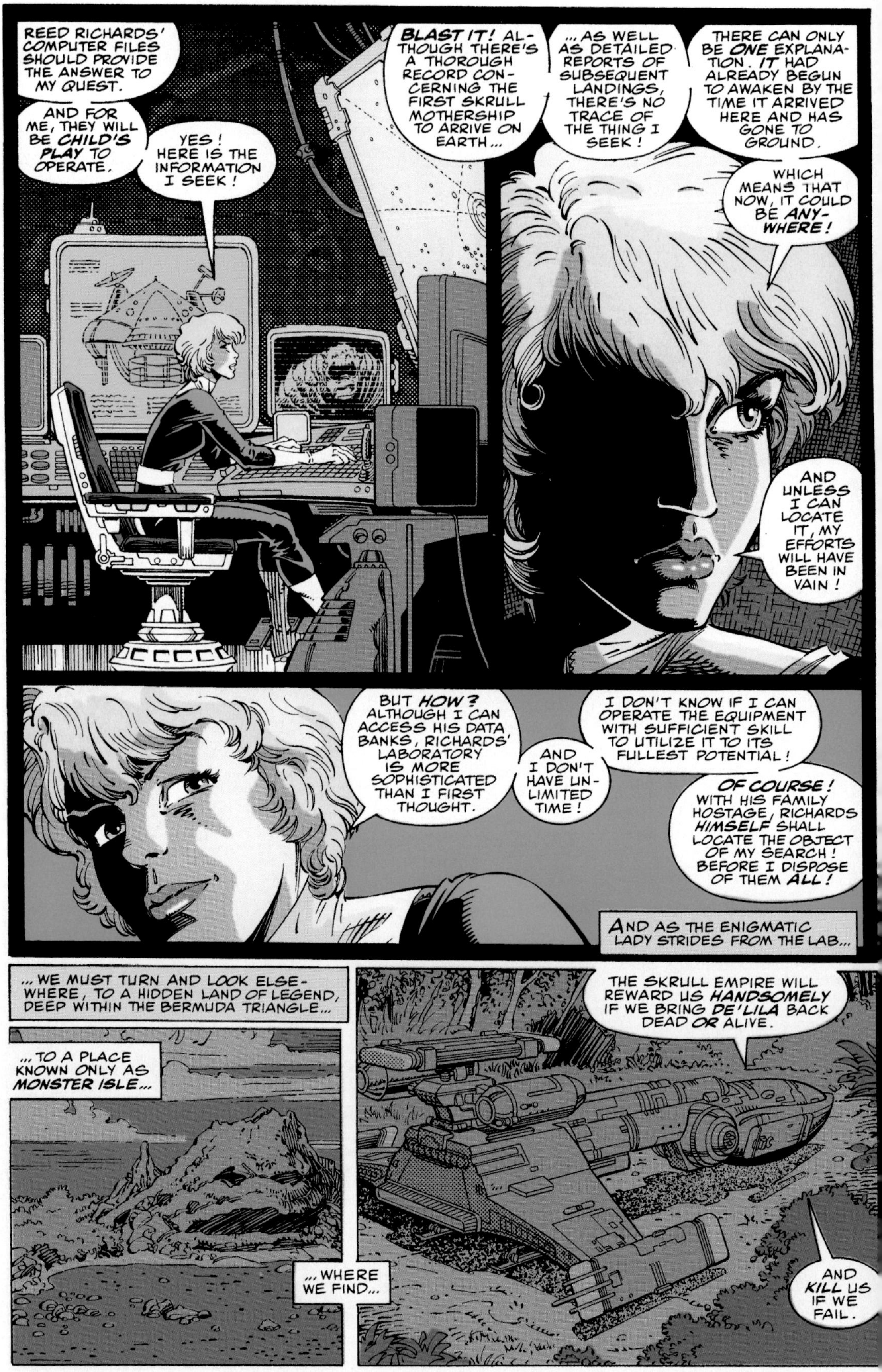
REED RICHARDS' COMPUTER FILES SHOULD PROVIDE THE ANSWER TO MY QUEST.
AND FOR ME, THEY WILL BE CHILD'S PLAY TO OPERATE.
YES! HERE IS THE INFORMATION I SEEK!
BLAST IT! ALTHOUGH THERE'S A THOROUGH RECORD CONCERNING THE FIRST SKRULL MOTHERSHIP TO ARRIVE ON EARTH...
...AS WELL AS DETAILED REPORTS OF SUBSEQUENT LANDINGS, THERE'S NO TRACE OF THE THING I SEEK!
THERE CAN ONLY BE ONE EXPLANATION. IT HAD ALREADY BEGUN TO AWAKEN BY THE TIME IT ARRIVED HERE AND HAS GONE TO GROUND.
WHICH MEANS THAT NOW, IT COULD BE ANYWHERE!
AND UNLESS I CAN LOCATE IT, MY EFFORTS WILL HAVE BEEN IN VAIN!
BUT HOW? ALTHOUGH I CAN ACCESS HIS DATA BANKS, RICHARDS' LABORATORY IS MORE SOPHISTICATED THAN I FIRST THOUGHT.
AND I DON'T HAVE UNLIMITED TIME!
I DON'T KNOW IF I CAN OPERATE THE EQUIPMENT WITH SUFFICIENT SKILL TO UTILIZE IT TO ITS FULLEST POTENTIAL!
OF COURSE! WITH HIS FAMILY HOSTAGE, RICHARDS HIMSELF SHALL LOCATE THE OBJECT OF MY SEARCH! BEFORE I DISPOSE OF THEM ALL!
AND AS THE ENIGMATIC LADY STRIDES FROM THE LAB...
...WE MUST TURN AND LOOK ELSEWHERE, TO A HIDDEN LAND OF LEGEND, DEEP WITHIN THE BERMUDA TRIANGLE...
...TO A PLACE KNOWN ONLY AS MONSTER ISLE...
...WHERE WE FIND...
THE SKRULL EMPIRE WILL REWARD US HANDSOMELY IF WE BRING DE'LILA BACK DEAD OR ALIVE.
AND KILL US IF WE FAIL.

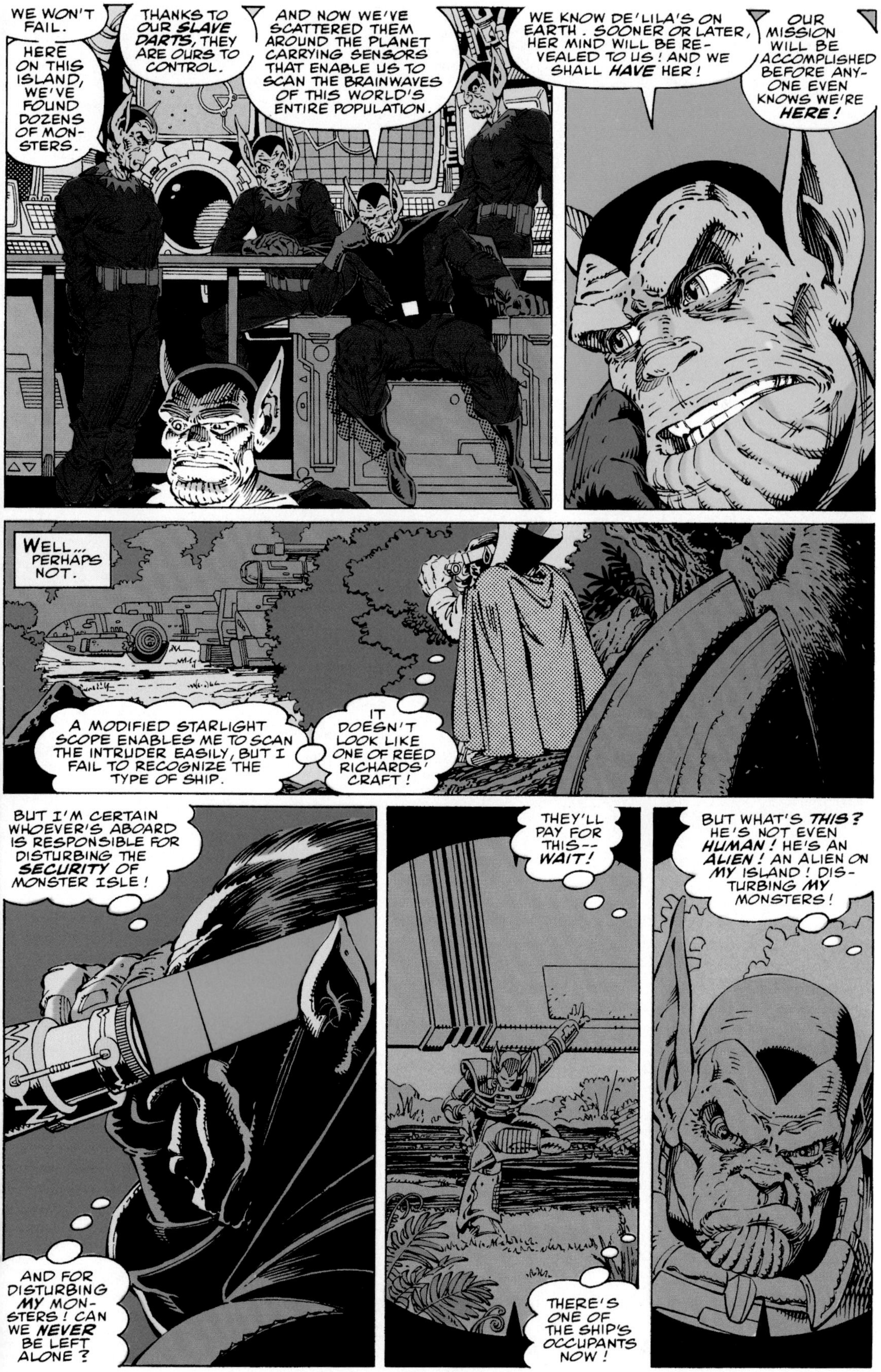
WE WON'T FAIL.
HERE ON THIS ISLAND, WE'VE FOUND DOZENS OF MONSTERS.
THANKS TO OUR SLAVE DARTS, THEY ARE OURS TO CONTROL.
AND NOW WE'VE SCATTERED THEM AROUND THE PLANET CARRYING SENSORS THAT ENABLE US TO SCAN THE BRAINWAVES OF THIS WORLD'S ENTIRE POPULATION.
WE KNOW DE'LILA'S ON EARTH. SOONER OR LATER, HER MIND WILL BE REVEALED TO US! AND WE SHALL HAVE HER!
OUR MISSION WILL BE ACCOMPLISHED BEFORE ANYONE EVEN KNOWS WE'RE HERE!
WELL... PERHAPS NOT.
A MODIFIED STARLIGHT SCOPE ENABLES ME TO SCAN THE INTRUDER EASILY, BUT I FAIL TO RECOGNIZE THE TYPE OF SHIP.
IT DOESN'T LOOK LIKE ONE OF REED RICHARDS' CRAFT!
BUT I'M CERTAIN WHOEVER'S ABOARD IS RESPONSIBLE FOR DISTURBING THE SECURITY OF MONSTER ISLE!
AND FOR DISTURBING MY MONSTERS! CAN WE NEVER BE LEFT ALONE?
THEY'LL PAY FOR THIS-- WAIT!
THERE'S ONE OF THE SHIP'S OCCUPANTS NOW!
BUT WHAT'S THIS? HE'S NOT EVEN HUMAN! HE'S AN ALIEN! AN ALIEN ON MY ISLAND! DISTURBING MY MONSTERS!

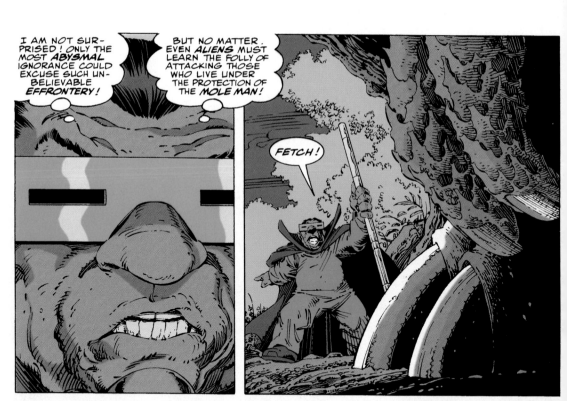

I AM NOT SUR-PRISED! ONLY THE MOST *ABYSMAL* IGNORANCE COULD EXCUSE SUCH UN-BELIEVABLE *EFFRONTERY!*

BUT NO MATTER. EVEN *ALIENS* MUST LEARN THE FOLLY OF ATTACKING THOSE WHO LIVE UNDER THE PROTECTION OF THE *MOLE MAN!*

FETCH!

MEANWHILE, BACK IN FOUR FREEDOMS PLAZA...

THAT SHOULD DO IT.

IF ANY OF THEM RECOVER CON-SCIOUSNESS AND TRY TO ESCAPE, THEY WILL *ALL* STRANGLE TOGETHER.

AND THE SIMPLE EXPEDIENT OF LEAVING THEM HIDDEN ABOARD THE FF'S PRIVATE ELEVATOR AT THE BOTTOM OF THE SHAFT WILL PREVENT ANYONE FROM DISCOVERING THEM ACCIDENTLY.

NOW I MUST AWAKEN MY HOST.

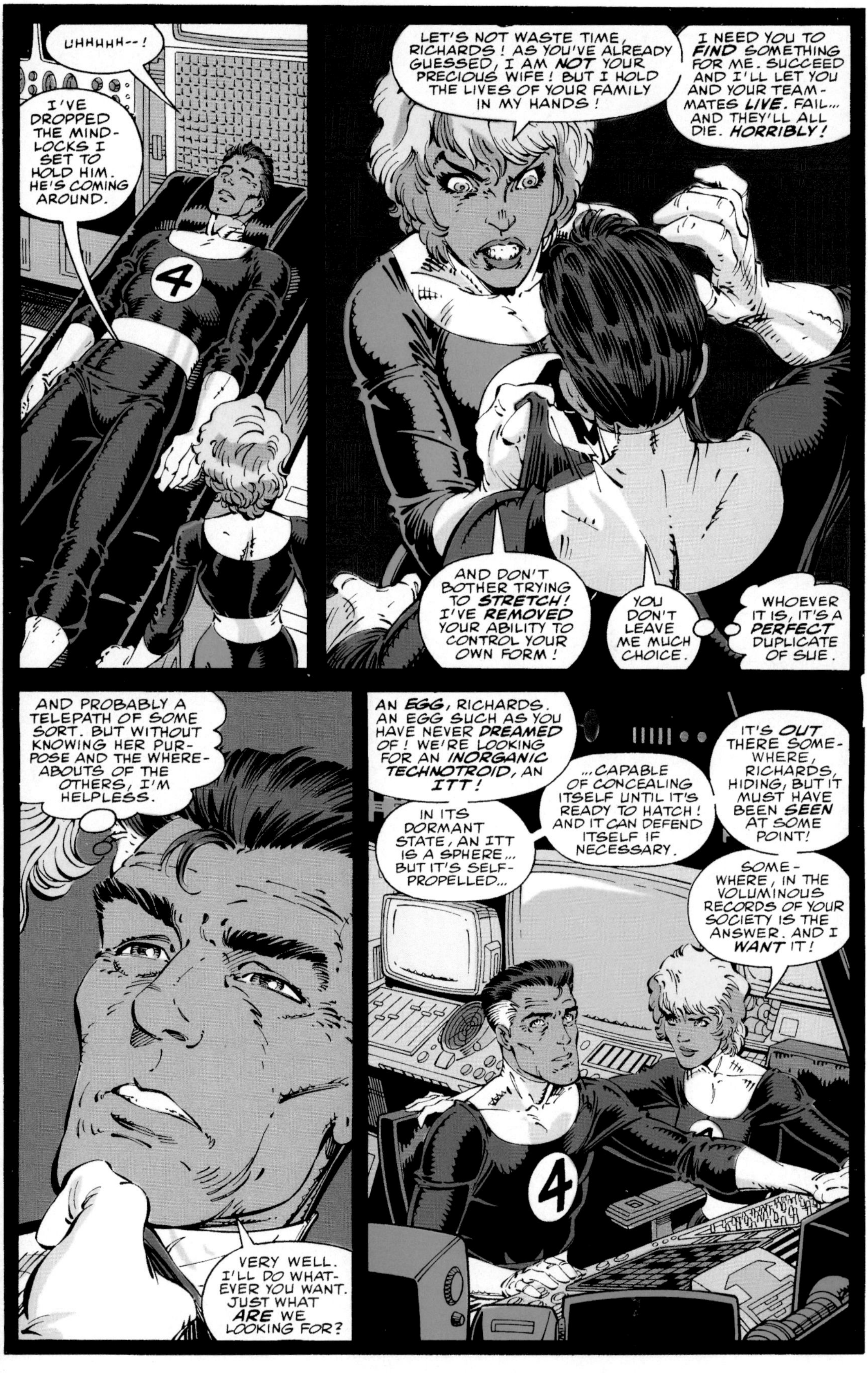
UHHHHH--!
I'VE DROPPED THE MIND-LOCKS I SET TO HOLD HIM. HE'S COMING AROUND.
LET'S NOT WASTE TIME, RICHARDS! AS YOU'VE ALREADY GUESSED, I AM NOT YOUR PRECIOUS WIFE! BUT I HOLD THE LIVES OF YOUR FAMILY IN MY HANDS!
I NEED YOU TO FIND SOMETHING FOR ME. SUCCEED AND I'LL LET YOU AND YOUR TEAM-MATES LIVE. FAIL... AND THEY'LL ALL DIE. HORRIBLY!
AND DON'T BOTHER TRYING TO STRETCH! I'VE REMOVED YOUR ABILITY TO CONTROL YOUR OWN FORM!
YOU DON'T LEAVE ME MUCH CHOICE.
WHOEVER IT IS, IT'S A PERFECT DUPLICATE OF SUE.
AND PROBABLY A TELEPATH OF SOME SORT. BUT WITHOUT KNOWING HER PURPOSE AND THE WHEREABOUTS OF THE OTHERS, I'M HELPLESS.
VERY WELL. I'LL DO WHATEVER YOU WANT. JUST WHAT ARE WE LOOKING FOR?
AN EGG, RICHARDS. AN EGG SUCH AS YOU HAVE NEVER DREAMED OF! WE'RE LOOKING FOR AN INORGANIC TECHNOTROID, AN ITT!
IN ITS DORMANT STATE, AN ITT IS A SPHERE... BUT IT'S SELF-PROPELLED...
...CAPABLE OF CONCEALING ITSELF UNTIL IT'S READY TO HATCH! AND IT CAN DEFEND ITSELF IF NECESSARY.
IT'S OUT THERE SOMEWHERE, RICHARDS, HIDING, BUT IT MUST HAVE BEEN SEEN AT SOME POINT!
SOMEWHERE, IN THE VOLUMINOUS RECORDS OF YOUR SOCIETY IS THE ANSWER. AND I WANT IT!

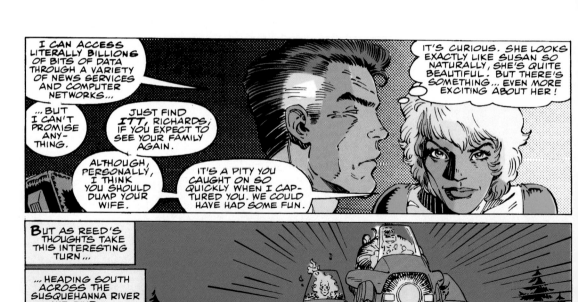

I CAN ACCESS LITERALLY BILLIONS OF BITS OF DATA THROUGH A VARIETY OF NEWS SERVICES AND COMPUTER NETWORKS...

...BUT I CAN'T PROMISE ANY-THING.

JUST FIND ITT, RICHARDS, IF YOU EXPECT TO SEE YOUR FAMILY AGAIN.

ALTHOUGH, PERSONALLY, I THINK YOU SHOULD DUMP YOUR WIFE.

IT'S A PITY YOU CAUGHT ON SO QUICKLY WHEN I CAP-TURED YOU. WE COULD HAVE HAD SOME FUN.

IT'S CURIOUS. SHE LOOKS EXACTLY LIKE SUSAN SO NATURALLY, SHE'S QUITE BEAUTIFUL. BUT THERE'S SOMETHING... EVEN MORE EXCITING ABOUT HER!

BUT AS REED'S THOUGHTS TAKE THIS INTERESTING TURN...

...HEADING SOUTH ACROSS THE SUSQUEHANNA RIVER WE FIND...

VARROOOUMM!

REPORTS'RE STARTIN' TA COME IN FROM ALL OVER.

LOOKS LIKE THE MONSTER MASH HAS HIT MOS-COW...

...SAN FRAN-CISCO...

...AND EVEN MEXICO CITY. THEY'RE ZEROIN' IN ON MAJOR POPULATION CENTERS!

WE'RE NEARING WASHING-TON, DC.

BUT I HAVE YET TO SEE ANY FIRST-HAND EVIDENCE OF THE MONSTERS' PRESENCE.

THEN TAKE A LOOK ABOVE US, GHOSTY! I THINK WE'RE ABOUT TO GET OUR FIRST TASTE OF TROUBLE!

WAKE UP AND SMELL THE COFFEE, CHUMPS! I'VE ONLY BEEN CLOSING IN ON HIM FOR THE LAST FIVE MINUTES!

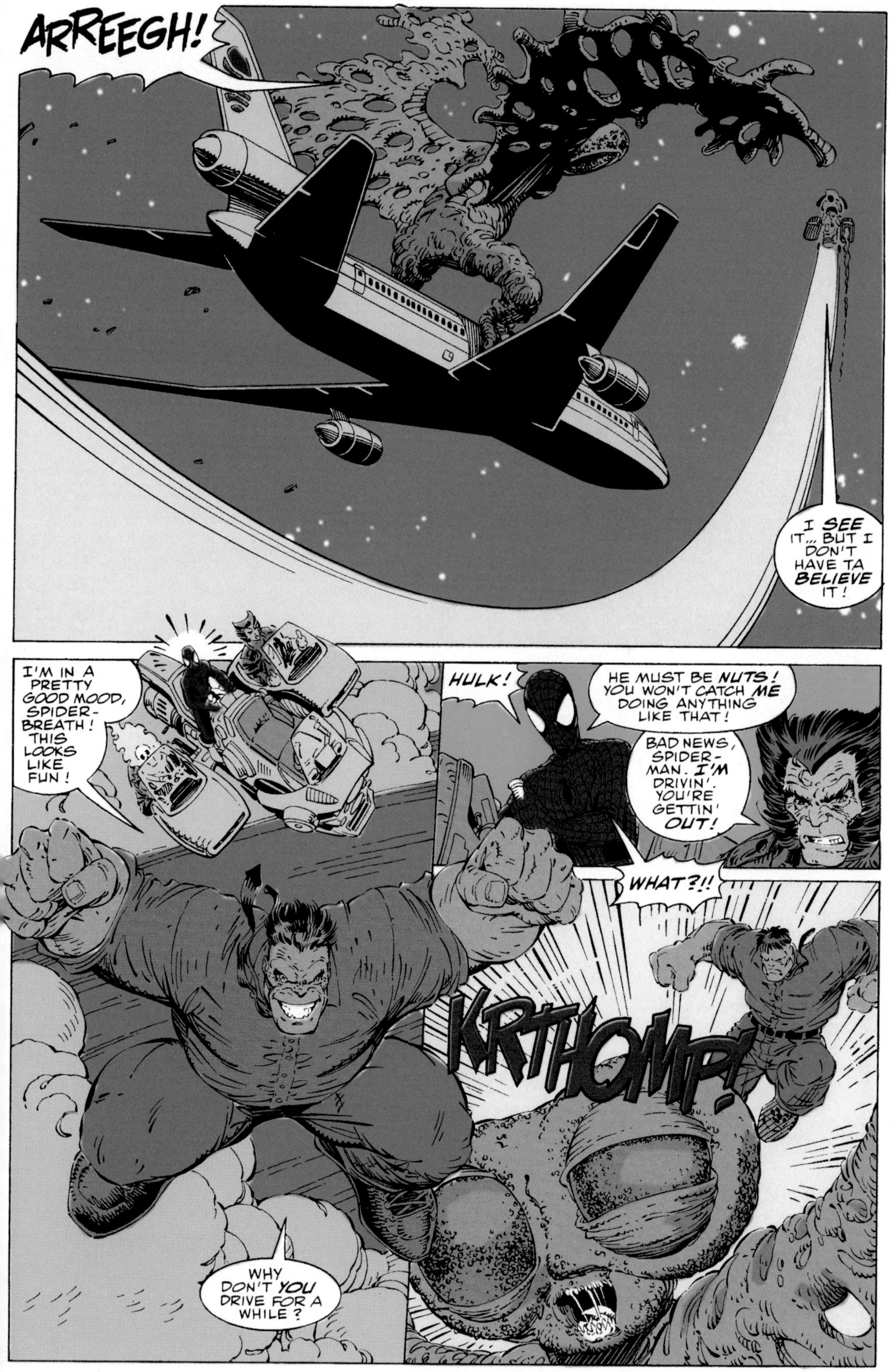
ARREEGH!
I SEE IT... BUT I DON'T HAVE TA BELIEVE IT!
I'M IN A PRETTY GOOD MOOD, SPIDER-BREATH! THIS LOOKS LIKE FUN!
HULK!
HE MUST BE NUTS! YOU WON'T CATCH ME DOING ANYTHING LIKE THAT!
BAD NEWS, SPIDER-MAN. I'M DRIVIN'. YOU'RE GETTIN' OUT!
WHAT?!!
KRTHOMP!
WHY DON'T YOU DRIVE FOR A WHILE?

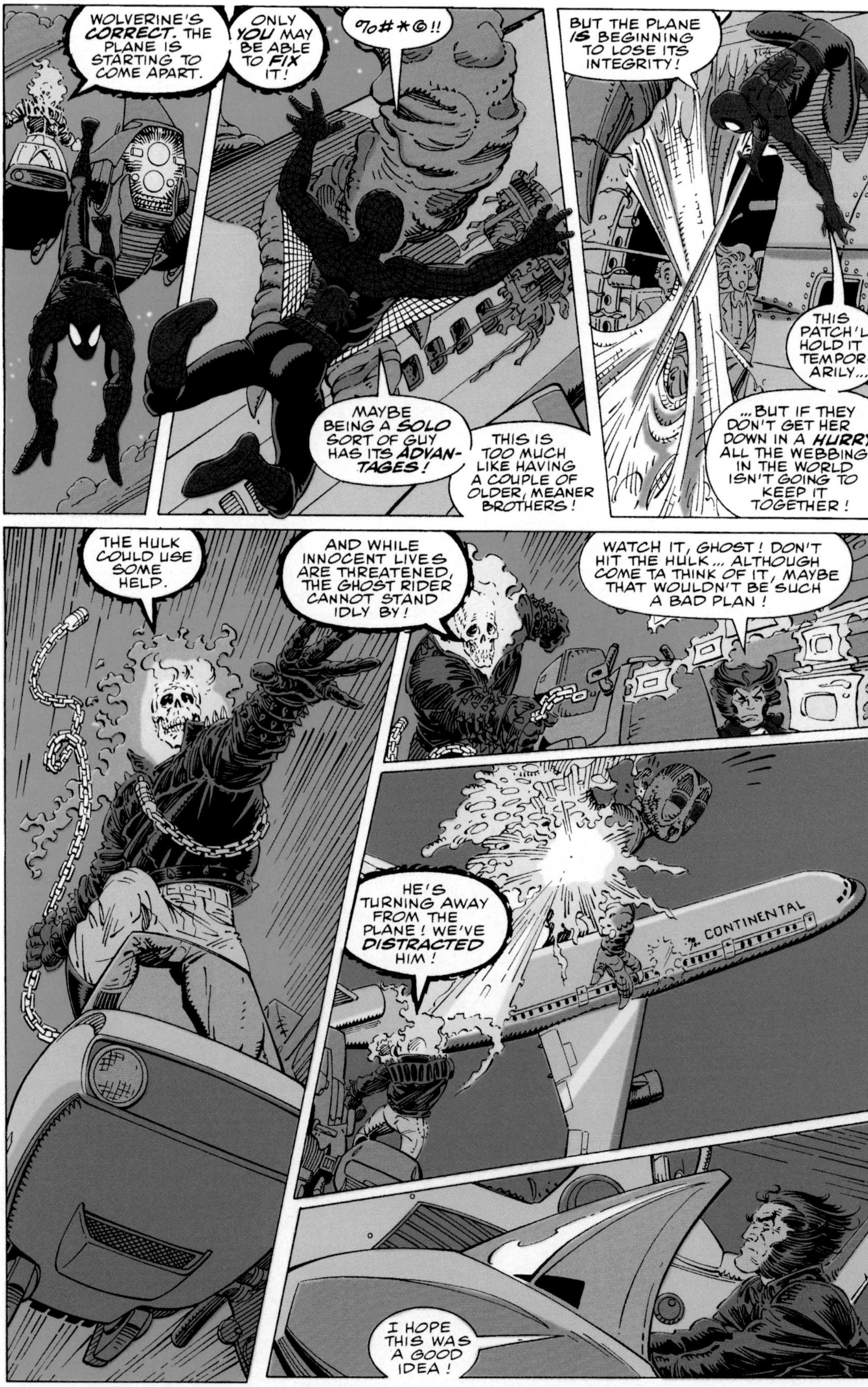
WOLVERINE'S CORRECT. THE PLANE IS STARTING TO COME APART.
ONLY YOU MAY BE ABLE TO FIX IT!
%#*@!!
MAYBE BEING A SOLO SORT OF GUY HAS ITS ADVANTAGES!
THIS IS TOO MUCH LIKE HAVING A COUPLE OF OLDER, MEANER BROTHERS!
BUT THE PLANE IS BEGINNING TO LOSE ITS INTEGRITY!
THIS PATCH'LL HOLD IT TEMPORARILY...
...BUT IF THEY DON'T GET HER DOWN IN A HURRY, ALL THE WEBBING IN THE WORLD ISN'T GOING TO KEEP IT TOGETHER!
THE HULK COULD USE SOME HELP.
AND WHILE INNOCENT LIVES ARE THREATENED, THE GHOST RIDER CANNOT STAND IDLY BY!
WATCH IT, GHOST! DON'T HIT THE HULK... ALTHOUGH COME TA THINK OF IT, MAYBE THAT WOULDN'T BE SUCH A BAD PLAN!
HE'S TURNING AWAY FROM THE PLANE! WE'VE DISTRACTED HIM!
CONTINENTAL
I HOPE THIS WAS A GOOD IDEA!

AND ELSEWHERE, ON MONSTER ISLE...

CAPTAIN! FULLY INTEGRATED SKRULL MINDWAVE READINGS! WE'VE FOUND HER! SHE'S IN THE MIDDLE OF NEW YORK CITY!

EXCELLENT! WELL DONE. RECALL THE SCOUTING PARTIES.

ANTI-MATTER GENERATORS ON LINE. ALL BOARDS TO GREEN.

WE DEPART IN FIVE MINUTES. WE'LL NAIL HER BEFORE SHE KNOWS WHAT'S HAPPENING. ARM THE BLOCKBUSTERS!

SIR! I'M GETTING ANOTHER SKRULL-TYPE READING! 63.02% SIMILARITY! RIGHT NEXT TO THE SHIP! BUT THERE'S NOTHING OUT THERE!

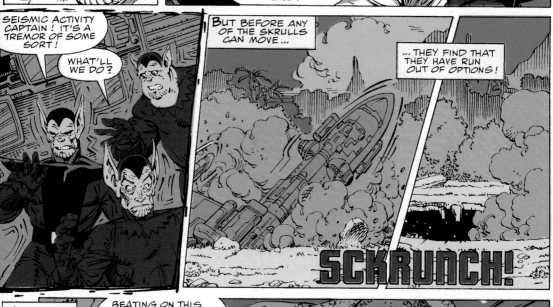

SEISMIC ACTIVITY CAPTAIN! IT'S A TREMOR OF SOME SORT!

WHAT'LL WE DO?

BUT BEFORE ANY OF THE SKRULLS CAN MOVE...

...THEY FIND THAT THEY HAVE RUN OUT OF OPTIONS!

SCKRUNCH!

AND SOME DISTANCE AWAY, NINE THOUSAND FEET UP...

BEATING ON THIS CLOWN IS LIKE HITTING A RUBBER WALL! HE JUST KEEPS BOUNCING BACK!

HUH? THE THING'S GONE STIFF ALL OF A SUDDEN!

SKREEEAL!

249

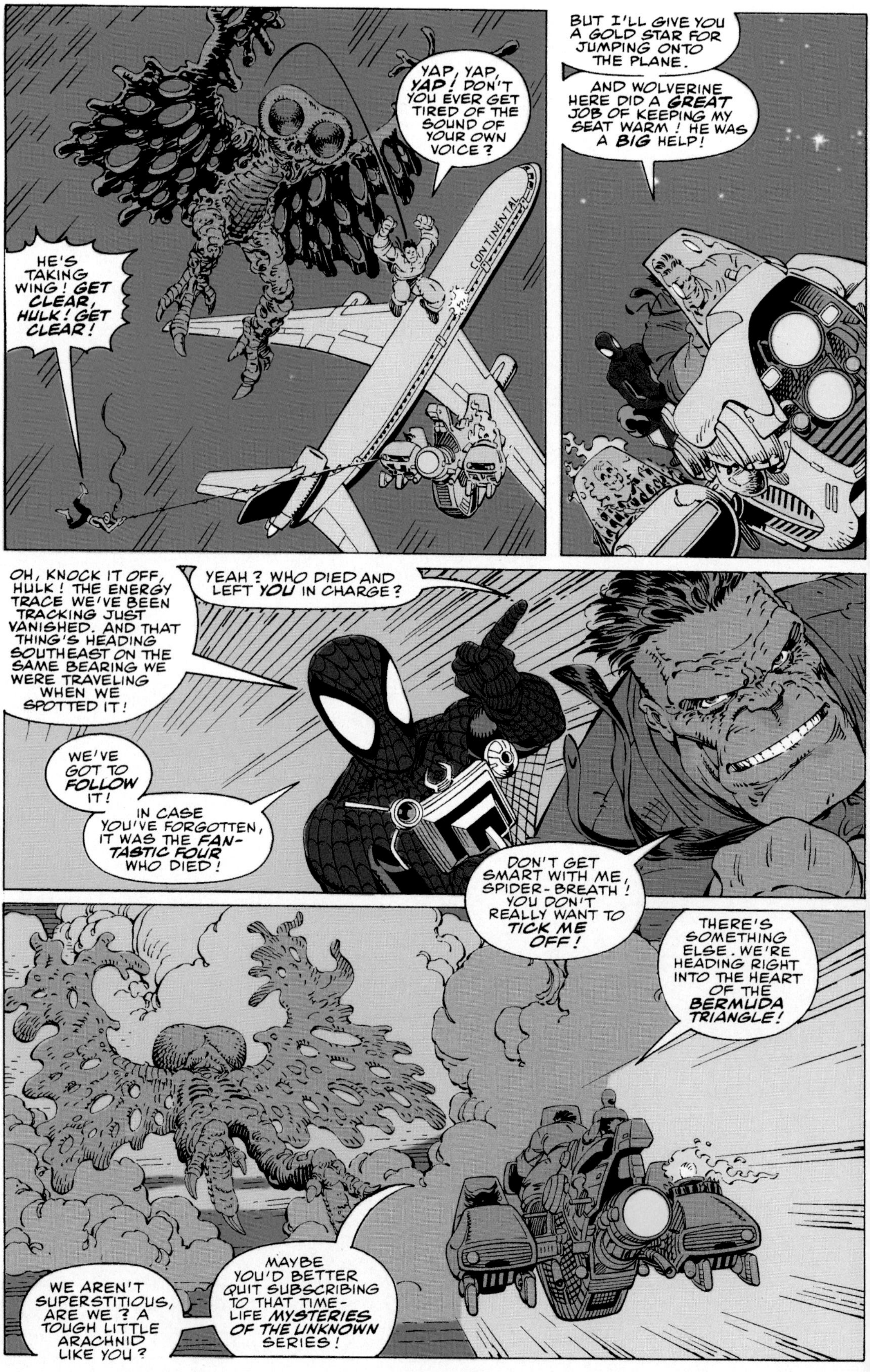
YAP, YAP, YAP! DON'T YOU EVER GET TIRED OF THE SOUND OF YOUR OWN VOICE?
HE'S TAKING WING! GET CLEAR, HULK! GET CLEAR!
BUT I'LL GIVE YOU A GOLD STAR FOR JUMPING ONTO THE PLANE.
AND WOLVERINE HERE DID A GREAT JOB OF KEEPING MY SEAT WARM! HE WAS A BIG HELP!
CONTINENTAL
OH, KNOCK IT OFF, HULK! THE ENERGY TRACE WE'VE BEEN TRACKING JUST VANISHED. AND THAT THING'S HEADING SOUTHEAST ON THE SAME BEARING WE WERE TRAVELING WHEN WE SPOTTED IT!
YEAH? WHO DIED AND LEFT YOU IN CHARGE?
WE'VE GOT TO FOLLOW IT!
IN CASE YOU'VE FORGOTTEN, IT WAS THE FANTASTIC FOUR WHO DIED!
DON'T GET SMART WITH ME, SPIDER-BREATH! YOU DON'T REALLY WANT TO TICK ME OFF!
THERE'S SOMETHING ELSE. WE'RE HEADING RIGHT INTO THE HEART OF THE BERMUDA TRIANGLE!
WE AREN'T SUPERSTITIOUS, ARE WE? A TOUGH LITTLE ARACHNID LIKE YOU?
MAYBE YOU'D BETTER QUIT SUBSCRIBING TO THAT TIME-LIFE MYSTERIES OF THE UNKNOWN SERIES!

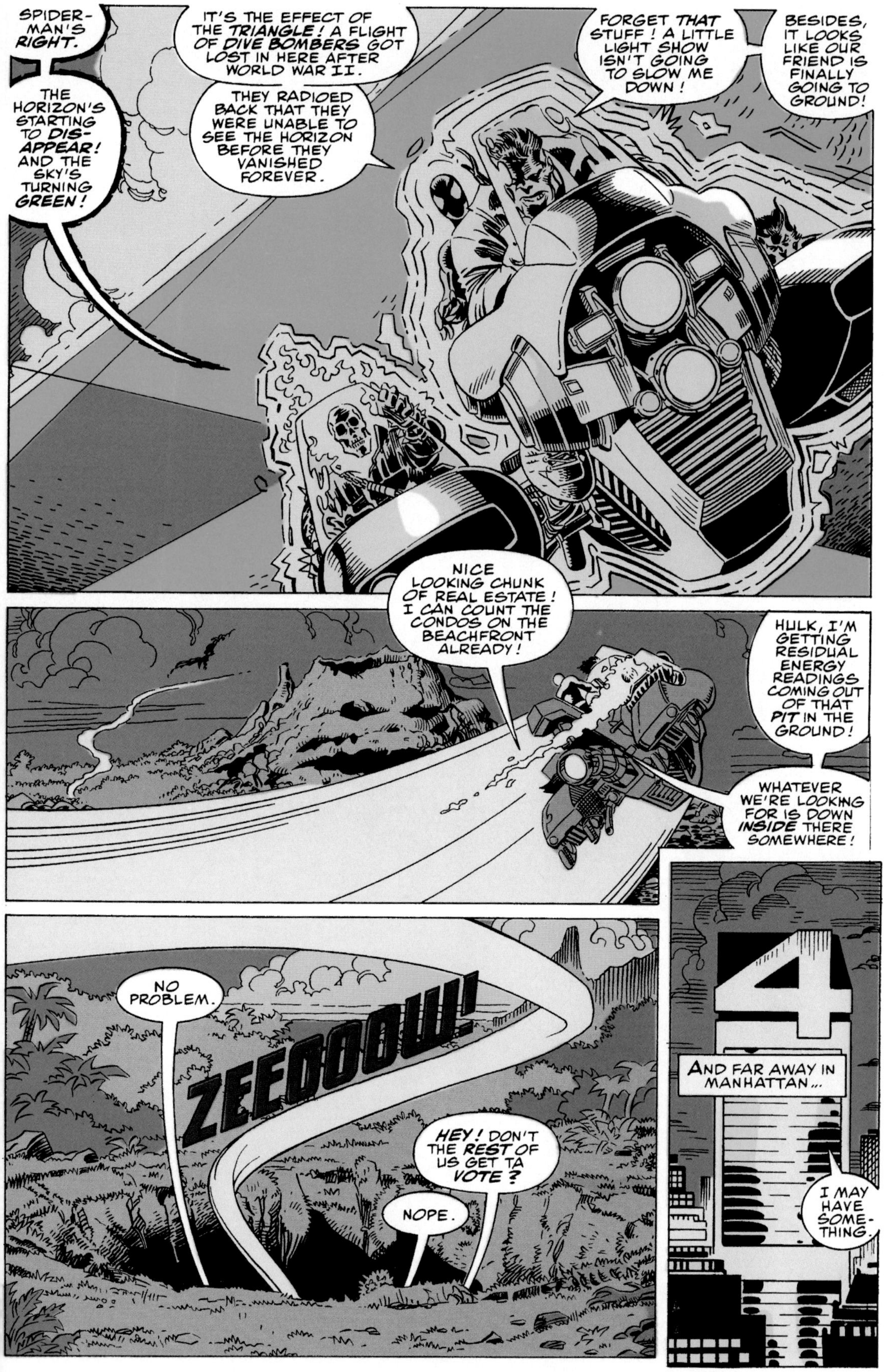
SPIDER-MAN'S RIGHT.
THE HORIZON'S STARTING TO DIS-APPEAR! AND THE SKY'S TURNING GREEN!
IT'S THE EFFECT OF THE TRIANGLE! A FLIGHT OF DIVE BOMBERS GOT LOST IN HERE AFTER WORLD WAR II.
THEY RADIOED BACK THAT THEY WERE UNABLE TO SEE THE HORIZON BEFORE THEY VANISHED FOREVER.
FORGET THAT STUFF! A LITTLE LIGHT SHOW ISN'T GOING TO SLOW ME DOWN!
BESIDES, IT LOOKS LIKE OUR FRIEND IS FINALLY GOING TO GROUND!
NICE LOOKING CHUNK OF REAL ESTATE! I CAN COUNT THE CONDOS ON THE BEACHFRONT ALREADY!
HULK, I'M GETTING RESIDUAL ENERGY READINGS COMING OUT OF THAT PIT IN THE GROUND!
WHATEVER WE'RE LOOKING FOR IS DOWN INSIDE THERE SOMEWHERE!
NO PROBLEM.
ZEEOOOW!
HEY! DON'T THE REST OF US GET TA VOTE?
NOPE.
AND FAR AWAY IN MANHATTAN...
4
I MAY HAVE SOME-THING.

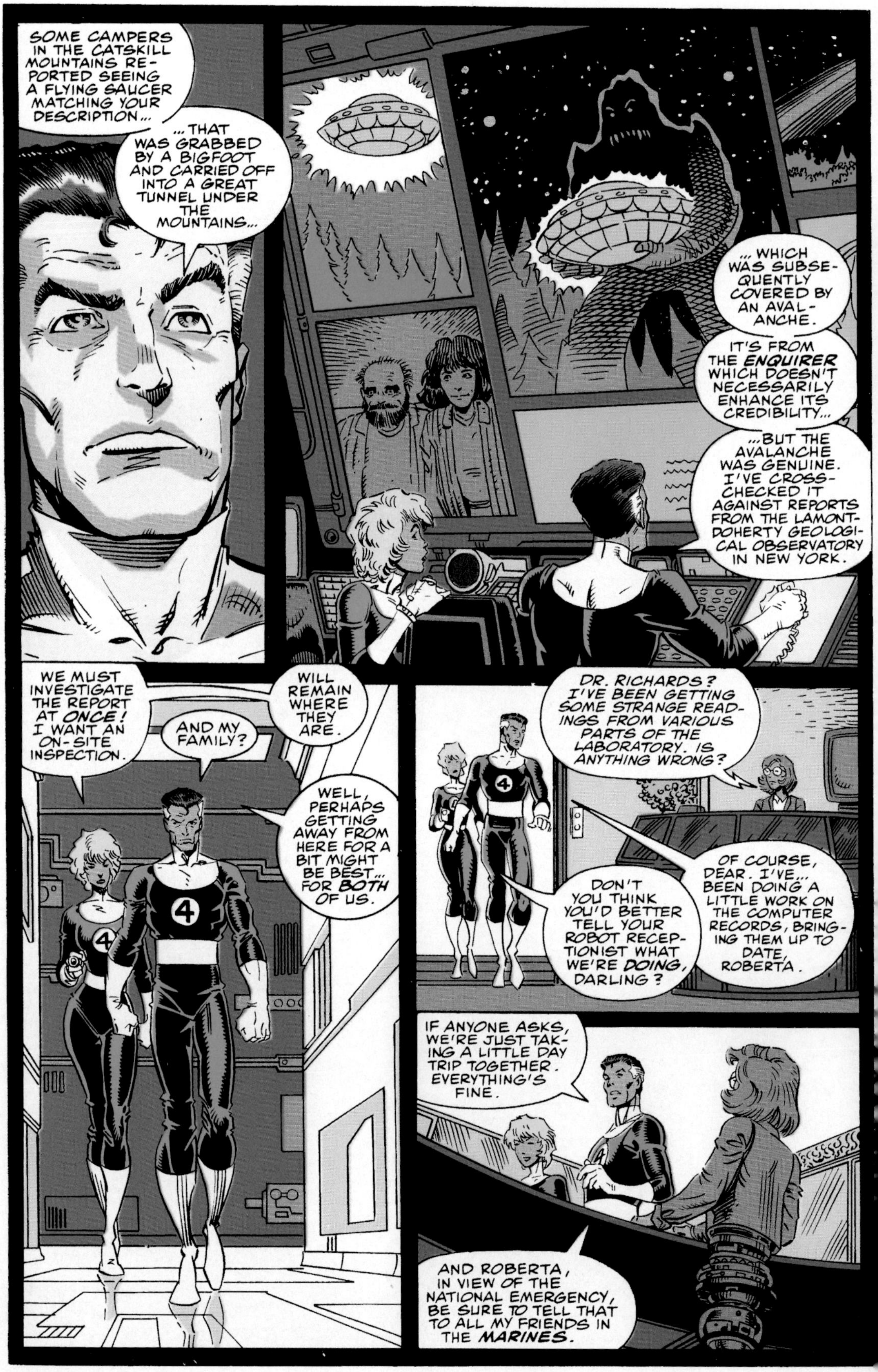
SOME CAMPERS IN THE CATSKILL MOUNTAINS REPORTED SEEING A FLYING SAUCER MATCHING YOUR DESCRIPTION...
...THAT WAS GRABBED BY A BIGFOOT AND CARRIED OFF INTO A GREAT TUNNEL UNDER THE MOUNTAINS...
...WHICH WAS SUBSEQUENTLY COVERED BY AN AVALANCHE.
IT'S FROM THE ENQUIRER WHICH DOESN'T NECESSARILY ENHANCE ITS CREDIBILITY...
...BUT THE AVALANCHE WAS GENUINE. I'VE CROSS-CHECKED IT AGAINST REPORTS FROM THE LAMONT-DOHERTY GEOLOGICAL OBSERVATORY IN NEW YORK.
WE MUST INVESTIGATE THE REPORT AT ONCE! I WANT AN ON-SITE INSPECTION.
AND MY FAMILY?
WILL REMAIN WHERE THEY ARE.
WELL, PERHAPS GETTING AWAY FROM HERE FOR A BIT MIGHT BE BEST... FOR BOTH OF US.
DR. RICHARDS? I'VE BEEN GETTING SOME STRANGE READINGS FROM VARIOUS PARTS OF THE LABORATORY. IS ANYTHING WRONG?
OF COURSE, DEAR. I'VE... BEEN DOING A LITTLE WORK ON THE COMPUTER RECORDS, BRINGING THEM UP TO DATE, ROBERTA.
DON'T YOU THINK YOU'D BETTER TELL YOUR ROBOT RECEPTIONIST WHAT WE'RE DOING, DARLING?
IF ANYONE ASKS, WE'RE JUST TAKING A LITTLE DAY TRIP TOGETHER. EVERYTHING'S FINE.
AND ROBERTA, IN VIEW OF THE NATIONAL EMERGENCY, BE SURE TO TELL THAT TO ALL MY FRIENDS IN THE MARINES.

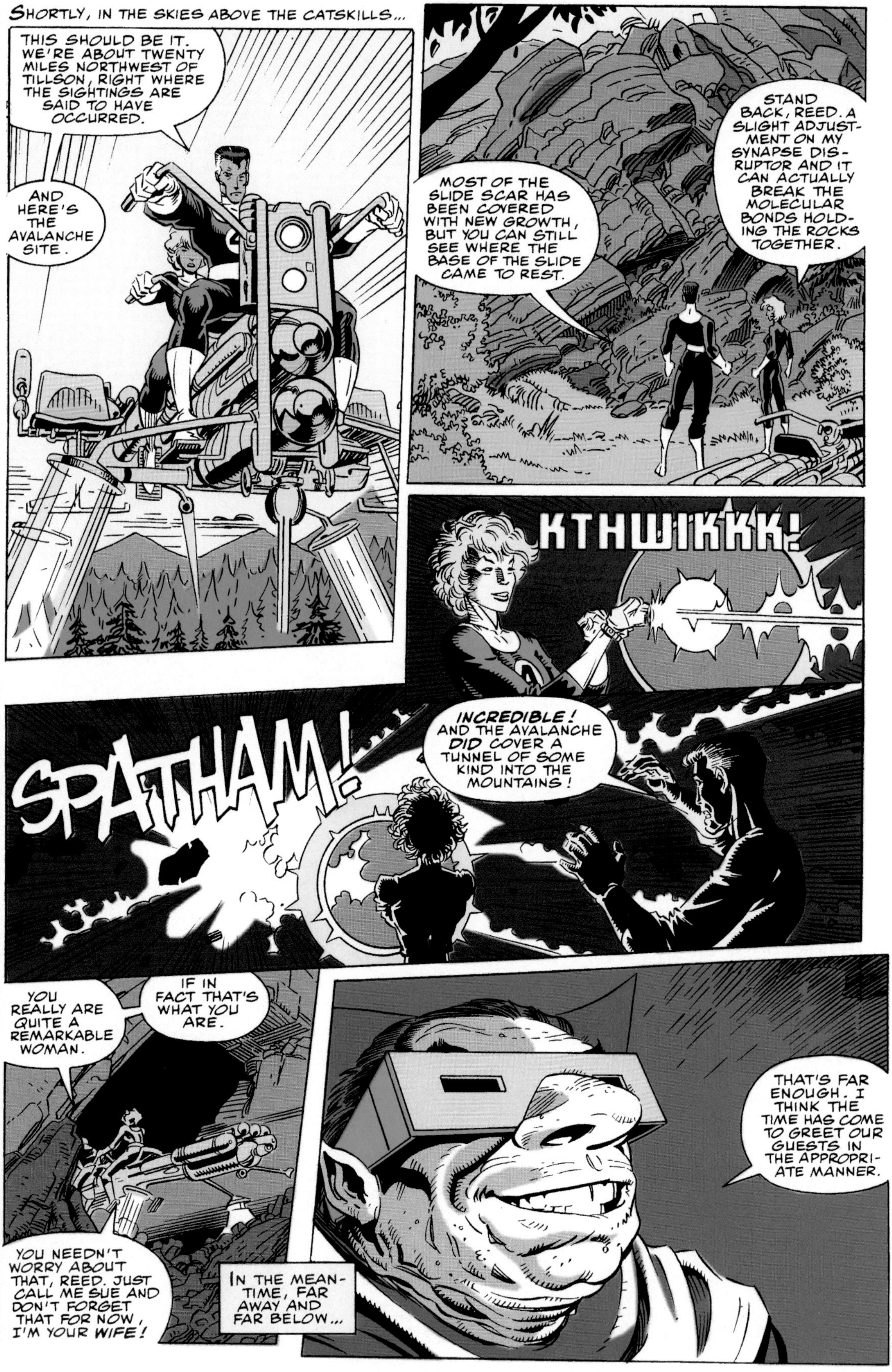
SHORTLY, IN THE SKIES ABOVE THE CATSKILLS...
THIS SHOULD BE IT. WE'RE ABOUT TWENTY MILES NORTHWEST OF TILLSON, RIGHT WHERE THE SIGHTINGS ARE SAID TO HAVE OCCURRED.
AND HERE'S THE AVALANCHE SITE.
MOST OF THE SLIDE SCAR HAS BEEN COVERED WITH NEW GROWTH, BUT YOU CAN STILL SEE WHERE THE BASE OF THE SLIDE CAME TO REST.
STAND BACK, REED. A SLIGHT ADJUSTMENT ON MY SYNAPSE DISRUPTOR AND IT CAN ACTUALLY BREAK THE MOLECULAR BONDS HOLDING THE ROCKS TOGETHER.
KTHWIKKK!
SPATHAM!
INCREDIBLE! AND THE AVALANCHE DID COVER A TUNNEL OF SOME KIND INTO THE MOUNTAINS!
YOU REALLY ARE QUITE A REMARKABLE WOMAN.
IF IN FACT THAT'S WHAT YOU ARE.
YOU NEEDN'T WORRY ABOUT THAT, REED. JUST CALL ME SUE AND DON'T FORGET THAT FOR NOW, I'M YOUR WIFE!
IN THE MEANTIME, FAR AWAY AND FAR BELOW...
THAT'S FAR ENOUGH. I THINK THE TIME HAS COME TO GREET OUR GUESTS IN THE APPROPRIATE MANNER.

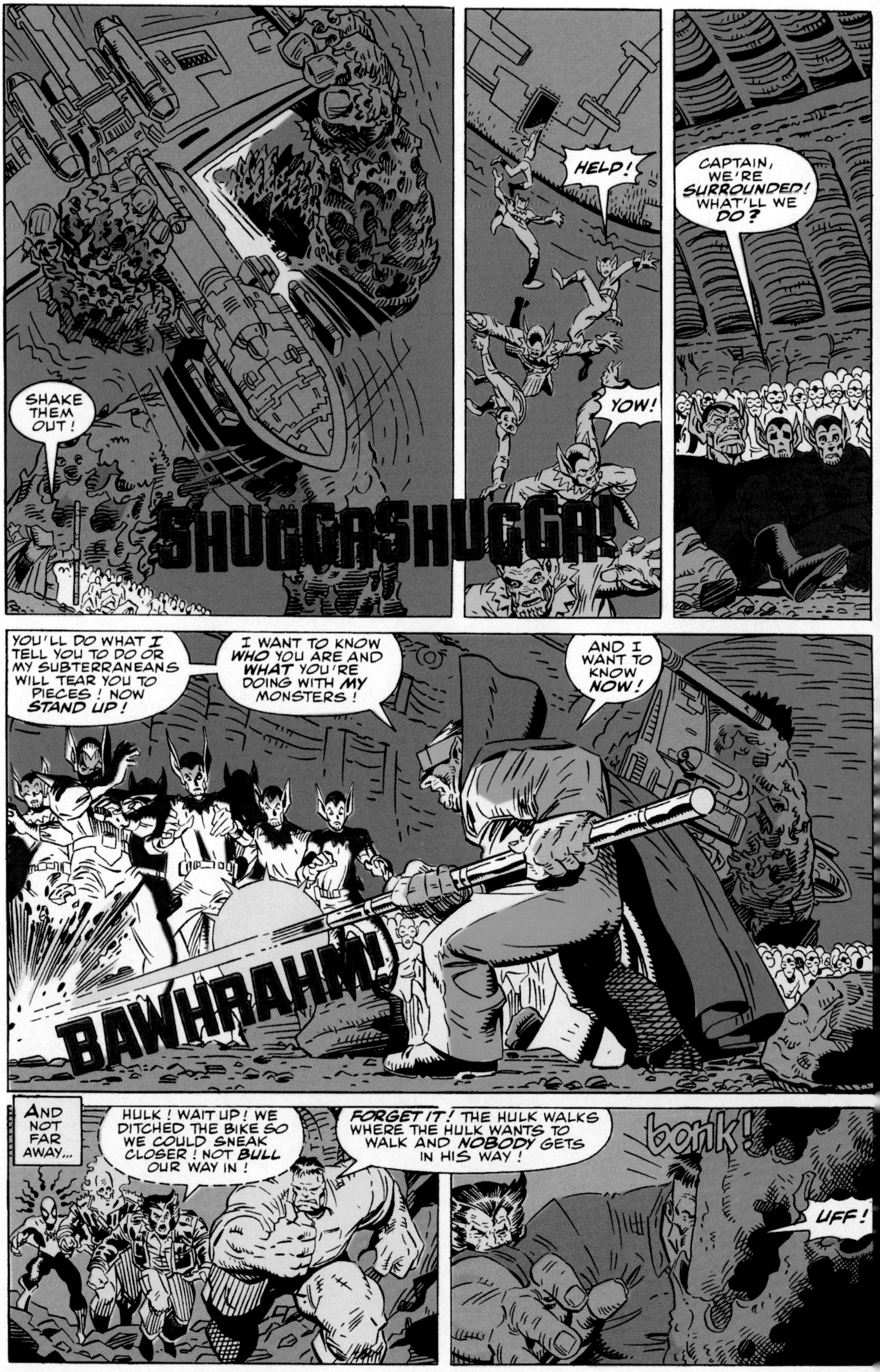
SHAKE THEM OUT!
SHUGGASHUGGA!
HELP!
YOW!
CAPTAIN, WE'RE SURROUNDED! WHAT'LL WE DO?
YOU'LL DO WHAT I TELL YOU TO DO OR MY SUBTERRANEANS WILL TEAR YOU TO PIECES! NOW STAND UP!
I WANT TO KNOW WHO YOU ARE AND WHAT YOU'RE DOING WITH MY MONSTERS!
AND I WANT TO KNOW NOW!
BAWHRAHM!
AND NOT FAR AWAY...
HULK! WAIT UP! WE DITCHED THE BIKE SO WE COULD SNEAK CLOSER! NOT BULL OUR WAY IN!
FORGET IT! THE HULK WALKS WHERE THE HULK WANTS TO WALK AND NOBODY GETS IN HIS WAY!
bonk!
UFF!

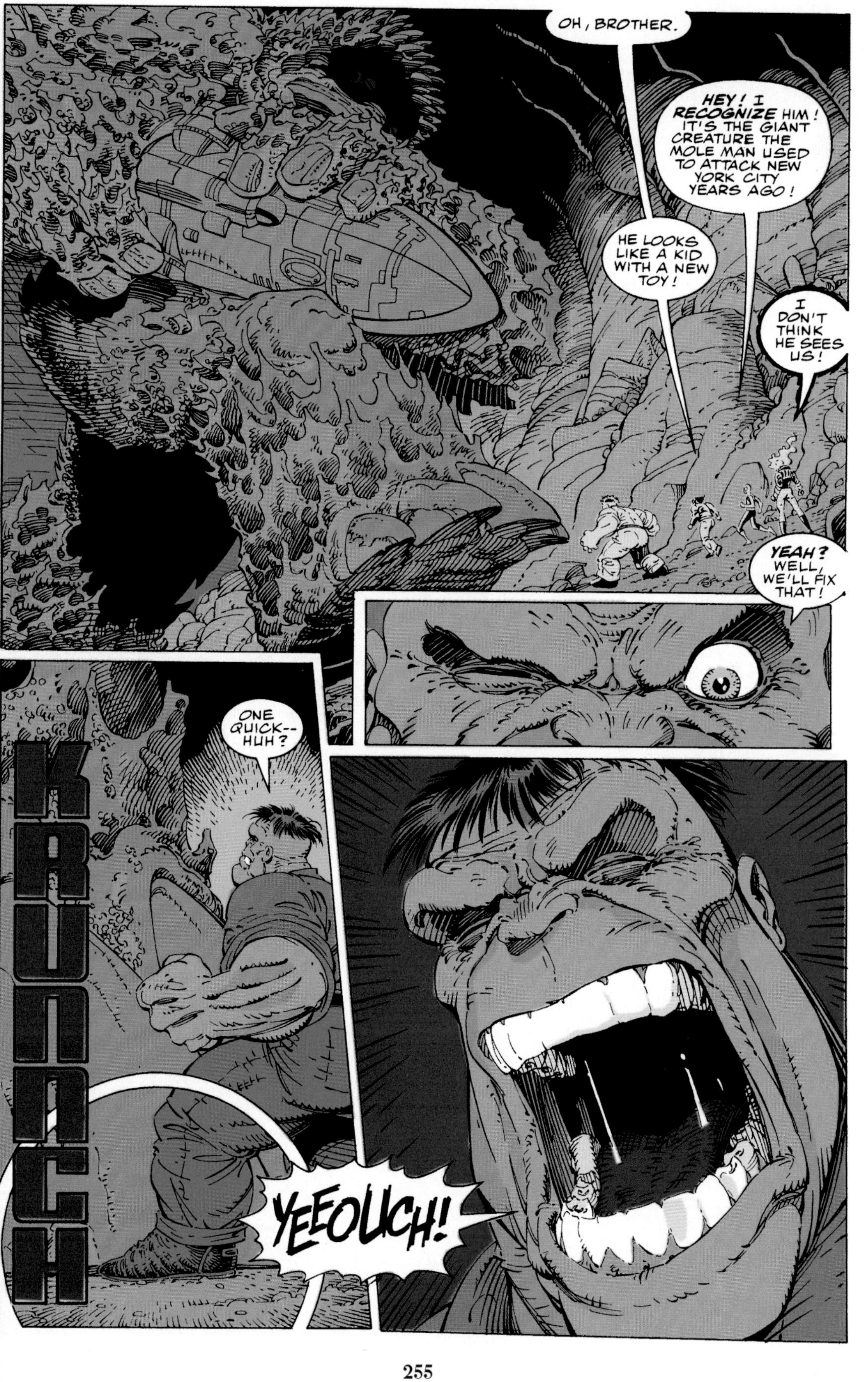
OH, BROTHER.
HEY! I RECOGNIZE HIM! IT'S THE GIANT CREATURE THE MOLE MAN USED TO ATTACK NEW YORK CITY YEARS AGO!
HE LOOKS LIKE A KID WITH A NEW TOY!
I DON'T THINK HE SEES US!
YEAH? WELL, WE'LL FIX THAT!
ONE QUICK-- HUH?
KRUNNCH
YEEOUCH!

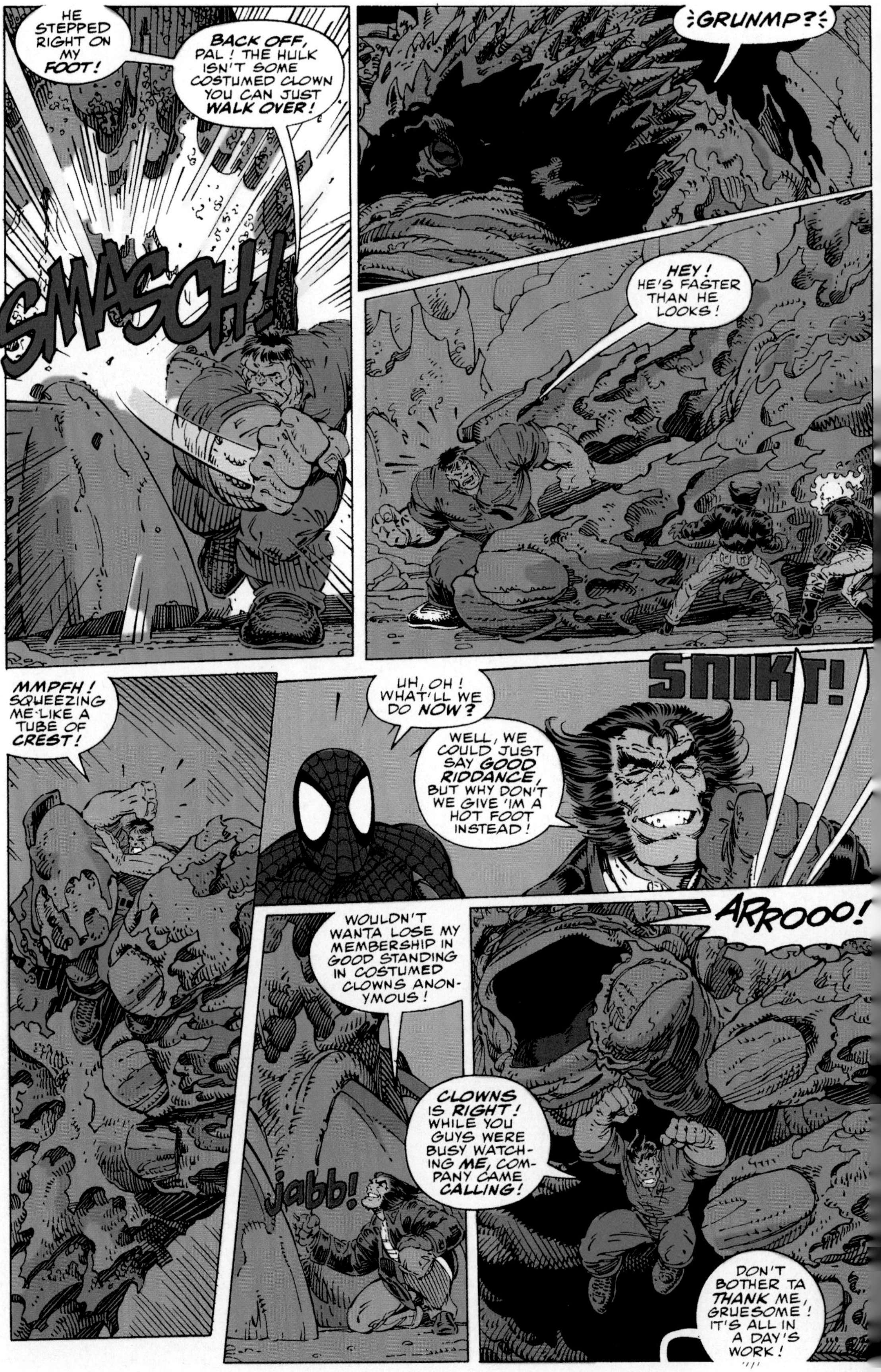
HE STEPPED RIGHT ON MY FOOT!
BACK OFF, PAL! THE HULK ISN'T SOME COSTUMED CLOWN YOU CAN JUST WALK OVER!
SMASCH!
¡GRUNMP?!
HEY! HE'S FASTER THAN HE LOOKS!
MMPFH! SQUEEZING ME LIKE A TUBE OF CREST!
UH, OH! WHAT'LL WE DO NOW?
SNIKT!
WELL, WE COULD JUST SAY GOOD RIDDANCE, BUT WHY DON'T WE GIVE 'IM A HOT FOOT INSTEAD!
ARROOO!
WOULDN'T WANTA LOSE MY MEMBERSHIP IN GOOD STANDING IN COSTUMED CLOWNS ANONYMOUS!
CLOWNS IS RIGHT! WHILE YOU GUYS WERE BUSY WATCHING ME, COMPANY CAME CALLING!
jabb!
DON'T BOTHER TA THANK ME, GRUESOME! IT'S ALL IN A DAY'S WORK!

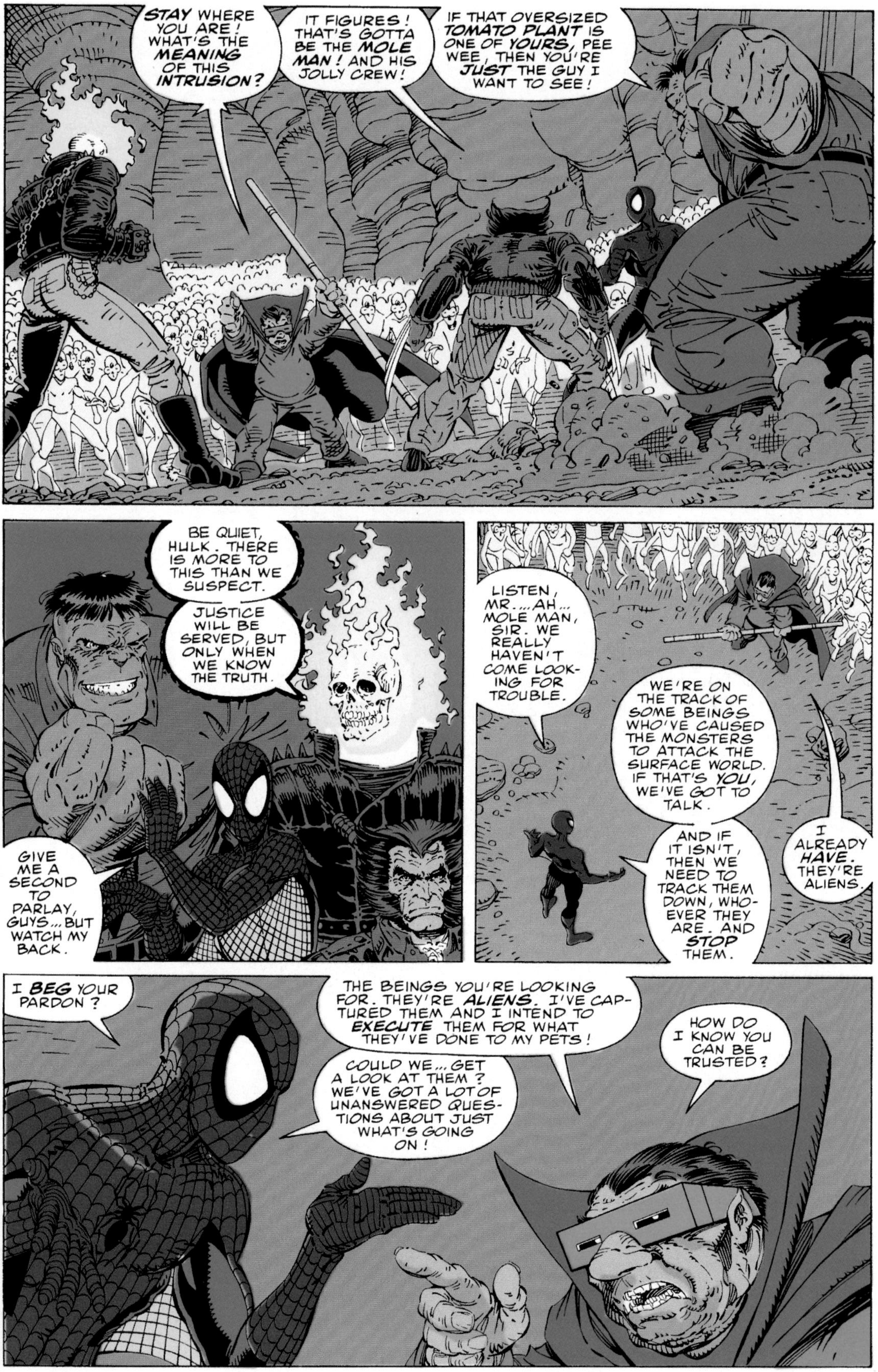
STAY WHERE YOU ARE! WHAT'S THE MEANING OF THIS INTRUSION?
IT FIGURES! THAT'S GOTTA BE THE MOLE MAN! AND HIS JOLLY CREW!
IF THAT OVERSIZED TOMATO PLANT IS ONE OF YOURS, PEE WEE, THEN YOU'RE JUST THE GUY I WANT TO SEE!
BE QUIET, HULK. THERE IS MORE TO THIS THAN WE SUSPECT.
JUSTICE WILL BE SERVED, BUT ONLY WHEN WE KNOW THE TRUTH.
GIVE ME A SECOND TO PARLAY, GUYS... BUT WATCH MY BACK.
LISTEN, MR.... AH... MOLE MAN, SIR. WE REALLY HAVEN'T COME LOOKING FOR TROUBLE.
WE'RE ON THE TRACK OF SOME BEINGS WHO'VE CAUSED THE MONSTERS TO ATTACK THE SURFACE WORLD. IF THAT'S YOU, WE'VE GOT TO TALK.
AND IF IT ISN'T, THEN WE NEED TO TRACK THEM DOWN, WHOEVER THEY ARE. AND STOP THEM.
I ALREADY HAVE. THEY'RE ALIENS.
I BEG YOUR PARDON?
THE BEINGS YOU'RE LOOKING FOR. THEY'RE ALIENS. I'VE CAPTURED THEM AND I INTEND TO EXECUTE THEM FOR WHAT THEY'VE DONE TO MY PETS!
COULD WE... GET A LOOK AT THEM? WE'VE GOT A LOT OF UNANSWERED QUESTIONS ABOUT JUST WHAT'S GOING ON!
HOW DO I KNOW YOU CAN BE TRUSTED?

QUITE HONESTLY, YOU DON'T. BUT YOU DO SEEM TO HAVE THE ADVANTAGE OF NUMBERS.

STRAY, HECK. THERE'S HARDLY ENOUGH ROOM TO WALK!

GOOD ANSWER. FOLLOW ME.

AND DON'T STRAY OFF INTO OTHER TUNNELS.

THERE THEY ARE. BUT WHAT'S GOING ON? THERE'S ONE MISSING! THE ONE THEY CALLED "CAPTAIN"!

GUYS, LOOK! THEY'RE ALIENS, ALL RIGHT! THEY'RE SKRULLS!

AND THERE'S NO OTHER WAY IN OR OUT.

WHAT DO YOU KNOW ABOUT SKRULLS, SHORTY?

JUST ENOUGH. WHAT ABOUT YOU?

SLATTSCH!

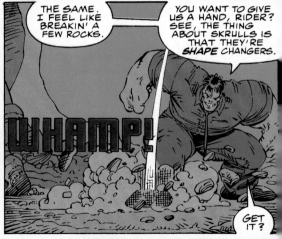

THE SAME. I FEEL LIKE BREAKIN' A FEW ROCKS.

YOU WANT TO GIVE US A HAND, RIDER? SEE, THE THING ABOUT SKRULLS IS THAT THEY'RE SHAPE CHANGERS.

WHAMP!

GET IT?

I'M BEGINNING TO.

BRAKGH!

HMM. THIS SEEMS TO BE THE LAST BOULDER. I'LL JUST--

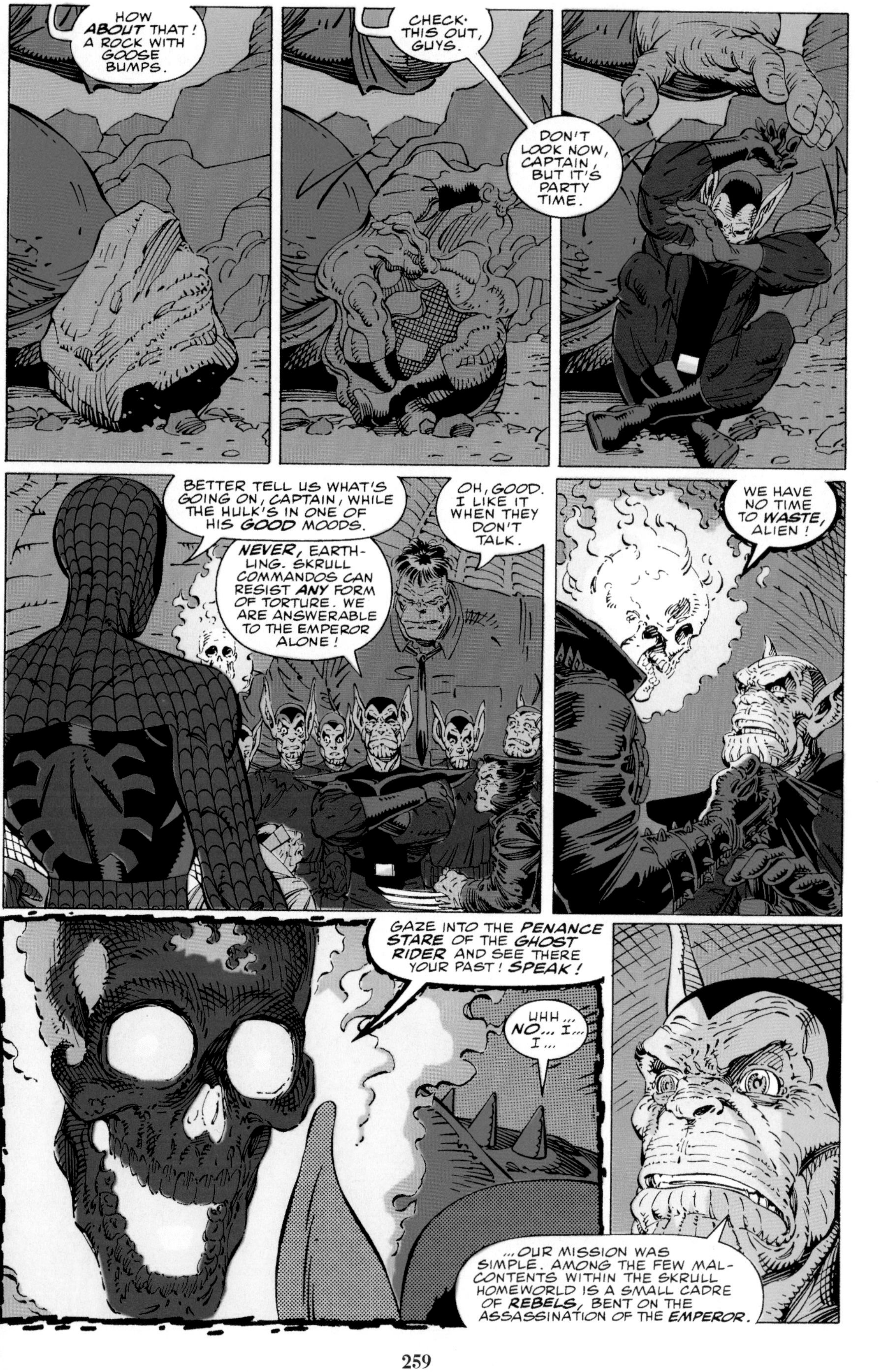
HOW ABOUT THAT! A ROCK WITH GOOSE BUMPS.
CHECK. THIS OUT, GUYS.
DON'T LOOK NOW, CAPTAIN, BUT IT'S PARTY TIME.
BETTER TELL US WHAT'S GOING ON, CAPTAIN, WHILE THE HULK'S IN ONE OF HIS GOOD MOODS.
NEVER, EARTHLING. SKRULL COMMANDOS CAN RESIST ANY FORM OF TORTURE. WE ARE ANSWERABLE TO THE EMPEROR ALONE!
OH, GOOD. I LIKE IT WHEN THEY DON'T TALK.
WE HAVE NO TIME TO WASTE, ALIEN!
GAZE INTO THE PENANCE STARE OF THE GHOST RIDER AND SEE THERE YOUR PAST! SPEAK!
UHH... NO... I... I...
...OUR MISSION WAS SIMPLE. AMONG THE FEW MALCONTENTS WITHIN THE SKRULL HOMEWORLD IS A SMALL CADRE OF REBELS, BENT ON THE ASSASSINATION OF THE EMPEROR.

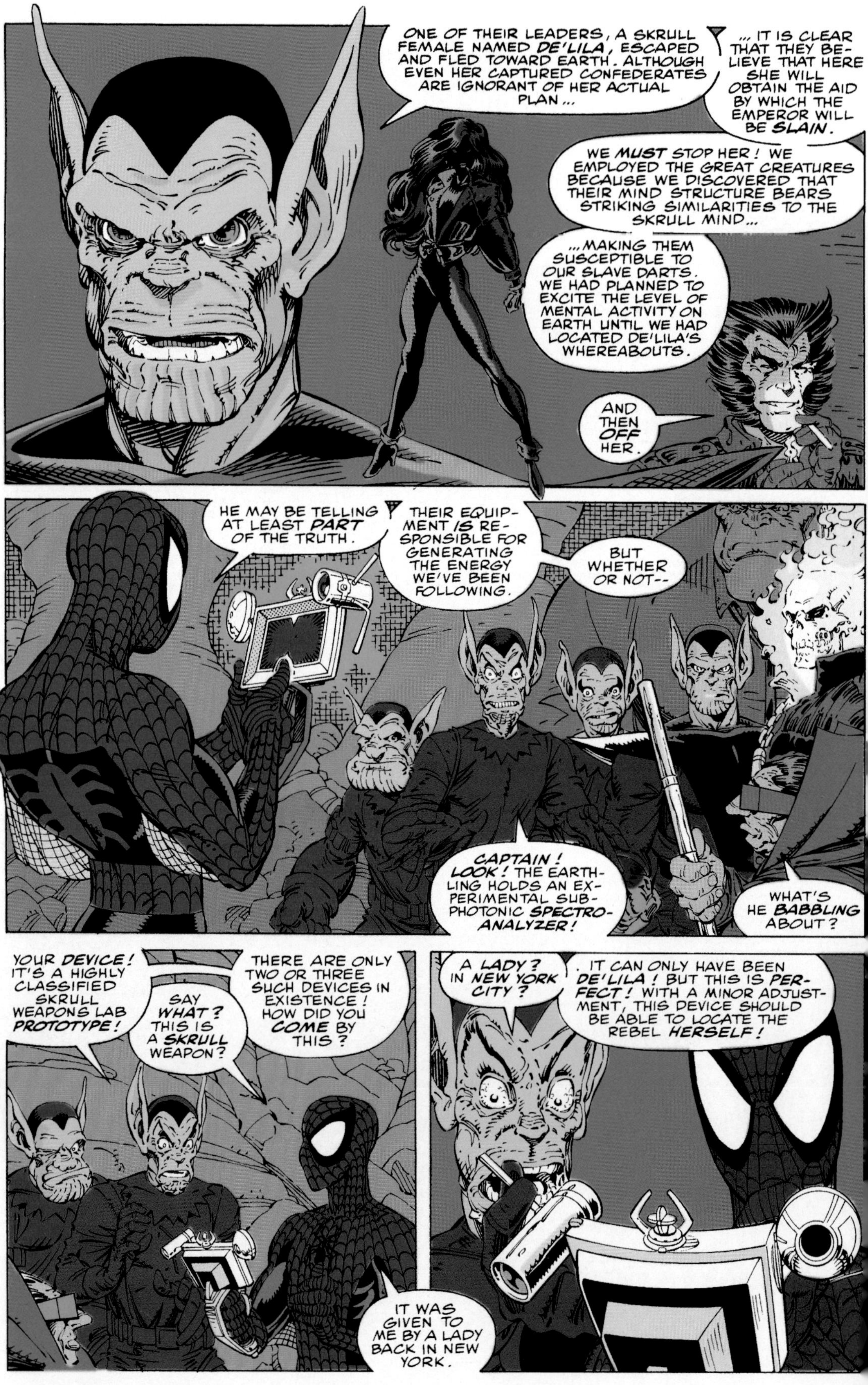
ONE OF THEIR LEADERS, A SKRULL FEMALE NAMED DE'LILA, ESCAPED AND FLED TOWARD EARTH. ALTHOUGH EVEN HER CAPTURED CONFEDERATES ARE IGNORANT OF HER ACTUAL PLAN...
... IT IS CLEAR THAT THEY BE-LIEVE THAT HERE SHE WILL OBTAIN THE AID BY WHICH THE EMPEROR WILL BE SLAIN.
WE MUST STOP HER! WE EMPLOYED THE GREAT CREATURES BECAUSE WE DISCOVERED THAT THEIR MIND STRUCTURE BEARS STRIKING SIMILARITIES TO THE SKRULL MIND...
...MAKING THEM SUSCEPTIBLE TO OUR SLAVE DARTS. WE HAD PLANNED TO EXCITE THE LEVEL OF MENTAL ACTIVITY ON EARTH UNTIL WE HAD LOCATED DE'LILA'S WHEREABOUTS.
AND THEN OFF HER.
HE MAY BE TELLING AT LEAST PART OF THE TRUTH.
THEIR EQUIPMENT IS RE-SPONSIBLE FOR GENERATING THE ENERGY WE'VE BEEN FOLLOWING.
BUT WHETHER OR NOT--
CAPTAIN! LOOK! THE EARTH-LING HOLDS AN EX-PERIMENTAL SUB-PHOTONIC SPECTRO-ANALYZER!
WHAT'S HE BABBLING ABOUT?
YOUR DEVICE! IT'S A HIGHLY CLASSIFIED SKRULL WEAPONS LAB PROTOTYPE!
SAY WHAT? THIS IS A SKRULL WEAPON?
THERE ARE ONLY TWO OR THREE SUCH DEVICES IN EXISTENCE! HOW DID YOU COME BY THIS?
IT WAS GIVEN TO ME BY A LADY BACK IN NEW YORK.
A LADY? IN NEW YORK CITY?
... IT CAN ONLY HAVE BEEN DE'LILA! BUT THIS IS PER-FECT! WITH A MINOR ADJUST-MENT, THIS DEVICE SHOULD BE ABLE TO LOCATE THE REBEL HERSELF!

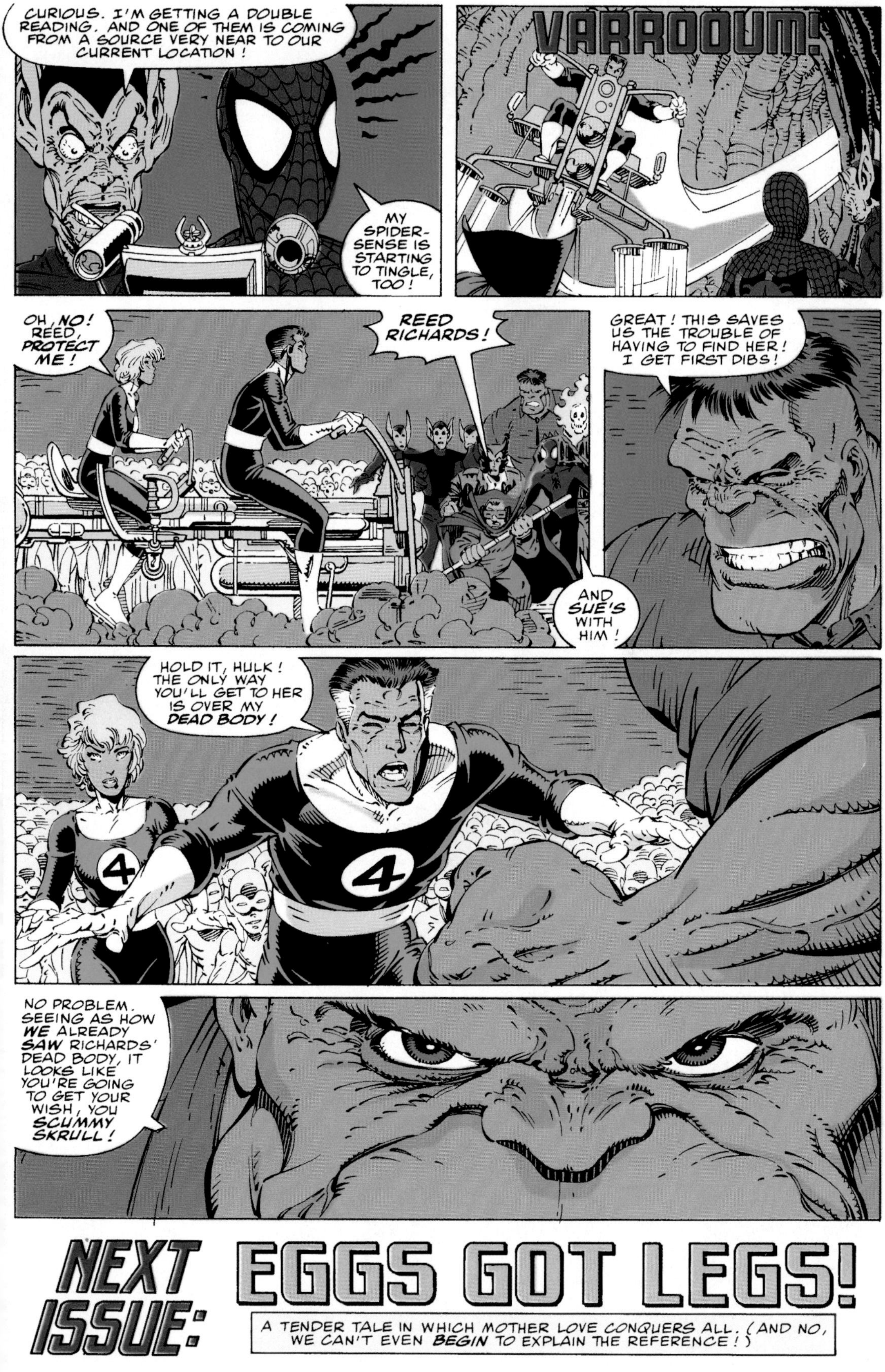
CURIOUS. I'M GETTING A DOUBLE READING. AND ONE OF THEM IS COMING FROM A SOURCE VERY NEAR TO OUR CURRENT LOCATION!
MY SPIDER-SENSE IS STARTING TO TINGLE, TOO!
VARROOUM!
OH, NO! REED, PROTECT ME!
REED RICHARDS!
GREAT! THIS SAVES US THE TROUBLE OF HAVING TO FIND HER! I GET FIRST DIBS!
AND SUE'S WITH HIM!
HOLD IT, HULK! THE ONLY WAY YOU'LL GET TO HER IS OVER MY DEAD BODY!
NO PROBLEM. SEEING AS HOW WE ALREADY SAW RICHARDS' DEAD BODY, IT LOOKS LIKE YOU'RE GOING TO GET YOUR WISH, YOU SCUMMY SKRULL!
NEXT ISSUE: EGGS GOT LEGS!
A TENDER TALE IN WHICH MOTHER LOVE CONQUERS ALL. (AND NO, WE CAN'T EVEN BEGIN TO EXPLAIN THE REFERENCE!)

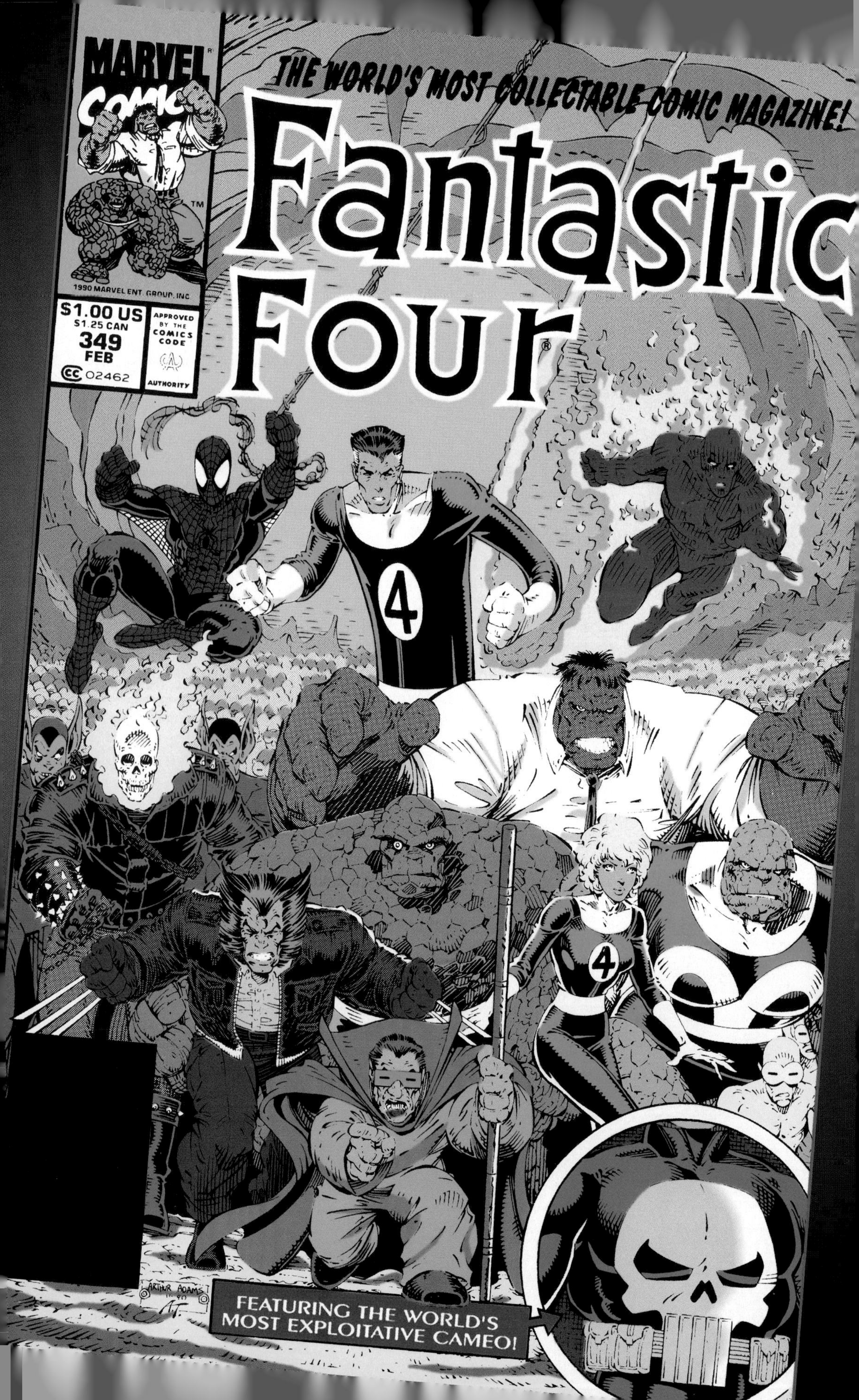

MARVEL COMICS
1990 MARVEL ENT. GROUP, INC.
$1.00 US
$1.25 CAN
349
FEB
02462
APPROVED BY THE COMICS CODE AUTHORITY
THE WORLD'S MOST COLLECTABLE COMIC MAGAZINE!
Fantastic Four
ARTHUR ADAMS
FEATURING THE WORLD'S MOST EXPLOITATIVE CAMEO!

EGGS GOT LEGS!

...OR **LOVE CONQUERS ALL!**

THE ***FANTASTIC FOUR*** ARE CAPTIVES BACK IN FOUR FREEDOMS PLAZA. BUT RIGHT HERE AND NOW, THE ***HULK***, ***WOLVERINE***, ***SPIDER-MAN*** AND ***GHOST RIDER*** ARE CAPTIVES OF THE ***MOLE MAN!***

SO ARE A BUNCH OF ***SKRULL WARRIORS*** WHO ARE CHASING A ***LADY*** SKRULL...

...AND SHE'S HUNTING FOR A MISSING SKRULL ***EGG*** WITH REED RICHARDS! (OKAY, SO HE'S ***NOT*** BACK AT FF PLAZA! ***SUE*** US!)

IN ANY CASE, THE HULK'S ABOUT TO PUNCH OUT HER ***LAMPS!***

STAN LEE PRESENTS:

WALTER SIMONSON -WRITING
ARTHUR ADAMS -PENCILING
GRACINE TANAKA -PENCILING ASSIST
ART THIBERT -INKS (P. 1-3)
AL MILGROM -INKS (P4-24)
BILL OAKLEY -LETTERING
STEVE BUCCELLATO -COLORING
RALPH MACHIO -EDITING
TOM DEFALCO -EDITING IN CHIEF

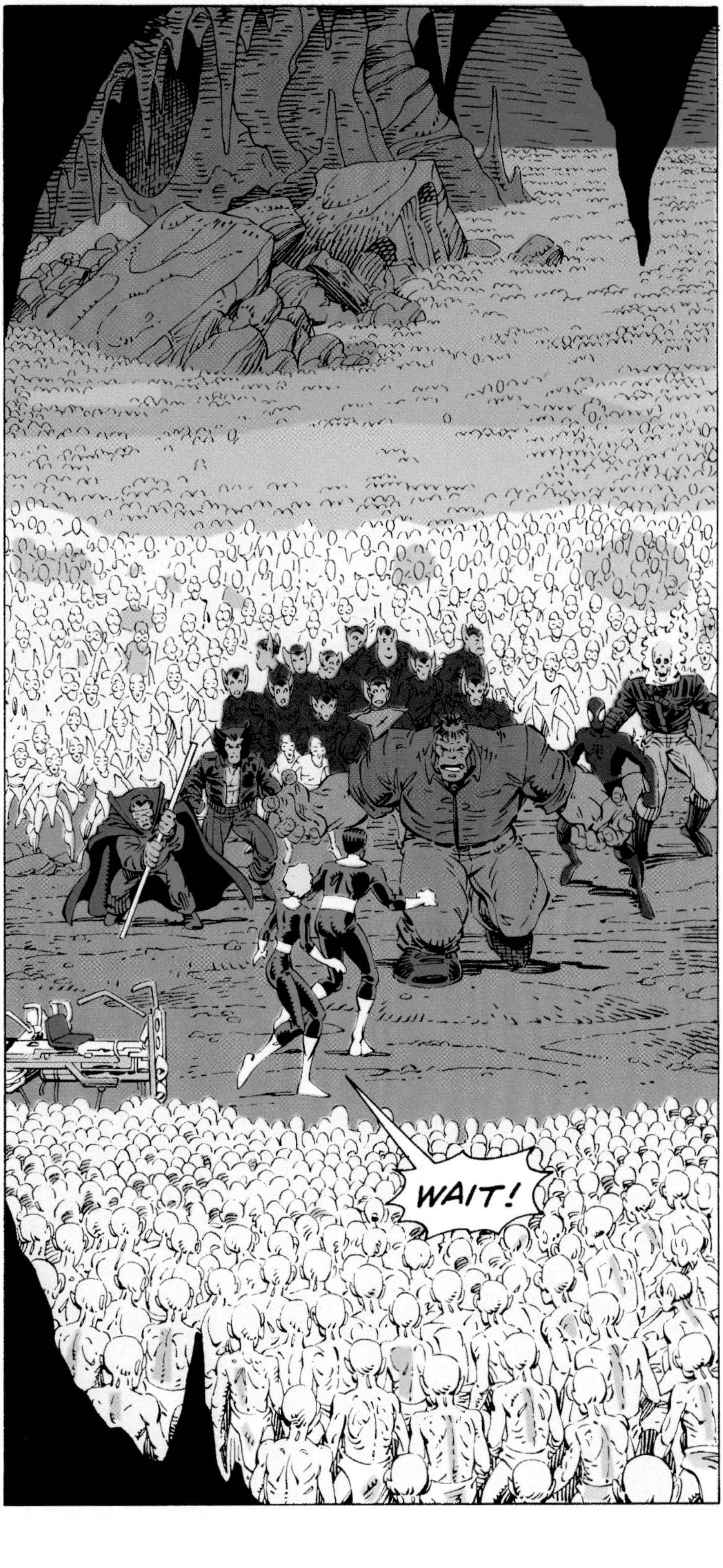
WAIT!

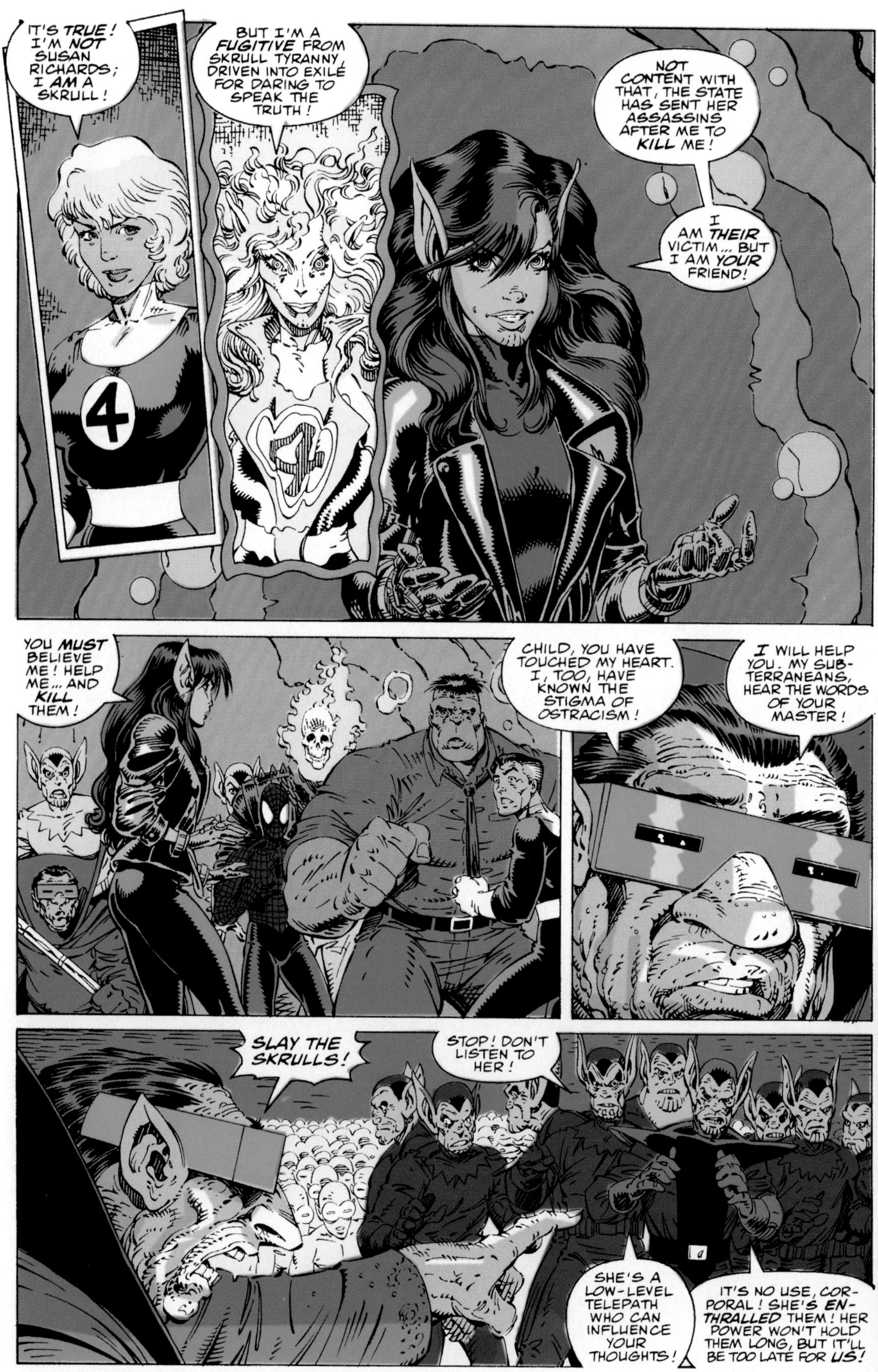
IT'S TRUE! I'M NOT SUSAN RICHARDS; I AM A SKRULL!
BUT I'M A FUGITIVE FROM SKRULL TYRANNY, DRIVEN INTO EXILE FOR DARING TO SPEAK THE TRUTH!
NOT CONTENT WITH THAT, THE STATE HAS SENT HER ASSASSINS AFTER ME TO KILL ME!
I AM THEIR VICTIM... BUT I AM YOUR FRIEND!
YOU MUST BELIEVE ME! HELP ME... AND KILL THEM!
CHILD, YOU HAVE TOUCHED MY HEART. I, TOO, HAVE KNOWN THE STIGMA OF OSTRACISM!
I WILL HELP YOU. MY SUBTERRANEANS, HEAR THE WORDS OF YOUR MASTER!
SLAY THE SKRULLS!
STOP! DON'T LISTEN TO HER!
SHE'S A LOW-LEVEL TELEPATH WHO CAN INFLUENCE YOUR THOUGHTS!
IT'S NO USE, CORPORAL! SHE'S ENTHRALLED THEM! HER POWER WON'T HOLD THEM LONG, BUT IT'LL BE TOO LATE FOR US!

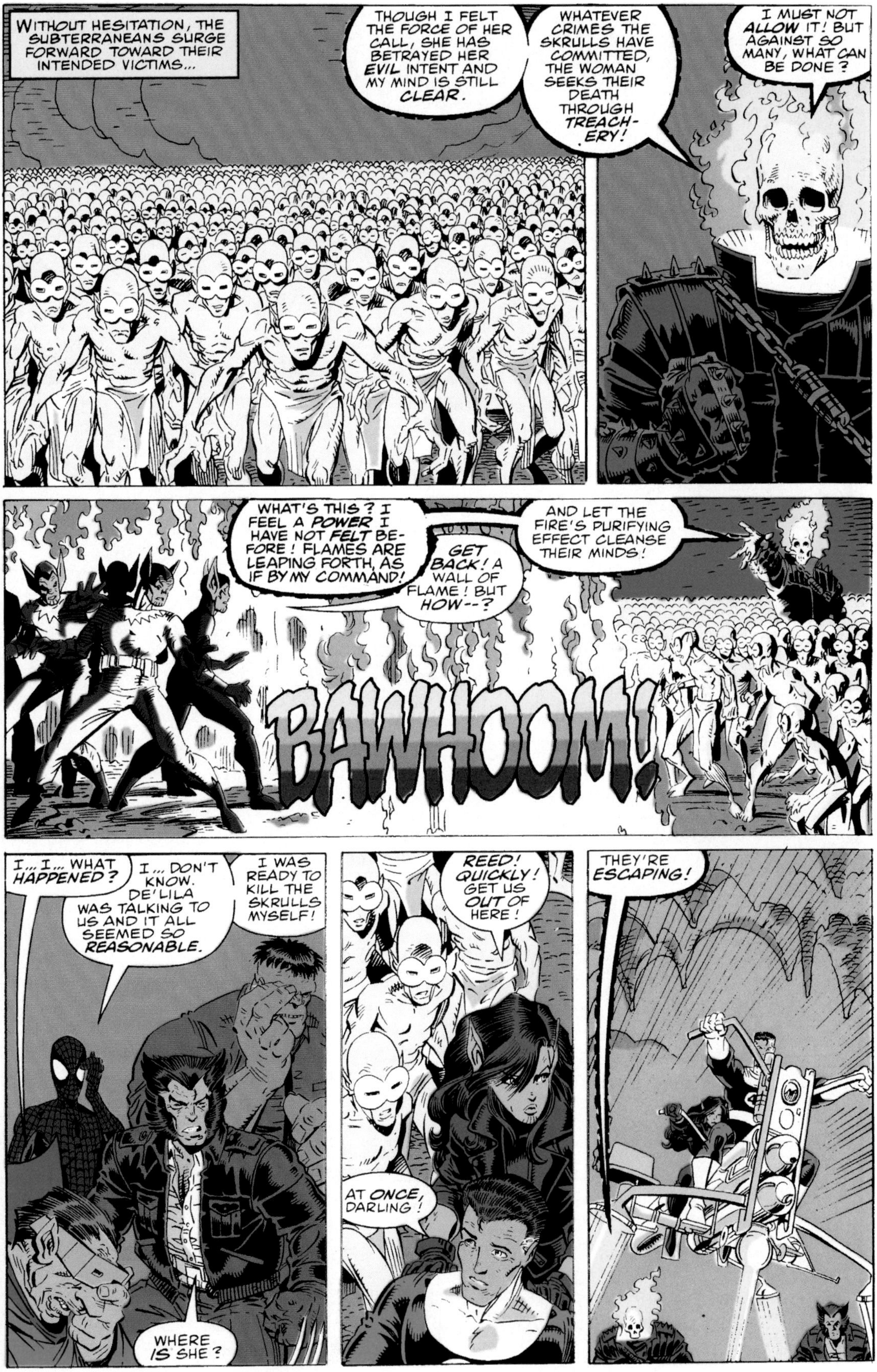
WITHOUT HESITATION, THE SUBTERRANEANS SURGE FORWARD TOWARD THEIR INTENDED VICTIMS...
THOUGH I FELT THE FORCE OF HER CALL, SHE HAS BETRAYED HER EVIL INTENT AND MY MIND IS STILL CLEAR.
WHATEVER CRIMES THE SKRULLS HAVE COMMITTED, THE WOMAN SEEKS THEIR DEATH THROUGH TREACH-ERY!
I MUST NOT ALLOW IT! BUT AGAINST SO MANY, WHAT CAN BE DONE?
WHAT'S THIS? I FEEL A POWER I HAVE NOT FELT BE-FORE! FLAMES ARE LEAPING FORTH, AS IF BY MY COMMAND!
AND LET THE FIRE'S PURIFYING EFFECT CLEANSE THEIR MINDS!
GET BACK! A WALL OF FLAME! BUT HOW--?
BAWHOOM!
I... I... WHAT HAPPENED?
I... DON'T KNOW. DE'LILA WAS TALKING TO US AND IT ALL SEEMED SO REASONABLE.
I WAS READY TO KILL THE SKRULLS MYSELF!
WHERE IS SHE?
REED! QUICKLY! GET US OUT OF HERE!
AT ONCE, DARLING!
THEY'RE ESCAPING!

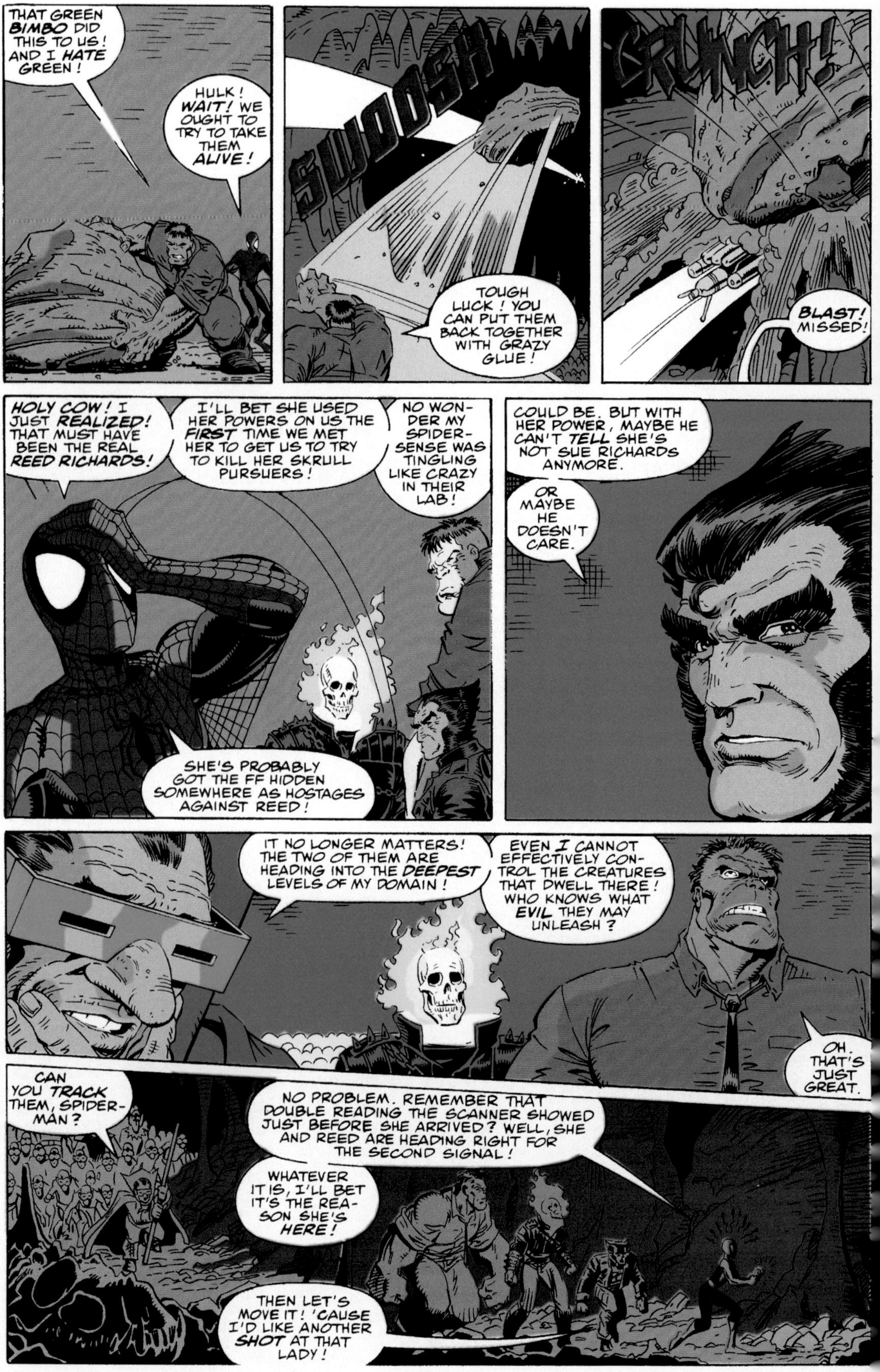
THAT GREEN BIMBO DID THIS TO US! AND I HATE GREEN!
HULK! WAIT! WE OUGHT TO TRY TO TAKE THEM ALIVE!
SWOOSH
TOUGH LUCK! YOU CAN PUT THEM BACK TOGETHER WITH GRAZY GLUE!
CRUNCH!
BLAST! MISSED!
HOLY COW! I JUST REALIZED! THAT MUST HAVE BEEN THE REAL REED RICHARDS!
I'LL BET SHE USED HER POWERS ON US THE FIRST TIME WE MET HER TO GET US TO TRY TO KILL HER SKRULL PURSUERS!
NO WONDER MY SPIDER-SENSE WAS TINGLING LIKE CRAZY IN THEIR LAB!
SHE'S PROBABLY GOT THE FF HIDDEN SOMEWHERE AS HOSTAGES AGAINST REED!
COULD BE. BUT WITH HER POWER, MAYBE HE CAN'T TELL SHE'S NOT SUE RICHARDS ANYMORE.
OR MAYBE HE DOESN'T CARE.
IT NO LONGER MATTERS! THE TWO OF THEM ARE HEADING INTO THE DEEPEST LEVELS OF MY DOMAIN!
EVEN I CANNOT EFFECTIVELY CONTROL THE CREATURES THAT DWELL THERE! WHO KNOWS WHAT EVIL THEY MAY UNLEASH?
OH. THAT'S JUST GREAT.
CAN YOU TRACK THEM, SPIDER-MAN?
NO PROBLEM. REMEMBER THAT DOUBLE READING THE SCANNER SHOWED JUST BEFORE SHE ARRIVED? WELL, SHE AND REED ARE HEADING RIGHT FOR THE SECOND SIGNAL!
WHATEVER IT IS, I'LL BET IT'S THE REASON SHE'S HERE!
THEN LET'S MOVE IT! 'CAUSE I'D LIKE ANOTHER SHOT AT THAT LADY!

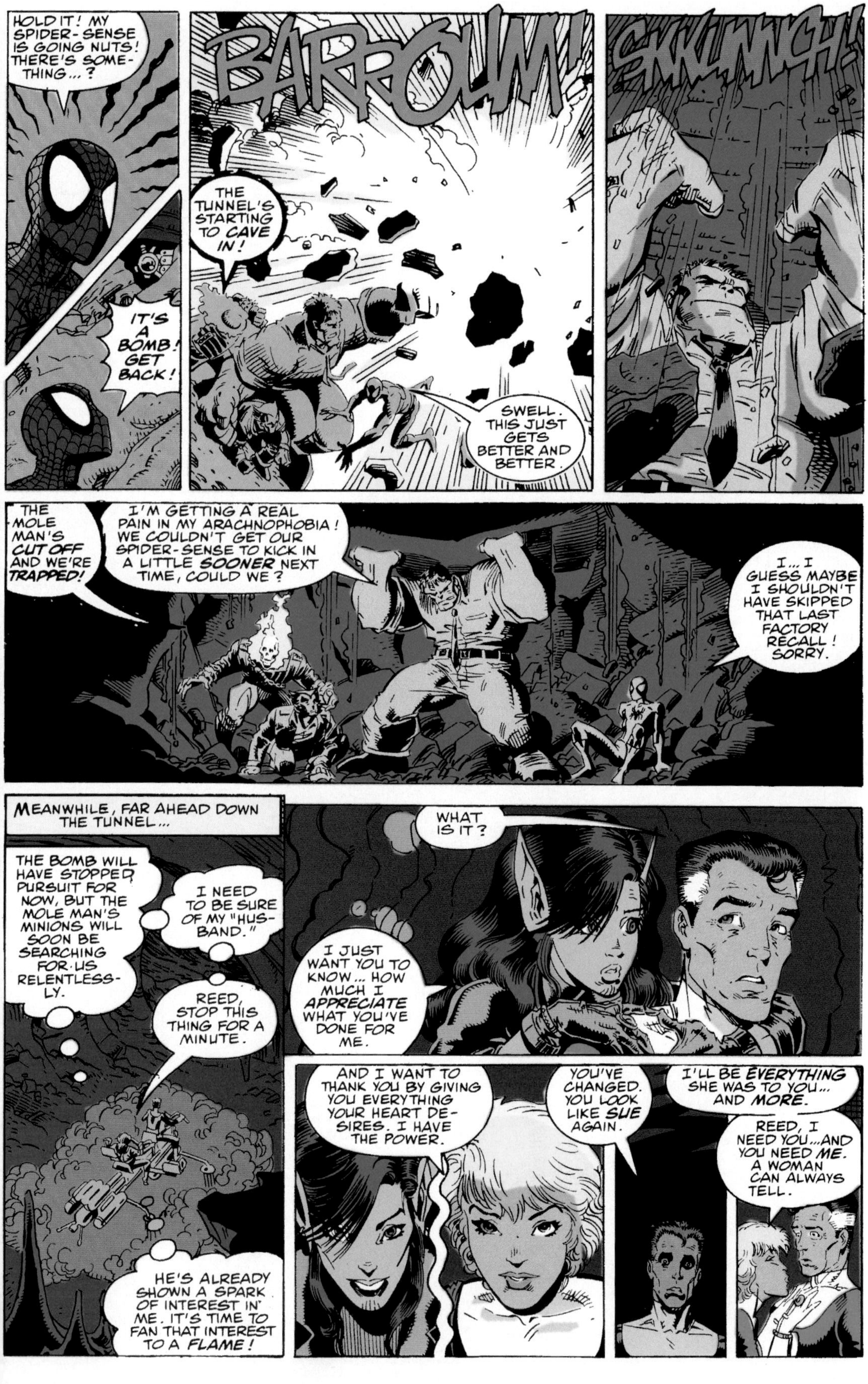
HOLD IT! MY SPIDER-SENSE IS GOING NUTS! THERE'S SOME-THING...?
IT'S A BOMB! GET BACK!
BARROUM!
THE TUNNEL'S STARTING TO CAVE IN!
SWELL. THIS JUST GETS BETTER AND BETTER.
SKKLUNNCH!
THE MOLE MAN'S CUT OFF AND WE'RE TRAPPED!
I'M GETTING A REAL PAIN IN MY ARACHNOPHOBIA! WE COULDN'T GET OUR SPIDER-SENSE TO KICK IN A LITTLE SOONER NEXT TIME, COULD WE?
I... I GUESS MAYBE I SHOULDN'T HAVE SKIPPED THAT LAST FACTORY RECALL! SORRY.
MEANWHILE, FAR AHEAD DOWN THE TUNNEL...
THE BOMB WILL HAVE STOPPED PURSUIT FOR NOW, BUT THE MOLE MAN'S MINIONS WILL SOON BE SEARCHING FOR US RELENTLESS-LY.
I NEED TO BE SURE OF MY "HUS-BAND."
REED, STOP THIS THING FOR A MINUTE.
HE'S ALREADY SHOWN A SPARK OF INTEREST IN ME. IT'S TIME TO FAN THAT INTEREST TO A FLAME!
WHAT IS IT?
I JUST WANT YOU TO KNOW... HOW MUCH I APPRECIATE WHAT YOU'VE DONE FOR ME.
AND I WANT TO THANK YOU BY GIVING YOU EVERYTHING YOUR HEART DE-SIRES. I HAVE THE POWER.
YOU'VE CHANGED. YOU LOOK LIKE SUE AGAIN.
I'LL BE EVERYTHING SHE WAS TO YOU... AND MORE.
REED, I NEED YOU...AND YOU NEED ME. A WOMAN CAN ALWAYS TELL.

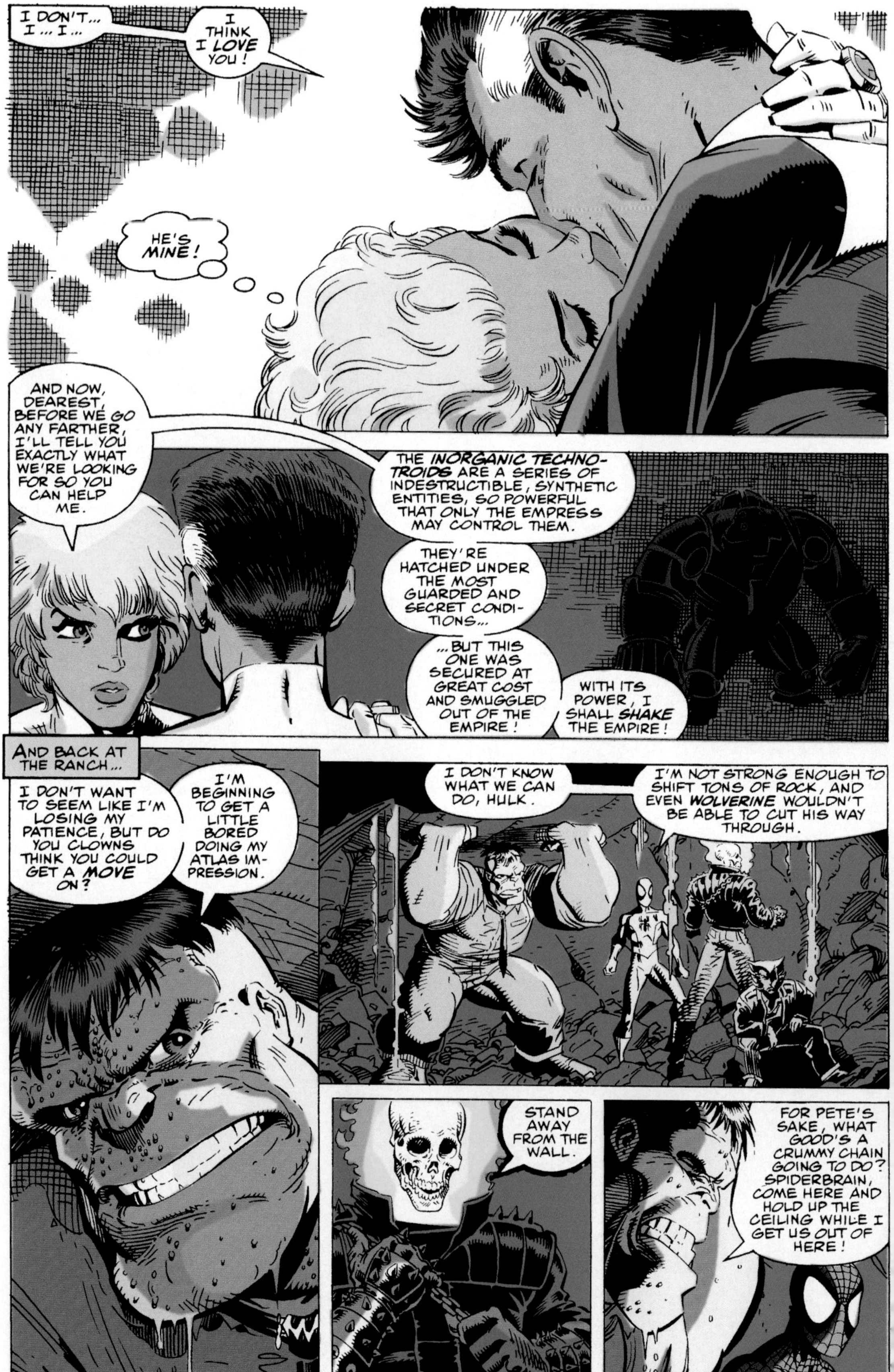
I DON'T... I ... I ...
I THINK I LOVE YOU!
HE'S MINE!
AND NOW, DEAREST, BEFORE WE GO ANY FARTHER, I'LL TELL YOU EXACTLY WHAT WE'RE LOOKING FOR SO YOU CAN HELP ME.
THE INORGANIC TECHNO-TROIDS ARE A SERIES OF INDESTRUCTIBLE, SYNTHETIC ENTITIES, SO POWERFUL THAT ONLY THE EMPRESS MAY CONTROL THEM.
THEY'RE HATCHED UNDER THE MOST GUARDED AND SECRET CONDI-TIONS...
...BUT THIS ONE WAS SECURED AT GREAT COST AND SMUGGLED OUT OF THE EMPIRE!
WITH ITS POWER, I SHALL SHAKE THE EMPIRE!
AND BACK AT THE RANCH...
I DON'T WANT TO SEEM LIKE I'M LOSING MY PATIENCE, BUT DO YOU CLOWNS THINK YOU COULD GET A MOVE ON?
I'M BEGINNING TO GET A LITTLE BORED DOING MY ATLAS IM-PRESSION.
I DON'T KNOW WHAT WE CAN DO, HULK.
I'M NOT STRONG ENOUGH TO SHIFT TONS OF ROCK, AND EVEN WOLVERINE WOULDN'T BE ABLE TO CUT HIS WAY THROUGH.
STAND AWAY FROM THE WALL.
FOR PETE'S SAKE, WHAT GOOD'S A CRUMMY CHAIN GOING TO DO? SPIDERBRAIN, COME HERE AND HOLD UP THE CEILING WHILE I GET US OUT OF HERE!

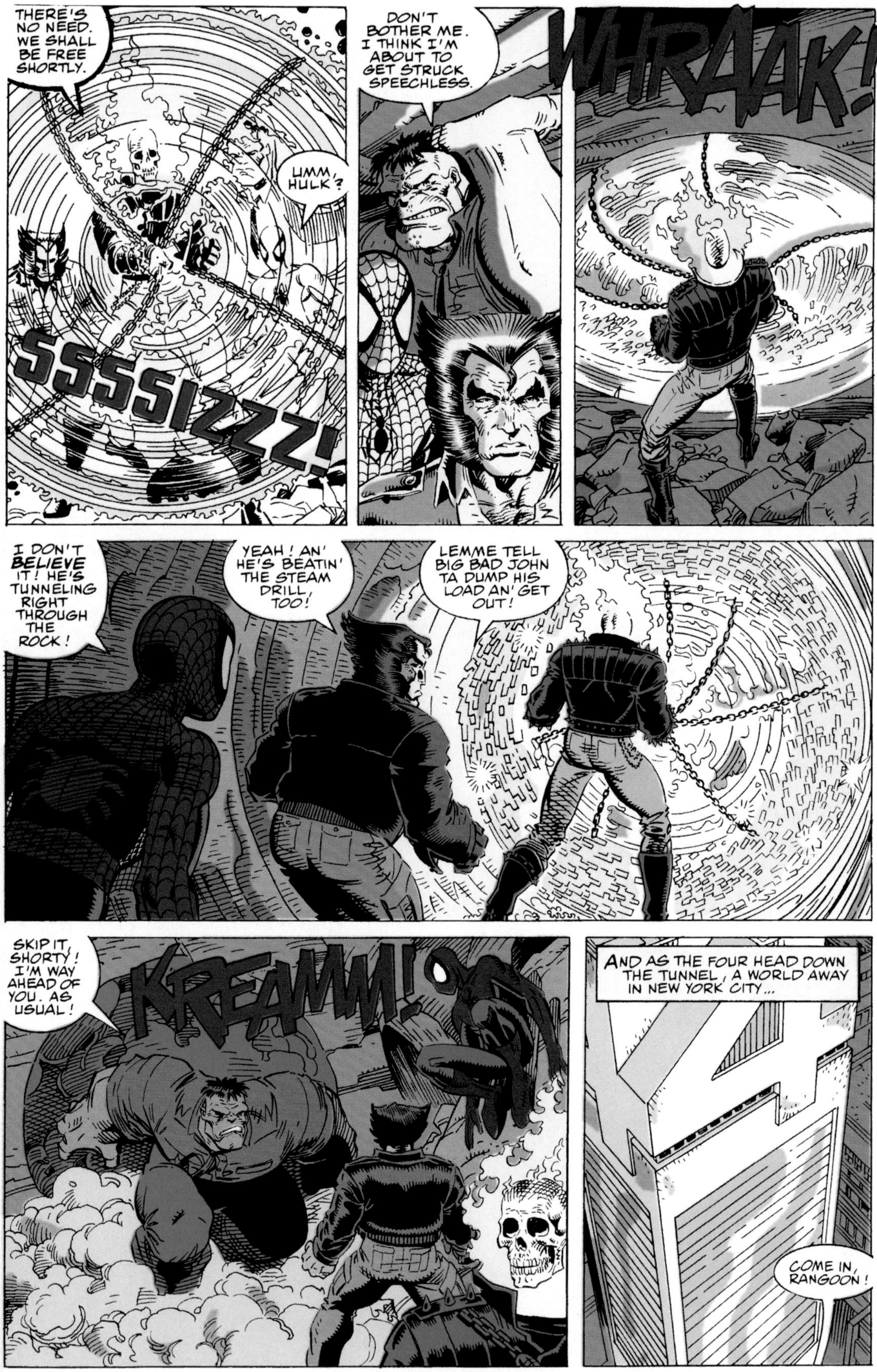
THERE'S NO NEED. WE SHALL BE FREE SHORTLY.
UMM, HULK?
SSSSIZZZ!
DON'T BOTHER ME. I THINK I'M ABOUT TO GET STRUCK SPEECHLESS.
WHRAAK!
I DON'T BELIEVE IT! HE'S TUNNELING RIGHT THROUGH THE ROCK!
YEAH! AN' HE'S BEATIN' THE STEAM DRILL, TOO!
LEMME TELL BIG BAD JOHN TA DUMP HIS LOAD AN' GET OUT!
SKIP IT, SHORTY! I'M WAY AHEAD OF YOU. AS USUAL!
KREAMM!
AND AS THE FOUR HEAD DOWN THE TUNNEL, A WORLD AWAY IN NEW YORK CITY...
COME IN, RANGOON!

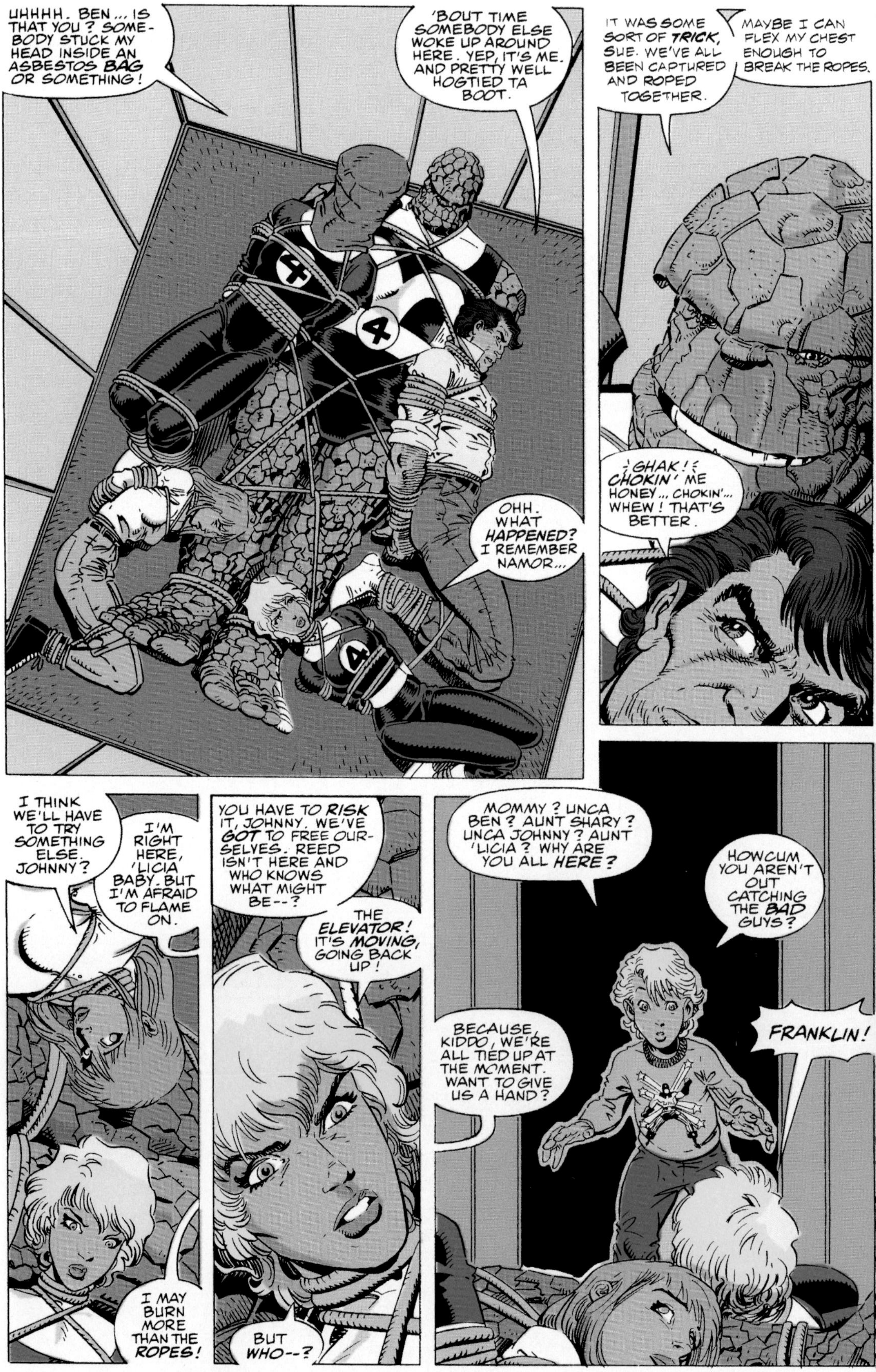
UHHHH. BEN... IS THAT YOU? SOMEBODY STUCK MY HEAD INSIDE AN ASBESTOS BAG OR SOMETHING!
'BOUT TIME SOMEBODY ELSE WOKE UP AROUND HERE. YEP, IT'S ME. AND PRETTY WELL HOGTIED TA BOOT.
OHH. WHAT HAPPENED? I REMEMBER NAMOR...
IT WAS SOME SORT OF TRICK, SUE. WE'VE ALL BEEN CAPTURED AND ROPED TOGETHER.
MAYBE I CAN FLEX MY CHEST ENOUGH TO BREAK THE ROPES.
GHAK! CHOKIN' ME HONEY... CHOKIN'... WHEW! THAT'S BETTER.
I THINK WE'LL HAVE TO TRY SOMETHING ELSE. JOHNNY?
I'M RIGHT HERE, 'LICIA BABY. BUT I'M AFRAID TO FLAME ON.
I MAY BURN MORE THAN THE ROPES!
YOU HAVE TO RISK IT, JOHNNY. WE'VE GOT TO FREE OURSELVES. REED ISN'T HERE AND WHO KNOWS WHAT MIGHT BE--?
THE ELEVATOR! IT'S MOVING, GOING BACK UP!
BUT WHO--?
MOMMY? UNCA BEN? AUNT SHARY? UNCA JOHNNY? AUNT 'LICIA? WHY ARE YOU ALL HERE?
HOWCUM YOU AREN'T OUT CATCHING THE BAD GUYS?
FRANKLIN!
BECAUSE, KIDDO, WE'RE ALL TIED UP AT THE MOMENT. WANT TO GIVE US A HAND?

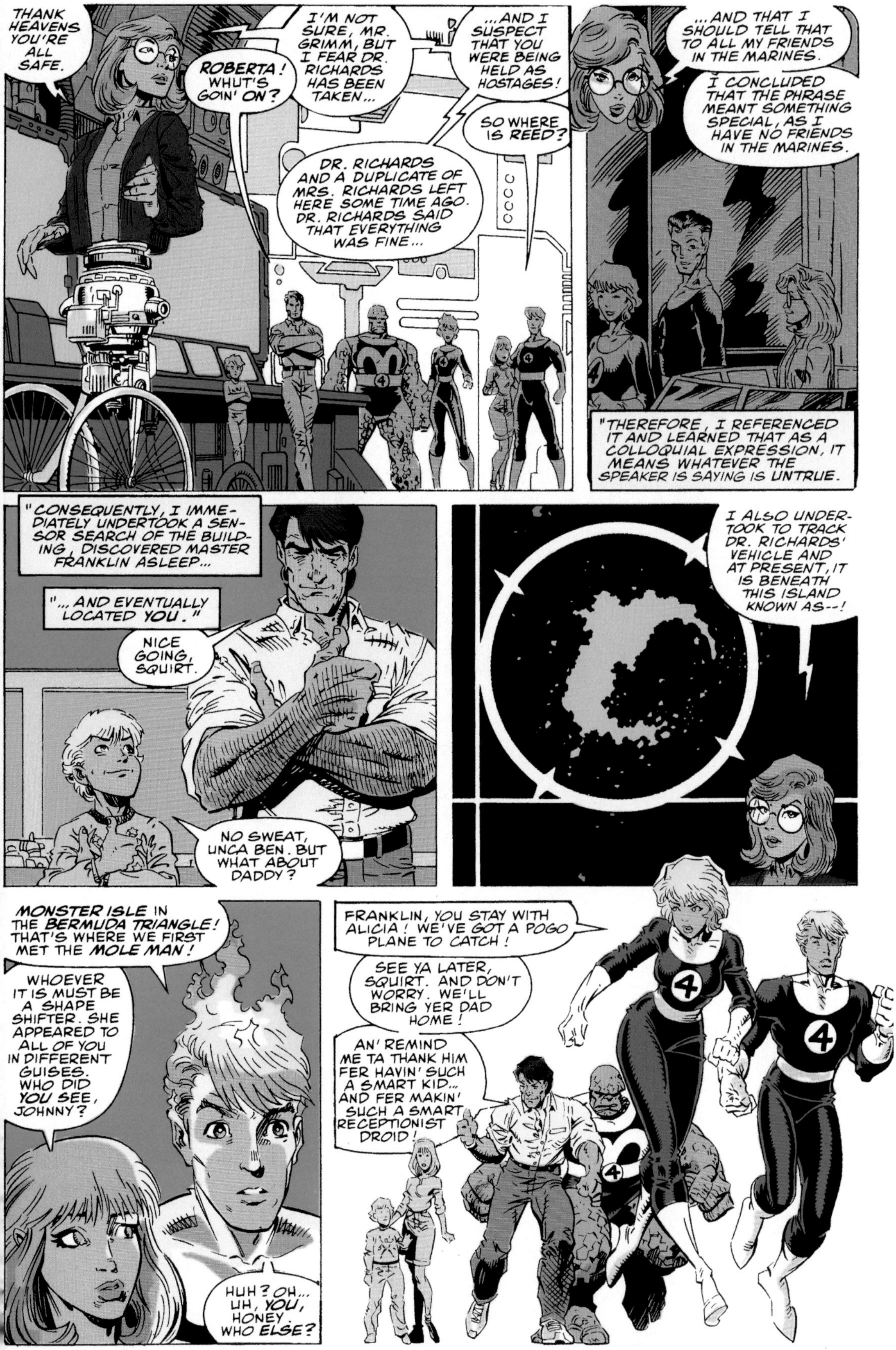

THANK HEAVENS YOU'RE ALL SAFE.
ROBERTA! WHUT'S GOIN' ON?
I'M NOT SURE, MR. GRIMM, BUT I FEAR DR. RICHARDS HAS BEEN TAKEN...
...AND I SUSPECT THAT YOU WERE BEING HELD AS HOSTAGES!
SO WHERE IS REED?
DR. RICHARDS AND A DUPLICATE OF MRS. RICHARDS LEFT HERE SOME TIME AGO. DR. RICHARDS SAID THAT EVERYTHING WAS FINE...
...AND THAT I SHOULD TELL THAT TO ALL MY FRIENDS IN THE MARINES.
I CONCLUDED THAT THE PHRASE MEANT SOMETHING SPECIAL, AS I HAVE NO FRIENDS IN THE MARINES.
"THEREFORE, I REFERENCED IT AND LEARNED THAT AS A COLLOQUIAL EXPRESSION, IT MEANS WHATEVER THE SPEAKER IS SAYING IS UNTRUE.
"CONSEQUENTLY, I IMMEDIATELY UNDERTOOK A SENSOR SEARCH OF THE BUILDING, DISCOVERED MASTER FRANKLIN ASLEEP...
"...AND EVENTUALLY LOCATED YOU."
NICE GOING, SQUIRT.
NO SWEAT, UNCA BEN. BUT WHAT ABOUT DADDY?
I ALSO UNDERTOOK TO TRACK DR. RICHARDS' VEHICLE AND AT PRESENT, IT IS BENEATH THIS ISLAND KNOWN AS--!
MONSTER ISLE IN THE BERMUDA TRIANGLE! THAT'S WHERE WE FIRST MET THE MOLE MAN!
WHOEVER IT IS MUST BE A SHAPE SHIFTER. SHE APPEARED TO ALL OF YOU IN DIFFERENT GUISES. WHO DID YOU SEE, JOHNNY?
HUH? OH... UH, YOU, HONEY. WHO ELSE?
FRANKLIN, YOU STAY WITH ALICIA! WE'VE GOT A POGO PLANE TO CATCH!
SEE YA LATER, SQUIRT. AND DON'T WORRY. WE'LL BRING YER DAD HOME!
AN' REMIND ME TA THANK HIM FER HAVIN' SUCH A SMART KID... AND FER MAKIN' SUCH A SMART RECEPTIONIST DROID!

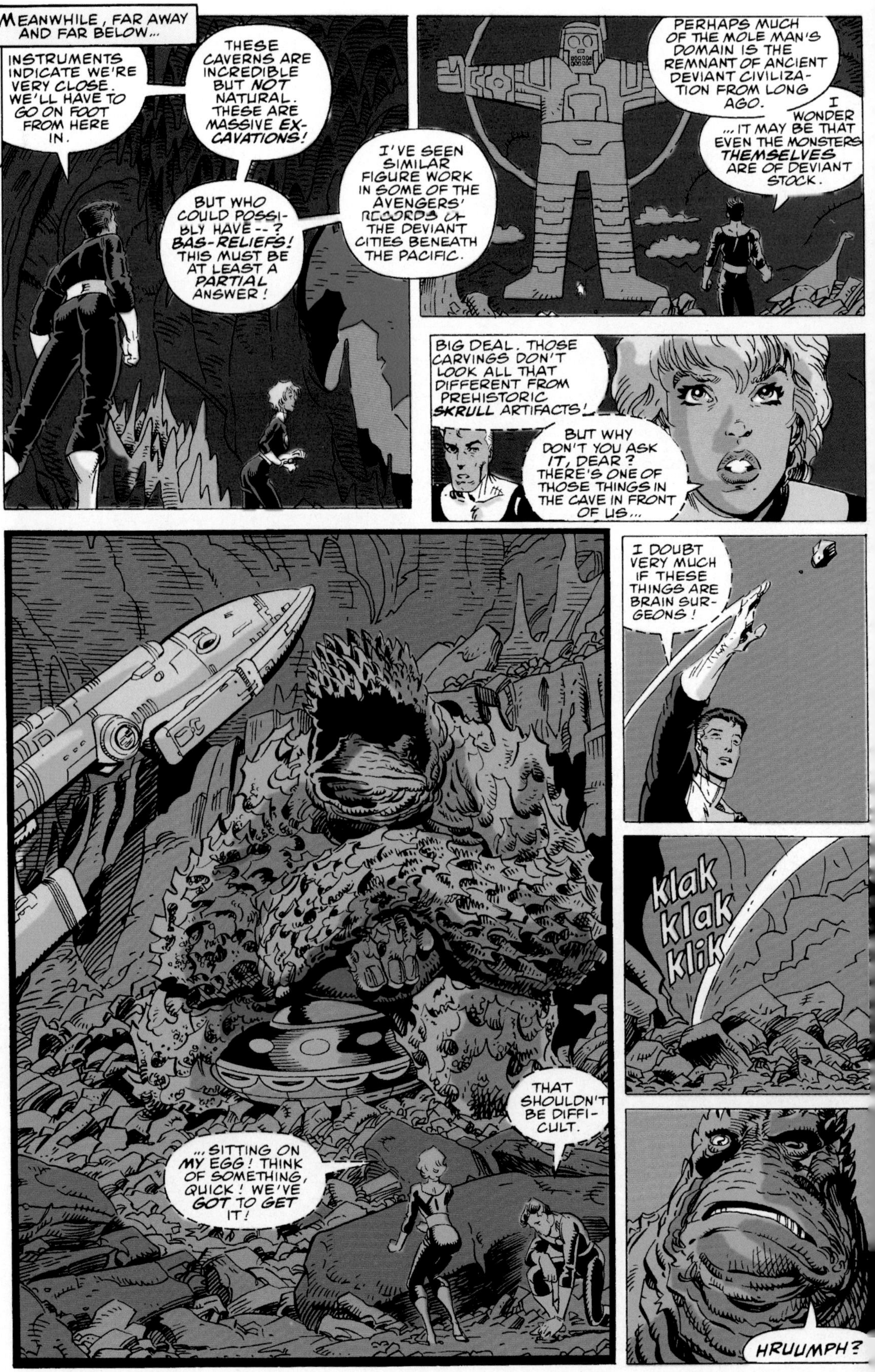
MEANWHILE, FAR AWAY AND FAR BELOW...
INSTRUMENTS INDICATE WE'RE VERY CLOSE. WE'LL HAVE TO GO ON FOOT FROM HERE IN.
THESE CAVERNS ARE INCREDIBLE BUT NOT NATURAL. THESE ARE MASSIVE EXCAVATIONS!
BUT WHO COULD POSSIBLY HAVE--? BAS-RELIEFS! THIS MUST BE AT LEAST A PARTIAL ANSWER!
I'VE SEEN SIMILAR FIGURE WORK IN SOME OF THE AVENGERS' RECORDS OF THE DEVIANT CITIES BENEATH THE PACIFIC.
PERHAPS MUCH OF THE MOLE MAN'S DOMAIN IS THE REMNANT OF ANCIENT DEVIANT CIVILIZATION FROM LONG AGO.
I WONDER ...IT MAY BE THAT EVEN THE MONSTERS THEMSELVES ARE OF DEVIANT STOCK.
BIG DEAL. THOSE CARVINGS DON'T LOOK ALL THAT DIFFERENT FROM PREHISTORIC SKRULL ARTIFACTS!
BUT WHY DON'T YOU ASK IT, DEAR? THERE'S ONE OF THOSE THINGS IN THE CAVE IN FRONT OF US...
...SITTING ON MY EGG! THINK OF SOMETHING, QUICK! WE'VE GOT TO GET IT!
THAT SHOULDN'T BE DIFFICULT.
I DOUBT VERY MUCH IF THESE THINGS ARE BRAIN SURGEONS!
klak klak klik
HRUUMPH?

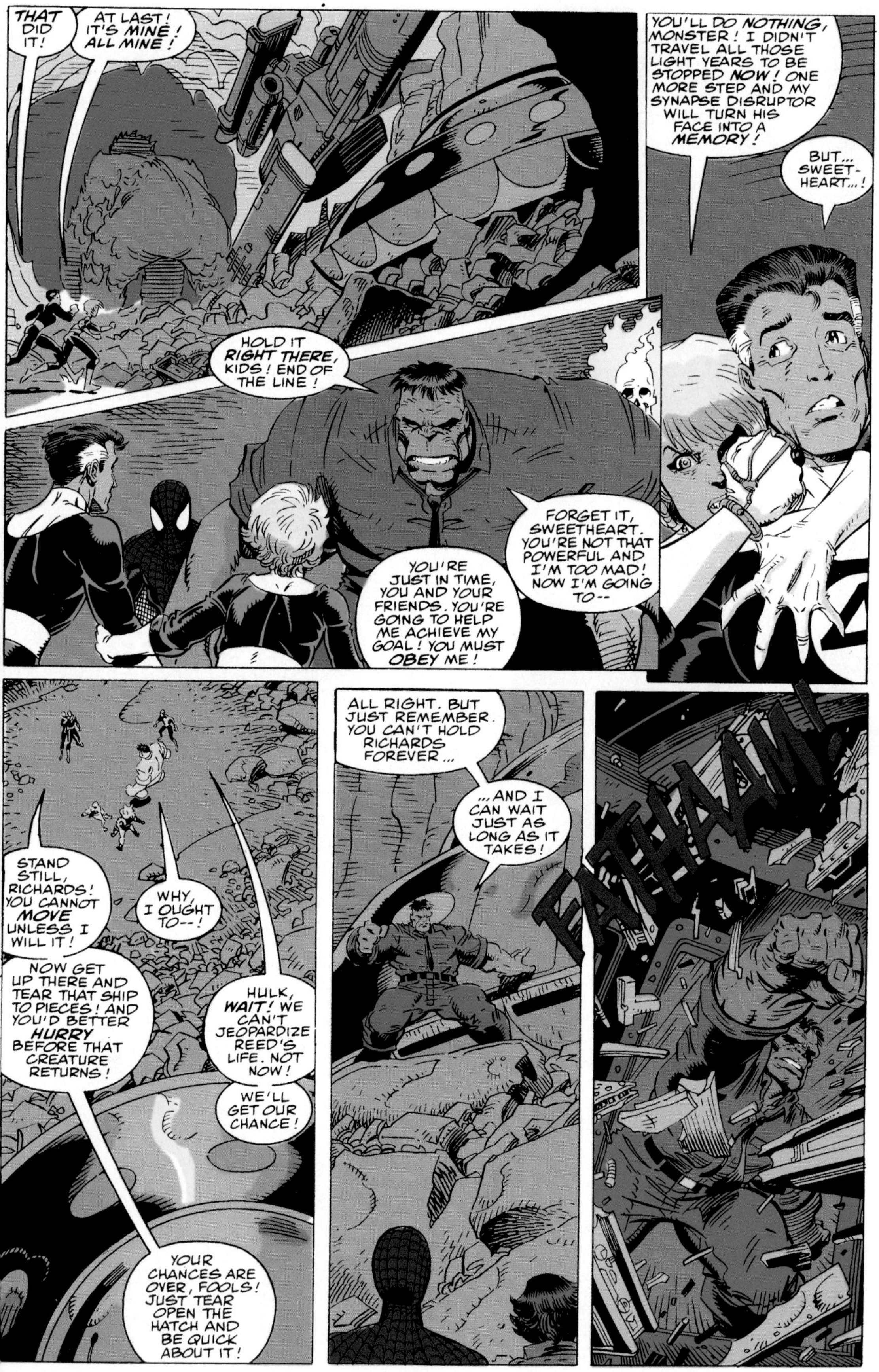
THAT DID IT!
AT LAST! IT'S MINE! ALL MINE!
YOU'LL DO NOTHING, MONSTER! I DIDN'T TRAVEL ALL THOSE LIGHT YEARS TO BE STOPPED NOW! ONE MORE STEP AND MY SYNAPSE DISRUPTOR WILL TURN HIS FACE INTO A MEMORY!
BUT... SWEET-HEART...!
HOLD IT RIGHT THERE, KIDS! END OF THE LINE!
FORGET IT, SWEETHEART. YOU'RE NOT THAT POWERFUL AND I'M TOO MAD! NOW I'M GOING TO--
YOU'RE JUST IN TIME, YOU AND YOUR FRIENDS. YOU'RE GOING TO HELP ME ACHIEVE MY GOAL! YOU MUST OBEY ME!
STAND STILL, RICHARDS! YOU CANNOT MOVE UNLESS I WILL IT!
WHY, I OUGHT TO--!
NOW GET UP THERE AND TEAR THAT SHIP TO PIECES! AND YOU'D BETTER HURRY BEFORE THAT CREATURE RETURNS!
HULK, WAIT! WE CAN'T JEOPARDIZE REED'S LIFE. NOT NOW!
WE'LL GET OUR CHANCE!
YOUR CHANCES ARE OVER, FOOLS! JUST TEAR OPEN THE HATCH AND BE QUICK ABOUT IT!
ALL RIGHT. BUT JUST REMEMBER. YOU CAN'T HOLD RICHARDS FOREVER ...
...AND I CAN WAIT JUST AS LONG AS IT TAKES!
FATHAAM!

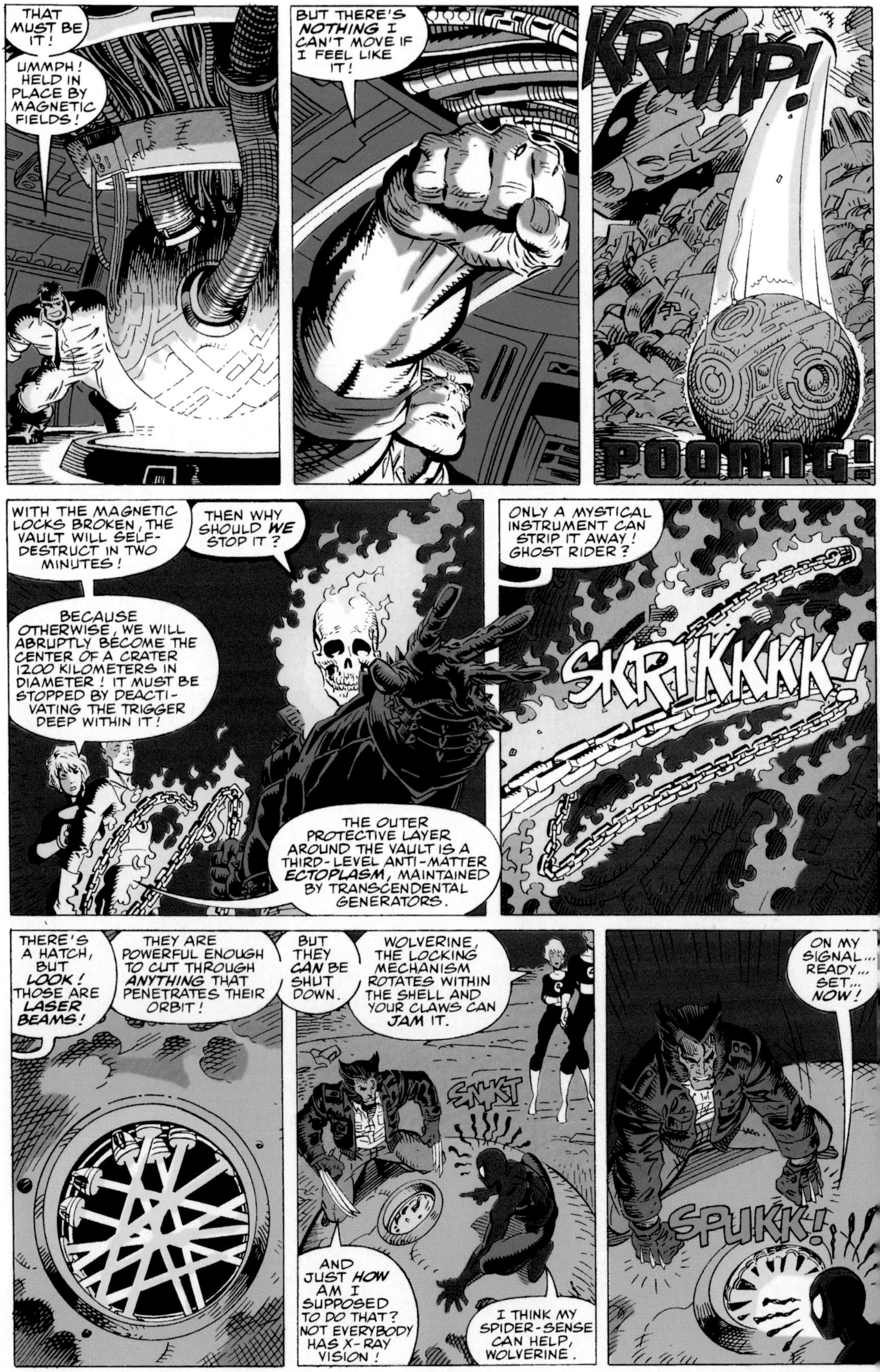
THAT MUST BE IT!
UMMPH! HELD IN PLACE BY MAGNETIC FIELDS!
BUT THERE'S NOTHING I CAN'T MOVE IF I FEEL LIKE IT!
KRUMP!
POONNG!
WITH THE MAGNETIC LOCKS BROKEN, THE VAULT WILL SELF-DESTRUCT IN TWO MINUTES!
THEN WHY SHOULD WE STOP IT?
BECAUSE OTHERWISE, WE WILL ABRUPTLY BECOME THE CENTER OF A CRATER 1200 KILOMETERS IN DIAMETER! IT MUST BE STOPPED BY DEACTIVATING THE TRIGGER DEEP WITHIN IT!
THE OUTER PROTECTIVE LAYER AROUND THE VAULT IS A THIRD-LEVEL ANTI-MATTER ECTOPLASM, MAINTAINED BY TRANSCENDENTAL GENERATORS.
ONLY A MYSTICAL INSTRUMENT CAN STRIP IT AWAY! GHOST RIDER?
SKRIKKKK!
THERE'S A HATCH, BUT LOOK! THOSE ARE LASER BEAMS!
THEY ARE POWERFUL ENOUGH TO CUT THROUGH ANYTHING THAT PENETRATES THEIR ORBIT!
BUT THEY CAN BE SHUT DOWN.
WOLVERINE, THE LOCKING MECHANISM ROTATES WITHIN THE SHELL AND YOUR CLAWS CAN JAM IT.
SNIKT
AND JUST HOW AM I SUPPOSED TO DO THAT? NOT EVERYBODY HAS X-RAY VISION!
I THINK MY SPIDER-SENSE CAN HELP, WOLVERINE.
ON MY SIGNAL... READY... SET... NOW!
SPUKK!

YOU DID IT, WOLVERINE! BUT IT'S GETTING READY TO BLOW!
THE LASERS ARE STILL ON BUT THEY'RE NOT ROTATING ANY MORE!
I CAN SEE THE TRIGGER!
GOT TO ADJUST MY WEB SHOOTERS TO MAXIMUM VISCOSITY. THERE'S TIME FOR JUST ONE SHOT!
BTHUK!
BULL'S EYE! JAMMED IT!
GET BACK! THE SHELL'S STARTING TA CRACK!
Krung! Krung!
YES! YES! YES!
KSSSSSHHHHHH!
AT LAST! THE EGG IS MINE!
SORRY, LADY. END OF THE LINE. I STILL DON'T KNOW WHAT THAT THING IS, BUT ANYTHING THAT CAREFULLY PROTECTED HAS GOT TO BE POWERFUL.
AND YOU'RE THE LAST PERSON WHO OUGHT TO BE GETTING IT. IF RICHARDS WAS IN HIS RIGHT MIND, HE'D AGREE WITH ME.

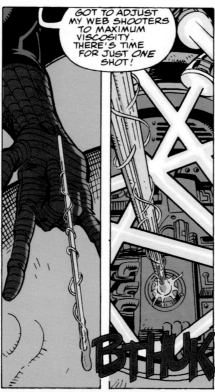

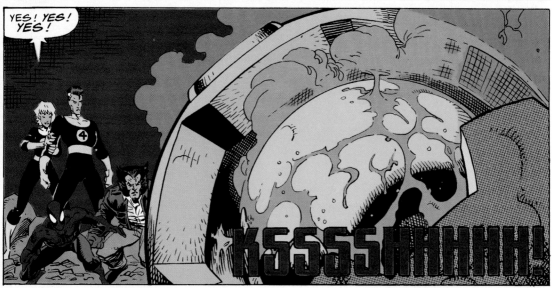

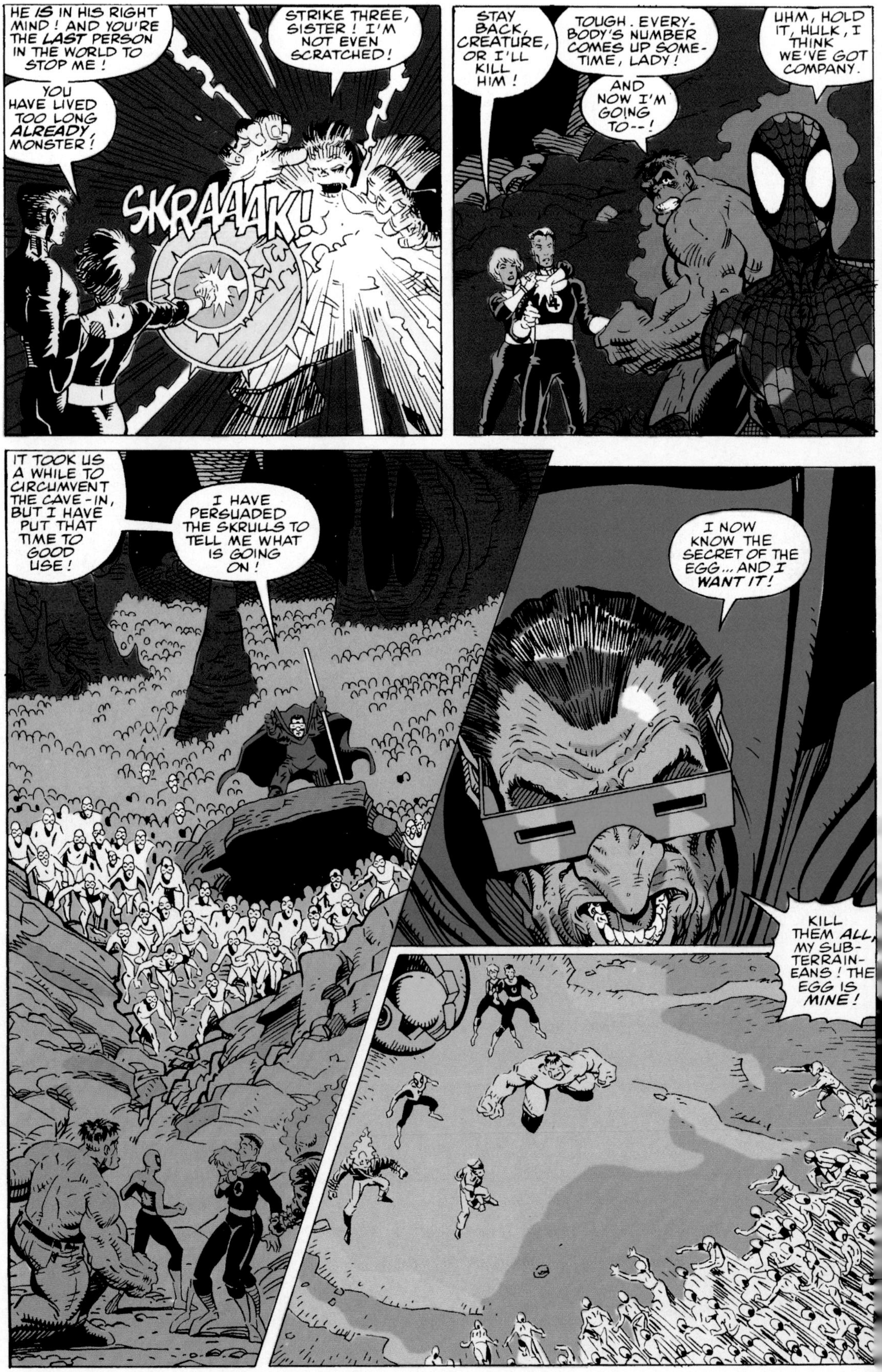
HE IS IN HIS RIGHT MIND! AND YOU'RE THE LAST PERSON IN THE WORLD TO STOP ME!
YOU HAVE LIVED TOO LONG ALREADY, MONSTER!
STRIKE THREE, SISTER! I'M NOT EVEN SCRATCHED!
SKRAAAK!
STAY BACK, CREATURE, OR I'LL KILL HIM!
TOUGH. EVERYBODY'S NUMBER COMES UP SOMETIME, LADY!
AND NOW I'M GOING TO--!
UHM, HOLD IT, HULK, I THINK WE'VE GOT COMPANY.
IT TOOK US A WHILE TO CIRCUMVENT THE CAVE-IN, BUT I HAVE PUT THAT TIME TO GOOD USE!
I HAVE PERSUADED THE SKRULLS TO TELL ME WHAT IS GOING ON!
I NOW KNOW THE SECRET OF THE EGG... AND I WANT IT!
KILL THEM ALL, MY SUBTERRAINEANS! THE EGG IS MINE!

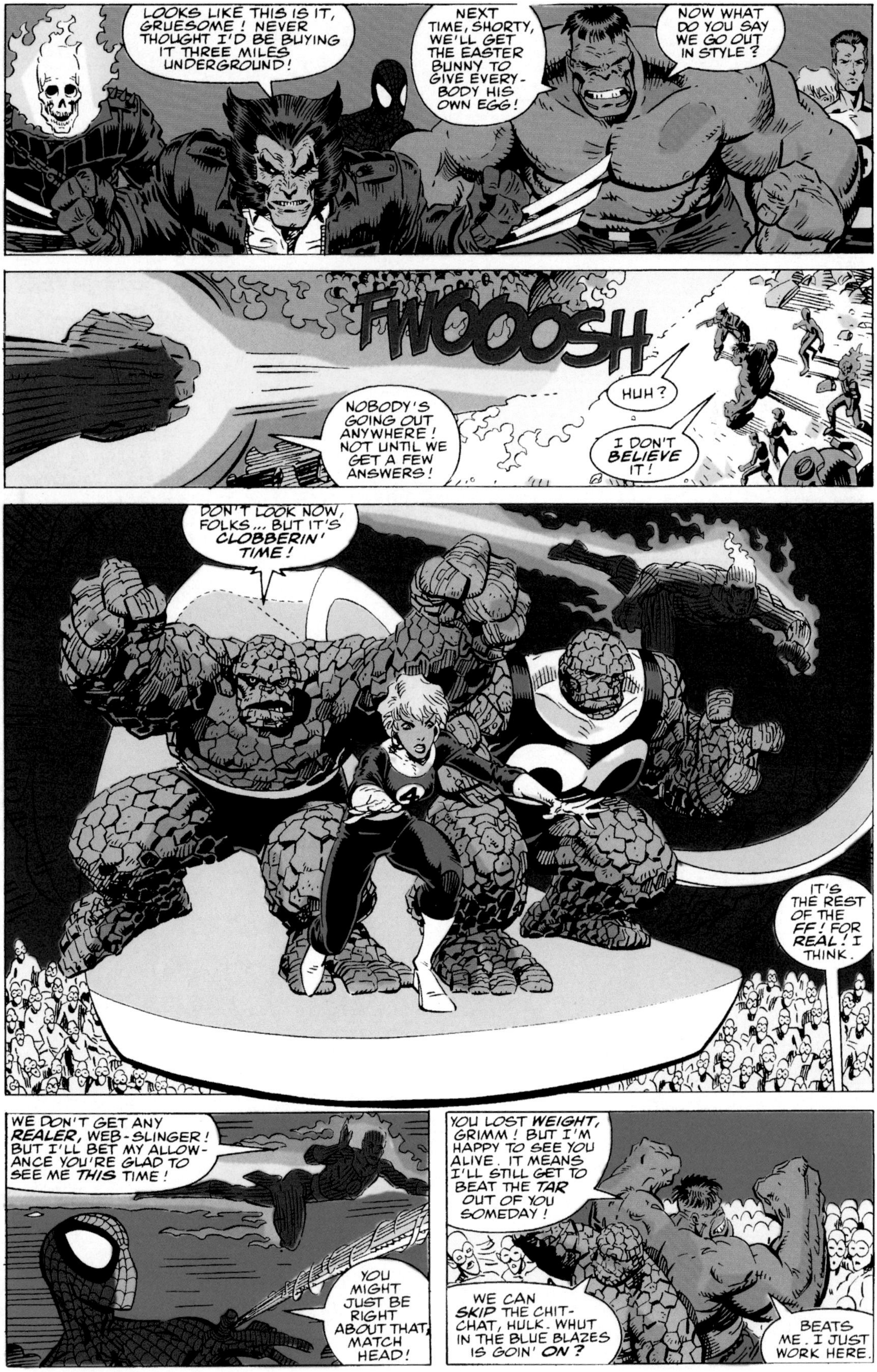
LOOKS LIKE THIS IS IT, GRUESOME! NEVER THOUGHT I'D BE BUYING IT THREE MILES UNDERGROUND!
NEXT TIME, SHORTY, WE'LL GET THE EASTER BUNNY TO GIVE EVERY-BODY HIS OWN EGG!
NOW WHAT DO YOU SAY WE GO OUT IN STYLE?
FWOOOSH
NOBODY'S GOING OUT ANYWHERE! NOT UNTIL WE GET A FEW ANSWERS!
HUH?
I DON'T BELIEVE IT!
DON'T LOOK NOW, FOLKS... BUT IT'S CLOBBERIN' TIME!
IT'S THE REST OF THE FF! FOR REAL! I THINK.
WE DON'T GET ANY REALER, WEB-SLINGER! BUT I'LL BET MY ALLOW-ANCE YOU'RE GLAD TO SEE ME THIS TIME!
YOU MIGHT JUST BE RIGHT ABOUT THAT, MATCH HEAD!
YOU LOST WEIGHT, GRIMM! BUT I'M HAPPY TO SEE YOU ALIVE. IT MEANS I'LL STILL GET TO BEAT THE TAR OUT OF YOU SOMEDAY!
WE CAN SKIP THE CHIT-CHAT, HULK. WHUT IN THE BLUE BLAZES IS GOIN' ON?
BEATS ME. I JUST WORK HERE.

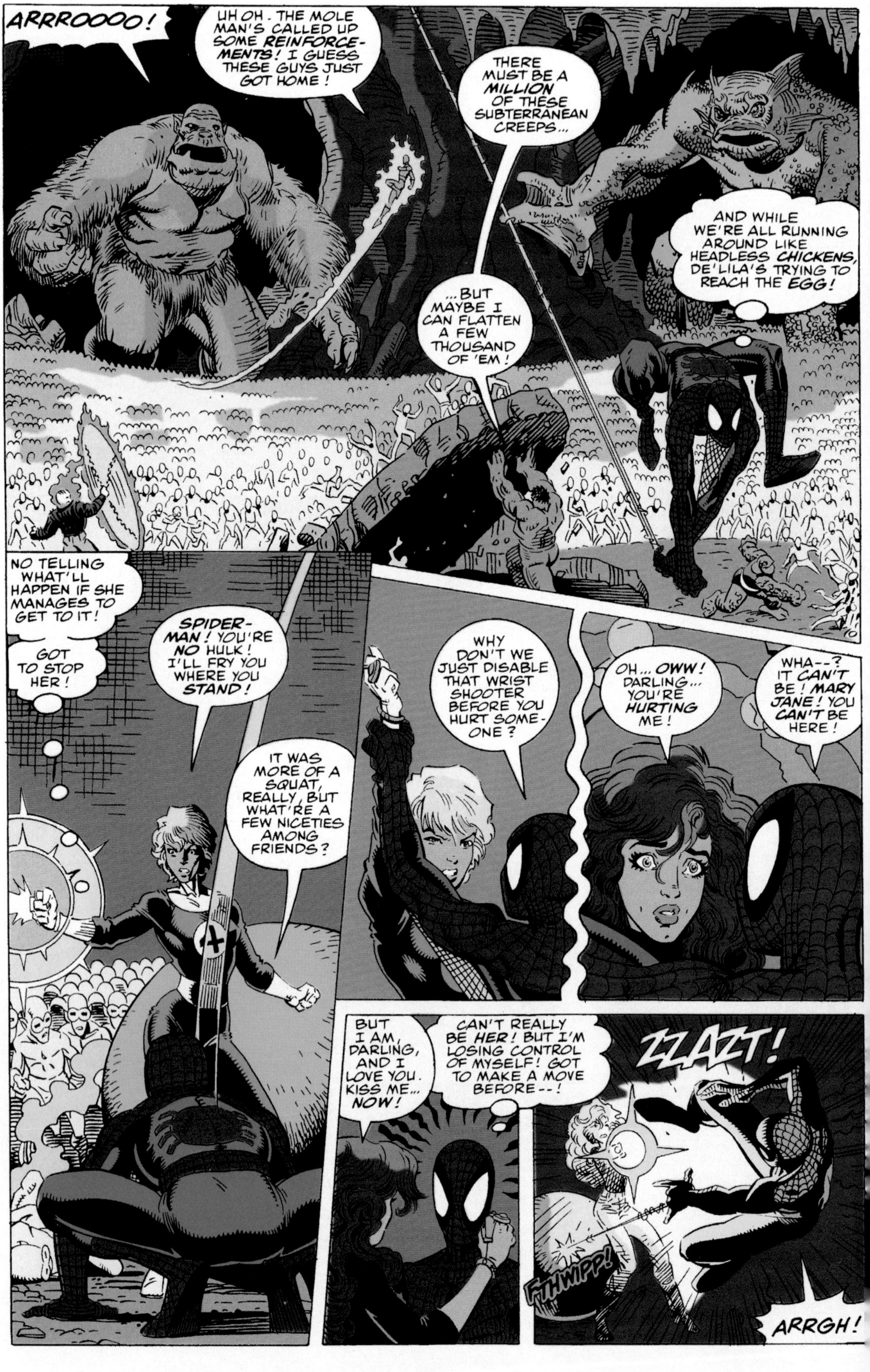
ARRROOOO!
UH OH - THE MOLE MAN'S CALLED UP SOME REINFORCE-MENTS! I GUESS THESE GUYS JUST GOT HOME!
THERE MUST BE A MILLION OF THESE SUBTERRANEAN CREEPS...
...BUT MAYBE I CAN FLATTEN A FEW THOUSAND OF 'EM!
AND WHILE WE'RE ALL RUNNING AROUND LIKE HEADLESS CHICKENS, DE'LILA'S TRYING TO REACH THE EGG!
NO TELLING WHAT'LL HAPPEN IF SHE MANAGES TO GET TO IT!
GOT TO STOP HER!
SPIDER-MAN! YOU'RE NO HULK! I'LL FRY YOU WHERE YOU STAND!
IT WAS MORE OF A SQUAT, REALLY, BUT WHAT'RE A FEW NICETIES AMONG FRIENDS?
WHY DON'T WE JUST DISABLE THAT WRIST SHOOTER BEFORE YOU HURT SOME-ONE?
OH... OWW! DARLING... YOU'RE HURTING ME!
WHA--? IT CAN'T BE! MARY JANE! YOU CAN'T BE HERE!
BUT I AM, DARLING, AND I LOVE YOU. KISS ME... NOW!
CAN'T REALLY BE HER! BUT I'M LOSING CONTROL OF MYSELF! GOT TO MAKE A MOVE BEFORE--!
ZZAZT!
FTHWIPP!
ARRGH!

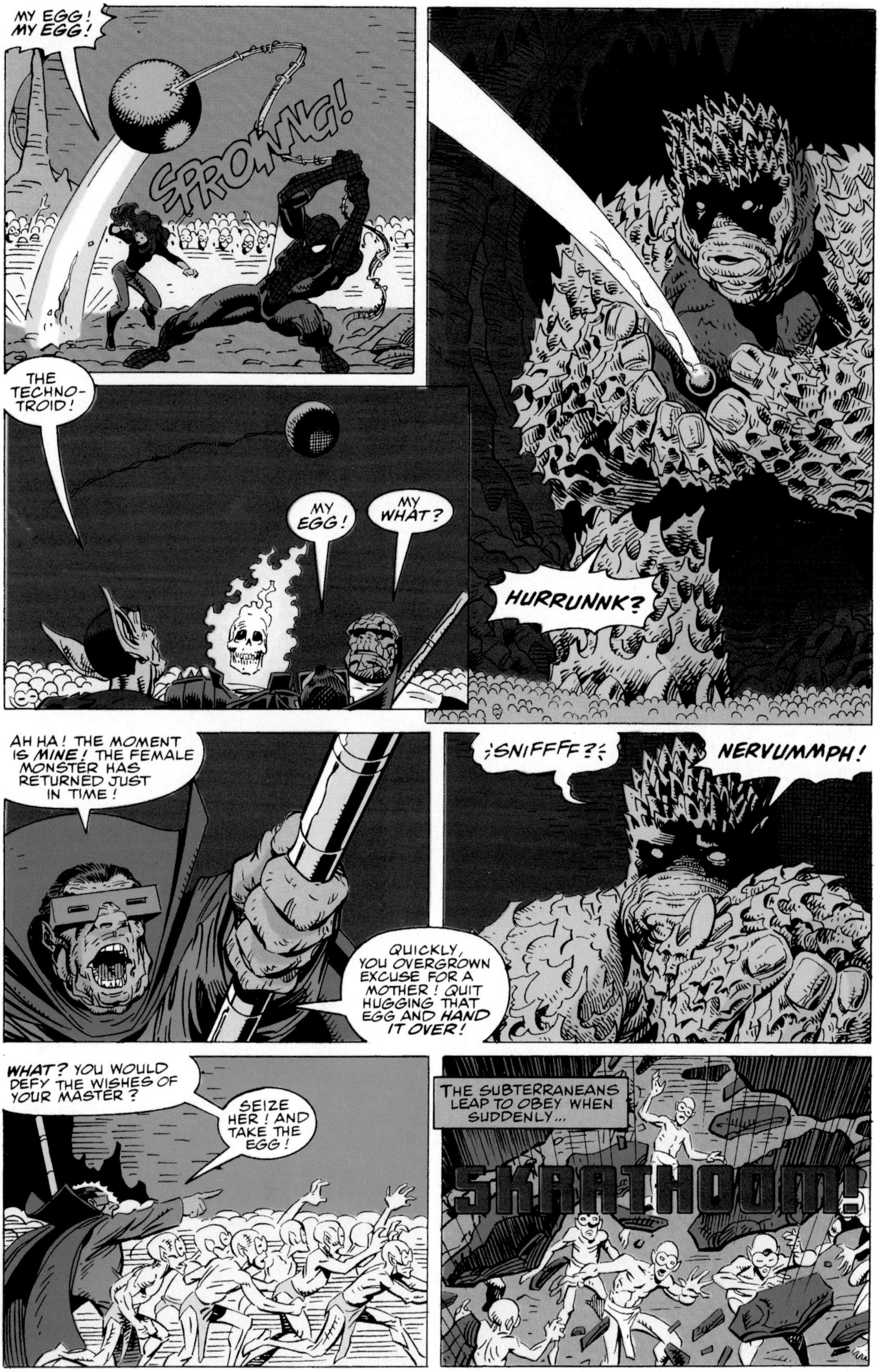
MY EGG! MY EGG!
SPRONNG!
THE TECHNO-TROID!
MY EGG!
MY WHAT?
HURRUNNK?
AH HA! THE MOMENT IS MINE! THE FEMALE MONSTER HAS RETURNED JUST IN TIME!
QUICKLY, YOU OVERGROWN EXCUSE FOR A MOTHER! QUIT HUGGING THAT EGG AND HAND IT OVER!
SNIFFFF?
NERVUMMPH!
WHAT? YOU WOULD DEFY THE WISHES OF YOUR MASTER?
SEIZE HER! AND TAKE THE EGG!
THE SUBTERRANEANS LEAP TO OBEY WHEN SUDDENLY...
SKRATHOOM!

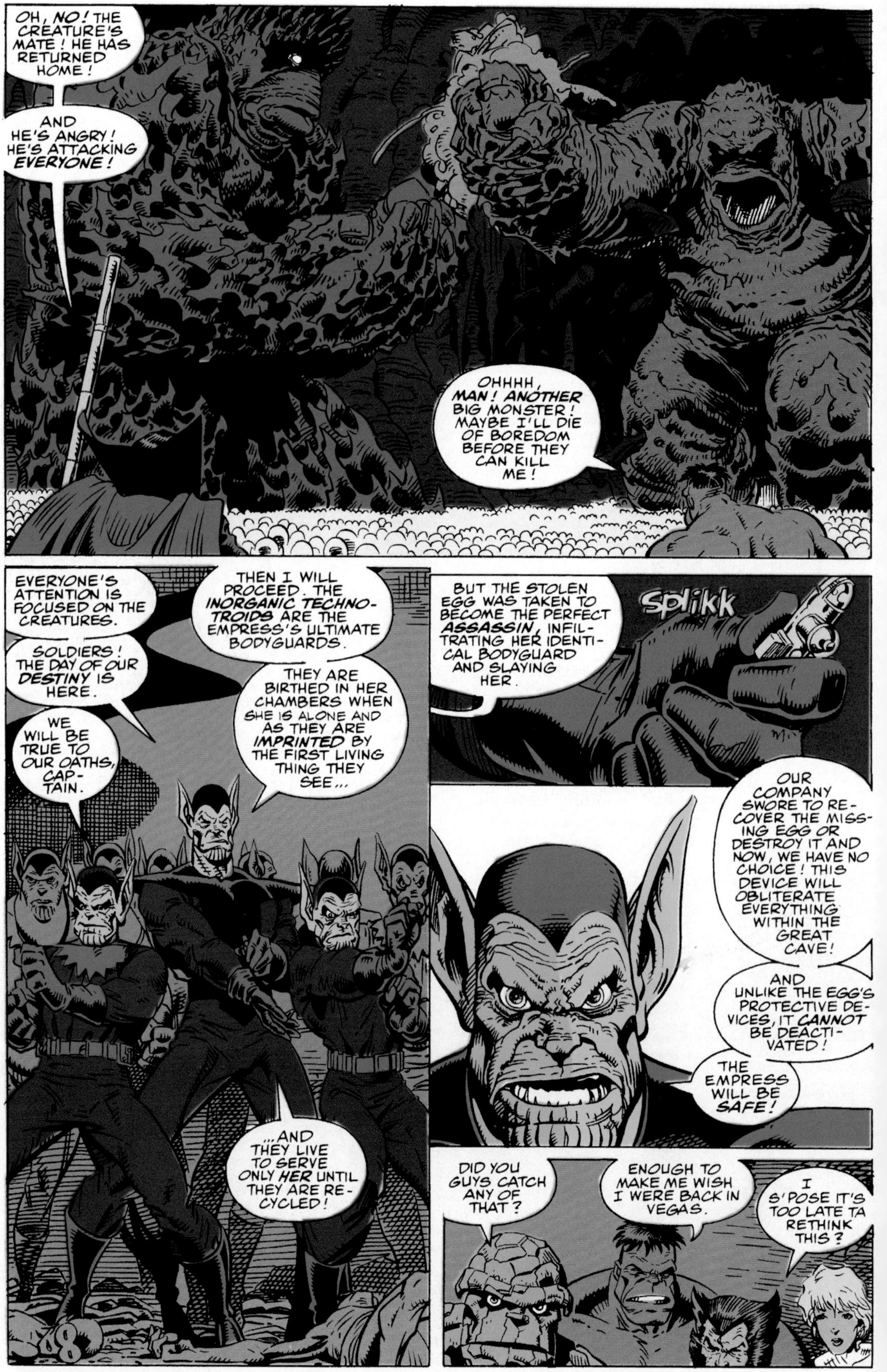

OH, NO! THE CREATURE'S MATE! HE HAS RETURNED HOME!
AND HE'S ANGRY! HE'S ATTACKING EVERYONE!
OHHHH, MAN! ANOTHER BIG MONSTER! MAYBE I'LL DIE OF BOREDOM BEFORE THEY CAN KILL ME!
EVERYONE'S ATTENTION IS FOCUSED ON THE CREATURES.
THEN I WILL PROCEED. THE INORGANIC TECHNO-TROIDS ARE THE EMPRESS'S ULTIMATE BODYGUARDS.
SOLDIERS! THE DAY OF OUR DESTINY IS HERE.
THEY ARE BIRTHED IN HER CHAMBERS WHEN SHE IS ALONE AND AS THEY ARE IMPRINTED BY THE FIRST LIVING THING THEY SEE...
WE WILL BE TRUE TO OUR OATHS, CAP-TAIN.
...AND THEY LIVE TO SERVE ONLY HER UNTIL THEY ARE RE-CYCLED!
BUT THE STOLEN EGG WAS TAKEN TO BECOME THE PERFECT ASSASSIN, INFIL-TRATING HER IDENTI-CAL BODYGUARD AND SLAYING HER.
SPLIKK
OUR COMPANY SWORE TO RE-COVER THE MISS-ING EGG OR DESTROY IT AND NOW, WE HAVE NO CHOICE! THIS DEVICE WILL OBLITERATE EVERYTHING WITHIN THE GREAT CAVE!
AND UNLIKE THE EGG'S PROTECTIVE DE-VICES, IT CANNOT BE DEACTI-VATED!
THE EMPRESS WILL BE SAFE!
DID YOU GUYS CATCH ANY OF THAT?
ENOUGH TO MAKE ME WISH I WERE BACK IN VEGAS.
I S'POSE IT'S TOO LATE TA RETHINK THIS?

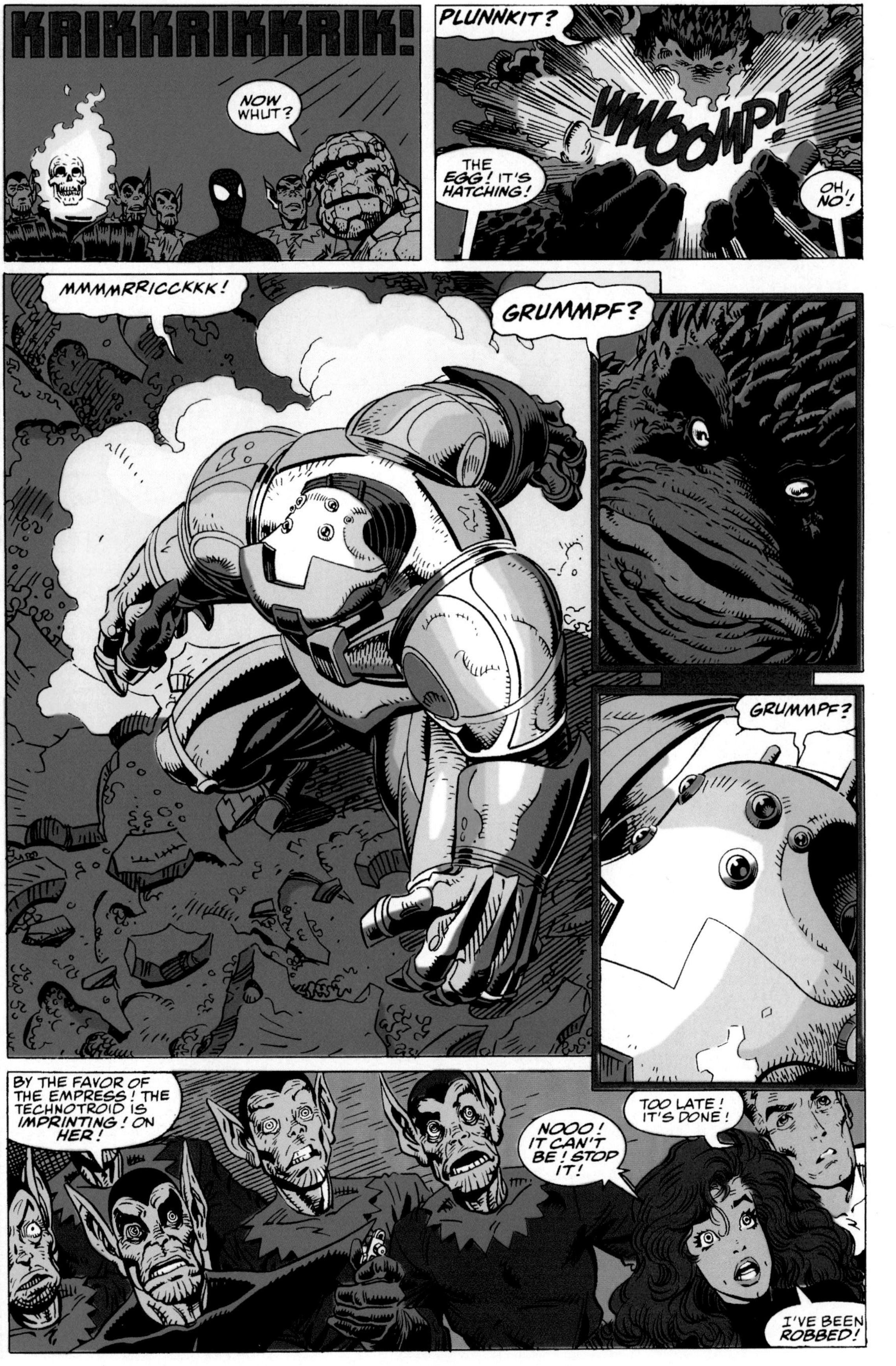
KRIKKRIKKRIK!
NOW WHUT?
PLUNNKIT?
WWOOMP!
THE EGG! IT'S HATCHING!
OH NO!
MMMMRRICCKKK!
GRUMMPF?
GRUMMPF?
BY THE FAVOR OF THE EMPRESS! THE TECHNOTROID IS IMPRINTING! ON HER!
NOOO! IT CAN'T BE! STOP IT!
TOO LATE! IT'S DONE!
I'VE BEEN ROBBED!

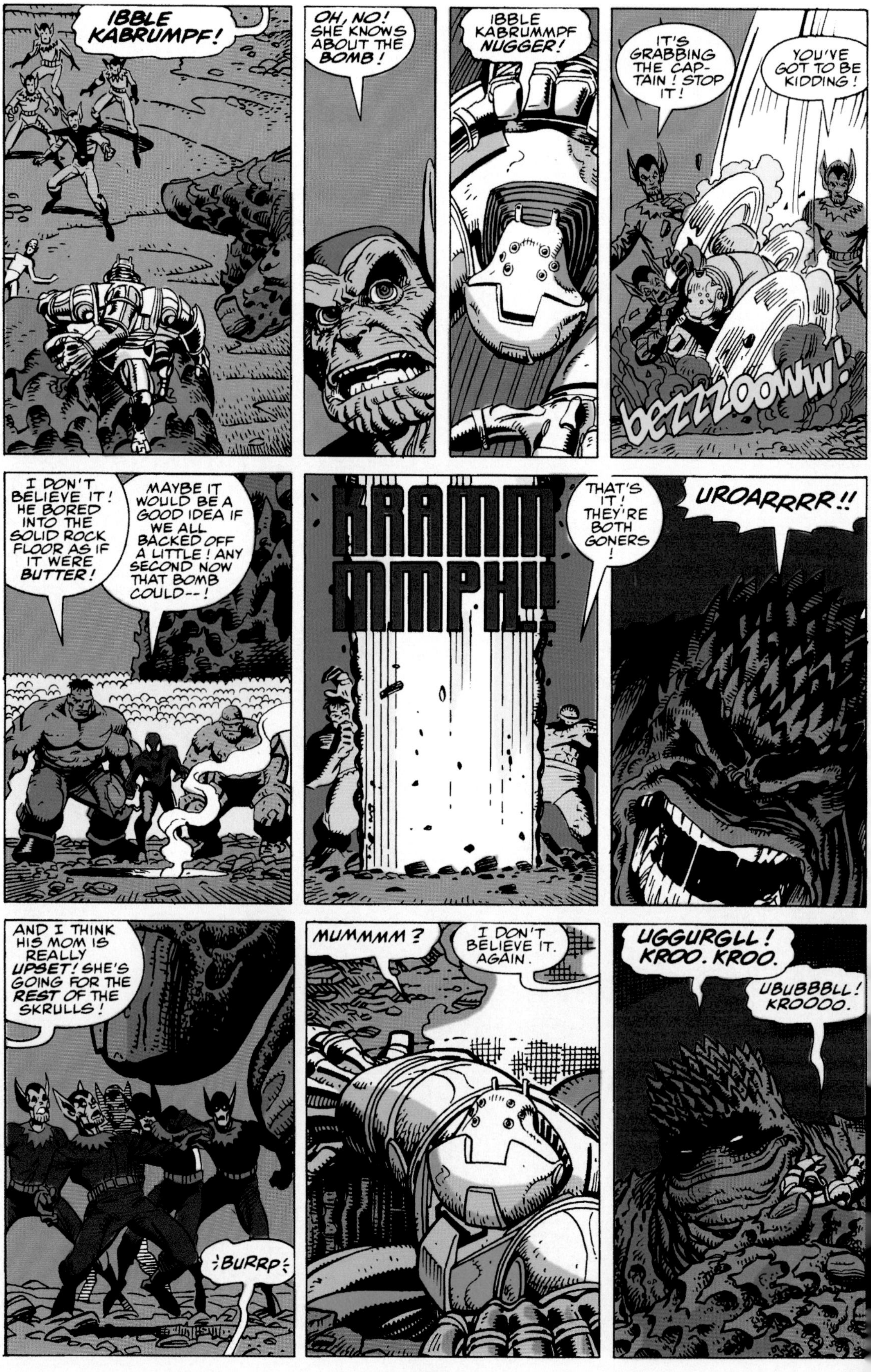
IBBLE KABRUMPF!
OH, NO! SHE KNOWS ABOUT THE BOMB!
IBBLE KABRUMMPF NUGGER!
IT'S GRABBING THE CAP-TAIN! STOP IT!
YOU'VE GOT TO BE KIDDING!
bezzzoowww!
I DON'T BELIEVE IT! HE BORED INTO THE SOLID ROCK FLOOR AS IF IT WERE BUTTER!
MAYBE IT WOULD BE A GOOD IDEA IF WE ALL BACKED OFF A LITTLE! ANY SECOND NOW THAT BOMB COULD--!
KRAMMM MMPH!!
THAT'S IT! THEY'RE BOTH GONERS!
UROARRRR!!
AND I THINK HIS MOM IS REALLY UPSET! SHE'S GOING FOR THE REST OF THE SKRULLS!
BURRP
MUMMMM?
I DON'T BELIEVE IT. AGAIN.
UGGURGLL! KROO. KROO.
UBUBBBLL! KROOOO.

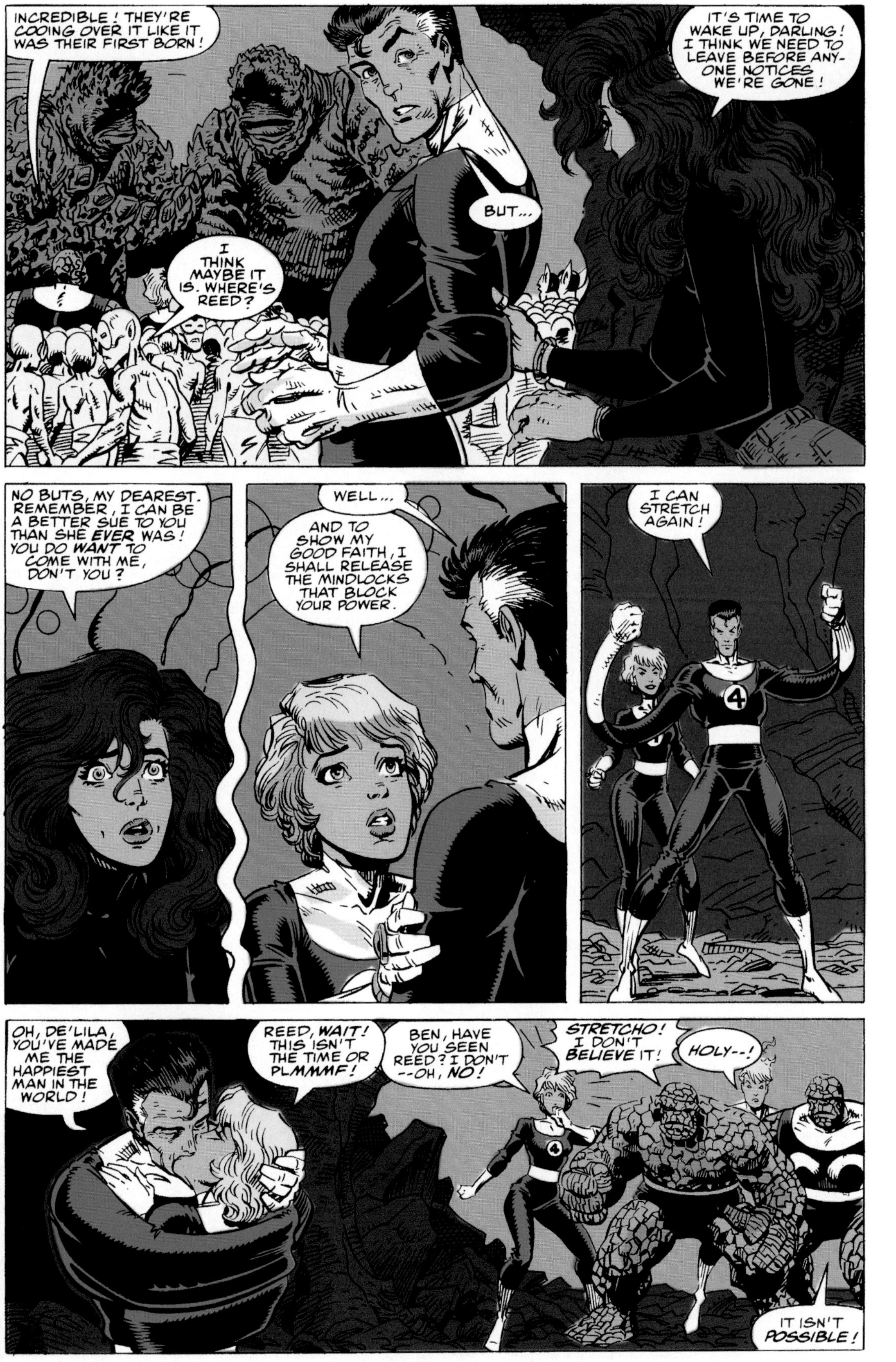
INCREDIBLE! THEY'RE COOING OVER IT LIKE IT WAS THEIR FIRST BORN!
IT'S TIME TO WAKE UP, DARLING! I THINK WE NEED TO LEAVE BEFORE ANY-ONE NOTICES WE'RE GONE!
BUT...
I THINK MAYBE IT IS. WHERE'S REED?
NO BUTS, MY DEAREST. REMEMBER, I CAN BE A BETTER SUE TO YOU THAN SHE EVER WAS! YOU DO WANT TO COME WITH ME, DON'T YOU?
WELL...
AND TO SHOW MY GOOD FAITH, I SHALL RELEASE THE MINDLOCKS THAT BLOCK YOUR POWER.
I CAN STRETCH AGAIN!
OH, DE'LILA, YOU'VE MADE ME THE HAPPIEST MAN IN THE WORLD!
REED, WAIT! THIS ISN'T THE TIME OR PLMMMF!
BEN, HAVE YOU SEEN REED? I DON'T --OH, NO!
STRETCHO! I DON'T BELIEVE IT!
HOLY--!
IT ISN'T POSSIBLE!

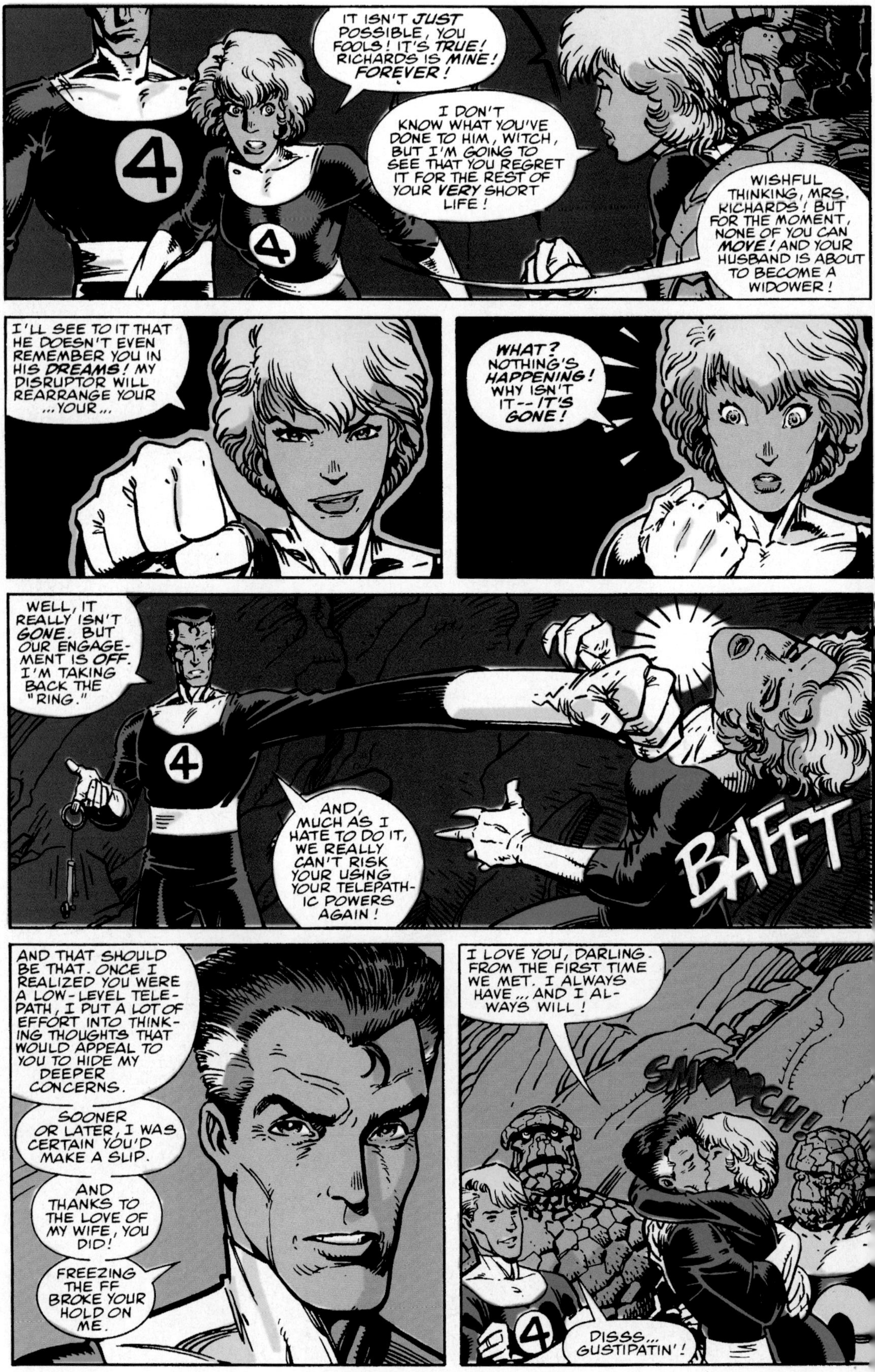
IT ISN'T JUST POSSIBLE, YOU FOOLS! IT'S TRUE! RICHARDS IS MINE! FOREVER!
I DON'T KNOW WHAT YOU'VE DONE TO HIM, WITCH, BUT I'M GOING TO SEE THAT YOU REGRET IT FOR THE REST OF YOUR VERY SHORT LIFE!
WISHFUL THINKING, MRS. RICHARDS! BUT FOR THE MOMENT, NONE OF YOU CAN MOVE! AND YOUR HUSBAND IS ABOUT TO BECOME A WIDOWER!
I'LL SEE TO IT THAT HE DOESN'T EVEN REMEMBER YOU IN HIS DREAMS! MY DISRUPTOR WILL REARRANGE YOUR ...YOUR...
WHAT? NOTHING'S HAPPENING! WHY ISN'T IT-- IT'S GONE!
WELL, IT REALLY ISN'T GONE. BUT OUR ENGAGEMENT IS OFF. I'M TAKING BACK THE "RING."
AND, MUCH AS I HATE TO DO IT, WE REALLY CAN'T RISK YOUR USING YOUR TELEPATHIC POWERS AGAIN!
BAFFT
AND THAT SHOULD BE THAT. ONCE I REALIZED YOU WERE A LOW-LEVEL TELEPATH, I PUT A LOT OF EFFORT INTO THINKING THOUGHTS THAT WOULD APPEAL TO YOU TO HIDE MY DEEPER CONCERNS.
SOONER OR LATER, I WAS CERTAIN YOU'D MAKE A SLIP.
AND THANKS TO THE LOVE OF MY WIFE, YOU DID!
FREEZING THE FF BROKE YOUR HOLD ON ME.
I LOVE YOU, DARLING. FROM THE FIRST TIME WE MET. I ALWAYS HAVE... AND I ALWAYS WILL!
SMOOCH!
DISSS... GUSTIPATIN'!

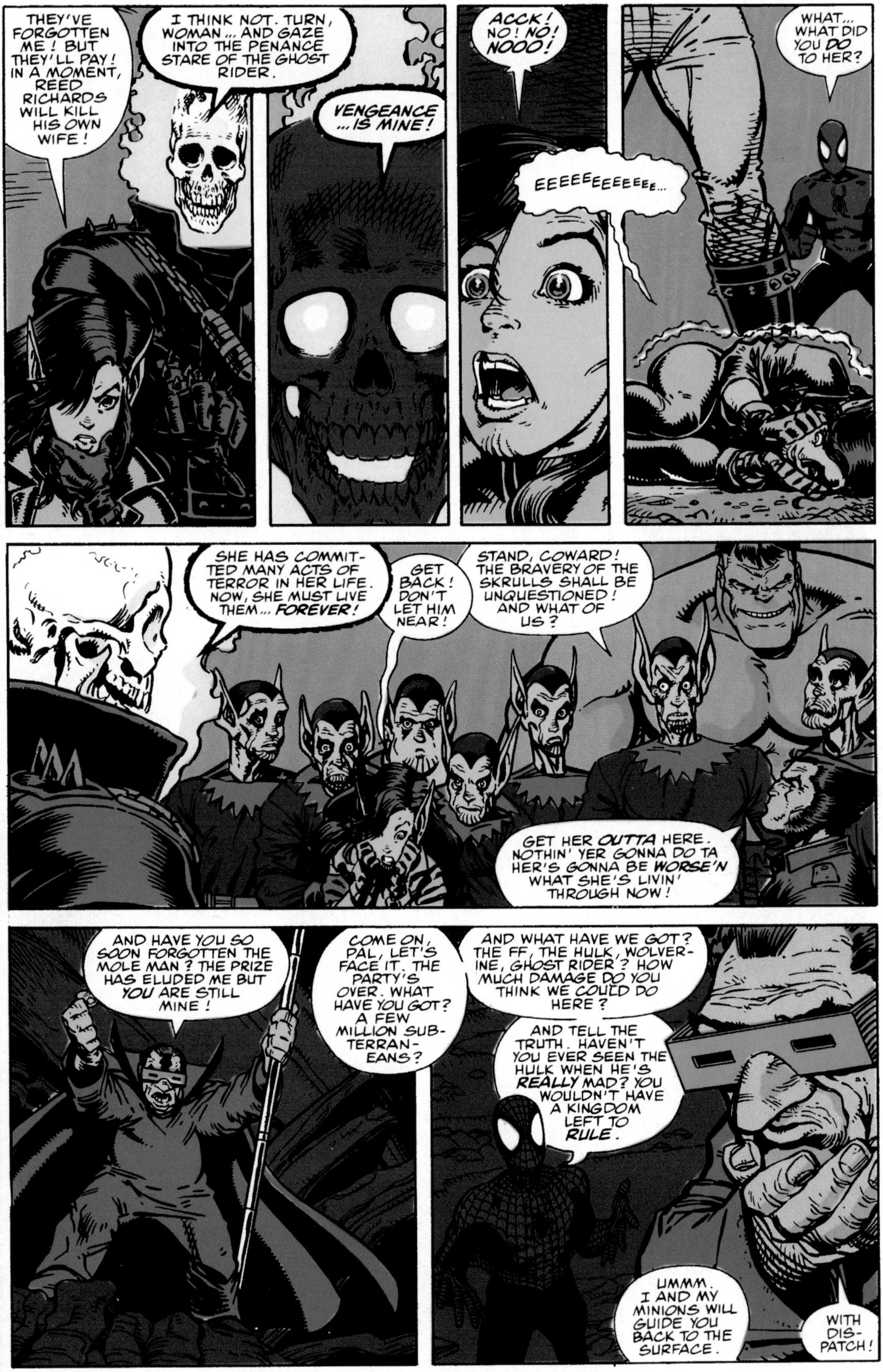
THEY'VE FORGOTTEN ME! BUT THEY'LL PAY! IN A MOMENT, REED RICHARDS WILL KILL HIS OWN WIFE!
I THINK NOT. TURN, WOMAN... AND GAZE INTO THE PENANCE STARE OF THE GHOST RIDER.
VENGEANCE ...IS MINE!
ACCK! NO! NO! NOOO!
EEEEEEEEEEEE...
WHAT... WHAT DID YOU DO TO HER?
SHE HAS COMMITTED MANY ACTS OF TERROR IN HER LIFE. NOW, SHE MUST LIVE THEM... FOREVER!
GET BACK! DON'T LET HIM NEAR!
STAND, COWARD! THE BRAVERY OF THE SKRULLS SHALL BE UNQUESTIONED! AND WHAT OF US?
GET HER OUTTA HERE. NOTHIN' YER GONNA DO TA HER'S GONNA BE WORSE'N WHAT SHE'S LIVIN' THROUGH NOW!
AND HAVE YOU SO SOON FORGOTTEN THE MOLE MAN? THE PRIZE HAS ELUDED ME BUT YOU ARE STILL MINE!
COME ON, PAL, LET'S FACE IT. THE PARTY'S OVER. WHAT HAVE YOU GOT? A FEW MILLION SUBTERRANEANS?
AND WHAT HAVE WE GOT? THE FF, THE HULK, WOLVERINE, GHOST RIDER? HOW MUCH DAMAGE DO YOU THINK WE COULD DO HERE?
AND TELL THE TRUTH. HAVEN'T YOU EVER SEEN THE HULK WHEN HE'S REALLY MAD? YOU WOULDN'T HAVE A KINGDOM LEFT TO RULE.
UMMM. I AND MY MINIONS WILL GUIDE YOU BACK TO THE SURFACE.
WITH DISPATCH!

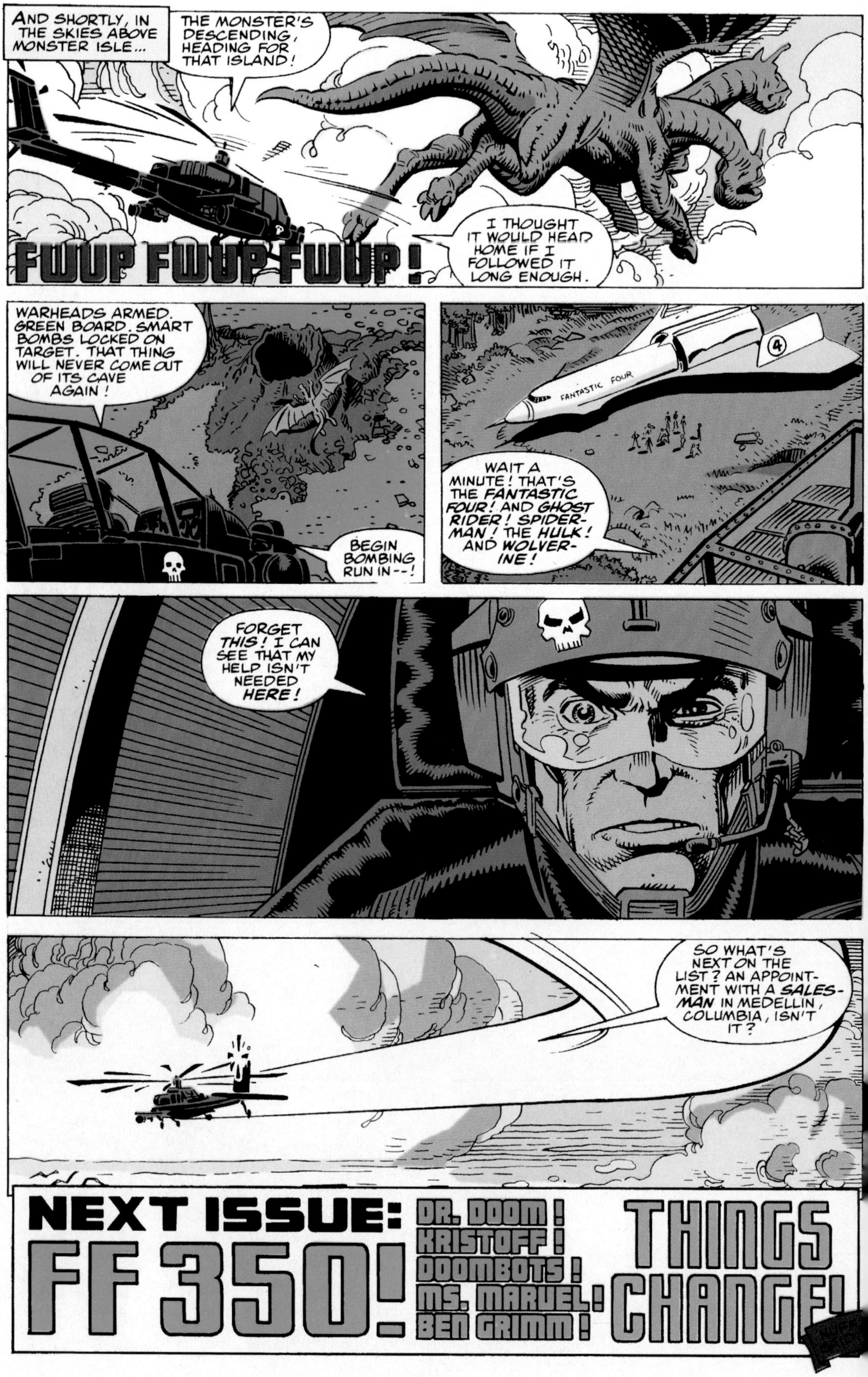
AND SHORTLY, IN THE SKIES ABOVE MONSTER ISLE...
THE MONSTER'S DESCENDING, HEADING FOR THAT ISLAND!
FWUP FWUP FWUP!
I THOUGHT IT WOULD HEAD HOME IF I FOLLOWED IT LONG ENOUGH.
WARHEADS ARMED. GREEN BOARD. SMART BOMBS LOCKED ON TARGET. THAT THING WILL NEVER COME OUT OF ITS CAVE AGAIN!
BEGIN BOMBING RUN IN--!
FANTASTIC FOUR
WAIT A MINUTE! THAT'S THE FANTASTIC FOUR! AND GHOST RIDER! SPIDER-MAN! THE HULK! AND WOLVERINE!
FORGET THIS! I CAN SEE THAT MY HELP ISN'T NEEDED HERE!
SO WHAT'S NEXT ON THE LIST? AN APPOINTMENT WITH A SALESMAN IN MEDELLIN, COLUMBIA, ISN'T IT?
NEXT ISSUE: FF 350!
DR. DOOM! KRISTOFF! DOOMBOTS! MS. MARVEL! BEN GRIMM!
THINGS CHANGE!

FANTASTIC FOUR THUMBNAILS

A special bonus from the archives:

Thumbnail sketches from Arthur Adams' uncanny take on the Fantastic Four.

MOLE'S BODY GUARD
MOLE
HEY! MOLE MAN! SOME ONE'S TAKIN' ALL THE MON STERS!
WE'RE OFF TO SEE THE LIZARDS...
MOLE

Fantastic Four #347, Page 15

HUH!
HEY GET OFFA MY FOOT... YA SON OF....
CRUNCH!

Fantastic Four #348, Page 17

SPIDER MAN
HULK DRESSED OR IN RAGS?
HULK
HI GUYS. WHAT'CHA DOIN IN THE BIG APPLE?
YEESH! TALK ABOUT GROUCHY!

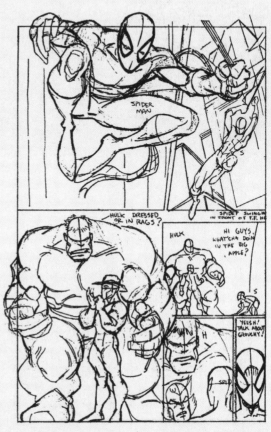

Fantastic Four #347, Page 17

CHARACTER DESIGN

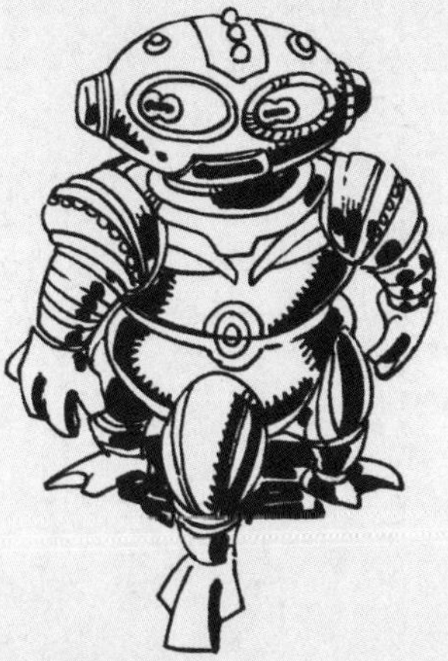

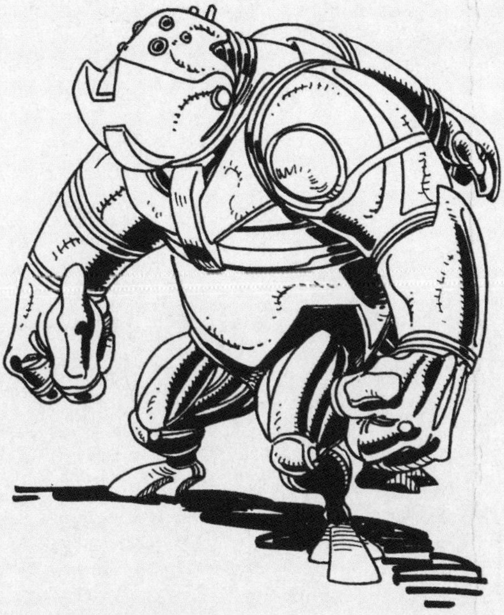

Arthur Adams' concept designs for the Skrulls' Inorganic Technodroid.

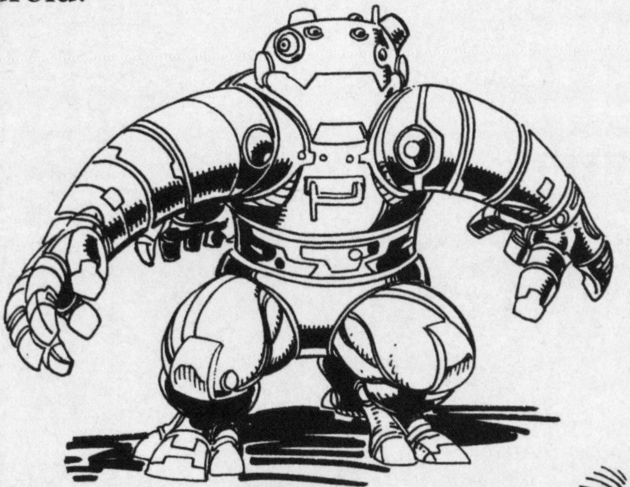

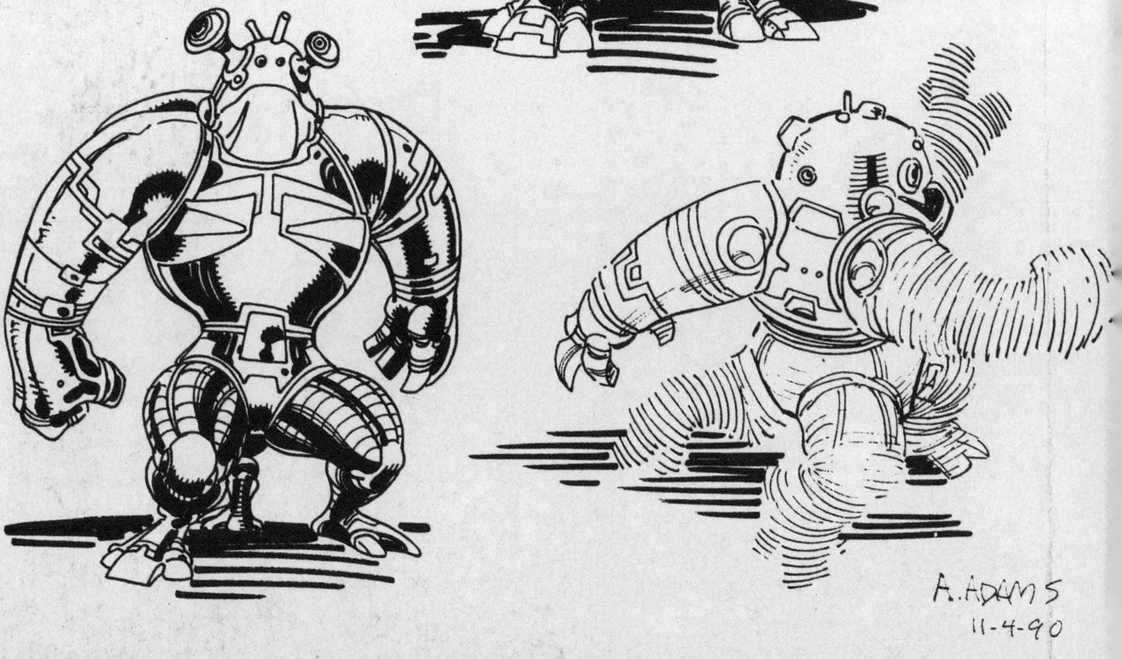
A. ADAMS
11-4-90